Teaching to Change the World

McGraw-Hill Higher Education

*A Division of The **McGraw-Hill** Companies*

TEACHING TO CHANGE THE WORLD

Published by McGraw-Hill, a business unit of The McGraw-Hill Companies, Inc., 1221 Avenue of the Americas. New York, NY, 10020.

This book is printed on acid-free paper.

2 3 4 5 6 7 8 9 0 FGR/FGR 0 9 8 7 6 5 4 3 2

ISBN 0-07-240738-7

Publisher: *Jane Karpacz*
Developmental editor II: *Cara Harvey*
Editorial coordinator: *Christina Lembo*
Media producer: *Lance Gerhart*
Project manager: *Ruth Smith*
Production supervisor: *Carol Bielski*
Coordinator of freelance design: *Mary E. Kazak*
Supplement producer: *Nathan Perry*
Photo research coordinator: *Alexandria Ambrose*
Cover/chapter opener photograhpy: *© Robert Pacheco*
Typeface: *10/12 Palatino*
Compositor: *GAC Indianapolis*
Printer: *Quebecor World Fairfield, Inc.*

Library of Congress Cataloging-in-Publication Data

Oakes, Jeannie
Teaching to change the world/Jeannie Oakes, Martin Lipton.—2nd ed.
p. cm.
Includes index.
ISBN 0-07-240738-7 (softcover : alk. paper)
1. Public schools—United States. 2. Education—Aims and objectives—United States. 3. Curriculum planning—United States. 4. Classroom management—United States. 5. Effective teaching—United States. 6. Educational change—United States. I. Lipton, Martin, 1942-II. Title.
LA217.2.O25 2003
371.01'0973—dc21

2002070283

www.mhhe.com

Teaching to Change the World

SECOND EDITION

Jeannie Oakes
University of California, Los Angeles

Martin Lipton
University of California, Los Angeles

Boston Burr Ridge, IL Dubuque, IA Madison, WI New York
San Francisco St. Louis Bangkok Bogotá Caracas Kuala Lumpur
Lisbon London Madrid Mexico City Milan Montreal New Delhi
Santiago Seoul Singapore Sydney Taipei Toronto

About the Authors

JEANNIE OAKES holds UCLA's Presidential Chair in Educational Equity. A nationally recognized education researcher and social justice advocate, Oakes is past director of UCLA's Teacher Education Program and now directs both UCLA's Institute for Democracy, Education, and Access, and the University of California's All-Campus Consortium on Research for Diversity. Among her many education policy services and distinctions Oakes serves as adviser to the California State Legislature in its work to develop the state's Master Plan for prekindergarten through university education. She frequently serves on national policy panels, most recently the National Academy of Sciences Committee on Programs for Advanced Study of Mathematics and Science in American High Schools.

Oakes's awards and distinctions include the Distinguished Achievement Award from the Educational Press Association of America, and the Ralph David Abernathy Award for public service, from the Southern Christian Leadership Conference. The American Educational Research Association (AERA) has awarded Oakes its prestigious Early Career Achievement Award and the Palmer O. Johnson Award for the Outstanding Research Article. Oakes is author of *Keeping Track: How Schools Structure Inequality* (1985), which was honored by the Museum of Education at the University of South Carolina as one of the most significant books on education in the twentieth century.

MARTIN LIPTON is an education writer and consultant and has taught in public schools for thirty-one years. He is coauthor with Oakes of *Making the Best of Schools* (1990). Oakes and Lipton recently received AERA's Outstanding Book Award for their publication of *Becoming Good American Schools: The Struggle for Virtue in Education Reform* (2001).

Brief Contents

Contents

Introduction

In 1997 there were 2.6 million public school teachers. The U.S. Department of Education estimates that the nation's schools will hire 2 million new teachers by 2007.

—U.S Department of Education

In fall 1997 William was five, and he was finishing his first week in kindergarten. First-year teacher Tracy Barnett was also finishing her first week, as William's teacher. When she announced that it was time for the class meeting, William asked, "Why do we have to do that again?" Mrs. Barnett answered obliquely with a question of her own, "Why, William, if we don't hear all the children's voices, how will we change the world?" William rolled his eyes upward, sighed with exasperation worthy of a teenager, and took his place in the circle. One week later, on a Monday morning, William walked into class and straight up to his teacher's desk. "Mrs. Barnett, what are we going to talk about today to change the world?"

In 2002 William was a fifth grader. This year his little sister entered kindergarten, but Tracy Barnett was not her teacher. Barnett had become a special education resource teacher at her school. Instead of spending her days with twenty rambunctious five-year-olds, she now works one-on-one with troubled learners. True to her commitment, she is determined that her students understand that they, too, are amazing learners who can strive to change the world.

By the year 2007 Tracy Barnett and others new to teaching at the turn of the twenty-first century will compose about half of all the public school teachers in the nation. During the course of their careers, these teachers will touch the lives of millions of children and adolescents with their skills, their knowledge, their talents, and their passion. This could be a good time to change the world.

The Book's Perspective

This book provides a comprehensive look at teaching for twenty-first century American schools. It is both practical and foundational. The chapters are organized around conventional topics—schooling, learning, curriculum, instruction, classroom management, and so on—with two themes that weave these chapters into a coherent story. The first theme is that learning is a social and cultural activity. The second theme is that the United States is a multicultural society. You will note, however, that there is no separate chapter here on multicultural education. Rather, we treat diversity as an integral part of all elements of education—of learning theory, curriculum and instruction, classroom management, assessment and testing, grouping, and the school culture.

The historical, philosophical, and sociological foundations of education are emphasized throughout the book. However, as with multicultural education, we do not include separate chapters on these foundations. While Chapter 1, "Schooling: Wrestling with History and Tradition," is heavily grounded in the history and ideas that help explain today's schools, the foundations are most powerful when people can use them to make sense of contemporary practices and concerns. For this reason, each chapter includes the history, philosophical positions, and social theories that help illustrate that chapter's topic—sometimes presenting entirely new background information and sometimes offering a new view of information presented earlier.

This book has a point of view. It takes the position that a hopeful, democratic future depends on whether all students learn and experience academic rigor and social justice in school. If only a few citizens have such teaching when they are small children, young boys and girls, and teenagers, there is no hope for change—just more of the same. This book aims to help teachers know why they should, and how they can, pursue social justice teaching and have sufficient hope to pursue it relentlessly.

We hope the book will help educators act on a commitment to social justice schooling. We define a *social justice perspective* on education as one that does three things: (1) It considers the values and politics that pervade education, as well as the more technical issues of teaching and organizing schools; (2) it asks critical questions about how conventional thinking and practice came to be, and who in society benefits from them; and (3) it pays particular attention to inequalities associated with race, social class, language, gender, and other social categories, and looks for alternatives to the inequalities. Acting to achieve social justice in schools is a struggle sustained by hope. Lacking hope, many thousands of promising teachers quit the profession within their first few years, unable to see how they can make a difference in students' lives. This book helps to build a foundation for hope by helping teachers understand and critique "commonsense" views of schools and conventional practices.

If good teaching and rigorous academic achievement do not reach every student in every class, we lock out the possibility of both social justice and excellence, even for a few. A common point of view, not ours, is that excellent teaching and social justice are distinct—that it is sufficient for good teachers to possess appropriate professional skills and impart the culture's knowledge and values to students. Daily consideration of social justice may or may not characterize such teachers, just as a passion for social justice may or may not characterize a good lawyer or businessperson. Again, this is not our perspective.

Throughout, we emphasize research and historical analyses that show how excellent teaching requires social justice.

Obviously, there are significant ideological differences in how people view educational practices both past and current. These ideologies are often consistent with political positions that bear the traditional political labels of conservative, moderate, liberal, and radical; and, as in politics, the ideological boundaries in education are often hard to pinpoint. Education uses similar labels and others—such as "progressive," "back to basics," and "traditionalist." If we had to label this book's perspective, we would call it "social progressive." Its roots lie in John Dewey's turn-of-the-twentieth-century learning theories and political sentiments, and its current frames of reference are the sociocultural and democratic theorists who are Dewey's intellectual descendants at the start of a new century.

Once labeled, however, educational perspectives are easily caricatured. Adversaries use the caricature in the manner of a *straw man* logical fallacy (constructing the opponent's argument in the worst possible light and then attacking what they, themselves, have constructed). Such has been the case with Dewey's progressive educational ideas and with current sociocultural theories. Over the years, educators have enacted a good many wrongheaded schooling excesses—many under the banner of progressive or child-centered education. Although the ideas of Dewey and of today's sociocultural theorists and teachers bear little resemblance to these caricatured practices, critics attempt to discredit—with some success—today's progressive reforms by portraying them as having a soft, "social agenda" free of rigorous academic content and skills. To these potential charges, we will leave it to the reader to decide whether the evidence we present would lead to "ratcheting up" or "dumbing down" the academic learning opportunities and outcomes for all students.

Unlike some introductory education texts, this book doesn't simply offer a smorgasbord of theory for readers to browse and then choose whatever suits their appetites. We try to help readers understand what is good in education and dissuade them from simply getting good at what is popular. So, for example, when teachers are troubled by misbehaving students, whether they should (a) struggle to build a caring classroom community or (b) work to perfect "assertive discipline" routines is not a neutral choice in this book. The correct answer to the "quiz" is (a): build a caring classroom community. It is correct because theory and substantial research evidence reveal how caring classroom communities support high-achieving, socially just, intrinsically motivated teaching and learning and reduce unproductive student behavior. Assertive discipline, on the other hand, is a commercially hawked scheme to control behavior, and it promotes an authoritarian, anticommunity, and less intellectually challenging classroom. Furthermore, it has no support in sound educational research and theory. It is neither honest nor objective to describe popular teaching practices in a neutral manner if they do not stand up to the standards of social justice or education research. We do not believe that the world is a neutral place or that teaching is a neutral profession.

Making choices on behalf of children and social justice requires personal qualities of integrity, decency, and the capacity to work very hard. We find these qualities in abundance in people who choose to be teachers. But making social justice choices also requires teachers to have a professional groundwork of social theory and educational research to make their efforts credible to others and sustainable for themselves. We would be very pleased if this book helps teachers get started in that direction.

Overview of Chapters

Each chapter describes a particular domain of school knowledge and practice. Throughout the chapters, we include the observations of first-year teachers—in their own words. We would expect these teachers to be struggling with lesson plans, discipline, paperwork, time management, school bureaucracy, and so on. And, of course, they are. But please listen carefully to their voices. What is crucial is not that they struggle, but the quality of the problems with which they struggle. For example, Dung Lam, first-year teacher of ninth-grade mathematics, confronts the problem of students who "are restless and would rather do other work or chat with their friends." She is devastated, not by students who do not behave, but by her own part in the "horror" of lessons that make it "so tempting and easy to cheat." "Sad and angry because this math year is virtually wasted," Dung Lam began teaming with a veteran teacher to revise the curriculum. These teachers belie one criticism of a social justice emphasis to a teacher's career—that these are soft "do-gooders" whose social agenda wipes out their obligation to teach. For readers who might need to ask, yes, these teachers have high expectations for their students; and the teachers are, indeed, very competent. They are among the most sought-after teachers in their communities because they expect their students to learn by thrusting themselves into a better, more humane, more equitable future.

Chapter 1, "Schooling: Wrestling with History and Tradition," explains how and why Americans are so conflicted as they both pursue and avoid the "common school." We probe four deeply held modern beliefs—based on the myths of merit, efficiency, competition, and progress—that insulate schools from the most promising research and practices that support all children learning well. First, *merit* is the belief that people deserve what they have, and if they have little, that is all they deserve. Second, *factory efficiency* is the belief that rational, scientifically run organizations geared to produce the greatest returns, outcomes, or "bottom line" benefit everyone working within that system. Third, *marketplace competition* claims that social benefits are fairly and justly distributed through unfettered competition. And, fourth, *progress* suggests that current practices result from a progression of improvements, which require only further improvement and "fine-tuning." The chapter concludes with arguments that each of these cultural beliefs has been tested in schools and is collapsing under global postmodern demands for a skilled, flexible, and diverse citizenry. Meeting these twenty-first-century demands in the democratic spirit of the common school requires the preeminence of a fifth cultural belief that comes to Americans from our shared heritage of slavery, *struggle. Struggle* is the directing of one's unflinching commitment, endurance, and hope in order to achieve social justice. In a world that does not promise moral victories, struggle promises a moral journey.

Chapters 2 and 3 explore theories of learning in their historical, philosophical, and social contexts. These contexts matter since humans quickly shape "scientific" findings to conform to prevailing social beliefs. Ours is a cultural and scientific heritage that too often clings to unproductive—frequently racist—psychological theory, often leaving little room for the hopeful and accurate theories that would allow schools to teach well and equitably. The challenge here is twofold. First, teachers need a critique of traditional psychology to help them examine school practices and to scour their common sense for naïve or destructive theories that govern learning—particularly conceptions of intelligence. This is primarily the intent of Chapter 2, "Traditional Learning Theories: Transmission, Training, and IQ." Reaching back to the European Enlightenment, we examine the hallmarks of belief that set the philosophical stage for the next three hundred years of Western thought. We then turn to the nineteenth century for the earliest attempts to study human behavior scientifically, and we continue with the twentieth-century emphasis on the social and scientific consequences of laboratory experimentation and scientific testing and measurement.

Chapter 3, "Contemporary Learning Theories: Problem Solving, Understanding, and Participation," asks readers to consider emerging theories that permit and direct us to equitable teaching. The most educationally relevant of these theories weave together knowledge from social science theory and research including sociology, anthropology, psychology, and education. Recent advances in these fields present learning as something that each learner must actively construct. We rely on empirically grounded work emphasizing that "intelligence" is constructed in developmental and social contexts. Within these contexts the overlapping notions of *learning, intelligence,* and *knowledge,* are given shape and power by the experiences, histories, languages and cultures of diverse groups of students.

Chapters 4 and 5 tackle the most enduring question of schooling: What should the curriculum be? Chapter 4, "Curriculum: Philosophy, History, and Politics: What Should Students Learn?," looks beneath the superficial consensus that all children need reading and writing, mathematics, science, and whatever else it takes to be responsible citizens. Like everything else about schools, the American curriculum is deeply rooted in history and politics, as well as in the intrinsic human eagerness to learn. Debates about what content best serves students and society and how teachers should organize and present that content reflect starkly different views of the nature of knowledge, the nature of humans, and the nature of a good society. Today, fierce political battles overwhelm professional curriculum debates. Political conservatives argue that schools must continue to transmit traditional knowledge, while political progressives assert that schools must reflect the multiple American cultural and linguistic traditions. Chapter 4 reviews these issues and sets the stage for the current controversies over local and national "standards" in the school subjects.

Chapter 5, "Curriculum: The Subject Matters," spells out how the professional and political curriculum debates surface in four major academic content areas, shaping what and how students learn in each. The standards movement, along with the emphasis on testing-based "accountability" has brought under the glare of the political spotlight discussions to determine exactly what math, language arts, science, and social studies students should learn. One side—political liberals, social progressives, and most experts on teaching the subjects—argues that a socially just curriculum provides every child access to the most important ideas of the core disciplines. This happens, they contend, when teachers emphasize meaning-making and understanding, and recognize that facts and skills can best be learned in the context of these important core ideas. The other side—political conservatives, traditionalists, and some scholars in the subject areas—focuses first on the mastery of basic facts and skills. They insist that basic facts and skills are prerequisite to complex ideas. These disputes have been intense and often referred to as history, science, math, and phonics "wars" as they are fought by local school boards and state and national policymaking bodies.

Chapters 6 and 7 explore classroom practice. Chapter 6, "Instruction and Assessment: Classrooms as Learning Communities," begins with pictures of past classrooms that, as archaic as they sound, have disturbingly familiar features. As in many of today's classrooms, the teachers' job was to transmit knowledge to students in an orderly sequence of steps. However, the narrow, unidimensional design of such lessons leads most students to conclude that they're just not very smart. In contrast, cognitive and sociocultural research presses teachers to focus less on transmitting knowledge than on developing learning relationships with students. These relationships allow students to engage knowledge in ways that transform their thinking, promote their development, and over time help them realize their potential to be fully participating members of the culture. Teachers who want to change the world strive to make their classrooms places where both they and their students can be confident about everyone's ability to learn. They structure active and interactive learning activities and assessment tasks that make learning accessible to culturally and linguistically diverse groups of students.

Chapter 7, "Classroom Management: Caring and Democratic Communities," surveys the legacy of management, discipline, and control that many contemporary teachers still rely on to organize classroom life. It also reviews a second tradition—caring and democratic classrooms—that, while less common, also has deep American roots. This second tradition is generally consistent with cognitive and sociocultural learning theories. The chapter concludes by calling attention to the important contributions of critical theorists who address classroom issues of power and domination and how teachers may respond to these issues as they attempt to make their classrooms socially just. This work argues that classrooms must allow children to experience democracy as well as learn about it, if they are to learn to be members of a culturally democratic community.

Chapter 8, "Grouping and Categorical Programs: Can Schools Teach *All* Children Well?," deals with the often-controversial ways that schools respond to differences in students' abilities, achievements, and behaviors. Schools commonly categorize and separate children into groups that appear to be similar—or homogeneous—in order to address their needs. Many times, these practices limit rather than expand students' learning opportunities, and children of color and those from low-income families disproportionately feel these negative effects. The chapter overviews the history and social theory that link race, class, and culture to these seemingly objective and technical practices of schooling. It also explores how educators attempt to give students the attention and resources they need without isolating and alienating them from the mainstream.

Chapter 9, "The School Culture: Where Good Teaching Makes Sense," identifies theory and research-based characteristics of schools that support excellent and democratic learning and teaching. These characteristics include opportunities to learn, an environment that makes learning seem inevitable, structures that allow teachers to know their students and their community well, and conditions that allow teachers to care and work hard. These cultural elements are necessary conditions for teachers to challenge all their students to do rigorous, intellectually demanding work. The chapter describes several current, progressive reform projects based around *inquiry*—a mode of conversation that elicits from all members of the school community their understanding of the school's environment for rigorous and socially just learning. These inquiry-based school reforms help individuals clarify others' and their own perceptions and help translate shared beliefs and values into democratic action.

Chapter 10, "Connections with Families and Communities," is new to this edition. In this chapter we consider two dominant (and contradictory) complaints about parents: (1) They neglect their responsibilities to participate and support their children's schools; and (2) they are disruptive and overly involved in schools. We also examine four types of constructive engagement: (1) parents supporting the work of schools; (2) schools serving families' and communities' need for health and social services; (3) bridging the cultures of home and school through curriculum; and (4) engaging parents directly in schools through community empowerment. The chapter argues that however teachers engage with families, their efforts will be most constructive if they enable them—poor, middle class, and rich—to exercise their rightful power over schooling as *citizens* who are responsible for the education of all children, not simply as parents looking our for their own children's interests. This means that parents who educators consider to be *too* involved, as well as those who seem not involved enough, must develop a very different concept of involvement. They must also come together with parents of different racial groups and socioeconomic positions and act together as citizens on behalf of all children.

Chapter 11, "Teaching to Change the World: A Profession and a Hopeful Struggle," draws parallels between teachers' work in American schools, John Dewey's progressivism, Paulo Freire's pedagogy of hope, the nation's social movements for civil and human rights, and Cornel West's prophetic pragmatism. The chapter grounds this struggle for high-quality and socially just schooling in current thinking about the future of democratic institutions in our postmodern world, and in the experiences of first-year teachers engaged in that struggle. It also describes the pressures that plague the teaching profession and details ways that committed new teachers do maintain their hope, their struggle, and their commitment to change the world.

Digging Deeper: Going Beyond the Text

Each chapter ends with a section called "Digging Deeper." Here we identify scholars who are studying or working on practical applications of the issues we raise, and we list a few of their books and articles that you might find interesting and useful. In some chapters, we also list professional organizations and activist groups working to make education policy or school practices more consistent with and supportive of socially just teaching. Wherever possible, we provide Internet sites that are good starting points for pursuing additional resources.

Perspectives of Those Engaged in Hopeful Struggle

The words of the first-year teachers whom we cite throughout the book come from the comprehensive portfolios they presented for their Master's Degree in Education at UCLA. We recommend that all potential teachers write about their experiences, thoughts, and observations. Whether a personal journal, or a portfolio that presents a full record of a teacher-candidate's intellectual and professional growth, a written record inevitably provides wonderful opportunities for reflection.

The Reader's Perspective

You will find that this book does not offer chapter-end questions and does not wrap up chapters with lists of "main points" to tell readers what the chapters say or mean. Instead, readers must furnish what the book itself cannot provide—lots of discussion and elaboration. Readers need to become engaged in the *social learning* the book describes in Chapters 3 and 6 and elsewhere. The discussions in those chapters apply to mature readers as well as to elementary and secondary school students.

Readers will find that reading and discussion groups or "book clubs" are excellent structures for forming and revealing their own perceptions as they pursue this book's issues in depth. A "jigsaw" approach with several people responsible for different supplemental articles or bodies of research and practice can enable readers to support or scaffold their own and others' sense-making. Readers who are fortunate to have access to other readers with diverse backgrounds, experiences, cultures, and lifestyles will have especially enriched learning opportunities.

Of course, there are some questions that, if not specific to a particular chapter, have good generic potential for sparking the reader's thinking. For example, What memories of your own schooling or other experiences does the book stir up? What connections can you make to your other knowledge? What makes you angry? What sounds reasonable, but you can't believe it is true? What have you always known, but you didn't know you knew it? What do you imagine your acquaintances would think about the material? And, of course, what are your questions?

Teaching

Finally, we suggest that a teacher's most important skill is finding the intelligence and understanding the knowledge that each student possesses. This is no easy matter when teachers are culturally very similar to their students; and, when the teacher is culturally different, it is a real challenge. To perfect this skill is a legitimate and fulfilling life's work. Mary Ann Pacheco, one of the first-year teachers you will meet in this book, put it this way:

I began the year afraid, and gradually developed a more solid sense of who I was, what my profession meant to me, and what I wanted for my students whose lives I would touch forever. Perhaps my views and practices will change in the future, perhaps they will not. What is important is that I developed a new identity through teaching, and this will sustain me. I expect that from a career in which I deal with real and diverse lives every day.

—Mary Ann Pacheco
First-year teacher, grades 1 and 2

Acknowledgments

The most immediate inspiration for this book was the courage, passion, and hard work of the wonderful UCLA teacher education graduates whose words and photographs appear throughout the chapters. We are enormously appreciative of their commitment to students, their struggle to create democratic schools and classrooms, and for their hard questions about how to make a socially just education real. We are indebted to UCLA's teacher education faculty, notably Eloise Metcalfe, Jody Priselac, Shelia Lane, and others who read and commented insightfully on the first edition, along with the novice and resident teachers at UCLA during 1999–2002 academic years. Their responses provided illuminating direction. McGraw-Hill editor Beth Kaufman remains a thoughtful and energetic champion, even though she spends much of her time these days with little Maisie. Cara Harvey and Jane Karpacz have ably assumed Beth's role marshaling the book through the complicated publication process. As with the first edition, Laurie McGee fine-tuned our words.

Finally, we would like to thank the instructors who made helpful substantive suggestions:

John R. Aston,
Southwest Texas State University
Deron R. Boyles,
Georgia State University
Wade A. Carpenter,
Berry College
Sheena Choi, *Indiana University–Purdue University, Fort Wayne*
Carlian W. Dawson,
Purdue University, Norht Central
Rev. Joseph A DiMauro,
DeSales University
Louise Flemming,
Ashland University
Kenneth Gold,
College of Staten Island
Sharon Hobbs,
Montana State University
Grace C. Huerta,
Utah State University
Charles E. Jenks,
August State University
Vicki LaBoskey,
Mills College
Richard D. Lakes,
Georgia State University
Luis F. Mirón,
University of California, Irvine

James Mitchell,
California State University, Dominguez Hills
Carolyn O'Grady
Gustavus Adolphus College
Karina Otoya-Knapp
Bank Street College
Jean Peterson,
Purdue University
Alfred A. Rocci, Jr.,
Simmons College
Susan Marie Rumann,
Northern Arizona University
Doug Sherman,
Portland State University
Barbara Tye,
Chapman University

We are also grateful to many scholars who, over the years, have contributed to the ideas and approach we take here. These colleagues' rich ideas and generous conversations have shaped our thinking in subtle and not-so-subtle ways. Among those, James Banks, Linda Darling-Hammond, Megan Franke, John Goodlad, Andy Hargreaves, Peter McLaren, Doug Pollock, John Rogers, Kenneth Sirotnik, Gladys Topkis, Amy Stuart Wells, and Anne Wheelock stand out as mentors and friends. We have also learned a great deal about schooling, multiple perspectives, and the struggle for social justice from former and current doctoral students whose scholarly work has enriched our own, most notably Susan Auerbach, Tony Collatos, Robert Cooper, Amanda Datnow, Diane Friedlaender, Laila Hasan, Diane Hirshberg, Rebecca Joseph, Makeba Jones, Michelle Knight, Ernest Morrell, Karina Otoya, Karen Hunter Quartz, Karen Ray, Steve Ryan, Irene Serna, Jamy Stillman, Linda Symcox, Kevin Welner, and Susan Yonezawa. Our appreciation to Jared Planas for his proofreading services. Thanks, too, are due the many generous funders who have sponsored Jeannie's research.

Our family provides a solid rock of support for which we are always grateful. Martin's parents, Irene and Nathan Lipton, were enthusiastic cheerleaders about the project, and Jeannie's mom, Martha Nall, read carefully and made thoughtful comments along the way. Jeannie's dad, Ron Nall, had a sense of humor that still echoes, keeping us from taking ourselves too seriously. Our four children contributed to the substance of this book in amazing ways: Lisa Oakes brought her considerable expertise as a developmental psychologist and provided many helpful suggestions and examples for Chapters 2 and 3; Tracy Oakes Barnett, now a special education resource teacher, offered inspiring anecdotes and the constant reminder of how much fun teaching for social justice can be; Lowell Lipton, teacher of rhetoric and composition, contributed a fresh look at the postmodern struggle for meaning; and Ethan Lipton, a fellow writer, extended knowing encouragement and good dinner company throughout the writing process. Finally, Emily and Haley Barnett, Alison Luck, Max Lipton, and the two expected new additions to our growing family remind us of why this matters so much. We thank them all.

CHAPTER 1

Schooling:

Wrestling with History and Tradition

Kelly Ganzell

First-year teacher, high school English

The class meeting was the first step in a long process that would allow the students to voice their concerns about the community where they lived. Before we began, I disclosed my personal reasons for having chosen such an activity. I explained that I decided to become a teacher because I wanted to change something about the world. I shared that I wanted them to understand that we have the power to change things. The students were very honest with their concerns: "gang bangers," shootings, robberies, dogs and cats (noisy), old people, homeless people, bad language, and kidnapping. It was a powerful experience to stand in front of a classroom full of young children and tell them that I wanted to change the world.

—*Mary Ann Pacheco*
First-year teacher, grades 1 and 2

Mary Ann Pacheco wrote these words as she finished her first year of teaching. She and many others in her teacher education program begin their careers committed to teaching in ways that will change the world. Their voices—scattered throughout this book—are hopeful and optimistic about the possibilities of education and social justice in a diverse, unpredictable world. These new teachers also reveal their struggle to bring their professional knowledge and unequivocal values to their practice as they strive to create classrooms and schools where students develop the academic and moral capacities and the commitment to shape their own places in a socially just future.

And what a struggle it is! Mary Ann Pacheco and her colleagues differ from many Americans who look longingly to a mostly imagined past, when the "good" life meant one without diversity, a life lived with people mostly like us. In this sense *us* has typically meant those at the center of society—a location that is white and middle class, with males in authority and women and children safely protected in heterosexual families. These new teachers also differ from some of their colleagues who are intent on returning to an imagined "good" past when children all spoke English, scored above average, and their parents only came to school to deliver cookies. The social justice these new teachers envision does not try to re-create the past. They know they must wrestle with traditions in schools and society that will obstruct their efforts and attempt to persuade them that their idealism is naïve or destructive.

The Teaching Challenge of the Twenty-First Century

Most of my students either are recent immigrants from Latin America (most from Mexico) with limited prior academic experience, or are low academic achievers for a variety of reasons. Out of twenty-nine students, one is vision impaired, three attend resource specialist classes daily, one attends speech therapy weekly, and two receive special math assistance two days a week. All of my students come from economically disadvantaged homes, every one receives either free or reduced price lunches at school, and 12 receive free breakfast. Twenty-eight are Mexican Americans and one is of Puerto Rican descent. Many of my students' parents have limited education; none attended schools in the United States. Two speak English.

What exactly is our obligation to prepare my students for the future? I hope that the everyday lessons of math, language arts, social studies, and science, which require the majority of my attention, are helping to prepare them for the world outside of our classroom. But I believe that becoming bicultural requires more than just readying the individual for the dominant society. It also requires preparing society for the minority members. I can only guide my students in their quest to become individuals. I can help them define valuable assets within their own culture, I can provide them with assistance in achieving personal success, but eventually they will have to face the rest of society without me or other educators at their sides.

—Michelle Calva
First-year teacher, grades 4, 5, and 6

Today, classrooms like Michelle Calva's are common in cities like Los Angeles, New York, Chicago, and Miami. By the mid–twenty-first century, a majority of all American schoolchildren will be nonwhite. For teachers today, *multicultural* cannot be a lesson, a curriculum, a teaching style, or even a philosophy. Multiculturalism neither strengthens nor dilutes our society. Multiculturalism is simply a fact—a condition of culture. Nonwhite and immigrant voices and languages will be either heard or ignored, but they will not be silenced or assimilated out of existence. Some teachers will struggle, like Michelle Calva, to construct something whole and wonderful that connects these cultures; some won't. We hope most do, because we believe that this is the only way to provide a free and equal education to all.

In the face of cultural diversity, school critics on the political right have openly launched what some call the "culture wars" by attempting to require teaching the mainstream culture and language and none other. They often favor "back to basics" and traditional teaching methods. Political moderates and liberals have sought ways to equalize students' chances for school success by giving them the same opportunities as white, middle-class students. To do this they promote equally high academic standards that depart significantly from traditional views, and they call for all students to have equally well qualified teachers and other resources. Progressive educators are cautious about the moderates' and liberals' programs unless these programs are accompanied at every step by tough cultural questions: Whose schools are these, and who benefits from them? Whose language may be spoken? Whose knowledge is important to include?

Finally, finding no hope in a common education, some individuals—on both the right and left—have carved out separate specialized schools to serve different "monocultural" communities. Many are giving up on public education, emphasizing the democratic right to be separate over the democratic ideal to stay together. This is not a quiet or passive withdrawal of support, but an active, complex, political battle.

Clearly, the broad mix of cultures and ideologies that shape our national character also shape today's schools and classrooms. At its core, this tradition represents Americans' commitment to values that always compete and sometimes conflict: from democracy, to capitalism, to individual freedom, and to the common good. This chapter provides an overview of links between schools and American traditions.

A Brief History of American Public Schools

Since the Republic's founding, Americans have placed their hopes for democracy on public schools. Americans are fortunate to have a school tradition that speaks—if not always loudly and clearly—to democracy's core values. And, in a uniquely American way, the nation keeps its democratic tradition alive through the hopeful and often angry voices of criticism. Today, more teachers than ever before are listening to these critical voices as they seek new ways to enhance the democratic tradition.

The Role of the Common Public School in Securing Democracy

Thomas Jefferson argued that democracy required citizens to deliberate publicly and to use their reason to decide among competing ideas for guiding the nation. Because a free press would circulate the ideas that Americans would debate, citizens must be able to read; therefore, Jefferson claimed that government should provide children with three years of schooling to ready them for citizenship. Jefferson advocated basic literacy—reading, writing, and mathematics—and beyond that students might also learn the rudiments of Greek, Roman, English, and American history.

In arguing for public schooling (and in criticizing those who saw no need), Jefferson acted on a view shared by late–eighteenth-century intellectuals: Creative and rational thought must be the foundation of orderly and stable modern societies. Jefferson articulated other ideas about democratic society that continue to shape American education today. Perhaps the most important is that democratic institutions must ensure individual liberties, even as they advance the common good. Perhaps the ugliest, at least partly attributable to Jefferson, is that race provides a meaningful and useful way to distinguish among people.

In the 1830s Horace Mann augmented Jefferson's vision of public schools. Mann argued compellingly that all Americans should be educated in "common" schools that would complement what families taught their children at home. Mann defined the essential characteristic of what would later be called, simply, the "public school." These would be *equal* schools. Of course, schools today are not equal (and were not then), but Mann gave the country a goal worthy of pursuing. These common schools were not charity schools for the poor, but free public schools for the sons and daughters of farmers, businessmen, professionals, and the rest of society.

Mann intended common schools to teach the knowledge and habits, as well as the basic literacy, that citizens needed to function in a democracy. He envisioned the common school as the "great equalizer" and the "creator of wealth undreamed of" and hoped it would eliminate poverty and crime and shape the destiny of a wise, productive country. Like other modern thinkers of the day, Mann believed that social improvement would follow from advances in knowledge and that schooling would extend individual rights and liberties to all.

> First and second graders can affect the conditions they live in—for at least half the day. . . . Throughout the year, voting and classroom meetings provided a medium for conflict resolution. The voting was not simply a hand poll. We visited polling stations, filled out registration cards, set up polls and an ongoing voting station in our classroom; we voted on specific units to study. I did anything possible to make students realize that they have a voice.
>
> —Sarine Gureghian
> *First-year teacher, grades 1–2*

Horace Mann would surely smile. As Sarine Gureghian's efforts illustrate, the young continue to learn, in school, the knowledge and habits of citizenship. Horace Mann's ideal for the common school, to advance liberty and democracy, persists in spite of dramatic social arguments over what makes up an essential, basic education.

Expanding Visions of Public Schools

Only a century ago, Americans hadn't added much time to their idea of how long it took to learn reading, writing, and arithmetic, and whatever else was needed to be well governed and prosperous. Five years was then considered enough time to prepare children, especially immigrant children, to learn the knowledge and habits necessary for social harmony. Policymakers did not think adolescents needed supervision other than what families and the workplace provided. Only those children interested in a gentleman's education or heading for the professions needed schooling beyond the age of 10 or 11, which they could get in less widely available public or private schools. The twentieth century brought increased years of education as Americans made new demands on schools.

Schools Must Preserve the Culture At the end of the nineteenth century, rapid industrialization, urbanization, and immigration placed incredible new demands on teachers and public schools. Social reformers wanted teachers to become the caretakers for youngsters who roamed footloose on city streets during their parents' long factory hours. Politicians pressed teachers to "Americanize" newcomers—especially immigrants from southern and eastern Europe, who seemed more "foreign" than earlier northern European immigrants. Now, in addition to the rudiments of citizenship and patriotism, students must be taught the habits, values, and language of the predominantly Anglo-Saxon Protestants, who considered themselves the trustees of American culture. When schoolchildren first recited the "Pledge of Allegiance" on Columbus Day in 1892, their teachers were told to have students follow the Pledge by shouting, "One Country! One Flag! One Language!"[1]

Schools Must Support Economic Stability As manufacturing boomed in the early twentieth century, the common school also took on the role of developing "human capital" for the American economy. Industrialists and labor unions asked teachers to prepare students with the skills needed in modern workplaces. Thus, by the 1920s, a major role of schools was to prepare workers with both the specific job skills and the dispositions (e.g., punctuality, following routines) for factory work. However, when the Great Depression in the 1930s made jobs scarce, students began staying in school longer. The once-easy transition from vocational classes to factory jobs disappeared. As the supply of workers outstripped demand, it made sense to conservative politicians and businessmen to cut back on education spending. Teachers' salaries fell and programs considered frivolous—including vocational education—were dropped. Fracturing their friendly alliance with business, reform-minded educators banded together to protect public spending on schools and to place schools at the forefront of economic reform. These "social reconstructionists" wanted schools to help create a new social and economic order, one that would reduce income inequalities and free the nation from the threat of depressions. Educators added social studies courses to the curriculum—some with quite explicit attacks on capitalism—hoping that these courses might prepare students to tackle the social and economic problems of the time. Whereas many progressive labor groups and social reformers supported these mid-century efforts, conservative political interests and business objected to what they saw as a blatant effort to undermine the free-market economy by indoctrinating students with socialist ideas. The two sides parted company over their views about how schools should connect students to the economy, although neither side doubted that control of the common school was key to shaping the nation's economic life.

Schools Must Ensure National Security It was not until midcentury that even a majority of students graduated high school. But by the 1950s a twelve-year education was an important public policy objective. And particularly after 1957, when Russia launched the first space satellite, Sputnik, those twelve years of school were expected to be academically rigorous. The press and politicians, anxious about falling behind the Russians, lambasted the flabby academic courses in American high schools and thrust upon teachers the job of developing the nation's capacity in science and mathematics to support cold war space and defense technology. Unquestionably, American schools demanded too little from all its students; however, mainstream critics neglected to see or mention that America's universities were the envy of the world, and America's elite (white and wealthy) high schools were producing the best and finest students anywhere. Certainly, the *least* likely explanation for America's lagging in space exploration was that America had too few smart scientists. Where it was willing to place its priorities and resources, America was perfectly capable of turning students into well-educated citizens with world-class science and mathematics skills.

Schools Must Solve Social Problems Throughout the twentieth century, society has expected the common school to help solve the social problems stemming from poverty, racism, inequality, urban decay, and the cultural unrest those conditions have brought. In the 1960s and 1970s these expectations increased as reformers began programs for school desegregation, compensatory education, Head Start, along with subsidized breakfast and lunch programs, and other cornerstones of the War on Poverty. Yet by the 1980s not only had the problems not gone away, new, more frightening ones had emerged. So, in the 1980s and 1990s, teachers' list of social responsibilities grew to include combating drug and alcohol abuse, preventing the spread of AIDS, and resolving gang conflicts. New laws required teachers to report evidence of physical and sexual abuse and harassment, including that which might occur on the campus; and they learned to screen students for weapons.

Even as the demands on schools grew, politicians and the public had little appetite for addressing those problems outside of school—increased law enforcement being the exception. Some saw the continued problems related to race and poverty as evidence that the 1960s and 1970s reforms that brought money and programs to bear on the problems had failed. For example, conservative economist Charles Murray argued in his best-selling book *Losing Ground* that these efforts, rather than helping, had created an unhealthy dependence on government assistance, had eroded families, and had undermined individual effort. As a result, during the Reagan and Bush administrations government would no longer "throw money" at correcting the social conditions that had appeared to give rise to social problems and poor school performance. Instead, schools were to provide "character education" and to instill "traditional" values including sexual abstinence outside marriage, disdain for welfare, exercise of will over the temptation of drugs, hard work, respect for public institutions, and so on. This values-based approach, conservatives argued, would restore the moral base to community and family life and enable individuals to solve their own problems. Although teachers' scope of social responsibility grew wider, their efforts were often constrained by requirements to follow narrow, dogmatic, and judgmental approaches to teaching. For example, they were asked to instruct about AIDS, but not mention condoms; teach about drug abuse, but avoid frank and confidential discussions; assert what makes a strong family, but not discuss single parent families or help students understand gay or lesbian parenting.

Schools Must Boost International Competitiveness In 1983 a government-commissioned report, *A Nation at Risk,* blamed public schools for the faltering U.S. economy and reeling national self-esteem in the wake of the 1970s oil crisis. *A Nation at Risk* called for increases in academic courses taken by all high school students: four years of English, and three years each of social studies, science, and mathematics; and it added computer literacy as a "new basic." In 1991 the Secretary of Labor's Commission on Achieving Necessary Skills specified what graduates need to succeed in the labor market and to enhance the nation's economic competitiveness in the tight global market. These workplace skills closely matched those advanced in *A Nation at Risk,* and policymakers and educators increasingly saw workplace preparation and intellectual development as complementary components of common schooling.

More recently, President Clinton elaborated and extended this definition of a competitive American common school. The Clinton-sponsored *Goals 2000: Educate America Act* passed by Congress in 1994 set as a national goal, "the high school graduation rate will increase to at least 90 percent." The Act specified that all students will leave grade 12 "having demonstrated competency over challenging subject matter including English, mathematics, science, foreign languages, civics and government, economics, the arts, history, and geography." It decreed that every school must ensure that all students learn to use their minds well, so they may be "prepared for responsible citizenship, further learning, and productive employment in our nation's modern economy." With much opposition, the Act funded the development of academic standards in a whole range of subject areas that specify what all students need to live and work in the twenty-first century.

As a teacher, I must question everything I do. All my classroom practices must be open to a critical examination. How do issues of race, class, language, and gender influence what I do? How does my classroom resist and perpetuate the institutional, racism, classism, linguicism, and sexism of education and society? I must ask myself who benefits from the structure of my class. Yet with this awareness, must also come action. I must commit myself to multiculturalism and a culturally relevant pedagogy that affirms and legitimizes the language and culture of my students. I must try to create a democratic classroom, where students actively construct their own knowledge. Finally, I must be a teacher who helps students discover their possibilities and urges them to claim their role as transformative members of society.

—Matthew Eide
First-year teacher, high school history

Matthew Eide, like every other teacher, has to solve the technical question "What do I teach on Monday morning?" But he poses other questions for himself that will ultimately determine the success and satisfaction he finds in his career. These are not the questions of beginning teachers but the concerns of every twenty-first-century educator wrestling with the traditions of American schooling.

The American Dilemma: Racial and Economic Privilege and Common Public Schooling

In 1997 President Clinton and the Congress agreed to extend public support for education for all students to include two years of postsecondary education. By the end of the twentieth century, then, college—once reserved for a tiny group of the nation's elite—had become part of the American ideal of a common education.

However, like the reforms that came earlier, the national reform initiatives at the end of the twentieth century expressed no outrage at inequality of opportunities among children of different races and in different communities. Rather, the reports and criticism focused on children's failure to achieve rather than society's failure to provide adequate conditions for learning. The start of the twenty-first century heard George W. Bush's conservative administration declare that it would "leave no child behind." Yet, while decrying the "achievement gap" between races, Bush promised even less than his predecessors to address comprehensively the race-based and income-based inequities that place enormous obstacles in the way of low-income students and students of color.

Actually, Bush's approach—advocating for all students' learning, but not challenging the disparities in resources and opportunities—is also part of the American educational tradition. Most notably, children of slaves were not to be educated at all. Further, even though Jefferson proposed that every nonslave child would have three years of public schooling, only the most "talented" would go to special regional grammar schools at public expense. Of these, educators would select a few for further education. Jefferson reasoned, "By this means twenty of the best geniuses will be raked from the rubbish annually, and be instructed, at the public expense."[2]

A History of White Privilege Long before Jefferson's plan for public schooling, structural inequalities related to race, ideology, and economics kept dim the prospects for common American schools. From the earliest colonial times, many Americans identified their prosperity with confiscated land and slave labor. Annihilation of Indians and the African slave trade were justified both on economic grounds and biblical explanations of white superiority. After the mid–eighteenth century, a new group of modern natural scientists—craniologists—offered empirical evidence, arguing that white superiority rested on racial differences in skull size, with the larger skulls of Caucasians proving their greater capacities. Some argued that hot African climates lulled blacks into inactivity and, over time, decreased their brain and skull size.

When he studied American society in the 1830s, French intellectual Alexis de Tocqueville noted, "The same schools do not receive the children of the black and European."[3] Widespread agreement about the moral and intellectual deficiencies of nonwhites justified denying them citizenship and prohibiting nonwhite landowners from passing property on to their heirs. Many Southern communities passed "compulsory ignorance" laws that banned schooling for slaves. Communities in the North established segregated schools because it was simply unimaginable that white children could be safe from sexual and other physical threats and moral corruption. Thus, by the time Horace Mann described his vision for a common public school, the country already had deep traditions that allowed the government to limit those it would include in the collection of persons called the "public." By the mid–nineteenth century, Darwin's *Origins of the Species* had established that all races were human, but it also spawned new theories of whites as a more highly evolved, cognitively superior, race. Even after the abolition of slavery, most white Americans viewed African Americans as inferior and supported racial segregation.

As the nation expanded westward, new groups were added to the American racial hierarchy, and from time to time groups would be reclassified. Whites migrating to the Southwest judged Mexicans to be "half-civilized" (in comparison to the uncivilized Indians) but "white," due to their Spanish language, Catholicism, and the presence of a property-owning elite that bespoke European as well as Indian heritage. On the other hand, Asian men, imported in the late nineteenth century to build California's railroads and work its mines and farms, joined the ranks of the black slave laborers brought from the American South and were disdained for their strange customs, "pagan" religions, and incomprehensible language. In the mid–nineteenth century, a California court classified the Chinese as Indians and, therefore, "nonwhite." Throughout the nation, laws limited occupational mobility and restricted access to schooling. Supporters of such policies took a Social Darwinist perspective, arguing that the economic and social disadvantage minorities faced stemmed from their genetically limited cognitive and sometimes moral deficiencies.

In 1868 the U.S. government declared "compulsory ignorance" laws illegal and extended citizenship to native-born nonwhites. Schooling, however, remained the province of the states, and states could choose whether or not to fund schools for nonwhite children. In 1896 the Supreme Court decided in

Plessy v. Ferguson that separate public facilities for different races could still be equal and upheld the right of states to segregate racial minorities in schools and other realms of public life. It was not until 1910 that the majority of black children attended school, and it was 1920 before the same was true for Mexican, Asian, and Indian children. Under the *Plessy* decision, they attended segregated schools. In spite of laws that limited freedom and opportunity, discriminated groups learned in rich educational environments, both exclusively within their own cultures and whenever a slight crack appeared in the wall of segregation. However, minorities' lack of prosperity and political power has nearly always limited their publicly supported educational opportunities and their school achievement. In 1944 Swedish social scientist Gunnar Myrdal's massive (more than 1,500 pages) study of race in America concluded that a deeply troubling *American Dilemma* was the fundamental contradiction between the nation's democratic ideology and its pervasive racism.[4]

The 1954 *Brown v. Board of Education* Supreme Court decision overturned the *Plessy* decision, ruling that separate is inherently unequal, and ordered schools to desegregate with "all deliberate speed." However, the initial promise *Brown* held for equal opportunity has never been realized. Today, black students in the United States remain nearly as racially isolated as before *Brown*, and Latino racial isolation increases steadily.[5] Just as good people look back at the pre-*Brown* days and are angered that a society would allow segregated and unequal schools, that cause for anger remains today.

Educating Immigrants and English Learners Every wave of immigrants to the United States has come seeking a new beginning—usually economic, often political. Also, every wave has struggled with the cultural question of how to become American while being so obviously from somewhere else. The current surge in immigration has brought unprecedented numbers of people from Latin America and Asia, many of whom are refugees from political turmoil or the devastation of poverty. Many have come illegally. Today's schools include more that four million students with native languages other than English; about three-quarters of them speak Spanish. Eight states, including California, Florida, Illinois, New York, Texas, Massachusetts, New Jersey, and New Mexico, have large numbers of Latino students.

For the past 100 years, schools have been asked to "Americanize" immigrant children. It is not surprising, then, that the school has also been the focus of the nation's ambivalence about immigration—pitting the principles of an equitable and welcoming society against the fear and hostility that arises out of differences. At the turn of the twentieth century, for example, President Theodore Roosevelt argued that the United States had room for only one language, English, and urged restrictive language policies. Now, in response to our most recent arrivals, several states and communities have sought and some have passed "English only" policies. Some have attempted to exclude undocumented immigrants from schooling, health care, and other public services.

In 1974 the Supreme Court ruled in *Lau v. Nichols* that the right to equal educational opportunity extends to those students not fluent in English. Later court decisions mandated that students be provided with programs to help them learn English, and that these students' language differences must not prevent them from learning academics comparable to their English-speaking peers. The 1994 Equal Educational Opportunities Act requires state departments of education to set standards for programs designed for English learners, and to monitor and enforce those standards. Nevertheless, these protections have faced enormous opposition. For example, the most recent of California's anti-immigrant measures, Proposition 227, prohibited instruction in languages other than English. Proposition 227 and a subsequent regulation requiring that all students take the state's achievement test in English limited teachers' ability to teach the state's large and growing number of students whose primary language is not English. For the most part, these students, like their African American counterparts, find themselves in racially segregated and under-resourced schools.

"Savage Inequalities" In the past thirty years, the geographic division of the nation into poor inner cities and more affluent outer-urban and suburban communities has further undermined the public school. The trends have been for middle-class families—minority and white—to move away from central cities, and for those remaining residents to face problems of unemployment, poverty, and racial isolation, and crumbling schools. Unemployment among black youth remains roughly double that of young whites.

As the new century begins, city smokestack-industry jobs continue to be "downsized," move to the suburbs, go overseas, or disappear entirely. "New economy" jobs in information and high-tech industries are even more difficult for urban youth to break into than the "old economy" factories. By the early 1990s, 97 percent of all new businesses formed were in the suburbs.[6] There are spotty trends for some businesses to move back toward city centers, but often this simply creates pockets of affluence that bring little opportunity to most inner-city residents. Few inner-city residents—especially the large number of newly arrived, hardworking immigrants—qualify for urban white-collar jobs. Most settle for irregular, part-time work in "services" and lack security, benefits, or a "living wage" (this is an income, calculated for each community, which assures that a person working full time will not fall below the poverty line).

For a time, government programs helped. Affirmative action (programs to employ or admit to colleges underrepresented minorities selected from pools of qualified applicants) enabled some minorities to gain access into the middle class and its generally superior schools. However, by 2001 affirmative action had been challenged in the courts and the ballot boxes in many states. Public universities in Texas and California felt the effects of anti-affirmative-action court cases and legislation in the late 1990s, with declines in their enrollments of African Americans and Latinos. Many fear that the U.S. Supreme Court will eliminate such policies altogether.

In the mid- and late 1990s, the centrist Clinton administration found common ground with conservative politicians and instituted significant welfare reforms. These reforms have been hotly debated as to their effect on the overall economy, but certainly they capped a trend to reduce benefits and institute more stringent eligibility requirements for Aid to Families with Dependent Children, food stamps, and other public assistance for poor children. The unprecedented prosperity of the late 1990s was accompanied by a widening gap between rich and poor. Also, more people who are fully employed do not earn enough to keep their families out of poverty (the "working poor"). At the century's end, a quarter of American children lived in poverty.[7]

I had heard horror stories about inner-city schools where the adults were the real culprits. Many days after school my teaching partner and I would walk over to the local community where most of my students live, and make home visits. This opened up a whole new perspective. It was one thing having a David Ferguson in my class. But meeting his parents, seeing the driveway where he hung out, and sitting on his living room couch while his mother admits that she also has trouble reading forces you to change your priorities.

—Janet Kim
First-year teacher, English, grade 7

Janet Kim's experience in a low-income urban neighborhood provides a glimpse of how the circumstances of urban life have profound implications for public schools. Overall, larger proportions of poor and minority children enroll in public schools each year. At the same time, more middle-class whites—often older and more affluent than earlier generations of parents of school-aged children—increasingly choose private education. Some of these seek private schools for the resources, status, and privilege. Others worry that racial integration triggers a decline in school quality, and many others, swayed by dramatic—if exaggerated—accounts of school violence, fear for their children's safety. The withdrawal of vital public support has left many urban schools inadequate and decaying. Contemporary schools, then, remain segregated not only by race but also by social class and family background. In 1997 the Harvard Project on School Desegregation reported that only 5 percent of segregated white schools face conditions of concentrated poverty, compared with 80 percent of segregated black and Latino schools.

The fifth-grade class was relocated into portables in October. The portables are half the size of the regular classroom. There is barely enough room to walk around because all books and supplies are nestled around the perimeter of the room on the floor. There are no cabinets. There are no windows. The district is in such dire financial straits that the teachers can't make photocopies; we don't have overhead projectors, nor do we have enough space for the children.

—Steven Branch
First-year teacher, grade 5

My boys' and girls' bathrooms have been flooded for over two months. Finally, after winter break, I decided that the janitors did not intend to fix anything, so I put in a formal request for work to be done. Last week, after I complained numerous times to the principal and vice-principal, the bathrooms were fixed. So, after two months of sickening smell and slimy scum (literally, the students were walking in slime), the bathrooms were fixed. But the way in which they were fixed was ridiculous. For two days straight, all day long, there was a jackhammer going off in the back of my room. Couldn't they have done this work after 2 p.m.? Or during recess and lunchtime? Or couldn't they at least have given me some advance notice that there was going to be a loud noise going off in my room for two straight days so that I could have made some outdoor plans? I lost two days. Learning can't take place in that sort of environment.

—Jennifer Haymore
First-year teacher, grade 4

Steven Branch's and Jennifer Haymore's experiences in impoverished city school systems are not unique. Jonathan Kozol's wrenching account, *Savage Inequalities,* vividly portrays inequalities that other studies have documented. Kozol found black and Latino students in dilapidated Camden, New Jersey, schools learning keyboarding without computers, science without laboratories, and other subjects without enough textbooks to go around. Seven minutes away in white, affluent Cherry Hill, students enjoyed well-kept facilities, including a greenhouse for those interested in horticulture, abundant equipment, and supplies.[8] Since its publication in the early 1990s Kozol's book has significantly increased the public's awareness of the enormous disparities in the conditions among schools in wealthy and poor communities, and, as we discuss in the following, activists in many states have pursued legal action to correct them.

Restricted Opportunities to Learn In 1997 the *Los Angeles Times* published a humiliating story of textbook shortages in the city's schools. Fremont High School, with mostly Latino, all minority students, reported needing 7,200 textbooks simply to comply with the state law. For its 1,200 tenth graders, Fremont owned only 210 English textbooks. Within a few weeks of the exposé, the newspaper filled with reports of school district money, private donations, action at the state level, and large photos showing stacks of new books at Fremont. The inescapable conclusion was that these stopgap measures solved the problem. Meanwhile, all of Los Angeles's schools faced serious problems. It is difficult to imagine that a school with mostly affluent white students, anywhere, would not have enough books. It is unthinkable that the nation would tolerate a lack of textbooks in an entire urban school district—one of the largest—if its children were white and not poor.[9]

Typically, schools attended by African Americans and Latinos offer very few critical college "gatekeeping" courses such as advanced mathematics and science. In 1999 Rasheda Daniel, a working-class, African American teenager, sued her school district and the State of California for not offering the advanced classes at her high school that she needed to attend the state's university as a science major. Nobody thought she was wrong; and nobody thought she was an isolated case. Daniel's suit prompted the state legislature to provide new funding to schools like hers—mostly in low-income communities and communities of color—to begin offering advanced courses.

But it's not just the lack of rigorous courses that limits students' opportunities. Teachers at schools in low-income communities tend to place less emphasis on having students develop inquiry and problem-solving skills, and they offer fewer opportunities for students to become actively engaged in learning. Making matters worse, students at these schools have fewer well-qualified teachers than their peers at affluent, white, suburban schools. High-poverty and minority schools suffer more teaching vacancies, and principals have a tougher time filling them. In a national study, 47 percent of children in poor schools (not the poorest, where the percentage was even higher) had teachers who lacked college degrees in the subjects they teach.[10] Even when schools in poor neighborhoods make some headway in providing new resources and college prep classes, the rate at which they improve their programs is typically outpaced by more advantaged schools. Even with resource and performance gains, achieving equity is a moving target, and the gaps between the wealthiest schools and the poorest continue to increase.

Within the same school, American students usually do not have a common experience. Educators divide students into ability-grouped classes and track them into programs that prepare them for different post–high-school experiences. Sometimes it is not clear to the students themselves or to their parents which track they are in. For example, while some tracks prepare students for success at four-year colleges, other tracks may offer classes called "college prep" that don't even prepare students for success at a two-year college. Schools separate students in special programs for "gifted" or "learning disabled." Those students who are not "high ability," "college prep," or "gifted" typically have much less exposure to rigorous content, and teachers seldom ask them to grapple with critical thinking or problem solving. Seldom do they experience engaging, hands-on lessons; more often they read texts or fill out worksheets—inactive and alone.[11]

These courses and programs, of course, are followed by all too familiar differences in schooling outcomes. From at least the fourth grade on, African American, Latino, and low-income children lag behind their white and better-off peers. They more often take low-ability and remedial classes, and they drop out of school at higher rates. They consistently score lower on measures of student achievement that schools claim are crucial. Far fewer take college preparatory classes and go on to college; fewer still earn college degrees.[12]

The way that society thinks about and justifies the differential treatment of its poor and nonwhite students has some surprising effects on children in suburban schools. Ironically, in many white, wealthy suburban schools a majority of students are treated as if they belong to an intellectual tier that is below the school's best and brightest students. Although achievement is generally higher in well-off schools, not all the students can be in the uppermost tracks. This means that no matter how competent many or most students at the school might be, many will be painfully aware that they are not the very brightest and that they should not aspire to the most demanding, rigorous education the school offers. Some teachers and principals, however—in well-off and poor schools—resist the tradition of offering a challenging education only to the top few students.[13] Theirs is a struggle worth emulating.

For example, the following poem comes from first-year teacher Jasper Bui's eighth-grade English class. Jasper Bui's class contained a mix of middle-class and poor students; whites, blacks, and Latinos; and high and low achievers—including Shana, an African American girl who, in Jasper's words, "rarely followed classroom rules or completed assignments." Rather than succumbing to low expectations and giving Shana and her classmates a low-level fare of worksheets, memorization, and drills, Bui offered a challenging academic program that connected with his students' lives. According to Bui, "As we studied different ways poets express themselves through metaphor, simile, hyperbole, images, memories, and other poetic techniques, I encouraged students to express their feelings and understandings—to use poetry to explore and to communicate issues that were important to them." His students responded. Shana put together a compelling collection of poems, including the following one.

"My Culture"

When
I think of my culture,
I think of the good things.
I also think about the bad things.
I think about how people make fun of my culture.
When people say, "Eeuuu, look at your hair.
It's all nappy
And kinky."
It makes me want to say,
"I know you aren't talking about my hair,
The curls, Afros, clothes and fashionable styles we wear.
It's the sisters and the brothers struggling for the cause,
Fighting economics, politics and unjust laws."

—Shana, grade 8

Through poetry, Shana was able to succeed in a class where she had always failed. The poetry project helped her to see value in herself and her culture, one of the first steps in fulfilling herself and making a change in society.

—Jasper Hiep Dang Bui
First-year teacher, English, grade 8

School Finance: The Struggle for Equity and Adequacy

Most low-income children and children of color attend schools that spend less than schools serving white students. The differences between states are also considerable. This means that children attending schools in the wealthiest communities in the country receive a public education that costs several times more than what children in the poorest communities receive. How does this happen in a country so committed to equal educational opportunity?

School finance is complicated and deeply embedded in the tradition of local control. Most school funding comes from state and local taxes on property, income, and sales and from state and local bonds. Arcane funding formulas determine how revenues are collected and allocated. School funding depends very heavily on local taxes on property and businesses, so high-wealth communities generate much more money than do low-wealth ones. Even if low-wealth communities tax themselves at higher rates than do high-wealth communities, which is often the case, they have far less money to spend on schools. These resource inequalities are exacerbated by the concentration of students with special and costly educational needs—for example, learning disabilities and language differences—in the lowest wealth areas. Although federal and state programs provide additional "categorical" funding for these students, the extra revenues rarely offset the extra financial burdens borne by school systems serving low-income students. And though the federal government has pursued the goal of educational equity over the past forty years, federal spending constitutes only a small share of schooling dollars—about 6 percent. These federal dollars have done little to equalize spending.

Since the 1970s civil rights lawyers and advocates have sought relief in courts from these resource inequalities, and nearly every state has experienced a fiscal equity lawsuit. Many of these cases have been successful; others have not. However, even the successful cases have not brought much real relief. Courts, reluctant to set specific finance policies, have asked state legislatures to do so. Facing tremendous political pressure to maintain the status quo, most legislatures have failed to make much change. In Texas and Vermont, to name only two states that have tried to equalize resources, prominent citizens have created a furor by denouncing equalization proposals as untenable "Robin Hood" schemes that steal from the rich. In California, a striking courthouse victory—promising a more equitable distribution of school funding—was quickly followed by an equally striking "taxpayer revolt." This resulted in the withdrawal of public support for educational spending. The state's school system was made more equal by the leveling down of spending, but it also plummeted from being one of the most generously funded educational systems in the country to being one of the least.

Discouraged by these results and by an increasing reluctance of federal courts to view unequal funding as a violation of the Constitution, advocates have turned increasingly to the concept of educational "adequacy" as a basis for their claims on behalf of low-income communities. These claims look to state constitutions, which almost always guarantee residents a right to an education.

Rather than seeking to equalize funding, adequacy suits ask for guarantees that each child in the state will have the resources required to meet the state's own standards for an adequate education. This was the basis of the 1989 decision that Kentucky's school system was unconstitutional. Following Kentucky's lead, advocates in several other states have brought similar cases. In a potentially far-reaching decision, a New York judge ordered the state legislature to do whatever it takes to ensure that every New York student has a sound basic education, defined as sufficient numbers of qualified teachers, administrators, and other personnel; appropriate class sizes; adequate and accessible school buildings with sufficient space for classes and curriculum; sufficient and up-to-date books, supplies, libraries, and technologies; suitable curricula, including an expanded platform of programs to help at-risk students by giving them more time "on task"; adequate resources for students with extraordinary needs; and a safe and orderly school environment. Although the New York case is being appealed by the state, it has fueled the hopes of advocates around the nation for more equitable schooling. However, making equity and adequacy a legal requirement is only the first step. Any fundamental and lasting changes must successfully confront powerful myths and metaphors that keep the current unequal status quo firmly in place.

Metaphors and Myths Have Shaped American Schools

Americans have constructed an odd mix of ideologies that both support and undermine their commitment to public schools. These ideologies, taken together, help explain how Americans can love all their children and want them to prosper while maintaining institutions and social structures that guarantee that some children won't. Nineteenth-century sociologist Max Weber used the term "ideology" to identify the self-serving interpretation of reality that powerful groups in societies use to make their dominance seem legitimate and that preserves social cohesion in face of clear inequalities. For an ideology to "work," both the powerful and those without power must believe that the distribution of power (and the benefits that result from power) is legitimate or inevitable. In the following sections, we explore four related ideologies—revolving around the myths of merit, scientific efficiency, competition, and progress—that characterize American culture and schooling and prevent society and schools from realizing their democratic possibilities. Teachers who sense the omnipresence of ideology—including their own—enlarge their ability to interpret the world of their schools and to succeed in their daily work.

The Myth of Merit: "Any Child Can Grow Up to Be President"

One source of enormous national pride has been that Americans, unlike their more aristocratic European cousins, forged a fair culture in which individual ability and determination, rather than wealth or personal connections, hold the key to success and upward mobility. This is what Gunnar Myrdal in 1944 called the "American Creed." It is also what Jay McLeod describes as the myth of merit in his book *Ain't No Makin' It,* which tells the story of the hopes and disappointments of young men growing up in a low-income neighborhood. As McLeod puts it:

> "Any child can grow up to be President." So says the achievement ideology, the reigning social perspective that sees American society as open and fair and full of opportunity. In this view, success is based on merit, and economic inequality is due to differences in ambition and ability. Individuals do not inherit their social status; they attain it on their own. Since education insures equality of opportunity, the ladder of social mobility is there for all to climb. A favorite Hollywood theme, the rags-to-riches story resonates in the psyche of the American people. We never tire of hearing about Andrew Carnegie, for his experience validates much that we hold dear about America, the land of opportunity. Horatio Alger's accounts of the spectacular mobility achieved by men of humble origins through their own unremitting efforts occupy a treasured place in our folklore. The American Dream is held out as a genuine prospect for anyone with the drive to achieve it.[14]

McLeod, of course, notes that "for every Andrew Carnegie" there are uncountable hardworking and able others who fare much less well, and that most Americans wind up in positions similar to their parents.

Do Ambition and Hard Work Really Matter Most? Like most myths, this one draws its strength from the grain of truth embedded in it. Among those students who have the resources, opportunities, and connections that come with privilege, the more ambitious and hardworking may well go farther than those who simply do okay in school. Nothing said here belittles the ineffable qualities of character, ambition, or even charisma. However, these meritorious qualities occur with no less frequency in low-income families and among blacks, Latinos, and immigrants. Yet these groups cannot parlay these qualities into economic success to the same degree that middle-class and wealthy whites can. (In fact, it is entirely possible that ambition and charisma without legitimate opportunity lead to decidedly antisocial outcomes when more legitimate paths to success are blocked.) When it comes to explaining "success," ability and ambition are often important, but that is not all there is to it.[15] Americans' belief that success in school (and life) follows from ability and aspirations masks the reality that schooling, within the broad social structure, favors children from privileged families.

In 1962 Michael Harrington's influential book *The Other America: Poverty in the United States* documented a huge underclass of unemployed and working poor.[16] He argued that this underclass, contrary to popular view, was not an artifact of temporary economic conditions. Rather, increasing numbers of people were locked into lifelong and intergenerational webs of poor education, housing, nutrition and health care, and more. Harrington's book arrived at the end of the post–World War II period of optimism and growth. These years were filled with unsettling discord, including the start of the cold war, America's

McCarthy-era political repression, and the Korean War. They were also years of undisputed American political and economic world dominance and unprecedented prosperity. The 1954 *Brown v. Board of Education* decision made it easy for those who saw themselves as fair-minded to feel satisfied that racial prejudice and the economic disparities that accompanied it were being addressed. In reality, by the 1960s the nation had made little progress toward a desegregated society. Most Americans were shocked and many were favorably disposed to social action when Harrington's book revealed that the national prosperity and well-being had missed or disillusioned so many. How could it be that such a large segment of society simply did not "earn" better conditions?

Inequalities associated with gender, social class, and age began to shape the social conscience and enrich the climate of social change. Women took stock of their lack of opportunity, their silenced perspectives, their physical domination, their lower wages, and more. College students reacted to what seemed to be a hypocritical gap between their lessons in democracy and the limits that college campuses placed on their free speech. When the student protesters wouldn't back down, they were both confused and energized by the power and force that their college administrators and state governors brought against them. Television viewers were horrified when nightly news programs exposed the dramatic violence of racism and, later, the horrible carnage of the Vietnam War. Nothing in most Americans' experience and little in our national rhetoric prepared the nation to witness how abusive some Americans with power could be. The American social fabric seemed to be disintegrating, and with it, the notion that Americans get what they deserve.

Can We Level the Educational Playing Field? It had become clear that regardless of their merit, some people could never overcome the disadvantages with which they began. It was as if they were playing on a field tilted in their opponents' favor—they might kick or throw farther and run faster, but their efforts reaped fewer positive results because the work was all uphill. It was time to fix what ailed the country—to repair the ideology of merit.

From the mid-1960s until 1980, the federal government pursued social policies designed to make the playing field level.[17] Civil rights and War on Poverty legislation sought to remedy the hunger, inadequate housing, and discrimination that diminish the power of ambition, effort, and school achievement. Other measures aimed directly at creating equal educational opportunity and making schools more powerful for disadvantaged children. Some of the better ideas and programs included free school lunches to the very poor, Head Start preschools for low-income children, funds to support desegregation, and extra academic programs for low-achieving poor children.

The War on Poverty did slow the widening gap between rich and poor—if only briefly. Programs fed hungry children and provided important learning experiences. However, they barely scratched the surface of the problems of poverty and unequal schooling. Moreover, the country lacked experience and expertise in formulating and administering antipoverty programs and equity-minded interventions, and national politics provided little room for error. When programs faltered or needed reworking, skeptics judged them as failures. Most pernicious of all, many well-off Americans saw "the problem" as poor people themselves rather than the social and economic conditions that made them poor. The country was not prepared to concede that larger social and economic structures, including schools, had to change fundamentally, and that the necessary changes would be costly and difficult.

Not surprisingly, the War on Poverty did not make the problems of poverty and inequality go away, and new, unanticipated problems emerged. Children, their families, and the institutions that tried to help them, such as schools, shouldered most of the blame. Today, many look back on this short-lived but significant national effort on behalf of the poor and interpret its disappointing results using the myth of merit. If the poor and poorly educated did not lift themselves with the aid of the national programs, then the fault lies with them and with their misguided helpers.

Others invoke the fact that some African Americans and Latinos achieve stellar successes in school despite the combined burdens of racism and poverty. Thus, a theoretically possible outcome—hammered home by highly touted examples—obscures what is actually possible for most children. For every General Colin Powell, there are thousands of black and Latino men and women whose success and achievements have been diminished by racial and meritocratic thinking. It strains credibility, however, to suggest that the few who manage to succeed under unlikely or miserable conditions provide evidence that *anyone* can succeed, and if they do not, it is their own fault. Yet that's exactly where the myth of merit leads.

When Merit Makes Inequality Acceptable Why does our culture support the convoluted logic that failure to "overcome" poverty or inferior education proves a lack of merit? The answer may be that people prefer believing that their own wealth stands on a moral platform of merit. Also, like many ideologies, the myth of merit depends on *everyone* believing in the myth just as strongly as those who benefit from it. Many poor and nonwhite Americans also believe schooling benefits are equally accessible to all. Students with dismal schooling experiences typically blame their own lack of ability, effort, or failure to take advantage of opportunities. Describing "the Brothers"—the young African Americans he studied—Jay McLeod put it this way:

> They blame themselves for their mediocre academic performances because they are unaware of the discriminatory influences of tracking, the school's partiality toward the cultural capital of the upper classes, the self-fulfilling consequences of teachers' expectations, and other forms of class-based educational selection. Conditioned by the achievement ideology to think that good jobs require high academic attainment, the Brothers may temper their high aspirations, believing not that the institution of school and the job market have failed them, but that they have failed themselves.[18]

In sum, merit permeates how Americans make sense about schooling—emphasizing the role of the individual, and de-emphasizing the responsibilities of school or society.

The Factory Metaphor—Making Schools Efficient

In the twentieth century, Americans sought to reach their idealistic goals by imposing tough-minded management practices borrowed from captains of industry. Schools inherited the factory model of production from theories about managing large-scale industrial production scientifically and efficiently—theories that revolutionized the workplace.

The Lure of the Assembly Line Industrial efficiency caught the public's imagination through the writings of Frederick Winslow Taylor and the example of Henry Ford. Taylor recommended time-and-motion studies to set standards of performance. Basing their practices on careful record keeping, managers established the "best methods," which replaced the rule-of-thumb approaches that workers had developed over time. Managers trained and supervised workers and were themselves trained in techniques of scientific control and efficiency. People called the techniques scientific because they were systematic and precise and allowed few individual judgments and little variability. Factory owners and managers centralized decision making and authority at the top, divided labor by specializing tasks, and governed every aspect of the enterprise with rules, regulations, and an impersonal (more efficient) attitude toward the individual. Ford's assembly-line autoworkers were easily trained and supervised by managers who used standardized methods to perform small tasks. In this way "Fordism" became the apex of scientific production and management.

By World War I school administrators began using similar methods to cope with problems facing schools. Immigration and urbanization had changed schools dramatically. Not unlike today, these shifts caught educators and politicians unprepared. Almost overnight, educators became responsible for providing eight to twelve years of education for large numbers of students—many of whom were immigrants.

As schools grew larger and more expensive, politicians, industrialists, and social reformers criticized them for their inefficient methods and dubious success. Many critics suggested that, like workers in all large enterprises, teachers could achieve greater success under factory-like management systems. University professors and school administrators set about conducting the same types of scientific studies of schools that Taylor had done in industry, and they developed schemes for making schools run more like efficient factories. To mention just a few of these new efficiencies, schools divided their large auditorium-like spaces for a hundred or more students into today's familiar classrooms that separate students by ages and subjects. Texts such as readers and spellers proliferated, making it possible to standardize curriculum. Colleges began to specify sequences of courses that would prepare students for admission. Normal schools (the first teacher education institutions) started training teachers in correct and efficient teaching methods.

Scientific Managers and the Feminization of Teaching Most educators of the day were not far removed from the dusty schoolmasters of earlier times. They undoubtedly knew something about different school subjects and about children from farms and small towns. Yet most were unprepared to run large, cost-effective operations involving hundreds or thousands of students. Many educators were staggered by the diversity of newly arrived southern and eastern European immigrants and viewed them as having educational and social deficits far more severe than those of other Americans. Industrial efficiency seemed to be the answer. Educators embraced scientific methods to impose order and rationality. As in business, people believed that the efficiency movement would produce school products—educated adults—at the lowest costs. In later years, this product would become even more scientifically standardized, and school "productivity" would be measured in test scores. Thus, there could be a standard for knowing when schools were successful.

Education administrators of the early 1900s, especially those in urban areas, relished scientific management partly because it cast them in the role of the expert and enhanced their personal status and political clout. A concurrent shift in the teaching force fit well with the new arrangement in which experts (school administrators) supervised low-skilled, low-paid workers (teachers). Increasingly, women, who would work for less money, who would not move on to better jobs, and who were thought to be "naturally" more nurturing, filled more of the teaching jobs. Men were principals, superintendents, and members of school boards; they were teachers of older students in elite schools and of subjects that required academic training.

Scientific management and the feminization of teaching combined to differentiate jobs, status, and authority and helped create today's bureaucratic schools and classrooms. Schools today still separate students into classes by age, grade, and ability. Most teachers teach all of the students in the room simultaneously—the same material at the same pace in the same way. Curriculum specialists, school district administrators, and even state legislators, acting like factory production designers, design the curriculum sequences and instructional processes for teachers and students to follow, subject by subject, grade by grade. Everyone specializes. One is a reading specialist, one is a third-grade teacher, one teaches social studies, and another is a giftedness expert. The various parts—skills and subjects—require careful administrative coordination to keep running smoothly. Report cards provide an efficient, if uninformative, shorthand of letter grades and checklists that sum up and communicate students' learning to parents. Standardized achievement tests (e.g., the Comprehensive Test of Basic Skills [CTBS], Iowa Test of Basic Skills, California's SAT 9; Texas's TAAS, etc.) report productivity with precision, if with little depth of understanding, to the "bosses" on school boards and in state legislatures, as well as "consumers" such as parents, real estate marketers, and so forth. The list of ways that today's schools are run like factories and, more generally, businesses, could go on and on.

Efficiency: From Judging Schools to Judging Students Certainly, some grudging credit is due the educators who attempted to apply scientific management to schools. Generally, educators coupled the new efficiencies with efforts to bring more and better education to greater numbers of citizens than most other countries could have imagined. However, scientific management styles and attitudes are as much responsible for promoting educational mediocrity as with remedying inefficiency. The legacy of scientific management is schools that are often huge and impersonal, rule dominated, slow to change, and top-heavy with administration.

Beginning in the 1960s, schools had to meet a heightened standard of cost-effectiveness. Do the time and money spent on actual practices and programs contribute to student outcomes such as academic achievement or job readiness? Do lower class sizes pay off? Do free lunches improve student performance? Increasingly, policymakers began to weigh the value of school expenditures in terms of the gains they produced in student outcomes.

Is Equity Cost-Effective? This refinement of scientific management in schools came about quite unexpectedly. Hoping that public schools could address problems of racial discrimination and poverty, the federal government in the 1960s commissioned sociologist James Coleman to survey educational opportunity. The government wanted to know the extent to which schools were racially segregated and whether resources and less tangible aspects of schooling, such as teacher morale, were distributed evenly across schools. Coleman and his team decided to augment the survey by investigating the relationship between these various educational "opportunities" and student achievement. They focused on determining whether countable school resources, such as buildings, library resources, teachers' qualifications, class size, and so on, were related to achievement test scores. Coleman hoped this approach would reveal just how inequalities in opportunities led to the educational gaps between well-off and poor students and between whites and students of color.

The study's findings surprised even Coleman. His now famous "Coleman Report" concluded that though there were differences in tangible school resources, they really *did not* matter. For example, more books in the library did not affect how poor and nonwhite students did in school. Also, better-trained teachers did not close the gap between high- and low-achieving schools. But if not resources, what then? The report argued that school resources matter far less than the students themselves—that is, their race and their parents' income and education. Family background seemed to determine how well students do at school.

Coleman was wrong. He failed to understand in this first report that most features of schooling that benefit students, taken one by one, are *helpful, but not sufficient,* to transform their education. For example, simply reducing class size may not be *sufficient* to improve educational outcomes if teachers continue to teach in the same ways as before. On the other hand, smaller classes are sure *helpful* if teachers take advantage of them to improve teaching methods and spend more time with individual students. Instead of understanding schools as complex human systems that could improve with attention to resources *and* democratic values and local politics, Coleman studied schools as if they were technical puzzles that could be solved one piece at a time.

Most policy analysts interpreted Coleman's findings through the lens of scientific management as well. His work seemed to argue that providing more resources for schools is inefficient and wasteful, since they are unlikely to improve schools' productivity. The study and recommendations appealed to policymakers who were more than willing to identify small problems or inefficiencies one by one and see what was cost-effective to invest in solving. Coleman's legacy continues. More than a generation of research and public policy have looked at educational "inputs" and "outcomes" to decide what is worth spending money on. Schools have tried to economically "spot-fix" or target specific school deficits without wasting money on things that couldn't be proven to raise test scores—the one outcome that has emerged in the public mind as really mattering. Invariably, proposals for increased spending on schools—whether to repair dilapidated buildings, increase teachers' salaries, reduce class size, or buy textbooks and materials—are greeted with an objection grounded solidly in the tradition of scientific efficiency. Policymakers shouldn't "throw money" at schools' problems, the argument goes, since the things money can buy don't really matter.

The Market Metaphor—Excellence through Competition and Choice

As schools struggled to meet the educational and social challenges of the 1960s and 1970s, traumatic events also were shaking American business. Business had been responding to changing world conditions and to national expectations with ever-greater reliance on rational, scientific bureaucracies and piecemeal changes. As with schools, it wasn't working very well. In the mid-1970s, upheaval in the Middle East created severe oil shortages. Images of American cars waiting in long, slow lines for rationed gas served as a wake-up call for American business and industry—and, eventually, to schools as well.

The demise of the belief that the United States completely dominated the global marketplace was powerfully symbolized by the Japanese and German car manufacturers who moved quickly to supply the American market with small, less thirsty alternatives to the Detroit gas guzzlers. These foreign competitors easily outpaced rigid, hierarchical Ford, GM, and Chrysler—companies whose highly rationalized approach to the organization of work and management made them extraordinarily slow to notice, let alone respond to, the crisis. American business finally did adapt to these new conditions, but slowly and in their uniquely American way.

American versions of the popular Japanese-style management designs included cooperative work teams, employee flextime, and paying closer attention to the ideas of workers. These ideas made strong inroads into Taylor's scientific management in business rhetoric and increasingly in business practices. Some of these innovations were implemented and judged successful; some were not. In most cases, however, they were driven and judged by the "bottom line." New management practices were worth doing only if they enhanced businesses' ability to compete and garner profits that might otherwise go to competitors. By the end of the 1990s, schools' own "bottom lines" were undergoing some slight shifts. Test scores mattered for their own sake, but increasingly, the "profit" of schooling was being measured, particularly by parents, in terms of whether grades and scores gained their children competitive advantage for admission into prestigious universities. These trends dampened enthusiasm for schools to adopt noncompetitive and less bureaucratic practices.

"A Nation at Risk" By the 1980s the percentage of Americans with high school diplomas had risen dramatically. This could have been heralded as a great educational success story, but it was not to be. Many business and political leaders explained the nation's perceived fall from world economic dominance by placing much of the blame on schools. At the same time, many believed education reform could help restore it.

The text of the 1983 *A Nation at Risk*—issued from the White House—leaves no doubt about the harshness of the judgment. In the twentieth century, no words uttered about schools were so widely quoted or so influenced the nation's perception of schools as these:

> Our Nation is at risk. Our once unchallenged preeminence in commerce, industry, science and technological innovation is being overtaken by competitors throughout the world. . . . The educational foundations of our society are presently being eroded by a rising tide of mediocrity that threatens our very future as a nation and a people. . . . If an unfriendly foreign power had attempted to impose on America the mediocre educational performance that exists today, we might well have viewed it as an act of war. As it stands we have allowed this to happen to ourselves. . . . We have, in effect, been committing an act of unthinking, unilateral, educational disarmament.[19]

"The Manufactured Crisis" Professors David Berliner and Bruce Biddle argue persuasively in their award-winning book *The Manufactured Crisis* that these hostile charges against schools were largely untrue, and that the critics deliberately ignored, distorted, and suppressed evidence that contradicted their conclusions.[20] Nevertheless, the highly placed school critics found a receptive public audience when they held schools to the same yardstick as business—excellence and mediocrity defined in terms of international competition. School critics gave enormous credence to international comparisons of eighth- and twelfth-grade students' scores on mathematics tests administered by a consortium of privately funded researchers in thirty-one countries at the beginning of the 1980s. Critics claimed that these comparisons proved that the U.S. education system lagged far behind other "highly developed" counties and many developing ones. Perhaps most disturbing in Berliner and Biddle's analysis is that "competitiveness" emerges as a substitute for fairness and as a justification for inequality.

With little evidence or logic, many education critics looked at two trends—the "decline" in school achievement and the decline in national economic preeminence—and decided that they were partly caused by an emphasis on equity issues such as desegregation and compensatory education. Schools were told that they must find new ways to raise test scores and improve students' achievements. Schools were told that their poor students and students of color must do better, but programs designed to help them do that were cut back. Wealthy communities vigorously fought efforts to equalize money and resources between rich and poor schools. Despite the Coleman study, people of wealth somehow knew that resources did matter and helped their children compete for jobs and admission to good colleges.

The New Competition: Optimism and Concern By the late 1990s America's overall prosperity was soaring again, with at least some credit due to the deft responses by American business. Many bureaucratic organizations had been replaced by more flexible staffing patterns, patterns of production, and labor markets. Niche marketing had replaced some large-scale mass production. Seeking to beat the global competition with quicker turnaround times and lowered labor costs, many industries had adopted new employment practices; for example, operating with smaller core workforces. Companies today rely on more fluid job descriptions and on temporary workers who replace salaried workers. And they "outsource" or contract significant portions of their product lines to other businesses, often to foreign manufacturers or businesses that pay lower wages.

The revolution in manufacturing is matched, if not outpaced, by the accelerated speed at which information, goods, and people travel. This trend liberates many from strictly local goods and ideas and allows small-scale enterprises to compete alongside large, centralized businesses. Complete businesses now operate out of single rooms in people's homes, and the human connections necessary for commerce are electronic instead of face-to-face. Students who formerly crowded into libraries after classes now log on to information sources in complete privacy or, some would say, isolation. These are indeed very different interaction processes than the previous ones.

However, the national prosperity and changes in work have not been kind to everyone. Amid reports of declining unemployment, many American workers are underemployed, have reduced hours, less job security, and fewer health benefits because of practices that businesses believe are necessary to be competitive. Data from the 2000 census reveal that more than eleven million children still have no medical insurance, and increasing numbers of adults are working more hours to make ends meet. Too little attention is paid to the cross-generational effects that these macro employment trends have on schooling, and the new round of challenges that teachers are asked to meet in classrooms. Even less attention is paid to the serious challenge to common schooling brought about by these events; namely, the increasing school opportunity gap for students that follows the increasing income gap of their parents.

Vouchers, Magnets, and Privatization Cures for low-achieving schools follow some of the same trends that manufacturing and business are following. These include deregulation and local control, accountability based on productivity (to be judged with tests of the quality of schooling outcomes), niche marketing, competition and choice, and increased privatization. As essential public enterprises, the public continues to hold schools strictly accountable for becoming more effective and more competitive. Get-tough policies in many states and schools dictate that failing schools be "taken over" by the state or "reconstituted" (current administrators and teachers removed and replaced by a new staff) by the school district. Thus, schools start the twenty-first century hearing a mixed reform message. Decentralization and deregulation promise to free schools from bureaucratic control and open up possibilities for innovative practice. Yet schools had better do well on external standards and traditional measures of achievement in comparison with other schools. Those that don't face public embarrassment, or worse. While many in schools and business struggle mightily to define and achieve "quality," "satisfaction," "security," "contributions to society," and a host of other intangible values, the surest guide to doing the "right thing" remains doing better than the others.

This desire to do better embodies the strength of the marketplace, of free enterprise, and of capitalism. However, in the late twentieth century, the accelerating confidence in competition and market forces brought proposals that would set schools loose from their connection to the larger community of public schools—proposals that threaten the public school itself. For example, one of the great schooling controversies of the new century is whether government should allow parents greater choice in where their children go to school. Some reformers advocate voucher plans where students take the government's financial support with them to the school of their choice. Others see hope in charter schools that operate independently from existing school districts and many laws. Many school districts promote magnet schools—schools with a special mission that attract students from many neighborhoods, often for the purpose of desegregation. Most magnet and charter schools are smaller, more autonomous, more responsive organizations than conventional schools. Their advocates hope that freedom from central authority and regulation will foster healthy competition and increase the quality of all schools. Parents typically play a much more important role in guiding these schools than they have in traditional schools. The logic is that with parents in charge—rather than big education bureaucracies—schools would move toward higher quality or lose their market share of students.

The marketplace theory behind these programs (to be sure, there are also other ways that people defend them) is that the most successful will thrive, and those that do a poor job will disappear. Skeptics point out, however, that in the traditional marketplace of goods and services, harmful or wasteful products do not necessarily disappear or improve but are often the most popular. "Rational choice," according to some social theorists, is a local and individual matter. For example, some parents might choose to send their children to a neighborhood school even though its test score averages are low and its resources limited. For these parents, having their children close to home instead of going to a neighborhood of strangers may be rational. Other parents might choose to send their children across town, in part because that is where the mayor's daughter attends. For them, this is rational input for their decision making.[21]

Finally, some point out that public schools are the strongest voice in society for the *common* good. Where else is there an entire profession with the goal of giving the best possible treatment to everyone, irrespective of whether they have a constituency that can support its own special school? They point out that free marketplace competition in a democracy *requires* common schools so that individuals can compete on even ground when they enter the market.

In short, teachers and the public must look both closely and broadly at any "noncommon" school. If the school thrives because of its focused sense of purpose and community, it may benefit its students *and* the community. But if the school's strength results from winning the local competition for scarce educational resources (i.e., support from politically powerful parents, money, and highly qualified teachers), then the community will soon suffer. If schools of choice succeed because their students forge closer links with the widest cross section of adults and other students in their communities, then they should be emulated for that reason. But if they serve elite or isolated interests that further divide communities, they will not serve social justice.

The Myth of Progress

Throughout the world's cultural and intellectual history, people have sought large, overarching, organizational principles to help make sense of the world. Whether from God, king, nature, science, humans' own intellect, or from political or economic systems, people have looked to consistent systems of thought and rules that freed them from meaningless chaos. American traditions and institutions, including schools, were born out of *modern* systems of thought that developed with the eighteenth-century European period known as the Enlightenment. The nation was founded as Western thought turned increasingly to science and reason as central organizing processes.

Much of the logic of modernism and modern progress involves bringing more and more of life's variables—in manufacturing, in warfare, in learning, and even in human relationships—under control. In this sense, progress is cumulative, with each generation becoming better because it controls more. As a nearly inexhaustible font of inspiration and optimism, a belief in progress imagines the present moment to be a high point that is built on past achievements and is destined to proceed in an ever-improving, incremental advance.

The God of Reason and Progress Benjamin Franklin, Thomas Jefferson, and other intellectuals at the time of the country's founding were influenced by deism, a religious perspective that saw God as the rational architect of an orderly world. After the initial work of creation, God had little to do with the day-by-day (or eon-by-eon) operations of the universe. Something like a "Master Watchmaker," God created a perfect mechanism and left the universe to run on its own. God was similarly absent from the daily affairs of people. Every human was born with all necessary spiritual knowledge, making the teachings of any church unnecessary. Only human reason was necessary to gain access to spiritual and physical truths. Of course, while the universe was complete and orderly, human reason was incomplete and imperfect. Thus, the modern era began, characterized by beliefs that humans, imperfect though they are, can, through science and reason, discover, organize, and control for their own benefit and enlightenment the mysteries of the universe and human existence.

Science and Reason Are the Instruments of Progress From the nation's beginning, schools have been at the center of efforts to create social progress out of change and upheaval. The main social task of common schools in the early nineteenth century was to impart to youth values such as honesty, civic loyalty, hard work, and charity—all considered essential for national unity, republican government, and social progress. Schools at the turn of the twentieth century sought to assimilate immigrants and teach the habits and skills needed for factory work. Throughout the twentieth century the country's middle- and upper-class decision makers would look back on their own education and conclude that schools had served them well (though they might feel that many other Americans did not take advantage of schools). Thus, while praise for American schools has never been extravagant, at midcentury Americans expected schools to be the primary place where social cohesion and progress were fashioned. And if the schools themselves were broken, rational and scientific methods, the instruments of progress, must be brought in to fix them.

It was in this tradition that the federal government, in the 1960s, asked James Coleman to study the problems of urban poverty, social protest, and racial insurrection in the cities. Just as advanced technology, physical science, and medical science could build roads and bridges, win wars, and cure polio, advanced social science and theory should be able to study, diagnose, and offer relief from social problems.

One of the more startling of Coleman's findings, presented in the previously mentioned Coleman Report, was that while more resources did not improve the education of African Americans, their achievement was higher when they attended the same schools as whites. Coleman and others proposed a host of reasons for African Americans doing better in integrated schools. None of the theories or explanations was ever entirely satisfactory, but most had one element in common. Somehow, "doing better" had more to do with the presence of white children than anything having to do with the tangible schooling needs of African Americans. Since most students in the country attended segregated schools, the study proposed that racial integration could improve African Americans' chances simply by placing them in schools that had white students. This conclusion boosted support for the federal government's and the courts' roles in busing students to equalize opportunities for black and white students.

The Ideology of Progress Ten years later, Coleman again reported—this time finding that court-ordered school integration actually produced few benefits and that it caused "white flight." Coleman had found that whites were moving to neighborhoods where neither their own children would be bused out nor black students would be bused in. What happened?

Coleman and the government went after progress for African American students while ignoring the country's entrenched beliefs about merit, competition, and efficiency. They approached segregation and desegregation as if they were technical problems, not ideological ones. Social change in the form of progress for the poor and minorities upset perceptions of the balance, or rather, imbalance, of relative social privilege. According to prevailing beliefs, "efficient" progress should be smooth, orderly, and quick, and not disrupt or frighten those who did not see themselves as part of the problem. Progress should not upset the relative social positions and privileges for those who believed their greater merit is what earned them their advantages. It didn't take long for many powerful Americans to make clear that desegregating schools was not their idea of progress. Conservatives in Nixon's and later administrations combined the results from Coleman's two studies. They argued against "wasting" money on resources that did not improve schools, and they argued against integration because it caused widespread social disruptions—primarily white protests. Scientific studies, they claimed, provided the proof.

Coleman and those who acted on his conclusions were guided by their ideology, not by the clear data. Racial integration, in fact, has brought considerable benefits to children of color who attended desegregated schools, particularly in terms of better life chances. They develop higher aspirations and know better how to achieve them. They are more likely to choose to go to racially integrated colleges and have greater educational attainment. As adults, they are more likely to be working in white-collar and professional jobs in the private sector, and to have racially mixed social and professional lives. Researchers Amy Stuart Wells and Robert Crain have concluded that school desegregation can indeed help "break the cycle of segregation and allow non-white students access to high-status institutions and the powerful social networks within them."[22] As such, desegregated schools seem to lead to the social progress the government had intended. However, no one should assume that students of color benefit simply because they are on the same campus as white students. More likely, the benefits come from the available resources, qualified teachers, and school cultures that expect and make possible higher aspirations and achievement.

A Crisis of Modernity By the 1970s signs of disillusionment with the ideology of twentieth-century progress were everywhere. Disillusionment was evident when the struggle for civil rights—a struggle benefiting from American political progress—ended with success for some and despair for many. It was obvious in the cynical "tune in, turn on, drop out" response of affluent white young people who, in an earlier generation, would have been eager college students. It rang loud and clear in the continued carnage of the Vietnam War, and in the anger of returning Vietnam War veterans who were greeted as dupes rather than heroes. The blows to the ideology of progress continued into the 1980s in the form of economic excesses and upheavals. Progress brought vast, highly publicized wealth to a few and slow decline to many. In *The Work of Nations,* former Secretary of Labor Robert Reich referred to these events, together with the changing world economy, as "the centrifugal forces of the global economy which tear at the ties binding citizens together."[23]

In recent years the advent of "informational democracy" has speeded up many Americans' disillusionment, making it undeniably clear that not everyone benefits from the dominant, traditional notion of progress, and that many are clearly oppressed by it. Television, universal education, travel, immigration, and the Internet provide evidence to vast numbers of people that the failings of progress around the world are often as profound as the advances, and sometimes the two are indistinguishable. At home, Americans have also recognized other examples of progress that bring questionable or mixed benefits. A college student thrills her family by being the first in the family to graduate. However, her job prospects may not be greater than an older generation of nongraduates who had better opportunities to enter the labor force after high school. A bookstore chain opens a new megastore, drawing sales from much smaller independent stores, forcing some to close. In the end, the selection of books for sale in the community narrows. A new highway opens, making affordable suburban housing accessible to the city. However, in a few years homeowners are spending long hours commuting in heavy traffic.

More and more Americans recognize that they do not or cannot make democratic choices about how progress will affect them. This recognition has led to cynicism and despair.

Hope and Struggle in a Postmodern World

Recent cultural, technical, and population trends, including technology's virtual shrinking of the globe and the increased diversity of the U.S. population, call into question basic social premises. Few advocate overorganized, bureaucratized, centralized, standardized factories and schools, and everyone welcomes flexible organizations that are responsive to human needs and efficient production. Yet high-quality work lives, a living wage, dignity, equity, and society's needs for community and a common school experience do not take care of themselves as natural outcomes of marketplace competition and laissez-faire government. These are matters that individuals and groups must struggle to enact.

Analysts from many different disciplines now view the linear nineteenth- and twentieth-century habits of thought borne of the "scientific method" as *one* of many ways of knowing, not the *only* way. Thus, we can no longer be so certain (or arrogant) about what is progress for others, and what seems good to others, or even what is real to others. Multiple versions of truth and goodness might be credible not only to different people but also to ourselves. Little by little, formerly unquestioned modern and Western ideas of universal truths, regularity, and progress are giving way to a *postmodern* emphasis on particularity, difference, and unpredictability.

But in the midst of well-justified worry, concern, and outrage, the twenty-first century also brings signs of an energizing hopefulness. The abundant daily evidence that the old fixed truths and habits are open to investigation emboldens groups and individuals to mount democratic challenges to the status quo. Groups are acting to liberate themselves and to liberate others in the process—this is an ideology of progress far different from one based on merit and competition. Feminist writers and theorists help women see that oppressive husbands and underemployment are not the natural order of the universe and autonomy and dignity are worth struggling for, if not easily achieved. The gay community rebels against hate crimes and more subtle discrimination, signaling to gays everywhere to defy conventional notions of power and progress in order to live dignified and fulfilled lives. Asian Americans upset notions of the "quiet minority" with militancy and active political engagement. Hope sustains their commitment to social justice, and struggle energizes their rejection of the dominant ideology of progress.

Doing Democracy Is the Alternative to Myths and Metaphors

As people come to understand the limits of the *modern* ideologies of merit, scientific efficiency, competition, and progress, they are also finding new ways to express and act on the positive and necessary human desire for betterment. Educational philosopher James Garrison reminds us that when John Dewey struggled with this problem early in the century, he distinguished between two different views of progress. Dewey denounced the conventional view of progress as a "false idea of growth or development that is a movement toward a fixed goal." For Dewey, the sense of "growth . . . as *having* an end instead of *being* an end," was purely illusion.[24] In contrast, Dewey argued that *being progressive* can focus efforts on the *process* of making the world better and on ensuring that the process is a good one. Hope rests on today's processes of working to change the world, rather than on the promise of a better world somewhere in the future. Importantly, being progressive in this sense is not an open-ended invitation to do whatever one feels like doing as long as it feels good. To the contrary, Dewey places heavy responsibility on progressive processes. He insists that the process of human betterment be democratic—not the "majority-rules" democracy, which certainly has its place, but "democracy in terms of dialogue and communication." According to Dewey, "A democracy is more than a form of government; it is primarily a mode of associated living, of conjoint community experience."[25]

Cornel West, professor of theology and Afro-American Studies at Harvard argues for a "prophetic pragmatism" that combines faith in democratic processes with a "critical temper." West argues that, in diverse cultures such as the United States, any democratic process must place its faith in "the abilities and capacities of ordinary people to participate in decisionmaking procedures of institutions that regulate their lives." So far, West's argument sounds like quite conventional democratic rhetoric. But, like Dewey, he adds a very tough responsibility to those who would live the process of a democratic life. The process is one that "keeps track of social misery, solicits and channels moral outrage to alleviate it, and projects a future in which the potentialities of ordinary people flourish and flower."[26] According to West, it is not enough to *favor* democratic processes. We must be sure the conditions exist so that everyone can participate fully. Democratic schooling is one of these conditions because of its unique capacity to keep track, solicit, channel, alleviate, and project a future.

Similarly, Brazilian educator Paulo Freire paired hope for better social conditions with an active struggle to attain them. Struggle is not simply the *instrument* that produces improved social conditions (a modern idea of progress), although improved social conditions is a critically important goal. Participation in struggle is also itself an "improvement." In arguing that hope is a fundamental human need, Freire cautioned against separating it from action. "The idea that hope alone will transform the world . . . is an excellent route to hopelessness, pessimism, and fatalism." Hope is what sustains the struggle for a better world. "[T]he attempt to do without hope, in the struggle to improve the world, as if that struggle could be reduced to calculated acts alone, or a purely scientific approach, is a frivolous illusion. . . . Without a minimum of hope, we cannot so much as start the struggle. But without the struggle, hope . . . dissipates, loses its bearings, and turns into hopelessness." Yes, it is circular. Hope sustains the actions, and people must act or the hope turns against them—empty. Freire tied all of this specifically to education, making him one of the most provocative, recognized, and influential educators worldwide: "One of the tasks of the serious progressive educator, through a serious, correct, political analysis, is to unveil opportunities for hope, no matter what the obstacles may be."[27] We will return to Dewey's and Freire's curriculum ideas in Chapter 4.

The Struggle for Socially Just Teaching

Schooling based on hope and struggles for social justice makes far more sense in postmodern America than the myths and metaphors that create and preserve social class distinctions.

Diversity opens doors of intellectual exploration and discussion; it should not close doors of opportunity and growth. My responsibility as an educator lies not only in opening doors of knowledge and opportunity for my students but in showing them how they are capable of opening such doors themselves. . . . It is my duty to ensure that my students will emerge as socially conscious and sensitive, and intellectually curious and competent. . . . I will encourage students to become active knowledge seekers and constructors, not passive or submissive participants who do not question and seek clarity and personal truth. . . . My students must enter the world with full knowledge of the social, political and economic realities that exist in order to rise above the inequalities and transform our world.

—Janene Ashford
First-year teacher, grade 6

Teachers like Janene Ashford struggle for socially just public schools that forge unity without diminishing difference. Their teaching recognizes the limits of "modern" theories of rationality and science as the keys to human progress. Yet it also holds onto the belief that schools and teaching can indeed change a world where lives are marked by poverty, discrimination, and injustice.

The postmodern world is abandoning the notion of progress though universals and predictability. However, the teacher just cited, like John Dewey, Cornel West, and Paulo Freire, finds a commonness of the human spirit across diverse cultures and languages. Today's teachers for social justice dispute modernistic "scientific" research that offers nuggets of certainty about what makes schools "effective." Instead, they embrace empirical research and theory that illuminate from multiple perspectives schooling dilemmas and their effects on particular students. They turn to colleagues and experts for critical dialogues about how to *think* about challenges, rather than turning to them to receive solutions. Just as teachers for social justice resist having themselves "fixed" and "improved" by tradition-minded experts and authorities, they are unwilling to become similar authorities for their own students.

My need to care for each student who walks into my classroom has driven me to educate myself about social justice education. As an educator, I can make a difference in students' lives. I can help them become transformative citizens in our society and liberate their minds to soar above and beyond the constraints of race, ethnicity, and social status. As I continue along my path as an educator, I carry with me the words of Alice Walker, "Keep in mind always the present you are constructing. It should be the future you want."

—Kelly Ganzel
First-year teacher, high school English

Digging Deeper

To learn more about the social and educational history and tradition issues raised in this chapter, we suggest you seek out work by the following scholars. Some are referenced in the text; others are not. They all provide highly regarded research and theory about American educational traditions. Their work can help you think deeply about the implications of these traditions for teachers' work in schools and classrooms.

University of Arizona professor **David Berliner** and his colleague, **Bruce Biddle,** at the University of Missouri provide detailed and hard-hitting analyses of the evidence underlying current criticism of public schools. In their book *The Manufactured Crisis: Myths, Fraud, and the Attack on America's Public Schools*

(New York: Addison-Wesley, 1995), they trace that criticism to its sources. They also provide evidence that, despite the barrage of criticism in the past two decades, American schools have actually improved. In 1996 the American Educational Research Association gave Berliner and Biddle's work its award for the outstanding research book of that year.

Raymond Callahan's classic text *Education and the Cult of Efficiency: A Study of the Social Forces That Have Shaped the Administration of the Public Schools* (Chicago: University of Chicago Press, 1962) still stands as the best work analyzing the impact of scientific management on American public schools.

Professor **Andy Hargreaves** of the Ontario Institute for Educational Studies in Toronto, Canada, has written thoughtfully on the conditions of postmodernity and their impact on schooling, and especially on teachers' work. This work can be found in *Changing Teachers, Changing Times: Teachers' Work and Culture in the Postmodern Age* (New York: Teachers College Press, 1994). His many other books and articles, especially recent ones on the emotions of teaching and educational reform, are well worth pursuing as well.

The *Kappan*, a monthly journal published by Phi Delta Kappa, an educational association, provides short readable articles on current education issues. Especially useful is **Gerald Bracey's** regular column on educational research, and his annual reports on the condition of public education. With Berliner and Biddle (mentioned at the beginning of this section), Bracey's voice has been one of the few countering the current attacks on schools with empirical evidence. His recent book *Bail Me Out!: Handling Difficult Data and Tough Questions About Public Schools* (Thousand Oaks, CA: Corwin Press, 2000) provides a very helpful guide to understanding how educational research data is used and abused in the political arena.

Jonathan Kozol, education writer and former teacher, has written a number of popular books about race, disadvantage, and schooling. His book *Savage Inequalities: Children in America's Schools* (New York: Crown, 1991) paints a vivid portrait of the discrepancies in resources and opportunities between the schools of rich and poor children.

Jay McLeod followed two groups of young men—one white, the "Hallway Hangers," and the other black, the "Brothers"—as they made the transition from high school to adulthood in the housing projects and schools of Clarendon Heights. McLeod's ethnography, *Ain't No Makin' It: Aspirations and Attainment in a Low-Income Neighborhood* (Boulder, CO: Westview Press, 1995), weaves a fascinating story. At the same time, it provides insightful analyses of the role of race, class, and the "achievement ideology" of schools in shaping low-income students' ambitions, effort, and life chances.

Gary Orfield, professor and director of the Harvard Civil Rights Project, is the nation's foremost authority on school desegregation. His books include *The Closing Door: Conservative Policy and Black Opportunity* (with Carole Ashkinaze, Chicago: University of Chicago Press, 1993) and, most recently, *Dismantling Desegregation: The Quiet Reversal of* Brown v. Board of Education (with Susan E. Eaton, Boston: New Press, 1996). This book details how the Supreme Court's recent decisions have opened the door for wide-scale abandonment of desegregation. Orfield and Eaton include stinging profiles of schools as they analyze this devastating trend, offering evidence and solutions guaranteed to stimulate national debate about the state of our schools today. Orfield's most recent studies expand his work beyond schooling for black children to focus on Latinos and other low-income immigrant groups of color.

Mike Rose, UCLA education professor, has written two very readable and compelling books about the problems and possibilities of schools for low-income children. His first book, *Lives on the Boundary: The Struggles and Achievements of America's Underprepared* (New York: Penguin, 1990), detailed how low-achieving and minority students have been disregarded and mistreated in schools. His most recent book, *Possible Lives: The Promise of Public Education in America* (Boston: Houghton Mifflin, 1995), provides rich portraits of schools, teachers, and classrooms across the country where similar students engage in socially and intellectually rich learning.

Joel Spring is professor of educational history at SUNY-New Paltz and author of numerous educational histories. Spring's work is especially helpful for understanding how schools have worked systematically to support the social, economic, and political status quo, and how the history of peoples of color in the United States connects with educational policies and practices. Of particular interest might be *Education and the Rise of the Corporate State* (Boston: Beacon Press, 1972), *Conflict of Interests: The Politics of American Education* (New York: Longman, 1988), *The American School, 1642–1990* (New York: Longman, 1990), *Deculturation and the Struggle for Equality: A Brief History of the Education of Dominated Cultures in the United States* (New York: McGraw-Hill, 1997), and *Education and the Rise of the Global Economy* (Hillsdale, NJ: Erlbaum, 1998).

David Tyack, Stanford education historian, has written a number of solid and engaging historical texts. Of particular interest is his *The One Best System: A History of American Urban Education* (Cambridge, MA: Harvard University Press, 1974), a history of how modern urban schools were shaped by a coalition of civic elites, reformers, and professional school administrators.

UCLA professor **Amy Stuart Wells** writes on a range of educational policy issues, paying particular attention to how racial and cultural politics interweave with the impetus for particular policy directions and with the outcomes of various policies. *Steppin' Over the Color Line* (New Haven, CT: Yale University Press, 1997) traces the course of the St. Louis, Missouri, school desegregation though the experiences of black students in the city school system. Her book *Time to Choose: America at the Crossroads of School Choice Policy* (New York: Hill and Wang, 1993) analyzes how market forces and theories of self-interest shed light on the current press for school choice and privatization. She is currently studying charter schools.

Cornel West, professor of theology and Afro-American Studies at Harvard, is a noted author, scholar, and social commentator on issues of race and the American culture. West first attained wide public recognition in 1993 with his best-selling book *Race Matters* (Boston: Beacon Press, 1991). His more recent books include *Keeping the Faith* (Boston: Beacon Press, 1993) and *The Future of the*

Race (Boston: Beacon Press, 1996), coauthored with his colleague in the Harvard Afro-American Studies department, Henry Louis Gates, Jr. Although West's specific focus is on race relations and the struggle of African Americans, he ties issues of race and freedom to questions of philosophy and to a belief in the power of the human spirit.

Harvard professor **William Julius Wilson** provides penetrating analyses of race, urban poverty, and public policy in contemporary America. Particularly worth reading are *The Truly Disadvantaged* (Chicago: University of Chicago Press, 1987) and *The End of Work* (Chicago: University of Chicago Press, 1997).

Notes

1. Who Built America? CD-ROM produced by the American Social History Project, City University of New York, as cited in *Rethinking Schools,* Summer, 1996. The project also can be located on the Internet at www.ashp.cuny.edu.
2. Thomas Jefferson, *Notes on the State of Virginia,* quoted in Joel Spring, *The American School* (New York: Longman, 1990), pp. 8–10.
3. Alexis de Tocqueville, *Democracy in America,* 2 vols. (New York: 1945, Originally published 1835), Vol. 1, pp. 373–374.
4. Gunnar Myrdal, *The American Dilemma: The Negro Problem and Modern Democracy* (New York: Harper & Row, 1944).
5. Gary Orfield, Mark Bachmeier, David James, and Tamela Eitle, *Deepening Segregation in American Public Schools* (Cambridge, MA: Civil Rights Project, Harvard Graduate School of Education, 1997).
6. 1997 report of the U.S. Department of Housing and Urban Development (23 June 1997) as cited in Ronald Brownstein, "Cities Still Carry Poverty Burden, HUD Study Says," *Los Angeles Times,* 23 June 1997, pp. A1, A12.
7. Bureau of the Census, *How We're Changing, Demographic State of the Nation: 1997* (Washington, DC: U.S. Department of Commerce, 1997).
8. Jonathan Kozol, *Savage Inequalities: Children in America's Schools* (New York: Crown, 1991).
9. Amy Pyle, "Attacking the Textbook Crisis," *Los Angeles Times,* 29 September 1997.
10. Data from the National Center for Educational Statistics, cited in Richard Whitmire, "Poor Students More Likely to Have Less Qualified Teachers" *Detroit News,* 1 August 1997.
11. Jeannie Oakes, *Keeping Track: How Schools Structure Inequality* (New Haven, CT: Yale University Press, 1995); Jeannie Oakes, *Multiplying Inequalities: Race, Social Class and Tracking on Students' Opportunities to Learn Mathematics and Science* (Santa Monica: RAND, 1990).
12. Jeannie Oakes, *Lost Talent: The Underrepresentation of Minorities, Women, and Disabled Persons in Science* (Santa Monica: RAND, 1990).
13. Oakes, *Keeping Track;* Oakes, *Multiplying Inequalities.*
14. Jay McLeod, *Ain't No Makin' It* (Boulder, CO: Westview Press, 1995), p. 3.

15. "Success" here means what readers commonly understand the definition to be—without looking into it too deeply—perhaps something like "the good life" or "middle class." Here, and throughout, we use terms that defy precise definition unless one is offered on the spot. When there is no compelling reason to define the term in a technical way, readers should apply a common or informal interpretation.
16. Michael Harrington, *The Other America: Poverty in the United States* (1962, reprint, New York: Collier Books, 1997).
17. Joel Spring, *American Education* (Boston: McGraw-Hill, 1996), p. 212. By the mid-1960s the federal government had responded to post-Sputnik concerns and had established The National Defense Education Act to address perceived weaknesses in math and science. The rationale was that these weaknesses jeopardized military readiness.
18. McLeod, *Ain't No Makin' It,* p. 126.
19. National Commission of Excellence in Education, *A Nation at Risk: The Imperatives for Educational Reform* (Washington, DC: U.S. Department of Education, 1983), p. 5.
20. David Berliner and Bruce J. Biddle, *The Manufactured Crisis: Myths, Fraud, and the Attack on America's Public Schools* (Reading, MA: Addison-Wesley, 1995).
21. Amy Stuart Wells, *Time to Choose: America at the Crossroads of School Choice Policy* (New York: Hill & Wang, 1993).
22. Amy Stuart Wells and Robert L. Crain, "Perpetuation Theory and the Long-Term Effects of School Desegregation," *Review of Educational Research* 64, no. 4 (1994), pp. 531–555.
23. Robert Reich, *The Work of Nations: Preparing Ourselves for 21st Century Capitalism* (New York: Knopf, 1991).
24. John Dewey, as quoted in Jim Garrison, "Deweyan Pragmatism and the Epistemology of Contemporary Social Constructivism," *American Educational Research Journal* 32, no. 4 (1995), p. 731.
25. Ibid., p. 730.
26. Cornel West, "The Limits of Neopragmatism," *Southern California Law Review* 63 (1990), pp. 1747, 1749.
27. Paulo Freire, *Pedagogy of Hope* (New York: Continuum, 1995), pp. 9–10.

CHAPTER 2

Traditional Learning Theories:

Transmission, Training, and IQ

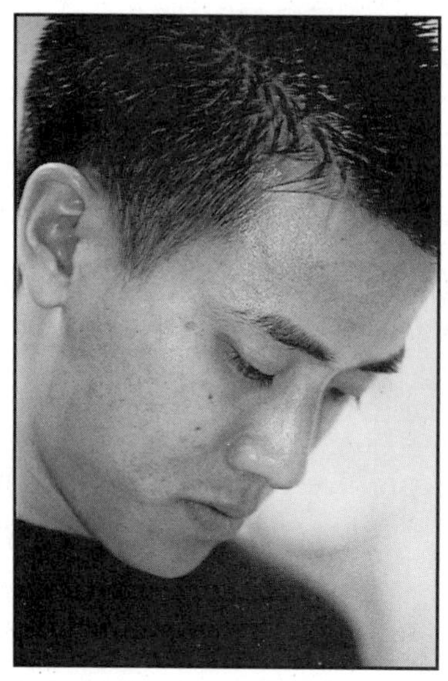

Benjamin Chang
First-year teacher, grade 1

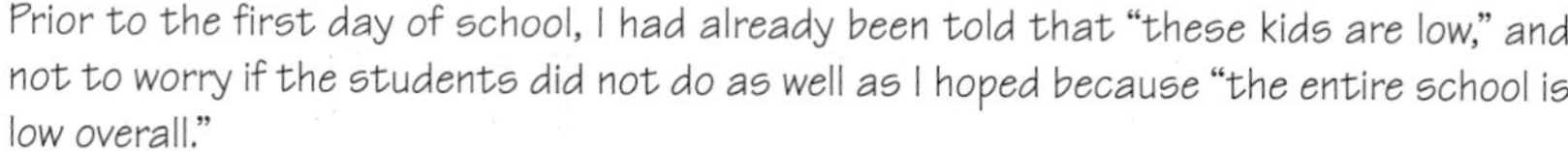

Prior to the first day of school, I had already been told that "these kids are low," and not to worry if the students did not do as well as I hoped because "the entire school is low overall."

—Rosalinda Perez Silva
First-year teacher, grade 1

Rosalinda Silva, who teaches a class of twenty 6- and 7-year-olds in a Spanish-speaking immigrant neighborhood, says that her young students are "brilliantly intelligent" but "already struggling." Certainly, a large part of their struggle is to overcome the judgments teachers have already made about them. Those judgments are not uncommon.

The Bell Curve: Debates Rage about Intelligence and Learning

In 1994, just two months after its publication, *The Bell Curve: Intelligence and Class Structure in American Life* had 400,000 copies in print. Richard Herrnstein and Charles Murray's best-selling book claimed to offer scientific proof that African Americans inherit lower IQs than white Americans and that these IQ differences are virtually impossible to change. Put bluntly, Herrnstein and Murray state that the average African American is less well educated and less wealthy than the average white because he or she is not born with the capacity to be as smart. Therefore, the authors also claim, social programs that attempt to close opportunity gaps—programs such as Head Start, compensatory education, and affirmative action—are costly and useless. They argue that (1) the programs hurt those people they are intended to help by steering them away from the lower-level aspirations and occupations that suit their abilities and (2) such programs harm society because they give less intelligent people access to social positions that require greater aptitude. The authors, well-known academics from prestigious universities, bolstered these claims with impressive-looking charts, graphs, and statistics in their 800-plus-page book.[1]

One Side: Some Children Simply Aren't Smart Enough

The Bell Curve has profound implications for schools and teaching. It argues that Americans need to face the reality that "in a universal education system, many students will not reach the level of education that most people view as basic."[2] Moreover, according to the authors, efforts to teach groups of children with low IQs (disproportionately, disadvantaged children of color) more than the most modest skills will benefit neither those children nor society. Rather, government and educators should shift most of their teaching resources and efforts from the disadvantaged to the intellectually gifted.

Readers of *The Bell Curve* and of the countless magazine and journal reviews that followed its publication, as well as listeners to TV talk shows and radio call-in programs about the book, were frightened and enraged. Those who liked the book were angry because it confirmed their political views about the futility (or worse) of social programs that aimed at improving the life chances of Americans of color. People who disagreed were furious because they found the book dishonest, unscientific, and morally offensive.

A book such as *The Bell Curve* appears every few decades or oftener. In 1969 Harvard psychologist Arthur Jensen argued that because national poverty programs did not appreciably raise children's IQs, children of the poor must be genetically intellectually inferior. Physicist William Shockley reemerged years after co-inventing the transistor to bring the authority of his scientific credentials to a proposal for reimbursing voluntarily sterilized individuals according to their number of IQ points below 100.[3] What is notable here is the instant popularity of such views. The findings in these reports made front-page headlines, and they gave eager readers permission to speak aloud their previously private convictions about race and the poor.

Even the most fair-minded teachers did not realize the extent to which *The Bell Curve's* old-fashioned, inaccurate (at best), and racist perspectives were present in the minds and hearts of their fellow Americans, including many of their colleagues at school. Respected scholars instantly refuted the books and reports, but they were consigned to smaller pieces on the editorial pages and to magazines and journals with smaller audiences than television or newspapers.

The Other Side: All Children Are Smart Enough, But Schools Aren't

Other books by distinguished scholars, many in recent years, tell a much different story about learning and intelligence. Stephen J. Gould, who teaches the history of science at Harvard, details the scientific and statistical flaws of intelligence testing and traces the links between IQ, bigotry, and oppression in his richly documented history *The Mismeasure of Man*. Howard Gardner and David Perkins, both at Harvard's education school, also dispute *The Bell Curve*. They offer evidence that the kind of intelligence that IQ represents pales in importance compared with other, more reflective mental processes. In *Frames of Mind,* Gardner argues that people are intelligent in many different ways, and in *Outsmarting IQ,* Perkins contends that the most important mental processes are learned, not inherited.

Jerome Bruner's *Acts of Meaning* and *Culture and Education* are just two of many recent books that draw from research in anthropology, linguistics, and psychology to show that learning is a social and cultural process. This sociocultural view, discussed more fully in Chapter 3 departs dramatically from views expounded in *The Bell Curve.* According to Bruner and many other scholars, learning takes place within the whole person's experience in society, not just inside the head; and learning is constructed and shaped through relationships, not determined by inherited aptitudes. That is, people learn as they interact with others to make sense out of the world and their experiences in it, and intelligence develops as people learn and grow. Because different cultures provide children with different learning situations, and because they value the mastery of different tasks, differences among groups of people in "native intelligence"—a much disputed concept—explains little about what they can and do learn.

That children can learn to be smart in school represents a dramatic shift from older views and is an idea gaining in popularity in schools' rhetoric. However, this perspective is too easily interpreted to mean that different children need dramatically different treatments in school because some get smarter faster. Given schools' legacy of scientific management, the temptation is great to judge how smart students are at a particular moment and to rank and sort them accordingly. These judgments soon trap educators into seeing intelligence as placing a ceiling on what students can learn. A fairer and more accurate view is for teachers and school policies to acknowledge that all students *are* smart, as opposed to *capable of being* smart. They may not be smart about the same things or in the same language. They may be smart about many things that others, especially adults, disapprove of or do not understand. But to respect the mental powers of students, teachers do not need to look at students' potential or their theoretical ability to reach the school's idea of what it means to be smart. Students are smart. They are smart now.

The views in books such as Perkins's and Bruner's are supported by far more reliable evidence from distinguished scholars and credible reviewers than are Murray and Herrnstein's arguments. But, typically, perspectives such as those of Perkins and Bruner do not make headlines, lacking the flashy claims that people's genes cause inequality or that buying off the less intelligent can purify the human race.

Theories and Debates Drive Practice

Neither my students nor I enter our classroom empty handed. We come, as Luis Moll says, "con nuestras mochilas llenas, no estan vacias (with our backpacks full, not empty)." How I view people directly impacts how I teach. I not only carry pedagogical theories about teaching and learning, but I also carry assumptions and ideas about people: what learning looks like, what a teacher looks like, what schooling looks like and why. . . . No classroom practice exists in isolation of a social and cultural history.

—Cindy Kauionalani Bell
First-year teacher, grade 2

The forces of inequity and democracy are perpetually in tension within our schools. . . . Ignoring the power that lies in our position as teachers, not examining our theories about children and learning, and ignoring the political dimensions of our work perpetuates in our own classrooms the social inequality that plagues our society.

—Laura Silvina Torres
First-year teacher, grade 2

The debates about learning and intelligence are more than intellectual disagreements among psychologists. Every school organization and teaching act is based on some theory—well founded or not—of how and why it will work well for students. This chapter looks at the theories of learning and intelligence that are embedded in *The Bell Curve* and, sadly, are alive and well in today's schools. Even this brief overview makes clear that theories about learning are not neutral and objective scientific discoveries. Rather, they reflect the beliefs and values of the times and of the Western and American cultures in which they develop. Typically, the theories that gain acceptance serve the interests of powerful people of the period.

Part of teachers' professional knowledge includes their ability to recognize, articulate, and weigh the theories that underlie their own and others' practice. Many new teachers will begin their careers in schools and communities where older, traditional theories still prevail. Understanding the historical, cultural, and political contexts of conflicting theories about learning helps explain why many people find traditional theories so appealing. It also sheds light on why some people resist newer, competing theories that support all students learning well. The next (more encouraging) chapter explores newer, sociocultural conceptions of learning and intelligence. Teachers committed to teaching for social justice can use these theories with confidence to guide their practice in diverse American schools.

Changing Conceptions of Learning

Although intelligence, learning, development, and psychology are distinctly different concepts, they are very closely associated, both historically and in common practice. In this chapter and elsewhere, *learning* refers to the processes and mental structures by which people accumulate experiences and make them into new meanings. The key is that learning theories attempt to explain a "process." *Intelligence* refers to mental power. The key to intelligence theories and measurements is that they try to determine "differences" among people; that is, no one is simply intelligent, he or she must be *more* or *less* intelligent than some comparison individual or group. *Development* refers to the relatively predictable changes everyone experiences throughout their lives. Theories of development attempt to explain how these changes take place. Most consider development to be a progression from one distinctly different stage to the next, rather than changes that are smooth and gradual. Although these changes are unique for each individual, there are certain consistent patterns of maturation, and social, personal, physical, and cognitive (mental or thinking) development.

Psychology is that field which investigates the mind and mental processes, and out of which come the most dominant understandings of the learning process. In many respects, over the last hundred years or so, the most powerful science and the most damaging misinformation have come from this field. However, while the science of psychology is relatively young, theories of learning have been around for a very long time. Before psychologists, theologians and philosophers explained the nature of knowledge and how humans came to know it.

One enduring controversy—debated long before the birth of psychology—is the degree to which nature and/or nurture best explains an individual's learning, intelligence, and development. *Nature* refers both to the particular genetic inheritance individuals receive from parents and to the general mental capacities held in common by the whole human species. *Nurture* refers to an individual's environment—essentially all that a person experiences after conception (environmental conditions in the womb may influence a person's development). Today, virtually everyone agrees that both biological inheritance (nature) and experiences (nurture) are very important and cannot be separated. But just as in the distant past, debates rage over which matters *most* in learning, intelligence, and development.

The Enlightenment: Reason for Thinking

The European Renaissance from roughly the fourteenth to the seventeenth century marked a transition from medieval to modern thought—from people as subjects in God's world to people as worthy of investigation in their own right. Easing into the modern era, philosophers began to seek answers by using means other than the authority of scripture. Although they did not discount God, the seventeenth- and eighteenth-century Enlightenment thinkers did take stock of the Renaissance achievements in architecture and art, mathematics, commerce, cities and government, and more. They asked what it was about humans that allowed those achievements, what the source of knowledge was that made the achievements possible. In a more technical sense, they pondered the processes that humans use to make knowledge.

Assuming that humans "make knowledge" is a particular and significant point of view. The prevailing alternative was, and often remains, that humans do not make knowledge—that knowledge is *there* (out *there* in the world or in *there* in the mind) already, waiting to be known. If scripture could not provide the large answers or the smallest details to these questions, what could? Enlightenment scholars concluded that *reason*, an inborn human capacity, is partly responsible for humans turning experiences into certain types or categories of knowledge.

The giants of Enlightenment philosophy—Rene Descartes (1596–1650), John Locke (1632–1704), Immanuel Kant (1724–1804), and others—proposed many of the perplexing questions at the heart of twentieth-century psychology:

> Are some forms of knowledge inborn or innate?
>
> What truths can be known through reflection, or examining our own thoughts?
>
> Is there a mind or soul that is spiritual or separate from the physical body? If so, do they interact?
>
> What is the difference between physical sensations and ideas?
>
> How do smaller bits of experience (I feel cold) turn into broad abstractions (Is it better to conserve energy, or should I turn on the heater and maybe avoid the stiff neck I get from the tension?)?
>
> How do we study something (like the mind) that we can't see?

Each of these Enlightenment thinkers came to somewhat different answers—answers that have influenced the direction of our ideas about human thinking and learning ever since. Descartes, who emphasized the mind as a region separate from the body that inspects ideas, argued that some forms of knowledge were inborn, and that the mind's reasoning was the most reliable source of that knowledge; he doubted the certainty—the reliability—of bodily sensations. Locke, in contrast, questioned the concept of innate ideas and turned to "empirical" evidence for knowledge—the reality that can be detected by the senses. He kept Descartes's notion of a mind but argued that the mind is a blank slate that only is written on through experience. Kant saw the mind as an organ that, rather than blankly awaiting experience, was equipped with processes that created orderly thought and understanding. The mind mediated, categorized, and represented the sensations and ideas, making sense out of more chaotic, concrete experience. For Kant, the outside world was not irrelevant to thinking, as it was to Descartes, because it provides the raw material that the mind organizes. Today's various perspectives on learning and teaching have deep roots in the past and draw their logic from these earlier modes of thinking. We also see these perspectives in today's arguments over curriculum, influences we return to in Chapters 4 and 5.

Interestingly, one concept that did *not* seem to trouble Enlightenment philosophers was individual differences in intelligence. On one hand, they certainly took note of the differences in people's social status, and they could not help but notice that some people performed their life's work with more or less skill or brilliance. On the other hand, their main task was to discover the meaning and the nature of knowledge. They had many other cultural ways to figure out who was worthy, who had merit.

Although most nineteenth-century teachers had little or no training in how to teach, metaphors drawn from the work of Descartes, Locke, Kant, and other

Enlightenment thinkers helped people "understand" the mystery of learning and helped shape classroom instruction. These metaphors portrayed young minds as "empty vessels" to be filled or as "blank slates" to be written on. Some educators used these ideas to develop "methods" for teaching. German educator Johann Herbart (1776–1841), for example, combined Enlightenment ideas of reason with the growing faith in systematic approaches, planning, and organization. He developed and popularized a design for classroom lessons that promised to bring order to instruction and standardization among classrooms. The Herbartian lesson plan included five steps: (1) Remind students of knowledge already learned; (2) present new material; (3) compare new material to prior knowledge; (4) generalize a central idea; and (5) apply the new knowledge to some other situation. These steps organized common teaching practices of the time into a rational, efficient, and easily monitored method of instruction. More important than the organization (steps) themselves, Herbart introduced many to the idea that teaching could be a highly orderly process.

Others took the ideas of Enlightenment thinkers, Locke, in particular, to mean that young children should learn from contact with real objects, investigating for themselves rather than being given verbal instruction. Maria Montessori, for example, combined hands-on investigation and a more nurturing, maternal approach to teaching (one accompanying the increased presence of schoolmarms) to create an early forerunner of twentieth-century progressive education—especially for the very young.

Most teachers, though, stuck with traditional methods for transmitting knowledge. Children spent their time memorizing, reciting, and reproducing their lessons to demonstrate that they had acquired knowledge. Some older people today may recall school days filled with copying long texts verbatim; memorizing poems, famous speeches, and Shakespearean dialogue; conjugating Latin verbs; and the class being called upon by the teacher to recite the lesson as a group. Their vessels (note the metaphors for foolishness: "empty-headed," "airhead") were being filled with knowledge, and their slates were being written on. Nurturing and "softer" views of teaching and learning would compete with, but never displace, the influence of the "mental disciplinarians." People were tremendously attracted to the belief that as children got older, "certain subjects had the power to strengthen faculties such as memory, reasoning, will, and imagination."[4] It is to this view that we owe the still popular metaphor of the "mind as a muscle" and the notion that the study of classical languages, geometry, and so on causes learners to "exercise their brains" and produces stronger, more capable minds.

The Nineteenth Century: From Reason to a Science of Psychology

The nineteenth century also brought some early scientific psychological studies—a curious mix of crackpot invention alongside more mature study of learning and intelligence. Phrenology, for example, represented an attempt to apply to practical use an early version of psychological theory. Yes, some believed that they could feel the bumps on one's skull and know something about that person's mental faculties and character traits. But Franz Gall, a noted nineteenth-century phrenologist (a practitioner of bump analysis), combined his nonscience with a systematic study of anatomy. Other investigators studied the brain and brain functions—sometime correctly identifying parts of the brain that had specific functions such as speech or sight.

What is most significant about these studies is that they signaled the beginning of the scientific study of behavior and, eventually, learning. No longer limited to thought scenarios, general scholarship, and study of the classics, scholars were becoming systematic in their observations, recording their findings, and building on, or refuting, the work of other observers. Furthermore, psychologists began to look at the general characteristics of mind and behavior that all members of the species hold in common. Throughout the 1800s enthusiasm mounted about the prospect of knowing with precision a person's mental and behavioral characteristics. Might scientists predict who was a person of compassion, a murderer, crazy, intelligent? Could there be certainty about how people come to know (learning), and could they compare their knowledge and reasoning to others (intelligence)? It would still be some time before these theories would become relevant for schools.

By the middle of the nineteenth century, Charles Darwin (1809–1882) had argued that intelligence transmitted by inheritance was central to human evolution; that is, as the human species, through natural selection, favored its most intelligent members, humans became increasingly distinct from apes. His nephew, Sir Francis Galton (1822–1911), used Darwin's notions to study the importance of intelligence in modern times. He gathered data about the British royal family to show that intellectual capacity runs in families. He also developed tests of sight, hearing, reaction time, and sensitivity to touch to measure intelligence. These were *empirical* studies—that is, they relied less on subjective judgments and more on objectively recorded observations. Empirical studies are likely to produce consistent data when experiments are repeated by different observers. Galton's pursuit of a measurement that would capture inherited abilities sparked a search that dominated much of psychology in the first decades of twentieth century.

The Promise of Scientific Schooling

Events of the late nineteenth century brought the first hints that the science of psychology could provide practical benefits to schooling. In spite of the horrendous social problems and inequality that accompanied industrialization, mass production, and urbanization—not the least of which was the challenge to educate so many from so many different places—Americans at the turn of the twentieth century were optimistic, believing the nation could overcome any harsh conditions that might eventually threaten social stability. After all, there was the myth, and for many the reality, of personal and public improvement, advancement, and progress. Further, new technological accomplishments were in evidence every day. If there was a problem worth fixing, then surely American know-how could fix it. Schools had many problems, and Americans would take to any scientific and technological solution that came their way as long as it matched common conceptions of who was smart and who was not.

G. Stanley Hall (1844–1924) used his pioneering theories and studies of child development to press for a more scientific approach to teaching. Founder of the "child study movement" at the end of the nineteenth century, Hall's research led him to argue that each stage of children's development mirrors that of social evolution. For example, Hall likened ages 4 to 8 to the hunting and gathering period of human history, and he saw ages 11 and 12 as paralleling barbarian life. Puberty brought a romantic stage of life when youthful passions could either be marshaled for the good of society or allowed to degenerate. For Hall, this adolescent stage represented either society's bright future or its demise.

Hall's stages are rooted in the naturalistic views of philosopher Jean-Jacques Rousseau (1712–1778), who believed in the inherent (natural) goodness and high potential of children—goodness and potential that must be protected from a corrupting society, especially from the babbling talk and teaching that keep the young from direct experience with the concrete world. Rousseau believed that, if left uncorrupted, children would develop naturally into the best possible adults. This idea of development in stages, during which children change in their deep and fundamental nature, gave Hall his greatest influence in education, although his specific logic and description of the stages did not last long. In particular, Hall provided the foundation for the idea of adolescence—a time of life when children had markedly different needs and required distinctive treatments in school. The invention of the junior high school as a separate institution with curriculum and instruction designed to match the young adolescent's developmental needs and interests followed directly from Hall's science.

Intelligence, Learning, and Merit: You Get What You Deserve

Historically, Western societies distributed wealth and privilege according to how close one was to an elite or ruling class. Prior to the surge of democratic thinking in the seventeenth century, royalty, church leadership, landowners, and wealthy merchants managed to have more wealth and privilege than artisans, peasants, and slaves. Not everyone thought it was fair, but few with power apologized or felt they had to justify it.

A central dilemma of modern and more egalitarian societies is how to explain disparities in wealth and privilege. Americans have always been disdainful of aristocracy, of publicly acknowledged ruling classes, and of social power as a birthright. Instead, the idea of merit, discussed in Chapter 1, substitutes for inherited privilege. Merit, which provides moral legitimacy to what might otherwise appear as unfair or undemocratic, explains why some citizens and their children are so well off generation after generation.

Who Is Deserving?

An early way to explain why some Americans had greater wealth—one that is still with us to some degree—was based on Calvinist and Puritan religious ideas. According to these views, those favored by God were prosperous and those not favored had less. Conversely, being poor was a sign of not being favored by God. Another explanation important from the earliest days was that hard work and ambition determined who deserves wealth and social advantage. Again, the unsuccessful could be seen as having less of these qualities. Additionally, although aristocracy and parentage were not useful ways to make sense out of significant social class differences, many other largely unquestioned group characteristics were indeed useful. It was obvious, with little explanation required, that racial minorities, immigrants, women, persons from rural areas, and others had no moral standing on which to base complaints against their social or economic status.

But over time, and slowly at first, the obvious would be challenged. In the late nineteenth century, scientists began the systematic study of intelligence as they sought to develop more rational and scientific explanations to explain and justify the social class differences between racial and other groups. They gave intelligence a home: the brain. It had origins: heredity. It had an amount measured in terms of IQ: a person could have 110 of it or 78 of it, and people and groups could on average possess more or less. They traced the lesser merit of the poor and of "other" races to their smaller brains, nefarious eyes, recent descendancy from apes, parents who were eastern or southern European, or religion. For many, grounding merit in the concepts of intelligence and achievement—measured by scientifically developed standardized tests—was attractive because it did not upset the prevailing distribution of wealth and privilege. In addition, intelligence testing demonstrated that though all might benefit from mental exercise, the mental muscles of some were inherently too weak for rigorous intellectual effort. Thus, within a few decades, Americans had accepted new definitions of learning and merit. Psychometrics—the measurement of mental traits, abilities, and processes—was applied quickly and widely throughout the country.

A brief historical sketch in the next section illustrates how intelligence and learning are social constructions laden with a history of racial and social class discrimination, rather than objective entities discovered by science.

A Science of Intelligence

At the end of the nineteenth century, the American school population swelled. In 1890 only 10 percent of young people pursued schooling beyond the basic primary years. But by 1920 that percentage had nearly quadrupled. France, too, had instituted mass education. French schools, like American ones, continued to educate children from prosperous families who learned easily; at the same time, they began struggling to teach children from families who had never attended school and who seemed unable to learn or behave. At the request of the

French government, French psychologist Alfred Binet (1857–1911) devised a test to help schools select those students who might benefit from greater help and attention in school—thus increasing their chances of succeeding in school. Binet's test included a range of questions designed for different-aged children. An 8-year-old who could pass most of the questions designed for a 12-year-old was said to have a *mental age* of 12. The reverse was true as well—a 12-year-old could have a mental age of 8, thus indicating a child who required special help. Binet cautioned that the test was strictly a screening device, not for use with "normal" children or to be applied broadly in schools.

Motivated less by sentiments of helpfulness or fairness than by needs for greater efficiency and social organization, Americans imported Alfred Binet's intelligence test. Within a few years, the field of psychology had made intelligence the cornerstone of a new scientific respectability. And, despite Binet's admonitions, educators had worked intelligence testing into the very structure and ideology of American schools. Many refinements of Binet's original tests followed, each one giving the test more power in the minds of the test givers and more power over the test takers. A significant change was to report the "result" (e.g., a 5-, 6-, or 7-year-old mental age) as a ratio of mental age to chronological age (actual age in years). Thus, a 6-year-old who scored a mental age of 4 received a score that was the quotient of 4 over 6, or a 67 intelligence quotient (after getting rid of the decimal). A 4-year-old with a mental age of 6 would have an IQ of 150. Of course, the test results did not really say anything more about a child than how many questions he or she could answer relative to other children of the same age. However, the convenient shorthand created the impression that IQ captured the essence of the child's prospects for school achievement, occupational fitness, and adult success.

Intelligence: The Clean Prejudice Binet's test did not remain a neutral device to identify a small population of students. The test immediately linked progress-minded, scientific authority to existing social power and prejudices. At the center of this process were men of high regard in the world of science. Their views and work employed statistical analyses along with novel, often twisted, interpretations of the evolution theories of Charles Darwin (1809–1882) and the inheritance theories of Gregor Mendel (1822–1884), two profoundly influential nineteenth-century scientists. H. H. Goddard (1866–1957), Lewis Terman (1877–1956), Charles Spearman (1863–1945), and others, along with the society they influenced, believed that science could fashion from theories of evolution and inheritance a progressively precise and scientific theory of eugenics. Eugenics was the use of selective breeding, including who should not be allowed to breed, to improve the mental and moral qualities of the human race.

Intelligence Is Inherited: H. H. Goddard Prior to World War I, psychologist H. H. Goddard used a version of Binet's tests on youngsters in a large New Jersey mental institution, as well as on their relatives, to explore whether "feeblemindedness" ran in families. His work was responsible for popularizing Binet's ideas in the United States. But Goddard went much further than Binet, by applying Mendel's ideas of biological inheritance to intelligence. Binet's scale provided Goddard a single number to represent how much intelligence a person inherited. Goddard concluded that the poor and criminals had low intelligence—a trait they passed on to their children:

> Our thesis is that the chief determiner of human conduct is a unitary mental process which we call intelligence: that this process is conditioned by a nervous mechanism which is inborn: that the degree of efficiency to be attained by that nervous mechanism and the consequent grade of intellectual or mental level for each individual is determined by the kind of chromosomes that come together with the union of the germ cells: that it is but little affected by any later influences except such serious accidents as may destroy part of the mechanism.
>
> How can there be such a thing as social equality with this wide range of mental capacity?[5]

Low-IQ Children Are Mostly Non-Anglo and Poor: Lewis Terman Terman, a professor at Stanford University, developed and promoted intelligence tests for U.S. schoolchildren. Although Terman purported that his Stanford-Binet IQ tests measured innate abilities, the following items taken from one section of his test make clear that children from educated, culturally mainstream families were more likely to earn high IQs:[6]

4. Most exports go from
   Boston San Francisco New Orleans New York

9. Larceny is a term used in
   Medicine Theology Law Pedagogy

16. A character in *David Copperfield* is
    Sinbad Uriah Heep Rebecca Hamlet

Because children from nonwhite and poor families scored lower than more socially advantaged ones, Terman used his IQ test results to confirm his view that heredity determined intelligence. He also used the test results to support his advocacy of low-level schooling for those who tested poorly as well as population control among the feebleminded. After testing a group of boys who lived in an orphanage, Terman wrote:

> The tests have told the truth. These boys are ineducable beyond the merest rudiments of training. No amount of school instruction will ever make them intelligent voters or capable citizens. . . . Their dullness seems to be racial, or at least inherent in the family stocks from which they came. . . . [O]ne meets this type with such extraordinary frequency among Indians, Mexicans and Negroes. . . . Children of this group should be segregated in special classes and be given instruction which is concrete and practical. . . . There is no possibility at present of convincing society that they should not be allowed to reproduce, although from a eugenic point of view they constitute a grave problem because of their unusually prolific breeding.[7]

Although IQ tests were periodically modified after the 1920s, they would continue to support views similar to Terman's.

IQ Predicts Almost Everything: Charles Spearman Spearman, an English military engineer before he was a psychologist, tested schoolchildren with a wide variety of measures to determine whether people who were good at one thing tended also to be good at others. Through statistical analysis of the results of the tests of different abilities, Spearman inferred an entity that he called *g*, for general intelligence. He conceived of *g* as a kind of inherited energy or power within the brain that activated other entities he called *s*, which referred to more specific abilities for which one could be trained. Without going through Spearman's inventive statistical methods, suffice it to say he made a big mistake. Stephen J. Gould, who does explain the methods very well, calls Spearman's *g* "the theory of intelligence as a unitary, rankable, genetically based and minimally alterable thing in the head." He also calls it "a bankrupt theory."[8] According to Spearman, in 1927:

> The general conclusion emphasized by nearly every investigator is that as regards "intelligence" the Germanic stock has on the average a marked advantage over the South European. And this result would seem to have had vitally important practical consequences in shaping the recent stringent American laws as to admission of immigrants.[9]

As this brief account makes clear, the twentieth-century Western world invented a peculiar way of thinking about a person's capacity for learning. This thinking gave psychologists, schools, the military, and even parents an instrument that could easily determine and communicate how smart a person was. Especially important, the tests appeared to be scientific and fair: The same tests were administered under the same conditions, with impartial mathematical formulas used to produce the final representation of a person's intelligence. In an even more potent development, groups of children now could be compared by averaging individual intelligence quotients.

Intelligence persists as a widely respected and legal marker in a society that wants to see itself as just and equitable. However, given its embeddedness in a history of racial and social class discrimination, no one should be surprised that using intelligence as an indicator of merit produces a distribution of power and privilege that bears striking familiarity to the explicit race and social class sorting of earlier times.

A Prejudicial Construct Becomes a Real Thing Very soon, IQ became firmly entrenched as the scientific measure of a real human attribute—the substance or quality of mind that defines the upper limits of learning ability. Those who have a lot of the substance have a high IQ, those with less, a low one. Because psychologists considered intelligence to be a natural endowment—like hair color or height—people were thought to be more or less stuck with the intelligence with which they are born. However, in the attempt to accommodate the role of nurture as well as nature, psychologists also argued that families quickly influence whether and how children use their intelligence for learning. Consequently, a highly intelligent child born to a supposedly culturally impoverished family might not blossom intellectually because the parents would not provide intellectual stimulation. By the time children reach age 5 or 6, schools, supposedly, could do little to alter the predetermined upper limits of what these children could accomplish in school. What began as Binet's highly specialized construct and measure for recognizing severe cognitive deficiencies had become a real thing.

Intelligence had become, in a word, *reified.* Reified ideas are not real in any material sense. Rather, they are ideas and abstractions about human attributes and behaviors—what social scientists call *constructs.* According to researcher and measurement expert Kenneth Sirotnik, many educational constructs begin as narrowly defined, highly specialized measures that researchers and theorists use for very limited purposes. Then, as these constructs make their way from research to professional journals and teacher preparation programs to popular media to the everyday talk of policymakers and the public, they lose their narrow definitions and specialized uses. "Pretty soon," Sirotnik notes, "people talk and make decisions about other people's *intelligence, achievement,* and *self-concept* as if these attributes really existed in the same sense as, for example, people's height and weight."[10] Sirotnik argues that this reification (treating abstract social constructs as if they have concrete, material reality) distorts people's thinking about education. Once reified, categories such as "gifted," "high ability," "average," and "retarded," whether they began with specific and technical definitions or as loose and informal concepts, become deeply embedded features of students' identities—in both their own and others' minds. Often, educators and others fail to examine the origins and limits of the specialized meanings of these labels, and they exaggerate and overinterpret them. These dangers of intelligence-related constructs have plagued makers and users of intelligence and similar tests from their beginning.

For example, in 1927 Harper and Brothers published a book, *Tisn't What You Know, But Are You Intelligent?* Its back cover proclaimed, "Rate yourself on the actual tests used in the Department of Applied Physiology at Yale University." The book consists of intelligence tests and a preface by a Yale psychologist explaining the concept of intelligence. A table provides the intelligence ratings that correspond with the test scores and a list of the average number of correct answers given by members of different occupations—from laborers at the bottom with "low average intelligence" to accountants and doctors at the top with "superior intelligence." The preface explains that intelligence is the "capability to do productive thinking" and that intelligence is not knowledge, but "an inborn capacity of the mind." In the section on feeblemindedness, the author declares, "By the principle of heredity, two feebleminded parents have nothing but feebleminded children and usually in large numbers."[11] Although no claims are made about the racial basis of intelligence, there are some rather amazing assertions about gender.

> The introduction of a strain of low mentality into an intelligent family sometimes shows up in later generations. This strain of feeblemindedness is usually introduced into the family on the female side. This statement is not one of misogyny. Its reason lies in the fact that many of the qualities in the male which make him a desirable mate, his abilities and his earning capacity for example,

are related to intelligence. These qualities are not always expected in the female. A girl of moron intelligence may have the physical beauty and grace that lead quickly to matrimony even though her conversation is limited to, "I've had a perfectly glorious time"; "Isn't it too wonderful"; "You dear"; and, "Oh, anything you say—!"[12]

What were the questions on the Yale tests like? Much like those included in Terman's early tests, and, perhaps not surprising, some are quite a lot like the questions that turn up on today's aptitude tests like the SAT. Here are some examples:

It is wiser to save some money and not spend it all, so that you may

- ❑ gamble when you wish
- ❑ prepare for old age and sickness
- ❑ collect all the different kinds of money

How long will it take a man to walk 42 miles if he walks at the rate of 3 miles per hour?

The Percheron is a kind of (a) goat, (b) horse, (c) cow, (d) sheep.

The idea of IQ and IQ tests gave educators and the public a way to measure any student's capacity for thinking and learning, and this capacity represented an upper limit, a ceiling, on how clever or successful a student might become. Schools and society even adopted a construct called "overachiever" to explain the exceptional and rare occasion of when a student's performance exceeds his *potential.* (Note the expression "fulfilling one's potential.") Because potential is established with intelligence tests, it too is commonly understood as an unchangeable human attribute.

Readiness, Aptitude, and Ability: IQ in New Guises

In recent years, IQ tests have justly fallen into disfavor. They are used more carefully now than in the past, but not before they spawned several variations of themselves—variations that are not quite the same as IQ tests, but not very different, either. IQ tests are *standardized* and *norm referenced,* characteristics that refer to the statistical procedures that give IQ tests their scientific validity, reliability, and credibility. The same statistical features characterize the many IQ "wanna-bes," with their pervasive educational and social influence.

Tests such as the Scholastic Aptitude Test (SAT), and many tests of "basic skills," have some questions that are closely aligned with schools, but like IQ tests, they measure very general knowledge and skills. The SAT argues that studying for the test is not worthwhile because the test measures a general human quality, not specific subject knowledge. In short, as an aptitude test, the SAT claims to predict future school success but does not claim to measure accurately what students have learned in school. The following SAT "mathematical reasoning" question is an example of the blending of school knowledge (math), reading ability (with a focus on vocabulary), cultural knowledge (familiarity with playing cards, and perhaps prior experience solving problems for no practical reason), and reasoning:

> "Seven cards in a pile are numbered 1 through 7. One card is drawn. The units digit of the sum of the numbers on the remaining cards is 7. What is the number of the drawn card?" (The choices are numbers 1, 3, 5, 6, or 7.)[13]

Other tests that have important reading comprehension components, such as the CTBS and the Iowa Test of Basic Skills, measure very similar skills as the SAT. In fact, since scores on reading comprehension tests typically correlate strongly with scores on IQ tests, the reading tests are often used to substitute for IQ tests. In other words, a high reading score is taken to mean high general ability—just as a high score on an IQ test is taken to mean high intelligence. This includes kindergarten reading readiness or prereading tests. So, although most students today are unlikely to be tested for IQ, their schools will have something very similar by which to judge them.

These tests owe their great social acceptance and influence—that is, their compatibility with cultural views of merit, efficiency, and competition—to their statistical (scientific) methods. Like IQ tests, all these tests are norm referenced; that is, scores on the test have meaning only in comparison to the scores of others who took the test. So, for example, a 500 on the SAT is an average score, just like 100 on an IQ test. It doesn't tell what a person knows but, rather, where he or she stands in comparison with others. The tests are constructed so that most people score in the average range, with fewer getting scores above and below average, and even fewer at the two extremes. This is why the scores on these tests can be described with a bell curve. The large number of average scores form the highest point of the bell, and fewer number of extremely high and low scores flatten out the curve on either side.

Cultures with fixed social hierarchies use class, race, gender, and so on, to determine who has merit or who deserves social advantages, privileges, and power. At a glance, people can legitimately judge others' merit. Therefore, there is less need to compare people to determine who most deserves rewards or social privileges. However, an egalitarian and democratic society frowns on such categories and cannot tolerate categories that are permanent. Thus, in the United States, intelligence has become a substitute for less acceptable indicators of merit. Hiding behind the intelligence/merit connection and the technicalities of testing makes it easier to confer benefits on people who are members of traditionally powerful and favored groups.

Learning as Behavioral Training

Much early psychology was a blend of folk wisdom, philosophy, anthropology, introspection, and biological science. Trying to rise above this ill-formed anarchy, psychologists in the early years of the twentieth century strove mightily to bring order and respectability to their discipline. In brief, they wanted a "scientific" field of study.

Laboratories and Psychometrics: The Trappings of Science

Much psychology in the first half of the twentieth century followed two traditional lines of scientific inquiry: (1) laboratory experiments with animals, often investigating response times and other physiological responses (blood pressure, respiration, eye blinks, etc.), and (2) psychological study with humans that was psychometric, that is, involving tests that could be scored and converted to statistics. In 1913 American psychologist John Watson argued against an approach being pioneered by European psychologists, where human participants might "cooperate" with investigators by reporting about their mental processes. He maintained that since impartial investigators could not observe the working of the mind, asking people about their own thinking produced horribly unreliable, unscientific information. Therefore, Watson contended that psychologists should stick to examining observable behaviors.[14]

Following Watson, American psychologists kept their studies in the laboratory or a carefully controlled setting, apart from messy "real-world" interference. The new experimental psychologists gathered information from groups of people to make inferences about individual psychological processes. They studied laboratory animals because data on animals were easier to refine or reduce to the simplest, isolated "psychological laws."[15] The study of animals was made legitimate via Darwin's notion that the difference between species is "one of degree, not of kind." Thus, mainstream psychology asserted that psychological laws apply across species. Once these laws were identified, psychologists, in the manner of the physical and biological sciences, asserted their universal application. That is, their laws would apply to all individuals in their natural or everyday settings regardless of how different the settings might be.

Conditioning through Stimulus and Response

In the 1920s Russian physiologist Ivan Pavlov's experimental studies laid out the principles of learning that became the foundation of behavioral psychology. Very briefly, Pavlov discovered that dogs he was using in experiments on digestion started salivating when the feeder approached. This accidental finding led to his classical studies of "conditioning." In these studies, he would produce a tone before feeding a dog and over time *condition*, or "teach," the dog to salivate in response to the tone—actual food no longer being required to get the dog's digestive system going. Pavlov thus proposed that learning at its most elemental level involved the involuntary (without a goal or purpose) association of stimuli (whatever prompts or activates behavior) and a set response.

Like Pavlov's work, behavioral learning theories of human learning focus on external events *before* learning (stimuli, input, causes) and observable actions *after* learning (responses, output, effects). Behavioral psychologists pay somewhat less attention to processes that occur at the moment of learning—tending to distrust drawing conclusions about processes they cannot observe or, in an experimental sense, carefully control. Applying behavioral principles is appealing because it seems to suggest a direct and relatively uncomplicated route to training. By training, we mean our ability to respond to situations—even complex ones—without having to figure them out, reason, or practice like we did the first times we faced the situation. For example, a driver of a car in a busy but familiar city, an expert piano player, and accomplished athletes are all engaging in complex, almost automatic, highly trained behavior. In these situations, people respond instantaneously to all but the most unexpected events, and they are usually not aware of any thinking at all.

For a more elaborate human example of this basic learning behavior (called *conditioned response*), imagine yourself having once been terribly embarrassed because your teacher asked you a question while you were daydreaming. Since then, whenever you catch yourself daydreaming in class, you jump back to attention with a sense of panic. You respond to the one stimulus (daydreaming) as if it were no different from the "actual" threat. You respond as if you had actually been caught and embarrassed.

Learning as Pursuing Rewards and Avoiding Punishment

Studies of stimulus and response dominated experimental psychology through the 1940s, but it was psychologist B. F. Skinner's theories in the 1950s that focused renewed interest on behaviorism and learning. Skinner built on the earlier work of Edward Thorndike, who conducted studies of animal learning early in the twentieth century. Thorndike discovered two important learning principles. First, he observed that animals *learned* to repeat intentionally a particular "accidental" movement (e.g., sliding open the bolt to a cage) when their action was *reinforced* by the reward of the food. Second, he found that animals improved the speed of their problem solving with "exercise," or *repetition.*

Like Thorndike, Skinner focused on prompting purposeful and voluntary behavior. Although he appreciated the enormity of the task, he believed, in principle, that by breaking down complex behaviors into their simplest component parts, it was possible to understand and take charge of one's own or another's behavior. Skinner's ultimate goal was to develop a science of behavioral control that would promote widespread happiness in a well-engineered society.

Classical conditioning theories had focused on reinforcing existing behaviors—such as Pavlov's salivating dogs. Skinner's goal, however, was to establish *psychological laws* for conditioning, or causing a subject to acquire new behaviors or stop undesirable ones. He developed a variety of strategies for reinforcing desired behaviors with rewards or by removing something negative; he also developed strategies for suppressing undesirable behaviors with punishments.

Schooling as Behavioral Training

Schools quickly saw behavioral psychology as enormously advantageous to their work. It helped make education more scientific at a time when being scientific brought increased respectability and higher status. Likewise, in an era when assembly-line efficiency had earned admiration throughout the culture, behavioral theories promised to help schools direct students' attention and energy toward classroom tasks and train them in the good habits that would be expected in the world of work. Finally, at a time of increasing uncertainty over *what* should be taught, behavioral methods exercised subtle but powerful influence over school curricula—causing schools to emphasize the type of knowledge suited to behavioral methods. Generations later, schools would still be trying to shake loose from behaviorism with calls to emphasize problem solving, critical thinking, and other "higher-order" tasks.

Teaching as Transmitting Knowledge Scientifically

Early in the century, Thorndike combined the results of his animal studies with philosopher and psychologist William James's theory that systematic exercise and drill could build proper habits of thought in humans. He applied his scientific "laws" of learning to classrooms, reasoning that drill and practice corresponded to his Law of Exercise; that is, the more often a child repeats a correct answer, the more likely that answer will be permanently "connected" to the question or problem. Thus, Thorndike recommended that teachers enhance children's language learning by exposing them to the same words over and over, and that they increase their pupils' facility with mathematics by having them practice common calculations repeatedly. Thorndike's Law of Effect, which was built on stimulus-response theory, held that if a child's correct response were rewarded with something pleasant—a smile or candy, for example—he or she would be more likely to repeat the response. Clearly, Thorndike saw teaching as a science aimed at efficiently controlling student learning. He believed scientific tests enabled teachers to address students' particular mental capacities and prepare students for particular social roles based on those mental capacities.

Like Thorndike, Skinner applied his behavioral theories to classrooms. He developed "teaching machines" that instructed by presenting knowledge in small chunks and providing constant rewards or reinforcement. Thorndike's behaviorist approaches formed the foundation for twentieth-century teaching theories, and Skinner's refinements were embraced enthusiastically in the late 1960s and the 1970s. Educational historian Joel Spring argues that Skinner's behavioral theories were widely applied, in large part, because they reflected the increasingly conservative tenor of the Nixon era. Behavioral theories supported greater control over the teaching process and over student behavior—both of which were seen by conservative critics as having run amok.[16] Interestingly, neither Thorndike nor Skinner had their work catch on outside the United States. Countries whose student achievement Americans came to envy in the 1980s and 1990s managed to be superior without paying much attention to America's behavioral reforms. However, so strong is this country's attachment to behavioral models that the back-to-basics movement of the 1990s would reassert these models in attempts to surpass the foreign "competition." These reforms are discussed further in Chapters 4 and 5 in relation to the school curriculum.

The first educational hallmark of behaviorism is the insistence that for learning (a behavior change) to take place, teachers must present students with the smallest and simplest units of complex behaviors. The second rarely questioned hallmark is that changing behavior (learning) requires conditioning through positive and/or negative reinforcement. Behaviorists have spun out an incredible variety of refinements to managing the rewards and punishments that presumably lead to desired goals. From these principles, psychologists and many others interested in understanding, controlling, or improving behavior draw their applications for education. They use them to explain how teachers can motivate students to learn, specify the details of what students should learn, reinforce correct responses, and manage student behavior in class.

Bloom's Taxonomy

Perhaps the most sophisticated explication of behavioral learning theory is found in Benjamin Bloom's taxonomy of the cognitive domain. In 1956 Bloom and his colleagues classified educational objectives into three domains—the cognitive, affective, and psychomotor. Although Bloom argued that all three were important, it was his hierarchy of cognitive objectives that came to dominate educators' rhetoric and practice of lesson planning. Bloom divided cognitive tasks into the following six types, ordered from the least to the most demanding:

- Knowledge: Rote learning of something, without necessarily making meaning of it
- Comprehension: Understanding something, but not necessarily in relation to other things
- Application: Knowing how to use an idea to solve a problem
- Analysis: Breaking a concept down into its component parts
- Synthesis: Combining parts into a new and meaningful whole
- Evaluation: Making judgments about the worth of how ideas or materials are applied

In the 1960s teachers all across the country began designing lesson plans that both specified a "behavioral objective" and identified where in Bloom's taxonomy the objective fit. Many teachers also designed their classroom tests to include tasks and items that could assess the "level" of cognitive knowledge their students had attained in the content they were expected to learn.

In Pursuit of Psychological Efficiency

Bloom's was not the only scheme that had an appealing blend of the scientific efficiency of modern production and the psychological efficiency of behaviorism. Since the 1970s, for example, hundreds of thousands of teachers have learned an approach called "Mastery Teaching" or "Clinical Instruction" developed by Madeline Hunter. Hunter's strategy, reminiscent of both Herbart and Skinner, specifies the steps of an "effective" lesson based on behavioral learning theory.

In Hunter's method, teachers begin each lesson by providing students an *anticipatory set*—a provocative question or activity to preview the information and tasks to follow. The second step conveys the learning objectives unambiguously, nearly always expressed as what teachers expect students to know or be able to do at the end of the lesson. Then teachers present the information or skill to students using a variety of materials and familiar examples. Next, the teacher or an already accomplished student would *model* the correct behavior or response. The teacher would give the students opportunities for *guided practice,* all the while monitoring and checking for understanding to determine whether students are acquiring the knowledge or skill. For example, before individuals are asked to demonstrate their knowledge, the teacher asks the whole group to respond—with either hand signals or choral recitation. Throughout the lesson, the teacher prompts and cues when needed and reinforces correct responses with praise. After most students seem to have "gotten it," the teacher provides them an opportunity for *independent practice,* and she gives feedback immediately. Although the preceding terms may sound unfamiliar, the lessons surely are not. These are the lessons that most adults today experienced, though few had teachers who actually "mastered" the complex orchestration of the methods and rules.

This approach seems logical to many teachers, and it actually helps them achieve certain behavioral objectives. Inexperienced teachers, in particular, seem to appreciate the security of concentrating on what they, the teachers, are supposed to do next, rather than the difficult and ambiguous job of constantly responding to what students are thinking and learning. However, research into the method has not provided evidence that it helps children learn, or be more effective citizens. There seems to be no substitute for keeping instruction focused on students' learning rather than teachers' teaching. Neither is there evidence that of the thousands trained in the method, any more than a small percentage of teachers continue to practice it.

Motivating with Rewards and Punishment

Adults often explain children's failure by stating that they lack motivation. People commonly assume that motivation comes and goes, as when they say, "I don't feel motivated today." Some see motivation as an action, like spanking or encouraging: "What can I do to motivate that child?" Clearly, motivation is a flexible and useful idea for referring to the unseen energy and determination that drive people to take charge of their actions. However, two people using the term may have very different premises about what it describes.

How people use the term *motivation* reveals much of what they believe about learning. Not surprisingly, the behavioral view of motivation rests heavily on reinforcement (reward and punishment). Its appeal is easy to understand. Long before first graders have a well-developed understanding of proper classroom behavior, teachers can motivate and train them with rewards and punishment not to talk while others are talking and to raise their hands before speaking. Teachers who are skilled classroom managers can accomplish this after a relatively short period. However, they run the risk that, if the rewards and punishments stop, so will the desired behavior. Often, maintaining good behavior requires increasingly large rewards or punishments.

Educators and psychologists commonly distinguish between *extrinsic motivation,* which comes from someone or somewhere else, and *intrinsic motivation,* which is generated from within. Rewards and punishments are associated with extrinsic motivation, and they can be efficient in starting or stopping simple, routine acts and habits. But as behaviors become more complex, systems for rewards and punishments must become equally elaborate. Rewards and punishments ultimately become harder to keep convincingly aligned with the behaviors they must influence.

Controlling Misbehavior with Behavioral Training

Thousands of teachers around the country have been trained in "assertive discipline," probably the most popular current behavioral strategy for keeping classrooms orderly. When teachers use assertive discipline, they establish a clear set of classroom rules and a highly visible schedule of consequences for breaking them. For example, at the first infraction, the teacher might warn the student verbally and write her name on the board; the second offense might bring a check mark next to the written name; at the third, the teacher would remove the student from the room or keep her after class. A telephone call home would likely follow, and so on, with more severe consequences if the misbehavior continues.

Many teachers find these behavioral management schemes useful, but often the benefits are temporary and the long-term consequences are negative. The following reflection from first-year teachers Julie McKay and Julie Bosustow tell just such tales.

I have about five students who already had been labeled as "problems" and who had gone through every assertive discipline plan imaginable. Daily contracts with teachers, yearly contracts with the principal, numerous parent conferences, and Student Study Team reviews had all been tried. The end result was merely that the students knew they were "problems." It was amazing to me to realize how savvy they were about the deals they had made with their teachers and administrators—how they knew the conditions of whichever contract they were on. Unfortunately, my realization came after I made the same type of contracts (upon the advice of administrators and past teachers), and once again the students fell into the same negative behaviors.

—Julie McKay
First-year teacher, grade 4

I have developed a system of sticker cards wherein the students can receive a sticker for each of the four periods of the day. Their name goes up in a happy face on the board if they are on task and following the rules. If their name stays in the happy face for the entire period, they get a sticker on their card. If they don't get a sticker, I write on the card the exact reason why they didn't. These cards go home every Friday (and are returned signed by the parents on Monday), and their parents can see exactly what has transpired with their child for that week in the classroom. I also give the whole class points for following the rules that can be applied to extra center time, and I give table points for the tables of students who stay on task and who are behaving properly.

So why is it that I resort to yelling and being angry sometimes instead of relying on the discipline methods that I have instituted? This is a question that I continually reflect upon. I have problems with extrinsic rewards and haven't been able to totally accept their effectiveness for first graders. I have problems with being consistent. The system of sticker cards that I have set up requires time and often I don't make that time available. But, most importantly, I think I'm still waiting for my students to respond from a more intrinsic perspective that I believe should come from their desire to learn and to be treated with respect.

—Julie Bosustow
First-year teacher, grade 1

These teachers' experiences are not unusual. Systematic studies of assertive discipline have not supported it or other behavioral schemes as helpful approaches to curbing most student misbehavior. It is certainly a legitimate human response to express delight with behavior that pleases and to sometimes ignore undesirable behavior. It is just not very useful to try to work these human responses into a rational scheme for controlling behavior. Education writer Alfie Kohn has written convincingly about the harmful effects of praise if the praise becomes more important than the intrinsic importance of acting correctly. Sometimes people get so accustomed to praise that if they do not get it, they cannot feel that the activity is worthwhile.

In school, rewards often become the objects of negotiations that distract from the particular learning focus at hand ("If you do this thing you don't want to do, I will reward you by letting you do something you like"). Sometimes negotiation becomes an end in itself—especially when trying to change the behavior of a skilled student negotiator ("OK, class, finish the book report for homework, and tomorrow we can watch the movie . . . OK, just a draft, but a really good one . . . OK, I'll check your progress on the draft tomorrow and I'll collect it on Monday"). Sometimes punishment or the threat of punishment makes a person feel so bad she wants to act in a way to avoid the punishment, but other times a punishment reinforces negative behavior ("You are suspended from school for a week").

Behavioral approaches do shape behavior; they work well for teaching small, discrete behaviors. They help to socialize children with habits approved by the culture. The behaviorists were also not wrong about the usefulness of conditioning for managing classroom discipline. If teachers want quiet and orderly students, at least in the short run, conditioning with rewards and punishment will help. Moreover, rewards and punishments seem so fundamentally engrained in human behavior that we cannot imagine the world or individuals functioning without them—at some level, they are here to stay. Visit most any classroom, and you'll see rewards and punishments aplenty. But if behavioral approaches to teaching succeed in limited ways, they are severely limited for promoting the deep understanding, the problem-solving skills, and the respectful relationships that are required to acquire complex knowledge and for democratic civic life.

The Limits of Transmission and Training

Remedial Math, called Math 1, is a thirty-year-old program that was said to be successful when it was first implemented. The individualized program allows the students to advance at their own pace in mastering the four basic mathematical operations: addition, subtraction, multiplication, and division. The four basic operations are applied to five main topics: Whole Numbers, Decimals, Percents, Fractions, and Measurements. Each of the five topics has its own workbook.

Students are to practice in their workbook, correct the work, and take the test when the teacher deems they are ready. If the student fails the test, then she/he does another practice page and retakes the test. There are days when they do not want to do the pre-made problems. These problems have absolutely no meaning or relevancy to their lives. The students have to do at least one page of work to master the concepts, correct the answers to the odd-numbered problems, then patiently wait for the teacher to correct the even-numbered problems. Much time is wasted waiting for the teacher, and many times the teacher has three to five students waiting to be checked. By then, the students are restless and would rather do other work or chat with their friends. (I do not blame them.)

This repetitious and tedious process continues with no change for the entire school year. What is more devastating is the fact that the majority of the students do not retain what they have learned. They only learn for the test, and forget almost instantaneously. The horror continues as all of the Math I teachers use the exact same set of tests. It makes it so tempting and easy to cheat. Tests have been stolen, as well as answer keys. Students will memorize the answers and give them to other students. This is the most ineffective method I have seen. There is very little teaching or learning taking place. It makes me sad and angry because this math year is virtually wasted.

—Dung Bich Lam
First-year teacher, mathematics, grade 9

Although all behaviorally based instruction is not as awful as the situation Dung Bich Lam describes, many teachers teach at schools where there is a heavy reliance on behavioral learning theories of instruction and on IQ. The *transmission* model of teaching and learning proposes that knowledge from the sender (teacher) is sent (transmitted) to the receiver (student). This model resembles a straightforward one-directional conduit or pipeline. The process asks the teacher to break down and organize the facts (curriculum and lesson planning), send the facts (teaching), monitor whether the facts have been received (testing), and try again if testing demonstrates that something was missed (reteaching).

Behaviorism Ignores Thinking

Sometimes theories and practices are instructive because of their failures. At the same time that B. F. Skinner's theories were refining behaviorism in classrooms, observers became increasingly aware of what behaviorism left out—thinking. Consequently, new theories of cognition (thinking) began to emerge. Along with the proliferation of behavioral methods came an equally vigorous critique from a group calling themselves cognitive scientists. But this was not just a battle between theorists in universities and laboratories, nor was it confined to educators and psychologists in opposing camps. The arena for the conflict was culture itself. To be sure, one found the debate about behavioral versus cognitive theories argued in scholarly journals and school faculty rooms, but it also took place in the highest policy forums in Washington, in state houses, at school board meetings, and across the dinner table when parents tried to understand Junior's homework. International events, political ideologies, and the results of national elections helped shape, and continue to shape, the development and practice of these and other theories of learning. For example, the former Soviet Union's launch of an unmanned spacecraft in 1957 boosted enthusiasm for Skinner's promise of orderly and scientific learning, especially in the technical skills that Americans seemed to lack.

Behaviorism Can't Prepare a Nation of Problem Solvers

Many new and diverse voices entered the public education debates during the late 1950s and throughout the 1960s. These were scientists who knew the kind of knowledge that was needed in laboratories, businesspeople who understood the demands on workers, and corporate leaders who appreciated the complex skills and relationships required in trade and finance. All concluded that citizens needed to be able to solve complex problems, not just step-by-step accumulations of simple ones. Students needed to draw knowledge from real life, not just learn the information "building blocks" provided in the classroom. Memorizing the pieces of knowledge produced by science was not enough; students must learn to think like scientists. These views had long influenced elite schools, but now the country sensed that elites alone could not keep the country apace with the rest of the world.

The environment during the liberal Kennedy and Johnson years encouraged breaking with traditions in social structures and thinking. For example, in the 1960s President Kennedy brought into the White House a "kitchen cabinet" of young, mostly Harvard-educated intellectuals to advise him about solving domestic social problems as well as managing international diplomacy; most stayed on to help Lyndon Johnson strategize in the Vietnam War and the war against poverty at home. Independent think tanks filled with social scientists who offered expertise and policy advice. If social science were to unlock the keys to international relations and remedy the ills of poverty and racial injustice, as well as enable the United States to compete in the arms and space race, then schools must produce large numbers of graduates who were thinkers and problem solvers.

Religious and political conservatism of the 1980s and 1990s supported traditional and behavioral preferences for schooling. And yet it was during these years that the "cognitive revolution" took over as mainstream educational theory. Of critical importance was that advocates for social justice were conducting powerful research and developing models for teaching to support a common school curriculum and multicultural perspectives. The promise of linking a good education and a good society seemed possible once again.

Digging Deeper

The scholars and works listed in this section should provide readers with a deeper understanding of the development of IQ and behavioral psychology and the limits of these approaches for today's classrooms. The "Digging Deeper" section at the end of Chapter 3 points to research and the teaching implications of newer, more hopeful conceptions.

Daniel W. Bjork, who teaches history at St. Mary's University in San Antonio, Texas, has written a well-reviewed biography, *B. F. Skinner: A Life* (Washington, DC: American Psychological Association, 1997), that traces the psychologist's life and work. Bjork draws on the Skinner collection in the Harvard archives and other sources to highlight the development of his thinking. **B. F. Skinner** explained his theories of behaviorism and his wish to improve society through systematic behavioral control and positive reinforcement in two widely read books, *Walden Two* and *Beyond Freedom and Dignity.*

Stephen Jay Gould's *The Mismeasure of Man* (New York: W.W. Norton, 1996) traces the history of efforts to classify and rank people according to their supposed genetic gifts and limits. This revised edition includes a new introduction telling how and why he wrote the book and tracing the subsequent history of the controversy on inherited characteristics, right through *The Bell Curve.* The book also includes five essays, dealing with *The Bell Curve* in particular, and with race, racism, and biological determinism in general.

Asa Hilliard is an educational psychologist and professor of urban education at Georgia State University in Atlanta. Hilliard served as an expert witness in several landmark federal cases on test validity and bias, including the *Larry P. v. Wilson Riles* IQ test case in California—a case that outlawed the use of IQ tests for classifying African American students as mentally retarded. His book *Testing African-American Students* (Chicago: Third World Press, 1996) explores issues of educational equity in assessment, particularly regarding the use of IQ tests with African American students.

Alfie Kohn's book *Punished by Rewards: The Trouble with Gold Stars, Incentive Plans, A's, Praise, and Other Bribes* (Boston: Houghton Mifflin, 1995) argues against the use of rewards in raising children, teaching students, and managing workers. Kohn makes the case that rewards, like punishments, are methods of controlling people (perhaps, a morally objectionable goal), and that, at best, they produce only temporary compliance. He traces the development of behaviorist doctrine and its widespread acceptance and examines the effect that rewards have on behavior, concluding that rewards fail for many reasons: They punish, rupture relationships, ignore underlying reasons for behavior, discourage risk-taking; and undermine interest in the task at hand. He also looks carefully at how behavioral approaches to learning and external motivation undermine students' intrinsic motivation to learn.

Journalist **Nicholas Lemann**'s 1999 book *The Big Test: The Secret History of the American Meritocracy* (New York: Farrar, Straus & Giroux) tells a fascinating story of testing and meritocracy in the United States. His revealing history of the SAT makes clear that American conceptions of meritocracy that lead to unequal and unfair opportunities are neither natural nor inevitable.

Elaine and **Harry Mensh**'s book *The IQ Mythology: Class, Race, Gender and Inequality* (Carbondale, IL: Southern Illinois University Press, 1991) reports a comprehensive, well-documented study of bias in mental testing and in IQ tests in particular.

Steven Selden, who teaches and coordinates the program for curriculum theory and development at the University of Maryland, has studied the eugenics movement in American history and traces how this strange mix of racism and science has influenced our conception of human abilities. His book, *Inheriting Shame: The Story of Eugenics and Racism in America,* was published in 1999 by Teachers College Press at Columbia University.

University of Texas at Austin educational psychologist **Richard Valencia** evaluates the validity and reliability of intelligence and achievement tests, particularly for use with Latino students. His work has traced the links between tests, test bias, and widely held conceptions of cultural deficits in students of color. Of particular interest is his book *The Origins of Deficit Thinking: Educational Thought and Practice* (London, England: Falmer Press, 1997).

Lelia Zenderland's book *Measuring Minds: Henry Herbert Goddard and the Origins of American Intelligence Testing* (Cambridge, England: Cambridge University Press, 1998) is a new, well-documented history of the development of IQ tests in early twentieth-century America.

Notes

1. Richard Herrnstein taught psychology at Harvard until his death in 1995; Charles Murray was for many years a professor of sociology at the University of Chicago.
2. Richard Herrnstein and Charles Murray, *The Bell Curve: Intelligence and Class Structure in American Life* (New York: The Free Press, 1994), p. 436.

3. Stephen J. Gould, *The Mismeasure of Man,* 2nd ed. (New York: Norton, 1996), p. 24.
4. Herbert Kliebard, *The Struggle for the American Curriculum: 1898–1958* (New York: Routledge, 1983).
5. Gould, *The Mismeasure of Man,* p. 190.
6. Excerpted from "Mental Ability Test, Stanford University, Test 1, Information (World Book Co, 1920), as reprinted in Bill Bigelow, "Testing, Tracking, and Toeing the Line," *Rethinking our Classrooms: Teaching for Equity and Social Justice* (Milwaukee, WI: Rethinking Schools, Ltd., 1994), p. 121.
7. Gould, *The Mismeasure of Man,* p. 221.
8. Moreover, Gould calls *The Bell Curve,* published in 1994, "little more than a hard-line version of Spearman's *g*." In Gould, *The Mismeasure of Man,* p. 35.
9. Gould, *The Mismeasure of Man,* p. 301.
10. Kenneth Sirotnik, "Equal Access to Quality in Public Schooling: Issues in the Assessment of Equity and Excellence," in *Access to Knowledge: The Continuing Agenda for Our Nation's Schools,* rev. ed., ed. John I. Goodlad and Pamela Keating (New York: The College Board, 1994), p. 162.
11. *Tisn't What You Know, But Are You Intelligent?* Preface by Howard W. Haggard (New York: Harper and Brothers, 1927), p. 8.
12. Ibid.
13. College Board Online, Test question of the day, 16 March 1998. (On the Internet at http://www.collegeboard.org).
14. Pioneering German psychologist Wilhelm Wundt introduced what might have become in America a third line of inquiry—the systematic analysis of the perceptions, interpretations, and judgments that people report. Wundt was influential in Europe, but American investigators found Wundt's procedures—talking to people and recording what they report—less than scientific.
15. Emily D. Cahan and Sheldon H. White, "Proposals for a Second Psychology." *American Psychologist* 47 (1992), pp. 224–235, as cited in Michael Cole, *Cultural Psychology: A Once and Future Discipline* (Cambridge: Harvard University Press, 1996).
16. Joel Spring, *The American School, 1642–1990* (New York: Longman, 1990), p. 364.

CHAPTER 3

Contemporary Learning Theories:

Problem Solving, Understanding, and Participation

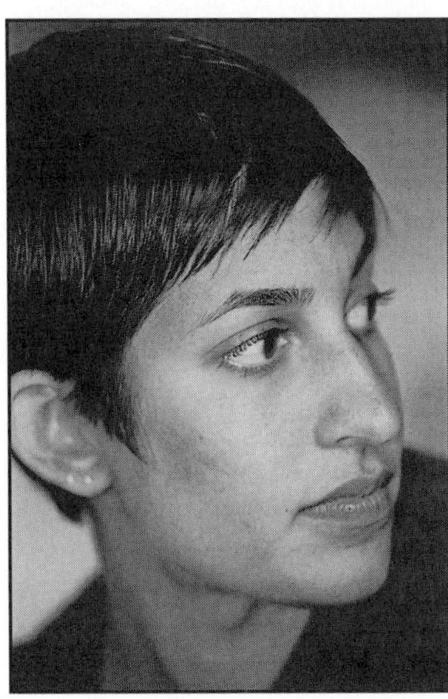

Zeba Palomino

First-year teacher, high school mathematics

The transmission view of knowledge doesn't lend itself to true understanding, but instead to memorizing random facts. Knowledge must be relevant and meaningful for children to acquire it and put to use. It seems like such an obvious strategy, yet I certainly never experienced it in school and do not know many who did.

—Lisa Trebasky
First-year teacher, science, grades 9–12

As politicians, scientists, and military leaders attacked the "flabby" school curriculum of the 1960s, the federal government responded to the education "crisis." The National Defense Act and the National Science Foundation distributed money, reports, and the views of scholars and scientists to change the nation's beliefs about what American students should learn. It was fine to prepare law-abiding citizens and workers who could read and do math, but that was not enough to fight and win the cold war. What the nation needed, these voices argued, was a nation of problem solvers.

Learning as Thinking and Understanding

This new demand on the common school raised serious questions, for psychologists at least, about the adequacy of the behavioral theories that dominated schools. Jerome Bruner was among the psychologists who disputed the behaviorists' transmission theories and proposed that it was possible to know more about how thinking and learning actually happened. Given that the country now saw the ideas of leading scientists and creative people as the most valued and practical kind of knowledge, Bruner proposed that it was *how* these people thought as much as what they knew that made their contributions possible.

So, instead of looking at the curriculum as a linear progression of adding facts upon facts throughout the grades, Bruner argued for a spiral curriculum. He suggested that all subjects had certain essential structures that children could learn at some appropriate level of sophistication at nearly any age. For example, children can begin learning fundamental ideas in physics even in the earliest grades, if teachers embed these concepts in concrete activities. First-year teacher Erik Korporaal acts on Bruner's ideas as he engages his students with the concept of wave formation, in a way appropriate to their age.

When learning about wave formation, the students engaged in an activity where they used their mouths to blow puddles of paint around on a piece of paper. The students then observed the tiny waves in the paint that resulted. Then, I deliberately connected the students' hands-on experience with wave creation to the ways in which wind forces create waves on the surface of the ocean.

—Erik Korporaal
First-year teacher, grade 6

Bruner's ideas influenced how people thought about science and mathematics and, eventually, other school subjects as well. His contributions foreshadowed, popularized, and even brought into public policy new theories of thinking and learning.

Of course, what psychologists were proposing in theory, many teachers already knew in practice: that teaching all the components of a subject did not add up to rigorous, complex learning—just lots of parts that frequently "turned off" students from the subject. Many teachers took readily to new curriculum materials that approached subjects from perspectives of large problems and hands-on projects. At the same time, psychologists tried to explain the processes people actually use to understand concepts, think critically, and solve problems. No longer were the invisible workings of the brain off-limits. Today we call this period of intellectual ferment the "cognitive revolution."[1]

What's Going On in the Mind?

Unlike their behavioral colleagues, cognitive psychologists paid attention to what goes on at the very moment of learning instead of looking solely at what happens before and after. It is often easy to see the *results* of learning. For example, we can watch a child sloppily bake his first cake, and we can identify at least a few of the many stimuli for this learning. We might credit the cake-baking modeling provided by parents, the child's sweet tooth, the attraction of a complex challenge, and the prospect of pleasing those who will eat the finished cake. Some popular theories spoke of inherent human "needs" such as the need for approval, the need to create, and so on, but identifying such stimuli or needs and suggesting that they "cause" the learning leaves unanswered too many questions about how and why the learning actually happens.

Cognitive theorists see children as active agents of learning—making sense, understanding, and creating knowledge—rather than as passive receivers or observers of outside events. Cognitive theorists also certainly consider how environmental conditions and biology affect those mental processes. But, knowledge is not "out there" in the world, waiting for us to nibble away in pieces until we are filled up. Knowledge is in us; we make it as we experience the world.

This powerful idea is of tremendous consequence for teachers, because the focus of education shifts to children's thinking; when this happens, the teacher's instruction is no longer the only variable we have to pay attention to. Now, the learner is at least an active, and some would say controlling, partner in acquiring school knowledge.[2] However, this element of cognition was also unsettling to many traditionalists—and not only teachers or psychologists. Some people "in charge" balked at the prospect of giving deep consideration to others who are younger, less powerful, or who "know less." Others who were perfectly willing to listen to children and those with minority viewpoints were not willing to concede their conviction that reality is more concrete than a human construction. Not just a few preferred to maintain the order and predictability of behaviorism.

Learning Is Active

A focus on learning as a process of making sense out of one's experience was not a new idea in the 1960s. At the turn of the century, philosopher John Dewey argued that children's learning is essentially problem solving, especially when they are engaged in devising their own experiments, building equipment, and cooperating with others in planning and doing projects. In the article "How We Think," published in 1910, Dewey railed against "the complete domination of instruction by rehearsing second-hand information, by memorizing for the sake of producing correct replies at the proper time."[3] Although Dewey didn't discount the importance of information, he maintained that information was acquired as children solved problems. Dewey's work provided a foundation for considering children's learning as an active mental process. However, it was radical for its time. It certainly failed to convey a sense of order and control over children and knowledge that many modern adults seemed to crave. Not until the 1960s did a theorist with similar ideas to Dewey capture the interest of psychologists and pique the curiosity of educators.

In the 1950s, at nearly the same time that B. F. Skinner was creating so much enthusiasm for behavioral studies, a group of American psychologists interested in child development "discovered" French biologist Jean Piaget's work. Piaget stunned them with his model for what humans actually did with all those inputs and stimuli that behaviorists discussed. He argued persuasively that behavioral psychologists were asking the wrong questions, and that even Dewey's suggestion that learning was a process of sense-making through action did not go far enough.

Learning Is the Construction of Meaning

Piaget had begun to observe children, including his own three, in the 1920s. Based on these observations, he developed learning theories that accounted for both human biology and experience. Piaget proposed that children are born with the drive—the curiosity—to construct new meanings. Learning or constructing new knowledge was the result of the mind's work, not an outsider's (whether the environment generally or a person in particular) manipulation. According to Piaget, children, like "little scientists," investigate and learn pretty much on their own, using the environment as their laboratory. Like real scientists, their explorations are partly self-directed and partly random or unplanned. Throughout childhood, they are curious and inclined to experiment. They not only take advantage of learning experiences but also create these learning opportunities for themselves.

For Piaget, it was not sufficient to explain children's increasingly sophisticated behavior simply on the basis that they accumulate more pieces of knowledge with which to work as they grow older. In other words, children's learning is not a simple process made more complex only because new details are added. Rather, Piaget argued that thinking and learning processes *develop* through particular stages—points at which children begin thinking about the world in fundamentally different ways.

Learning Reorganizes Our Minds To explain mental processes or structures of learning, Piaget proposed the interrelated ideas of schemes, assimilation, and accommodation. We can think of a *scheme,* roughly synonymous with a *template* (a pattern or mold to guide new work), as the mental framework that we use to organize our perceptions and experiences. Later "scheme theorists" propose that schemes enable us to connect the details of prior knowledge that are related in some potentially useful way. For example, schemes allow us to identify particular objects we have never seen before by connecting them with our experiences. We can identify chairs we have never seen before as chairs because we have a scheme that allows us to recognize an essential set of characteristics—general size and shape, suitability for sitting, and so on. In short, we have a sense of "chairness" that relieves us of the need to do elaborate figuring before we take a chance and sit down. It does not much matter if it is a rocking chair; a backless chair; or a leather, green, or broken chair. As soon as enough recognizable chair details fit our chair scheme, recognition is accomplished—we make a meaning. We make the object into a chair.

Piaget saw assimilation and accommodation as the processes through which children develop and alter their schemes. When we ask children "What did you learn today?" we seem to ask what new facts they added to their existing ones. Piaget called this adding on, or blending, *assimilation.* It is much less common for us to ask, "How did you change today?" And, of course, this is a much harder question to answer. For example, compare these two questions and the answers you are likely to get: (1) "What did you learn about the Civil War?" and (2) "How do you understand the Civil War differently?" The first question asks, in effect, for added knowledge. The second question presumes that additional knowledge requires alterations in what the student already knows. This second process—the changing or altering of schemes to accept new experiences—Piaget called *accommodation*. While assimilation and accommodation follow from experiences, experiences may include one's own thoughts. Just sitting and thinking can generate new (mental) experiences and trigger assimilation and accommodation.

A familiar example may help make this a bit clearer. You probably have a scheme for driving. That is, you have lots of driving information (e.g., traffic rules, judgments of space and speed, recognition of sounds, and the feel of the wheel and road). You learned and now remember and make use of all these bits and pieces of information when you need them only because you have them organized or packaged into a driving scheme. So when you get into your car, you simply drive off without thinking consciously about all of the judgments you make and specific operations you perform. If you drive a different but fairly similar car, you could use your existing driving scheme by assimilating a few new bits of information about the new car. The turn indicator switch might be in a different spot, the steering wheel might be a bit more or less sensitive, and the brake pedal might be a somewhat farther reach. But your driving scheme does not have to change. Now, consider what would happen if you went to England and had to drive on the "other" side of the road and you had to use a stick shift for the first time. Would your existing driving scheme work? Probably not. You could not simply add on, or assimilate, a few more pieces of information to make it work. More likely, you would have to reorganize the way you think about driving, in some respects starting from scratch. You might feel like and drive like an English beginner, chugging and weaving, until you could accommodate your driving scheme sufficiently to account for the differences in the new driving conditions. You would think about driving, and about yourself as a driver, in quite a different way.

Learning Unsettles Us Consider those people who love the challenge of their job, or working a puzzle, or going to a higher, more difficult level (more tension) in a computer game. A boring job is one that provides little new information to either relieve tension or create new challenges. Piaget used the concepts of *disequilibrium* and *equilibration* to explain the energy, tension, sense of balance and imbalance, and even the motivation (and sometimes resistance) that drives the whole cognitive process. Just think about how you would feel as you were adjusting to driving a manual transmission in England. Uncomfortable. Unbalanced! That same process happens as children develop new ways of thinking about the world. Needless to say, no good is served by having children flounder in the midst of unsuccessful problem solving. Unless resources are handy to support the problem solving, a student might learn to avoid problems. However, disequilibrium in children may needlessly "trick" well-meaning adults to step in and smooth the waters—get rid of the discomfort. It is important for schools to help students identify the tension of "not knowing" as curiosity or a "drive" or a need to know. This is a productive and necessary element of learning and is probably what most people experience as "motivation."

Equilibration is the lessening of tension as more information is acquired, and as the balance between what one knows and needs to know stabilizes—perhaps a point when the job or game teeters between the feeling of mastery and the beginning of boredom. Fortunately, a new "solution" is just as likely to set off a new imbalance as it is to put all questions and tension to rest. So, once again, just as we approach a tolerable balance we may seek more information, see more complex problems, accept new challenges. Confident learners identify disequilibrium as something positive—even addictive.

When everyone including our supposedly "best" student is struggling, we tend to think that we are expecting too much from them. I asked students not only to recite the formula, but also to derive it and understand where it came from. It was no longer enough just to memorize the formula. Students had to make sense of the formula. I nearly succumbed to the belief that the lesson was too difficult for them. Then I realized that I was not thinking about Piaget's theory. When I did, I realized I was not expecting too much from them, just something new.

—Marilyn Cortez
First-year teacher, mathematics, grade 9

Old Meanings Can Get in the Way Humans can get very set in their mental ways and erect barriers to further learning. In individual children and adults, it is tempting to see this as a character flaw. "Stubborn," we say of children; or "ignorant," we call adults. But schemes may take time to change to enable us to accept new information. Instead, people often alter their perceptions of information or experience to make them compatible with their existing schemes. For example, most children and adults have incorrect but fixed schemes for many of the physical laws of the universe. They naïvely experience the sun as moving across the sky instead of attributing the apparent motion of the sun to the earth's rotation. It is so difficult to develop a practical or experiential scheme for the earth spinning (none of our physical sensations support this) that we continue to perceive the sun as moving.

Stubborn schemes extend to social phenomena as well. For example, like other adults, teachers often have narrow, even prejudicial, schemes for forming conclusions (making sense or meaning) about who will be successful or unsuccessful students. A teacher might notice the race, language, dress, friends, standardized test scores, school label ("slow" or "regular"), or initial assignments of a student. If any one or combination of these observations fits in with a scheme for a child who "can't learn," the teacher is likely to act on this wrong conclusion—a conclusion that can be as hard to change as the conclusion that the earth stands still while the sun moves across the sky.

Once the teacher has made sense of the student, let us say as a low achiever, the teacher is likely to notice additional characteristics that fit the teacher's scheme or "frame of mind" for low achievers (i.e., "This kid is absent a lot—just like the rest of them"). On the other hand, what happens to information that contradicts the scheme, such as a high grade on the first test or perfect attendance? Initially, the contradictory information might cause disequilibrium—tension that needs to be resolved. Because schemes are difficult to recognize and difficult to change, perfect attendance might simply pass unnoticed or be dismissed as not important; a good grade might be seen as one exception to the scheme or cause to wonder if the student cheated.

Minds Develop in Stages

Can you bring to mind medieval paintings that portray children with adult faces on top of chubby child bodies? If so, you have an idea of how people understood learning well into the twentieth century. Historically, society thought children had the same mental capabilities for learning as adults—they just weren't as good at it. Even today, many adults look at children and see miniatures of themselves.

One of Piaget's most important contributions was his theory that children think in fundamentally different ways from adults and that their thinking *develops* as they make sense of experiences. Children represent the world differently as they proceed through developmental stages. They do not simply accumulate knowledge or get faster at figuring things out. It might help to think about a caterpillar transforming itself into a butterfly. A butterfly is not simply a larger, quicker, more complex caterpillar; it is a fundamentally different creature. So, too, with the fundamental differences Piaget saw in children's cognitive transformations between one stage and another.[4]

Consider a child's experience in the sandbox—pouring sand back and forth between a small pail and a larger one. This experience adds to his growing understanding of *conservation,* a fundamental physical law that says that altering the shape or position of something does not change its volume or quantity. Piaget used this law as an example of an understanding that cannot take place until the child is developmentally ready. A younger child will conclude that a small pail filled to overflowing contains more sand than a large pail only partly filled. This child will not conclude that the amount of sand remains the same whether it fills a small container or half-fills a larger one. Only later, when he is old enough and experienced enough, will he develop the concept of conservation.

Piaget argued that making new meanings—developing schemes—requires a complex interplay among broad concepts (such as conservation) and small bits of information (sand filling or not filling the pail), as well as sufficient age or maturity. An 18-month-old will not "get" conservation because she does not yet have the right kind of biological apparatus to acquire that mental understanding—just like the caterpillar can't fly and the tadpole can't hop. On the other hand, simply maturing physically does not fully account for development. The child's experiences and social interactions also play powerful roles. Taken together, new biological capacities and information set into motion the imbalance/balance tensions of equilibration, and the child learns from physical and social experiences when she is ready. Regarding the concept of conservation, an 18-month-old needs time (age). And she needs experience with sand and pails, water and buckets, getting into a full bathtub, trying to squeeze an extra toy into a suitcase, and the like. She also needs to feel all the possible attendant emotions—playing with sand is fun, approved by parents, feels good, and so on.

Stages and Personal, Social, and Moral Development

Following Piaget, two prominent psychologists have contributed intriguing analyses of how certain personal, social, and moral development also proceeds in stages. Erik Erikson identified eight stages of personal and social development that help us observe social growth. Five of the stages take place before the age of 18. These stages are flexible and overlapping, and they vary considerably among individuals. Erikson's contribution was to portray many of life's growing-up struggles as healthy development instead of aberrations that alarm parents and annoy schools. Erikson's stages consider children's maturation, experiences, and social interactions. When combined with an understanding of intellectual development, his stages help fill out a picture of the whole child.

During the child's first eighteen months, more or less, his essential developmental task is learning to rely on his mother. He also must learn to trust himself not to disappoint her. When mother cares for her baby and responds to him with pleasure, he trusts both her and his own worthiness. If mother is uncaring, her child will not trust others and, inevitably, he will lack confidence that others will care for him. Trusting oneself is closely linked to trusting others at this early age. As in all of his childhood stages, Erikson connects developing personality with social interactions. In the second stage, children explore possibilities for acting on their own. During the "terrible twos," power struggles frequently take place. Children slowly learn that sometimes they get what they want and sometimes they don't. During this stage, Erikson suggests, too few adult-imposed limits can cause children to feel out of control or have an unrealistic sense of their own autonomy. In contrast, too firm a hand can cause them to feel powerless and incompetent. The essential struggle between risk and security parallels children's needs for both autonomy and guidance. Between ages 3 and 6, children act and talk vigorously and spontaneously. They are full of energy and initiative. They develop a sense of comfort with their ability to make things happen—to be a force in the world and have others pay attention to them. But they may also feel unsure of their natural urges and guilty about them. This can happen if worried parents—afraid that their children will become uncontrollable—become too restrictive or punitive. During children's elementary school years, their developing self-concepts take on important new dimensions. Some children begin to define themselves as learners, workers, and people who accomplish things. Successful experiences promote such positive self-perceptions. Failure, on the other hand, can lead children to doubt their learning capacity. They may place responsibility for failure on circumstances beyond their control. Or they may attribute their success to the teacher or to luck rather than to their own efforts. Neither belief helps them learn. Teenagers struggle to resolve both the old conflicts of childhood and new trials of adulthood. They must assert themselves as independent individuals; at the same time they crave support and acceptance. In the process they may test, challenge, and shock others, especially their parents, but also their teachers and friends and anyone else they meet. They try to imagine themselves as adults. As they do they will often idolize adults (or even slightly older teenagers) whom they fantasize as having perfect or at least conflict-free lives. Many teenagers feel emotionally battered by their own conflicting wishes—security versus independence; recognition as a humanitarian versus having power over others; intimacy versus undemanding social and sexual relationships. The resolving of these conflicts helps generate very rapid development and makes these years both joyous and painful for adults to watch.

Lawrence Kohlberg studied stages of children's and adults' moral decision making. He focused primarily on reasoning—the process by which people make ethical choices. Like Erikson's, Kohlberg's distinctions line up in fairly recognizable ways. The simpler, more concrete moral reasoning appears earlier in life; the more sophisticated and abstract reasoning develops in adulthood, if at all. Kohlberg relied on Piaget's ideas of cognitive development to identify stages of moral decision making. Anyone who has tried to play checkers with a 3-year-old knows that the child's concept of rules is different from that of most adults. Young children can learn to state the rules. However, they may not be able to act upon them if losing a point or a game doesn't make sense. Kohlberg did not produce a scientific hierarchy of moral decision making that we can apply to individuals. Rather, he offered a wide range of processes (we might call them moral schemes) that people use to arrive at their moral choices. The following list shows the variety of logic that is possible. Note how difficult it is to assign a child to a single stage and how even adults make decisions in each or most of these ways. According to Kohlberg:

- Children make their early moral decisions out of habit or fear of punishment. They follow the rules made by authorities. These decision-making processes have a decidedly behavioral flavor. That is, children don't make sense out of the rules. They follow them because "that's just the way it is."
- Later, children interpret externally imposed rules to make them consistent with and satisfy their own needs. Children practice their developing understanding of fairness, especially when it does not conflict with their self-interest.
- Later still, children learn to override or reinterpret self-interest to make decisions that please others and gain approval. They attempt to make sense out of what other people define as right.
- For some people maintaining the social order and respecting authority define what is right and good. They obey laws, not out of blind acceptance, fear of punishment, or desire for social approval, but because they understand rules to be essential for a moral and orderly society.

- People reason that rules need to serve society, and they believe that reasonable people can decide on what is best. Values and ethical principles take precedence over tangible gains and losses to the individual. Laws may be disobeyed if they conflict with one's highest principles.

A few implications of Piaget's, Erikson's, and Kohlberg's work warrant emphasis here. At each stage of their development, children have particular learning and growing-up work to do. Much of the time they experience a natural state of struggle, conflict, or disequilibrium. Adults must participate in these experiences at times, and at other times they should keep their distance. Sometimes children's struggles are obviously painful; sometimes children seem inappropriately blasé. Aside from not allowing self-destructive behaviors, there are few hard-and-fast guidelines to help teachers decide whether to step in or hold back. However, it's nearly always appropriate to listen nonjudgmentally as children explain their reasons and tell more about their feelings; it's nearly always inappropriate to attempt to push children from one stage to the next.

The Cognitive "Revolution"

Since the 1960s psychologists have modified and refined Piaget's work. In a manner of speaking, the field of psychology took inspiration from Piaget and ran off in several directions, gaining more or less distance from behaviorism. Even so, cognitive psychology continues to reflect Piaget's observations about fundamental mental processes. All now agree that learning is developmental, though the stages are much less clearly defined than people first understood them to be. And all agree that learners are active creators, builders, or constructors of their own knowledge, rather than passive receivers.

The consequences of this *constructivist* model of learning are significant. Learning is much less a process of passively accepting knowledge that has been transmitted by teachers or through experiences than it is a process of selecting and transforming experiences to serve new information needs. Drawing on Dewey and Piaget, contemporary constructivists—including teachers—focus on how new information and novel situations affect what we already know, and how we apply what we already know to novel situations. First-year history teacher Matthew Eide could have had his students memorize important facts about turn-of-the-century immigration but instead chose this constructivist approach.

I had students interview a recent immigrant, ideally a family member or a close friend. About 80 percent of my students were able to interview a family member. The students asked how the immigrants navigated a new life in a sometimes hostile environment, and specifically how they used their family and social networks to survive. The students then wrote essays comparing the experiences of the immigrants they interviewed with those of the turn-of-the-century immigrants. This essay had the highest completion rate of any I had assigned. I believe that's because they used their cultural and linguistic knowledge in a way that was legitimate in the classroom.

—Matthew Eide
First-year teacher, high school history

Similarly, first-year teacher Maria Hwang helped her students learn about Mexico in light what they know about where they live.

My curriculum on Mexico begins in Los Angeles, a point of reference for the students. They explore and rediscover the familiar in order to establish a foundation for new information that will be introduced in their [studies about] Mexico. Understanding the influences of Mexico manifested in Los Angeles, students can absorb the authentic source from which the influence derives.

—Maria Chiping Hwang
First-year teacher, high school ESL

Constructivists suggest that, like most of real life, thinking is complex and disorderly. Sometimes we take years to make sense of ideas and experiences; sometimes making sense happens overnight. That's what we really hope for when we tell someone to "sleep on it." And sometimes understanding happens in a flash. Not surprisingly, this real-life, real-people learning can wreak havoc with teaching strategies that rely on tight schedules and precise five- or seven-step lesson plans with a tidy progression from presenting new information to practice to reinforcement to learning.

The Mind as a Computer

It is not surprising that in the 1960s cognitive psychologists would look to the most astonishing invention of the mid–twentieth century—the computer—for ideas about how the human mind works. *Information-processing* theorists, who compare the most elemental, biochemical workings of the brain with basic computer design, have pushed beyond Piaget's general theories about meaning making to investigate how humans acquire, process, and use information. They theorize that, like computers, people have the capacity to "input" information, code and store it for both short and long-term retrieval, process and manipulate it internally, and produce "output." Over time and use, these information-processing capacities gain efficiency, power, and complexity, enabling what people in other fields and disciplines may call "high-level," "critical," or "executive" thinking. Information-processing theory explores a narrower scope of learning than other theories that purport to be more comprehensive (i.e., behaviorism or the sociocultural theory that follows in this chapter). Although information-processing research reveals some basic insights about cognition, it has limitations similar to behaviorism. It often ignores the social contexts that children and adults always use to make sense. Fascinating and, perhaps, invaluable as a research tool, its findings do not apply easily to human behavior and thinking in messy, real-life settings like classrooms.

What Makes a Mind "Smart"?

Today most cognitive theories depart to various degrees from the view that intelligence is an inherited general attribute or property (as Spearman argued when he developed the concept of *g*) that powers or drives other abilities. Most emphasize that individuals call upon multiple processes, which vary in individuals because of differences in their development, experience, and biological disposition. Some emphasize that differences in intelligence stem from the speed, power, or efficiency of mental processes. Others stress that experiences shape and promote development.

Racial Differences Are Irrelevant Generally, cognitive psychologists disagree with *The Bell Curve's* authors and others who use IQ test scores as evidence that people of different races inherit more or less thinking ability. They consider that conclusion scientifically unwarranted and socially irresponsible. They find human thinking a far richer and deeper collection of abilities than IQ can explain, even if there were to be widespread agreement on the meaning of IQ. Poverty and oppressive social conditions (factors that do vary in the United States according to race) significantly affect the few abilities that IQ tests purport to measure. Jerome Bruner reports an interesting cross-cultural example of the interplay between social conditions and IQ: Korean immigrants to Japan scoring fifteen points lower on average on IQ tests in Japan than Korean immigrants score in the United States. Bruner attributes this gap to the two cultures' treatment of the Korean immigrants: In Japan, they are denigrated as ignorant; in the United States, they are stereotyped as smart.[5] Other differences, addressed later in this chapter, can be attributed to social and cultural differences not associated with poverty or oppression.

Intelligence Is Multidimensional A number of contemporary psychologists have developed theoretical models of multidimensional intelligence. For example, Robert Sternberg proposes three types of intelligence that vary in strength among people. One intelligence promotes analytical and critical thinking, one leads to the development of creative new ideas, and one enables humans to respond quickly and productively to everyday events and experiences. Together, these intelligences include many more cognitive abilities than are captured in the concept of IQ. Sternberg argues that intelligence which is not encompassed in IQ may be more important for success at school and on the job. He suggests that rather than being strictly innate, these intellectual skills can be taught "to at least some of the people, some of the time."[6]

Howard Gardner moves even further than Sternberg from the idea that intelligence is a trait. Like Sternberg, Gardner discounts a *single* intelligence and emphasizes the many mental abilities and intelligences we all use. Gardner identifies intelligences that include but are not limited to language, mathematics and logic, visual and spatial perception, control over one's own movements, sensitivity to others, and knowledge of oneself. He considers these intelligences as mastery of competencies or skills, rather than underlying abilities or the quality of one's mind. His theory of multiple intelligence stresses the flexibility and variety of children's proclivities for learning.

Gardner suggests that everyone inherits the capacity to develop each of these intelligences, although individuals vary, and he notes that different cultures and subcultures stress certain kinds of intelligence. In the school culture, for example, survival and success depend more on language and mathematical abilities than on other abilities. Out of school, other domains are often as or more desirable than the skills that earn success in school. The most successful corporate CEO, schoolteacher, or surgeon may have gotten the very best test scores in school, but school success typically does not predict one's ability to seize a business opportunity, ask a good question at just the right moment, or hold a scalpel steady.

Children Learn to Be Intelligent in Multidimensional Classrooms These cognitive theories tell us that students learn to be intelligent as they experience the world. This is extraordinarily positive and reaffirming for teachers. Classroom experiences that allow for meaning-making in the variety of ways that students have available to them do help students become smart. However, theories of multiple intelligence have sent educators off in two directions. The more sensible of the two is to develop complex, realistic, multidimensional assignments and projects so all children can discover and combine their particular strengths with areas where they are not strong or lack experience. The other direction is to search for and label a student's one particular kind of intelligence and prepare activities that tap into that intelligence. But treating these multiple intelligences as traits that characterize children is ridiculous. Cognitive psychologists disagree among themselves about many things, but they shudder collectively when they hear teachers talk about their "spatial" children or their "bodily kinesthetic" learners.

Brain Science and Learning

In the past decade, advances in neuroscience (brain research) have begun to converge with the findings of developmental and cognitive psychology. Neuroscientists study the brain's anatomy, physiology, chemistry, and molecular biology. Often using imaging technologies to observe learning directly, these brain scientists ask questions quite similar to those of psychologists: How does the brain develop? Does development occur in stages? Are there critical developmental periods? How does the brain program information? What role does experience play in the developing brain?

Together, with psychologists, neuroscientists are beginning to give a more complete picture of how people think and learn. As summarized in a report from the National Academy of Science, *How People Learn: Brain, Mind, Experience, and School,* neuroscience has revealed that learning changes the physical structure of the brain; through these structural changes, learning organizes and reorganizes the brain; and different parts of the brain may be ready to learn at different times.[7] This work in neuroscience, together with work of developmental and cognitive psychologists, also supports some ideas of great importance in education:

1. The functional organization of the brain and the mind depends on and benefits positively from experience.
2. Development is not merely a biologically driven unfolding process, but also an active process that derives essential information from experience.
3. [S]ome experiences have the most powerful effects during specific sensitive periods, while others can affect the brain over a much longer time span.[8]

Perhaps most important, brain research has answered the puzzling question "What counts most in learning and intelligence—nature or nurture?" with a resounding answer of "both."

As these and other findings from brain research develop, they will likely bring fascinating insights into the process of teaching and learning in classrooms. However, we're not there yet. Despite some popular professional development material for teachers offering "brain-based" learning, little work in neuroscience has reached a point where specific implications for teaching can be derived.

Learning Is Social and Cultural

Learning, remembering, talking, imagining: all of them are made possible by participating in a culture. (p. xi)

So, in the end, while mind creates culture, culture also creates mind. (p. 166)

—Jerome Bruner
Culture and Education, 1990

The cognitive learning theories we have considered so far emphasize learning as an individual activity that takes place in the mind. According to these theories, individuals may differ in the particulars of *what* they learn, but mental processes are essentially the same across individuals and cultures. However, a growing number of psychologists, anthropologists, and linguists are finding these theories inadequate. Their work shows how cognitive processes differ in cultures that stress different kinds of knowledge, values, social organization, or work. Their *sociocultural* and *sociohistorical* theories argue that society and culture determine learning as much as mental activities, or rather, learning and mental activities *are* cultural. These scholars go beyond simply saying that culture *influences* thinking. Like Bruner, they maintain that society and culture are indistinguishable from learning or thinking. People cannot separate *how* thinking takes place from *what* knowledge is available in the place *where* learning happens. Drawing heavily from cross-cultural studies of learning (comparing how people think and solve problems in different societies), sociocultural theories fuse learning, intelligence, and culture into a single entity.

Families, Communities, and Cultures

It is easy enough to recognize that different cultures teach different knowledge in different ways. Within our own society we have an abundance of ethnic, regional, and neighborhood cultures in which common knowledge, customs, and how people express themselves are very different. If learning and intelligence were independent of culture, we could conclude that all knowledge is equally accessible to everyone, and a single standard for learning, ability, achievement, and merit would be warranted. But what happens when a theory of learning integrates culture with thinking processes? In that case, being smart by the standards of one culture is not comparable to being smart by the standards of another culture. In highly competitive societies such as ours, who is the "smartest" is determined by whichever culture has the power to set the cultural standards that the smartest people (those who learn "best" or "fastest") are supposed to reach. Therefore, in diverse societies students can reach society's highest standards for knowledge and skills only when schools allow them to use all the knowledge (from all the cultures) they have experienced and when standards are not so narrow as to exclude the value of that knowledge and experience.

Building on Students' Cultural Knowledge Students must be able to use their own social and cultural thinking processes to make sense of *any* new knowledge, whether it is knowledge derived from their "home" culture, the larger societal culture, or some combination. But schools often send the message that a student's existing cultural tools for learning and solving problems are inferior to those of the dominant (or school) culture. If we do not encourage students to develop and use all the cultural background they possess, we deny them, according to sociocultural theories, a substantial part of their available intelligence.

Again, cross-cultural comparisons provide some of the clearest examples. A child from a culture that does not have a formal number system would not think about *quantity* in the same way as a child from a culture with such a system. That is, those difficult-to-budge schemes for numbers and quantity, established early in life, might not easily accommodate Western mathematics. Western mathematics can be learned, but the people cannot be thought of as less intelligent because of some initial difficulty.

Culturally sensitive teachers keep in mind that important cultural differences often go undetected or misunderstood. All teachers will lack some cultural knowledge and miss cultural cues, but respectful teachers can make it clear to even the youngest students and their parents that the teachers themselves are in many ways cultural beginners and are eager to learn. For example, the degree to which students ask questions or remain quiet and observe can be a culturally shaped trait. However, many teachers might view constant questioning as aggressive or dependent behavior or interpret a reflective, observing child as withdrawn or slow. It is typical for white, middle-class, school-minded parents to constantly ask their children questions that they already know the answers to: "What do you call this?" "What kind of a car is that?" "What is this color?" "Is this my nose?" Children with other backgrounds may not be used to an adult asking questions unless the adult does not know the answer. In some cultures, if adults want to find out whether a child knows something, they are likely to be more imperative and business-like: "Tell me what the teacher said." "Show me how you do this problem." Imagine the potential for such a child's bafflement (and a teacher's misperception about the child's intelligence) when a teacher says "And where do we go now?" "And how are you going to leave?" instead of "It's time for recess. Please do not run until you are on the playground."

Whose Culture Is Best? A Political, Not a Learning Issue Sociocultural theories integrate social, historical, and cognitive processes. They recognize multiple ways of thinking and multiple definitions of important knowledge; they support a wide range of cultural perspectives and practices in the school curriculum; and they justify using social interaction as the primary medium of instruction. Suddenly, the political implications of sociocultural theories leap out at us. Sociocultural theories threaten those who want schools to represent only one culture's view of the world—only one group's shared ways of knowing and making sense. These theories also call into question traditional teaching practices such as lecturing and having students work alone. Sociocultural theories of learning and intelligence open the door for sociocultural interpretations of merit and progress. They admit a diverse range of hardworking, socially productive, creative, and very smart people.

A Socially Just Learning Theory Sociocultural theories are important twenty-first-century theories because they shift the burden of low achievement from culturally and linguistically diverse groups of children to where it belongs: on schools and the larger society. The strength of sociocultural perspectives is that social theory and learning theory at last converge in ways that will allow differences among Americans to strengthen, rather than weaken, our social, economic, and political life. Although students outside the dominant culture carry the greatest burdens from schools that ignore the social and cultural elements of learning, white and middle-class students do not escape damage. They, too, are victims of narrow and limited conceptions of learning and intelligence.

Sociocultural theory supports teachers who believe their job is to help all students develop the understanding and problem-solving skills necessary to fill important roles in a diverse and democratic society. No longer must these teachers endure the charge that they are naïve idealists who ignore the real-world lessons of "scientific" theory. Instead, teachers and others are now obliged to confront traditionalists with the obvious and documented failures of traditional theory and practice. They can now "answer back" with a theory of their own, one more consistent with their moral and ethical convictions and more relevant to today's practice.

In 1896 philosopher John Dewey wrote an essay for *The School Journal* called "My Pedagogic Creed." In it, Dewey ties children's learning to the social context in which they learn. Dewey wrote:

> I believe that all education proceeds by the participation of the individual in the social consciousness of the race. This process begins almost unconsciously at birth, and is continually shaping the individual's powers, saturating his consciousness, forming his habits, training his ideas, and arousing his feelings and emotions. Through this unconscious education, the individual gradually comes to share in the intellectual and moral resources which humanity has succeeded in getting together. He becomes an inheritor of the funded capital of civilization. . . . I believe that the only true education comes through the stimulation of the child's powers by the demands of the social situation in which he finds himself. . . . Through the responses others make to his own activities, he comes to know what those mean in social terms. . . . I believe that the psychological and social sides are organically related and that education can not be regarded as a compromise between the two, or a superimposition of one upon the other.[9]

Learning through Participation

> No matter how student-centered the classroom may be, I still have an important job to facilitate discussion and cognitive conflict by asking a tough question, or challenging their conjectures. In knowing my students and where they are, I must know how to support the "stretching of their minds." I know I need experience. One never knows how students will respond—that is the excitement of education.
>
> —Juliana Jones
> *First-year teacher, mathematics, grade 6*

Innovative Soviet psychologist Lev Vygotsky was born the same year as Jean Piaget—1896. However, most of his work was not translated or published in

English until the late 1970s, when it sparked the interest of American psychologists and educators. Like Piaget, Vygotsky devoted himself to understanding how children develop cognitively. However, Vygotsky was especially interested in the social origins of children's thinking. He saw learning as a process of children "appropriating" their culture and making it their own.

Whereas Piaget saw the child as very much an independent learner, already equipped to draw in and make sense of the environment (including relationships with others), Vygotsky stressed a much more essential and interdependent relationship between child and adult. Vygotsky blurred the distinction between social experiences and mental processes. He emphasized learning and solving problems as that which happens *between* a learner and others, rather than something having a direction as with the teacher-to-learner transmission model of behaviorists and some cognitive psychologists. Social participation does not simply provide external stimulation for one's own thought; it is part of and in some respects indistinguishable from one's own thinking process. Vygotsky claimed that all meanings stem from interactions.

To explain why some social environments and interactions—including classrooms and learning opportunities—support learning far better than others, Vygotsky proposed the *zone of proximal development* (ZPD). He conceptualized this zone as containing the knowledge that a student can learn when assisted by or collaborating with an adult or more knowledgeable peer. The zone's boundary on one side is the knowledge the student already has or the problems she can solve alone. On the other side of the zone is knowledge and problem solving for which the student is not developmentally ready. Students who are within but close to this "edge" of the zone might be able to participate in an activity, but they need involved and active assistance. For example, the student with beginning writing skills might benefit from a question such as "Is there something important that this sentence needs at the beginning?" Or he might benefit from straightforward information such as "This sentence says, 'ran home' but I could understand it better if it told who or what ran home." As skills develop, the more knowledgeable person models increasingly sophisticated questions and problem solving. Some call this learning relationship *scaffolding,* because it provides a temporary structure around the "construction" of the student's learning and helps hold concepts together during the early stages of "sort of" knowing something, but not having it "all together."

Like Dewey, Vygotsky places great importance on the teacher's role of arranging activities and social groupings that keep students stretching within their zone. Obviously, students who do not enter the zone where they are challenged will only attempt problems they already know how to solve; students beyond their zone cannot learn well in spite of the help available. First-year teacher Cindy Bell's approach to mathematics instruction places scaffolding at the center. Not only does she assist her students' mathematical learning by asking questions that enable them to do what they could not have done alone, she has created a classroom where students continuously scaffold one another's problem solving.

By analyzing students' strategies, I can begin to understand my students' reasoning, which helps me know where I can focus my lessons and dialogue to assist them in developing more efficient ways of solving problems. To do this, I use frequent "on the spot" check-ins. The knowledge I collect serves as a springboard for my interactions with my students because I know what questions to ask them. For example, I posed the following math problem to the class:

210 students will be going on a field trip next week. If a school bus can hold 20 people, how many school buses will they need to take?

One of my students, Victoria, had difficulty understanding that one of the 11 buses would only be half filled (i.e., it would have 10 instead of 20 people on it). When I looked at her strategy, she had drawn 10 buses with 20 people in each, making the total number of people going 200, instead of 210. So my question to her was, 'What happens to the other 10 people left over?' She replied to me saying that they didn't get to go on the bus. Marisol and Catalina, overhearing our discussion, told her to put them on another bus. Victoria then tried to add another bus, drawing 20 seats (people) on the new bus. I could see here that Victoria didn't know how to account for the remaining 10 people because she was adding another full bus. I then asked her to count how many people she had going on the field trip. When she counted to 220, I asked her to check the problem again and see how many people the problem said were going on the field trip. In response, she said, "210" and then paused again, showing me she was thinking about how to resolve the remainder of 10 people. Eventually, Victoria decided to change her strategy.

—Cindy Kauionalani Bell
First-year teacher, grade 2

By setting classroom norms to guide math talk, Bell has developed a community of math learners whose members scaffold one another's understanding of mathematics strategies, explanations, and algorithms. These norms are consistent with Vygotsky, who proposed that learning and cognitive development were nearly indistinguishable from interactions with others—that learning occurs "out there" as much as inside the head. More precisely, Vygotsky viewed thought as the internalization of experiences in the social context. Thus the "location" of Cindy Bell's students' mathematical learning and knowledge cannot be specified as being in individual students' heads, in the classroom culture at large, or in the relationship among students. It is, in a word, sociocultural. The internalization of the social interaction *becomes* the cognitive process.

Social learning is not random. Relationships that can enhance or inhibit learning are organized or structured in families, schools, the workplace, and so on. In other words, when we organize a classroom and the interactions within, we are structuring learning. As explored in following chapters, many teachers, following Vygotsky, have come to think of their classrooms as "learning communities" where they pay special attention to relationships that give students access to adults and knowledgeable peers who scaffold one another's learning. For example, history teacher Mikel McBride uses both peer and teacher scaffolding as he engages students in constructing their own understanding of historical events.

I hope that I'm creating a new community in which my students will acquire historical literacy by interacting with others in activities. For instance, the students go through a simulated immigration process at Ellis Island. They must get their passports stamped a number of times in order to finish the activity, and this turns out to be very difficult. The wrap-up is a short discussion on how they felt and what they were thinking as they were doing the activity. The students, even the ones who cannot write very well, are literate in terms of what the immigrant experience was like at Ellis Island and are able to express this. However, if I didn't ask them about the experience, many of my students would have a very difficult time writing about it. I hope that this "guided participation" makes the learning process personal and that the students take ownership of it.

—Mikel McBride
First-year teacher, history, grade 9

Learning Is Becoming Part of a Community

Psychologists today continue to explore the fusion between social settings and mental processes. As they do, they have returned to Dewey's notion that children learn as they participate in social settings—not as they interact with knowledge but as they interact with their culture's use of knowledge. Jerome Bruner has become increasingly convinced that people create and transform meanings (learn) as members of particular cultures.[10]

Becoming Somebody Learning has much to do with developing one's *social identity*. The roles and competencies we gain depend on developing the knowledge, ways of thinking, and behaviors of more mature members of the community. For example, college students—even successful ones—take a long time to develop as scholars. Some never do. Only gradually do they come to see themselves as serious, knowledge-hungry students who live, work, study, and associate with others in the "community of scholars." When that happens, the nature and quality of their learning and much else is quite different from their "prescholar" period. Equally important are interactions with others who do or do not see these students as scholars. Both "developments"—that which occurs within the person and that which involves the social or cultural acceptance—are interdependent. Whether it is taking oneself seriously as a student, parent, teacher, or even friend, cognitive development requires a community of others who support a person in that role. When that happens, mastering the particulars of "how to act" is much enhanced.

An Apprenticeship Some sociocultural theorists view the learner as an apprentice—a cognitive apprentice. A cognitive apprenticeship guides a novice learner toward mastery of intellectual tools through social activity and relationships. It provides appropriate situations in which learners get help and are challenged by increasingly sophisticated skills and responsibilities until they are "mature" members of a culture and community. Novices learn as they participate in the actual work, beginning with small, even peripheral contributions that are nevertheless a real part of the task at hand.[11] Learning through such apprenticeship is, at its root, "identity construction." As anthropologist Jean Lave puts it, "Crafting identities is a social process, and becoming more knowledgeably skilled is an aspect of participating in social practice. By such reasoning, who you are becoming shapes crucially and fundamentally what you 'know.'"[12]

Cognition Is Cultural Good places to search for insights into cognition are cultures with social conventions that are most different from our own. For example, cultural psychologist Michael Cole studied Kpelle farmers in West Africa. Cole and his colleagues found that when asked to sort objects into groups that made sense to them, the farmers placed a hoe and a potato together and a knife with an orange. The farmers explained that these are the groupings that a "wise" person would make.[13] Of course, these groupings differed from the ones Americans typically consider wise. Americans are more likely to put the foods together in one group, and the tools in the other; the Kpelle farmers considered those arrangements ones that only "fools" would make. Clearly, a fundamental human mental process, grouping, makes sense according to the context and culture.

Similarly, Europeans who learned their mathematics in schools considered these same Kpelle people mathematically inept. However, the Kpelle were highly skilled at measuring, estimating, and calculating when conducting their business of buying and selling rice. In fact, they outperformed comparison groups of American workers and students on mathematics tasks related to their cultural practices.[14] Likewise, streetchildren in Brazil who have never been to school learn and use sophisticated mathematical processes to support themselves as vendors of candy, coconuts, and other commodities—processes they cannot perform successfully as school mathematics problems.[15] Meanwhile, American math students who were successful in the classroom performed poorly when asked to solve simple practical problems "on their feet." Clearly, while mathematical problem solving may have some universal elements, people's true mathematical abilities are strongly shaped by having a good match between the contexts in which they learn and the contexts in which they apply their knowledge.

Researcher Luis Moll assessed the enormous knowledge resources that Mexican American children had available to them *outside* their school. Because of the low expectations held for children of poor and working-class parents, these Tucson, Arizona, children performed "as expected." They had low achievement, and they found in school little relevance to their lives. As Moll studied the children's extended families, however, he found rich funds of knowledge. Each household was a place that developed expertise in particular domains (Moll identified nearly fifty, including soil and irrigation systems, minerals, renting and selling, budgets, design and architecture, first aid, folk cures, moral knowledge and ethics, etc.). Together, the households formed a community for the exchange of information and resources. Children participated in the exchange, by doing tasks and chores, all the while observing, asking questions, and being assisted by adults. For example, a son may indicate interest in fixing a car by asking his father questions. The father, taking his cue from the child, decides what level of participation is appropriate. Although the son's help may be minimal, such as helping to put in screws or checking the oil, he feels he participates in the whole task, because he is allowed to attempt tasks and to experiment without fear of punishment if he fails. In such families, learning and questioning are in the hands of the child. Moll believes that schools could use these cultural funds of knowledge and practices to enrich both culture and intelligence, instead of the current practice, which is to see cultural knowledge as not useful or as an obstacle.[16]

Language Communities and Learning Chapter 1 noted the increasing diversity of U.S. schoolchildren, in particular, students from Asia and Latin America. Providing scaffolding for these children requires strategies that connect the culture they bring to school with the academic content of the curriculum. This is especially challenging when students' primary language is not English, particularly in schools where there are "English only" policies.

Because language is at the very heart of culture, educators must pay attention to both first and second language learning. Vygotsky made clear that learning language and literacy is a never-ending process of communicating with others and internalizing content, meaning, and feelings. Drawing on Vygotsky's ideas, linguist Jim Cummins has developed the principle of "additive bilingual enrichment," based on the theory that language is learned in contexts where communication is meaningful, purposeful, and has social value. Additive bilingual enrichment argues that primary languages are essential and authentic aspects of culture and means of communication in communities and families. Thus, children can best learn second languages in highly interactive social contexts where they learn a new language as they simultaneously strengthen and enrich their primary language. In other words, students use the experiences and meanings in their primary language to scaffold their learning of the new one. Cummins contrasts this approach with a "subtractive" approach in which one language *replaces* the other and often results in little more than minimal literacy in either language. Cindy Bell, whose classroom is in a Latino immigrant community, used this work to guide interactions and learning in her classroom.

When my students talk to each other, they engage in purposeful conversation. Whether to help a friend find a word in the dictionary or to discuss what game they will play at recess, they talk to communicate. They know that they must speak to be understood and they must listen to understand. The students develop their speaking and listening skills by developing conversational strategies. They ask each other questions. They repeat the most important points. They emphasize words and give them meaning. They also identify their audience and tailor their words by switching between English and Spanish depending on with whom they are talking. This last practice is most obvious when we welcome new students into our classroom's Community Circle. Lali, who recently arrived in the United States from Mexico, joined our classroom in November. As our class introduced ourselves to her, the students immediately changed from their usual English welcomes to Spanish greetings, because, as they discussed, Lali wouldn't understand if they spoke in English. Even Maria, my one mono-literate English student, recognized the value of communicating for meaning and asked someone to translate so Lali would understand. In this group interaction and in many others, language acts as a functional social skill that develops oral literacy skills. My students understand that both English and Spanish are social tools because they are valuable and meaningful forms of communication.

—Cindy Kauionalani Bell
First-year teacher, grade 2

Learning theorist Steven Krashen adds an affective dimension to this work on language learning by arguing that negative feelings inhibit students when they are learning a new language, especially if their primary language itself is disparaged. First-grade teacher Benjamin Chang describes the learning challenges he faced in his first year in his diverse classroom, and how his understanding of what Krashen calls "affective filters" supplemented more general theories of learning as problem solving, understanding, and participation.

Two days before school started, I finally received my class roster. Four of my students are African American with roots in Texas, Georgia, and Alabama. Seven are Latino, with parents born and raised in Guatemala, El Salvador, and Mexico. Other families come from countries in Asia and the Pacific, such as Vietnam, Cambodia, Thailand, Hong Kong, the Philippines, and China. Six of my students are biracial or triracial, with families from all of these areas, as well as Belize and Puerto Rico. Within each category of race and ethnicity, I also learned about substantial linguistic diversity in my class (ten languages). . . . I was surprised, but it was a challenge I was eager to take. One idea that supported my effort to research and access my students' languages and cultures is Krashen's concept of the "affective filter." As I have come to know more about my students and their families, I have been able to connect what I learned outside the classroom with what we are doing in the classroom. For example, to learn about nouns and adjectives, I asked students to pretend they were going to the store with their lola (Tagalog for grandmother) or some other family member. With all of the different domestic practices and foods in my students' homes, this context for learning about different word types also became a social studies lesson. The end result was a group of engaged students learning about and appreciating their differences as well learning the official language arts curriculum. A simple assessment lets me know if I have been successful in lowering affective filters. It is the twinkle in their eyes, and the smiles on their faces. Their faces light up in a way that is unlike anything else. Neither ice cream, nor stickers, nor extra recess minutes can duplicate the expression on my students' faces when I ask them how to say a high frequency word in their own language or when they answer questions in the context of their homes and families.

—Benjamin Chang
First-year teacher, grade 1

Who Is Intelligent?

Typical conceptions of intelligence do not hold up well in sociocultural theories. Why bother trying to figure out intelligence differences between a Kpelle farmer and an American accountant? It makes more sense to pay attention to a person's particular competencies.

Intelligence Is Culturally Specific Intelligence is hard to pin down, changing as it might from activity to activity and culture to culture. Moreover, intelligence does not operate "inside the head" but develops as people interact using the tools and symbols of their culture. Although innate and universal predispositions may enhance the development of some abilities, most people are more concerned about whether or not children develop those abilities and values the culture wants. For example, Americans have learned to value people who can troubleshoot a crashed computer. The ability to do it well makes one intelligent in that matter, and there are many people with that intelligence. On the other hand, fewer people than in the past seem to be able to make up long narrative stories to tell to their families. If and when the culture truly values storytelling, more would do it. In the meantime, the few people who tell stories well are especially prized for the uniqueness of their talent.

Again, it is instructive to look at cross-cultural examples. Middle-class Americans often associate problem-solving speed with intelligence; Ugandan villagers, however, describe intelligence with words such as *slow* and *careful.* The Chinese place a high value on the ability to memorize facts; Australians consider this trivial. Middle-class Americans consider intelligence to encompass technical and abstract skills; Kenyans and Maylans see intelligence as comprising social and personal responsibility as well as cognitive skills. Ugandans and the Ifaluk people of the western Pacific consider intelligence to include both knowing socially responsible actions *and* actually acting that way.[17] Researchers Harold Stevenson and James Stigler illustrate how intellectual capacity is constructed differently from culture to culture. Comparing American, Chinese, and Japanese cultures, Stevenson and Stigler show that American culture constructs intelligence as a function of innate ability far more than do Asian cultures that emphasize effort and persistence in explaining what accounts for being "smart."[18] Clearly, different cultures see the relationship between effort and ability differently, and in America's diverse culture there are distinctly different views. Some see effort and ability as unrelated. Some see effort as something that compensates for lack of ability (the prevailing American view—as when one says, "Yes, she gets A's, but the poor thing has to work so hard"). Some see effort as something that increases ability (the prevailing Asian view, and one that is, perhaps, more consistent with cognitive and sociocultural theory).[19]

Intelligence Is Distributed Whatever else intelligence might be, an especially useful concept for teachers is that intelligence is *distributed* throughout a person's social world—home and community, the workplace, and school. If a preliterate or tribal culture has its shaman, competent hunters, a storyteller, and a rich cultural tradition that includes getting along with others, providing food, and so on, then it has all the necessary competencies and, collectively, quite a lot of intelligence. Similarly, the productivity of a typical American workplace may depend less on highly knowledgeable *individuals* than on the productive social arrangements that make it possible to use all that intelligence. Finally, a classroom that has a helpful teacher, social structures that allow for productive interactions, and students with different backgrounds and knowledge who can be called together to solve academic and other problems might be seen as a class with lots of intelligence distributed across many people. As Jerome Bruner puts it, intelligence includes the "toolkit" of "reckoning devices and heuristics and accessible friends that the person could call upon . . . the reference books one uses, the notes one habitually takes, the computer programs and data bases one relies upon, and perhaps most important of all, the network for friends, colleagues, or mentors on whom one leans for the feedback, help, advice, even just for company."[20]

I have five students in my class who speak only Spanish and are working to acquire English as their second language. My challenge is to create a community where these five students are not seen as inferior or less intelligent because of their inability to speak English but are respected and admired as individuals who are pushing and challenging themselves to take on a learning task. One day I brought in two different books, both written in Korean. One was a very visual picture book with simple words and phrases; the other was a Korean novel with no pictures and sophisticated writing. I asked the class to imagine that they were just starting to learn Korean and that they had to choose one of the books in order to begin. I asked the class which one they thought would give them more understandable information, and all of them said that the picture book with illustrations and simple phrases. I then asked the students if choosing the easier book in any way made them less intelligent or incapable, and they said no. Since they were only beginning to learn Korean, it would be impossible for them to read anything any more advanced. I told them that our five language learners were not any different. They, too, would be reading picture books in English with easy words and lots of pictures while the rest of the class would be reading novels and chapter books.

—Amy Lee
First-year teacher, grade 6

Sociocultural theories emphasize the inextricable connectedness of the mind and culture. Along with cognitive understandings of *constructed* sense-making, these theories offer a promising, but for many an unsettling, concept of learning. As we discuss more in the next section and in the chapters to follow, the implications of these ideas for teaching in culturally diverse societies are enormous.

Why Do Children Learn?

One of the wonders of being human is that we learn so much so easily and have so much fun doing it—outside of school, anyway. Children naturally feel competent. They tackle difficult tasks on their own and have no natural inclination to feel discouraged by mistakes. Just think of the number of times that small children try new and difficult tasks. From climbing stairs to buttoning clothes to making sentences, they keep plugging away until they get it right. Indeed, patience seems far more natural than impatience. A child's face lighting up spontaneously as he masters a task reminds us of the sheer pleasure learning brings, and how learning can be its own reward. Perhaps most important, neither psychologists nor teachers can predict with much accuracy who will accomplish what and when. History abounds with stories of early-blooming Mozarts and late-blooming Einsteins.

Intrinsic Motivation

When explaining why people learn, cognitive theorists, in contrast to behaviorists, emphasize intrinsic motivation (that which comes from within) rather than extrinsic motivation (i.e., rewards and punishments). They see intrinsic motivation as tension, a sense of imbalance, the drive or desire to make sense of something that is confusing, to bring order to a mess, to fit in or find acceptance where acceptance is not complete. This is not the negative tension that we associate with psychological stress. It is perhaps closer to curiosity, but so much more. Cognitive theorists reason that if such productive tension is present in lessons, children will work hard even without consistent outside reinforcement. Think about reading a novel and wanting to know how it ends. Consider the fun of learning and figuring something out—apart from the instrumental goal of passing a class. Performing acts of charity, keeping oneself studying hard day and night while some classmates are not, working with others cooperatively, and so on require resources from within. External rewards can help, but they can't carry the whole motivational load. Rarely can students draw on their full measure of resources if they attribute their successes to conditions beyond their control rather than resulting from their own volition and efforts.

Self-Concept, Identity, Motivation, and Learning

We can't separate children's feelings about themselves, that is, their self-concept or their identity, from their other cognitive processes. We use the term *self-concept* to include students' global judgments about themselves: "I am good." "I am competent." "I am clumsy. "I am skilled at having people like me." Self-concept has much to do with our sense of efficacy—whether we think we can have things go our way. Students draw these conclusions from their experiences at home, at school, and at play and use them to guide their future actions: "Since I am a likable person, I will introduce myself to those strangers and make new friends." With *identity*, we refer to slightly more external and specific roles: "I am a student and therefore act in studentlike ways." "I am a goof-off, so I make a joke in class." "I am going to be an engineer." "I am the team captain." "I am a 'hot' date." Here, we are looking at cultural categories of behavior that are accompanied by a set of behavioral standards. We all use these identities to guide our behavior.

Identity and self-concept are powerful organizers of people's lives. People could hardly get along if they had to stop at every moment to think, What am I good at? How should I act as a new member of this group? Will I succeed? Like a powerful magnet, our own sense-making draws us to situations that fit our self-concept and identity. Similarly, we are cautious or resistant if we cannot make sense of our participation. The desire to be in situations and act in ways that fit one's identity is an important motivator.

But how can we account for successful students and adults performing many tasks with enthusiasm and competence even when the task itself is not pleasurable or satisfying? Traditionalists often ridicule intrinsic motivation—calling it overrated in importance and asserting that little would get done if everyone waited to "feel like" doing life's necessary, if unpleasant, activities, especially those in school. Some psychologists who have studied these processes in classrooms use the concept of *achievement motivation* to describe a more general enthusiasm for acting with competence just for its own sake, rather than a drive that is necessarily related to *either* extrinsic rewards or to pleasure derived from doing a specific school task. Traditional theorists may acknowledge this more general drive as an individual, family, or cultural trait; those with a cognitive perspective, however, see high achievement motivation as something people learn—something very close to having developed an identity as a "high achiever."

Students with high achievement motivation feel competent and in charge; they expect valuable successes, and they exert the time and energy to learn. Children who don't feel competent often assume that no amount of effort will lead to success. They often display a *learned helplessness.* That is, *not* being successful makes more sense to them, so even when the teacher or others can demonstrate that they are competent, these students treat their success as an exception or mistake.

Motivation and Relationships

As we might expect, sociocultural theorists add a social dimension to motivation, although they rarely use the term itself. Learning to do what the more capable members of a community do is the essential route to being and remaining a member of the community. Cultural theorists Jean Lave and Etienne Wenger note, "Acceptance by and interaction with acknowledged adept practitioners make learning legitimate and of value from the point of view of the apprentice."[21] Through apprenticeship, younger members work alongside older ones on tasks that are valued for their own sake by the whole community. The actual tasks that the learners do are real, and they contribute something of value, however small, to the group's work. Wanting to do work that the community values, by any other name, sounds a lot like motivation.

Cognition, Culture, and Teaching to Change the World

Students who are free from serious neurological disorders can learn rich and challenging knowledge and skills at school. Yet some students achieve very well while many others barely achieve at all. These differences in school success—which cannot be explained adequately by innate intelligence traits or cultural differences—tell us far more about how teachers and schools respond to students than they tell us about how capable the students are.

The path is rocky for teachers and schools pursuing sociocultural theories of learning. To appreciate the obstacles, it is worth keeping in mind this rule of thumb: When a promising theory comes along, people will try to understand it in terms with which they are most familiar. A less generous statement of this "rule" is that the dominant culture in society will try to discredit the theory or use the theory to maintain the status quo. Some parents, policymakers, and even other educators demean the idea of socially constructed knowledge as something that is "just made up"—not factual, or not based on scientific evidence.

Cognitive and sociocultural theories *do* argue that students' social interactions within their culture shape what they know and how they come to know it. But that doesn't mean that American students do not need to learn the "facts" of science, mathematical algorithms, the conventions of formal and informal language, and other school knowledge. Much of this knowledge is not negotiable if one wants to participate fully in the American culture. However, new learners in each generation must make knowledge and the facts personally meaningful through interactions with peers or teachers, or through experience.

All cultural knowledge has been constructed at some point, over time, and is always subject to revision. It may be helpful to remember that after the best and wisest scientific minds decided that the earth was not flat, it took a very long time before most of the world could make sense of or reconstruct this "fact." Concepts of race and gender superiority are examples of societal constructs we hope are collapsing today. Still, people are uneasy because they fear that if each person makes sense anew of the culture's knowledge and beliefs, society will lose its venerable values and the knowledge of the ages.

American schools emphasize fitting children's ways of knowing to the needs of the culture, and the culture is not so ready to adjust to fit the needs of its diverse members. But in the twenty-first century, people will be increasingly challenged to make sense of diverse knowledge and in diverse social settings. Changing the world might well begin with changing views about whose culture belongs in "the" culture, whose intelligence is valuable to us all.

Digging Deeper

You might want to read work by researchers currently investigating the social and cultural dimensions of learning and intelligence. Their work can help you think deeply about the implications of the sociocultural perspective for teachers presented in this chapter.

Stanford University psychologist **Albert Bandura** developed social learning theory that draws both from behavioral and cognitive theories. Social learning theory focuses on the consequences (including rewards and punishments) of experiences; however, it steps outside the behavioral realm to suggest that people engage in a meaning-making process as they observe—a cognitive view. Social learning theory has been used to explain why children are likely to do well in school if they grow up around adult role models who turned their own school achievements into high-paying jobs. Bandura's book *Social Foundations of Thought and Action* (Englewood Cliffs, NJ: Prentice-Hall, 1986) provides a good overview of his work.

Jerome Bruner, research professor of psychology and senior research fellow in law at New York University, has a long and distinguished career. His work investigates how cognitive psychology and child development can inform teaching so that all children can become highly competent and fully participating members of their cultures. Books you might want to read include *The Process of Education* (1960), *Toward a Theory of Instruction* (1966), *The Relevance of Education* (1971), *Acts of Meaning* (1990), and *The Culture of Education* (1996)—all published by Harvard University Press. Bruner's most recent books are helpful for thinking about the shortcomings of cognitive psychology, especially when it fails to account for the importance of culture in thought, language, and learning. Bruner suggests the possibilities for schools and teaching that derive from these sociocultural perspectives.

Stephen Ceci, professor of psychology at Cornell University, argues in *A Bio-ecological Treatise on Intellectual Development* (Cambridge: Harvard University

Press, 1996) that traditional conceptions of intelligence ignore the role of society in shaping intelligence and underestimate the intelligence of non-Western societies. He offers a "bio-ecological" framework of individual differences built on his studies of how children's prior knowledge and familiarity with a context affect how they process information intelligently.

Michael Cole, a professor of communication and psychology and the director of the Laboratory of Comparative Human Cognition at the University of California, San Diego, has conducted cross-cultural research on cognitive development. Cole currently leads a project called UC Links that pairs undergraduate students with elementary school children in after-school activities, including working with computers, telecommunication, and educational games. Building on cultural psychology, Cole hopes the partnership will create a context that supports and motivates learning and gives underrepresented minority children resources and impetus for pursuing higher education. You might want to read Cole's latest book, *Cultural Psychology: A Once and Future Discipline* (Cambridge: Harvard University Press, 1996), and an earlier work with Peg Griffin, *Contextual Factors in Education* (Wisconsin Center for Educational Research, University of Wisconsin, Madison, 1987).

Mihaly Csikszentmihalyi, a professor of human development and education at the University of Chicago, studies how the experience of learning becomes its own reward—a state he calls "flow." His work is devoted to examining how flow comes about and how it can be facilitated. His books include *Optimal Experience* (with Isabella Csikszentmihalyi, Cambridge: Harvard University Press, 1988) and *Flow, The Psychology of Optimal Experience* (New York: Harper & Row, 1990).

Harvard education professor **Howard Gardner's** many books range from explications of his own theories of multiple intelligence (e.g., *Frames of Mind* [New York: Basic Books, 1983, 1993]), to a history of the cognitive revolution (*The Mind's New Science* [New York: Basic Books, 1985]), a textbook providing a comprehensive overview of intelligence (*Intelligence,* with Mindy L. Kornhaber and Warren K. Wake [Orlando, FL: Harcourt Brace, 1995]), to the implications of cognitive psychology for teaching (e.g., *Multiple Intelligences: The Theory in Practice* [New York: Basic Books, 1993] and [New York: Basic Books, 1991]).

Stanford anthropologist and sociolinguist **Shirley Brice Heath** spent several years living in two unnamed poor communities—one largely white, the other largely black—in a rural mountain area near southern mill towns. In her book *Ways with Words: Language, Life, and Work in Communities and Classrooms* (New York: Cambridge University Press, 1983), Brice Heath documents differences in the way the two communities used questions, told stories, reared children, and used toys and reading material. In a more recent book, *Children of Promise* (Berkeley: University of California National Center for the Study of Writing and Literacy, 1991), written with teacher Leslie Mangiola, she provides practical ideas for classroom teachers who want to develop activities that can help all students to achieve their full potential.

Jean Lave and **Etienne Wenger** have developed the idea of learning as occurring within a "community of practice." Lave, a professor of anthropology at the University of California at Berkeley, has developed theories of "situated" cognition, and learning as identity development. Her studies contrast the informal (and usually productive) ways that people learn skills with how schools teach. For example, she compares the math calculations Americans do when buying groceries or figuring their Weight Watchers' diets with the formal algorithms learned in school. She has studied the effectiveness of apprenticeship training including that of tailors in West Africa. Her most available book is *Situated Learning: Legitimate Peripheral Participation* (with Etienne Wenger [New York: Cambridge University Press, 1991]). Wenger's book *Communities of Practice: Learning, Meaning, and Identity* (Cambridge, England: Cambridge University Press, 1999) provides a comprehensive framework for learning in social contexts and the relationship between learning and identity, drawing on his extensive studies of people interacting and learning at work.

Luis Moll, an education professor at the University of Arizona, studies learning and knowledge in the lives of working-class Mexican American students and their families in the barrio schools of Tucson. You may find the following articles particularly useful: "Bilingual Classroom Studies and Community Analysis: Some Recent Trends," *Educational Researcher* 21, no. 2 (1992), pp. 20–24, and "Funds of Knowledge for Teaching: Using a Qualitative Approach to Connect Homes and Classrooms," *Theory into Practice* 31, no. 2 (1992), pp. 132–141. Moll has also edited a very helpful collection of articles by leading sociocultural theorists, *Vygotsky and Education: Instructional Implications of Sociohistorical Psychology* (Cambridge, England: Cambridge University Press, 1992).

David Perkins of Harvard's Graduate School of Education studies human capacities and their development. He has studied thinking and understanding in Venezuela, Colombia, Guatemala, and South Africa as well as in the United States. His most recent book, *Outsmarting I.Q.* (New York: The Free Press, 1995), argues for a "new science of learnable intelligence." Readers might also be interested in his earlier book, *Smart Schools: Better Thinking and Learning for Every Child* (New York: The Free Press, 1992).

Barbara Rogoff is a professor of psychology and education at the University of California, Santa Cruz. She studies how children's development occurs in the context of their relations with other people (especially parents and peers) as they participate in activities of social and cultural origin. She also investigates the variation and similarities across diverse cultural communities, as well as schools, children's museums, and families. Rogoff's book *Apprenticeship in Thinking: Cognitive Development in Social Context* (New York: Oxford University Press, 1990) provides an in-depth look at how social context affects thinking and learning.

At Yale, psychologist **Robert J. Sternberg** develops models of multidimensional intelligence. His Triarchic Theory of Intelligence includes "componential" intelligence—the linguistic and logical-mathematical abilities that most traditional intelligence tests assess; contextual intelligence (the source of creative insight), and experiential intelligence (the "street smarts" of intelligence). He argues that the latter two are of enormous value, yet are not given much opportunity to develop in traditional classrooms. His books include *Beyond IQ: A Triarchic Theory of Human Intelligence* (1985) and *Metaphors of the Mind: Concep-*

tions of the Nature of Intelligence (1990). Cambridge University Press published both.

Deborah Stipek, dean of Stanford's School of Education, is also a psychologist who studies developmental issues related to achievement, motivation, and achievement-related emotions. She has been especially interested in children's perceptions of competence, their perceptions of the cause of achievement outcomes, and their understanding and experience of such emotions as pride and shame. Her achievement motivation research focuses directly on preschool and elementary school–aged children, and classroom conditions that affect effort and interest in academic tasks. Her book *Motivation to Learn* (Needham Heights, MA: Allyn & Bacon, 1993) provides a thoughtful overview and discussion of motivation and school learning.

The following are some classic works that spawned much of the interest in cognitive and sociocultural theories. You may want to read them in the original.

John Dewey

Democracy and Education. New York: The Free Press, 1906.

Experience and Education. New York: Macmillan, 1938

How We Think. Boston: D.C. Heath, 1910

"My Pedagogic Creed" in *The School Journal,* 1896, reprinted in *John Dewey, Early Works,* Vol. 5. Carbondale, IL: Southern Illinois University Press, 1989.

Jean Piaget

The Construction of Reality in the Child (M. Cook, trans.). New York: Basic Books, 1954.

The Science of Education and the Psychology of the Child. New York: Orion Press, 1970.

The Equilibrium of Cognitive Structures (T. Brown and K. L. Thampy, trans.). Chicago: University of Chicago Press.

Lev Vygotsky

Mind in Society. Cambridge, England: Cambridge University Press, 1978.

Notes

1. In his book *Cultural Psychology: A Once and Future Discipline* (Cambridge: Harvard University Press, 1996), psychologist Michael Cole relates that one of the founders of the discipline of psychology, Wilhelm Wundt, proposed, in fact, two psychologies. The first would address the mind in the manner of other respected scientific endeavors. In this case, "the mind, it was believed, could now be measured and explained according to the

canons of experimental science" (p. 6). The "second psychology" would have the task of understanding how culture enters into psychological processes" (p. 6).

2. By contrast, behaviorists' insistence on "objective" observations of behaviors leads them to distrust for scientific purposes the mostly unobservable events of the mind. Consequently, behavioral approaches are likely to emphasize how the teacher teaches—manipulates the environment with particular stimuli—rather than how the students are learning (not to be confused with tests of what the students have learned).
3. John Dewey, "How We Think," in *John Dewey, the Middle Works,* Vol. 6 (Carbondale, IL: Southern Illinois University Press, 1989), p. 338.
4. In babyhood, what Piaget called the *sensorimotor* stage, children make sense of the world in terms of behavioral representations. For example, let's return to the example of chairs. Babies in modern Western cultures probably develop a chair scheme at a young age. However, Piaget argued that at this early stage that babies only think about, or "represent," chairs in terms of how babies behave in relation to the chairs. They conceptualize chairs as things to sit on. Later, as toddlers, children enter what Piaget calls a *preoperational* stage where they can begin to think about or represent things symbolically. That is, they can close their eyes and imagine a chair that is in front of them. A bit later, about the time they begin school, children develop the ability to perform *concrete operations;* that is, they can mentally rearrange things that they've actually seen. For example, a child in a living room with a red plaid couch and a plain green chair could imagine what the chair would look like if it were reupholstered with the red plaid fabric. Sometime in early adolescence, children enter the stage where they will remain as adults—a stage Piaget called *formal operations,* when logical and abstract thinking develop. A child at this stage would be able to imagine chairs in all sorts of configurations, even those highly unlikely in the real, concrete world. For example, an adolescent could conjure up a chair made of ice cream—a logical but hardly realistic possibility.
5. Jerome Bruner, *Culture and Education* (Cambridge: Harvard University Press, 1996), p. 77.
6. Robert Sternberg, "Myths, Countermyths, and Truths About Intelligence," *Education Researcher* 25 (March 1996), pp. 11–16, 13.
7. John D. Bransford, Ann L. Brown, and Rodney R. Cocking (Eds.), *How People Learn: Brain, Mind, Experience, and School* (Washington, DC: National Academy Press, 1999).
8. Ibid., p. 114.
9. John Dewey, "My Pedagogic Creed," 1897, *Early Works,* Vol. 5 (Carbondale, IL: Southern Illinois University Press, 1989), p. 93.
10. Bruner, *Culture and Education.*
11. Jean Lave and Etienne Wenger, *Situated Cognition: Legitimate Peripheral Participation* (Cambridge, England: Cambridge University Press, 1991).
12. Jean Lave, "Teaching as Learning in Practice," *Mind, Culture, and Activity* 3, no. 3 (1996), pp. 149–164.

13. Joseph Glick, as cited in Barbara Rogoff, *Apprenticeship in Thinking: Cognitive Development in Social Context* (New York: Oxford University Press, 1990), p. 57. Note: Michael Cole was also part of this work.
14. Cole, *Cultural Psychology,* pp. 75–76.
15. Geoffrey Saxe, *Culture and Cognitive Development: Studies in Mathematical Understanding* (New York: Erlbaum, 1990).
16. Luis Moll, "Funds of Knowledge for Teaching: Using a Qualitative Approach to Connect Homes and Classrooms," *Theory into Practice* 31, no. 2 (1992), pp. 132–141.
17. Rogoff, *Apprenticeship in Thinking,* p. 58.
18. Harold Stevenson and James Stigler, *The Learning Gap: Why Our Schools Are Failing and What We Can Learn from Japanese and Chinese Education* (New York: Touchstone, 1994).
19. University of Pittsburgh cognitive theorist Lauren Resnick made this point in an invited talk at UCLA in September 1997.
20. Bruner, *Culture and Education,* p. 132.
21. Lave and Wenger, *Situated Cognition,* p. 112.

CHAPTER 4

Curriculum: Philosophy, History, and Politics:

What Should Students Learn?

A. Dee Williams

First-year teacher, high school social studies

One of the most daunting experiences for a teacher, new or seasoned, is to scan a classroom of faces during a lesson, call on a student with a raised hand (hoping for a probing question or comment that gets to the heart of the topic), and hear the question "Why do we have to learn this?" On the one hand, there can be no more fundamental and legitimate question—one that we hope students are constantly raising, mulling the answer, and revising their own conclusions. On the other hand, well . . . why do they have to learn this English, this math, and so on? A number of answers float around society and schools:

- You'll need it later (in more advanced grades or subjects; to get into college; to get a good job)
- To keep you out of trouble (recognize dangerous combinations like electric currents and water; prevent AIDS)
- For the good of the country (productive workforce, informed voters, patriotic citizens)
- Because it's good for you (builds character, self-discipline, and persistence)
- Because everybody learns it (the culture, history, traditions, the "classics")

These answers, or at least some of them, may be true. But they miss the life and essence of the subjects to which students are exposed—the delight of reading a story that places the character in danger of falling into a vat of chocolate, the satisfaction of understanding why their parent might favor one political candidate while they favor another, or the excitement of re-creating a rain forest in a corner of the classroom. So how compelling will these answers be to that inquiring student with his hand raised? Not very. Largely external and instrumental, they reflect adult conclusions about what makes a good society—conclusions that are rarely examined and sometimes not even true.

Beyond a superficial consensus that everyone should learn reading and writing, mathematics, science, and whatever else it takes to be a "responsible citizen," agreement about the curriculum is hard to find. Psychologists, curriculum specialists, and teachers debate about what content will best lead students toward a solid understanding of the subjects and how that content can best be organized and presented in classrooms. But these *professional* debates pale in comparison to the fierce *political* battles over what American students should learn at school, how they should learn it, and why.

This chapter treats the political and professional debates as inseparable. They both flow from dramatically different philosophies about the purposes of education. The teachers cited in this chapter and throughout this book recognize that teaching is a political act. They apply sociocultural learning theory to engage students with ideas and values that reflect multiple cultural and linguistic traditions. Teaching that examines the power that holds traditional theory and culture in place and the actions that change the distribution and effects of power are easily understood as political. But what of those teachers, guided by traditional theory, who teach only the dominant culture? By exercising the power that holds the traditional culture and practices in place, they are no less political than those who seek change.

A passion for teaching and for students' learning knows no political bounds. Even amid the technical challenges and political discourse, all teachers can cherish moments of classroom life when they share their own enthusiasm for discovering, theorizing, and knowing mathematics, language, science, and the other school subjects. This common ground must be kept in the forefront, but it cannot be allowed to obscure teachers' important role of bringing reform to schools. If teachers are to contribute to the public debate, they must bring to the forum more than their enthusiasm for students and their knowledge of subjects. It helps to know about the social and political traditions that lie behind the curriculum debates. The remainder of this chapter reviews those traditions. In the next chapter, we consider how these traditions, pressures, and struggles emerge in four major academic subjects that students learn at school.

Philosophies of Education: Some Basics

Just as the twentieth-century theories of learning we discussed in Chapters 2 and 3 can be traced back to the ideas Locke, Descartes, and Kant espoused about the nature of mind, so, too, can today's ideas and debates about curriculum. Reduced to their bare essentials, these centuries-old arguments stake out different positions on (a) the nature of reality, (b) humans' ability to "know" it, and (c) what's worth knowing. Idealists argued that reality is essentially spiritual and knowledge is a product of human reason; the ideas of most value are those that have stood the test of time. Realists countered that reality exists "out there" and humans come to know it by examining the empirical world; what's most worth knowing are the universal laws that govern the working of the universe. Humanists paid less attention to the nature of reality than they did to the amazing capacity for humans to develop and learn and make sense of the world. These fundamental positions were challenged in the late nineteenth century by a new set of ideas—pragmatism—promulgated by John Dewey and his American colleagues. Pragmatists too believed in a reality that exists in the world and in the power of humans to know it through interacting with it. However, unlike realists who placed the greatest value on knowing the unchanging laws of nature, the pragmatists emphasized the importance of understanding how the physical world changes and knowing how to solve problems. Midcentury, these philosophical positions were joined by another set of fundamental ideas about the nature of reality and humans' interactions with it—existentialism. Existentialists disdained the attempt to identify a universal reality; rather, they argued that individuals face an infinite array of choices in a world devoid of meaning. Humans must craft their own meaning by exploring possibilities for their lives and developing personal responsibility. Each of these preceding philosophies has spawned theories of how society should educate its young people. Debates among them foreshadowed today's arguments over what and how students should learn at school.

The following chart depicts the usual way that four of the most influential educational philosophies can be categorized.

	Education's Purpose	Preferred Curriculum	Role of the Teacher	Role of the Student
Perennialism	To cultivate the mind, instill timeless virtues, and advance the search for truth	Enduring ideas, universal truths, and classic intellectual achievements—e.g., the "Great Books"	The authority in the classroom and the conveyor of received wisdom and knowledge	Receiver of knowledge transmitted—i.e., an "empty vessel." They may think critically but not challenge authority
Essentialism	Transmitting the culture from one generation to the next; training in the intellectual basic skills	Knowledge and basic skills necessary to preserve the culture and to enable constructive participation of the individual	The authority in the classroom, the conveyor of knowledge, and the administrator of tests to ensure that knowledge has been acquired	Receiver of knowledge transmitted—i.e., an "empty vessel"
Progressivism	Learning to solve problems of democratic society	Problems engaged by society and by children; problems that interest children	Creates an environment rich with opportunities for student-directed learning and group problem solving	Active engagement in deciding what to study and in learning by doing, rather than listening
Social Reconstructionism	Solving critical problems to promote equality, justice, and democracy in the social environment	Community and larger social problems that are amenable to social and political action	Raise students consciousness about social problems and provide the tools for social critique and social action	Active engagement in understanding social problems and taking action to solve them

With the exception of social reconstructionism, these educational philosophies are not typically described as being political. However, as the remainder of this chapter makes clear, our view is that each is quite consistent with the deep political differences that also permeate our debates about schooling. The debates about educational philosophy, as often as not, are also debates about political ideology.

Why Do We Have to Learn This? History and Political Debates

In preliterate societies, teaching the young was so thoroughly integrated into the culture that one cannot imagine sustained arguments into the content or methods of how, what, or why the children should learn; for example, how to build a canoe or how to prepare the meal. What we think of today as planned *lessons, objectives,* and *education* would be largely a matter of growing up and participating in society. Moreover, for most of western European history, the formal overarching educational traditions were so engrained that only a few members of the elite—primarily scholars and clergy—might propose institutional reforms to education.

Like other modern societies, the United States presents a different picture. Since the American Revolution we Americans have locked ourselves into a struggle between stability and reform. We want schools to reflect *both* how we think society used to be *and* how we think it ought to be in the future. We want our schools firmly rooted in venerable traditions, and we want flexible institutions that we can shape to realize complex social purposes.

Since the arrival of the first European settlers Anglo-Americans have tended to believe that they were absolutely and exclusively correct in matters of religious and social interpretation, including how schools should operate. That is fair enough; it makes this country no better, worse, or different from every other culture that values its own customs. On the other hand, Americans also value individual liberty and rights and argue that it is inadvisable or futile to try to force "others" to change their ways—especially if others' ways do not tread on one's own. These two honored American traditions make deciding what to teach far more than a technical matter of choosing the most important topics. At every turn, every curriculum choice (even the supposedly scientific ones like mathematics) also becomes a cultural question and often a political decision.

Offering Opportunity and Maintaining Privilege

One defining purpose of American public schools is that they serve everyone. Yet scholars—even politically moderate ones—agree that Americans have never acted energetically on the view that everyone needs or deserves the same knowledge. Educational psychologist Lauren B. Resnick, for example, notes that Americans "have inherited two quite distinct educational traditions—one concerned with elite education, the other concerned with mass education. These traditions conceived of schooling differently, had different clienteles, and held different goals for their students."[1] Complicating matters further is that Americans are unique in insisting that everyone have *opportunities* to get the elite education.

These "distinct educational traditions"—elite and mass—existed from the start, with schools affecting students' life chances by opening up or closing off access to universities and jobs. It is not surprising that Americans with wealth, power, leadership, higher education, and so on would want to transfer to their children these elite privileges. And it is not surprising that they would expect the schools to play a role.

Indeed, the American schooling tradition accommodates parents who exercise their democratic and parental prerogatives to give their children the same or more advantages than the parents have. On the other hand, much in our democratic rhetoric—including having public schools for everyone—seeks to diminish the power of social class at school. Even the most privileged Americans argue that every child must have the opportunity to parlay education into upward social and economic mobility. Adding the nation's ambivalence about ethnic and linguistic diversity to this mix of traditions and sentiments exacerbates class-related tension. Inevitably, many of the most powerful members of the community make individual and school policy decisions that ignore, distort, or do not fully represent the heritage, perspectives, or aspirations of all the community's students.

Mass and Elite Education

In the fifty years following the Revolution, much of America's population either dispersed through westward expansion or concentrated in urban clusters to work in a rapidly expanding trade and manufacturing economy. Fully tax-supported schools were still a long way off, and communities that had compulsory education rarely enforced it.

Mass Education Is Moral and Political All students, including the masses, were expected to learn their sums and perhaps a little accounting; read well enough to understand the Bible, newspaper, and almanac; understand a smattering of natural history (biology); and be familiar with at least some national, European, and classical stories or history. This emphasis on the basics makes clear that an essentialist approach to curriculum prevailed. But, most important, the community expected teachers to transmit the prevailing moral and religious predilections—typically those of northern European Protestant denominations.

In the 1780s Noah Webster—of dictionary fame—authored an enormously popular series of textbooks, notably the "blue-backed speller." Commonly referred to as the "Schoolmaster of America," Webster was passionately committed to an America free of decadent European influence and with strong, uniquely American citizenship and institutions. Starting as a schoolteacher himself, he fashioned a system of instruction that, in addition to providing lessons in reading and writing, aimed at developing patriotic Americans and creating a unified national spirit. The speller attempted to instill respect for hard work and property rights. Its political and moral catechism required students to memorize the following series of questions and answers:

- What is a moral virtue? It is an honest upright conduct in all our dealings with men.
- Can we always determine what is honest and just? Perhaps not in every instance, but in general it is not difficult.
- What rules have we to direct us? God's word contained in the Bible has furnished all necessary rules to direct our conduct.
- In what part of the Bible are these rules to be found? In almost every part; but the most important duties between men are summed up in the beginning of Matthew, in Christ's Sermon on the Mount.[2]

By 1875, 75 million copies of Webster's blue-backed speller had sold. Its incredible popularity attests to its match with what people already thought children should learn. Once the speller became the standard (there were not many choices), it set a curriculum pattern—of infusing political and moral content into teaching basic skills—that would persist in American schools until the present. For example, in the 1990s former U.S. Secretary of Education William Bennett decried what he saw as the erosion of explicit moral content in schools. His best-seller, *The Book of Virtues* (1996), spawned a series of videotapes for children that used classic stories and fairy tales as the vehicle for teaching morals to children. Bennett's book was simply a highly visible manifestation of a resurgence of interest in "character education." At the turn of the twenty-first century, that interest has become an educational policy priority under George W. Bush and Secretary of Education Rod Paige. As we note later in this chapter, the ideas of virtue and character have become integral to a conservative turn in education policy. However, character education is now and has been in the past a hotly contested topic. Of course, no one speaks against character and virtue as being part of education. Rather, the battle wages over whether these qualities are derived from particular interpretations of written works and codes (the conservative position) or whether virtue and character are qualities held in common by a good society in which individuals and groups must continually reexamine and make sense anew of their moral and behavioral precepts (a more progressive view).

Elite Education Is Classical, Preparatory, and Practical In the 1800s more-advanced education was largely distributed along the lines of social class, available only to those who could pay for private tutors and schools. Most private schools favored a classical European education and prepared students for high schools and universities. Typically, they offered mathematics, science, Latin, Greek, English grammar, geography, perhaps rhetoric, and so on. For elites, too, an essentialist approach to education prevailed.

However, some private schools took on a more distinctively American character. Benjamin Franklin and other rationalists of the revolutionary period urged a departure from traditional courses in religion and classics and favored useful and practical studies. Franklin, not surprisingly, envisioned an education consistent with his own values for self-improvement. These values depended less on mastering facts through rote learning than on accumulating learning processes that would serve, as they did in Franklin's own case, a lifetime of learning. Franklin favored a breadth of utilitarian knowledge such as modern languages and the study of commerce and trade. Thus, Franklin advocated an education for elites that would later hold strong appeal for the masses. He also provided some of the earliest hints of a curriculum that could serve social justice goals—one that is process oriented and focused on complex and practical knowledge.

That the first public high school was not established until 1821, however, bears witness to the prevailing view that an education beyond basic literacy and moral training was a matter of private, elite interests, not of mass public concern. When public high schools did begin to appear, schoolmasters patterned them after the private academies, and few children had access to them.

The Common School Curriculum

In the 1830s and 1840s the idea of the common school took hold, bringing with it two meanings of the word *common.* On the one hand, these were schools in which all shared a common interest—schools that would provide the same curriculum to all. But these schools were also tinged with another meaning—schools for those who were of low or common rank, as when people speak of someone as a common laborer.

The common school appealed to nearly everyone, but for very different reasons. Working-class people, immigrants, and those outside the dominant culture who lacked resources for their own private schools saw the common school as a path (a narrow one, to be sure) to the American dream. People of greater wealth and status saw their own well-being enhanced by common schools, even if their children did not attend them. Everyone would benefit, they reasoned, if schools could turn out productive workers and good citizens. Some literacy and some math were required of all, but when determining "how much" and "for whom" Thomas Jefferson's view prevailed: More elite private schools would meet the country's intellectual needs.

National Textbooks for Literacy and Social Distinctions Moral truths, cultural certainty, nationalism, capitalism, Protestant Christianity, and the view of children as "empty vessels" reinforced one another in the common school. Imagine the overlapping influence of Webster's blue-backed speller and another 122 million copies of *McGuffey's Readers.* Between 1836 and 1920 *McGuffey's Readers* taught rules for reading and proper speech; practical moral precepts; God's active participation in death, nature, and distribution and withholding of wealth; the rules of capitalism; and—in a time before separate textbooks for different subjects—science, history, biography, geography, and more. *McGuffey's Readers* did it all. Elites could be comforted since the readers, though educating large numbers of previously uneducated classes, offered academic and social lessons that preserved important social class distinctions. Consider historian Joel Spring's comments and selections from two stories and what both rich and poor children would learn from them.

> In "The Rich Boy," students learned that the rich boy knows "that God gives a great deal of money to some persons, in order that they may assist those who are poor." In keeping with the idea that the rich are elected by God, the rich boy is portrayed as being humble, kind to servants, and "careful not to make a noise in the house, or break any thing, or put it out of its place, or tear his clothes." The reader is also told that this model of virtue "likes to go with his parents to visit poor people, in their cottages, and gives them all the money he can spare."[3]

In "The Poor Boy," Spring tells us that

> unlike the rich boy wanting to help the poor, the poor boy dreams of earning his own living. He likes his food of bread and bacon and does not envy the rich little boys and girls "riding on pretty horses, or in coaches." At the end of the story, the poor boy states his acceptance of his social position: "I have often been told, and I have read, that it is God who makes some poor, and others rich—that the rich have many troubles which we know nothing of; and that the poor, if they are but good, may be very happy. Indeed, I think that when I am good, nobody can be happier than I am."[4]

During the latter half of the 1800s, Webster's spellers and *McGuffey's Readers* amounted to national textbooks, with the readers remaining popular until World War I. These texts helped unify social, moral, political, and educational values, just as their authors had very pointedly intended. Educational and political leaders educated according to these values retained power and influence well into the twentieth century. Many were active in resisting change or in shaping reforms to keep schools aligned with nineteenth-century educational values. Further, throughout most of the twentieth century, the public, generally, would continue to see as sensible McGuffey's and Webster's rote learning and their heavy-handed political and moral indoctrination with its male, Anglo, and Protestant orientation.

Will Curriculum Challenge or Confirm the Social Order? Horace Mann had hoped that the common school would "contribute substantially to fashioning an emerging social order governed by a new public philosophy."[5] But Mann's view competed unsuccessfully with those who saw schooling as supporting the status quo. For example, William Torrey Harris, respected scholar and philosopher as well as superintendent of St. Louis schools and United States Commissioner of Education from 1889 to 1906, argued persuasively that schools could best pursue democratic principles "by confirming an order that had already come into existence."[6] Harris advocated strict discipline, orderly behavior, and mastery of the school subjects that we recognize today as the core of the modern essentialist curriculum: mathematics, geography, literature, art, grammar, and history. If schools were scientifically and rationally organized, Harris claimed, this curriculum would produce better people for the American democracy. What did such a curriculum look like? In 1893 pediatrician and school critic Joseph Mayer Rice gave the following description of a geometry lesson in a New York City school:

> Before the lesson began there was passed to each child a little flag, on which had been pasted various forms and colors, such as a square piece of green paper, a triangular piece of red paper, etc. . . . Upon receiving the signal, the first child sprang up, gave the name of the geometrical form upon his flag, loudly and rapidly defined the form, and fell back into his seat to make way for the second child, thus: "A square; a square has four equal sides and four corners; green" (down). Second child (up) "A triangle; a triangle has three sides and three corners; red" (down). . . . The rate of speed was so great that seventy children passed through the process of defining in a very few minutes.[7]

In 1893 an influential report from the National Education Association's "Committee of Ten" recommended that secondary schools teach a highly academic, that is, humanist, curriculum to all students.[8] Like Harris, the Committee argued that all students—regardless of their future station in life—would benefit from a mix of classical and modern studies that would transmit the western European intellectual tradition. However, this would not be.

Separate Schooling under One Roof By 1918 vast numbers of workers' and immigrants' sons and daughters were attending public secondary schools, where they joined a much smaller group of students from more-established, elite families. Here, the tradition of separate mass and elite education established itself under one roof.

Most educational leaders believed that only the elites had the mental capacity to learn a rigorous academic curriculum, and only they would occupy the social roles that require such knowledge. *Social efficiency* advocates sought a scientifically designed curriculum that would provide students direct instruction in the specific skills that they would use as adults. Thus, children of the elites would have an academic curriculum; children of the masses (including most immigrants) would learn practical and vocational knowledge and skills, infused with a heavy dose of American patriotism. For that vast majority of students, a 1918 NEA Commission on the Reorganization of Secondary Schools established seven curricular goals: (1) health, (2) command of fundamentals (basic skills), (3) worthy home membership, (4) vocation, (5) citizenship, (6) worthy use of leisure, and (7) ethical character. The Commission tied the loftiest attributes of democracy—especially freedom and self-determination through effort and merit—to schools teaching the mass of citizens practical competencies and sound moral character.

By the mid-1920s, most secondary schools managed to satisfy both the advocates of traditional academics and those who wanted a curriculum tailored to students' future social roles. Sociologists Robert and Helen Lynd found twelve different programs of study when they studied Muncie, Indiana's, high school in 1924. Of the twelve, only one had an "elite" academic college preparatory curriculum. The others included a general course of study, specialized programs oriented toward music and art, and a set of programs more closely allied with the tradition of "practical" education—shorthand, bookkeeping, applied electricity, mechanical drawing, printing, machine shop, manual arts, and home economics. This differentiated design of the high school curriculum, which has persisted in nearly every American high school throughout the twentieth century, is a topic explored in greater detail in Chapter 8.

Progressive Impulses

Sociocultural and cognitive theories of learning assert that students must understand knowledge, rather than simply acquire it, and social justice teaching requires that students experience democratic values, rather than simply being told how good citizens behave. But understanding through experience is not a recent invention. Although often buried and nearly silent, experiential learning is a value that has nagged at the practice and conscience of American schooling since the late 1800s. At that time, progressive educators grappled with the challenge of mass public education and sought new ways to counter social and schooling disorder. Some advocated scientific and social efficiency. They stressed preparing students for adulthood according to their particular talents or abilities and ensuring efficiency by rationally planning the entire curriculum in detail from beginning to end. One influential reformer, Franklin Bobbitt, thought that a curriculum designer should be like a "great engineer." Those following in Horace Mann's tradition, the "social meliorists," emphasized schools' role in social reform by addressing the social ills associated with poverty, poor health, and lack of education. Supporters of the child study movement, which was inspired by Stanley Hall, advocated a curriculum based on the emerging science of child psychology.[9]

Even though these reformers differed considerably from one another, they all countered the traditional humanist curriculum with confidence that their perspectives were bolstered by a good dose of rational, scientific organization and development. In that sense, they were all "progressive," but quite unlike another progressive philosopher and reformer whose name today is most closely associated with the term *progressive education,* John Dewey. Like other progressives of the time, Dewey emphasized the social nature of schooling and learning. However, recognizing that children's development and learning were anything but rational and orderly, he and his followers advocated a "child-centered" curriculum to give students experiences that make rigorous intellectual demands in the contexts of democratic social living.

Child-Centered Curricula Child-centered reforms emerged as early as 1873 in response to the results of an examination given by the school board in Quincy, Massachusetts. Historian Lawrence Cremin relates, "The results were disastrous. While the youngsters knew their rules of grammar thoroughly, they could not write an ordinary English letter. While they could read with facility from their textbooks, they were utterly confused by similar material from unfamiliar sources."[10] Shocked by these results, the Quincy board, under the leadership of Superintendent Francis Parker, made a number of changes. Cremin goes on to note:

> [The] set curriculum was abandoned, and with it the speller, the reader, the grammar, and the copybook. Children were started on simple words and sentences, rather than the alphabet learned by rote. In place of time-honored texts, magazines, newspapers, and materials devised by the teachers themselves were introduced into the classroom. Arithmetic was approached inductively, through objects rather than rules, while geography began with a series of trips over the local countryside. Drawing was added to encourage manual dexterity and individual expression. The emphasis throughout was on observing, describing, and understanding, and only when these abilities had begun to manifest themselves—among the faculty as well as the students—were more conventional studies introduced.[11]

In short, Parker had introduced a curriculum that "began" with the child's learning and then sought out appropriate content, materials, and experiences to make the learning happen. This differed markedly from conventional approaches that began with content, materials, and traditional approaches and expected the student to adjust to them. After only a few years Quincy students achieved excellent scores in reading, writing, and spelling on a second exam, this one administered by the Massachusetts State Board of Education.

Parker moved on to train teachers as head of the Cook County Normal School in Chicago, where only a few years later, he stated explicitly that his academic goals had a clearly social character. The school, he argued, should be a "model home, a complete community, and an embryonic democracy."[12] In Parker's experimental school, children created stories that became their "texts" for reading, spelling, penmanship, and grammar. Science took the form of nature study, including field trips to Lake Michigan, where the students observed, wrote descriptions, and made drawings of what they saw. Back in the classroom, these observations became the basis of "laboratory" work, where the children also learned mathematics as they constructed the "equipment" they would use in scientific study. Teachers introduced all subjects by connecting them with activities or experiences that already had meaning for the children.

It was to Parker's Chicago school that University of Chicago philosopher John Dewey sent his own children, and there Dewey gathered ideas for the University Laboratory school that he began in 1896. As at Parker's school, Dewey introduced children to learning through familiar activities of the family. An early account gave this description of Dewey's classroom for 4- and 5-year-olds following a trip to a farm:

> Part of the group played grocery store and sold fruit and sugar for the jelly making of the others. Some were clerks, some delivery boys, others mothers, and some made the grocery wagons. The clerks were given measuring cups with which to measure the sugar and cranberries and paper to wrap the packages to take home. . . . A wholesale house was constructed out of a big box. Elevators would be necessary, a child volunteered, for storehouses have so many floors; and these were made from long narrow corset boxes, a familiar wrapping in every household of the day.[13]

Dewey anticipated the sociocultural idea of expert scaffolding of learning. He stressed that a deep and thorough knowledge of the academic disciplines allowed the teacher to identify the particular help children needed and to devise activities to lead them to deeper understanding. So although many critics (and some advocates) accused Dewey of abandoning the academic disciplines in favor of a child-centered classroom, this was not the case. Dewey had such high regard for knowledge and knowledgeable teachers that he was supremely confident that an avenue or activity or opportunity could be found for each child to get to the heart of the academic discipline.

As students grew older, Dewey's teachers guided them through integrated activities filled with increasingly sophisticated opportunities to learn mathematics, science, and the other disciplines. Six-year-olds constructed a model farm and planned and raised wheat. Seven-, 8-, and 9-year-olds explored the history of Western civilization and the United States through concrete human activities, such as occupations, trade, and building cities. Teachers integrated these thematic activities with lessons in the arts, science, music, history and geography, foreign language, and literature. History illuminated human successes and failures; and literature conveyed the hopes of people in various social contexts. The oldest children specialized in a particular discipline, developing in-depth, yearlong projects.

Thus, Dewey's curriculum began with experiences immediately familiar to the child, then moved students to more distant and abstract ideas, and finally led them to grapple with broad social themes. Such an approach, Dewey argued, would prepare students to improve society as well as understand it.

Curriculum for a Progressive Democracy Dewey was no less interested in shaping character than those who preceded him—Webster, McGuffey, or Harris, for example. However, progressive reformers such as Dewey were less interested than others had been in preventing or correcting undesirable traits. Rather, progressive child-centered reformers sought a curriculum to develop in students a character that would build democratic and interdependent communities. Not surprisingly, given the emphasis on learning through activity, Dewey argued that schools should themselves be miniature democratic societies—places where children *live,* rather than "only a place to learn lessons."[14]

Dewey and other early-twentieth-century reformers also argued for cultural pluralism in the curriculum. In 1899 Jane Addams founded Chicago's Hull House, the best known of the big city settlement houses that helped immigrants adjust to American life. Addams created a community in the Chicago slums that was rich in intellectual and cultural opportunities. Together she and Dewey sought ways to help immigrants adapt to the American culture without losing contact with the cultures they left behind. They argued that while everyone should learn the common culture—English, American history, and the American political system—immigrants should also retain their home cultures. Thus, while helping immigrants learn what they needed to adjust to life in Chicago, part of the program at Hull House sought to teach them about their home cultures and to foster pride in those cultures.

Schooling figured prominently in Jane Addams's reform efforts. She argued that education for immigrants must go beyond the basics of English language instruction and civics, to provide for the social and moral well-being of the poor. That meant attending to their social and aesthetic needs with lectures, discussions, concerts, and art gallery visits; providing vocational training; and giving workers an understanding of the history and significance of the industrial life to which they and their families belonged. In 1908 Addams explained in an address to the National Education Association how schools should address social concerns:

> The schools ought to do more to connect these children with the best things of the past, to make them realize something of the beauty and charm of the language, the history, and the traditions which their parents represent. . . . If the body of teachers in our great cities could take hold of the immigrant colonies, could bring out of them their handicrafts and occupations, their traditions, their folk songs and folk lore, the beautiful stories which every immigrant colony is ready to tell and translate. . . . Give these children a chance to utilize the historic and industrial material they see about them and they will begin to have a sense of ease in America, a first consciousness of being at home. I believe if these people are welcomed upon the basis of the resources which they represent and the contributions which they bring, it may come to pass that these schools which deal with immigrants will find that they have a wealth of cultural and industrial material which will make the schools in other neighborhoods positively envious.[15]

In the 1920s Dewey and other intellectuals became increasingly outspoken about social and economic injustices. By the 1930s progressive reforms had taken an even more political turn. As the Great Depression made injustice highly visible, George Counts, professor at the University of Chicago, and Harold Rugg of Teachers College, Columbia University, with Dewey's support, captured the curriculum reform spotlight with their calls for a "social reconstructionist" curriculum. In a manifesto called "Dare the Schools Build a New Social Order," Counts railed against capitalism's emphasis on property rights over human rights and the culture's overemphasis on the individual. He indicted both the traditional humanist curriculum and the push for scientific efficiency, calling them ideally suited to cementing the status quo of unequal economic and social power. Counts argued that democracy must exert greater control over capitalism, that the school curriculum must critique social institutions that did not further democracy, and that teachers must act as a militant force for change. The traditional curriculum alone could not accomplish this, in Counts's view.

Although Counts and the social reconstructionists struck a responsive chord in American social thought, they barely penetrated the school curriculum. Their most salient contribution came with the widespread adoption of Harold Rugg's textbooks. These texts were the first that wove together the disciplines of history, geography, civics, economics, and sociology—all previously taught as separate subjects—as integrated "social studies." Rugg believed that a curriculum centered on real social problems, informed by ideas from the social sciences, would lead students to independent thinking and social action. For example, Rugg's books described the plight of African slaves and included vivid descriptions of conditions on the slave ships. His unit on economic disparity included photographs of wealthy and poor neighborhoods in the nation's capital.

Although Rugg's textbook series proved enormously popular during the 1930s, most educators and the public did not sympathize with the social reconstructionists' anticapitalistic ideology. And with World War II bringing both economic prosperity and a resurgence of American patriotism, Rugg's texts came under attack by conservative newspapers and organizations such as the American Legion and the Daughters of the Colonial Wars. Attacked as un-American (one column blasting Rugg in the *American Legion Magazine* was called "Treason in the Textbooks"[16]), the ideas of Rugg and Counts, and even Dewey, stood little chance. That would not change until the 1960s and 1970s when the civil rights and anti–Vietnam War movements brought widespread public political critique and pressure for social activism to universities and, soon after, high schools. Even then, however, little social critique actually made its way into school textbooks. Still today, social conservatives continue to prefer a sequence of fact-based courses in history, geography, economics, and so on, instead of integrating these topics for the sake of larger meanings and social theory in courses called "social studies." Today, the "critical pedagogy" movement, which we discuss later in this chapter, echoes this progressive political agenda.

Sputnik and Curriculum Crisis

The 1940s and 1950s brought little curricular ferment other than a continuing, rather academic debate between traditional and progressive educators. Preoccupation with World War II, followed by the business of returning the country to normal, in turn followed by complacency with postwar affluence meant that little public frustration was directed toward schools. The most salient reform was called the "life adjustment" movement, which argued that the highest curriculum priority should be teaching about the practical concerns of daily living, for example, the chemistry of detergents, driving and servicing an automobile, and how local utility services work. The life adjustment movement warranted criticism, but its most severe and successful critics were able to discredit by association two threats to the status quo. They successfully connected the public's general distrust of the progressives' agenda with the life adjustment movement's sometimes-frivolous curriculum that indeed lacked intellectual rigor.

The cold war of the 1950s, marked by the virulent anticommunist sentiment of the McCarthy period and the horrific oppressions of Stalinist Russia, made an inhospitable climate for pursing progressive schooling. It was a time when the vocabulary of progressives, including "reform," "social justice," "democratic," and "progressive," could taint the speaker with suspicion of un-American sympathies. The launching of *Sputnik* in 1957 silenced further debate between the progressive and traditional camps, at least temporarily. That the Russians—source of cold war anxieties and the ever-present communist threat—could beat the Americans into space could only mean that U.S. schools had failed. Many citizens believed that only the imposition of high academic standards and rigorous curriculum, particularly in science and mathematics, would restore the nation to its rightful place in the world order and ensure the preeminence of democracy. High school graduation and college entrance standards were raised, and mathematicians and scientists around the country turned their energies toward developing rigorous new courses of study for elementary and secondary schools.

Drawing from the new, cognitive learning theories of Jerome Bruner and the developmental theories of Jean Piaget, the "new" math, science, and social studies programs asked students to engage with the central concepts of the disciplines in an increasingly sophisticated "spiral" curriculum. Bruner contended that children at every stage of cognitive development could learn some form of the most important ideas of the disciplines if the curriculum mirrored the structure and the inquiry processes of the discipline.

Implementation of these new, more academic curricula was spotty, however, and interest in them was short-lived. The country's regained prowess in space, coupled with the social activism and civil unrest of the late 1960s and 1970s, brought a curricular swing toward social relevance followed by a backlash of "back to the basics." These swings were in no small part prompted by the feeling that the briefly and barely implemented curriculum of the new math, new science, and new social studies actually caused the student activism that so shocked much of the nation. And, as described later, Ronald Reagan's presidential victory in 1980 brought dramatic changes in social and educational policies and renewed noisy debate about the American school curriculum.

The Struggle for a Twenty-First-Century Curriculum

As Chapter 1 described, national uncertainties, a shrinking world community and global economy, dramatic demographic shifts, and struggles for racial and gender equality have disrupted modernists' confidence in the nation's progress toward a dominant and tightly unified American culture. Exposure to the broader world and different points of view, as well as expanding notions of democracy (often presented through the media rather than formal schooling), have revealed the limits and fallibility of much that Americans have taken as unquestioned. Such fundamental ideas as scientific progress have moved from being unquestioned truths to artifacts of Western Enlightenment thinking.

The modern school curriculum considers knowledge to be truth discovered by and recorded by experts, and teaching as the transmission of that knowledge to students. It is modern because it considers learning as a building process that starts with the simple and moves to the more complicated, proceeding from the parts to the whole. Thus, according to the modern view, the mastery of basic skills or facts becomes a necessary foundation for learning more complex processes and concepts, and the curriculum should break down whatever is taught into its smallest constituent parts. Today, however, faith in the modern perspective is waning, as evidenced by the extent to which the whole society is intensely engaged in debating the questions "What knowledge and skills are most worth learning?" and "Whose culture and whose character should we pass on to the young?"

Postmodern conditions, including increased ethnic diversity of the population and women's increasing economic and political power, have challenged the dominance of the modern ways of thinking described in the last paragraph. Reformers see no risk that core moral commitments (for truth, family, charity, etc.) shared across cultures would be endangered by meanings and actions that may seem strange to Americans accustomed to mainstream culture. Moreover, they argue that a central concern for social justice in schools and society is a powerful guide for developing curricula that is useful, intellectually rigorous, culturally cohesive, and accessible to all. Today's reformers maintain, therefore, that the hallmarks of the modern curriculum—absolute certainties and universal truths as mined from the depths of white, Western culture—are weak and limiting guidelines for deciding what and how students will learn in the twenty-first century.

These attempts at reform have triggered virulent reactions from traditionalists and have resulted in what is popularly known as the *culture wars.* A hallmark of reactionary conservative initiatives has been the campaign to standardize the curriculum around a *canon* or set of indisputable, unchanging ideas, values, facts, and particular works found in past generations of history, literature, and even science and mathematics instruction. Although many of those arguing for the canon place a high value on depth of thinking and interpretation, most of today's traditionalists lobby for curricular basics and emphasis on the rules governing correct procedures and right answers. Some propose and achieve a rigidity and control over curriculum that exceeds anything the nation has experienced in the past.

Matching Content to Cognition

Sociocultural theorists begin with the view that knowledge has meaning in existing cultural contexts, not in some idealized past. The curriculum and pedagogy that follows from this perspective bears a strong resemblance to that John Dewey posed a century ago. The resemblance is not lost on Dewey's critics, who believe cognitive and sociocultural innovations sacrifice intellectual and moral rigor by catering to children's interests.

Learning Is Constructing Knowledge in Contexts The main point of departure from centuries-old modern ideas to postmodern ideas—from traditional notions of learning to sociocultural approaches—is the concept of *construction.* Construction is central to both learning and knowledge. It is so central, in fact, that learning and knowledge become inseparable. Knowledge (or subject matter or content contained in the school curriculum) is not fixed but varies in important ways in different contexts and over time. This claim, that knowledge is a human construction, gives people fits. "What about 2 plus 2 equals 4?" Yes, there are multiple ways to construct even this simple equation, and here are just three of many: First, as young children we had to make sense of it as a simple sum of quantities, otherwise we would just parrot the sound of words. Second, the question has a symbolic, cultural meaning to represent what people commonly take as a "no-brainer"—an example of how some things are just "true facts" that never change. Finally, there is a meaning in the particular context of this page.

One profound consequence of constructed learning and constructed knowledge is that the request "Would you explain what you mean by that?" competes with "What is the answer?" as essential questions for teaching and learning and human relations as well. *What do you make of that? Can you help me make sense of the way you see it? Can you explain how you solved this?* These questions do not suggest a relationship of ignorance and intelligence. Rather, they acknowledge that knowledge can be constructed in multiple ways. Even when two people (or two cultures) hold a construct in common, it is possible that shades of difference exist that are important to include as shared knowledge.

A constructivist approach to learning, knowledge, and teaching can dramatically alter the academic and social environment of the classroom; it also presents several challenges to teachers as they develop and implement such a curriculum. For example, many students find the traditional curriculum more comfortable; it is familiar and predictable, even if it doesn't help them learn as much. Teachers like first-year teacher Marilyn Cortez (see the following) worry that the blizzard of facts and drills in the traditional curriculum overwhelms students. Many teachers see few opportunities for students to struggle for new meanings or gain firsthand experience making sense of new and complex ideas. Further, as a practical matter, often this blizzard is simply never learned!

My students . . . frequently complained about this "discovery" approach and about justifying their answers. Many complained about discussions. "Why don't you just give us the assignment out of the book?" or "Why do I have to justify the formula if I still remember what it is from my other class?" or "Why do we have to work in groups?" or "This is too confusing; why don't you just tell us the answer?" I began to see how they really are convinced that "school math" is something algorithmic. It is something that holds true on its own without any need for justification or understanding, and school math is something that could be and should be done individually. If students come across an obstacle, the teacher is the fountain of solutions. I think that the preconceptions students have about mathematics are just as important [as the new knowledge they learn].

—Marilyn Cortez
First-year teacher, mathematics, grade 9

Cortez reveals one of the great delights and intellectual challenges awaiting teachers who match cognitive and sociocultural theories to teaching practice. These are not curriculum theories in the modern sense of curriculum; that is, they do not prescribe for the teacher what, when, and in what order to transmit particular knowledge. Instead, these theories pose knowledge as a social construction and teaching as assisting students to make meanings. This approach demands a far deeper knowledge of subject matter and a far wider range of instructional interactions with students than a traditional curriculum does. Also, it requires considerable forethought and planning. "Teaching on autopilot" is a condition described by some traditional teachers, but never by constructivists. Since every class and every child is different, teaching becomes less a matter of applying protocols and following plans and directions than applying theory and processes to fluid, ever-changing conditions—namely, different students' needs for assistance and guidance. Since the teacher cannot personally, moment by moment, be part of every question or be involved in every conversation, the teacher seeks to provide a classroom environment and learning culture that is also responsive to students' learning.

A Thinking Curriculum A child-centered, constructivist curriculum focuses on children's thinking and learning. Throughout this book, there are many references to ill-advised behavioral practices such as relying only on drill and practice and memorizing, sometimes to the exclusion of complex real-life issues. The alternative to this approach is to offer curriculum material and assistance that guides students toward understanding and stretches their thinking. For example, psychologist Lauren Resnick argued compellingly in her 1983 book, *Education and Learning to Think,* that because most learning happens when we solve problems, the curriculum should model real-world problem solving.[17] Only with such a curriculum will students develop their capacity for "higher-order" thinking. Resnick defines higher-order thinking as follows:

- *Nonalgorithmic*—the path of action is not fully specified in advance
- *Complex*—the total path is not "visible" (mentally speaking) from any single vantage point
- *Yields multiple solutions,* each with costs and benefits, rather than unique solutions
- *Involves nuanced* judgment and interpretation
- *Applies multiple criteria,* which sometimes conflict with one another.
- *Involves uncertainty*—not everything that bears on the task at hand is known
- *Self-regulating*—we do not recognize higher order thinking in an individual when someone else "calls the plays" at every step
- *Imposes meaning,* finding structure in apparent disorder
- *Effortful*—there is considerable mental work involved in the kinds of elaborations and judgments required[18]

When teaching is guided by these ideas, students learn to be problem solvers; but just as important, they learn to be problem finders. This skill is essential in a world in which obstacles to technical solutions and social justice remain hidden from all but the sharpest eyes. One caution, however. So powerful are the behavioral, progress-driven, rational-scientific traditions in schools that some tradition-minded educators simply cannot resist designing programs, protocols, steps, and rules for how to get students to be creative, divergent, problem-solving, and higher-order thinkers.

My students are often frustrated when I answer their questions by posing another question and resist telling them the "right" answer. I want them to think. I do not ask them to memorize a lot of names and dates, although they need to refer to events to respond to questions. For example, one question on the Scientific Revolution asked whether it was a good idea for the Church to have so much power in those days. To answer that question students referenced their knowledge that Galileo's theory went against the Church's and that the Church tried him and kept him under house arrest. I am proud to say that my students themselves are able to develop penetrating questions. For instance, one student wanted to know, "If they could, would white people bring slavery back?" When developing questions for the Mexican Revolution, students wanted to know about life after the revolution, women's participation, weapons, and the fate of various participants; their questions reflect their individuality and inquisitiveness.

—Jeffra Becknell
First-year teacher, social studies, grade 9

Jeffra Becknell's approach contrasts with the more traditional curriculum process of diagnosing students' existing knowledge and skills (though this rarely happens more than superficially), then teaching students, step-by-step, the facts and skills they need to solve a problem. The traditional curriculum would not necessarily ask students to apply the facts and skills to real and important problems. However, a curriculum focused on thinking through important questions, like the ones Jeffra Becknell and her students ask, also emphasizes the complicated nature of such problems and teaches that they don't go away easily.

Consider also the hypothetical case of two students writing on global warming. Chris began her essay, "There are no easy solutions to the problem of global warming." Julie began, "There are three important steps to solving the problem of global warming." Chris has as much data about the problem as Julie does. Nonetheless, in a traditional classroom Chris may receive the poorer grade if she reveals some of her struggle over her ideas in the paper itself. Julie may have an easier time because her essay lends itself to a certain tidiness of structure and organization. Having read thousands of such beginnings, we predict that of the two, Chris will be more likely to make sense of the problem as an environmental, human, and personal issue. Chris will correctly and realistically approach the problem as one that is not about to go away soon. She is more likely to go home full of passion regarding this real-life concern. In years to come she will probably follow this issue and be receptive to new developments. On the other hand, Julie may be more likely to set this topic aside once she has done the assignment. She may see her entire involvement with it as a school problem or a writing problem—not a social or personal one.

Knowledge in Context: Making the Abstract Concrete Learning within meaningful contexts is essential. Remembering facts—names, events, dates, formulas, and algorithms—is far easier if they are presented within the context of ideas, narratives, or experiences that already mean something to students. Educational and social critics frequently wave surveys showing that a shamefully low percentage of teenagers know basic historical facts, such as the century in which the American Civil War was fought. It isn't that they were never taught. More likely, they learned the dates outside of any meaningful context and promptly forgot them. That's the problem that first-year teacher Zeba Palomino struggles with as she helps her ninth graders think about solving algebraic equations—a topic typically taught with even fewer connections to meaningful contexts than history.

As difficult as it has been for me to find or design contextualized math lessons, they have worked much more effectively than boring and meaningless lectures about a rule or algorithm. In the unit on solving equations, my students became very familiar with the idea of balance scales, and with keeping the scales balanced by doing the same thing to both sides of the balance scale. They also became comfortable with the concepts of "variables," "like terms," "distributive property," and "opposite operations" through using manipulatives including teddy bears, number blocks, and visual balance scales. Gradually, all of them, at their own pace, "weaned" themselves off the manipulatives and became comfortable solving equations with just pencil and paper. We did not talk about rules or algorithms such as "to undo an operation you must perform the opposite operation to both sides of the equation." Instead, we discovered easy, logical ways to figure out an unknown amount on a balance scale without throwing the scale off balance.

—Zeba Palomino
First-year teacher, high school mathematics

Building on What Students Know Students bring to classrooms a store of informal knowledge, which is the *personal context* children use to get started making sense of new ideas. This prior knowledge and experience is a valuable curriculum resource, as first-year teacher Ramon Martinez discovered when he began a geography unit with his first graders.

My students are Latino first graders who have been classified as Limited English Proficient. All of them come from low-income homes, and most live in the projects. My unit "Donde Estamos?" builds on my students' knowledge of their community to help them understand basic concepts in geography. We made a "mural map" as the centerpiece of the unit. Instead of telling my students what to include, I allowed them to decide. Many students supplied me with details about their community that would have otherwise gone unnoticed. One saw that I had forgotten to put a particular store on the map. I encouraged her to make it and put it where it belonged, which she did in amazing detail. Another noticed that the Chinese restaurant near her house did not appear. Not surprisingly, she knew exactly where to put it. My students began noticing maps everywhere. Once my students realized that I welcomed their knowledge, they began to participate more actively. They showed me maps in the hallway and interrupted during journal time to show me maps in books. One brought back a map from Disneyland and insisted on sharing it. After I introduced the cardinal directions, they were constantly notifying me every time that they saw the cardinal directions in print.

—Ramon Martinez
First-year teacher, bilingual grade 1

Teachers in multilingual schools also find ways to use students' prior language as a bridge to understanding of concepts.

One day a student who has a lot of difficulty speaking English spoke. I did not understand him and was reminded of the trouble he had acquiring English in my class, while speaking mostly Spanish at home and studying Cantonese at Chinese school. As I often do, I replied to him in his home language, saying "What?" in Spanish. He then rattled off a beautiful description of a bird building its nest on a rooftop, and he connected it to an integrated lesson we had a month earlier. To the casual observer, it might not have seemed like any success in developing language. For me, it was poetry—the student's description of a bird building a nest to take care of eggs that would someday hatch. He engaged his classmates in a real-life situation and connected it to what we had done in class. He not only got his Spanish-speaking peers to speak in their home language, the rest of the class became interested. Despite not being able to understand Spanish, other students were excited and tried to figure out what was being said. This led the Spanish speakers to explain in English and Spanish. As I looked at this class at that moment, I saw twenty smiling faces engaged in a spontaneous language arts lesson led by a peer who was speaking just two of the languages he was going to master.

—Benjamin Chang
First-year teacher, grade 1

Much current curriculum reform, like the curriculum of Dewey's laboratory school, attempts to build on the world students already know, including family, neighborhood, and city. Many traditional classrooms do include informal knowledge but stop short of making that knowledge central to rigorous academic learning. So, for example, we can point to the ubiquitous "family tree" lessons that start out so many school years. These are wonderful foundations for building on students' informal knowledge throughout the term. Unfortunately, they are too often simply a nod toward "diversity," an opportunity to decorate the bulletin board, and are quickly abandoned. Teachers could explore many school projects of this sort as a foundation for yearlong development that could include placing the student's background in ever-widening social, historical, literary, geographical, and technological contexts. Many students whom schools identify as less able—often because they are culturally or linguistically "different"—make important contributions, and their sense of competence is enhanced when teachers value these students' informal knowledge. These children are as clever at bringing useful informal knowledge to a problem as their classmates who may be quicker to learn the formal knowledge in traditional ways. Building on *prior knowledge* presents a challenge to many teachers who are not used to valuing all knowledge or in whom it is engrained that classroom knowledge must not depart from the subject matter in texts and curriculum guides.

In one sense, *all* of a person's knowledge is prior knowledge. And in one sense we might see learning as a process of "updating" or *re*constructing that prior knowledge. As students mature and gain experience, they are capable of bringing new, richer interpretations to past knowledge and experience. Thus, recall and review are rarely just reminders or transitions to next lessons. In particular, cognitive and sociocultural perspectives point to new ways for teachers to address "wrong content," misperceptions, and naïve and prejudicial views. Thus, teaching with cognitive and sociocultural theory in mind means that the teacher will be prepared to listen carefully to a student's explanation of why 5 + 5 = 55, why "poor people are lazy," in what sense Columbus "discovered" America. Simply telling a student that he has the wrong answer and moving on to the next lesson is a poor way to replace incorrect with correct knowledge. The curriculum must provide for undoing misconceptions as well as for teaching correct ones.

Multiple Entry Points Howard Gardner, a leading psychologist who relates cognitive theory to learning and teaching, offers five entry points or ways of connecting with students' learning strengths and prior knowledge. He shows, for example, how the topic of democracy might be presented to students through narrative (e.g., the story of its beginnings), a logical-quantitative consideration (e.g., analyses of voting patterns), a foundational approach (e.g., beginning with the roots of the word and idea), an aesthetic approach (e.g., listening to a string quartet play together without turning over control to a conductor), and an experiential approach (e.g., having students make decisions under both democratic and undemocratic conditions).[19] Similarly, psychologist Robert Sternberg advocates a curriculum that presents students with information in ways that tap into four different modes: memory, analysis, creativity, and practical thinking. Like Gardner, Sternberg believes that framing knowledge from multiple perspectives allows far more students to learn successfully.[20] Of course, to do this well, teachers themselves need a deep reservoir of content knowledge and teaching skill in order to scaffold, match, question, suggest, and interpret in ways that build on diverse groups of students' learning strengths. The key to these approaches is that the entry points are multiple—students benefit more when many are available and used. The entry points are not items on a menu from which the teacher or student makes a single choice. Notice the multiple entry points Lucy Patrick incorporated into her lesson on the gold rush.

After reading about the lifestyle and struggles of forty-niners coming to California, students in "mining groups" of five or six reenacted the day in the life of a miner and tried their hand at "panning" for gold—experiencing firsthand some of the thrills and hardships that gold miners felt. I buried false gold nuggets in the kindergarten sandbox, and students used pan sifters to look for gold. We discussed how finding gold was thrilling, yet it was not until students were under the hot sun, with dust in their eyes, that they were able to make real connections to the physical hardships of the miners. We constructed rules for the mining, rather than having the rules imposed. I pointed out that stealing and robbery were common during the gold rush. We talked about fair punishment for someone who would jump claims. Three students (unplanned by me) trespassed onto the kindergarten yard after school to find more pieces of gold, much as the claim jumpers did. The class then came up with punishments for the "wanted" people. The consequences would depend on whether or not the criminals would come forward and confess. Luckily, the students surrendered and apologized for their wrongdoing.

The true excitement of the lesson came as students made connections. I could see them trying to make sense out of what we had read and reflecting on the ethics of people's actions during the gold rush era. They learned about a different time and place by reenacting some of the miners' daily activities. The textbook provided a knowledge base, so that students could connect what they were doing with the facts and figures about that era.

—Lucy Patrick
First-year teacher, grade 4

Is the Answer Right or Right? In everyday life, there is seldom one right resolution to most real problems. Similarly, most real-life problems lack definitive resources like a spell checker or dictionary that give an answer that is (somewhat) indisputable. Real-life solutions have to be compatible with so many ideas, fit so many contexts, and suit the knowledge and opinions of so many people that two people rarely enact the same resolution. Furthermore, the same person often will not select the same solution twice if given the chance to change her mind or learn from her experience. In the real world, people need to figure things out by using trial, success, and error, as well as by relying on memorized and automatic routines.

In contrast, traditional school problems usually have right procedures to follow and right answers to find, and certainly standardized tests presume a curriculum built around right answers. Curriculum reformers do not dispute that single right answers have their place—spelling, math facts, and so on—but they do object to a curriculum where attention to narrow, single-answer tasks displaces opportunities for multiple right answers or selecting among approaches to solving problems. And although reformers welcome multiple meanings that students offer, they don't just accept any answer. Typically, the multiple meanings students offer don't diverge dramatically, and when they do, they are negotiated. When older students offer meanings that are clearly off the mark, they are strongly and adequately challenged both by teachers and by other students.

Culturally Democratic Curriculum

Despite the fact that my school is 70 percent Latino and 90 percent minority, the English department's list of ninth-grade core novels includes *To Kill a Mockingbird, Of Mice and Men, The Great Gatsby, The Scarlet Letter, Wuthering Heights,* and *Brave New World,* all works written by white authors. I knew I was going to have to provide my own texts and materials to have any kind of multiculturalism in the classroom. I found some Latino and African American poetry and just added it into what I was already doing. I did nothing radical, to say the least—almost everything we read was by a white author. However, toward the end of the first semester, two students questioned my choices. First an African American student asked me why I always chose Latino literature for the class, and then a white student asked why everything we read was racial. I could not understand where these questions were coming from. Why didn't the African American student ask me why I always chose white literature for the class? The answer to this has to do with how our culture naturalizes whiteness. We do not give students a sense of whiteness as an ethnic identity. White middle-class culture becomes an invisible norm. This young student did not question the use of white literature because she sees it as the norm—what she has come to expect from school.

—Michael Alvarez
First-year teacher, middle-school English

A culturally democratic curriculum helps students know and value the diverse traditions that enrich and dignify the nation's heritage and engages them in learning and maintaining their own heritage and language. A culturally democratic curriculum also acknowledges the very practical matter that social and economic power come primarily to those with a command of Anglo-American traditions and standard English. A culturally democratic curriculum confronts the visible and invisible norms that perpetuate racism, classism, sexism, and other "isms" so that students can act on their knowledge—become transformative. Teachers cannot expect that these diverse traditions will sit quietly side by side in students' minds. Different traditions are not cold historical paragraphs, but current realities that can inflame students' passions for justice and demands for justification. By employing reforms typically called a "multicultural curriculum," teachers acknowledge many cultures, help the less powerful acquire the cultural tools of the dominant Anglo-American culture, and create a democratic forum for exploring conflict and oppression.

Including Everyone Jane Addams's voice echoes in much multicultural and bilingual curriculum today. Like Addams, contemporary multiculturalists press for curriculum that includes the "handicrafts and occupations, their traditions, their folk songs and folk lore, the beautiful stories which every immigrant colony is ready to tell and translate" of nonwhite and immigrant students. We also hear W. E. B. DuBois's passionate plea:

> We should fight to the last ditch to keep open the right to learn, the right to have examined in our schools not only what we believe; not only what our leaders say, but what the leaders of other groups and nations, and the leaders of other centuries have said. We must insist upon this to give our children the fairness of a start which will equip them with such an array of facts and such an attitude toward truth that they can have a real chance to judge what the world is and what its greater minds have thought it might be.[21]

Like DuBois, many of today's multiculturalists engage students with the ideas and "truths" of diverse people.

However, what typically passes for a pluralistic or multicultural curriculum is little more than a mention of the "place" of minorities and immigrants in the unquestioned story and content of American culture. For example, schools may celebrate (or simply announce) "ethnic" holidays like Cinco de Mayo and Ramadan to acknowledge non–Western European immigrants. They may use Black History Month to recognize events such as Harriet Tubman's nineteenth-century smuggling of slaves to freedom on the underground railroad or to play a few seconds of Martin Luther King's "I Have a Dream" speech. Even these modest inclusions may result only after hard-won curriculum battles against forces who would claim that "foreign" celebrations have no place in American schools. And although King and Tubman—as modified by white curriculum writers—are considered appropriate historical representatives of African Americans in American history, W. E. B. DuBois and Malcolm X usually are not. Not only is their social criticism more difficult to make palatable to mainstream tastes, many teachers and curriculum planners have only superficial knowledge of their contributions. Sonja Nieto stresses that the curriculum must relay not only how nonwhites have contributed to mainstream American history, literature, arts, sciences, ideas, and so forth but also how groups develop culture "in their own terms."[22]

First-year teacher Laila Banani Taslimi shows how social justice priorities can influence curriculum in ways that go far deeper than simple mentions, tributes, and food tastings. A yearlong curriculum emphasis for her racially mixed class of first graders—developmentally appropriate for their age—is perspective taking. The following excerpt is from her letter inviting the superintendent to participate in an event that was well integrated into her ongoing curricular objectives:

> We have been learning about Dr. Martin Luther King, Jr. and the peaceful fight he led to change the unfair laws that kept people separate and unequal. As a culminating activity we are marching with messages (penned by the students) about friendship, equality, and brotherhood, etc. to the local McDonald's to enjoy lunch together. The celebration is because, thanks to Dr. King and those who fought with him, we are now able to sit down in the same restaurant together.

More ambitious school and district efforts are possible, if beyond the scope of an individual teacher's decision making. An example is two-way bilingual programs, where native English–speaking children and those with another primary language—Spanish, for example—become fully literate in both languages. These programs don't consider the "other" language as a problem or regard bilingual education as a way of remediating language deficits of children whose first language is not English. In a number of cases, these two-way programs have become quite popular with English-speaking, affluent families who see learning a second language as worthwhile for their children.

Whereas conventional teaching might *enrich* lessons by acknowledging diverse and multiple cultures, sociocultural theory invites teachers to place inclusive and democratic elements at the center of their curricula and from that core let develop the daily learning opportunities. Professor Luis Moll's research at the University of Arizona explains how diverse students bring knowledge and experiences to school that provide a rich and valid basis for learning. Moll contends that the secret to literacy instruction is for schools to investigate and tap into the "hidden" home and community resources of their students. Moll, who studied Mexican American families in Tucson's impoverished barrio, discovered that clusters of these households had developed rich "funds of knowledge" about agriculture, mining, economics, household management, materials and science, medicine, and religion. However, the schools neither knew about nor used this knowledge base to assist students with academic skills.[23]

First-year teachers Wendy Herrera and Megan Ward followed Moll's approach as they created a curriculum for their bilingual K–1 class where learning developed through cultural interactions.

> We chose *Dia de los muertos* instead of Halloween. We wanted our students to understand better the tradition that stems from their own history and culture, and choose whether or not they want to embrace it for themselves. We asked the students, *"Que es el Dia de los muertos?"* so we could create a brainstorm web of their ideas. Students responded to the question with a blank stare, and later made comments such as, *"Es cuando la gente se muere y los gusanos se los comen"* ("It's when people die and the worms eat them"). Another comment was, *"Es como Halloween cuando la gente se viste de monstruos"* ("It's like Halloween when people dress up as monsters"). So, we asked that parents share what they know with their children, and students drew and wrote

about what they had learned from their parents. The students compiled their drawings into a big book.

We created a classroom altar. Students went home and discussed with their parents what meaningful artifact they would like to share and place on the altar. Each time that a student brought something in for the altar, we would sit in a community circle and the student would share its significance. The altar and the walls were filled with student work, and we encouraged the students to decorate and add their personal objects on the altar that reminded them of someone or something that had passed away. Many students brought in photographs and drawings. Some students placed stuffed animals that reminded them of a pet that had died.

Dia de los muertos was an open invitation for parents and school community members to become a part of our learning process. One woman in the community who knew a lot about the celebration demonstrated making paper flowers for the altar. She also offered insights into the meaning behind items that go on the altar. She gave the students *calavera* rings that she painted representing an aspect of *Dia de los muertos*. Throughout the month, we had read books that illustrated the various items that could be placed on the altar, and the students brought in flowers, plants, fruit and candles. Mothers gave suggestions and reminded us of things that needed to go on the altar. We painted, colored, and made various art projects, including puppets and masks and even making our own *Pan de Muertos*. One could walk into our classroom and feel the students' energy.

—Wendy Herrera and Megan Ward
First-year bilingual teachers, grade K–1

Wendy Herrera and Megan Ward, like Louis Moll, identified the funds of knowledge in their students' families and communities. In doing so, everyone learned to do far more than simply identify a few features of the *Dia de los muertos* tradition.

In rural, low-income Appalachia over the past thirty years, the Foxfire project has engaged high school English classes in the study of Appalachian customs and traditions. Students read books by Appalachian authors, such as Thomas Wolfe and James Agee; they conduct interviews with community elders and publish their writing in their own quarterly magazine, *Foxfire.* Some of the students' work has also been collected into a popular book. *A Foxfire Christmas: Appalachian Memories and Traditions* celebrates the holiday traditions of Appalachian families as passed from one generation to the next.[24] Interviews with neighbors and family members include instructions for re-creating many of the ornaments, toys (e.g., cornhusk dolls and hand-whittled cars), and recipes (e.g., chicken and dumplings, and black walnut cake) from local families. The students shot and developed most of the photographs for the book and edited the final manuscript.

One of the core principles of the Foxfire project is that students reveal their attitudes and values through schooling activities in order to use those attitudes and values in the students' critique of essential community issues. Thus, Foxfire teachers use culturally relevant curriculum, not to keep their students provincial but to appreciate various groups' commonalties and unique features and to examine local conditions.

A less common approach to curriculum that reflects cultures other than the white mainstream is an ethnocentric approach that places nonwhite cultures at the center of the curriculum. Several big school systems (e.g., Detroit, Milwaukee, Washington, D.C., and Baltimore) have developed special Afrocentric elementary schools for black students—sometimes just for black boys—in racially isolated city centers. Elsewhere, even without an official "mandate" for an ethnic emphasis, individual schools and teachers have shifted the school curriculum to reflect the special relevance of the students' culture. Often, this shift takes place under the leadership and scholarship of the school's teachers of color. Policymakers have been willing to try these controversial schools and/or willing to overlook curriculum variations given the overwhelming evidence that the typical traditional curriculum does not work well in inner-city neighborhoods. Teachers in these schools hope that their students can break the persistent pattern of low academic achievement and antischool attitudes. The teachers' approach is to offer a curriculum that better matches students' home culture and provides knowledge of students' own heritage, race, and culture. For example, teachers at Detroit's Malcolm X Academy wear African dress; the hallways display African murals, posters, and flags; and the curriculum gives prominence to African and African American history, culture, and current events as students learn basic academic skills. Few secondary schools have adopted ethnocentric curricula wholesale. However, many in racially mixed as well as racially isolated communities have developed Black studies and Chicano studies courses to balance the Western ethnocentric mainstream with knowledge of other American cultures. These schools are worth watching. They certainly pose no greater a threat to the tradition of the common school than schools focused exclusively on "mainstream" culture, and they may also reveal new and more powerful ways to incorporate diverse groups into new expressions of a culturally democratic common school curriculum.

Teaching the "Codes of Power" In Gloria Ladson-Billings's book *The Dreamkeepers,* which is about outstanding teachers of African American children, she cites teacher Patricia Hilliard, whose multicultural classroom attends to the power of standard English as well as respects the Black English her students speak outside of school:

> "I get so sick and tired of people trying to tell me that my children don't need to use any language other than the one they come to school with. Then those same people turn right around and judge the children negatively because of the way they express themselves. My job is to make sure that they can use both languages, that they understand that their language is valid but the demands placed upon them by others mean that they will constantly have to prove their worth. We spend a lot of time talking about language, what it means, how you use it, and how it can be used against you."[25]

Hilliard's teaching reflects recent sociological theory and research about how both the content and the structures of schooling connect with social class and race stratification. Perhaps the single most important finding of this research is that possession of what sociologists call *cultural capital* is often used to justify and legitimize the uneven distribution of wealth and power among racial and social class groups. Just as dollars have purchasing power, certain cultural knowledge, tastes, and habits have exchange value. (In the United States, the cultural capital that is most highly prized for high-wealth jobs and professions and for high-status colleges is white middle- and upper-class knowledge, dispositions, and values.) In the market, dollars may be exchanged for goods or services. In schools, jobs, and social interactions generally, certain habits and knowledge "buy" acceptance or favored treatment. First-year teacher Kay Goodloe is determined not to perpetuate this pattern.

As an African American female, and a product of the public school system, I am bidialectical. But do not jump to conclusions and assume that Black English was my primary home language. It was not. I learned Ebonics on the playground and on the streets of Los Angeles. Our working/middle-class community expected children to use mainstream English. I use the word "community" because all of the mothers shared the duty of policing our language. I have clear recollections of being reprimanded by a neighbor for using "slang" and being questioned as to where I had learned such language. As children, we became adept at code switching. We used mainstream English at home and in the presence of our parents and other authority figures, but we used Ebonics freely among our peers and at school. To be able to talk "jive" became a sign of group membership and demonstrated an individual's level of "coolness." It was also a form of resistance. We could communicate with our peers, ridiculing whites and other authority figures with the realization that they were absolutely clueless.

I vowed never to deliberately silence my students' voices. This vow is not easy to keep; it is something I struggle with daily. I am committed to creating a safe environment within my classroom, where my students feel comfortable expressing themselves regardless of the language that they bring with them, be it Ebonics, Spanglish, or other English dialects. But, to facilitate my students' acquisition of mainstream English, all of their assignments must be written in "standard" English. The majority of the time, I communicate with my students using standard English, but I feel that it is also necessary to model code switching in the classroom.

To achieve success in mainstream American society, bicultural students need to acquire "mainstream" English. But in exposing bicultural students to standard English, we also need to expose the relationships of power inherent in these forms of discourse. When standard English is discussed as "proper," society fails to acknowledge the cultural hegemony implicit in this definition. An effective teacher cultivates a classroom in which all student voices are valued.

—Kay Goodloe
First-year teacher, history, grade 11

Much cultural capital is wrapped up in students' language. Standard English and formal diction are quickly judged indicators of social class, parental influence, aspirations, school behavior, and academic potential. Cultural capital may be as simple as the good impression created by a young student knowing and being willing to say "please," and "yes, ma'am" (and knowing when it is not worth the bother). It may be as subtle as a middle-school student's degree of inoffensive confidence when asking for clarification about a grade.

Cultural capital also comes in nonlinguistic forms. It may be as trivial as a high schooler knowing that wearing a sweatshirt with an Ivy League university's logo is somehow better than wearing one from the local community college. It may be as significant and as profoundly complex as a parent providing his elementary school-aged child with private music lessons. Playing an oboe or violin may be a value in itself, but the parent may also know how this hobby—this skill—contributes to the child's continued acquiring of cultural capital. For example, students in the middle-school orchestra may be more likely to end up in the advanced academic track at the high school. Since nearly all of the students in orchestra are college bound, the school arranges its schedule that way. Students firmly ensconced in the school culture of "orchestra" may be less likely to work after school, have very poor parents, play in a counterculture (rock, punk, grunge, etc.) band, and so on. A student's identity as a scholar is certain to be shaped differently when others respond to her with preconceived judgments about what "types" of student spend after-school time in orchestra or cheerleading, soccer or baby-sitting, volunteering at the senior citizen center or "hanging out."

Large or small, the coins of cultural capital add up, giving an extra edge over and over again. Findings that cultural capital is so pivotal in gaining wealth and power have prompted some reformers to reassert the value of teaching nonwhite and low-income students the formal, traditional knowledge and skills of white middle- and upper-class culture as well as the less formal knowledge and skills that privileged children learn at home.

These reformers are not traditionalists in the usual sense, however. Most strongly support a multicultural curriculum, and they disdain the usual approaches to teaching mainstream culture to nonmainstream students as *assimilationist*—or designed to obliterate other cultures and preserve white middle- and upper-class privileges. Instead, they are suspicious of curriculum that cultivates students' own language and culture *to the exclusion* of the mainstream. Researcher Lisa Delpit framed it as well-intentioned liberalism run amok in her book *Other People's Children,* when she asks, "Will black teachers and parents continue to be silenced by the very forces that claim to 'give voice' to our children?"[26] Delpit and teachers like Kay Goodloe believe that all children should have access to the knowledge and skills that they will need to participate fully in the culture—as long as they understand that they are learning a particular code of power and not simply the "right" or "best" culture and language.

An interesting example of teaching students how to acquire the high-status cultural capital is San Diego–based AVID, a program that helps high school students of color from non-college-going families to prepare for college. Like many other such programs, AVID provides academic tutoring and encouragement. Unlike most other programs, AVID explicitly teaches what it calls "the hidden curriculum of the college track." This hidden curriculum includes some of the cultural capital—for example, the skills, manners, dress, and styles of interaction with teachers—that most college-bound students learn at home. So, for example, much like a middle-class, white parent would, the AVID teacher might coach a student about how to approach a teacher to question a grade with which the student disagrees. AVID also teaches the test-taking strategies, note-taking skills, and other "basics" of college preparation often not taught explicitly in class.[27]

Critical Pedagogy Critical analysis is a powerful tool for revealing the cultural content in school curricula and in the community. Students at all grades can use critique as a filter that preserves the best of democratic traditions while it identifies oppression. Teaching critical analysis, most often called *critical pedagogy,* links knowledge of diversity and inequality with actions that can make the culture more socially just. From this perspective, typical multicultural curricula appear superficial because they fail to consider institutionalized racism and other oppressive social structures. For the teacher, critical pedagogy means that classroom procedures and relationships as well as subject-matter content are continually subjected to questions designed to reveal bias, favoritism, or single perspectives (usually, not always, those of the dominant culture).

The questions that teachers consider when they plan their curriculum from a critical perspective include: Who benefits from the lesson being taught this way (i.e., the projects, worksheets, lectures, discussions, testing, grading, etc.)?, Who benefits from this version of the story (i.e., manifest destiny, Japanese internment camps, the Bill of Rights, AIDS, Martin Luther King, etc.)?, and Whose prior knowledge and cultural experiences are best matched to the most important principles of the lesson, and whose are excluded? Questions such as these become cultural tools that teacher and students use to examine the fairness and the multiple understandings of the curriculum as they learn and teach what is conventionally understood as "subject matter."

Sonja Nieto and others advocate a critical curriculum that teaches students about the systematic discrimination that people of color have faced in the past and present. The goal is not merely to expose injustice (or to generate guilt among white and affluent Americans). Rather, it is to help students see that possibilities for liberation exist side by side with oppression. Advocates of critical pedagogy argue that the study of liberation and oppression is basic for everyone. Any student who does not experience it is being *mis-educated,* to use the term that African American educator Carter Woodson used when he introduced this idea in 1933. Nieto observes:

> Textbooks in all subject areas exclude information about unpopular perspectives, or the perspectives of disempowered groups in our society. For instance, there are few U.S. history texts that assume the perspective of working-class people, although it is certainly true that they were and are the backbone of our country. Likewise, the immigrant experience is generally treated as a romantic and successful odyssey rather than the traumatic, wrenching, and often less-than-idyllic situation it was and continues to be for so many. . . . And finally, we

> can be sure that if the perspectives of women were taken seriously, the school curriculum would be dramatically altered. Unless all students develop the skill to see reality from multiple perspectives, not only the perspective of dominant groups, they will continue to think of it as linear and fixed and to think of themselves as passive in making any changes.[28]

First-year fourth-grade teacher Lucy Patrick used her gold rush lesson, described earlier, to draw students into taking the perspectives of others.

We also dealt with power and justice. After the excitement of panning for gold, I asked the students, "How do you think the kindergarten children felt when you took over their sandbox, and what happened when they wanted to play, too?" We discussed our greediness and how we can all get caught up with "gold fever," but we had taken over an area that really did not belong to us. When the kindergartners saw us, they were intimidated, and one fourth grader snatched a gold piece from a kindergartner. I asked my students to connect this oppression to our readings about the people from the east taking over parts of California inhabited by the Spaniards, Mexicans, and Indians. My students made some powerful statements:

- "We took over the kindergarten yard like the forty-niners did from the Indians. In a way, we were greedy, greedy for gold. . . . We were greedy, we didn't care, but we didn't realize whose 'home' we were actually destroying."
- "Now I know how the Indians and Spaniards felt when pioneers took over their land."
- "Today we went mining for gold in the kindergarteners' sandbox. It was just like what the forty-niners did to the Spaniards and Indians. I don't think it was fair!"

Students considered the issue in depth, exchanged views and opinions, and debated the implications. Through role playing and class discussions, students were able to generalize principles, such as fairness and justice, and apply them to present situations.

—Lucy Patrick
First-year teacher, grade 4

Lessons like Lucy Patrick's draw on the curriculum theories of Brazilian educator Paulo Freire, as well as a postmodern view of knowledge as a social and political construction. This critical pedagogy asks students to reflect on what they learn by examining its history and politics, by generating alternative explanations, and by acting on what they learn. Freire's curriculum for helping poor Brazilian farmworkers focused literacy instruction on the social, political, and economic circumstances of their lives, particularly on the oppression that kept them poor and made wealthy landowners even wealthier. Applying these ideas to the American culture, critical multiculturalists argue for *praxis*—that is, a curriculum that teaches students the knowledge and skills of recognizing and combating racism and discrimination.

Peter McLaren's book *Life in Schools* describes a role for teachers as social agents who help students analyze the relative power that people hold. Power imbalance is a phenomenon inherent, but seldom discussed, in all social contexts (e.g., marriages, classrooms, and school faculties). The concept of power differences can be revealed as students examine the commonly accepted meanings of ideas such as democracy, equal opportunity, and fairness. Critical pedagogy aims to help students become efficacious in the face of cultural oppression or power imbalances.

English teacher Michael Alvarez found ways to infuse a critical perspective into the standard high school literature curriculum in his school—helping his students to see power relations that they otherwise might have missed.

I made attempts at critical teaching with *To Kill a Mockingbird*. If one of the reasons to teach this novel is to expose students to the racism African Americans have had to deal with, I think we could find better choices. We see the effects of racism not through the eyes of someone who has experienced it, but rather through the eyes of a white narrator and white author. We only see African American characters such as Tom Robinson and Calpurnia through the eyes of a young white girl.

I wanted my students to explore issues of race and power by looking through the eyes of Tom and Calpurnia. Do we think Tom would really be so pleased to help Mayelia Ewell after she had called him a nigger? What about Calpurnia? I asked my students how these characters might be different if an African American had written the novel. My fifth-period class, which has the largest percentage of African American students of my classes, gave me some of the most revealing answers. One girl responded that Calpurnia probably would not be so happy to raise two children other than her own, but would feel that it was the only job she would be able to get because of racism. Another student said that while Tom would probably be grateful to Atticus, he would not act so inferior to him and always refer to him as "Sir."

—Michael Alvarez
First-year teacher, English, grade 9

Critical pedagogy goes beyond analysis to include action. Teachers teaching from this perspective incorporate community projects or ask students to participate in local political processes, adopting a Deweyan view that the curriculum should require students to enact as well as learn about such ideas. That way, students learn to contribute to social change and struggle for social justice by doing it. For example, first-year teacher Armi Flores describes how she helped her students act on their growing knowledge of racism.

In the past year, we have had many bouts with racism in our classroom. Light-skinned students have ganged up on darker-skinned students. And those who are more "American" by virtue of the amount of time they have been in the United States have a higher social status within our classroom. . . . When I informed them that the entire class was designated "Latino or Hispanic," the majority of the light-skinned students were outraged. They didn't want to be associated with "Latinos": They believed that they were "white." In an attempt to create some sort of wall of protection around themselves from the dark-skinned students, one student called out, "Well, what about Douglas? He's not Latino, he's black." When I informed the class that Douglas, although he was dark-skinned, was also Latino, the class fell silent. They couldn't believe that they were all Latino and not "white."

This discussion launched us into discussions about definitions of race and ethnicity, and about discrimination. The concepts (i.e., discrimination, protest, and segregation) were straight out of the social studies book. Then, the students took part in a simulation. The entire class took a brief math assessment. One third sat in front and received preferential treatment (i.e., clean sheets, candy, privileges, teacher attention, and encouragement). Those in the back had to share ripped-up copies of tests; I made discouraging comments and gave them little positive attention. Afterward, the students talked about what it felt like to be discriminated against. Then, I invited the students to examine other examples of discrimination they have seen or experienced.

We discussed issues of discrimination we saw in the media or in our city. After the simulation and discussion, I was amazed at the range of topics they wrote about. Students raised topics such as slavery, the 1992 LA riots, gang warfare, and deportation. They were making connections from history, from the social studies text, from their personal experiences, from the media, and then wrestling with the issues orally and in writing. Marcos wrote a letter to the president voicing his concern about the current issue of the burning of black churches. When I asked him why he thought this happened he answered, "Well, I'm not sure . . . but I read this book before about how a long time ago, white people used to buy black people and make them work for them." I asked him, "Do you think that's connected to the churches being burnt down now?" He answered, "Yes, I think so." Marcos connected the content of the lesson, the media, a book he had read and then made a huge critical jump to posit a historical rationale for the prevalence of hate crimes today.

Finally, they all wrote letters to influential people who they thought could ameliorate the problems of discrimination. Students wrote to Bill Clinton, the marines, the police, a judge, God, or their parents. One student suggested that the answer was within themselves—that they had to take responsibility for discrimination and act against it. They weren't writing hypothetically.

—Armi Flores
First-year teacher, grade 4

Current Debates about Constructivism and Multiculturalism

Most adults—and among them, many teachers—still consider children's learning as something like a sponge sopping up knowledge. Despite enormous attention to cognition and reform, the most persistent curriculum consists of prescribed sequences of facts and skills and conforms to traditional subjects and grades. Additionally, most Americans find discussions of racism and classism—let alone activism for social justice—extraordinarily threatening in any setting, and in schools, seditious. So it's not surprising that multicultural and constructivist curricula rarely go beyond including the contributions of nonwhite groups in the mainstream curriculum. Next we describe how even moderate efforts to reform the curriculum toward cognitive, sociocultural, and multicultural perspectives have triggered a virulent backlash.

A Violation of Common Sense—and More

Given the way most Americans think about learning, it has seemed a violation of common sense to consider a curriculum based on the social construction of learning and knowledge. In the late 1960s and 1970s, when curriculum materials began to tentatively encourage attention to the social nature of learning and knowledge, critics worried that programs such as the "new math" and discovery-oriented social studies were flaky and devoid of familiar facts and skills. They also worried that teachers were reluctant to teach traditional tenets of right and wrong.

Back to Basics The backlash was a back-to-basics movement that, in a return to a strong essentialist philosophy, prescribed a skills-based curriculum that would be enforced through tests of students' competencies. With a traditional curriculum, critics hoped to restore stability and predictability to society through the schools.

This "basic" and skills-oriented curriculum quickly found allies among Americans who believed that through "technology," scientific methods could bring advanced order to skills instruction. For example, reading labs sprang up in reforming schools throughout the land. Spurred by reports that President Kennedy endorsed a popular, widely advertised speed-reading method for White House staff, capable readers along with nonreaders were soon exposed to expensive programs that promised to increase reading speed a hundredfold or more. The labs and classrooms filled with "controlled readers"—machines that would flash word groups on a screen to train readers' eyes to take in more words, faster. Tachistoscopes would blink words or numbers on a screen for a similar effect. "Programmed" and individualized reading and math kits turned teachers into monitors. They spent the lion's share of their class time administering diagnostic tests that placed students at the right starting point in the kit, handing out and scoring worksheets in the proper sequence, giving mastery tests, and keeping extensive records of students' progress. The instructions and practice exercises in the kits did the teaching. As usual, the benefits of these methods were most loudly proclaimed for students who were poor, of color, had "learning disabilities," or otherwise did not fit in with conventional schooling. Not unlike the hoped-for "computer revolution" a generation later, this earlier version of technology reform produced limited benefits.

Back to Basics, Again. Ronald Reagan's 1980 election brought a new and extremely hostile assault on American schools. Eager to end federal government involvement in education, particularly programs providing additional resources for low-income children and support for racial desegregation, Reagan's administration sought to discredit the education system as a whole. Efforts to promote equality, Reagan and his advisers argued, had eroded the quality of American schools. The "rising tide of mediocrity" in the schools heralded by the administration's *A Nation at Risk* (discussed in Chapter 1) required tough-minded reforms that would restore excellence to American schools.

The curriculum was attacked first. *A Nation at Risk* called on the states to enact higher graduation standards based on a more rigorous set of "new basics"—four years of English in high school; three years each of mathematics, science, and social studies; and a half year of computer science. It also argued that state policies should compel elementary teachers to spend more time on these basics. States quickly rallied to the reform call, enacting more stringent high school graduation and college entrance requirements and lengthening the school day and year.

In the rush to restore excellence—as well as economic competitiveness and national security—few noticed that the National Commission of Excellence in Education overlooked data that might have softened their conclusions. For example, when the Commission members decried declines in SAT and ACT scores, they didn't consider that those declines might have complex causes, including a greatly expanded pool of test takers. At the beginning of the period of "decline," only a small fraction of high school seniors took these exams, and they were among the most qualified of all seniors. The dramatically larger group of test-taking students at the end of the period included a much larger percentage of students who were not nearly as well prepared. Additionally, the lower ranking of U.S. schools in international comparisons can be substantially attributed to the way American schools sort students into an "elite" academic and a more practical "mass" curriculum. Thus, smaller proportions of U.S. students (only those in the elite curriculum) were in classrooms where teachers taught the material on the test, compared with many other countries.[29]

Restoring Cultural Certainty

Shaken by the highly visible public pronouncements that schools were mediocre, much of the public welcomed the late E. D. Hirsch's less upsetting, essentialist explanation for the problem. In his 1988 best-seller, *Cultural Literacy,* and his more recent 1997 book, *The Schools We Need, and Why We Don't Have Them,* Hirsch argues that progressive reformers' emphasis on projects, "discovery learning," and other "anti-subject matter" methods have brought curricular anarchy to U.S. schools. Teachers working from a constructivist and social justice perspective are the primary targets of Hirsch's outrage. Hirsch saw such "curricular anarchy" at the root of the nation's low educational quality and, by extension, its flagging international competitiveness.

"Core Knowledge" In response, Hirsch attempted to restore uniformity and predictability to the curriculum by proposing the "core knowledge" that all American students should learn. In a series of books entitled *What Your First Grader Needs to Know: Fundamentals of a Good First Grade Education,* and so on, Hirsch provided the lists of the essential names, phrases, dates, and concepts that children should learn at each grade. Topics are carefully sequenced in the books so that students can master the simpler parts of content before they are exposed to more complex knowledge. And rather than having students "discover" this knowledge through a problem-based approach, Hirsch preferred classrooms where teachers present the information they expect children to practice and memorize.

Hirsch's ideas proved enormously popular and were widely promoted by the Reagan and Bush administrations. While Hirsch must be credited for his insistence that all children be given access to "high-status" knowledge, his popularity among political conservatives came mostly from the comfortable familiarity of his lists of content and because his approach keeps teachers firmly in charge of meaning. In turn, the lists also keep teachers from straying too far from dominant community interests. Hirsch neither encourages students to be skeptical nor challenges them to generate alternative meanings of what they are taught. So, in literature, for example, what the author of a work *intended* is far more important than the meanings students might find in it.[30] In a very modernist way, Hirsch argues for an unambiguous, "correct" curriculum that students acquire rather than construct.

Goals 2000 and the Standards Movement In 1989 President George Bush and the fifty state governors held an educational "Summit" to set goals for the year 2000 that would spur the nation to improve students' academic performance. Among the goals was to have U.S. students be first in the world in their mathematics and science achievement. Although the year 2000 has come and gone without those goals being met, Goals 2000 had an enormous impact on the debates around what students should know and be able to do. Perhaps most important, the Summit spawned the "standards movement" that has engaged policymakers, businesspeople, and educators in defining what students should learn in each of the subject areas. The idea of standards, it turns out, appealed to nearly everyone. Traditionalists like E. D. Hirsch believed that they would restore clarity and correctness to the school curriculum. Many progressives—especially those who had fought hard for civil rights—believed that setting high standards for all children and holding schools accountable for reaching them might be the best tool for gaining equitable schooling for minority students.

To establish standards, teachers and subject-matter experts gathered throughout the 1990s at national, state, and local meetings to deliberate and write long reports detailing the standards in each subject. These groups offered the results of their work as the new standards to guide curriculum and testing programs. But rather than following Hirsch's example or other traditionalist conceptions of the curriculum, these expert groups framed the standards, by and large, in the form of a "meaningful" curriculum that matches cognitive and sociocultural learning theories. As each of these expert-informed consensus reports came forth, conservatives were further outraged. They saw that the new standards for tough, rigorous learning had strayed even further from a familiar fact- and skills-based curriculum. In fact, instead of turning back the direction of reform, the reports encouraged schools to move faster and far beyond where reform had taken most schools.

To prevent these reforms from being adopted as policy, conservative groups mounted an aggressive campaign to persuade policymakers and the public that such standards were dangerous. Their tactics included belittling "expert" involvement in favor of common sense, and then calling upon their own "experts" to support their views. They garnered considerable media attention as they caricatured the social constructivist approach as nothing more than mindless games, "invented" spelling, and math without numbers. Illogically, they blamed these "new" methods for the persistent low standardized test scores of students who had been taught with mostly conventional approaches. But the attack didn't stop there. In testimony before the California State Board of Education, for example, E. D. Hirsch railed against the most-distinguished educational researchers, subject-matter specialists, and stellar teachers who helped frame the new standards. These experts (such as Lauren Resnick—identified earlier as very influential in curriculum reform) certainly did not fit the caricature of valueless demons who would seduce the nation's young with play, low standards, and mathematics where correct answers don't matter. Nevertheless, Hirsch looked for a conspiracy that silenced dissident opinions. He likened the aims of these moderate reformers to the state-controlled "party line" in the Stalinist Soviet Union: "The dominance over this ideology . . . not only retarded Soviet biology, it caused mass starvation."[31]

By the mid1990s, the backlash against cognitively and socioculturally oriented curricula had captured enormous public sympathy and policy clout. Antireform advocacy groups such as "Mathematically Correct" in California and "Arizona Parents for Traditional Education" began using the Internet as a forum to fight the standards. As we'll describe in more detail in Chapter 5, these battles continue to wage today. By 2001 forty-nine states had academic standards in at least some subjects, in large part because Clinton administration initiatives required that they do so in order to qualify for federal education dollars. Most states have also moved very rapidly to align the school curriculum, testing, and teacher training and certification to those standards. Most teachers support the standards, but, as we detail in Chapter 6, most also believe that the tests that accompany the standards have had negative effects on instruction and that their states have been far too slow in providing the resources they need to ensure that schools fulfill the promise of standards—that all children can learn at very high levels.[32]

The Culture Wars

In the late 1980s Allan Bloom, author of the influential book *The Closing of the American Mind,* wrote, "Culture means a war against chaos *and* a war against other cultures."[33] Although Bloom directs his declaration of cultural war most pointedly at mid- and late-twentieth-century liberal reformers, these cultural battles grow out of the country's cultural ambivalence that began in its earliest days. In prerevolutionary days, there was frequent controversy over religious interpretation and the treatment of secular topics even within a locale's single religious school. At the end of the eighteenth century, Noah Webster argued that children should be educated in uniquely American language and social perspectives to distinguish our culture from less acceptable European ones. Gradually, throughout the 1800s, social leaders turned to public schooling as the battleground on which to wage their cultural war, and the preferred arsenal would be the school curriculum. Later, even as Americans cherished the sentiments written on the new Statue of Liberty in 1886, welcoming the "poor, . . . huddled masses, . . . wretched refuse, . . . homeless, . . . and tempest tossed," they recoiled at the undesirable traits and ideologies that they perceived invading and weakening American culture. From the beginning, most Americans took an assimilationist view—maintaining that other citizens with other languages and cultures would undermine national unity unless their language and culture faded into the American background.

Preserving the Canon Allan Bloom and other late-twentieth-century conservatives have argued for an elite curriculum focused on what they believe are the enduring, unchanging social "truths" embedded in a classical or liberal arts education. This curriculum has come to be called the *canon*, or a binding and unchanging set of core principles and works. Bloom and others argue that Western literary classics, capitalism, the practice of American government since its earliest days, the nuclear family, and so on constitute the curricular canon. Without this body of principles and standards (as determined by Bloom, Hirsch, and others of whom they approve), Bloom argues, American students will continue their decades-long lapse into a relativism that undermines the moral grounding of the nation.

If Bloom's prescriptions for what college undergraduates should learn were to be translated into a curriculum for late elementary and secondary schools, it would look quite a lot like Hirsch's *Cultural Literacy* lists. Although Hirsch's curriculum would acknowledge "contributions" from African Americans and Native Americans, it would not consider multiple perspectives or permit debate about the dominant perspective. Rather, Hirsch seeks a curriculum that will be fair and democratic because it enables "others" to adopt the traditional, largely Anglo-American culture (including both facts and interpretations) as their own. This becomes particularly problematic when one looks at the items on Hirsch's lists. They seem to convey that Hirsch would have all children accept—without deliberation or debate about alternative interpretations—the idea that the land Columbus came to was a "new" world, that manifest destiny was a progressive national expansion, and that civil rights law (though not the civil rights "movement" that brought the laws about) has solved the racial problems in America.

Battling "Retrogressive" Multiculturalism Hirsch argued that there are two forms of multiculturalism: the ethical, progressive, and cosmopolitan form that he advocates; and a retrogressive and ethnocentric form that "tends to set group against group" and "hinders the educational excellence and fairness it was conceived to enhance."[34] The progressive form, as embodied in Hirsch's core knowledge curriculum, considers ethnicity an accident of history, having little to do with defining one's identity and cultural essence. Consequently, according to Hirsch, the progressive form encourages sympathy for other cultures and respect for one's own, but it stresses "competence in the current system of language and allusion that is dominant in the nation's economic and intellectual discourse."[35] The regressive form, Hirsch claimed, emphasizes ethnic loyalty. It allows children to learn a lot, for example, about their African and African American past, at the expense of learning to read, write, solve mathematical problems effectively, and understand natural science. This regressive multiculturalism, he argued, victimizes minority children by preventing them from participating in the mainstream culture.

English Only? Perhaps the most dramatic example of the battle against "regressive multiculturalism" has been the "English for the Children" movement. Led and funded by California software developer Ron Unz, English for the Children mounted successful campaigns in California (1998's ballot Proposition 227) and in Arizona (2000's Proposition 203) to replace bilingual education with English-only instruction and aims to do the same in Colorado in 2002 and elsewhere. Under the banner "Let's teach all of America's children English and end bilingual education nationwide," Unz and his followers argue that no matter how well intentioned, bilingual education has been a "dismal practical failure." "For decades," they argue, "millions of mostly Hispanic immigrant students have remained trapped in these Spanish-almost-only classes." Yet Unz and his followers tell only part of the story. True enough, many bilingual programs have not been, by anyone's measure, successful. Progressive educators and critics of English-only argue that bilingual education was rarely implemented in ways that lived up to its promise. And, like so many reforms, bilingual education is necessary, but by itself, not sufficient to deliver a good education to non-English speakers. Rather than rejecting immigrants' language as having no place in American schools, they struggle to help students become bilingual, biliterate, and bicultural.

Eighty percent of the students at my school are Latino, many of whom are recent immigrants or speak a language other than English at home. The other 20 percent are African American whose English is often discriminated against and devalued. There are many teachers here who believe that students should transition completely into Standard English and, in the process, divest themselves of their linguistic and cultural rights. Several students have complained about teachers who permit no talk in any language other than Standard English. One P.E. teacher publicly humiliates any student who speaks Spanish in her presence. Another veteran advised me that the only way to create a positive classroom environment is to only permit English to be spoken, even in informal small group conversations. Students report that teachers penalize their participation grades. . . . Perhaps the most pernicious aspect of this linguistic repression is that many students have internalized the negative attitudes about their native language. I began teaching aspiring to resist the hegemony of English in my classroom by creating an environment that supported, respected, and valued my students' first language while developing their academic English. Were it only so easy.

—Matthew Eide
First-year teacher, high school history

Educating the "Right Way"

In 2001 curriculum scholar Michael Apple wrote a remarkable book, *Educating the "Right" Way: Markets, Standards, God, and Inequality*, documenting the process by which conservative movements have shaped current school reforms. Apple traces how a disparate set of conservative social movements—including neoliberals committed to markets and competitive individualism; neoconservatives committed to traditional culture, knowledge, and behavior (like Bennett, Hirsch, and Bloom); "authoritarian populists" who promote Christian fundamentalist ideas; and the "new middle class" of professionals and managers—have come together to forge a "mainstream" reform agenda of standards, testing and choice. In the process, and more consequentially, these groups have also redefined how Americans think and talk about democracy, freedom, morality, and culture and changed the relationship of these ideas to the marketplace. These redefinitions and changed relationships undergird the growing political appeal of vouchers and other strategies for privatizing public education. Apple helps us understand how this new coalition and new meanings have brought a "conservative modernism" (a phrase consistent with the discussion of modernism in Chapter 1) that poses serious, ongoing challenges, not only to multicultural curriculum, but to all the related efforts to create socially just schooling.

A familiar example for this reform direction is illustrated by the much-touted "Texas miracle" of raising achievement and narrowing the minority-white achievement gap. Indeed, much has happened in Texas that can be admired, such as a surge of grassroots political organizing for better schools in low-income communities. (We explore that dimension of Texas reform in Chapter 10.) Yet beneath the miracle is a less happy story of huge increases in the number of elementary school children being retained, soaring middle and high school dropout rates, and the dominance of a low-level, skill-based, "test prep" curriculum schools attended by poor children.[36] Nevertheless, what George W. Bush and other conservatives currently emphasize is the power of state standards and testing.

Struggling for a Socially Just Curriculum

Today's teachers sit at the center of a curriculum battle—a battle shaped by traditional American understandings of merit, efficiency, competition, and progress—that extends far deeper than their classrooms. The modern curriculum does not match the way students learn, and it favors Americans of wealth and power. But it could be otherwise. Each day American teachers confront and win, over and over, the battle against the modern curriculum, as they engage students with rich and powerful ideas that touch their lives. That is one reason they return to school each day. The struggle waits for them.

Digging Deeper

A number of curriculum theorists and curriculum historians have delved deeply into the philosophical, cultural, and political underpinnings of the U.S. school curriculum. We list a few here whose work might be particularly interesting to teachers. We also list a professional organization for multicultural curriculum whose membership includes both university faculty and educators who work in elementary and secondary schools.

University of Wisconsin professor **Michael Apple's** books *Ideology and Curriculum* (New York: Routledge, 1990), *Cultural Politics and Education* (New York: Teachers College Press, 1996), *Official Knowledge* (New York: Routledge, 1993), and others provide analyses of how politics and ideology pervade curriculum. Another book with Linda Christian-Smith, *The Politics of the Textbook* (New York: Routledge, 1991), examines how the content of textbooks reflects the dominant perspective in ways likely to maintain the national status quo of power and privilege. Of particular interest is his newest book, *Educating the "Right Way": Markets, Standards, God, and Inequality* (New York: Routledge-Falmer, 2001).

Professor **James Banks** of the University of Washington was instrumental in developing the idea of a multicultural curriculum. Banks has edited two of the most complete sources on multicultural education history and research: *The Handbook of Research on Multicultural Education* (New York: Macmillan, 1995) and *Multicultural Education, Transformative Knowledge, and Action: Historical and Contemporary Perspectives* (New York: Teachers College Press, 1996). Additionally, Banks is author of books for teachers on social studies curriculum, including *Teaching Strategies for the Social Studies: Inquiry, Valuing, and Decision-Making*, with Ambrose A. Clegg, Jr. (New York: Addison-Wesley, 1990).

John Dewey's writings on curriculum provide the foundation for current social constructivist curricula. Especially relevant for this chapter are his 1897 essay, "My Pedagogic Creed," and his books *The Child and the Curriculum* and *The School and Society* (reprinted, Chicago: University of Chicago Press, 1991).

Professor **Carl Grant,** University of Wisconsin-Madison, and Professor **Christine Sleeter** of California State University at Monterey Bay have written some of the most helpful books for teachers on developing multicultural curriculum. Their 1989 book, *Making Choices for Multicultural Education: Five*

Approaches for Race Class and Gender (Columbus, OH: Merrill/Prentice-Hall, 1989), is a classic explanation of the theories grounding multicultural education. Their most recent book, *Turning on Learning: Five Approaches for Muticultural Teaching Plans for Race, Class, Gender, and Disability* (Upper Saddle River, NJ: Prentice Hall, 1998), translates those theories into a practical guide to planning multicultural lessons. Additionally, Sleeter has recently produced an e-book, *Culture, Difference, and Power* (New York: Teachers College Press, 2001), that helps teachers understand the theoretical underpinnings of a critical approach to multiculturalism.

Elliot Eisner, Stanford University professor of education, has written on various conceptions of the curriculum in the twentieth century, particularly in *Conflicting Conceptions of Curriculum* (with Elizabeth Vallance) (San Francisco: McCutchan, 1974), and about the relationship between curriculum and representations of knowledge in *Cognition and Curriculum: A Basis for Deciding What to Teach* (New York: Longman, 1982).

Brazilian adult educator **Paulo Freire** developed "critical pedagogy," an approach to informal adult education that has influenced thousands of grassroots organizations, college classrooms, and, most recently, school reform efforts in major urban areas. Freire's best-known book, *Pedagogy of the Oppressed* (New York: Continuum, 1970), argues that education is a path to permanent liberation; that is, through critical pedagogy, people become aware of their oppression and transform it. Exiled from his native Brazil for his educational work among the rural poor, Freire continued working in Chile and throughout the world. In 1969 he taught at Harvard University; ten years later he returned to his own country under a political amnesty. In 1988 he became Minister of Education for the City of São Paulo—a position that made him responsible for guiding school reform within two-thirds of the nation's schools. His recent book, *Pedagogy of Hope* (New York: Continuum 1994), reexamines his work in critical pedagogy twenty-five years after *Pedagogy of the Oppressed*. His most recent, posthumously published book is *Teachers as Cultural Workers* (New York: Routledge, 1998).

Henry Louis Gates, Jr., W. E. B. DuBois professor of the humanities and chairman of the Afro-American Studies Department at Harvard, offers some of the most cogent arguments for multicultural curriculum. His book *Loose Canons: Notes on the Culture Wars* (New York: Oxford University Press, 1992) includes a series of essays that argue for a curriculum that respects both the diversity and commonalties of human culture. That curriculum, according to Gates, provides the best hope for forging a civic culture that respects both differences and similarities.

Herbert Kliebard, a professor at the University of Wisconsin, stands out as the nation's most astute curriculum historian. His book *The Struggle for the American Curriculum: 1893–1958* (New York: Routledge, 1995) provides an insightful analysis of the multiple forces that shaped the curriculum in the twentieth century.

UCLA professor **Peter McLaren** is one of the nation's leading thinkers and writers on critical pedagogy. *Life in Schools: An Introduction to Critical Pedagogy in* *the Foundations of Education* (New York: Longman, 1998), one of his many books, is an excellent resource for American teachers struggling with how to teach students to question the structures and power relations that limit their lives. McLaren includes a journal of his own teaching in an inner-city school as well as his analysis of that experience. He places both the journal and the analysis in the context of scholarship in the local tradition.

The **National Association for Multicultural Education** (NAME) was founded in 1990 to bring together educators who have an interest in multicultural education. NAME's quarterly magazine, *Multicultural Education,* features sections with promising practices and resources for teachers. The organization's annual conference provides an opportunity for intensive discussion and learning. NAME's Internet address is http://www.inform.umd.edu/NAME.

Professor **Sonja Nieto** is on the education faculty at the University of Massachusetts, Amherst, where she studies multicultural and bilingual curriculum issues. Her book *Affirming Diversity: The Sociopolitical Context of Multicultural Education* (New York: Longman, 2000) is a highly readable overview of the theory and practice of multicultural education. The text comes alive with Nieto's inclusion of case studies of twelve diverse students and how schooling intersects with their lives. Additionally, her other recent book, *The Light in Their Eyes: Creating Multicultural Learning Communities* (Teachers College Press, 2000), provides a review of the research on multiculturalism and powerful reflections on multicultural teaching by teachers engaged in it.

Notes

1. Lauren Resnick, *Education and Learning to Think* (Washington, DC: National Academy Press, 1983), p. 3.
2. Joel Spring, *The American School: 1642–1990* (New York: Longman, 1996), p. 41.
3. Ibid., p. 149.
4. Ibid.
5. Lawrence Cremin, *The Transformation of the School: Progressivism in American Education, 1876–1957* (New York: Vintage Books, 1964), p. 17.
6. Ibid.
7. Jacob Mayer Rice, *The Public School System of the United States* (1893, p. 34), as quoted in Herbert Kliebard, *The Struggle for the American Curriculum: 1893–1958* (New York: Routledge, 1995).
8. Although definitions of humanism vary widely, the term has been assigned two broad meanings (and both of these have broad and arguable meanings themselves). The humanism of Harris and Allan Bloom (at the end of the twentieth century) has strong elements of an idealist philosophy. Idealism proposes that a thing, practice, or idea has a best or ideal form and that the job of civilized (another problematic term) persons is to discover that form and try to achieve its perfection. One of the subtle features of idealism is that the perfect form of a thing, practice, or idea is

something like an enduring and unchanging Truth. Thus, according to this philosophy, if we are interested in finding the best (ideal) way of educating, we should do well to look for the ideals and enduring Truths of civilization and education of the past; and we should probably reject newer, less trustworthy conceptions. Herein lies a central departure point for how people respond to dilemmas of education, and more particularly, to the pitched battles over the curriculum—battles over what and how we should teach.

9. For a detailed analysis of these movements, see Kliebard, *The Struggle for the American Curriculum.*
10. Cremin, *Transformation,* p. 130.
11. Ibid.
12. Francis Parker, *Talks on Pedagogies* (New York: E. L. Kellogg, 1894, p. 450), as quoted in Cremin, *Transformation,* p. 132.
13. Katherine Camp Mayhew and Anna Camp Edwards, *The Dewey School* (New York: Appleton-Century, 1936, pp. 65–65) as quoted in Cremin, *Transformation,* p. 137.
14. Dewey, *School and Society,* p. 28, as quoted in Kliebard, *The Struggle for the American Curriculum,* p. 69.
15. Jane Addams, "The Public School and the Immigrant Child," in Daniel Calhoun, ed., *The Educating of Americans: A Documentary History* (Boston: Houghton Mifflin, 1969), pp. 421–423.
16. O. K. Armstrong, "Treason in the Textbooks," *The American Legion Magazine,* September 1940, pp. 8–9, 51, 70–72, as cited in Kliebard, *The Struggle for the American Curriculum.*
17. Resnick, *Education and Learning to Think.*
18. Ibid., p. 3.
19. Howard Gardner, *The Unschooled Mind* (New York: Basic Books, 1991).
20. Robert Sternberg, "A Waste of Talent: Why We Should (and Can) Teach to All our Students' Abilities," *Education Week,* 3 December 1997, p. 56.
21. W. E. B. DuBois, "The Freedom to Learn," in *W. E. B. DuBois Speaks,* ed. P. S. Foner (New York: Pathfinder, 1970), pp. 230–231. This 1949 speech came to our attention because Linda Darling-Hammond uses it to set the tone of her book *The Right to Learn.*
22. Sonia Nieto, *Affirming Diversity: The Sociopolitical Context of Multicultural Education,* 2nd ed. (White Plains, NY: Longman, 1996), p. 312.
23. Luis Moll, "Funds of Knowledge for Teaching: Using a Qualitative Approach to Connect Homes and Classrooms," *Theory into Practice* 31, no. 2 (1992), pp. 132–141.
24. Bobby Starnes and Eliot Wigginton (Eds.), *A Foxfire Christmas: Appalachian Memories and Traditions* (Chapel Hill, NC: University of North Carolina Press, 1996).
25. Gloria Ladson-Billings, *The Dreamkeepers* (San Francisco: Jossey-Bass, 1994), p. 82.
26. Lisa Delpit, *Other People's Children: Cultural Conflict in the Classroom* (New York: The New Press, 1995), p. 46.

27. Hugh Mehan, Lea Hubbard, Irene Villanueva, and Angela Lintz provide a comprehensive analysis of how AVID works to teach cultural capital and support college-going in their book, *Constructing School Success* (Cambridge: Cambridge University Press, 1996).
28. Nieto, *Affirming Diversity*, p. 319.
29. Curtis McKnight, F. Joe Crosswhite, and John A. Dossey, *The Underachieving Curriculum* (Indianapolis: Stipes, 1987).
30. Walter Feinberg, "Educational Manifesto and the New Fundamentalism," *Educational Researcher* 26, no. 8 (1997), p. 32.
31. E. D. Hirsch, "Address to California State Board of Education," April 10, 1997.
32. Education Week. *A Better Balance: Standards, Tests, and the Tools of Reform. Quality Counts 2001* (Washington, DC: Author, 2001).
33. Quoted in Lawrence W. Levine, *Opening of the American Mind: Canons, Culture, and History* (Boston: Beacon Press, 1996), p. 19.
34. E. D. Hirsch, "Toward a Centrist Curriculum: Two Kinds of Multiculturalism in Elementary School," Charlottesville, VA: Core Knowledge Foundation, 1992. Located on the Internet at http://www.coreknowledge.org.
35. Ibid.
36. Linda McNeil, *The Contradictions of School Reform: Educational Costs of Standardized Testing* (New York: RoutledgeFalmer, 2000).

CHAPTER 5

Curriculum:

The Subject Matters

Laura Torres

First-year teacher, grade 2

Don't all educated adults know and agree about the knowledge that belongs in each school subject? Haven't we all been to school? Haven't we all taken English, math, and so on? Don't all of the states have a set of agreed-upon academic standards? It turns out, in fact, that Americans *do not* agree about what schools should teach. And when a school departs from what one side or another approves of, many people become angry. These battles put teachers squarely in the fray, asking them not only to know *what* to teach and *how* to teach but also to articulate persuasively *why* to teach it. This chapter, which highlights the content of the most common academic subjects taught in schools, also uncovers the background for controversies that rouse Americans' interests, passions, and fears about what schools teach.

What Knowledge? Whose Knowledge? Knowledge for Whom?

The question "What knowledge?" inevitably becomes entwined with the question "Whose knowledge?" These questions prompt more than philosophical musing. They are asked and answered in explicit, practical detail every day in the political world; in textbook selection committees; in teacher education courses; in the "common sense" of opinion leaders; in professional communities of historians, scientists, writers, and mathematicians; in teacher's lesson plans; in classroom dialogues; in newspaper editorials; and in every other corner of the culture where people form opinions and make decisions about schools. Curriculum controversies can be a distraction, and most teachers have their moments when they utter a teaching mantra, "Why don't they just let me do my job?" And yet these controversies underscore that teachers are not merely social technicians parceling out a commodity called knowledge. Curriculum issues place professional teachers at the vital edge of the disciplines they teach—a very exciting place to be.

"Course content" is one way that a society expresses the version of culture that it wants its young people to learn. All societies do that. The unique American challenge is that America is multicultural and rich with multiple versions of knowledge, versions that often conflict and often exclude. The expression "dominant culture" is useful to identify those elements of the general culture that consistently prevail over others. For example, in U.S. culture, competition prevails over cooperation in most school activities, uniformity carries more weight than diversity, and so on. A dominant culture also pervades the specific content of the subject matters in different ways; for example, by preferring literature that expresses perspectives and experiences of males and people of European descent and accepting the knowledge in textbooks over teachers' and students' own study and experience. As a result, a curriculum that consistently favors the dominant culture must ignore much valuable knowledge and silence many knowledgeable voices.

Still another debate about subject-matter content centers on the question "Knowledge for whom?" Americans struggle with competing answers. On one hand, a common curriculum in each of the subjects is enticing if it could help achieve the American quest for a common culture across the diverse population. On the other hand, providing different content to different students is attractive if the different content really could accommodate relevant differences among students. When does a common curriculum lock students into unproductive uniformity? When does a differentiated curriculum hide bias and favoritism? This debate taps into deep philosophical, political, and cultural divisions about the meanings of equal access, opportunity, and difference.

People we will call "traditionalists" (because they hold conservative views of culture and essentialist views of education) and those we will call "progressives" (because they hold sociocultural views of learning and postmodern views of culture) consistently, but not always, take different sides in these debates. Put simply, traditionalists argue that teachable knowledge consists of basic facts, skills, and accumulated wisdom—of great discoveries and works. They are generally committed to transmission views of teaching and learning. Progressives, on the other hand, view knowledge as a social construction—a human invention within a particular historical, social, and political context. Traditionalists maintain that the established canon of Western scholarship, science, and art constitutes the knowledge that schools should transmit to students. They tend to see students' different abilities and backgrounds as requiring highly differentiated content because some students are suited for more demanding intellectual work than others. Progressives argue that a multicultural society requires multiple perspectives, including a critique of the Western canon. They believe that common understandings of "ability" rarely justify different curricula. Cultural conservatives assert that traditional versions of knowledge in the subjects, especially in language arts and social studies, support traditional codes of decency and moral behavior. Only by having a single dominant version, they claim, will society have the moral stability that makes it strong. Progressives argue that decency and moral behavior follow from multiple traditions, and they find a decent and moral center in all traditions that are committed to democratic participation. Thus, they envision multiple centers from which society gains stability.

These weighty issues weave their way—sometimes quite invisibly—through the decisions about what students should learn in mathematics, in English language arts, in social studies, and in science. The following discussion places these subject matters in the context of school traditions and politics. Not covered in the discussion is a close look at other central disciplines—the arts and foreign language, for example. No less critical to a democratic education and to social justice, these disciplines often fall victim to the narrowing, testing-obsessed debates that surround English, math, social studies, and science. It is hard to find anyone actually *opposed* to teaching, for example, music or foreign language, but our culture is all too ready to treat these disciplines as "extras"—the first to be cut when budgets or reading scores are seen as inadequate. And although sound arguments can be made that school graduates and society benefit equally from multilingual citizens who understand and create music and art as they do from citizens who can solve quadratic equations, it is success in algebra that is a social justice gatekeeper, and it is "verbal analogies" that suppress scores on gatekeeping tests such the SAT. For this reason, we focus our attention here on the subjects that determine which students' schools will consider the "good students."

Mathematics

In August 1997 Lynne V. Cheney was a senior fellow at a conservative Washington think tank, the American Enterprise Institute. Cheney, who would later become the nation's second lady as wife of Vice President Dick Cheney, achieved prominence on her own as head of the National Endowment for the Arts. Writing about mathematics curriculum reform, Mrs. Cheney used the following anecdote to make a rather caustic judgment:

> "They lied to me," says Madalyn McDaniel of Atascadero, California. "They completely betrayed me." At parents' night at the local high school, McDaniel was told about a great opportunity for her son: *The Interactive Mathematics Program,* in which he would be learning everything taught in traditional math courses only in a more effective way. But after signing him up, McDaniel realized the program was not at all what it was advertised. Instead of learning rules and formulas, her son and his classmates were presented with problems and expected to invent their own ways of solving them. "He was very frustrated," McDaniel says. "I'd say, 'Look in the book, it will explain.' He'd say, 'Mom, there is not a book.'"
>
> McDaniel had encountered "whole math." Also known as "fuzzy math" or "new-new math," whole math is based on the idea that knowledge is only meaningful when we construct it for ourselves.
>
> . . . The whole-math disaster began in 1989 when the National Council of Teachers of Mathematics issued a set of standards declaring a new approach to be in order. No more "drill and kill," as whole-math people like to call traditional teaching. Instead, from kindergarten on, there would be a calculator in

every hand so that young minds would be free of irksome chores like addition and multiplication and thus able to take on higher-order tasks such as inventing their own personal methods of long division.[1]

Cheney's story provides a glimpse of both the substance and the rancor of the debate still raging about mathematics in K–12 schools, and of the dilemmas that debate creates for teachers.

The Math Crisis

In the early 1980s the widely publicized Second International Study of Science and Mathematics Education rocked the math education community and the public.[2] That study showed American eighth graders lagging far behind their counterparts in nearly every other developed nation. The math and science communities swung into action, as they had during past crises. In 1989 the National Research Council (NRC), the research and policy arm of the National Academy of Sciences, published a report, *Everybody Counts,* advising the nation to overhaul mathematics education. That same year, the National Council of Teachers of Mathematics (NCTM) concluded a consensus-building process involving thousands of math teachers and mathematicians and published a set of "standards" defining what Americans should know and be able to do in mathematics. The NCTM believed that these standards would raise the quality of mathematics teaching and learning dramatically.

Within a decade, traditionalists like Lynne Cheney were engaged in (and, by many accounts, winning) a full-scale war against the NCTM standards. What had been widespread agreement in early 1980s about the need for reform had dissolved by the late 1980s into acrimony that extended far beyond the technicalities of mathematics curriculum and teaching, into conservative and progressive politics. The two groups interpreted the problem and its solutions very, very differently.*

What's the Problem?

For most Americans the problem that the international study brought to light seemed straightforward. The curriculum simply wasn't rigorous enough, and

*Much of the following discussion is framed in terms of differences between traditional and reform points of view. This is not to characterize a "party line" for either position, but pedagogy, multicultural perspectives, learning theories, approaches to discipline, and now, curricular content, do follow certain tendencies to group according to traditional or reform ideologies. It is important, too, to distinguish between the progressive and liberal views that developed over much of the twentieth century, and the provocative and hopeful views of the critical multiculturalists referred to in the previous chapter. These progressive, liberal, and critical (some say, radical) views all call for reform, and their proposals have much in common. At the risk of even greater oversimplification, we might say that the traditionalists have in mind a strong image of the educated Americans that all children ought to become. They believe that by looking to schools of the past, methods and curriculum can be found to achieve that image. The liberals and progressives tend to share much of the traditionalists' image of an educated American citizenry, but they believe that the methods of the past and much of the content must change.

American teachers weren't pressing students to learn as much math as they could. The solution, in this conventional view, was to establish high standards, upgrade teachers' knowledge, spend more school time on math instruction, and hold schools and teachers accountable (have some kind of negative consequences for schools and teachers whose students do not perform).

For the most part, the mathematics education community saw the problem differently. Many of these educators felt that the traditional emphasis on prescribed rules and methods for solving problems prevents students from understanding math principles, which in turn explained why so few students remember and use the mathematics they are taught.[3] They argued that even students who are proficient at remembering facts and performing algorithms—and who score well on tests—actually understand little. Moreover, reformers pointed out that the international study showed the U.S. curriculum to be fragmented and incoherent, especially when compared with countries like Japan and Germany where math achievement is very high. One of the nation's foremost experts on math and science education observed, "We teach a little of everything, but nothing in great depth."[4] They also implicated the U.S. system of ability grouping that keeps many students from being taught higher-level math, noting that most high-scoring countries shun that practice.[5] In other words, reformers argued that the "cure" that the traditionalists were recommending was very close to what schools were actually doing and was responsible for holding down improvements in math education. The solution, reformers concluded, was to have students work together in groups, to construct a core of deep mathematical understandings, rather than cover a broad array of rules and procedures.

These different diagnoses of what was and is wrong and how to fix it touch deep cultural misgivings about the nature of knowledge, the definition of mathematics, and how people learn. Progressives continue to upset traditionalists partly because they question the Enlightenment notion of mathematics as a fixed body of knowledge and a set of natural facts. In a world where many believe that age-old order and truths are unraveling, the claim that mathematics is a human invention—a social construction—is too much to bear. Those who claim that each child has to make sense anew of the simplest indisputable truths, and that math is not the same unchanging truth that previous generations thought, are seen as enemies of truth and order.

Traditional Mathematics: Skills-Based and Sequential

Mathematics is conventionally considered an orderly, enduring set of facts and logic that describes patterns and relationships in the physical world—arithmetic operations, algebraic manipulations, geometry terms and theorems, and so forth. Traditional math curriculum lays out a hierarchical sequence of topics and skills that allows students, step-by-step, to master this body of mathematical knowledge.[6] For example, a conservative member of California's standards commission argued in 1997: "Mathematics is a cumulative, hierarchical subject; learning new skills and concepts often depends on mastery of previous ones. . . .

[Students] must enter each grade in possession of all the prerequisite skills."[7] The prerequisite skills—or the basics—of math are math facts and the rules (or string of rules) known as algorithms. For example, long division is an algorithm composed of orderly steps that include basic mathematical skills such as multiplication and subtraction.

Traditionalists usually argue for "balanced instruction in mathematics: basic facts and skills, conceptual understanding; and problem-solving ability."[8] But "problem-solving ability," like many catchphrases in the curriculum controversies, means different things to different people. Unlike progressives, traditionalists place problem solving *after* the mastery of basic skills, or "building blocks." Traditionalists maintain that because complete accuracy is possible, it is of the highest value, and correct answers are the only confirmation of a student's mathematical knowledge. Although no progressive would deny that mathematics offers useful and precise solutions to certain problems, most also see estimation as integral to mathematical reasoning.

In line with tradition, elementary schools target instruction toward the number facts and algorithms necessary to add, subtract, multiply, and divide and to compute fractions, decimals, and percentages. Most middle-school math programs review these basic operations to ensure students' mastery. Beginning in middle school, however, the curriculum diverges dramatically for different students. Those who catch on to basic math skills move into the sequence of algebra, geometry, and a second year of algebra. The "best" math students eventually take courses in trigonometry and calculus. Those who haven't mastered the basics take general math classes, where they review the basic math skills of elementary school. They may also learn practical skills like balancing checkbooks and figuring interest rates. More recently, under both progressives' and traditionalists' severe criticism of these dead-end remedial courses, many schools have channeled low-achieving students through separate and slower pathways that may include first-year algebra. For example, as of the fall of 2001, the curriculum in the Los Angeles Unified School District now includes an algebra course for every eighth grader.

Progressive Mathematics: Meaningful Learning in Context

At the end of her first year of teaching Zeba Palomino wrote a letter to her high school students explaining why she teaches math.

> Mathematics has a history, and it is deeply rooted in cultures all over the world. Mathematics is logical and controversial at the same time. Mathematics is a beautiful cycle of connections; it is not a linear study of fragmented pieces. Mathematics is connected to, a foundation for, and dependent upon philosophy, communication, art, science, language, and more. Mathematics is not just numbers and letters, and it is not a set of rules to be memorized; it is a world of ideas and patterns to be discovered and played with. Mathematics is not a right or wrong answer; it is an infinite collection of strategies from which to choose to use as we develop our own ideas and make our own sense of the world. It is

because these beauties exist within and around the field of mathematics that I choose to use mathematics as a means for critical education.

My intention is to use a constructivist approach to mathematics and the power of collaborative learning to help you develop the intellectual and moral capacities and the commitment to help you shape your places in the world. Through your own construction of mathematics knowledge, you can become experts in understanding, reasoning, communicating, analyzing, imagining, examining, connecting, and proving. And by learning collaboratively, you learn and achieve more, you respect and care more about each other and your communities, and you take more pride in your responsibilities and capabilities. As you build these academic and moral capacities, my hope is that you are opening doors for yourselves to countless possibilities.

This ideal guides me in my practice. It requires a great deal of research, experimentation, reflection, persistence, and patience, especially within the discipline of mathematics. It does not go hand in hand with the way mathematics has traditionally been defined or taught. I believe that it is for that very reason that the majority of students in every generation has hated and "failed" mathematics. Most of you see math as so distant from your lives, so boring, so removed from emotion and people, and so abstract. Math does not have to be that way.

My biggest struggle is staying true to these goals. I know that I often fall into just teaching mathematics skills and concepts because it is much easier to do. I know that many of you would prefer that I continue to do it that way—just let you sit in rows, give you the algorithms, and give you individual work to practices those new math rules. But, please understand, it is unfair and unjust of me to do that to you. When I "teach" that way, you are not truly learning or empowering yourselves. You are only "learning" a meaningless concept with no deeper significance to you and which you will soon forget. You are not building or exchanging ideas, and you are not participating in a critical transformative education.

The approach that Zeba Palomino takes to mathematics teaching embodies much of the reform advice of the NRC report *Everybody Counts.* Mathematicians today have achieved (with the aid of computer technology) breakthroughs in number theory, logic, statistics, operations research, probability, computation, geometry, and combinatorics that expand far beyond the traditional areas of mathematics (algebra, analysis, and topology).[9] Such dramatic changes in the discipline, the NRC reasons, mean that mathematics education must also change:

The transformation of mathematics from a core of abstract studies to a powerful family of mathematical sciences is reflected poorly, often not at all, by the traditional mathematics curriculum. One can hardly blame students if they rarely see evidence of its full power and richness.

As mathematics is more than calculation, so education in mathematics must be more than mastery of arithmetic. Geometry, chance, and change are as important as numbers in achieving mathematical power. Even more important is a comprehensive, flexible view that embodies the intrinsic unity of mathematics; estimation supplements calculation; heuristics aid algorithms; experience balances innovation. To prepare students to use mathematics in the

> twenty-first century, today's curriculum must invoke the full spectrum of the mathematical sciences.
>
> [C]hildren should use calculators throughout their schoolwork, just as adults use calculators throughout their lives. . . . Real measurements from science experiments can be used in mathematics lessons because the calculator will be able to add or multiply the data even if the children have not yet learned how. Many adults fear that early introduction of calculators will prevent children from learning basic arithmetic "properly," as their parents learned it. The experiences of many schools during the last fifteen years show that this fear is unfounded. Students who use calculators learn traditional arithmetic as well as those who do not use calculators and emerge from elementary school with better problem-solving skills and much better attitudes about mathematics.[10]

The NRC also identified as a *myth* the common view that "[t]he best way to learn how to solve complex problems is to decompose them into a sequence of basic skills which can then be mastered one at a time." *Everybody Counts* argues that "[t]here is abundant evidence that mastery of necessary skills is rarely sufficient for solving complex problems."[11]

Mathematics as Purposeful Activity Consistent with *Everybody Counts,* the standards created by the NCTM in 1989 defined mathematics as an active process of using mathematical algorithms and ideas in the course of some *purposeful activity*—that is, across many disciplines and in real-life situations.[12] The NCTM standards emphasized mathematics as problem solving, communication, reasoning, and making connections, as well as that *knowing* math is inseparable from *doing* math. The NCTM further contended in the standards that computer technology is fundamental to mathematics—expanding the most basic mathematical ideas beyond those traditionally taught, changing the nature of the most important problems, and altering the methods mathematicians use to solve them.

> Although computation is important in mathematics and in daily life, our technological age requires us to rethink how computation is done today. Almost all complex computation today is done by calculators and computers. In many daily situations, answers are computed mentally or estimates are sufficient, and paper-and-pencil algorithms are useful when the computation is reasonably straightforward.[13]

The NCTM spelled out in its 258-page document what mathematics teaching and learning might look like. Throughout the grades, mathematical ideas should be embedded in problems that are familiar and meaningful to students. Teachers must show the links between math ideas and procedures rather than teaching a topic and then dropping it, never to be seen again. From kindergarten on, students should engage with the ideas and strategies of whole numbers, fractions and decimals, geometry, measurement, statistics and probability, patterns and functions. Number systems, number theory, algebra, trigonometry, discrete mathematics, and calculus can be added as students' mathematical understanding grows. Computers and calculators should be at the core of instruction instead of being used only as timesaving aides after students prove their proficiency with paper-and-pencil calculations. That calculators and computers are an *escape from* or *a way to avoid* rigorous mathematical work is an idea that begins with adults in our schools and communities, not with students.

The math standards made clear that learning mathematics is no more linear or sequential than learning how to dance. Certainly, there are concepts. There are big ideas. There are facts and processes that will be memorized over time and eventually become automatic (i.e., performed without conscious thought). And it is definitely best to approach certain ideas after one is competent with previous ones. That said, learning mathematics through traditional instruction might be compared to learning to dance from a lecture and a book. In both cases, it is not quite the "real thing," and only a few will rave about how much fun they had.

Mathematics for Everyone On the question of *mathematics for whom?* the standards were unequivocal. The core mathematical ideas are necessary and appropriate for *all* students. Schools cannot use the differences in students' talents, achievements, and interests as excuses for some students not learning math. Pedagogical strategies must reach out to African Americans and Latinos, groups that have been underrepresented in mathematics. Special efforts must be undertaken to respond to the fact that girls, whose participation in advanced math courses equals and often surpasses that of boys, are still underrepresented in mathematics, engineering, and other math-intensive careers. Mathematics also must be made accessible to students who schools judge as "slow" in math and to nonmath teachers and school personnel who sometimes boast of their lack of math knowledge.

The idea that every child could and should become highly competent in mathematics has become a reform mantra. A number of progressive groups have sought ways to overcome the particular difficulties that have constrained the mathematics achievement of low-income students of color. In 1999 the board of directors of the NCTM charged a special task force with studying and making recommendations about the teaching and learning of mathematics in poor communities. That task force found that the mathematics achievement is constrained by inequalities in curriculum, instruction, and expectations for student performance. Believing that low-achieving students have low math ability, educators have thought it sensible to teach these students low-level math. This approach has both rationalized the uneven distribution of qualified math teachers and depressed students' math achievement. The reformers were intent on changing all of this. Their goal has been adopted by everyone but the most conservative pundits. In fact, in 2001 Los Angeles Superintendent former Colorado governor Roy Romer, a person not known for radical educational views, borrowed a phrase promulgated by 1960s civil rights activist Bob Moses to characterize algebra "as" a "civil right" of all his city's students. However, the gap between this reform rhetoric and schooling reality remains cavernous.

Learning Mathematics by Constructing Solutions

> [S]tudents learn mathematics well only when they construct their own mathematical understanding. To understand what they learn, they must enact for

> themselves verbs that permeate the mathematics curriculum: "examine," "represent," "transform," "solve," "apply," "prove," "communicate." This happens more readily when students work in groups, engage in discussion, make presentations, and in other ways take charge of their own learning. All students engage in a great deal of invention as they learn mathematics; they impose their own interpretation on what is presented to create a theory that makes sense to them.
>
> —*Everybody Counts*, 1989, pp. 58–59

Mathematics reformers want students to construct mathematical understandings because that is how they learn. They want students to understand that mathematics knowledge is a human construction rather than facts that always exist "out there" whether or not anyone notices or uses them. *Everybody Counts* noted that "mathematics is one way we make sense of things."[14]

To support their position, progressive reformers call attention to Japanese students who solve problems in order to construct the students' mathematical understanding. In the United States, math lessons stress the reverse: Teachers first explain steps of the construction and then apply the construction to practice problems. Students focus on remembering the steps and rules instead of understanding the problem. Similarly, U.S. teachers usually stress a single "best" method for solving particular types of problems. When they demonstrate an alternate method, they typically do not emphasize the decision making that goes into choosing one or the other method.

In contrast, Japanese teachers typically begin math lessons by asking students to invent their own solutions (often collaboratively) to a problem they haven't encountered before. Then the students spend the rest of class sharing those solutions and working together to understand the underlying mathematical concepts.[15] Unlike American classes, where incorrect information and naïve reasoning often remain hidden, Japanese students reveal and challenge their unsuccessful "inventions." When multiple successful solutions arise, there is the opportunity for subtle and deeper probing into the principles behind the problem. Because American students are asked less often to explain or defend the processes they use, they acquire just enough superficial understanding to solve the more basic forms of the problems at hand. Only in the distant future (next week on the test, or next year in the next course) do students face the consequences of their thin or superficial knowledge.

The U.S. practice of creating fast and slow classes works against asking questions and probing for meaning. In Japan, rather than separating elementary- and middle-grade students according to estimates of their ability, students are taught the same math curriculum in the same classrooms. The Japanese assume that some will catch on quickly and some will struggle. Those who are faster at grasping the ideas probe more deeply into the concepts—often by finding ways to help and explain them to other students. Americans presume that students who catch on quickly benefit more from accelerating through the curriculum than from taking extra time to explore a concept deeply.

First-year teacher Marilyn Cortez used an approach with her ninth-grade class that was very much like that used by Japanese teachers.

I began the semester with area and perimeter. During the first activity, I didn't give the students the formula for area of a rectangle. Rather, I gave them paper and asked them to draw several rectangles, labeling the base and the height. I then asked them to find the area of each of the rectangles and then, eventually, the formula relating the base, height, and area. After the activity with the rectangle, I asked students to draw several parallelograms and, using what they know about rectangles, to find the formula for the area of a parallelogram. I allowed them to use grid paper, scissors, and each other to accomplish the task.

Students had an easy time establishing the formula for the area of a rectangle. Many of them began by counting the squares on the grid paper but later saw a pattern developing between the base and the height. Other students saw multiplying as a way of counting all the squares inside the rectangle. That is, they saw the reason why there was a relationship between the base and the height. The relationship between the parallelogram and the rectangle was not evident for many students, and they struggled with this activity for several days. Then, several students began to see a relationship develop between the rectangle and the parallelogram. By drawing cuts and inserts, manipulating their parallelogram until they formed a rectangle, the students developed the formula for area of a parallelogram. We discussed the students' findings in class, and although I thought students were exhausted with the topic, they were intrigued by the simple manipulations that helped establish the relationship.

The students' success with the parallelogram carried over to the next activity on finding the formula for the area of a triangle. During the triangle activity, several students found different and creative ways of finding the area. They worked with each other, cut and pasted, and drew multiple diagrams on paper. They were able to use similar strategies performed on the parallelogram.

Asking students to come up with the formula was something very new. The thinking required to do such an activity was unfamiliar to them. But this activity opened the door to a new way of learning. When students were able to discover the different formulas, they were able to see why and how certain formulas came to exist. They began to see mathematics as a subject that has reason and logic to it.

—Marilyn Cortez
First-year teacher, mathematics, grade 9

Like Marilyn Cortez, progressive teachers help students borrow, invent, and select among strategies—always asking for explanations and descriptions, thinking processes, reasoning, and whether there are equally appropriate or better ways to solve a problem.[16] The NRC called this approach "[r]obust arithmetic," noting that people use a variety of strategies to accomplish even relatively simple math tasks like adding long lists of numbers. "A dozen different people do it in a dozen different ways—top down, bottom up, grouping by tens, bunching, and various mixtures. There is no single correct method."[17]

Multiple Representations, Not "Anything Goes" Using a variety of strategies engages students in "doing" math in a way that more closely resembles how both mathematicians and ordinary people outside of school do mathematics. Further, as first-year math teachers Zeba Palomino and Lauren Garrott discovered (see the following quotes), when students explore multiple ways of representing a problem, they invent a variety of strategies for solving it, and they understand and remember better. Not incidentally, using different strategies also maximizes the likelihood of accuracy. After all, if a student doesn't really understand a problem, but simply applies an algorithm to it, she is less likely to catch obvious errors or cross-check a seemingly reasonable but incorrect answer.

In the beginning of the year when my students were learning about absolute value, I simply repeated what the book said. "If you see those absolute value bars," I would say, "just take the positive value of the number." Not surprisingly, most of them answered the more complex test questions on that concept incorrectly. However, when I had students stand at different numbers on the number line and discuss the distance between people, and then see that as an example of "absolute value," they seemed to have a much better grasp of the concept.

—Zeba Palomino
First-year teacher, high school mathematics

My students told me that they had done integers during the last portion of their seventh-grade year, but the majority could not perform basic operations using positive and negative numbers. When asked what they knew about integers, they would begin to spout off a list of jumbled rules they said their previous teacher made them memorize. When given the following problem, $-1 + -3$, my students insisted that the answer was $+4$ because their teacher had said that two negatives equals a positive.

I decided to focus on understanding integers, rather than memorizing rules. I showed the students how to manipulate red and blue chips to represent integer problems. I questioned them about the similarities between the methods they used to solve different problems. I then asked the students to create a few rules to describe how the integers worked. They tested the rules by using them to predict an answer to a problem and then checked their prediction using the chips model. After sharing ideas and listing conclusions, students tested their classmates' conclusions. A few of the students continued to use the chips to model their integer problems, but the majority relied on the rules they had created, returning to the chips only to clarify occasional confusions or disagreements. As the year progressed, fewer and fewer students returned to the physical model because they had internalized the ideas of the model.

These rules, similar to those their previous teacher had them memorize, have new meaning.

—Lauren Garrott
First-year teacher, mathematics, grade 8

Both Zeba Palomino and Lauren Garrott engage their students in what theorists call knowledge *construction.* It contrasts sharply with the *replication* that occurs when students simply follow the rules. When a student repeats what another has done, or copies what he has been told, the process is much less engaging, more easily forgotten, and more boring, than when he can say, "I figured it out on my own." Of course, relying on his best thinking and prior knowledge, a child might also "invent" 5 times 5 equals 55—an invention with serious consequences if left standing. But rather than allowing students to invent and retain the "wrong rules," as many traditionalists fear, progressive teachers press students to question their inventions in ways that generate deeper and correct understandings.

Learning Mathematics through Interaction Learning in reform math classes is also very social.

I gave each student $2 in fake coins to go shopping at our classroom "junk store" set up with recyclables and art materials. Students figured prices and calculated correct change, thereby practicing addition and subtraction of money. Students interacted as shoppers and storekeepers in this simulated environment.

Tenisha taught Eloise and Roberto the "counting on" strategy without formally labeling it. They wanted to buy something for 26 cents and handed her one quarter and one dime. She told them, "Start with 26 and count up to the full amount of money. Then you see how much change you get." Eloise and Roberto used a counting on strategy with the guidance of an expert. They completed the task and learned a strategy to take control of the same task in the future.

—*Jessica Seiden*
First-year teacher, grades 1–2

Jessica Seiden's students benefit, even at their very young age, from having willing listeners to whom they can explain problems and from opportunities to work with others who arrive at different answers. According to sociocultural learning theory, these students—by helping, asking, explaining, reviewing, and most of all doing—*scaffold* one another in a community of mathematics users. In other words, their classroom becomes not more "scientific" and rational, but more like real life where people learn by work and play. What school adds to these more natural processes of work and play is a teacher. Teachers organize the environments in which students can learn academic knowledge together.

However, the constant interaction among students in classrooms like Jessica Seiden's also worries traditionalists. What reformers call scaffolding, traditionalists often consider "the blind leading the blind" or exploiting able learners whose time is wasted in "tutoring" those who haven't caught on.

The "New" Math Standards: Politics and Mathematics Teaching

I had the good fortune to take part in College Preparatory Mathematics (CPM)—a very student-oriented course of study in algebra, geometry (which I taught this year), and intermediate algebra. CPM is driven by a discovery approach and group work.

Rather than being "taught" new material by the teacher, students follow the text as it guides them through a series of mathematical observations and has them make conjectures. Students then test these conjectures by measurement and observation to make and justify conclusions. Finally, they apply their conclusions in problem solving. My main role is facilitator, floating around the room among the buzz of the diverse groups, challenging and redirecting thinking. Problems are usually many layered and require students to discuss creative approaches with each other, rather than mimic the teacher's execution of a formula.

CPM never expects students to master the material after the first exposure. The book spirals and constantly revisits previously covered material. Even the previous year's material shows up to keep it fresh.

—Steve Rupprecht
First-year teacher, mathematics, grades 9–12

The reform movement of the late 1980s paved the way for the lessons of many of today's first-year teachers, who emphasize basic skills along with broad math concepts. Integration of algebra, geometry, trigonometry, and calculus concepts blurs traditional divisions. Active problem solving focuses on math applications in physics, economics, and other fields and helps students understand how and why mathematics is useful and works as it does.

Schools and teachers have not implemented the reform approaches to mathematics perfectly. It is safe to say that some places have implemented it quite poorly. For example, some teachers and some materials have emphasized fun activities over the mathematical ideas that the activities were intended to illuminate. Some professional development courses have given teachers script-like lessons to follow, rather than an understanding of how to interpret and respond to students' mathematical thinking. Too many teachers lack the mathematical knowledge themselves to guide students' conceptual understanding. Frequently, teachers, parents, students, and school administrators lack patience during the inevitably rough transitions between familiar practices and new approaches—especially those emphasizing cooperative work among students instead of lecture formats.

Traditionalists have fought vigorously against the new curriculum. They oppose the ideas of the reforms, even in very well implemented programs. In one of the most highly visible examples, traditionalists and progressives went head-to-head over California's effort to develop mathematics standards for the state. By 1996 lobbying groups had organized to see that the state adopt a set of back-to-basics mathematics standards. One group, called Mathematically Correct, established an anti-reform Internet site to marshal opposition to the NCTM standards and to fight curriculum materials using progressive methods.

Accusations flew back and forth across the Internet and in letters to newspaper editors. California teachers were attacked for teaching math without numbers, denying children access to standard methods of multiplying and dividing, and paying more attention to how students feel than to whether or not they can do math. Mathematically Correct and other conservative groups escalated the debate about the nature of mathematics and how best to teach it into a statewide, political "math war" that degenerated into a highly charged battle over, believe it or not, verbs!

In proposing standards to guide the state's mathematics curriculum and textbook adoptions, California reformers made generous use of the following verbs: "model, estimate, interpret, classify, explain, and create."[18] Each points to a different strategy for thinking about, learning, and solving problems using mathematics. However, before adopting the standards, the conservative State Board of Education revised them, rejecting these verbs in nearly every case. One board member declared that the way to "get children to do more and better and higher math" is with such phrases as "do it, solve it, know it."[19]

The revised standards embodied the traditional view of mathematics education. An assistant director at the National Science Foundation (NSF) wrote a letter to the California board stating that the California board's action "is, charitably, shortsighted, and detrimental to the long-term mathematical literacy of children in California."[20] The revised standards emphasize basic skills and memorizing and practicing and discourage invention, estimation, and solving nonroutine problems. They deny the early use of calculators and caution about their later use. So, for example, California's third graders will memorize the multiplication tables, fourth graders will master carrying and borrowing in subtraction without calculators. Seventh graders are expected to do the following:

> Use the inverse relationship between raising to a power and extracting the root of a perfect square integer; for an integer that is not square, determine without a calculator the two integers between which its square root lies and explain why.[21]

But the Mathematically Correct group has gone further in its efforts to rid the schools of what they call "fuzzy math." Among other strategies, they have sought to remove the College Preparatory Mathematics (CPM) texts from the state's classrooms. Perhaps the nastiest argument they make against the CPM materials takes the evidence that CPM has been effective with low-income students and students of color to mean that the materials sacrifice the math learning of more-advantaged student on behalf of less-advantaged ones.

California did not experience this mathematics backlash in a vacuum. Similar campaigns took place around the nation and included a direct assault on the NCTM standards themselves. Responding to the pressure, NCTM issued a set of revised mathematics standards in 2000. Called *Principles and Standards for School Mathematics*, the revised standards place more emphasis on memorizing and rote computation than did the earlier set of standards. However, NCTM insists that the revised standards remain consistent with the theories of mathematics and mathematics learning that underlay the first set. Glenda Lappan, the president of NCTM when the new standards were released, emphasized, "NCTM believes that children should know arithmetic cold. . . . We also believe that crunching numbers isn't enough, but kids have to understand the underlying concepts in math." [22] All the political meddling is having its negative effects in many classrooms.

Yet even under the worst political deluge, teachers can weather the storm and teach math well. Perhaps the best defense, and weapon as well, against political maneuverings is an articulate generation of teachers of mathematics—elementary and high school—who know more about math and how to teach it than their ill-advised critics. Not only do students need expert scaffolding—parents, colleagues, and local school boards need it as well, and there is no better place to get it than from a teacher.

English Language Arts

Webster's Encyclopedic Unabridged Dictionary of the English Language gives twenty-eight definitions of the word *read.* The first two sum up conventional notions of what it means to read: 1. To peruse and apprehend the meaning of (something written, printed, etc): *to read a book;* 2. To utter aloud or render in speech: *reading a story to his children.*[23] Progressive English language arts teachers and theorists also pay substantial attention to the other twenty-six definitions. A few examples make clear how varied and deep this broader conception of reading really is:

> 5. To make out the significance of by scrutiny or observation: *to read the dark and cloudy sky as the threat of a storm.* 6. To foresee, foretell, or predict: *to read a person's fortune in tea leaves.* 7. To make out the character, motivations, desires, etc. . . . as by interpretation of outward signs. 8. To infer (something not expressed or directly indicated) from what is read or considered. . . : *He read an underlying sarcasm into her letter.* 25. To admit of being interpreted: *a rule that reads two different ways.* 26. (Of an electronic computer) to read data. 27. Read in, to introduce information into a computer.

Webster's gives a similarly long list of definitions for *write.* And just as with reading, traditional educators prefer a narrow conception of writing—rejecting the many writing-related activities and competencies that progressives favor.

The conventional curriculum frames reading as acquiring a set meaning off the printed page, and writing as mastering the conventions of spelling, grammar, and form. However, teachers with a sociocultural perspective see young readers and writers as already having—bringing to school with them—the resources, background, personal history, and individual voices they need to be fully literate.

Traditional Language Arts: Mastering Skills, Rules, and Forms

Traditionally, schools expect young children to learn the rules (and many exceptions) that govern how letters and combinations of letters translate into sounds. Teachers emphasize the skills to decode letters, combinations of letters, and whole words. They work to help students learn a hierarchy of discrete skills—from recognizing beginning consonants, to consonant blends, to reading inexplicable words like *cough* and *height.* They expect students to master the conventions of Standard English by memorizing correct spellings; dividing words into syllables; alphabetizing; capitalizing; punctuating; recognizing synonyms, homonyms, and antonyms; and identifying parts of speech and sentences. They ask students to practice writing sentences, paragraphs, stories, and reports.

Building from Parts to Whole These basics cycle and recycle throughout the grades. Middle-school and senior high teachers layer on harder spelling, vocabulary, capitalization, punctuation, usage, and grammar lessons. They add new writing algorithms—topic sentences, supporting paragraphs, three and five (but rarely four) paragraph essays, and, finally, the research paper. Students try out the conventions of common writing styles—descriptive, persuasive, analytic, critical, personal, "practical" (business letters), and narrative. College-bound high school students memorize sophisticated vocabulary words—partly to ready them for college entrance exams like the SAT. And since approximately 40 percent of the questions on the verbal section of the SAT I are asked in the form of analogies, as much time may be spent on becoming comfortable with these puzzlelike challenges as on learning the words themselves. Here is a sample SAT analogy:

NASCENT:: MORIBUND

A. sophomoric : puerile

B. covetous : greedy

C. sycophantic : servile

D. shrewd : disingenuous

E. germinal : senescent

As in mathematics, tradition dictates that reading and writing are composed of parts—essential elements—that combine into wholes. For example, the alphabet is more specific, and therefore more basic, than recognizing the sounds of parts of words, which are more basic than whole words. Letters are analogous to numbers. Phonics, or the sounds of letters and groups of letters, is elemental, perhaps similar to counting or even addition and subtraction. Grammar and sentences are akin to more complex algorithms, such as algebraic formulas. Once students master the basics, they are ready for more adultlike, sophisticated tasks. The conventional curriculum also treats reading, writing, and speaking as universally applicable skills that (like mathematics, in the traditional view) do not change much in different contexts.

Extracting Meaning from Traditional Texts Literature also weaves its way through the traditional curriculum. Elementary students learn basic literary genres—stories, poems, newspaper articles, and novels (known to many younger students as "chapter books"). Older students learn Western literary conventions, like plot, setting, characters, theme, and so on, and they read classics and established twentieth-century writers who are part of the cultural canon: William Shakespeare, Charles Dickens, Ralph Waldo Emerson, Emily Dickinson, John Steinbeck, Ernest Hemingway. Teachers stress discovering the author's intended meaning, and students learn to identify conventional literary devices (irony, foreshadowing, and metaphor, etc.). This is not to say that traditional approaches *never* allow "contemporary" literature; but when contemporary works are taught, their relevance and value are likely to be subordinated to the canon. Often, what passes for contemporary turns out to be twenty to fifty years old.

Textbooks form the traditional curriculum's bedrock. Basal readers and language arts texts provide simple stories and practice exercises to support young students' sequential development of decoding, vocabulary, comprehension, and other skills. In later grades, the basal reader merges into the familiar anthology that contains longer and shorter works, fiction and nonfiction, and includes poetry, drama, and essays. Some anthologies feature themes such as exploring life in cities; others focus on particular traditions, such as American, British, or world literature. Like basal readers, anthologies target particular grades and include particular pieces according to their reading difficulty. Because these particular texts are adopted to serve all the students in a particular grade, and therefore must be comprehensive enough to suit the tastes of school board members, teachers, parents, and so on, the books are often very large. Because marketing these books often emphasizes colorful graphics or photographs on every page, their costs can be enormous. Because of the financial investment in these adoptions, few schools can change their books as often as they need to, and because some students inevitably lose or, shall we say, are less than fully respectful of their books, the burdens on parents to pay for replacements are great.

Some textbooks provide detailed manuals that offer teachers step-by-step "direct instruction" strategies, including questions to ask, ways to motivate, assignments, tests, worksheets, posters, overhead projections, video recordings and disks, software, websites, and more. Some publishers provide consultants to train teachers, and some furnish detailed, scripted lessons. These highly structured formats are well suited for enforcing a basic skills and comprehension emphasis, but they may not be well matched to the particular needs of students in a particular class. Moreover, these expensive textbook series may leave little money for instructional resources that teachers could purchase at their discretion. State legislatures and local school boards often select traditional texts to ensure that teachers teach reading and writing comprehensively, competently, and uniformly. However, with an increasing shortage of qualified teachers, especially in overcrowded urban communities, many decision makers see scripted approaches to reading as "damage control" in classrooms where teachers know little or nothing about teaching reading. It's not surprising, then, that many urban school districts have adopted these materials.

Literacy as a Cognitive and Sociocultural Activity

Since the 1960s critics have faulted the traditional language arts curriculum on two related counts—its inconsistencies with cognitive and sociocultural and cultural-historical theories of literacy development, and its solid grounding in the elite, white cultural canon. Reform-minded educators worry that a narrow focus on the mechanics of reading, writing, and speaking may cause some students to miss the essence of language—the pleasure and power of expressing and understanding ideas. Even skilled students often miss the central purpose of writing, which is to enable others to understand something important to the writer and to enable the writer to engage in a thinking process that clarifies and orders her own sense-making. Progressive educators find it helpful to think of literacy *practices* rather than literacy skills—to think of literacy as something that people *do* rather than learn about and store for future use.

All students have profoundly fertile literacy possibilities. Some whose language, backgrounds, and family norms are similar to their schools' and teachers' barely have those possibilities scratched. As long as these students become proficient at decoding, vocabulary, and age-appropriate writing conventions, society considers them competent. If they continue on to college, they are considered a success. Other students whose language, backgrounds, or family norms are not similar to the schools' may suffer a much worse fate: They are likely to have their literacy possibilities actively denied. Schools often treat these students' language and experiences—so valuable in their own right and so necessary to develop formal literacy competence—as characteristics to overcome rather than resources to develop.[24] In the hands of many traditionalists and in monolingual environments dominated by standardized testing, the traditional approach ignores many of the literacy strengths all students bring to school.

Making Meaning in Context In the past thirty years, cognitive research has shown that learning is a process of meaning-making, and sociocultural studies have shown that social contexts not only influence but also *become* what students learn. These two areas of research and theory give English language arts educators overwhelming evidence that all students come to school with sociocultural, meaning-making experiences that prepare them for full adult literacy. This includes *cultural literacy* for rich cultural lives and *formal literacy* for successful and powerful economic and political participation.

All students have experience and proficiency with language, symbols, and communication. Professor David Pearson, former director of the National Center for the Study of Reading and now dean of the Education School at University of California, Berkeley, notes: "Even the three year old who recognizes that if an arch is in sight, a hamburger is not far away has learned the basic principle of signs—that our world is filled with things that 'stand for' other things."[25] Similarly, the 3-year-old who sees his parent pick up a book knows that sitting on a lap and being told a story are soon to follow. This child can read the environment long before he can read the book. Also, the child has learned that he is an active agent in determining the full meaning of his "reading." How he sits—still or squirmy—and how he "rewards" his parent—by pointing to the illustration that matches the text being read—show that relationships are inseparable from this and most literacy events. When teachers build their literacy lessons on their belief that children are already literate, Pearson argues, they are more likely "to engage them in tasks in which they can demonstrate their literacy and use those successes as bridges to even more challenging literacy activities."[26]

Teaching Skills in Meaningful Contexts Teachers and researchers have devised new methods to embed literacy in meaningful contexts. Attention to realistic and useful reading and writing experiences, starting in the earliest grades, is at the heart of "whole language" and "literature-based" approaches to language arts. Teachers also have begun to focus on writing as a multistepped, repeating process of reflection, drafting, editing, getting feedback, more reflection and drafting, and so on. These processes are not linear, have no clearly defined beginning and end, and at their best are intensely interactive.

Central to these new approaches are principles of integration and authenticity.[27] *Integration* means that literacy events and acts are not broken down into subskills (thus the whole in whole language); that reading, writing, speaking, and listening are treated as different aspects of the same fundamental linguistic and cognitive processes; and that every school subject makes important literacy contributions. *Authenticity* means that students should engage in literacy activities that allow them to communicate about real things of interest and that have relevance beyond school. From the earliest grades, young children should read and produce real stories and other forms of genuine communication—even if they don't have all of the conventional "skills." For example, first-year teacher Chrysta Bakstad integrated her literacy lessons into her first graders' study of mountains.

To learn more about bears, we read and listened to the storybook tape/book *Bear Facts*, by Norma L. Genter and Phillip Howe. After we got to know this book well, and the students had an opportunity to read it independently, we made our own reproduction of the book as a class. This process helped strengthen their story sense and gave them ownership of the book. The book pages were displayed on the wall and then bound and put in the classroom library.

In small groups, led by a parent volunteer, students created their own original *Bear Facts* book to take home. Taking books home is a great way for students to build a home library of books that they can read.

If there is a negative result of making books, it is that the students fight over who gets to read them at B.E.A.R. (Be Enthusiastic About Reading) time. All of the students, at all reading levels, enjoy reading the books they have created.

—Chrysta Bakstad
First-year teacher, grade 1

Central to authenticity, as well, is that the language and traditions of children's homes and communities be extended into schools to connect school and home, formal and informal literacy.[28] For example, first-year English teacher Kelly Ganzel used Laura Esquivel's novel *Like Water for Chocolate* as a bridge to help her Latino ninth graders gain access to Shakespeare's *Romeo and Juliet*.

Pairing classic texts with contemporary, ethnically diverse, young adult literature is valuable. Such pairing affords the opportunity for teachers to collaborate with their students in choosing a contemporary novel to study. Through multicultural literature, I invite my students to share their knowledge about the history, traditions, and community of their own culture.

Similarly,

As I prepared to teach Harper Lee's *To Kill a Mockingbird*, I decided to capture my students' attention through a portrayal of African American women's experiences in the South during the Depression. After showing "I Know Why the Caged Bird Sings," the film version of Maya Angelou's youth, Nancy [an African American student with a history of school failure] was bursting with questions and comments. Her interest was authentic and consuming. I was ecstatic when Nancy approached me after class with a smile on her face. "I'll do my homework tonight, Ms. Ganzel. I really like that stuff." The next day, Nancy entered the classroom eager to know if we were going to share our writing. She had written a reflection about how she would have felt had she been in Maya Angelou's shoes.

—Kelly Ganzel
First-year teacher, high school English

Multicultural texts like the Esquivel novel and Angelou's filmed biography, Ganzel believes, allow her students to "celebrate their distinct human experiences" and "liberate them to find meaning in the literature as they define it."

National Standards in the Language Arts

Consider the fact that nearly every student in kindergarten through twelfth grade has a reading or English teacher. This adds up to a very large number of teachers whose interests are represented by one or both of two professional organizations: the International Reading Association (IRA) and the National Council of Teachers of English (NCTE). In 1992 the IRA and the NCTE took the lead in the federal government's effort to describe and establish what students should know and be able to do in English language arts. By standards they meant "what is valued" and "descriptions of what is considered quality work."[29] In 1994 the writers circulated drafts of the *Standards for the English Language Arts* to hundreds of review groups, including literacy organizations, state departments of education, and scholars and practitioners. As the standards group was receiving overwhelmingly—but not exclusively—favorable comments from reviewers, the federal government suddenly refused to continue sponsorship of this standards effort. The government cited "nonperformance," but some organizational leaders believed that politics was to blame.[30] With private funds and their own resources, IRA and NCTE continued developing the standards, seeking widespread reviews and building a consensus. In 1996 they published the standards.

The standards developed by the IRA and NCTE (reproduced following this paragraph) show the influence of sociocultural research on understanding how students construct literacy within their school environment. These standards press schools to respect, and help students to use, the literacy they have constructed elsewhere. Notice how many of the following standards are expressed in terms of what might be called *practices* ("apply," "adjust" "conduct," "develop," etc.), as distinct from the traditional idea of acquiring *skills*. Whereas skills are typically "taught" or "shown" by a book or teacher, these practices require that students read and write in order to "do" as well as to "learn." *Teaching* and *showing* place the emphasis on teachers; *doing* and *learning* emphasize students. The standards ask teachers to establish conditions for student's active engagement rather than telling students what they should know. Of course, a world of professional knowledge and values underlies each of the twelve standards, and these standards in no way represent the "last word" on what and how English classes should be taught.

> The vision guiding these standards is that all students must have the opportunities and resources to develop the language skills they need to pursue life's goals and to participate fully as informed, productive members of society. These standards assume that literacy growth begins before children enter school as they experience and experiment with literacy activities—reading and writing, and associating spoken words with their graphic representations. Recognizing this fact, these standards encourage the development of curriculum and instruction that make productive use of the emerging literacy abilities that children bring to school. Furthermore, the standards provide ample room for the innovation and creativity essential to teaching and learning. They are not prescriptions for particular curriculum or instruction.
>
> Although we present these standards as a list, we want to emphasize that they are not distinct and separable; they are, in fact, interrelated and should be considered as a whole.
>
> 1. Students read a wide range of print and nonprint texts to build an understanding of texts, of themselves, and of the cultures of the United States and the world; to acquire new information; to respond to the needs and

demands of society and the workplace; and for personal fulfillment. Among these texts are fiction and nonfiction, classic and contemporary works.

2. Students read a wide range of literature from many periods in many genres to build an understanding of the many dimensions (e.g., philosophical, ethical, aesthetic) of human experience.
3. Students apply a wide range of strategies to comprehend, interpret, evaluate, and appreciate texts. They draw on their prior experience, their interactions with other readers and writers, their knowledge of word meaning and of other texts, their word identification strategies, and their understanding of textual features (e.g., sound-letter correspondence, sentence structure, context, graphics).
4. Students adjust their use of spoken, written, and visual language (e.g., conventions, style, vocabulary) to communicate effectively with a variety of audiences and for different purposes.
5. Students employ a wide range of strategies as they write and use different writing process elements appropriately to communicate with different audiences for a variety of purposes.
6. Students apply knowledge of language structure, language conventions (e.g., spelling and punctuation), media techniques, figurative language, and genre to create, critique, and discuss print and nonprint texts.
7. Students conduct research on issues and interests by generating ideas and questions, and by posing problems. They gather, evaluate, and synthesize data from a variety of sources (e.g., print and nonprint texts, artifacts, people) to communicate their discoveries in ways that suit their purpose and audience.
8. Students use a variety of technological and informational resources (e.g., libraries, databases, computer networks, video) to gather and synthesize information and to create and communicate knowledge.
9. Students develop an understanding of and respect for diversity in language use, patterns, and dialects across cultures, ethnic groups, geographic regions, and social roles.
10. Students whose first language is not English make use of their first language to develop competency in the English language arts and to develop understanding of content across the curriculum.
11. Students participate as knowledgeable, reflective, creative, and critical members of a variety of literacy communities.
12. Students use spoken, written, and visual language to accomplish their own purposes (e.g., for learning, enjoyment, persuasion, and the exchange of information).[31]

A Conservative Backlash

Shortly after the NCTE and the IRA published the standards in 1996, a professor from Missouri wrote an angry commentary for *Education Week* (a weekly newspaper with wide circulation to those interested in education events and policies):

> One would have hoped that the leading language-arts standards-setting group in the country would have stated in plain English that our schools expect all students to use proper spelling, grammar, and punctuation in written commu-

> nication. Indeed, any normal person would have assumed that such fundamental matters would have been at the top of the list of concerns treated by language-arts teachers. However, if one reads the roughly 100-page document, one finds virtually no mention of such things.[32]

This critic closed by noting,

> I am a product of the "drill and kill" school of literacy training complete with weekly spelling and vocabulary tests throughout K–12, along with 20- to 30-page research papers done on weekends at the public library (as opposed to the one- to two-page journal-writing exercises that now dominate English instruction). I, like so many others, somehow managed to overcome this seemingly "stifling" and "boring" education to develop a love for the written word and to author several books and numerous other publications.[33]

A professor of education commented, "I can't imagine any other profession promulgating a practice that ends up harming literally hundreds of thousands of children."[34] These professors joined a rising chorus of educators and others who attributed all manner of social and educational ills to a supposed departure from skills-based instruction in language arts.

As with mathematics, the debate about how to teach language arts has gathered advocates and resources far afield from the public schools and their mission to educate everyone well. Commercial companies like Sylvan Learning Centers filled the airways trying to "educate" the public to believe that schools have neglected an easy method to improve reading. Right-wing entities like the Blumenfeld Education Letter and the Eagle Forum Education and Defense Fund became strong back-to-basics advocates and helped to draw political and religious agendas into learning and teaching debates.

Researchers Constance Weaver and Ellen Brinkley, professors at Western Michigan University, spoke about the religious connection with language arts teaching at the 1996 NCTE convention. They concluded from their studies that many conservative Christians worry about what will happen if children are encouraged to construct their own meaning and do not turn first to adults and the Bible as exclusive, authoritative sources for facts and meanings.[35]

The opposition to whole language has made its way into policy as progressive and conservative groups jockey to have their views represented in the new state content standards. In California, Nebraska, North Carolina, Massachusetts, Texas, and Ohio, traditionalist have mounted concerted efforts to mandate explicit phonics instruction and to eliminate the use of whole language instruction, and some, as in California, have succeeded.[36]

Phonics or Whole Language? Seeking Balance

For a month, my eighth-grade students explore contemporary issues, such as teen pregnancy, suicide, gangs, and AIDS, that impose harsh choices upon young adults. They use a research process that engages them in accessing information, analyzing and organizing facts, and generating a written research report. They discover the power of information through research, and they also read realistic fiction that deals with the same contemporary issues. Coupling issues that are important to teenagers with literature helps students to see the relevance of reading, writing, and studying and education in their lives.

Several of my activities, such as the "Dear Friend Letter" and "Tea Party," provide a social setting in which students communicate their ideas, analyze new perspectives, and think about the impact their research might have in their lives. In the "Dear Friend" letter, students individually describe their topics, relate one important fact about their topic, and explain what they have learned and what they still wonder. Each student exchanges his or her letter with a peer and writes a letter in response. At the "Tea Party," students mingle and share one startling or important fact about their research topic with other students. After the party, students complete a quick-write responding to the question: "Why is it important for middle-school students to research these issues? Give specific reasons and examples for your answers." Through these activities, I expand the notion of literacy from isolated reading and writing events to a social practice involving reading and writing as well as thinking in new ways.

—Jasper Hiep Dang Bui
First-year teacher, English, grade 8

Jasper Hiep Dang Bui is teaching literacy to his students—a practice related to but quite different from teaching the discrete skills of decoding words and correct spelling. But what about those *skills?* Isn't there something to be said for phonetic decoding, for having both a subject and verb in one's sentences, for conventional spelling, for learning the protocols for writing research papers? Of course. These narrowly defined literacy skills and the more broadly understood literacy *practices* must work together in a just and democratic school. They are also clearly stated in the IRA/NCTE standards (items 3, 4, and 6, in particular). Scholars Gloria Ladson-Billings and Lisa Delpit, both who have studied teaching and learning in classrooms with African American students, warn that all students must be able to use the skills of accurate decoding and conventional writing to bring power and social advantage to their literacy. Ladson-Billings, Delpit, and others worry that if teachers don't teach the "codes of power"—including the conventions of reading, writing, and speaking in Standard English—they further limit the opportunities of students of color whose families and communities may speak Ebonics, or Spanish, or speak in some way other than formal Standard English.[37] Nothing in the IRA/NCTE English standards, nothing in a sociocultural perspective, nothing in a concern for social justice can ever justify an education that denies students the power to communicate skillfully to all people.

This "balanced" perspective is quite compatible with recent reports from panels of highly regarded scholars in the teaching of reading. The National Academy of Sciences and other groups agree that the explicit teaching of phonics is only one of a comprehensive set of strategies needed to assist young children to become literate.[38] Effective teachers use multiple approaches to teach content and skills, integrate test preparation into lessons, make connections between what students learn at school and their lives outside of classrooms, teach strategies to help students think about their work as they are doing it, and press students to probe deeper into what they have learned. At best, teachers and students engage in "cognitive collaboration" to "push one another's thinking, challenge one another, or bounce ideas off one another."[39]

Contrary to the fears and accusations of traditionalists, most researchers as well as progressive policymakers and teachers seek a "balanced approach" to literacy that neither neglects skills nor discounts the knowledge of the past thirty years about learning.

David Pearson places the search for a balanced approach to language arts instruction in a historical perspective:

> I am convinced that we are capable, as a profession, of developing an approach to phonics that is respectful of the journeys we have taken since . . . the early 1980s [when] phonics was a major component of literacy instruction. We are not the same profession now as we were then. Our views of reading have changed. In the 1960s, we regarded reading as fundamentally a perceptual process—taking in visual stimuli and recording them into verbal representations. In the 1970s, we discovered that reading was a cognitive process. In the 1980s, we added a distinctly socio-cultural perspective. And in the 1990s, we discovered a literary perspective. Today we are learning more and more about reading as a political phenomenon. We need a phonics that respects these roads we have traveled.[40]

We see this balance at work in first-year teacher Benji Chang's struggle to infuse his sociocultural understanding of how students construct literacy into the highly prescriptive, direct-instruction reading program he is required to use with his first graders.

Initially, I was overwhelmed and sometimes fell into the trap of just following along with what the Open Court teachers' guide told me to do. Because the program required my students to sit still for extended periods of time, I found myself thinly disguising its rote phonics drills and dry grammar lessons as games or with the use of a puppet. Although these strategies did not put lessons in the context of my students' lives nor tap into their background knowledge, they were somewhat successful at engaging my class.

By late November, I was more familiar with my students and the Open Court structure, and I had learned to work my way around the program's subtractive nature. I developed integrated lessons using multicultural literature. For example, I used *The Legend of Hua Mu Lan* to engage students in practicing synonyms by trying to retell the story. Because the students were exposed to different types of literature, by mid-January they were able to take a critical look at some of the literature provided by Open Court. In the basal reader, there is a story about an African boy named Jafta. It is one of the first encounters that students have with a character of African descent in the reader and one of the rare stories that identifies the ethnic or racial background of a character. The notes about the story state that the author wrote it so his white daughters could get a better understanding of South African life. It seems that the author thought that a better understanding would come from a story of a black male child, dressed only in his underwear, who does nothing but daydream and emulate the wild animals around him. During a shared reading of the story, I asked the students if they thought the story was fantasy or reality and why. Students said the story was fake because a little boy would not run around with hippos and elephants in his underwear. They said that he would probably have to help out his family at home and do homework because that is what they have to do. My students were not simply reciting the words on the pages of a story that reinforces stereotypes of black Africans. They were developing a critical lens through which to view the world. My students were not just developing literacy, but critical literacy as well.

—Benji Chang
First-year teacher, grade 1

What Texts? Whose Voice?

The debates over how students should develop linguistic proficiency might be seen as a *technical*, "how to go about it" matter of developing students' skills. The related *cultural* struggle over whose perspective, whose voice, and whose knowledge belong in the curriculum is at least as loud and contentious. In the English language arts curriculum, the outcome of this second struggle is clear. In spite of some recent progress, the ideas and voices of white males dominate the literature that most American students read. Despite the vibrant tradition of black American literature and a growing group of American Latino writers (as well as an extensive body of Latin American literature), U.S. students rarely hear these voices in school. As recently as January 1998, two different Maryland school systems removed books by African American authors from the curriculum—one, Nobel Prize–winning Toni Morrison; the other, poet Maya Angelou—after parents complained that the works were "trash" and "anti-white."[41] This struggle, too, is one that teachers committed to social justice will inevitably confront.

My ninth-grade classes are 50 percent Latino, and I purposely loaded my curriculum with Latino literature. I taught Cisneros's *The House on Mango Street*, a unit on Latin American magical realism, Esquivel's *Like Water for Chocolate*, and Rodriguez's *Always Running*. These works are all on the ninth-grade reading list, but I decided to forgo some of the traditional canon—*Great Expectations* and *Fahrenheit 451*, for example—to accommodate the Latino writers on the list.

I wanted my Latino students, in particular, to see themselves in the literature. Additionally, there is some Spanish included in many of the works I've taught this year, and I don't speak Spanish. My students (including students who are not Latino but are taking Spanish classes) love to show what they know, and they have been very helpful with pronunciation. I often ask my Spanish speakers for help, and I think they appreciate having their bilingualism acknowledged and used.

In the unit on magical realism, I wanted the students to experience the pure enjoyment of the stories. I also want them to understand what magical realism is (the imaginary becomes real), and why it originated in Latin America (according to Gabriel García Márquez, events in Latin America have been so extraordinary that realism was not adequate to describe people and events). The culminating project for the unit was a research project on an author, an event, or a historical figure. They needed to find the connection between their topic and the events or circumstances in Latin America that led to the development of magical realism.

The strength of this unit is the material—the students really liked the stories because they were unusual, lyrical, and challenging. In addition, my Latino students in particular enjoyed the opportunity to explore aspects of their heritage that they wanted to know more about (the slaughter of Mayans and Aztecs were popular topics for the research project). I also think that this approach is powerful because it combines students' home culture and high-status knowledge in an English curriculum. In an urban school, we need to acknowledge our students' home communities, but not at the expense of access to an honors-equivalent curriculum.

—Jessica Wingell
First-year teacher, English, grade 9

The growing popularity of multicultural language arts curriculum has not made it any less contentious. An instructive case in point was the 1998 decision by the San Francisco Board of Education to require teachers to assign books by nonwhite authors to high school students. At the time, the only required books were Chaucer's *Canterbury Tales,* Shakespeare's *Romeo and Juliet,* and Mark Twain's *Huckleberry Finn.* Board members thought the proposed policy reasonable, particularly since only 13 percent of the district's students are white. However, the news of the proposal exploded onto headlines nationwide and became the target of derision by talk-show hosts. The president of a conservative San Francisco think tank told a *New York Times* reporter, "They [students] have to go on to college and the work world, and this would destroy their opportunities." The board member who proposed the new policy described the event as the most difficult time of his life.[42]

Social Studies

Hannah Cha had just begun teaching first graders in a low-income, Latino immigrant neighborhood in Los Angeles. In the fall, Hannah, like most American first-grade teachers, wanted to teach her students about Thanksgiving and to tie her reading and writing lessons to the Thanksgiving theme. But Hannah's understanding of children's learning led her in an untraditional direction. Even first graders, as Hannah's teaching demonstrates, can engage with rich and complex ideas as they practice the fundamentals of literacy.

Thanksgiving is more than just the picturesque scene of European pilgrims sitting at a table eating turkey with Native Americans standing, almost hiding or blending, into the background. It was not only the first multicultural event celebrated in this country, it was the beginning of mixing, sharing, and appreciating one another's differences. My class considered the Pilgrims as immigrants seeking a life of more opportunities. They concluded that we are all pilgrims. Our families journeyed here from another country in search for a better existence. Further, we can celebrate Thanksgiving in our own cultural fashion and not feel marginalized if we do not have turkey for dinner.

We had just read *How Many Days to America?* by Eve Bunting, and Marissa strongly identified with the story. It is a book about a Latino family that underwent many tribulations to immigrate to America. Although Marissa did not remember [her immigration], the experience was very alive to her through her mother's stories. She shared some of these stories with the whole class, and concluded that she is American and Mexican—she is American even though people tell her that she is not. When a writing activity followed the story, Marissa went straight to work. Usually she is easily distracted because her reading and writing skills are so low, but she connected with this activity and took some risks. She achieved the critical awareness that she is just as much an American pilgrim as the traditional European Pilgrims. I believe this was Marissa's start to becoming literate.

—Hannah Cha
First-year teacher, grade 1

In social studies lessons, students can be historians, political scientists, geographers, anthropologists, sociologists, and economists. They can use history and social commentaries to observe and make sense of their own lives. And they can explore their personal and family histories to help make sense of traditionally taught events and historical figures. They can do original research and reenact society's decision making and problem solving around critical social issues. It can be liberating to students and society when teachers help students pursue these activities—these identities.

However, Freire, McLaren, and other critical multiculturalists remind us that the models we have for historians, geographers, and anthropologists, are largely men who learned and worked in the tradition of the European Enlightenment.[43] Teachers at the start of the twenty-first century have few models and scant social support for easing their students into the world of critical ideas that can liberate them from the cultural and psychic pigeonholes that come with minority status. For example, first grader Marissa seems on her way to developing a sense that she is not "less than" but "as good as" American first graders who are Anglo and not immigrants. It may be "progress" for Marissa to identify with the traditional Pilgrims, but is it liberating? Will Marissa's identity continue to develop *in relation* to the dominant Anglo-American story—either less than, or as good as, but never standing entirely on its own? The answer to these questions may depend on whether and where Marissa has access to historical knowledge about Americans who are Latinos, Indians, Africans, Chinese, Arabs, and others *in their own terms* instead of simply fitting into certain historical moments in Anglo-American history. In Hannah Cha's words, this was a "start to becoming literate," but Marissa will need support throughout her schooling before she stands on her own.

How Do We Teach the Past?

Do we revise and reinterpret the past to tell previously ignored stories because they reflect present-day values and speak to the issues of our own time? Or do we believe that the primary role of schools, textbooks, and museums is to preserve traditional versions of the past, to teach the basic facts, and to instill patriotism in our students?

These questions speak directly to the dilemma first-year teacher Hannah Cha faces. They are asked on the dust jacket of *History on Trial: Culture Wars and the Teaching of the Past,* a book that chronicles the background and writing of national standards for the history that students should learn.[44] Without discounting the importance of tradition, basic facts, and patriotism, the authors, who also oversaw the writing of the national standards, favor the approach suggested by the first question over that suggested in the second. The political fallout over these standards—"ones in which all citizens of the world's most diverse democracy can see their struggles, aspirations, contributions, and sacrifices"[45]—was intense and included their condemnation by the United States Senate.

Traditional Social Studies for Patriotic Citizenship In actual practice, the teaching of history, government, geography, and other social studies does change somewhat to reflect changing scholarship, values, and attitudes. But some find even these slight changes unacceptable and vow to fight further change while returning the school curriculum to reflect that which was taught at an earlier time. History, along with literature, carries most of the explicit responsibility for explaining and passing on the society's culture. It is not surprising, then, that literature and history—subjects that are actually seen as the proper domain for inculcating culture—are at the vortex of the larger society's cultural battles.

As far back as the 1830s, Americans thought social studies was particularly important for teaching the knowledge and values of citizenship. Then, as now, most believe that the study of history, economics, and government should help students become responsible political decision makers who understand the traditions of a free, democratic society. Therefore, the social studies curriculum typically combines information about government structures and processes, with appreciation for citizens' rights and responsibilities, and with the basic values and ideas in the nation's core documents—the Declaration of Independence, the Constitution, and the Bill of Rights. History, then, often traces how government and the values embedded in its founding documents have evolved over time. This history has always had a point of view; that is, schools have always intended to cultivate students' commitment to American institutions, processes, and values by presenting stories about how American leaders and heroes used solid values and courage to shape this country.[46]

In most elementary and middle schools, the social studies curriculum includes a grab bag of ideas and subjects: history, economics, geography, government, anthropology, psychology, and sociology. Typically, elementary school teachers teach units such as The Founding Fathers and The Westward Movement. Most middle schoolers study American history and government, including a hefty unit or whole course on state history. Nearly all high school students take required courses in American history and government, supplemented by electives in psychology, world history, economics, sociology, and law.

Traditionalists want students to focus on a body of enduring historical facts—what they see as the building blocks of cultural literacy. They prefer direct instruction of these facts in the traditional disciplines of history, geography, and government (civics), and they are critical of schools that focus on current values and issues while neglecting historic events. Some lament that essential historical content is no longer preeminent in the curriculum. They suggest that progressives' emphasis on process, attention to out-of-school meanings, and interest in constructive teaching methods (simulations, projects, etc.) all help to slight the traditional history content. Other traditionalists see social studies education as morally flabby and relativistic. They prefer that teachers teach values as absolutes—not as issues that students explore, discover, or clarify.

Progressive Social Studies to Understand "The Human Story" Progressive educators want students to "go beyond a study of the disciplines to develop an understanding of human commonalties."[47] They prefer a social studies curriculum that teaches about the diversity and similarities among the world's people—one that helps students "place the human story in larger context."[48] And they favor giving greater attention to the role of women and minorities and to a variety of interpretations and points of view about human events. Progressives believe that a true multicultural social studies curriculum is an interaction among representations of the world, the nation, and the students' own cultural backgrounds and experiences. Even when the curriculum dictates that teachers cover material not directly related to students' own backgrounds, progressive teachers seek to make connections. As with other subjects, a teacher's own curiosity, interests, and knowledge make these connections more or less possible.

Teacher Erik Korporaal's class brought together 10- and 11-year-old Latino Catholics and African American Protestants and Muslims. He connected the standard sixth-grade social studies unit on Egypt with the rich and complex knowledge that the children could share with one another and with him about their own cultures.

My students were learning about Egyptian burial practices. They researched the burial customs of their own families and cultures, shared information, and compared their own customs with those of other students. The students now had real-life contexts that they could relate to new understandings of Egypt. They were able to critically analyze their burial customs and form deeper understandings about their history and origin.

—Erik Korporaal
First-year teacher, grade 6

Jeffrey Madrigal used a similar approach with his fourth graders.

The study of music quickly expanded into a study of international and domestic politics and geography. The class explored the African roots of Hip Hop and learned about the trials and accomplishments of Nelson Mandela. We used the strong social commentary present in some music to study the politics of South Africa (South African revolutionary music), to learn about the Rastafarian religion of Jamaica (Reggae), and to look at Black Nationalism in America (Rip Hop). After the lesson, a simple Rap song took on historical roots and sociopolitical meaning. We explored social commentary [in] Jazz and Middle Eastern music. The levels of understanding by each student varied, but the children were always attentive, and they even learned to take notes.

—Jeffrey Madrigal
First-year teacher, grade 4

Enriching students' already rich cultural literacy may be the surest way to introduce new insights into enduring human themes. Both Korporaal and Madrigal demonstrate that engaging students' literacy and drawing them into these themes helps them remember historical details and chronologies in two ways: (1) through the students' seeking out facts they want to know about and (2) through placing these facts in a context.

Teaching about the "Other" Progressive educators stress that *all* students—not just students of color, not just older students—need an approach to social studies that goes beyond the typical noncritical "let's-include-everyone" multiculturalism. Noncritical multicultural lessons supply answers rather than raise questions; they close social investigations rather than open new areas for inquiry. As a result, typical approaches fail to position students as solvers of social problems. Consider that when schools typically deal with these social issues, they treat the issues in the following ways: segregation as a solved problem, the Japanese internment as a mistake our forefathers made, homophobia and AIDS as having no historical and political contexts, drug and alcohol use and sexual behavior as character flaws. These approaches are not invitations to explore issues or to solve problems as much as conclusions and behavioral prescriptions the school asserts unconditionally. An older generation may criticize youth for being apathetic and cynical, but students may legitimately ask, "If you already have all the answers, how can you expect us to contribute?" One review of research on multicultural social studies classrooms noted:

> [S]tudents have little knowledge of the history of race relations in the United States. What they do know is the character of the relations between enslaved African Americans and their White masters. Focussing on the "evils" of slavery—cruel masters, the brutal treatment of slaves, belief in the inferiority of slaves—is important to be sure. But it provides a history that is too narrow and limited to be of much use in discussing contemporary American society. It provides very weak links to issues of racism, discrimination, and the denial of political and civil rights.[49]

In one of the studies cited in this review, students revealed how the curriculum limited their understanding of African Americans' experiences with racism. For these students, racial segregation and prejudice are not enduring social problems, but anomalies—historical moments that came and went.

> Jean wrote about southern slavery as the "era of racism, prejudice, and slavery"; Eric wrote, "less than ninety years later [after the Civil War], black people were the target of racism once again"; Diana wrote, "that was the past"; and Sue, summing up African Americans' experiences, wrote "in the end, as you know, there is no more slavery anymore."[50]

Although the treatment of race may represent the most glaring omissions or misrepresentations in social studies, the perspectives of all working people, whatever their race, have also been slighted. Traditionalists claim that history is told best from the perspectives of the great and powerful. And though some of these presidents, generals, tycoons, and inventors did have humble origins and may have improved the lot of "common folks," school history generally provides few insights into what it was like to live an ordinary working-person's life (of all races) during the 1950s, the Great Depression, the Reconstruction South, and so on. This reflects a common pattern of how schools treat social issues, including problems of schools themselves: in the context of their historical or contemporary *solution.* This attention to solutions and victories is consistent with a mythology of progress that treats history as if it were a forward moving time line—a history with consequences but not with roots. School history distances students' current experiences from their own personal or social class history. Poor students learn little about multigenerational poverty. They may learn how Cesar Chavez was a great Mexican American who led protests to improve conditions of migrant farmworkers but learn little about the conditions themselves before or after. They learn even less about the related roles of California's agriculture industry and California politics.

Moreover, schools typically do little to help middle-class students situate themselves in realistic socioeconomic contexts. Students are left to develop on their own a personal historical context to explain their relative advantages—that is, their parents work hard, their families or ethnic groups have always valued education. At worst, middle-class students believe that their own social position is the social norm and therefore requires no explanation at all.

A more balanced and just view is to add the perspectives or at least raise questions about those who may not have benefited from the technological advances, territorial expansion, and economic progress that highlight history. When first-year teacher Jennifer Garcia taught her eleventh graders about the end of the nineteenth century, she stressed how the industrial age affected workers and immigrants. She included their stories alongside more conventional accounts of the rise of industrialists' power and the making of new economic policy.

Throughout the unit on "Industrialization, Unionism, and Immigration," I attempted to incorporate critical multiculturalism—not in one or two activities but as a central theme. The goal was for students to be exposed to and appreciate the period's social complexities. Activities and discussions based on themes such as factory life, union organizing, political machines and corruption, and urban living conditions challenged students' preconceived notions about workers, immigrants, and politics. By the end of the unit, students had not only been exposed to the social complexities of the late 1800s but developed a measure of empathy with the people and issues through critically examining social, political, and economic issues.

—Jennifer Garcia
First-year teacher, history, grade 11

Traditionalists may accuse progressives like Jennifer Garcia of "tearing down" the country by exposing students to unsolved dilemmas, real or imagined, in the American culture. But she and her students draw energy and optimism from grappling with the issues of the day. They think that schools have an important activist role in challenging and improving society. They learn that an objective pursuit of social justice does not require one to be dispassionate, passive, or neutral. As one social studies educator framed it:

> In this milieu of disillusion and discontent, teaching that piously expounds on values as ideas in unexamined classroom discourse and texts risks further reinforcing the alienation of youth who have already experienced discrepancies between these ideas and the social, economic, and political realities of their world.[51]

Textbooks as a Conservative Force

My unit on slavery begins with the idea that historical texts give diverse subjective and objective information. My goal is to encourage students to begin questioning information that commonly remains unexamined. Thus, students are asked to consider who writes history, who is excluded from history, and why is history written as it is. We analyze history by looking at slavery as an economic mode of exploitation. Students examine how slavery is depicted by different authors. I explained the difference between primary and secondary sources. In groups students analyzed firsthand accounts of African American slaves. By looking at these primary documents, we validated the history and culture of our ancestors. As a class, we outlined the textbook section on slavery. We then compared the different ways that slavery was presented.

—Martha Guerrero
First-year teacher, high school history

I seek to make the hidden, visible, so before I even set foot in the classroom I interrogate my curriculum. I ask myself, whose interests does it serve? Upon what assumptions does it lie? Why have I chosen to teach this particular fact or subject? Consider my unit on Imperialism in Nigeria. I realized that it did not examine the pernicious effect of imperial policies on the colonized peoples. Instead, it focused on what allowed the Europeans to dominate. As I should have expected, history was written from the Europeans' point of view. Apparently, history did not begin in African until the Europeans arrived. As the book discussed how Social Darwinism was a motivating factor for the Europeans, it seems to perpetuate it by relegating the Africans to the status of those who are acted upon, instead of those who act. The textbook's version perpetuates a blind allegiance to racist and classist institutions. Therefore, our first act in the unit was to examine the textbook and unpack the hidden curriculum. This, in itself, is an act of empowerment. The curriculum is not to be blindly accepted, it is to be challenged, interrogated, and compared to alternate perspectives.

—Matthew Eide
First-year teacher, high school history

Guerrero and Eide are thinking carefully about how to use textbooks that reflect the "official," mainstream, and generally acceptable versions of history and social science. Although these two teachers thoughtfully press their students to think beyond these versions, many teachers teach little other than what the text provides. The following examples from textbooks that were used until recently reveal how the dominant culture can shape attitudes by telling biased versions of history:

> Indians helped the settlers, and the settlers helped the Indians. The Indians had better food and clothing than they had ever had. They were more comfortable than they had ever been.
>
> Once in a while a mission Indian had to be punished for something he had done. Sometimes such Indians ran away. Some of them took guns with them. Sometimes they took horses with them, too. The runaway Indians taught the wild Indians how to steal animals and other things from the missions. Once in a while soldiers had to protect the missions from an Indian raid.[52]

> The Indians at the missions ate more regularly than they had when they were wild. The padres took care of them in many ways. . . . They learned to do many things as the Spaniards did. They learned many new skills.[53]

Children who learned these facts and attitudes in their fourth-grade classes are now in their forties, close to the height of their economic, social, and political influence. They are parents of today's students, and veteran teachers and curriculum designers. We must wonder when and how and if they have changed their views of history, conquest, and Indians, and if more accurate renditions of history will seem strange and upsetting to them. We hope that their reflections on the California missions do not bring forth images of happy, grateful, wild men who sometimes were very bad and had to be punished.

The 1991 revision of the California text just cited showed some improvement. Or did it? The revised text that follows still situates Native Americans in the White American story of the westward expansion that brought progress to the wilderness:

> Although some Indians were content on the missions, many others were unhappy with this new way of life. By living at the missions the Indians gave up their own culture, the way of life they had known in their tribal villages. They could only leave the mission grounds with permission from the padres. They were not free to hunt or to pick berries.
>
> Mission Indians were not allowed to return to their tribes once they agreed to take part in mission life. Some ran away. But soldiers usually brought them back and sometimes whipped them. Others wanted to revolt. They wanted to rise up against their leaders, the Spanish padres and the soldiers at the mission communities.
>
> Sometimes Indians revolted violently. Six years after its founding, the San Diego Mission was attacked by Indians. They set the mission on fire and killed one of the padres.
>
> Many Indians died of diseases brought by the Spanish. When crops failed, Indians didn't have enough to eat. Some became sick from the change in their diet on the missions. By the end of the Mission period, the California Indian population was half the size that it had been when Father Serra raised his first cross at San Diego Mission.[54]

Even this version, twenty-five years later, waffles as it portrays the stunning violations of decency and human rights that California Indians endured. That "some Indians were content" must be seen as the moral equivalent of references to happy Negro slaves on the plantation. That the Indians "gave up" their culture seems close to a free and neutral choice. The text explains offenses against the Indians in the familiar language of what grownups do to naughty children—whippings, not being able to leave without permission, not free to hunt or pick berries. Indian deaths seem sanitized, kept a safe distance from the killers; disease, crop failure, and a change in diet reduce the Indian population by half, not theft of land and enslavement. On the other hand, Indians, with *their* offenses, are downright uncivilized; they violently revolt, attack and burn missions, and kill padres.

Many conservatives worried that this most recent California text was too liberal in its depiction of California history. However, progressive teachers want to believe an equitable and excellent education confronts truth, myth, and controversy. They argue that even fourth graders "are intelligent enough to read about how [Father Junipero] Serra has become controversial . . . you give them a sense of what he thought he was doing and how the Indians experienced his role."[55]

Seeking a Middle Ground: The National History Standards

The historians and educators at UCLA's National Center for History in the Schools knew they had walked into the middle of the traditional/progressive debate when they launched their project to develop a set of national history standards. Seeking to avoid being labeled as part of either camp, the Center included both traditional and progressive groups in the standards-setting process. In 1994, after two years of work, the group had framed standards for teaching U.S. and world history from kindergarten to twelfth grade.

Historical Thinking and Historical Understanding Following tradition, the standards document outlined familiar goals for history in the schools and specified two types of standards:

> *Historical thinking skills* [our emphasis] that enable students to evaluate evidence, develop comparative and causal analyses, interpret the historical record, and construct sound historical arguments and perspectives on which informed decisions in contemporary life can be based.
>
> *Historical understandings* [our emphasis] that define what students should know about the history of their nation and of the world. These understandings are drawn from the record of human aspirations, strivings, accomplishments, and failures in at least five spheres of human activity: the social, political, scientific/technological, economic, and philosophical/religious/aesthetic. They also provide students the historical perspectives required to analyze contemporary issues and problems confronting citizens today.
>
> Historical thinking and understanding do not, of course, develop independently of one another. Higher levels of historical thinking depend upon and are linked to the attainment of higher levels of historical understanding. For these reasons, the standards . . . provide an integration of historical thinking and understanding.[56]

The Center's effort to forge a middle ground between traditional and progressive camps was futile.

"The End of History"—Conservatives Attack the Standards Two weeks before the public release of the standards, Lynne Cheney (the same Lynne Cheney who railed against the NCTM math standards), published a *Wall Street Journal* editorial, "The End of History." In it, she accused the National Center for History in the Schools of writing standards that promoted a left-wing political agenda. Among other things, she complained that Harriet Tubman was mentioned six times, while Ulysses S. Grant was named only once, and Robert E. Lee not at all—evidence, she argued, of a politically correct emphasis on women and minorities.[57] Rush Limbaugh, perhaps the nation's most popular conservative radio talk-show host, picked up the attack, saying the standards should be flushed "down the sewer of multiculturalism."

> When you bring [students] into a classroom, and you teach them that America is a rotten place, . . . and they don't have a chance here . . . you have a bunch of embittered people growing up, robbing and stealing and turning to crime because they've been told all their young lives that there's no future for them. . . . This country does not deserve the reputation it's getting in multicultural classrooms, and the zenith of this bastardization of American history has been reached with the new standards.[58]

Not all of the criticism came from such reactionary voices, but those with antigovernment, pro–free market, and fundamentalist religious ideologies generated much of the high-visibility criticism. Former Reagan White House policy adviser Gary Bauer declared:

> It is hard to overstate the magnitude of the failure. For the Department of Education, this embarrassing public fiasco is indisputable evidence of bureaucratic ineptitude. If we adopt these amnesiac history standards, we will succumb to a kind of national identity crisis. We will cease to remember who we are and why it matters that there is an America.
>
> [T]here is an anti-free enterprise bias to the history standards. Students are encouraged to put John D. Rockefeller on trial for his sharp business tactics. But where do the standards lead young Americans to an understanding of the most productive and free economic system in history? Nowhere.
>
> It goes without saying that the history standards' emphasis on race, gender, and class forces young Americans to accept a secular world view. The history standards panel clearly failed to comprehend the influence of religion in American life.[59]

What called forth such impassioned concern? Were the writers of the standards that ill-informed, that un-American, and that irreligious? Following is a brief sample of the kind of language in the standards that set off the critics. Indeed, not only does it encourage questioning, but questioning values:

> Value-laden issues worthy of classroom analysis include not only those irredeemable events in human history from which students can most easily draw clear ethical judgment—the Holocaust, for example, or the Cambodian genocide under the Pol Pot regime. These analyses should also address situations of lasting consequence in which what is morally right and wrong may not be self-evident. Was it right, for example, for Lincoln, in his Emancipation Proclamation, to free only those slaves behind the Confederate lines? Because of the complicated way values act upon people confronted with the need to decide, the full moral situation in a past event is not always immediately clear. Students should understand, therefore, that their opinions should be held tentative and open to revision as they acquire new insight into these historical problems. Particularly challenging are the many social issues throughout United States history on which multiple interests and different values have come to bear. Issues of civil rights or equal education opportunity, of the right of choice vs. the right to life, and of criminal justice have all brought such conflicts to the fore.[60]

Clobbered by the political backlash, the Center agreed to revise the standards and in 1996 issued a document that fared better with conservatives. The story of American history was cast in a more positive light, and many previously absent names were included.[61] The Center dropped the "teaching examples" and some of the more offensive language. Unlike the fate that met the English language arts standards, the revised history standards have retained their U.S. Department of Education sponsorship. Yet states' textbook publishers have shied away from using the controversial standards as a blueprint for standards and curriculum.[62] Those that have have been lambasted by traditionalists as extreme. The debate about what social studies and whose history should be taught will not likely be settled soon. The best hope, as always, lies with teachers who acquire the confidence and commitment that comes with training, experience, and scholarship. Teachers who want to press their students to think deeply and ask hard questions about the rhetoric and realities of social life may have to look elsewhere—besides standards and textbooks—for help. Used with care and thoughtful scholarship both by teachers and their students, the Internet can be a rich resource for escaping the chilling effects of curriculum and standards battles.

Science

Long-standing debates similar to those in the other subject matters confound curriculum decisions about science.

- Should the science curriculum focus on depth or breath of coverage of science topics?
- Should schools teach the traditional science disciplines—earth science, biology, chemistry, and physics—separately or integrated around themes or concepts?
- Should lessons connect science with related social issues?
- Should all students learn the same science, and can they learn it?

These questions relate directly to theories about knowledge and learning, they speak directly to social justice values, and responses line up roughly on the two sides of a traditional/progressive divide.

Progressive and constructivist views hold that science is a product of human understanding and subject to constant revision. Most contend that scientific "truth" lies on a continuum from pretty good hunches to long-enduring, seemingly unassailable (but always open to reinvestigation) facts. Progressives emphasize teachers' roles in helping students reconcile their naive ideas about phenomena with "scientific" conceptions and stress learning processes that replicate the unfolding of scientific discovery. This scientific *methodology*, progressives believe, is closer to the work of actual scientists than the highly over-rationalized schoolbook versions many have learned as *the scientific method*.

Traditionalists stress a more empirical view of science as an objective explanation of "the way things are," and they see teaching as transmitting this knowledge through explanation, demonstration, and practice. They prefer to approach each science discipline separately, with a systematic introduction and treatment of the major questions and findings. Many traditionalists, as well as some with more constructive views, favor a science "pipeline" that identifies scientific talent and interest early in school and accelerates some middle- and high school students into different, more-advanced study in preparation for science careers.

National Standards: Deep, Integrated, Socially Relevant Science for All

As happened in the other subjects, the extensive deliberations of the National Academy of Sciences (involving scientists, science educators, and policymakers) yielded a set of standards that leaned far more toward the progressive conception of science education than the traditional one. In part, this stance is not surprising, since previous groups including some of the nation's most prestigious science organizations had already offered similar reform standards. The National Science Foundation and the American Association for the Advancement of Science were already on record as endorsing progressive views.[63]

The *National Science Education Standards* place less emphasis on knowing scientific facts and more on understanding concepts and developing inquiry abilities. Those who developed the standards prefer science studies that probe deeply into fewer thematic and fundamental scientific ideas rather than skimming the surface of many topics. They favor integrating content that is often kept separate in courses such as biology, physical science, and chemistry, and they call for learning science in socially relevant contexts rather than as disciplines "for their own sake."[64] And, perhaps most important, they emphasize *inquiry,* or learning that is guided by asking increasingly refined scientific and social questions.

Joining Content and Process The national standards for science specify eight content categories that are necessary for a high-quality science program. Physical science, life science, earth and space science, and science and technology are four categories that sound familiar, and their adoption into school programs would not upset traditional views of teaching science. However, the remaining four categories—unifying concepts and processes, inquiry, societal challenges, and the history of science—would, indeed, turn science education on its head. These "new" conceptions of science content are provocative and exciting:

- The content of science cannot be placed outside of science's unifying concepts and processes.
- Participation in inquiry is scientific content, not just process.
- Scientific knowledge is not distinct from societal challenges.
- The history of science is science content that underscores science as a human and social enterprise.

Each of the standards specifies core skills and concepts. For example, upon entering high school, students will develop and enact the following abilities for scientific inquiry:

- Identify questions and concepts that guide scientific investigations.
- Design and conduct scientific investigations.
- Use technology and mathematics to improve investigations and communications.
- Formulate and revise scientific explanations and models using logic and evidence.
- Recognize and analyze alternative explanations and models.
- Communicate and defend a scientific argument.

In addition to these "abilities to do scientific inquiry," the standards also specify the *understandings* that students should develop. For example, students in grades 9–12 will understand how substances exist in or are represented by "three domains of thought—the macroscopic world of observable phenomena, the microscopic world of molecules, atoms, and subatomic particles, and the symbolic and mathematical world of chemical formulas, equations and symbols."[65]

Although many individuals in the business or political communities have voiced fears (unsubstantiated, to be sure) that a lack of scientific knowledge threatens national defense or global competitiveness, such warnings do not stir up citizens or embarrass them as easily as low rankings in reading or math skills. Perhaps this is because many Americans see science as less "basic" than reading or math. Perhaps because the country's "scientific literacy" is so limited, citizens feel less confident joining the debate. Then, too, the National Academy of Sciences's high credibility and political weight with conservative politicians may have contributed to the standards' milder reception.

Making Standards Real in the Classroom First-year teacher Jennie Lee captured the spirit of the standards as she taught her ninth-grade students a unit on plant structure.

My integrated, coordinated science class is centered on a "Survivor" theme. The students and I are stranded together on Santa Rosa Island—one of the larger channel islands off the coast of California. The first day of class I introduced the situation, showed them a map, and asked them what they wanted to learn. My students brainstormed topics that they wanted to study that would better equip us for survival on the island. They decided on three topics: water, food, and shelter. We decided that we needed to farm in order to sustain ourselves, and that to be efficient farmers we needed to be experts on plants. The students also wanted to study medicinal plants so that we could make medicine. Every lesson we did was tied to surviving on the island.

I wanted my students to be able to describe why humans and plants are dependent on each other, and what a plant needs in order to photosynthesize. Students should be able to trace the path of a water molecule from outside the plant to its transformation into glucose. The primary concept was that plants needed to use carbon dioxide, water, and energy in order to make glucose. My students should understand that on Santa Rosa Island, we provide the carbon dioxide and water, and the sun provides the energy. In order to understand the process of photosynthesis, my students needed to learn about the separate functions of roots, stems, and leaves. If we understood how plants work, then we would be good farmers on the island. My objectives matched the district standards.

On the first day of the unit, I asked my students to tell me what they knew about plants. I had them record their initial conceptions and prior knowledge. Before I did any experiment in class, I asked them to hypothesize about what would happen. Tapping into prior knowledge allowed me to incorporate their lives into the curriculum. It also revealed areas of weakness that needed more content instruction. My students were strong at identifying parts of a plant, but few had accurate ideas about the functions of those parts.

My goal for scientific literacy guided many of my activities. I wanted my students to acquire the academic language needed to talk about plant structures and their role in photosynthesis—terms including absorption, xylem, phloem, and glucose. The students learned by doing, and the content was learned as students used materials to test out hypotheses. The experiments forced students away from passive listening to active participation.

Because the students chose their own curriculum, it was relevant to their lives, and they were motivated to learn. Having an overarching theme of "survival" helped my students to understand scientific principles. Facts they learned were not discrete bodies of knowledge, but rather related principles that supported each other. There was always a purpose to learning. Having a theme also helped me to select science concept depth over breadth.

—Jennie Lee
First-year teacher, high school science

My insect unit introduces students to the life sequences of a number of insects. Darkling beetles, milkweed bugs, silk moths, and painted lady butterflies are a few of the organisms observed over time. Students observe and compare insect structures and behaviors in different stages of the life cycle. They discuss and record findings and pose questions to be resolved. Students experience complete and simple insect metamorphosis and are introduced to a sampling of the diversity in the animal kingdom. The center of the unit was keeping a record of various insects' life cycles. Students kept their own insect journals in which they recorded observations and conclusions.

I decided to teach the unit in the spring so students could follow up on their own over their summer vacation. Also, by spring, students could write a bit better.

Spring came as did the insects and the time to teach the unit. Although emergent writers in my classroom had developed their writing skills a great deal, it was not sufficient to express their findings. Unless I found a way to help them, they would feel less capable than the other students whose writing was stronger. I decided to write key words, concepts, vocabulary, and scientific names on the board for all students to use in their journal.

Throughout the unit, the students drew ladybugs, ants, caterpillars, and butterflies. As a final project, they created their own insects out of papier mâché. The only restriction was that the "invented insects" had to have the basic characteristics of real insects: two antennae, two eyes, six legs, three body parts, and wings if needed. Students worked in heterogeneous cooperative groups and built on one another's knowledge. Together in these groups students learned to take responsibility in caring for and respecting the insects, in creating and maintaining appropriate habitats, and in respecting one another as colearners/coexperts. The students not only developed science skills and concepts throughout the unit, they learned to respect life and accept death.

—Rosalinda Perez Silva
First-year teacher, grade 1

Is Less, More?

Many scientists and science educators assert that students learn more science by studying fewer topics *in* depth.[66] However, teachers also face enormous pressure to provide students a taste of many science topics, even if students can't stop long enough to get a confident understanding of science principles. A 1996 report, *A Splintered Vision: An Investigation of U.S. Mathematics and Science Education,* found that the average American ninth-grade science student covers nearly fifty-five topics. Most of the other fifty nations in the study offered far fewer topics while their students learned as much or more science.[67]

Sometimes lessons trivialize science. Science activities in the early grades often focus more on making something fun happen than on making scientific observations and judgments. For example, one teacher we know likes to save science activities for Friday afternoons. He has a bag of science tricks that keep children entertained at the end of the long week. One afternoon, for example, he had the children make "soda pop" in the classroom. The children loved it, but they learned little science. The teacher asked few questions and provoked little discussion of what had happened. We suspect the children saw the fizzy drink as something produced by magic without understanding what happened or why.

Secondary school science gets trivialized in other ways. For example, nearly all students learn the steps of the scientific method. Yet few have a chance to apply principles of scientific inquiry to real situations. Students doing "experiments" in class often follow prescribed routines and try to reproduce expected results. Their task is clear: Get the results the teacher or lab manual is looking for. This cookbook approach to science bears little resemblance to the process scientists actually use. Students' dexterity in handling equipment, their reading skills, and their speed often count more than their understanding. Often, girls' contributions are diminished or discounted, because students typically are socialized to treat science, especially when working with equipment, as a male domain. Thus, girls may defer to boys' more "authoritative," or aggressive behavior, and boys may miss the relevance of careful reflection to laboratory science.

Going Deep The following examples contrast the traditional with a more progressive approach. In traditional science programs, students study some botany during their school years—whether as a course in its own right, a unit in a biology class, or part of general science. The traditional science course follows an outline that incorporates the textbook's and teacher's complete command of the domain. This outline—topics, subtopics, and facts—makes wonderful sense to those who already understand the whole subject—biology. They can look at the textbook, the topics, the facts, and the course activities and see immediately how each piece fits—how each is important. But this approach asks students to make a giant leap of faith—"trust us and remember all this information; it will make sense to you some day." Thus, most students define and memorize terms (e.g., photosynthesis, osmosis, deciduous) and memorize important principles in their briefest form (e.g., plants are green because they contain chlorophyll, plants produce oxygen). Lessons are short term, often lasting as little as one class period, and the class moves on regardless of whether the students understand it. The teacher typically has overarching concepts in mind, but students hardly notice connections among lessons. This cycle repeats throughout the year until the teacher has covered all the objectives.

Contrast this with a semester-long or yearlong assignment in which students observe and make sense of the processes by which plants grow. An actual garden that provides students a place to cultivate and observe a variety of plants anchors this lesson. Each student participates in hands-on work (e.g., altering light, water, nutrients, and other growing conditions) and works with others while observing, recording, and forming and testing hypotheses. Each shares prior experiences and offers growth predictions based on articulated reasons. Many different experiments occur simultaneously, and students follow the progress of those that relate to their own hypotheses.

In such a lesson, the teacher also may ask the students to write creatively; to listen to music; and to draw, read, and talk about themes having to do with plant growth and the science of plants. When students ask what such activities—typically found in English, art, and music classes—have to do with science, the teacher encourages the vigorous class discussion that follows.

Students also investigate real-life consequences of plant growth for farmers, the public, the environment, businesses, and government. Each student considers the careers and lifestyles of those whose work centers on plants: farmworkers, growers, wholesalers, retailers, experimental botanists, chemists, conservationists, rangers, teachers, florists, and so on. Each student presents a formal oral report of his or her observations and work and participates in a group effort to present conclusions. The teacher holds all students accountable for core concepts that they can reasonably master (photosynthesis, osmosis, the nature of cells, plant reproduction, etc.) and for the concepts and foundations of their independent research.

What About Coverage? So what's the controversy? It is hard to imagine that anyone could prefer the first lesson to the second. In fact, other than critics who would seize on the writing and music as proof of "fuzzy" science, few would object. But the press to rush through large numbers of topics presented in disconnected lessons happens in subtle ways. Textbook publishers compete for the approval of teachers and school boards who, because of local control and individual experiences and histories, may have science programs that emphasize quite different topics and skills. Therefore, the books must include all the familiar topics, as well as the newest ones. To avoid making the texts even larger and more expensive than they already are, no topic receives treatment in depth. Such texts encourage superficial coverage, especially if teachers' own science knowledge limits their ability to extend lessons beyond what the text provides.

Should the Sciences Be Integrated and Taught in a Social Context?

Progressive science educators argue strongly that the old distinctions among the science disciplines should no longer drive the curriculum. Paul DeHart Hurd, perhaps the dean of American science education, argues that the move toward integrating the science curriculum reflects important changes in science:

> Disciplines have been replaced by research fields, and most research is done by teams of investigators. A team represents a cognitive system that is phasing out the traditional notion of scientific inquiry. Much of scientific research is strategy or problem oriented rather than theory stimulated. For example, the Hubble telescope has made a wealth of observations, and it may take scientists a century or more to find theoretical explanations for them. A blending of science disciplines is taking place, such as biophysics, biochemistry, and biogeochemistry. The most active areas of research today are cross-disciplinary.
>
> . . . Changes in the practice and culture of today's science go unnoticed. Professional science educators, as well as most scientists, pay little attention to what these revolutionary transformations in science ought to mean for a citizen's education in the sciences.[68]

In the past decade or so, many secondary schools have integrated their science curriculum—converting the traditional "layer cake" of separate physical science, biology, chemistry, and physics courses into a sequence of integrated classes organized around themes.

The *National Science Education Standards* press for integration across disciplines. Although they don't completely blur the distinctions among physical science, life science, and earth and space sciences, the standards do emphasize the following crosscutting themes—what the document calls unifying concepts and processes:

- Systems, order, and organization
- Evidence, models, and explanation
- Constancy, change, and measurement
- Evolution and equilibrium
- Form and function

These crosscutting ideas "provide students with productive ways of thinking about and integrating a range of basic ideas that explain the natural and designed world."[69]

However, just as in mathematics, traditionalists view efforts to integrate the sciences and to place them in a social context as disturbing signs of curricular softness. They fear that such moves both erode the rigor of students' academic studies and undermine the structure of the knowledge that has developed through scientific discovery.

Debating Darwin

Perhaps the most enduring controversy in curriculum has been over the science of evolution. Almost seventy-five years after biology teacher John Scopes was arrested for teaching evolution in violation of Tennessee law, the state board of education in Kansas voted in 1999 to remove evolution from the state's science standards. Although the board did not ban the teaching of evolution outright, it did eliminate evolution from the topics on which Kansas students would be tested. One argument made by the conservative board majority was that evolution is not a proper science topic. Science, they argued, is the investigation of the natural world, whereas evolution examines mankind's origins—a supernatural topic that falls under the purview of the supernatural. One board member said, "I don't want my children's biology teacher talking about religion."[70] On the other hand, Kansas governor Bill Graves called the board's decision an "embarrassment," and most school districts ignored it. In 1925, at the end of his famous "monkey trial," Scopes had to pay only a small fine for breaking the law, and the state supreme court instructed prosecutors not to bring charges against anyone else under its anti-evolution law. In November 2000 Kansas voted in new board members who promised to restore evolution to the state's standards, and in February 2001 the new board reversed the anti-evolution decision of 1999. However, the Kansas controversy was just the most-noticed clash in the creationism versus evolution conflict in science. Following Kansas's lead, Nebraska eliminated evolution from its state science guidelines, and Alabama required that science textbooks note that the theory of evolution is "unproven." In other skirmishes, New Mexico banned the teaching of creationism (after voting to allow it four years earlier), and Louisiana upheld teachers' rights to not read a disclaimer that evolution is an "unproven" theory.

Who Can Do Science?

For what grade is the long-term botany lesson described earlier appropriate? What should be the ability level of the students? Must students speak English in order to learn and contribute to their student groups? Nothing about age, skills, or language fluency need prevent students from working and making sense together. In fact, in a lesson with such a diverse set of tasks, diversity among students enriches the learning opportunities.

The *National Science Education Standards* authors' make clear their position about who can do science:

> The intent of the *Standards* can be expressed in a single phrase: Science standards for all students. The phrase embodies both excellence and equity. The *Standards* apply to all students, regardless of age, gender, cultural or ethnic background, disabilities, aspirations, or interest and motivation in science. Different students will achieve understanding in different ways, and different

> students will achieve different degrees of depth and breadth of understanding depending on interest, ability, and context. But all students can develop the knowledge and skills described in the *Standards*, even as some students go well beyond these levels.[71]

Similar statements appear in the reform documents of the National Science Foundation, the National Academy of Sciences, and the American Association for the Advancement of Science.

When controversy began to brew over California's science standards, the nuclear physicist who was leading the standards-writing group expressed the view that a major problem in science education is that too many students—particularly low-income and minority students—give up and never become scientifically literate.[72] He said that California's standards must change a curriculum that currently leaves behind "all these kids who don't get it."[73] And yet, in the midst of widespread agreement among scientists and science educators, skepticism about "who can do science" prevented a strong unified effort to reform science education. In 1997 three Nobel laureates, led by Glen Seaborg, protested California's plan to model its science standards on the national standards.[74] They charged that the progressives writing the California document were bent on "dumbing down" science to make science appealing to students. The laureates claimed that the standards expressed a philosophy of science education that would compromise rigor and undercut learning about great, though difficult to understand, scientific discoveries. One charged, "Educational content is continually diluted in a failed effort to produce palatable bits of information for progressively less skilled students. It is essential that we take a stand and insist on educational standards with greater content."[75] These traditional critics appeared to be judging the quality of the curriculum based on who they expected to master it. At the end of a rancorous process, Seaborg and his group were successful in securing a set of standards far closer to traditional science curriculum than what the national standards had sought to inspire.

Will Anybody Do Science?

The most serious problem with science may be that schools teach so little of it. For example, a 1987 National Center for Educational Statistics survey found that children in elementary school averaged only two and a half hours a week learning science.[76] More recent evidence suggests that little has changed, despite concern about our nation's increasing need for scientific workers.[77] Part of the problem is that many elementary teachers have little more scientific knowledge than the general public, and they feel uncomfortable teaching science. The same may be true of those who teach older students, many of whom are not science majors or not credentialed to teach science. Because basic reading and math dominate the movement for contemporary elementary school "accountability," science rarely shows up on basic skills tests and teachers may be less motivated to teach it. Many middle-school students can take science for only one semester, and many senior highs require only one science class for those not planning to attend college.

Journal Entry:

An area not much larger than a classroom is gated off from the rest of the schoolyard. An older woman proudly walks our group over to the metal fence to peer through the seemingly well-placed holes. I convince myself that I see some kind of brownish-greenish plant growing out of a wooden box that sits flush to the asphalt, but I cannot be sure. To the right of the box, a few potted plants appear to be flourishing, but it is awfully difficult to determine from behind the metal barrier. We are then encouraged to look at the roosters as they aimlessly roam through the area, in the hopes that they will perform for us on cue; but unfortunately, it appears as if they are saving their vocal cords for the next sunrise. I continue to gaze through the fence, not quite sure of what I am looking at or why I am looking at it, and I wonder if the children are as bewildered as I. The woman informs us that the special education teacher and her students are the main force behind the development and maintenance of the garden. She beams with pride as she shares this information. Before I can process and truly reflect upon and understand the episode, we are whisked off into our individual classrooms. I am given a chair next to the sink on the far side of the room. I complete the requisite once-over of the bulletin boards, checking for student work and any indications of subject-specific centers. I do not observe a science center, nor are there any science textbooks on the bookshelves. Although the sink next to me functions and is equipped with a metal workspace, it is clear that it is not used for science activities. It is covered with dust and dried paint splatters that are beginning to peel and flake with age. To the right of the sink, an outdated Macintosh computer sits, unplugged.

Upon reflection, I have conflicting thoughts and feelings about science education. The metaphor of the gated garden can represent the visions of science that I observed, and that students are presented with daily. The gate represents access, the wilting plant the students. The few blossoming potted plants represent hope. This image of the gated garden has remained with me throughout my first year. It is my responsibility, passion, and goal to equip students with the keys to unlock the gates of science knowledge, and to show them how they are capable of creating such keys themselves.

—Janene E. Ashford
First-year teacher, grade 6

Often, even science teachers who are skilled cannot develop their science programs because they have little time and few resources or well-equipped labs. Thus, they, along with less-skilled teachers, often resort to science shortcuts. They may simply *tell* students about science rather than let them *do* science. When this happens, science often boils down to memorizing names and facts. Given these conditions, the authors of the *National Science Education Standards* went beyond what the standards for other subject matters proposed, by creating standards for the entire science education system. In addition to content standards, the document includes standards for what teachers should know and be able to do, for professional development activities for teachers, for judging the quality of science assessments, for judging the conditions of school science programs (including resources and learning opportunities), and for judging policies related to science education. With this comprehensive set of standards, the science community highlighted crucial needs that apply to all the subject matters. In science, as in all of the disciplines, the content of the curriculum must be considered in light of who teaches the subject, how they teach and assess it, and what conditions prevail for students to learn.

The Struggle for the Subject Matter

Professional responsibility obliges teachers to be articulate participants in *both* the public and professional arenas of curriculum inquiry and debate. Sheridan Blau, president of the National Council of Teachers of English, cautions and advises:

> Our profession as seen from inside teachers' lounges and in the conversations of professionals and in the presentations and workshops at conferences . . . is not a bloody battleground of competing ideas, but it has been made to appear so by a press hungry for dramatic stories and by impatient policy makers and a frustrated public looking for the same kind of simple answers that popular opinion often demands—answers that offer scapegoats and saviors. . . . The true ideological battleground for our profession, then, is not in the field where teacher-educators and teachers debate about the most effective teaching strategies nor in the labs and research sites where scholars offer different theoretical perspectives, different methodological procedures, and competing findings. Disagreements in these arenas can and do lead to dialogue and thereby to the advancement of learning.[78]

Dialogue and advancement of learning in the subjects—in the classroom and out: This is the work of teachers.

Digging Deeper

The authors and organizations in this section provide rich detail on the issues described in this chapter, and many also provide specific guidance about translating curriculum reforms into practice. Each can provide an introduction to the wealth of resources available in each of the school subject areas.

Lucy Calkins, an education professor at Teachers College, Columbia University, is founding director of the Teachers College Writing Project, a coalition of teachers, teacher-administrators, professors, and writers, which provides professional sustenance and hope—roots and wings—to literacy educators across the country. Her publications include *Lessons from a Child* (Portsmouth, NH: Heinemann, 1983), *Living Between the Lines* (with Shelley Harwayne, Portsmouth, NH: Heinemann, 1990), and *The Art of Teaching Writing* (Portsmouth, NH: Heinemann, 1986, 1994). Calkins is widely respected for her ideas on how to teach children to read and write. A whole language advocate who also attends to fundamentals such as spelling, she has inspired a generation of teachers to help the youngest children become confident writers.

Facing History and Ourselves is a nonprofit organization that offers an innovative, interdisciplinary approach to teaching citizenship. It connects history to the day-to-day experiences of students by revealing the way violence and hate can destroy a society, and how the decisions of ordinary people shape an age and ultimately history. Facing History's resource center has a lending library of relevant books, periodicals, and videos. Resource books include *Facing History and Ourselves: Holocaust and Human Behavior, Elements of Time,* and seven study guides. The Facing History and Ourselves National Foundation is located at 16 Hurd Road, Brookline, MA 02146. The project can be reached by telephone at (617) 232-1595 or on the Internet at www.facing.org.

In their review of the research on mathematics learning, "Teaching and Learning with Understanding" in the *Handbook of Research on Mathematics Education* (New York: Macmillan, 1992), **James Hiebert** of the University of Delaware and **Thomas Carpenter** of the University of Wisconsin provide a comprehensive explanation of how students develop mathematical understanding, how conventional approaches to mathematics in school inhibit understanding, and how more progressive approaches can foster it. Hiebert and Carpenter review cognitive science and sociocultural learning theories applied to mathematics learning as well as studies of mathematics teaching.

Paul DeHart Hurd is professor emeritus of science education at Stanford University. Throughout his career, Hurd has argued that science does not and cannot proceed outside of the societal context. His most recent book, *Inventing Science Education for the New Millennium* (New York: Teachers College Press, 1997), elaborates on his claim that the first step to inventing new science curricula is the linking of science and technology to the welfare of students and to the economic and social progress of the nation. Such a curriculum, according to Hurd, is one that can be experienced by students; it is a body of subject matter that students recognize they can use; and it is in harmony with the findings of the cognitive sciences for improving learning.

The **International Reading Association** (www.reading.org) includes classroom teachers, reading specialists, consultants, administrators, supervisors, college teachers, researchers, psychologists, librarians, media specialists, students, and parents. Association journals include *The Reading Teacher,* directed toward preschool, primary, and elementary school educators, and the *Journal of Adolescent & Adult Literacy,* directed toward middle school, secondary, college, and adult educators.

Judith Langer, professor of education at the State University of New York at Albany, is the director of the National Research Center on English Learning and Achievement. Langer focuses on how people become highly literate, how they learn through reading and writing, and what this means for future instruction. Her work helps teachers understand how context and culture interact to affect thinking and learning. Langer's books for teachers include *Envisioning Literature: Literary Understanding and Literature Instruction* (New York: Teachers

College Press, 1996) and *Literature Instruction: A Focus on Student Response* (Champaign, IL: National Council of Teachers of English, 1992).

Lawrence Hall of Science at the University of California-Berkeley offers an exciting collection of hands-on science and math activities and materials, for preschool through high school, that emphasize the "learning-by-doing" approach pioneered at the Hall. One project, EQUALS, strives to increase access and equity in mathematics for students in traditionally underrepresented gender, race, class, and cultural groups. FAMILY MATH encourages underrepresented groups (especially girls and minority students) to pursue mathematics by engaging their families in mathematics activities. FOSS is an elementary-school science program with twenty-seven modules that incorporate hands-on inquiry and interdisciplinary projects, building on recent advances in the understanding of how youngsters think and learn. The Lawrence Hall of Science Internet site address is www.lhs.berkeley.edu.

The **National Center for History in the Schools,** housed at UCLA's Department of History, publishes the national standards for U.S. history, world history, and K–4 history. It also has available *Bring History Alive!*—two sourcebooks that offer teachers ideas for bringing history alive in the schools. The teaching examples are arranged by grade level and are keyed to the revised national history standards. The leaders of the Center, **Gary Nash, Charlotte Crabtree,** and **Ross E. Dunn,** have written a fascinating account of the political battles over the history standards in *History on Trial: Culture Wars and the Teaching of the Past* (New York: Knopf, 1997). The Center can be found on the Internet at www.sscnet.ucla.edu/nchs.

The **National Council for the Social Studies** serves as an umbrella organization for elementary, secondary, and college teachers of history, geography, economics, political science, sociology, psychology, anthropology, and law-related education. The group developed *Expectations of Excellence: Curriculum Standards for Social Studies* (Washington, DC: National Council for the Social Studies, 1994), which defines and presents each of ten thematic strands and correlated performance expectations for three distinct levels: early grades, middle grades, and high schools. Included is a special supplement on powerful teaching and learning. The Council can be found on the Internet at www.ncss.org.

The **National Council of Teachers of English** (www.ncte.org) provides a forum for the profession, an array of opportunities for teachers to continue their professional growth throughout their careers, and a framework for cooperation to deal with issues that affect the teaching of English. NCTE publishes three monthly journals: *Language Arts, English Journal,* and *College English.* It also publishes position papers, teaching ideas, and other documents on professional concerns such as standards.

For more than seventy-five years, the **National Council of Teachers of Mathematics** (www.nctm.org), the largest nonprofit professional association of mathematics educators in the world, has been dedicated to improving the teaching and learning of mathematics. NCTM provides professional development opportunities through annual, regional, and leadership conferences and publishes journals, books, videos, and software.

The **National Geography Standards,** *Geography for Life,* are available from the National Council for Geographic Education at the Indiana University of Pennsylvania or at www.oneonta.edu/~baumanpr/ncge/rstf.htm.

The **National Science Teachers Association** (www.nsta.org) offers curricular resources based on *A Framework for High School Science Education,* an NSTA publication. The microunits, composed of labs, readings, and assessments for teachers and students, form a complete curriculum that was developed and tested to meet the national science education standards. The NSTA-initiated project—*Scope, Sequence, and Coordination of High School Sciences* (SS&C)—is a major curriculum project, funded by the National Science Foundation and coordinated with the *National Science Education Standards.*

The **National Writing Project,** which brings teachers together in summer and school-year programs around the country, is led by classroom teachers who have been trained by the writing project to talk with one another about teaching. Close to 1,250,000 teachers have participated in the Writing Project's teachers-teaching-teachers programs since 1974. The National Writing Project is housed at the University of California-Berkeley in 5511 Tolman Hall, #1670, Berkeley, CA 94720-1670 and can be reached by phone at (510) 642-0963 or on the Internet at www-gse.berkeley.edu/Research/NWP/nwp.html.

Project 2061 (project2061.aaas.org) of the American Association for the Advancement of Science has developed books, CD-ROMs, and online tools to help teachers work toward science literacy for all high school graduates. Project 2061, which began as Halley's comet was flying by in 1985, aims to make everyone science literate by the time the comet returns in 2061. The 1989 publication *Science for All Americans* outlines what all high school graduates should know and be able to do in science, math, and technology and lays out some principles for effective learning and teaching.

Reading Recovery is a widely used program developed by New Zealand psychologist **Marie Clay** in the 1970s. The approach in this program is to intervene early and provide intensive literacy experiences for students who appear to be at risk for failing to learn to read in the first grade. The individualized approach infuses direct skill teaching into sessions where children read real books, write, and play with letters to form words. Marie Clay's book *Reading Recovery: A Guidebook for Teachers in Training* (Portsmouth, NH: Heinemann, 1993) offers practical suggestions for teaching problem solving while reading, teaching writing, vocabulary, and even phonemic awareness.

Linda Symcox, historian and teacher educator at California State University at Long Beach, has written a compelling history of the controversy surrounding the National History Standards. The book, *History Under Fire,* provides both an insider's view and a fascinating cultural analysis of how the school curriculum is highly political.

Deborah Schifter, senior scientist with the Education Development Center in Newton, Massachusetts, has written helpful accounts of teachers who use constructivist approaches to mathematics. Her books *Reconstructing Mathematics Education: Stories of Teachers Meeting the Challenge of Reform* (with Catherine Twomey Fosnot, New York: Teachers College Press, 1993) and *What's Happening* *in Math Class?* (New York: Teachers College Press, 1996) provide narratives from elementary teachers who are shifting their mathematics curriculum away from traditional lessons and focusing more on understanding children's mathematical thinking.

Notes

1. Lynne V. Cheney, "The Latest Education Disaster: Whole Math," *Weekly Standard,* 4 August 1997.
2. Curtis C. McKnight, F. Joe Crosswhite, and John A. Dossey, *The Underachieving Curriculum: Assessing U.S. School Mathematics from an International Perspective* (Indianapolis: Stipes, 1987).
3. For example, K. M. Cauley's study, "Construction of Local Knowledge: Study of Borrowing in Subtraction," in the *Journal of Educational Psychology* 80 (1988), pp. 202–205, found that third graders lacking conceptual knowledge of the multidigit subtraction procedure were more likely to make performance errors, such as subtracting the top smaller digit from the bottom larger digit.
4. Richard Shavelson, "The Splintered Curriculum," *Education Week,* 7 May 1997, p. 38. Shavelson places some of the blame on textbook publishers who "produce textbooks that are a mile wide and an inch deep" to promote sales across the diverse U.S. market and some on standardized tests that cover a wide range of material. Shavelson's essay draws on material in William Schmidt, Curtis C. McKnight, and Senta Raizen, *A Splintered Vision: An Investigation of U.S. Science and Mathematics Education* (Dordrecht: Kluwer Academic, 1997).
5. McKnight, Crosswhite, and Dossey, *The Underachieving Curriculum.* For a comparable, more recent international comparison and analysis, see the report from the Third International Mathematics and Science Study, William Schmidt, *Facing the Consequences: Using TIMSS for a Closer Look at U.S. Mathematics and Science Education* (Dordrecht: Kluwer Academic, in press).
6. National Council of Teachers of Mathematics, *Curriculum and Evaluation Standards for School Mathematics* (Reston, VA: Author, 1989), p. 7.
7. "Mathematics Content Standards for Grades K–12," Submitted by Bill Evers, Commissioner to California State Academic Standards Commission, September 15, 1997; on the Internet at http://www.rahul.net/dehnbase/hold/platinum-standards/altintro.html.
8. Ibid.
9. National Research Council, *Everybody Counts: A Report to the Nation on the Future of Mathematics Education* (Washington, DC: National Academy Press, 1989), p. 34. The National Research Council is a group established in 1916 by the prestigious National Academy of Sciences, whose own mission is furthering knowledge and advising the federal government.
10. National Research Council, *Everybody Counts,* p. 43.
11. Ibid., p. 60.

12. National Council of Teachers of Mathematics, *Curriculum and Evaluation Standards for School Mathematics*, p. 7.
13. Ibid. pp. 44–45.
14. Ibid., p. 59
15. James Stigler and James Hiebert, "Cameras in the Classroom: International Video Survey Examines Mathematics Teaching Practices in Three Countries," Connections (UCLA Graduate School of Education, Spring 1977), pp. 1–5; also included on the Internet Web page of the Third International Mathematics and Science Study at http://www.ed.gov/NCES/timss/video.
16. James Hiebert and Thomas Carpenter "Teaching and Learning with Understanding," in *Handbook of Research on Mathematics Teaching and Learning*, ed. Douglas A. Grouws (New York: Macmillan, 1992), pp. 65–97.
17. National Research Council, *Everybody Counts*, p. 60.
18. Richard Lee Colvin, "State Endorses Back-to-Basics Math Standards," *Los Angeles Times*, 30 November 1997, pp. 1, 18, 19, 26.
19. Ibid.
20. Luther S. Williams, letter to the California State Board of Education, 11 December 1997.
21. California Mathematics State Standards—Grade Seven. California Department of Education, 2000.
22. Glenda Lappan, as cited in "Revised Mathematics Standards Provide More Guidance," *Education Week*, April 19, 2000; on the Internet at http://www.edweek.org.
23. *Webster's Encyclopedic Unabridged Dictionary of the English Language* (New York: Gramercy Books, 1989), p. 1195.
24. Courtney Cazden, *Classroom Discourse* (Portsmouth, NH: Heinemann, 1988); Shirley Brice Heath, Ways with Words (New York: Cambridge University Press, 1983).
25. P. David Pearson, "Reclaiming the Center: The Search for Common Ground in Teaching Reading"; on the Internet at http://ed-web3.educ.msu.edu.cdpds/pdpaper.rtc21197.htm.
26. Ibid.
27. Ibid.
28. Luis Moll, "Funds of Knowledge for Teaching: Using a Qualitative Approach to Connect Homes and Classrooms," *Theory into Practice* 31, no. 2 (1992), pp. 132–141.
29. International Reading Association and National Council of Teachers of English, *Standards for the English Language Arts* (Champaign, IL: Author, 1996), p. 75.
30. Karen Diegmueller, "English Group Loses Funding for Standards," *Education Week*, 30 March 1994; Miles Myers, "Where the Debate About English Standards Goes Wrong," *Education Week*, 15 May 1995.
31. Ibid., p. 25.
32. J. Martin Rosser, "The Decline of Literacy," *Education Week*, 15 May 1996.
33. Ibid.

34. As quoted in Karen Diegmueller, "The Best of Both Worlds," *Teacher Magazine,* March 1996.
35. Karen Diegmueller, "War of Words," *Education Week,* 20 March 1996.
36. Ibid.
37. Ladson-Billings's and Delpit's work are discussed in more detail in Chapter 4.
38. National Academy Press. *Preventing Reading Difficulties in Young Children* (Washington: The National Research Council, 1998).
39. Judith Langer, as quoted in Deborah Viadero, "Researchers Flag Six Elements of Good Secondary English Instruction," *Education Week,* 14 June 2000; on the Internet at http://www.edweek.org.
40. P. David Pearson, "The Politics of Reading Research and Practice," a presentation at a conference in Houston, Texas, May 15, 1997; on the Internet at http://ed-web3.educ.msu.edu.cdpds/pdpaper. politics.html.
41. Annie Gowen, "Maryland Schools Remove 2 Black-Authored Books," *Los Angeles Times,* 11 January 1998, p. A6.
42. See, for example, "Multicultural Book List Proposed in San Francisco," *New York Times,* 11 March 1998, and "S.F. Board OKs Reading of Works by Nonwhites," *Los Angeles Times,* 21 March 1998, p. 1.
43. More discussion of Freire and McLaren can be found in Chapters 4 and 7.
44. Gary B. Nash, Charlotte Crabtree, and Ross E. Dunn, *History on Trial: Culture Wars and the Teaching of the Past* (New York: Knopf, 1997).
45. Ibid., p. xi.
46. Charlotte Crabtree, "A Common Curriculum for the Social Studies," in *Individual Differences and the Common Curriculum,* ed. Gary D. Fenstermacher and John I. Goodlad (Chicago: University of Chicago Press, 1983), pp. 248–281.
47. As quoted in Ron Brandt, "On the High School Curriculum: A Conversation with Ernest Boyer," *Educational Leadership* 46, no. 1 (September 1988), pp. 4–9.
48. Ibid.
49. Hugh Mehan, Dina Okamoto, Angela Lintz, and John S. Wills, "Ethnographic Studies of Multicultural Schools and Classrooms," in *Handbook of Research on Multicultural Education,* ed. James A. Banks and Cherry A. McGee Banks (New York: Macmillan, 1995).
50. John S. Wills, "The Situation of African Americans in American History: Using History as a Resource for Understanding the Experiences of Contemporary African Americans" as quoted in Hugh Mehan, Dina Okamoto, Angela Lintz, and John S. Wills, "Ethnographic Studies of Multicultural Schools and Classrooms," in *Handbook of Research on Multicultural Education.*
51. Crabtree, "A Common Curriculum for the Social Studies," p. 250.
52. California State Department of Education, *California: A History* (Sacramento: Author, 1965), quoted in "Tragic Side of Mission Era Being Told," *Los Angeles Times,* 2 September 1997.
53. California State Department of Education, *California's Own History* (Sacramento: Author, 1965).

54. *Oh, California* (New York: Houghton Mifflin Co., 1991) as cited in "Tragic Side of Mission Era Being Told," *Los Angeles Times*, 2 September 1997.
55. Gary Nash, as quoted in "Tragic Side of Mission Era Being Told," *Los Angeles Times*, 2 September 1997.
56. National Center for History in the Schools, *National Standards for United States History* (Los Angeles: UCLA National Center for History in the Schools, 1994).
57. Lynne Cheney, "The End of History," *Wall Street Journal*, 20 October 1994, p. A26.
58. Rush Limbaugh, as cited in Nash, Crabtree, and Dunn, *History on Trial*, p. 5.
59. Gary L. Bauer, "National History Standards: Clintonites Miss the Moon," Washington, DC, Family Research Council, 1995; on the Internet at http://www. frc.org.
60. National Center for History in the Schools, *National Standards for United States History*.
61. The United States is not the only society that struggles to protect a spotless version of its history. Perhaps we can have a higher regard for teaching new insights into our own past, when we see the dissembling (happily, corrected in this case) of another country. The following appeared in "Japan's High Court Rules Against Rewriting History," *Los Angeles Times*, 30 August 1997: "[The Japanese Court] ruled that the Education Ministry acted wrongly in ordering a textbook writer to delete accurate descriptions of Japanese atrocities during World War II, including a mention of the notorious Unit 731 that conducted gruesome medical experiments on human guinea pigs . . . and quoted one of Japan's most famous novelists, Ryotaro Shiba: "A country whose textbooks lie . . . will inevitably collapse."
62. Kathleen Kennedy Manzo, "Glimmer of History Standards Shows Up in Latest Textbooks," *Education Week*, 8 October 1997.
63. The AAAS considers science literacy as (1) being familiar with the natural world and recognizing both its diversity and its unity, (2) understanding key concepts and principles of science, (3) being aware of some of the important ways in which science, mathematics, and technology depend on one another, (4) knowing that science, mathematics, and technology are human enterprises and knowing what that implies about their strengths and limitations, (5) having a capacity for scientific ways of thinking, and (6) using scientific knowledge and ways of thinking for individual and social purposes. See AAAS, *Science for All Americans* (Washington, DC: Author, 1989).
64. National Research Council, *National Science Education Standards* (Washington, DC: National Academy Press, 1996), p. 113.
65. Ibid., p. 177.
66. A similar position is taken by the AAAS's reform 2061. Its "recommendations cover a broad array of topics. Many of these topics are already common in school curricula (e.g., the structure of matter, the basic functions of cells, prevention of disease, communications technology, and different uses of numbers). However, the treatment of such topics tends to differ

from the traditional in two ways. One difference is that boundaries between traditional subject-matter categories are softened and connections are emphasized. Transformations of energy, for example, occur in physical, biological, and technological systems, and evolutionary change appears in stars, organisms, and societies. A second difference is that the amount of detail that students are expected to retain is considerably less than in traditional science, mathematics, and technology courses. Ideas and thinking skills are emphasized at the expense of specialized vocabulary and memorized procedures. The sets of ideas that are chosen not only make some satisfying sense at a simple level but also provide a lasting foundation for learning more. Details are treated as a means of enhancing, not guaranteeing, students' understanding of a general idea. For example, that basic science literacy implies knowing that the chief function of living cells is assembling protein molecules according to instructions coded in DNA molecules, but that it does not imply knowing such terms as 'ribosome' or 'deoxyribonucleic acid.'" See AAAS, *Science for All Americans* (Washington, DC: Author, 1989).

67. William Schmidt, Curtis McKnight, and Senta Raizen, *A Splintered Vision: An Investigation of U.S. Mathematics and Science Education* (Boston: Kluwer Academic, 1997).
68. Paul DeHart Hurd, "Science Needs a 'Lived' Curriculum," *Education Week*, 12 November 1997, p. 48.
69. National Research Council, *National Science Education Standards*, p. 115.
70. Janet Waugh, as quoted in "Kansas Restores Evolution Standards for Science Classes," CNN.com/U.S., February 14, 2001; on the Internet at http://www.cnn.com/2001/02/14/Kansas.evolution.02/.
71. National Research Council, *National Science Education Standards*, p. 2.
72. Roland Otto, as quoted in Richard Lee Colvin, "Spurned Nobelists Appeal Science Standards Rejection," *Los Angeles Times*, 17 November 1997, p. A25.
73. Ibid.
74. The group, composed of Glen Seaborg, Dudley R. Herschbach, and Henry Taube, filed a formal appeal to the state Commission for the Establishment of Academic Standards in November 1997. See, Richard Lee Colvin, "Spurned Nobelists Appeal Science Standards Rejection," *Los Angeles Times*, 17 November 1997, p. A25.
75. Colvin, "Spurned Nobelists Appeal Science Standards Rejection," p. A25.
76. National Center for Education Statistics, *Time Spent Teaching Core Academic Subjects in Elementary Schools* (Washington, DC: U.S. Department of Education, 1997).
77. Ibid.
78. Sheridan Blau, "Toward the Separation of School and State," Inaugural address, 1997 NCTE Convention, Detroit, MI, November 20–25, 1997.

CHAPTER 6

Instruction and Assessment:

Classrooms as Learning Communities

Christina Haug

First-year teacher, grade 2

If you were a city schoolteacher in the early 1800s, you would likely sit on a raised platform at the front of a cavernous room designed for 450 students of various ages. Below your desk are three rows of monitors' desks, and, behind them, rows and rows of students in assigned seats. You direct the monitors who, in turn, instruct and hear recitations from platoons of students who march forward, slates in hand, to the monitors' desks. In precise sequences, students march, listen and recite—all under your watchful eye. You "motivate" with awards and punishment, including administering the rod, to keep your charges orderly and industrious. Your lessons focus on basic skills—for example, arithmetic, reading, spelling, and penmanship—but your primary interest is not students' intellectual development. Your work is part of the city's effort to keep the poor from evil influences, inculcate in them habits of good moral conduct, and ameliorate the problems they would otherwise cause by disease, clinging to foreign or rural habits, and so on. You were hired for being "of pure tastes, of good manners, of exemplary morals,"[1] and you see yourself as a model student

A century later, as a teacher in an early 1900s urban public school, you would be following new "scientific" and efficient school reforms. Pupils are divided by age into grades and by ability into classes, and you have forty to fifty of them sitting in rows of desks bolted to the floor. Since you have been to a normal school for your teacher preparation, you know some theory (e.g., that the mind needs exercising as if it were a muscle) and pedagogical skills (drill and recitation) to guide your teaching. But you follow a uniform curriculum and classroom routines dictated by your principal. The rules might be like these expected of Bronx teachers in the 1920s: (1) Size the children and assign seats, (2) make a seating plan of the class, (3) drill on standing and sitting and putting the benches up and down noiselessly, (4) place your daily lesson plan and your time schedule on the desk where you can refer to them frequently.[2] You help students build strong habits of mind through drill and repetition. You reward correct answers with grades, approval, and preferred seating. You measure progress with tests. Any fact the curriculum specifies as important, your students memorize and recite in unison. However, there are increasing pressures for you to teach silent analyzing and decoding of texts. You're also expected to give some attention to how well students communicate with and persuade others, as these become important business skills. You follow popular classroom management methods such as lining students up and marching them with good posture to assigned spots at the blackboard during instruction and to the lavatories at recess. Like your counterparts a century earlier, you are more concerned about developing character than intellect. Your focus is mostly utilitarian, preparing students—many who are immigrants—with the habits, language, and dispositions for industrial urban life.

As archaic as these pictures of past classrooms strike us, something about them is also disturbingly familiar. Tables and chairs may have replaced bolted desks, and desks in U shapes or groups of four may have replaced rows. However, individual teachers still instruct large groups of students, and students mostly work alone. Teachers transmit knowledge to students in an orderly sequence of steps, often prescribed in school or whole school district policy and watched for in observations by superiors.[3] Students drill and memorize and recite answers, and the mind-as-a-muscle metaphor still holds sway. End-of-unit tests assess whether learning took place. Mastery is rewarded, mistakes are corrected, and unlearned material is retaught. Then everyone moves on to the next topic or skill.[4] Although today's "time-outs," "behavior cards," and student behavior contracts are improvements over corporal punishment of the past, the theory of why such controls "work" is still the same. With low-income, culturally and linguistically "different" students, teachers stress language, basic skills, and good work habits rather than high intellectual achievement. Mostly, children of the wealthy and children of the poor sit in different classrooms, even when they go to the same schools.

Seeking a Sociocultural Pedagogy

Contrast the preceding classroom images with the context for children's learning in societies without mass schooling. Although children's learning in such societies can be difficult, even oppressive, their learning is not set apart from the activities of daily life but takes place in the context of what adults do. Adults generally believe that *all* children can learn everything they need to know. They also assume that children want to learn what the adults know and that they will learn it by observing and participating in adult daily life. When individual children need help, an adult or capable peer provides direction. Learning in such settings is essentially social—what sociocultural researcher Jean Lave calls "participation in communities of practice . . . . that increases gradually in engagement and complexity."[5] It is encouraging that new generations of teachers can introduce many of these features and assumptions of good learning environments and relationships that are excluded from most modern classrooms.

Given new understandings of learning, it's not surprising that teachers entering the profession today seek new, community-like images of classroom life that are similar to how children learn in societies without mass schooling rather than the factory-like settings of the past. By following Dewey, Piaget, and Vygotsky (and their current counterparts), teachers focus on developing classroom learning relationships that allow students to use knowledge in ways that transform their thinking, promote their development, and over time help them to participate in and benefit from society's multiple cultures.

Teaching for Authentic Achievement

There is no sociocultural pedagogy. In fact, some sociocultural theorists make clear that their work is meant only to describe the process of human learning as it occurs "naturally," not to prescribe how to make learning happen in classrooms.[6] Moreover, society expects classrooms to be quite different from more naturally occurring learning settings. Yet to set students apart and perhaps shield them from adults' work does not mean that students must accomplish all of their learning through a formal, academic curriculum and distant personal relationships. Indeed, much of what schools hope to accomplish could be accomplished more readily by using community life and work life as models.

In the past several years, researchers and teachers have sought to align classrooms more closely with the settings where people learn naturally, and, at the same time, to accomplish the academic goals of schooling. In one such effort, a team of researchers headed by Fred Newmann at the University of Wisconsin spent five years studying hundreds of classrooms, trying to understand what particular classroom conditions enhance the intellectual quality and the authenticity of students' schoolwork.[7] By "authentic," the researchers meant that students' classroom accomplishments were worthwhile, significant, and meaningful in the real world. They distinguished authentic student achievement from mastering bits and pieces of information—quite possibly important information—that becomes trivial and forgettable because it has little direct, concrete value outside schools unless it is embedded in daily activities and the solving of interesting problems. The concept of authenticity brings classroom information and practices far closer to the less formal settings in which people learn.

The Wisconsin team identified three characteristics of teaching that promoted both authenticity and high intellectual quality in classrooms: (1) Teachers engaged in helping students *construct knowledge,* (2) teachers helped children to use *disciplined inquiry,* and (3) teachers ensured that what students were learning had *value or meaning beyond school.* Having students construct knowledge brings school learning closer to the kind of activities that scientists, craftspeople, novelists, entrepreneurs, and most other successful adults do. Disciplined inquiry presses students to build on their own existing learning and experiences, striving to understand it deeply and communicate it in their own work. All this promotes students' engagement and effort, in part because it seems more likely that they will use what they learn in life outside school.

My vision: When you enter the classroom, it is not immediately apparent where the teacher is. Small heterogeneous groups of students are working purposefully and independently on a variety of authentic tasks. More academically able students provide encouragement and support to their classmates, allowing all to feel a sense of pride in the work being completed. Students move around the classroom freely. When the teacher needs the students' attention, she simply raises her hand; within moments, she has their undivided attention. A few students ask clarifying questions, and the work continues. The teacher circulates from group to group, providing suggestions and encouragement. Students and teacher feel they are part of a team. Students are working so intently that the teacher has to tell them when the period is coming to an end. Students turn in high-quality work. All students are aware that they are learning. Nobody is failing.

—Jeffra Ann Becknell
First-year teacher, high school social studies

Jeffra Ann Becknell creates her vision from her knowledge of learning theory and from her commitment to fairness. However, she and other new teachers learn quickly that their students, colleagues, and communities (and, sometimes, even they themselves) don't really expect that today's classrooms will be very different from those in the past.

Battling Myths and Metaphors

Why, in the face of cognitive and sociocultural research that has made such strides unraveling the mystery of learning, are conventional classroom practices so hard to change? Traditional teaching practices remain in schools partly because they are familiar and comfortable; they are what most adults think that school is supposed to be like. It should be remembered that behaviorism, which is the foundation of traditional teaching, offered a scientific rationale for what already made sense and still makes sense to most people. Behaviorism did not have to overturn prevailing views of learning and motivation; it simply gave theory and structure to informal and naïve conceptions. Teachers may have resisted parts of B. F. Skinner's sterile, scientific behavioral applications, but few disputed that rewarding and punishing students was a good way to "motivate" them. In addition to behaviorism, prevailing notions of merit, efficiency, competition, and progress are other features that smoothly adapt to and influence classrooms. Thus, cognitive and sociocultural practices have a long way to go before they can match the power of entrenched conventions.

Skeptics argue that basing teaching practices on sociocultural and cognitive research may work "in theory" but that real classrooms require traditional practices that generations of teachers have refined. Such lofty ideals, they assert, are hardly realistic in a culture where individuals compete to get ahead and where students must be controlled. Skeptics point out that teachers must prepare students to work, to sustain the economy, and to be solid citizens. Sure, students should work together, but they also must learn to be independent and not sacrifice individual achievement for the common good. Sure, teachers should assist students as they learn, but schools also must assess students' merit and sort them into different educational, social, and economic opportunities. Further, efficiency and merit dictate that those who learn on their own are more valued than those who "need" help.

Under these circumstances, many view social constructivist approaches to teaching as naïve, inappropriate, or worse. Some teachers who begin with a strong vision have their hope shaken, especially as they discover that a sociocultural perspective cannot be substituted seamlessly to replace the status quo. Jeffra Ann Becknell counters her vision with her struggle.

The reality: "We are going to do group work." Immediately there is a chorus of "I don't want to work with___. He never does anything." . . . . Because no one was listening during the explanation, the teacher has to explain the assignment to each group individually. After a few moments, a hand goes up. A question perhaps? "Teacher, tell him to give me my pencil." . . . By the time the bell rings most of the students are standing within two feet of the door. They race out leaving crumpled paper, cups, and candy wrappers all over the place. The teacher is discouraged, noting that more than half of the students are failing the class.

—Jeffra Ann Becknell
First-year teacher, high school social studies

The Struggle for Authentic and Socially Just Classrooms

Basing classrooms on cognitive and sociocultural learning theories and principles of social justice is an ideal in much the same way that democracy is an ideal—something to be pursued, but something never quite good enough to suit us. And so it's not surprising that teachers who act on what they know about learning and what they believe about social justice are often dismayed by the gap between their ideal and the classroom world they live in—a classroom where they must extricate teaching from the demands of a competitive modern society. Even so, such teachers can and do create environments consistent with what we know about learning and a commitment to social justice.

Each year Jeffra Becknell will modify her vision, as all fine teachers do. Her challenge will be to enrich her vision and support it with experience, reflection, educational research, and her commitment to social justice. She will have to resist the steady pressure to align her vision with the status quo of teaching. She cannot decide that certain practices are *good* because her colleagues or her students are more comfortable with them.

I have gone from being upbeat to discouraged to upbeat again. I have shown my students I care, but it is not enough. . . . On the other hand, there have been successes. Some students have made awesome connections and produced superb work. Others seem more competent, more tolerant, more independent than they were in September. Moreover, I may be planting ideas that will not surface again for years.

—Jeffra Ann Becknell
First-year teacher, high school social studies

Teachers who struggle to keep their vision don't create perfect classrooms. But they do close the gap between vision and practice by being strategic, opportunistic, and creative. They are strategically sensitive to how the power and politics of the school and community connect with their teaching; they watch, volunteer, and propose. They seize opportunities when they unexpectedly arise, forging alliances with colleagues who are also eager to change, and they creatively experiment with alternatives to traditional practice, fashioning them to fit unique contexts.

What classroom practices are these teachers struggling toward, since, as mentioned earlier, no single formula exists for authentic and socially just pedagogy? Unlike the scientific management tradition of specifying a proven set of "best" classroom practices, authenticity and social justice are not properties of particular techniques. Rather, they are qualities of the learning relationships among teachers and students. Classroom practices cannot be judged independent of the cultural knowledge students bring with them to school. Neither can these practices be separated from the curriculum.

However, the following are principles that teachers can use as guidelines as they construct authentic and social justice classroom learning communities:

- Teachers and students are confident that *everyone* learns well.
- Lessons are active, multidimensional, and social.
- Assessment enhances learning.
- Relationships are caring and interdependent
- Talk and action are socially just.

Each of these principles draws from a distinct body of research on teaching that is consistent with cognitive and sociocultural views of learning. But practices grounded in these principles act synergistically; that is, together the whole of the classroom community is more than the sum of its individual parts. Together with rich content, these principles support students' conceptions of themselves as competent learners, encourage effort and persistence, and promote high intellectual quality and democratic dispositions. They help make schooling socially just. In the remainder of this chapter, we explore the first three of these principles. In chapters that follow, we examine caring social justice.

Confidence in a Context of Difference

I focus on what students can do instead of focusing on what they are not doing yet. Then I give my students space to recognize their strengths and work on their needs in a supportive context that pushes them to think critically. A colleague of mine, who explicitly and subtly reveals his deficit thinking, approached me frustrated with his students' writing. He asked what we were doing, and I explained my students' analytical writing. He immediately said, "Oh, you guys are doing that? That is way too sophisticated . . . my kids are not going to be able to do it." He glanced over my students' work and asked, "So, what's the trick? If there are any tricks you can tell me, I'd love to hear them." I was upset with his implication that my students could not think at those levels without having some trick taught to them, so I said, "Well, it's not about any tricks, it's starting from a belief that they can do it. The lessons and scaffolds only complement my belief, and then the kids take off. It's the trusting and believing them that has been fundamental to our learning."

—Laura Silvina Torres
First-year teacher, grade 2

When it comes to learning, one of the most important things is attitude. If teachers can contribute to turning negative attitudes around, they have conquered a major hurdle. I feel I was able to do this by having my students engage in activities that required creative problem solving. Discussions that focused on logic and reason helped students to make sense out of mathematics. The challenges students faced in my classroom gave them a sense that their math class was no longer a place for "dummies." Rather, it was a place that stimulated their minds and challenged them to reason things out. I would hear them bragging about this to their friends outside of our class. Although several students would complain about the difficulty of the work, they were proud to be doing it.

—Marilyn Cortez
First-year teacher, high school mathematics

Whereas traditional pedagogy works against confidence, sociocultural learning theories and a value for social justice fosters confidence, hard work, persistence, and learning. How and why this is so has a great deal to do with how teachers respond to students' differences.

Even in the most homogeneous communities, schools, and classrooms, students are different. Much of the delight of teaching comes from observing and interacting with these differences. Prior experiences, attitudes and expressions, charm and sociability, shyness and silliness, mastery of sophisticated knowledge, and astonishing and hysterical misunderstandings and gaps in what they "should" but do not know all vary among the students in any classroom. In many classrooms, students also differ in the languages, cultures, and community resources they bring to school. These differences influence how students approach classroom learning, but they bear little relation to whether or not they are capable learners.

Narrow Expectations Constrain Confidence

When teachers teach as if they expect few differences among students, the inevitable differences that do exist become transformed into problems. It is not that teachers are surprised by student differences and therefore unprepared—it does not take too much experience to be able to anticipate the range of attitudes, language, and prior experiences one is likely to find in a community's schools. No, when teachers teach as if there are few differences, they do so because that is the way that they, the school, and school traditions decide is the correct way to teach. And if teaching is correct, but students do not respond well to it, then what is the problem? It must be the attitudes, language, prior experience, and other student characteristics that do not match the narrow range of the school and teacher's expectations.

Transmission Teaching Allows Few Differences Traditional pedagogy makes students acutely aware of how their personal characteristics are problems for themselves and for the teacher. Conventional transmission approaches call for lessons that assume that all students *should* learn the same things in the same way at the same time. Teachers give everyone the same homework and assess what students have learned with the same test, on the same day. This virtually guarantees that many children won't match up with the limited opportunities to develop or display competence in a way that the teacher or classmates are prepared to value. Those students who do not find a success opportunity disrupt the flow of instruction, and the teacher must either stop and try to modify instruction (perhaps grudgingly) to accommodate their "difference" or simply move on without them. These one-dimensional lessons make students' differences conspicuous and troublesome. This virtually guarantees that both the teacher and class will lose confidence in at least some students' capacity or willingness to learn.[8]

Public Comparisons Undermine Confidence and Effort All of this learning and succeeding (or not) is very public. The differences among students—for example, who finishes quickly, who gets the most correct answers, who never seems to be able to respond when the teacher calls on her—are obvious to everyone in the room. Even when teachers succeed in constructing activities that place students at the edge of their capacity (in Vygotsky's terms, their zone of proximal development)—with or without assistance—students risk making mistakes and suffering public humiliation. Thus, students' engagement is always "audienced"—not only by teachers but also by classmates. Students are constantly aware of the teacher's attention to their behavior and their displays of knowledge and skill.

Countless unquestioned classroom routines expose students' flaws to public examination. For example, in many classrooms, teachers post grades and other symbols of students' progress: letters, numbers, stars, smiley faces, racehorses, and halos, along with sad faces and zeros. A glance at student work stuck on the wall immediately tells who are top students and who are not. In addition, teachers sometimes read scores aloud or permit student helpers to return graded papers to their classmates. Gradebooks are often open for students to peruse classmates' grades. Results of aptitude, achievement, and other standardized tests become public when students or their parents offer their scores voluntarily. Informal assessments can easily serve as proxies for academic standing and social standing as well. In some schools, student aides call students out of class, and the color of the pass (from the principal's or dean's office) instantly informs everyone if this student is in disciplinary trouble or on his way to a special "gifted" activity. Students are often allowed to exchange gifts in the most open and public way. A teacher's public display of annoyance is noted by all; and signals sent by peers are always salient, especially to older students. In the world of these evaluative acts and symbols, students quickly sum up their own ability in a class and their schoolworthiness in general.

Of course, extraordinarily sensitive teachers, even if they follow largely traditional ways of teaching, can mitigate some of the destructive effects of public comparisons. But this is a very large hurdle, and few are entirely successful. More likely, teachers, just like students, drift toward coherent practices that integrate the culture, the pedagogy, and personal attitudes. Students themselves join in to cement the behaviors and achievement they expect of one another: As they are treated, so they treat their peers. For example, the disruptive student may receive encouragement as a prize ally from those who value the disruption or may become a pariah among those whose self-concept depends on associating with high achievers. Individual interactions—teacher-student, student-student—soon solidify as a shared classroom perception, that is, a consensus. Each day further refines the distinction between those students whom the classroom culture expects to meet the class's highest standards and those from whom that culture expects little. These class- and school-generated status differences trigger easy social comparisons of who in the classroom is "smart" and who is not. Then it is only a short step for the teacher to conclude that some students simply can't (or won't) learn well.[9] Worse, it's the students' differences that everyone blames for expected failure, not the classroom routines.

In a climate of comparison, attention to differences puts students constantly at risk of being publicly identified as "wrong" or "stupid." That undermines confidence, effort, and persistence. In spite of the cultural bromide that says "All anyone expects is that you try your hardest," students know better. When trying their hardest results in public identification as being wrong or not intelligent, students see little logic in further effort. Again, none of these consequences is inevitable.

Learned helplessness, a phenomenon psychologist Carol Dweck identified, can be another effect of public comparisons in classrooms. When students do not feel competent and have low status (i.e., their classroom peers also see them as less competent), they may assume that no amount of effort will lead to success. Each time they try to act competently, they risk making their incompetence more visible.[10] Gradually, they decide that the hard work needed for success only makes their shortcomings appear worse. It is safer for them to consider their failure as an unchangeable condition than to continue a cycle of trying and failing. Having decided before trying a task that they probably cannot succeed, they turn specific self-doubts into global judgments about their overall worth. They may begin by saying or thinking "I don't understand the problems on the test" and end up believing "I am not smart at math" or "I'm not much of a student."

Finally, the most far-reaching, as well as ironic, effect of public comparisons in the classroom is that these comparisons communicate that school is a place where imminent failure is possible for *any* student, not just those currently out of favor. The very existence of the status hierarchy that comparisons create may affect negatively the highest-achieving students. They may be chiefly motivated by a desire to "not fall" to a level where they are treated like others. They may become so invested in their high status that it becomes the primary focus of their attention and effort. Such conditions do not help students become fully engaged in their own learning or care about others' success. No wonder so many students, older ones in particular, spend their time acting on some of school's "real" lessons: Work hard for others' approval, and if that does not produce results, find another "game" you can win—disrupt, resist, or fail.

Beliefs and Expectations Matter The belief that students' intellectual capacities differ widely means that many students, including some of the highest achievers, will feel inadequate. The assumption that poor and minority children have additional disadvantages that hinder learning means that their chances for feeling successful are slim.

That teachers' beliefs about children's ability to learn have such power was first documented in Robert Rosenthal and Lenore Jacobson's landmark study, *Pygmalion in the Classroom*.[11] In their study, Rosenthal and Jacobson told a group of elementary teachers that a few students in their classes were "late bloomers." They said that although these students were not exceptional now, they would make substantial strides in the future. In fact, the researchers randomly selected students who were neither more nor less ready to bloom than the others. By the end of the year, the students who had been labeled late bloomers and expected to shine academically outperformed their classmates.

The study's central assertion—that teachers' expectations influence students' performance—has held up over the years. Adults respond to initial cues from students about what to expect from them and how much to push or encourage them. Experienced teachers often comment on how their first impressions of students are misleading, but sometimes those same teachers report that they can predict how well a student will do in class after a first meeting. Teachers often judge children as less capable when they are less adept at behaving in ways that make traditional lessons move smoothly (e.g., showing rapid recall, being motivated for grades, sitting still, working neatly). Unkempt appearance, behavior taken as disruptive, and cultural meanings ascribed to a student's accent can also be negative cues. Positive cues can include courteous behavior and a well-groomed appearance. A student's race can also matter when adults make judgments about students. In a recent innovative study, for example, Derek Mitchell asked teachers to recommend students for advanced or slower classes. The teachers were given student files that included photographs as well as information about the students' background and achievements. However, the files were actually fakes, designed so the teachers made judgments about students with identical background characteristics but with photos showing different races. Butler found that high school teachers judged African American and Latino students less likely to be suited for challenging mathematics courses than identically qualified whites.[12]

Teachers communicate expectations in many subtle ways. For example, a teacher may give some students a bit of extra time if they are confident of a correct answer, while quickly moving on from students whose hesitation matches the teacher's view that the student is "slow." Sometimes, to avoid embarrassing a student judged as having little to offer, a teacher will skip over the student or supply a correct answer or quietly accept a partial answer instead of probing for a fuller explanation. Which distracted student gets a good-natured call back to the task and which receives a scolding glare can influence a student's developing concept of himself as a learner. Myra and David Sadker's research offers fascinating documentation on the extent to which teachers communicate different expectations for boys and girls. Particularly in math and science, teachers, both men and women, enact the larger society's gender stereotypes in subtle ways that, when pointed out, are astonishing to the teachers themselves. For example, teachers ask boys more questions and allow them to dominate laboratory experiments. In addition, when students encounter difficulties, teachers encourage boys to press on and try harder but are more likely to console and comfort girls.[13] Low-income children and children of color face similar expectation barriers.[14] Such responses certainly affect a student's willingness to become engaged, to participate, to take risks, and to work hard.[15]

Stereotypes and Vulnerability Any time a student takes a test, especially one that compares her with other students, and any time her performance is public, such as when she answers aloud in class, this student is vulnerable to the judgments of others. However, there can be an added burden of vulnerability when the student is acutely aware that her lack of knowledge or difficulty with language is associated with all the negative judgments about her race, speakers of her first language, or others of her social class. Makeba Jones, an educational researcher at the University of California, San Diego, describes her personal experience with this phenomenon:

> As a teenager, I remember questioning my own abilities in comparison to my peers. Despite the fact that my large public high school was racially mixed, I was the only person of color in my white and affluent Honors level courses. I

> recall feeling conspicuous and out of place, or rather misplaced. When I did not understand an assignment, I felt sure my peers could see both the confusion on my face, and that I was only pretending to write an essay when I was staring at a blank page.
>
> I took mostly advanced and honors courses and adapted to the individualistic and competitive environment. I accepted the belief that only individual ability and merit would bring high grades and teacher praise. I was naïve about race as an adolescent. I am not sure if I felt so inadequate because I was the only black girl in the class. But looking back, I realize that I felt self-confident outside of my advanced classes. Although no one explicitly treated me as though I did not belong, there was a contradiction I felt in those classrooms. I battled the contradiction between what I knew in my heart was true about me, Makeba, and what I perceived that my peers and teachers thought about me and my "place." This struggle of identity and self-examination pushed me to drop out of Honors English my senior year. I felt relieved the second semester as I passed by the Honors English classroom on my way to a classroom that didn't suddenly fall silent when a student answered a question wrong. But I also felt as though the American Dream only applied to those whose stamina and ability allowed them to flourish under such pressure, and not those, like me, who needed more reassurance and sensitivity.[16]

As Makeba Jones observes, schools do not have to be overtly prejudiced to participate in social stereotypes. For example, although few schools tell girls to avoid advanced mathematics classes, many schools do not make a special effort to overcome the social stereotype that girls are less well suited for math. Thus, when a girl decides to avoid advanced math, the counselor may say (and believe), "OK, that's your choice." On the one hand, it *is* a free and individual choice; on the other hand, it is a choice that is informed by cultural knowledge that translates into limited opportunity. Further, the girl who does decide to take advanced math may frequently be aware that her performance in class not only carries the usual risks of exposing flawed math knowledge but also makes others see her, as one of the few girls in math class, as a representative of girls who take math. Finally, she is aware that she, personally, may reflect society's low estimate for girls' suitability for math. Stanford University professor Claude Steele argues that this combined awareness may impinge on a girl's concentration and her confidence, despite other evidence that she is well suited for success in math.[17]

Steele's studies help explain how stereotypes that exist in the larger social culture interact with school and classroom practices and result in limited opportunities. In one of his experiments, high-achieving African American men and women did less well on tests after they were told that the test could measure intelligence or when they were asked to specify their race. Other similar students who were given no indication that their scores might be judged according to racial stereotypes did as well as high-achieving whites on very challenging tests. Steele also found that everyone is vulnerable to stereotypes. For example, in another experiment, white males—unaccustomed to being intellectually stigmatized—were told that Asians achieved higher scores than Americans on a mathematics test. This group of white males achieved lower scores on that test than a control group of white males who were not told anything about previous test results. Importantly, like other social science research, Steele's findings are not meant as predictions for what will surely happen in particular cases. That is why his term *vulnerability* is so apt. Although everyone is vulnerable, *how* vulnerable probably depends on the prevalence and depth of the stereotype as well as a host of individual, nongroup characteristics. But clearly, some groups are going to be affected more than others—African American students because of the depth and history of prejudice; gay and lesbian students because families and other adults, along with play and peer groups, may not be available as sources of comfort and understanding; and other groups with multiple vulnerabilities such as Latinos whose first language is Spanish and whose families are very poor.

Blacks and other low-status minorities may have, like their white teachers, few mental images of academically successful minorities to call upon. Steele points out that this lack of images puts minority children in jeopardy not faced by whites. Not only do minority children risk being devalued for any particular mistake or failure they might make in class—for example, being not so good at spelling or multiplication—they also risk confirming the broader racial inferiority that others suspect of them—low intelligence. Steele writes, "Thus, from the first grade through graduate school, blacks have the extra fear that in the eyes of those around them their full humanity could fail with a poor answer or a mistaken stroke of the pen."[18]

Prejudice and stereotypes typically are not expressed as simple exclusionary rules or hateful epitaphs. They are often cultural beliefs subtly enacted by well-meaning classmates and teachers, and their most devastating effects work from within the psyche of the affected person. Sociologist Daniel Solorzano uses the term *microaggressions* to indicate how the real damage comes from racially laden attitudes, comments, and actions of peers and teachers who would deny that they were prejudiced or acting hurtfully. Solorzano offers many examples such as these:

> "When I talk about those Blacks, I really wasn't talking about you."
>
> "You're not like the rest of them. You're different."
>
> "If only there were more of them like you."
>
> "I don't think of you as a Mexican."
>
> "You speak such good English."[19]

Sociocultural Pedagogy Expects Difference

One way to think of difference is to contrast it with whatever is *not* different or normal. In this sense, African Americans are different from whites (who are *not* different). Many men treat women as different but do not see *themselves* as different. In America, Muslims are different, Jews are somewhat less different, and Christians are least likely to be considered different. Students with average test scores are not different, but those with very high or low scores are different.

Each of these common interpretations of difference requires a comparison with something normal.

Another way to think about difference is to presume there is no central "normal" by which others are compared and judged. Such a position does not mean that one is color-blind, ignores another's religious practices, or pretends that different gender preferences do not exist. But a conception of difference that doesn't have some idealized "normal" student as a reference point makes for very different classrooms.

In a multidimensional classroom, many dimensions of difference can exist in their own right, and differences (and students) do not have to be judged on how close to "normal" they are. Such a classroom becomes a community of very diverse learners where everybody is smart, and differences are the source of rich learning interactions. Teachers make each student's particular competence visible and available to others as learning resources. Social interactions allow students to scaffold one another's learning, and to combine their different knowledge and experiences into the learning community's knowledge and experience. Such lessons set in motion a far more positive cycle of confidence, effort, persistence, and learning.

Constructing Confidence in Classrooms Racial and other stereotypes along with perceptions of academic ability and acceptance of diversity are all tightly linked. Most teachers value and want to be sensitive to student differences, but they need experience and support to work productively with the social world of their classroom. Their skills and sensitivity need to take them far beyond simply having a logical lesson plan and caring about the well-being of their students.

Sociologists Elizabeth Cohen and Rachel Lotan have worked for more than twenty years identifying classroom practices that can interrupt low expectations for students' performance by responding directly to the "public" (visible to all) construction of their competence and status. Their studies of elementary- and middle-school classrooms affirm fundamental principles that teachers should follow to create lessons that sustain everyone's confidence. Cohen and Lotan have taken one of these principles—engaging students with rich and complex knowledge—and made it the foundation for their program called Complex Instruction. We examine a second principle—a focus on student interactions—later in this chapter. Complex Instruction requires lessons that include a variety of student abilities and special attention to students' status as learners and class members.

Constructing Competence with Multiability Lessons "Read the chapter and answer the questions at the end. Test on Tuesday. Don't forget the vocab." This is not a multiability lesson. Low-level reading comprehension and memorization are the intellectual skills required. The test will measure those skills alone, and who in the class scores high and who scores low is predictable. By the third month of school, the teacher and every student in class will know who is smart on this kind of test and who is not.

A multiability lesson can be short range and relatively simple. However, a richer, more complex lesson is long range, often a project that may involve a number of tasks and subassignments. It has some elements requiring distinctly different levels of skills and other elements that highly skilled and less-skilled students benefit from. It requires work that students can do individually and other parts that students must work on together to accomplish. It involves hands-on activity and traditional book-and-paper scholarship and research and makes use of students' informal and prior knowledge. All students participate in all elements of the lesson, and each student can find areas in which she has particular strengths. The teacher or other knowledgeable helpers are ready to step in when some students struggle or others are ready to forge ahead. Clearly, no such lesson ever reaches an ideal. There is always another activity, another opportunity for a student experiment, another theme to explore, more resources to add, and a teacher's wish for just a little more time.

Cohen and Lotan propose that with a multiability approach, teachers can engage the class in discussions that explicitly probe the many different intellectual abilities and other skills the lesson will require. Teachers can assure students that although no one in the class will be "good on all these abilities," each student will be "good on at least one." Cohen and Lotan found that when teachers do this consistently, students begin identifying each other and themselves as "smart" on a wide range of attributes, weakening the power of the more common negative expectations. Of course, the goal of identifying this wide range of abilities is not to assign or label individual students as being good at one thing and not another. Rather, the goal is for students to assume that everyone is competent, that it is everyone's job to help everyone contribute, and that individual competence results from *participating* in the classroom learning community.

Elizabeth Cohen's research has consistently found positive results in the attitudes and achievement of white, Asian, and Latino students (some with limited English) in elementary- and middle-school classrooms. Uri Treisman, a mathematician at the University of California-Berkeley, found similar positive achievement results in workshops teaching calculus to African American college freshmen.[20] In both settings, teachers saw students—and the students came to see themselves—as capable and valued for their intellectual potential, even if they currently lacked particular skills.

Stanford professor Jo Boaler's research in two English high schools documented superior mathematics achievement in multiability high school classes. She describes her study in the following:

> In one [high school], the teachers taught mathematics using whole-class teaching and textbooks, and the students were tested frequently. The students were taught in tracked groups, standards of discipline were high, and the students worked hard. The second school was chosen because its approach to mathematics teaching was completely different. Students there worked on open-ended projects in heterogeneous groups, teachers used a variety of methods, and discipline was extremely relaxed. . . . One of the results of these differences was that students at the second school—what I will call the project school, as

opposed to the textbook school—attained significantly higher grades on the national exam. This was not because these students knew more mathematics, but because they had developed a different form of knowledge.

At the textbook school, the students were motivated and worked hard, they learned all the mathematical procedures and rules they were given, and they performed well on short, closed tests. But various forms of evidence showed that these students had developed an inert, procedural knowledge that they were rarely able to use in anything other than textbook and test situations. In applied assessments, many were unable to perceive the relevance of the mathematics they had learned and so could not make use of it. Even when they could see the links between their textbook work and more-applied tasks, they were unable to adapt the procedures they had learned to fit the situations in which they were working. . . .

The students themselves were aware of this problem, as the following description by one student of her experience of the national exam shows: "Some bits I did recognize, but I didn't understand how to do them, I didn't know how to apply the methods properly."

In real-world situations, these students were disabled in two ways. Not only were they unable to use the math they had learned because they could not adapt it to fit unfamiliar situations, but they also could not see the relevance of this acquired math knowledge from school for situations outside the classroom. "When I'm out of here," said another student, "the math from school is nothing to do with it, to tell you the truth. Most of the things we've learned in school we would never use anywhere."

Students from this school reported that they could see mathematics all around them, in the workplace and in everyday life, but they could not see any connection between their school math and the math they encountered in real situations. Their traditional, class-taught mathematics instruction had focused on formalized rules and procedures, and this approach had not given them access to depth of mathematical understanding. As a result, they believed that school mathematical procedures were a specialized type of school code—useful only in classrooms. As one girl put it, "In math you have to remember; in other subjects you can think about it."

The math teaching at this textbook school was not unusual. Teachers there were committed and hard-working, and they taught the students different mathematical procedures in a clear and straightforward way. Their students were relatively capable on narrow mathematical tests, but this capability did not transfer to open, applied, or real-world situations. The form of knowledge they had developed was remarkably ineffective. At the project school, the situation was very different. And the students' significantly higher grades on the national exit exam were only a small indication of their mathematical competence and confidence.

The project school's students and teachers were relaxed about work. Students were not introduced to any standard rules or procedures (until a few weeks before the examinations), and they did not work through textbooks of any kind. Despite the fact that these students were not particularly work-oriented, however, they attained higher grades than the hard-working students at the textbook school on a range of different problems and applied assessments. At both schools, students had similar grades on short written tests taken immediately after finishing work. But students at the textbook school soon forgot what they had learned. The project students did not. The important difference between the environments of the two schools that caused this difference in retention was not related to standards of teaching but to different approaches, in particular the requirement that the students at the project-based school work on a variety of mathematical tasks and think for themselves.

When I asked students at the two schools whether mathematics was more about thinking or memorizing, 64 percent of the textbook students chose memorizing, compared with only 35 percent of the project-based students. The students at the project school were less concerned about memorizing rules and procedures, because they knew they could think about different situations and adapt what they had learned to fit new and demanding problems. On the national examination, three times as many students from the heterogeneous groups in the project school as those in the tracked groups in the textbook school attained the highest possible grade. The project approach was also more equitable, with girls and boys attaining the different grades in equal proportions.[21]

Constructing the Competence of Low-Status Children As Cohen's and Boaler's work makes clear, competence and participation should not be distinguishable concerns. A student's degree of competence does not matter as much as her degree of engagement in activities that scaffold her learning. In an ideal participatory setting, everyone's status would be that of a highly competent learner. However, students themselves have much to say about the classroom's learning environment. The combination of their existing self-concepts with their habits of judging others is so powerful that teachers must attack status and self-concept issues head-on. Thus, Cohen and Lotan encourage teachers using Complex Instruction to assign competence to low-status students explicitly. To do this, teachers watch for instances of capable performance on various intellectual tasks relevant to the classroom learning activities from students whose status and/or expectations of themselves are low. The teacher then gives the student a "specific, favorable, and very public evaluation," pointing out to others in the class that the student can serve as a resource to others in that area. First-year teacher Cindy Bell used just this strategy to boost her students' confidence.

"Asking a friend" is an important strategy that I encourage my students to use. To reinforce the importance of this, I've incorporated expert roles throughout all parts of the curriculum so that each student has an expert role in math, writing, and reading. In math we have different strategy experts who explain to the class their strategies for solving a problem. In writing we have editing experts such as "title titans," "main idea masters," "detail detectives," "super spellers," "handwriting experts," and the "capital letter crew" who assist in the second editing of our writing process. Every student is assigned a role because they all have something authentic to contribute. No matter where a student's overall literacy development is, each one plays an important role as an expert. I have one student, in particular, who has a diagnosed learning disability and is reading at a first-grade level. However because she has a role as a "handwriting expert," when our class is writing, she is seen as an expert. . . . Being identified as an expert by peers reaffirms my students' opinions, feelings, and prior knowledge as valid and even necessary resources.

—Cindy Bell
First-year teacher, grade 2

The assignment of competence directly disrupts the cycle of low expectations, low status, and low participation that students get caught in. Of course, the assignment of competence must be genuine and credible—like the competence that Cindy Bell assigns to her students. Quick praise for something mediocre or not central to the task (such as decorating the cover of a science project with cartoon characters) will not convince anyone of a student's competence. It may well have the opposite effect. Admittedly, these public evaluations carry some of the risks associated with rewards and praise. However, if the teacher has established his role in class as a "broker" of knowledge—one whose main job is not to evaluate but to ask questions and point out knowledge sources—then he can present the student as a resource rather than as a shining example.

But Can I Teach Them?

Perhaps the most critical factor in constructing confident classrooms is teachers' own confidence or efficacy—their confidence that they can teach all students successfully. Teachers' efficacy is undermined by lockstep curricula, fixed time limits, and customary grouping practices, and it is crucial to understand how these elements can get in the way of the teacher's intentions to construct multiability lessons. The real challenge is to keep pursuing such lessons while teaching, as most teachers are, within a traditional school culture. Teachers whose own education was in the traditional mold (nearly everyone) may have initial difficulty identifying and building on student successes within multiability lessons. Tradition-minded colleagues are not much help in this matter. They are more likely to suggest traditional solutions than to show enthusiasm for scaffolding and participating in the less-experienced teacher's crisis.

The remainder of this chapter and the next look more closely at the strategies Laura Torres, Cindy Bell, and many other teachers use to make their classrooms places where both they and their students can be confident about everyone's ability to learn. These strategies include creating active, multidimensional, and interactive lessons; making assessments an integral part of learning; and fostering caring, interdependent, and socially just classroom relationships.

Active, Multidimensional, and Social Instruction

Most teachers, striving for quiet and efficient classrooms, organize their instruction to control or minimize activity and social interactions. Teachers talk to the whole class at once, and they walk around the room giving individual help. They call on students to read aloud to the class, answer questions, or write on the board. Students quickly learn to identify the behaviors that school adults want from them. Children who can, or who decide they can, learn to listen for the answers that please adults, and they become skilled at repeating them, even when they haven't learned the underlying concepts. After only a short time in school, students decide that the real learning is what they do by themselves.

In contrast, the power of active, multicultural, and social instruction in learning is virtually uncontested by research. This research has been summed up in a new book by Roland Tharp and his colleagues at the Center for Research on Education, Diversity, and Excellence (CREDE)—a federally funded national research center at the University of California, Santa Cruz. In *Teaching Transformed: Achieving Excellence, Fairness, Inclusion, and Harmony,* Tharp and his colleagues offer five principles that describe the characteristics of classroom lessons that promote both academic excellence and extending that excellence to all students. These principles are (1) teachers and students producing together, (2) developing language and literacy across the curriculum, (3) making meaning—that is connecting school content to students' lives, (4) teaching complex thinking, and (5) teaching through conversation. Enacting these principles in classrooms, according to Tharp, requires that teachers create settings where multiple, diverse activities occur simultaneously. That requires that students be arranged in small groups. It is most likely in these small-group settings that students can actually work together, that teachers can draw upon student's experience out of school, and that teachers can converse with diverse groups of students in ways that challenge all of them. At the same time, the diversity among students becomes a strength rather than a problem, as it broadens the range of experiences from which they can learn. In short, these classrooms are active, multidimensional, and very social places.

Learning Together

Traditional modes of classroom interaction are supported by beliefs that each student must do his or her own learning and that the benefits of education accrue through individual accomplishment. These individualistic practices and norms reflect powerful cultural traditions and learning theories. Beliefs about intelligence as an inherited trait that governs how quickly and easily individuals learn, conceptions of teaching and learning as transmission and behavioral conditioning, the quest for efficiency and merit—all add up to a preference for looking at the individual rather than the culture to explain why people act as they do. Schools abound with admonitions that reflect these individualistic values about learning and achievement, such as "Be sure to do your own work!," "You need to become an independent thinker," and "He's just not a self-starter." In stark contrast, sociocultural theories lead teachers to structure classroom lessons that are active and social.

Two Lessons Consider how two different teachers might approach teaching measurement to upper elementary school students. The first teacher—one who is grounded in traditional theories and practice—explains to the class how to add feet and inches and demonstrates the process by working through several sample problems step-by-step on an overhead projector she keeps at the front of the room for math lessons. As she goes through the examples, she elicits students' ideas about what comes next, and as many as half the class get to respond at least one time. A handful of students is clearly enthusiastic and would answer every question if allowed. The teacher then gives the students a few minutes to do another problem by themselves at their desks and asks two volunteers to come to the board to model how they worked the problem. She corrects any errors they make and asks the rest of the class if they understand. Seeing mostly positive head nods, she assigns a page of twenty practice problems (e.g., 6' 4" + 2' 10" = ?) for them to work on quietly for the rest of math time, while she circulates and monitors their work.

The second teacher proceeds quite differently. She had a measurement lesson planned, but she modified it two days earlier, after one of her students came late to class, having been delayed in the school office while getting his cut knee bandaged. On the way to school the student was running across a littered empty lot and fell. The class talked about the problems of the lot, and the teacher asked them to imagine what could be done with it to solve the problem and improve the community. The students decided that a playground would be nice, with benches for old people to sit on. Enlisting the supervision help of two parents, the teacher took her class, organized into teams, to the lot to measure its dimensions and locate and sketch topographical features (a small hill, an abandoned refrigerator, etc.). Back in the classroom the students designed and located play equipment, paths, perimeter fencing, and other features. They calculated amounts of materials and costs—in some cases enlisting the help of parents with construction experience—telephoned and visited lumberyards, and so on. They figured costs and prepared a budget. To some degree, this teacher used the same instructional strategies as the first teacher: lecture/demonstration, question/answer, drill and practice. But these strategies were used more sparingly and in the context of solving real problems. Never did she allow them to become ends in themselves or to dominate large blocks of time. Often she used them with just a portion of the class.

Learning as a Community Activity If this second lesson doesn't seem entirely strange, it's because many teachers do use strategies in their classrooms that intuitively or purposefully are very consistent with cognitive, sociocultural, and social justice perspectives. Advocacy for classroom learning as an active and social process has a long, if not dominant, history in American schools. For example, early in the twentieth century John Dewey not only theorized about learning and curriculum, he pioneered progressive approaches to teaching that were consistent with his view that learning happens as students experience and interact with the world. Dewey believed that classroom learning activities should prepare children to solve the problems of a democratic society. What's more, he maintained that classrooms themselves should be democratic. Rather than places where adults retain all of the authority and dictate to students, classrooms must allow students' active learning in the context of a cooperative, democratic community.

Dewey's presence has been felt in education throughout the century. Although some Dewey-like practices have become commonplace—such things as field trips and science projects, for example—few schools or teachers promote lessons like the preceding one on measurement. And fewer still contemplate a social action project outside the school.

By teaching lessons such as the preceding one, the teacher allows the students to become members of a mathematical community. As members of that community, students see themselves as math-using specialists in a real and practical math-using world. The lesson invites instructional assistance, encourages the relationships and support that one finds in caring communities, and allows the class to enact social justice behaviors and values.

Many elements of active and social classrooms make them consistent with cognitive and sociocultural learning theories and principles of social justice. Three explored here stand out as particularly important: multidimensional tasks (of the sort recommended for authentic lessons and Complex Instruction), instructional assistance or scaffolding, and cooperative group work.

Multidimensional Tasks

The more elaborate measurement lesson just described, unlike the first teacher-at-the-board lesson, provides mathematical tasks in abundance and allows all students to succeed with what they know. The multiple tasks permit students to tackle problems, with help, just beyond their abilities to solve independently—in their zone of proximal development. Opportunities for the teacher to explore what and how much students learn (called "authentic assessment") are embedded within the tasks themselves.

The following lesson that Kim Pham describes has similar advantages. Her class had just finished investigating how the United Farm Workers Union fit into the Chicano Movement, and they were working in small groups preparing to present to the class what they'd learned.

The room is alive with activity. Desks are pushed to the edge of the classroom, accommodating various groups. Some students discuss how to share their recent experience of working with migrant farmworkers in the fields. One student patiently charts a graph showing the economic breakdown of maintaining a large farm. Two students and I plan the presentation order. Other students complete a poster on the United Farm Workers, focusing on the leadership of Cesar Chavez and Philip Vera Cruz. Their photographs, news clippings, and markers are sprawled across the floor. Laughter erupts from the back of the room where four students debate the idea of dressing up as fruit while presenting information on the movement of farmworkers across the state following the peak harvest times of the fruit and vegetable season. Someone asks me if she can give her classmates a test after the presentation. "Certainly," I reply, "but consider—'What do you want them to know?'" The student thinks about the question while slowly returning to the group. Activity continues unabated until the final minutes. I remind students to document progress with a short journal entry highlighting individual concerns and feelings. Students write until the end of class.

—KimMan Thi Pham
First-year teacher, history, grade 11

Elizabeth Cohen has drawn the following characteristics for multidimensional tasks from her own and others' research:

- Include more than one answer or more than one way to solve the problem
- Are intrinsically interesting and rewarding
- Allow different students to make different contributions
- Use multimedia
- Involve sight, sound, and touch
- Require a variety of skills and behaviors
- Require reading and writing
- Are challenging

Cohen gives as examples tasks that ask students to create a role play, build a model, draw a mind map of the relationship among ideas, or discover and describe relationships by manipulating equipment or objects—activities like those Kim Pham planned for her students. Cohen notes how "hands-on" science lessons that ask students to observe, carefully manipulate, collect and record data precisely, hypothesize causes and effects, and write up the report fit her notion of multidimensional. Cohen believes that basic skills are an important part of multidimensional classrooms, but she notes that learning these skills can be enhanced by multidimensional tasks. Cohen advises teachers that if tasks have a single right answer, can be done more quickly and efficiently by one person than by a group, and involve simple memorization or routine learning, teachers can be pretty sure the tasks are unidimensional and will inhibit many students' learning.[22]

Scaffolding through Classroom Interaction

Classroom social interactions include all the ways students and the teacher relate to one another about academics, behavior, and social matters. Teachers can design and organize all of these interactions in ways that lead students to develop new insights, deeper understandings and greater thinking skills. Thus, academic learning and classroom relationships are not separate; they occur simultaneously whenever a student is pressed by the teacher or a classmate through questioning and sharing of ideas to go beyond his current thinking. This concept of teaching as interactions that assist learners to become competent stems from Vygotsky's theories (see Chapter 3 for additional discussion). Specifically, the role of the teacher is to support, or scaffold, students as they move through their zone of proximal development, defined as the knowledge and skills that the student cannot learn on his own but can learn with the assistance (scaffolding) of someone who is more capable. As with an apprentice's relationship to an accomplished member of the community, these relationships value any contributions a novice might make—no matter how small.

A Focus on Questions Math teacher Juliana Jones, quoted next, is mindful of these interactions as she guides her students through social learning. Her work underscores how a teacher's active involvement has to rest on both her specific lesson preparation and her on-the-spot reliance on theory. There is no way for a teacher's plan alone to prepare her for the spontaneous and idiosyncratic questions and responses her students are likely to offer. Theory without preparation (and subject knowledge) will fall flat. Experience helps, too.

No matter how student-centered the classroom may be, I still have an important job to facilitate discussion and cognitive conflict by asking a tough question or challenging their conjectures. In knowing my students and where they are, I must know how to support the "stretching of their minds." I know I need experience to learn how to do this effectively, but it also takes preparation. Before a lesson, I can brainstorm ways to extend understanding, or compose questions to push students a little farther. I can think about questions they may ask and devise ways to help them come to an understanding. One never knows how students will respond—that is the excitement of teaching.

I have gotten the students to volunteer ideas and conjectures, and some of them ask the most wonderful questions. However, I must facilitate the discussions by asking rich mathematical questions and posing interesting problems. This requires my knowledge about how to illustrate concepts. I must field their wonderful questions (and by wonderful I mean they stop me in my tracks and leave me wondering how in the world I can answer them) by using a counterexample and asking questions, or articulating why what they say is correct or incorrect. And I must rely on what I know about the student's personality and prior struggles to figure out where they are getting lost, ask them a question that lets them rethink the situation, use a manipulative or drawing to clear something up, or tell them, "You know, that is a really good question, and I'm not sure how to answer it, so let's explore some possibilities. What does the class think?" I learn so much as I try to be the facilitator of rich mathematical discourse. The fodder for years of reflection lies in these class discussions.

—Juliana Jones
First-year teacher, middle-school mathematics

Juliana Jones combines her theoretical understanding of instructional scaffolding with her firsthand knowledge of her students and her sense of her own strengths and limitations. Impressively, she does not treat her question-asking casually but as a central element of her teaching that requires careful planning, execution, and reflection.

Janene Ashford used much the same strategy when she feared she would slip into traditional teaching.

At the end of a lesson on volcanoes, Pete raised his hand and innocently asked, "Ms. Ashford, why are volcanoes tall?" "Ha!" I thought to myself, "I am one step ahead of you." I had just set up the overhead projector and had placed a multilayer transparency on top that provides a clear representation of what happens when volcanoes form. As my finger hovered threateningly over the "on" button, I paused, caught myself, and thought about the value of this question and how I believe students learn. I was very tempted to take the "easy" route, which would have been to tell Pete the answer he, and presumably other students, wanted to hear. However, I refrained. I believe students develop an understanding of a concept through exploration, guidance, and by constructing knowledge through experience. So I positioned Pete's question at the center of the curriculum, and from that moment, his question drove the content. . . . So my response was, "Well, what do you guys think? Why are volcanoes tall?"

A few hands raised without hesitation. Ariana suggested that it had something to do with the plates pushing together and pushing the earth up higher and higher. She was taking the knowledge that she had learned during our unit on plate tectonics and applying it to a new situation. Samir thought that volcanoes are tall because they are formed on mountains. I asked the class if all volcanoes were formed on mountains. While a few students agreed with Samir, most did not. Some responses showed incredible conceptual understanding, while others demonstrated terrific gaps. However, the discussion that followed proved to be a wonderful example of how knowledge is constructed and how conceptual understanding is mediated. . . . By engaging with peers and actively working to make sense of why volcanoes are tall, the students were empowered to reflect on their theories and prior knowledge and then construct new and meaningful understandings tempered by scientific reasoning.

—Janene Ashford
First-year teacher, grade 6

Three Research-Based Scaffolding Strategies Teachers and classroom researchers offer additional ways to think about and use instructional scaffolding. The following three strategies are not teaching recipes but solid research-based principles that enrich a teacher's repertoire when they are combined with firsthand experience and knowledge of a particular class.

Substantive Conversation The Wisconsin project described earlier in this chapter identified teaching strategies that promote intellectual quality and authenticity. Fred Newmann and his colleagues found that one of the most powerful strategies was the "substantive conversation." By that, the researchers meant "students engage in extended conversational exchanges with the teacher and/or their peers about subject matter in a way that builds an improved or shared understanding of ideas or topics."[23] They stress that such subject-matter conversations go far beyond reporting facts, procedures, or definitions; they focus on making distinctions, applying ideas, forming generalizations, and raising questions. Teachers do not script or control substantive conversations. Rather, they flow from a sharing of ideas among the participants who are working to understand a concept or finish a project. The teacher's skill, art, and knowledge both of the students and the subject guide the conversation and return it to the teaching goals and extend important themes and principles. These conversations may appear to be self-sustaining—requiring little more than the students' interest and urge to participate. But the teacher's role is no more "effortless" than that of skilled athletes (say, a diver, a golfer, or a tight end) at the peak of their performances. Again, knowledge, experience, and relationships are what lie behind these lessons.

Reciprocal Teaching The late Ann Brown and her husband, Joe Campione, both professors at University of California-Berkeley, and Annemarie Palinscar, professor at the University of Michigan, developed strategies that use cognitive and sociocultural learning theories as a basis for teaching reading. These research-based principles have great relevance for adolescent and adult learning as well as for elementary students. One of their strategies, *reciprocal teaching,* teaches children to ask for assistance when they encounter unfamiliar words, to stop and summarize the text periodically, to ask questions about the content, and to predict what they expect to find next. Students work in groups of six or so. Each member takes a turn leading the discussion about an article, a video, or other material they are using to gather information. The leader begins by asking a question and may ask the group to make predictions. Clarifying and summarizing help ensure comprehension. Brown, Campione, and Palinscar believe this strategy works because it "provokes zones of proximal development within which readers of varying abilities can find support. Group cooperation, where everyone is trying to arrive at consensus concerning meaning, relevance, and importance, helps to ensure that understanding occurs, even if some members of the group are not yet capable of full participation. . . . The task is simplified by the provision of social support through a variety of expertise, *not* via decomposition of the task into basic skills."[24] Besides, reciprocal teaching takes advantage of the learning power that relationships bring to school work.

Cognitively Guided Instruction A third approach comes from University of Wisconsin researchers, Tom Carpenter and Elizabeth Fennema, and from Megan Franke, at UCLA. *Cognitively Guided Instruction (CGI)* is not a teaching strategy per se. Rather, the researchers provide groups of teachers information about cognitive theories of learning. Teachers learn how to investigate their students' thinking about mathematics. In other words, teachers learn all they can about how students are making sense or facing obstacles as they use various strategies for problem solving. From this understanding of *how* students are thinking about mathematics (rather than simply assessing "what they know"), teachers plan their lessons. CGI teachers develop their skills to make explicit the knowledge and strategies the students use to solve problems. Teachers ask students to explain, to show how, and to suggest different ways that might work. That is, teachers learn how to ask and students learn how to tell about their learning. Together, students and teachers explore what new strategies are worth trying. As the teachers focus less on what they are transmitting to students and more on how the students are thinking, instruction becomes more closely aligned with the help that students need. Also, the classes become alive with mathematical talk and activity as "figuring out" becomes an interactive or relational rather than an individual experience. In fact, "figuring out" becomes the heart of mathematics and replaces the old paradigm of "doing problems."

Productive Small-Group Work

In the first activity of the Pythagorean theorem unit, I gave students a chance to explore the relationships in the theorem by making sense out of it through their own investigation. Working in pairs and trying to convince each other of their responses, students helped each other see things from different perspectives. It was interesting to watch and listen to students claim their version had more area. It was more interesting to hear their reasons why. Because they were required to explain why and how they knew, students needed to fully analyze the situation while forming their final responses. They were confronted with situations where problem solving was difficult to do alone. I saw students working together and expanding each other's ideas. There appeared to be both a competitive spirit and a cooperative one at the same time. Although students worked together on finding solutions, they still wanted to be the first ones to discover them and explain them to the class.

—Marilyn Cortez
First-year teacher, high school mathematics

Considerable classroom research documents the advantages of students' working together in small groups.[25] In fact, while there remain vigorous disputes over how and when groups ought to work and how groups ought to be formed, there is simply no disagreement among researchers and education policy advisers over whether a substantial amount of group work should occur in classes. Sharing, talking, and working with others should be central to lessons, not by-products or behavior violations. As students work together, they take charge of the assignment. They help divide the lesson into tasks and decide how, when, and who will do each task. In such group work, each student has an opportunity to make valuable contributions to classmates' work. All students can have their work appreciated by others. Despite (or perhaps because of) all the interactions among students, any one student's strengths and weaknesses need not become fodder for comparison or embarrassment. While working with others, students can safely watch and learn how others become successful. Not surprisingly, students in these kinds of classrooms learn more.

Shared Expertise Ann Brown and Joe Campione combined the idea of cooperative group work with Vygotsky's and Piaget's theories of cognitive development. In a project called "Fostering a Community of Learners," Brown and Campione used the following "jigsaw" group strategy in science lessons for low-income African American elementary school students in Oakland, California. In an effort to develop expertise that is both individual and shared by the class, students select a topic for their own "research" that is related to the scientific idea that the class is learning. Then the children work in small groups sharing their expertise with one another. For example, in one class of second graders, the children studied the relationship of animals to their habitat. Some students became experts on how animals protected themselves from predators; others studied animal communication or reproduction. Then design teams composed of experts in each of the areas shared their knowledge to design a habitat or invent an "animal of the future." The teacher's role is that of a more knowledgeable person who guides the individual and group activities with questions and prompts.

In a similar vein, high school teacher Douglas Pollock assigns heterogeneous groups in his twelfth-grade composition classes to write a documented critical essay on a single author. Students in a group read different combinations of, for example, James Baldwin's works. Each student is responsible for his or her own independently produced paper, but the group develops a shared online database of research and support articles brought in from library research and from the Internet. Students reading these articles are quick to point out useful information for others' projects, and considerable common knowledge and cross-fertilization of ideas takes place. Various editing, critiquing, and interim reporting requirements keep students in tune with others' ideas and progress. Students are quickly and easily impressed with the power and extent of their group's literary "intelligence," and how that intelligence becomes the most important resource for their own work. Pollock's conversations with students help them articulate their problems and frustrations and formulate questions that the data or other students can help answer.

Cooperative Learning Well-designed cooperative lessons offer a variety of tasks and paths to success, so they stand a good chance of accommodating students' differences.

Since the mid-1970s several researchers have developed and studied a number of different approaches to cooperative learning. In addition to Elizabeth Cohen's Complex Instruction, strategies that have become popular with teachers include team learning approaches developed by Robert Slavin and his colleagues at Johns Hopkins University, learning together strategies developed by

David and Roger Johnson at the University of Minnesota, and jigsaw methods developed by independent researcher Spencer Kagan. Although all these approaches differ in their particulars, they all enact a common set of principles:

- Positive interdependence—students engage in a task that cannot be successfully completed without cooperation, and each individual's success is dependent on the success of the group.
- Talking together about what is being learned—asking questions and providing explanations to one another is central to the learning process.
- Individual accountability—each student is responsible for his or her own learning and for making a contribution to the group.
- Group social skills—knowing how to work together is not taken for granted but is an explicit part of what students must learn.
- Debriefing the group process—students discuss and evaluate how well they have worked together as a group, as well as judging how well they have learned.

Regardless of the particular strategy a teacher decides to use, good cooperative lessons are nearly impossible unless the knowledge they contain is complex and rich in meaning. Productive cooperative groups must seek rewards from achieving a group goal—a goal that students cannot reach unless each group member does his or her own best work. Such lessons challenge better-skilled students more than competitive lessons do. Simply doing better than others no longer brings easy rewards. All students, regardless of skill level, are able to contribute in areas of their strength, and all can receive help in areas in which they do less well. In cooperative lessons, students have the opportunity to elaborate on the ideas that come easily to them. They can explain and demonstrate their knowledge to others, and they can ask specific questions when they don't understand. All these opportunities help students master difficult concepts. When lessons include these opportunities, the commonly expressed fear that working with others will slow down the progress of better students is unwarranted. Even the strongest students make considerable intellectual gains when they work with students of all skill levels.

However, organizing students for productive group work requires attention to details and to sociocultural principles that make the experience different from what most students, parents, and teachers are familiar with. Especially troublesome may be the concerns of those students, parents, and teachers who previously worked in groups that were haphazardly designed and paid too little attention to the overall learning climate. For four or five students to work together they need to cooperate, but most students, accustomed to competing against their classmates, have few skills for cooperation in classrooms. For example, to work with others productively, students can't keep their ideas a secret, wish their neighbor would fail so that their own efforts will look better, or insist on personal victories. In addition, students can't keep offering excuses if several others have high expectations for them to perform. They have to help others, risk exposing their mistakes, feel safe with their peers, and be able to receive help from them. Moreover, they have to find value in what others offer and view their own success as interdependent with theirs. Without doubt, they need the social skills to resolve the inevitable conflicts that occur. Teachers cannot simply tell students to move their chairs and work together. They must gradually help students develop social skills, and they must design lessons carefully to take advantage of those skills. Absent these steps, group work may not be an improvement over working alone.

I began by having my students work on simpler, shorter activities in teams of two. For instance, I had the small groups of students work together on a set of math problems that they were already familiar with. I did this deliberately so that the students could then focus on working together rather than struggling to understand the problem. After providing various opportunities to work in these two-person groups, I increased the difficulty of the tasks as well as the size of the groups. I continually reinforced positive behavior and pointed out the types of interactions that led to successful groups. Over time students began to realize the sorts of interactions (e.g., effective communication, listening, delegation of responsibilities, and attention to each member's contributions) that needed to occur in order for their group to be successful.

Once my students had learned specific strategies to work collaboratively, I began to expand their responsibilities and increase their role in shaping their own learning experiences. For example, during a science unit, I assigned my students a project that focused on learning scientific methods within a unit on plant biology. Every team or group was responsible for developing its own question to investigate, designing a project, and then implementing it. I felt that if students could choose a topic that interested them, they would have an increased interest in answering it. I wanted the groups to feel as if they were undertaking a common pursuit, and that every team member had to help in order to get the answer they all wanted.

—Erik Korporaal
First-year teacher, grades 4 and 5

A Sample Lesson: To Kill a Mockingbird What does an academic and socially productive cooperative lesson look like? No single lesson can cover the entire range of possibilities, but a literature unit—only briefly sketched here—illustrates some essentials. In a ninth-grade English class, groups of four students had worked together for nearly ten weeks. They had practiced the necessary social skills—how to ask for help and give explanations, share ideas and not dominate, withhold judgments and not put down their classmates and others—and, although certain groups still had problems to work out, most had achieved easy familiarity. The teacher had balanced each group as far as possible, mixing students who differed in race, boys and girls, highly skilled and less-skilled students. She also had mixed high-energy social students with shy, quiet ones.

The class read *To Kill a Mockingbird,* an engaging and intellectually demanding book that is nearly always on the high school reading list. The novel includes themes of racism (including whether the book's treatment of racism is itself racist), justice, early education, one-parent families, small-town life, courage, sexism, maturation, assuming the perspectives of others, and more. Soon after the class started the novel, the special-education resource teacher (who had several students "mainstreamed" in the class) arranged a lunchtime showing of the movie adapted from the novel. Most students didn't want to give up their lunch periods, but several did—including all the special-education students. These students had an easier time reading the book after they had seen the movie. Furthermore, because they had an overview of the novel, they could make valuable contributions in their groups.

After reading about one-third of the book, each group member adopted a different character to follow. As they finished reading, the students wrote short compositions describing their characters and linking them to the book's themes. They took notes on their reading and exchanged ideas with "expert groups." That is, they conferred with their classmates from other groups who had chosen the same character. Although the students could get help and ideas from their classmates, the teacher held all students individually accountable for their brief composition.

The next part of this assignment emphasized group interdependence; that is, no student could successfully complete his or her own work without the participation and cooperation of the student's groupmates. The students wrote a longer composition, entitled "Exploring Themes in *To Kill a Mockingbird* through Four Characters," using the short pieces that each of the four group members had written as source materials. In the longer assignment, the most-skilled students found sophisticated differences and commonalties as they explored the characters and themes. They practiced research conventions by attributing ideas to their sources—quoting from both the novel and their classmates. Less-skilled students stretched beyond their first inclination simply to summarize their group's four papers and attempted to do what their more highly skilled classmates did.

Throughout, the interaction was intense—questioning, explaining, and arguing. The students had pragmatic reasons for engaging others and expecting good work from their fellow group members. As the individual compositions neared completion, the students grew increasingly interested in what their peers were writing. After all, their own ideas were being represented. It's hard to squelch your curiosity when you see your own name in the text or footnote!

When they had finished their compositions, each group wrote a skit loosely based on their characters. Each picked a common conflict at school that concerned them. The groups selected such problems as social cliques, dating, drug use, grade pressure, intimidation and violence, and parent-student trust. Then each student conjectured about how his or her character would fit into the school conflict. (They could take liberties with the character's age or gender.) Each student wrote the dialogue for his or her own character. Finally, the groups performed the skits for the class. Because the skit had a group rather than an individual goal, the group shared a single grade. As with the compositions, each student achieved something by working with others that could not have been achieved by working alone.

Work in small cooperative groups will not solve all the problems that ail typical classes. Nonetheless, successful cooperative groups enable learning to take place while presenting the fewest limits to students, and they help ensure many essential conditions for learning. They also make it more likely that teacher and students will believe that all can succeed. Cooperative lessons, which work best with rich and complex knowledge, provide multiple paths to success, and they promote evaluations that lead to more learning. Importantly, cooperative groups are like barometers that measure much else of what is important to an excellent and equitable class. When cooperative groups are successful, it is likely that there is a teacher who has a deep knowledge of the subject, who has designed rich and complex multiability lessons, who models scaffolding, who deals openly with his values for treating others with respect and dignity, and who frequently engages students in democratic participation and decision making.

How Does Technology Fit?

There is no doubt that technology has become a fundamental part of education. Not only does nearly every school across the nation see computers and the Internet as basic equipment for teaching and learning, students increasingly use computers to learn at home. In 2001, 73 percent of American middle and high school students reported having Internet access, 94 percent of them said they use the Internet for school research projects, and 78 percent said that the Internet helps them with homework.[26]

Just like books, paper, and pencils, however, electronic technologies can serve either traditional or progressive approaches to teaching and learning. Many software packages for classrooms, integrated learning systems with fully developed curriculum on the computer, "distance learning" opportunities beamed in by satellite, and educational Internet sites provide nothing more than traditional instruction wrapped up in electronic packages. On the other hand, used in the context of authentic and active learning communities, these same technologies can scaffold learners' explorations beyond the bounds of their current knowledge and provide multidimensional routes of investigation.

Technology as Scaffolding As with any other instructional materials and activities, teachers' choices of what technology to use and how to use it should be choices about learning, not choices about technology. The U.S. Department of Education has funded the North Central Regional Educational Laboratory (NCREL) to provide technology guidance to teachers and schools around the country. Their charge is to translate the best research on the educational uses of technology into practical guidelines for schools. One of their online publications, *Plugging In,* offers teachers' guidelines for judging whether any particular technology will promote students' active engagement.[27] Their technology "engagability indicators" tap into the dimensions teachers seek when they attempt to create active, multidimensional lessons that scaffold students' learning. To be worth bringing into classrooms the technology must do the following:

- Provide challenging tasks, opportunities and experiences. For example:

  Complex problems and cases; links to unique resources such as museums and libraries; opportunities to examine contrasting events or databases

  Access to experts, peers, and community members who can guide, mentor, tutor, broker, share, inform, and involve students in meaningful ways

  Access to rich media sources for data manipulation or presentations

  Tools for interactive browsing, searching, and authoring

- Allow students to learn by doing. That is, it engages students in planning, reflecting, making decisions, experiencing consequences, and examining alternative solutions and ideas.
- Provide guided participation and provide customized content to suit the particular needs or interests of students. This might include

  Socratic questioning

  Intelligent tutoring

  Diagnosing and guiding an analysis of mistakes

  Adaptations or changes that respond to students' actions.

One example of technology that provides rich, multidimensional tasks and scaffolds students' learning is the *Adventures of Jasper Woodbury* series developed by cognitive psychologist John Bransford and his colleagues at the Cognition and Technology Group at Vanderbilt University. The Jasper adventures are a series of twelve multimedia adventures designed for students in grades 5 and up. Each consists of a videodisc and supporting materials that center on a short video adventure that ends in a complex challenge. For example, in one adventure, Jasper travels upriver to buy an old boat that has no running lights and a small, temporary fuel tank. Students help Jasper determine whether he can make it home before dark without running out of gas. In another adventure, Larry's grandfather has been kidnapped but is able to get a message out, which students must decipher. They help rescue Grandpa by using algebra to decode the note that tells the location of the secret hideout.

The designers of the Jasper adventure series followed the model of good detective novels where all the data necessary to solve the adventure (plus additional data that are not relevant to the solution) are embedded in the story. Jasper adventures also contain "embedded teaching" episodes that provide models of particular approaches to solving problems. The materials are consistent with the National Council of Teachers of Mathematics (NCTM) standards. Teachers can use the adventures as tools to help students develop cognitive skills such as planning, formulating problems, finding and constructing information, mathematical calculation, and decision making. The Jasper series also seeks to bridge the gap between natural learning environments described by sociocultural research and school learning environments. The adventures provide a common context for instruction, an authentic task, and a chance to see that school knowledge can be used to solve real problems.[28]

The Vanderbilt group has followed its Jasper series with a new "Scientists in Action" project, a video-based science problem-solving program aimed at middle schoolers. This new series provides video-based materials that allow students in classrooms to work alongside the student and scientist characters in the video to solve problems that have real meaning for the students. The activities emphasize scientific processes of data collection, analysis, problem formulation, and hypothesis testing, and the materials focus on what the creators call the "deep principles" of science. By this they mean the conceptual understanding of larger science principles, in contrast to simply learning a list of science terms. The video portrayals of scientists also emphasize that scientists in the real world often work outside of laboratories in cooperative groups and that they are representative of the diverse American population.

In one Scientists in Action episode, "The Stones River Mystery," students in the field and in an electronically connected classroom have been monitoring a local river for pollution. During one sampling trip they notice that the measures they are monitoring have begun to change. The students and scientists must work together to determine where the pollution in coming from. In another, "The Lost Letters of Lazlo Clark," a time capsule has been found during a renovation of the local high school. In it are letters and a map from Lazlo Clark, a local philanthropist who had donated a large tract of land to the area almost 100 years ago. Students and their science teacher set out to find some Native American petroglyphys mentioned in Clark's letters. Although their initial trip is not successful, it helps them understand the importance of planning to make such a trip and how much science is needed.

Following guidelines like those developed by NCREL, teachers will be able to discern high-quality technology like the *Adventures of Jasper Woodbury* and the Scientists in Action project from the overabundance of low-level, trivial applications. This will allow them to bring technology to bear on their efforts to develop a sociocultural pedagogy.

The Digital Divide As with many other things, however, the widespread and creative use of computers in education is not evenly distributed across students and schools. Even though the most recent numbers suggest that schools serving low-income students and students of color have nearly as many computers as schools serving more-advantaged students, we also know that minorities remain among the "least connected" at home and school. According to a recent study, white students—even when income is taken into account—were more than twice as likely to have access to home computers as black students were. Moreover, white students who didn't have home computers were more likely to log on to the Internet at other locations than their black peers who didn't have access at home. And while the percentage of classrooms with Internet access in the nation's wealthiest schools rose from 62 percent to 74 percent in one year, students in many remote rural areas attend schools where telecommunications companies have yet to lay the fiber-optic cable necessary to run high-speed Internet. In some of these schools, slow Internet lines make it very difficult to download a few e-mail messages, and downloading video and audio clips is out of the question.[29]

Within schools, other divides remain. Janet Schofield's ethnographic study of how computer instruction was received and used in an urban midwestern high school found the computing lab to be claimed by a subset of white gifted boys who used it as their lunch room, gathering there during free periods and after school.[30] The computer lab became their "turf." Ownership was further bolstered by teachers who often relied on these students to help set up equipment, troubleshoot, and teach. In a variety of subtle and not-so-subtle ways, women and African American students were made to feel unwelcome in the lab.[31] Other evidence suggests that teachers tend to infuse technology into lessons much less with low-achieving students than with high achievers and that computer use is often limited for students learning English.

Gender differences in access and use of technology are not trivial. UCLA researcher Jane Margolis and her colleagues studied college students for four years and found that both male and female students, as well as teachers, expect males to be better at computing. Not surprisingly, they also found that these technology settings that expected girls to be inept also damage girls' confidence.[32] Some politicians and educators argue that the digital divide is really a result of personal preference rather than discrimination. However, it's a bit hard to believe that some students' choices can account for the limited access their schools provide. What we do know is that as technology gets more sophisticated, the divide is less about whether a machine is available than what the machine is connected to and how that machine is used for teaching and learning. Finally, there are important social justice implications to this "personal choice" argument. The proper role for schools must be to find the ways to prepare all students well and equally, not for schools to "excuse" themselves by saying that some don't want to learn.

Assessment for Learning

The excretory organelles of some unicellular organisms are contractile vacuoles and

A) Cell membranes
B) Cell walls
C) Ribosomes
D) Centrioles

—From the study guide for the 1995
New York Regents test in high school biology

Researcher Linda Darling-Hammond cites this typical example of a test question that focuses learning, instruction, and curriculum only on "the trappings of intellectual rigor" and crowds out the opportunity and motivation for making knowledge meaningful and useful.[33] The question is technical and specific, seems difficult, and appears to be measuring important knowledge. However, it really measures nothing more than whether a student has memorized definitions of words unique to the discipline (i.e., *organelles, ribosomes*).[34] And yet this type of assessment has a firm grip on the world of schools and the public's imagination. The ability to answer questions such as these shapes judgments about what students have learned, how they compare with other students, and what their future schooling opportunities will be. How well all students do with such questions becomes the basis for society's evaluation of the goodness of its schools.

The terms assessment, testing, and evaluation have overlapping meanings, but they also have some important distinctions. Generally, *assessment* implies gathering all the relevant information that can inform decisions about teaching, including information about the students and conditions for learning. This information may include test results. *Testing* is a more specific, more formal procedure by which a teacher obtains a sample of what a student knows or can do and generalizes about the student's broader knowledge—as when a few multiplication problems indicate whether the student understands multiplication or when a composition reveals the student's writing skills. *Evaluation* includes a judgment of the student's performance and involves some element of whether the performance is *good.* Grades are typically evaluations.

Tests: The Assessment That Counts

The nation looks to tests to tell it what is happening in schools. The senator looks at international comparisons in math scores; the governor proclaims a crisis when her state's achievement scores are lower than other states; the real estate salesperson touts the local school's test scores; the parent comes to school and wants to see the teacher's answer key or dispute his daughter's essay grade; and the student wants to know, "How many points is it worth?" Parents and policymakers are less willing to accept assurances that—given the resources they have to work with—schools and teachers are doing a good job, or even the best possible job. It seems that everybody wants a test to settle their concerns efficiently, scientifically, and fairly. Nearly every day each student is tested, results are reported, judgments are made, and actions are taken.

Tests Compare As structurally different as tests such as the SAT and Iowa Test of Basic Skills are from the teacher's spelling quiz and essay, all tests have in common the element of comparison.

- Tests that compare student performance against a standard of particular knowledge and facts are called *criterion-referenced* tests, or more recently, just *standards.* For example, on a spelling test the student's answers are compared with the correct version of the words that were assigned.

- Tests that compare students' performance with that of other students are called *norm-referenced* tests. For example, on the SAT the most relevant scoring information reveals how the student did in relation to the performance of other students. In the classroom, teachers typically do not use sophisticated statistical designs, but they may have an informal protocol (or "curve") for giving the top few performances A's and the lowest scores D's and F's—based as much on how the class as a whole performs as on the student's actual number of correct answers.
- Tests that compare student performance on a simulated, real-life task with the performance of an already accomplished person are called *performance* assessments. For example, a student group designs and maintains its own stock market "mutual fund," gaining specific economic and investor knowledge; at the end of the semester they prepare a prospectus to report on their fund and convince new investors to join. Or more simply, the teacher has students write a letter to the principal complaining about cafeteria hamburgers and evaluates writing skills exhibited in this "real" activity.

These are not precise categories. For example, all three of the preceding types of tests can be guided by standards, and any type of performance can be "normed" or statistically manipulated for comparisons among the test takers. One important distinction (others will be discussed later) is that performance tests are much less easily *standardized*—making them less useful for many traditional testing purposes.

Tests Claim Objectivity A second element that these tests have in common besides comparisons is that they rely on a particular "technology"—a defined set of practices, rules, and standards. The traditional trappings of scientific efficiency are required to make this technology trustworthy and legitimate, valid and reliable.[35] These include objectivity (the answers or judgments are not open to interpretation, bias, or dispute) and the requirement that test performances be reducible to statistical representations (scores, grades, averages). Even so-called subjective tests—essays and performance tests, for example—become objectified in their scoring and reporting processes. Thus, the teacher's reading of the essay test may be translated into points (87), the points into a grade (B plus), the grade into a class grade (B), which goes back into points before it can be averaged into the grade point average. As a practical matter, awareness of the essay's subjectivity evaporates just a few steps into the process. Likewise, there is nothing especially objective about a multiple-choice test other than the fact that a machine can score it. The decisions to include particular questions, the grading scale, the amount of time given for instruction and to take the test, and the weight or importance given to the test are all subjective decisions.

Tests Sort for Future Opportunities A third common element of traditional assessments is their claim to be fair and accurate tools for sorting students for future schooling opportunities. For example, will the student be promoted, go to an honors class, get into algebra in the seventh grade? Will the student repeat a class or be assigned to a class more likely to be taught by an uncredentialed teacher?

Today's teachers must use and respond to tests of all sorts—their own and those that others design and administer. As a result, they need a thorough understanding of the technologies of assessment, testing, and evaluation—more thorough than what is sketched here. If teachers accept uncritically these three common elements of tests (they compare, they claim scientific accuracy, and they sort) they step into a value-laden territory that defies teaching for all students' success.

Assessment as Integral to Learning

All tests have one other element in common. Tests proceed from an assumption of a *test giver*—powerful with knowledge and licensed to judge others—and a *test taker*—without power and submitting to judgment. In this respect conventional tests are consistent with traditional behavioral and transmission models of learning. By contrast, many teachers today are struggling hopefully with alternatives to conventional testing.

I have come to believe that assessment is one of the most overlooked challenges, especially if one departs from the multiple-choice/pencil-and-paper/procedural tests that are nicely provided in the Teacher's Edition. Do I just walk around the room and give grades based on content of discussion? How do I respond to the author of a journal entry who already understood the concept versus the hardworking author who finally achieved some degree of understanding? Do I respond differently? Will it take me a solid week to grade the test with open-ended questions? What if a good student does a poor job when editing another student's paper? How do I use the results of assessments to guide my teaching or grade student achievement? As a new teacher, I tried a variety of methods to begin learning how to assess my students' mathematical understanding and use the information to inform my instructional practices.

I used writing as an assessment tool as much as I could. (Next year, I know I can use writing even more.) Students had to write about their process of solving the problem. Strategies, false starts, steps they took, diagrams that helped—all these items and more were part of the process about which I wanted students to write. Not only did I want to know what they were doing and why, I wanted them to have to reason and justify their thought process. I did learn an incredible amount about how students think about mathematics. By giving students an opportunity to articulate their internal thought processes, I was able to assess understanding of the problem. I could identify strengths or weaknesses in their logic and help them, or comment accordingly.

—Juliana Jones
First-year teacher, middle-school mathematics

Learning that proceeds from a sociocultural and social justice perspective is not compatible with the unbalanced and coercive relationships that traditional testing fosters. Ideally, a sociocultural vision of assessment is seamlessly integrated with the student's learning. In this ideal vision, assessment and the scaffolding by which the student and teacher co-construct the student's new knowledge are indistinguishable.

Somewhere between this ideal and the social and educational conventions within which today's teachers must work are nontraditional assessments that bring teaching substantially closer to productive learning relationships. Teachers like Jennifer Garcia, who see knowledge and learning from a constructivist perspective, emphasize different elements for assessment than those discussed earlier. Constructivist teachers take note of the knowledge and skills students display when they participate in class. They observe how students interact and how they solve problems. They follow closely the nature and appropriateness of students' reasoning as well as the correctness of their answers. These teachers may well give assignments and tests, but they analyze students' responses to uncover gaps and errors in students' thinking about what they are learning and to help frame new strategies for pushing that thinking further.

I used concept maps in a variety of circumstances—from a quick comprehension check to an alternative way of assessing at the end my unit on World War I and Progressive Politics. Concept maps allow teachers (and students) to determine whether critical historical connections are being made. They test comprehension, not facts, and focus on what students know and the connections they can make, instead of what they don't know. They ask students to demonstrate historical understandings at a deeper level than a more traditional objective form of assessment (i.e., multiple choice, matching) because they must relate concepts to each other. One student, for example, connected the events of World War I pre–U.S. involvement to events in World War I post–U.S. involvement. However, his concept map told me that while he was able to recall many specifics from this historical period, he did not address the larger concepts. This format leaves plenty of room for individual differences; students realize that there is no one "correct" answer and that there is room for individual interpretation and analysis. Allowing for this type of maximum freedom (as much as is possible in a formal assessment situation) allows students of all abilities and types of intelligences to succeed academically.

—Jennifer Garcia
First-year teacher, history, grade 11

Assessments of this sort promote learning and social justice in classrooms because they can support teachers' beliefs that all students can learn, and students' beliefs that their hard work will bring success. These assessments can lead to instruction that is increasingly rich, complex, and full of meaning. Traditional comparison testing undermines lessons that offer authentic tasks with a variety of routes to success. Further, authentic assessments help teachers avoid the easy comparisons made possible by grades, numbers, and rankings and that everyone in the classroom and throughout the school can transform into destructive judgments about who is smart and who isn't. The following sections elaborate principles for assessment that supports authentic learning and is socially just.

When Assessment Is "Authentic" Linda Darling-Hammond proposes that assessments should be based on "meaningful performances in real-world contexts," and that these performances should be so "closely entwined as to be often inseparable" from the curriculum itself.[36] She points to schools that engage students in demonstrating their learning in exhibitions and portfolios with "products like mathematical models, literary critiques, scientific experiments, dance performances, debates, and oral presentations and defense of ideas." In such performances, rich conceptual knowledge, understanding, and problem-solving skills do not have to be broken up into small bits that can be easily measured with conventional testing.

Recall the University of Wisconsin researchers' definition of *authentic* (noted at the beginning of this chapter) as the extent to which a lesson, assessment task, or sample of student performance represents construction of knowledge through the use of disciplined inquiry that has some value or meaning beyond success in school.[37] *Disciplined inquiry* means that students work within the conventions of the scholarly discipline of the topic they are studying. Thus, the biology student would present her findings as a biologist might, by writing her findings in a report or demonstrating and discussing an experiment (this, of course, during and after her authentic learning/instruction, in which she learned as a biologist learns—reading, working collaboratively, reporting and checking findings, etc.).

When Assessment Is Interactive At best, "What did you learn?" is a question that should generate a narrative where students put some of their thinking into language. This is true even in those disciplines that are not primarily represented in spoken or written language—for example, music, mathematics, art, and so on. However, visual and symbolic representations are also useful for assessments in traditionally "language-only" subjects such as English and social studies. Even so, most of our school and interpersonal interactions rely on language to communicate how we have sorted knowledge into sequences and formed whole impressions and conclusions. As students construct logical answers that include descriptions, facts, experiences, and problems, they *use* their knowledge to sort, form, and conclude. This process makes their knowledge richer and more complex than if they had simply repeated facts or tried to recognize and choose the correct answer on a paper-and-pencil test.

When teacher and student go back and forth during assessments, the teacher can adjust on the spot to help the student express what he knows. Only in a spoken exchange can a teacher sense when it is appropriate to say, "Take a few more seconds to think about it" or "Let's skip that for now; we can come back to it later." Interactions can be open-ended. When teachers ask students probing questions like "What do you think of that?," "What will you do next?,"

"Why did you do it that way?," and "How did you figure that out?," they get as close as they can to the heart of the students' learning. Then students' responses will reveal their sense-making—not just their conclusions.

Interactive assessments generate responses that guide teachers as they help, explain, and provide feedback. Both teachers and students can make "course corrections" when students get stuck. These exchanges can help students become more comfortable with assessment and increase their efforts to do better. Students can begin to see assessment as a process by which a friendly person helps them identify and overcome roadblocks to learning. First-year history teacher Jennifer Garcia used journals as a forum for such "informal and comfortable" dialogues.

I used journal entries as a continuous form of informal assessment, and as a means of communicating more personally with students about what they were learning and how they felt about it. The goal was not to elicit any particular "correct" response, but to allow students to find their own voices and write about what interested them in that historical unit. Keeping the journal provided an opportunity for students to take time to reflect and opened up an informal and comfortable dialogue between the students and me (particularly for those learning English as a second language who are often reluctant to participate in other ways). Many commented that they appreciated time to reflect and ask questions in a private way, and even that they appreciated the response comments by me. This form of informal assessment can help develop self-confidence and student voice.

—*Jennifer Garcia*
First-year teacher, history, grade 11

If students receive feedback in the form of new questions and subtle encouragement, it prompts them to explore beyond their first hunches. Unlike conventional testing, or classroom question-response teaching—where a common first inclination is to give up, to say "I don't know," or to select any answer just to get over the discomfort—students raise their own questions as they explain what they have learned. They can elaborate and clarify. For example, both student and teacher might discover that the multiplication a student thought she knew (and passed a test on) last week has been forgotten. A question might uncover that *transcendentalism*—an awkward definition in yesterday's class—is now an intriguing idea (even if the definition is *still* awkward). The next steps in learning become more clearly focused and continue from where these answers end.

Teachers can keep interactive assessment nonthreatening and nonjudgmental, in part, because it can be negotiable. That is, teachers don't need to ask all students the same questions. Furthermore, they can accept many answers at many different levels of sophistication, depending on the question and on students' prior knowledge. For example, students often seem to know very little when their teachers or classmates first ask a question. If the teacher (or the test) accepts the first response as the final answer, this may confirm that the student knows very little. Given the chance to think about the question and receive some clarification, however, the student might reveal more knowledge than anyone thought he had, including himself. Such interaction invites follow-up questions and additional elaboration. Not only do teachers gain more insight into the student's knowledge, they elicit important misinformation that can create obstacles if not corrected.

Authentic and interactive assessments keep students working. Nobody gets off the hook by giving perfunctory, if correct, answers. Authentic assessments make it difficult for students to excuse themselves by quietly accepting a bad grade *before* the exam even takes place. Moreover, reasoning and figuring out take place *as a part of* the learning and assessment process, not at the end of the unit and just before the test. Ongoing assessments challenge students to go beyond the usual classroom study habits of skimming the chapters, doing problems, and studying before a test, and never again bothering with the material. Last, authentic assessments have a way of permeating the classroom culture. Students' interactions among themselves begin to take on many of the teachers' values, habits, and skills for authenticity that contribute to a learning-assessing community.

When Assessment Provides Multiple Routes to Success

I created a demonstration project assessment to assess students' historical understandings of the connections between the concepts of industrialization, unionism, and immigration (i.e., how they could tie together themes such as immigration trends, political machines, early union efforts, factory conditions, production changes, changes in gender roles, etc.). I did not set limits on the format, but I suggested some possible ideas. Students created immigrant journals, posters and advertisements, and original songs that showed they were able to incorporate both the historical evidence and creativity and originality at a deeper intellectual level. In the immigrant journals, students assumed the persona of an immigrant who came to the United States during the 1880s. Common themes included descriptions of what countries they immigrated from, why they immigrated, their immigration journey, the processing (Ellis Island), living conditions in urban areas, factory working conditions (union vs. nonunion), and so on. These journals were not re-creations or copies of texts/outside resources—they were original stories that students developed from lectures and their impressions of what experiences real people went through. This was a new form of assessment for many students and I was unsure about how seriously students would take it. I was impressed with the success, particularly for those who do not test well. I learned that it is a good teaching strategy to give students a variety of ways to be assessed so that each student can succeed, allowing their individual strengths to shine through.

—Jennifer Garcia
First-year teacher, history, grade 11

First-year teacher Christopher Yusi also found that some students can become as engaged in and learn as much from the assessment as the lesson itself—all the more reason for seeing the two as inseparable.

As a final project, the class made mobiles to hang around our room. Each mobile consisted of two main characters, two settings, and one plot. Each piece of the mobile was shaped and illustrated on one side to match what they represented, and on the other side students wrote a description or narrative. This was a great final project, because it afforded students the opportunity to use different modalities to show what they had learned. Most of the unit consisted of reading and writing, with too few creative, artistic exercises. But when we developed the rubric for the final mobile project, some students' motivation seemed to skyrocket.

—Christopher Yusi
First-year teacher, grades 4 and 5

When Assessment Is Personalized Teachers can assess individual students' progress and avoid public comparisons. However, most teachers still work in schools with policies that require traditional evaluations and record keeping. A goal, then, is to use authentic assessments while promoting a classroom culture that both cares about students' progress and protects privacy. One high school teacher discussed privacy concerns with his class, and the class agreed to this policy. "*Do* inquire about classmates' grades if you are genuinely interested in their progress, if you have worked with or helped them on the assignment, and you care about them. If you do inquire, do so outside of class. *Do not* sneak a look at someone's grade or shout out 'Wadja get?' "

Increasingly, teachers are balancing traditional evaluations and grades with strategies for students to demonstrate to others their growing competence. When others can witness and then respond to one's work, assessment occurs *and* learning continues. For example, many teachers ask their students to collect samples of their work over time in a *portfolio*—like artists who keep samples of their work. Students might include a series of writing samples, experiments, lists of books they've read, math problems that they've solved, and more. Portfolios work well when they go beyond simple collections of all of the student's work and instead allow students to assess and select work that represents their best achievements and growth. Teachers, parents, classmates, and students themselves can reflect and discuss the portfolio. This would be most productive if each piece of work were not identified with a score or grade—something that defeats much of the usefulness of the portfolio. Many teachers, though, do find a way to give feedback for each or most of the students' work as it is accomplished, making sure that students know well the specific criteria for quality work. For example, one criterion might be that the work demonstrates a strategy that the student has not attempted previously. Personalized methods of evaluating and reporting student learning also communicate substantive and meaningful information to parents about what their child has learned, and how well.

Assessment with High Stakes

In the past decade, large-scale, standardized "high-stakes" tests have become the single most popular policy instrument for raising academic standards in schools. The idea of "high stakes" is that performance on the test has important consequences—so-called carrots and sticks that will entice or prod educators and students to perform well on tests in order to reap rewards or avoid punishing sanctions. For students, the rewards are mostly the right to be in a high-level class or program, to be promoted to the next grade, to graduate from high school, to qualify for college, and, in a few cases, to win scholarship money. The sanctions for students who perform badly are being retained in grade or being denied a high school diploma. These are the strategies that politicians advocate to end so-called social promotion—the much lambasted practice of promoting students according to their age, rather than their achievement. The use of social promotion as the problem to be corrected reveals that the imposition of high-stakes testing is largely political rather than educational. Notably, social promotion has not been formal educational policy, and few educators even think it's a good idea.

High-stakes decisions for schools and principals are those that label them as "good" or "bad" relative to other schools and principals. The carrots for educators in a growing number of states include cash payments for score increases, being assigned a "grade," and the pride that comes with being at the top of very public rankings. The sticks include such things as being humiliated as a low-performing school, or, at worst, being taken over by the state or shut down altogether. Some policies also provide "targeted assistance" (what UCLA law professor Gary Blasi has called "hard carrots") giving students and educators a chance to improve before sanctions are levied. Such assistance for students includes their being placed in a special segregated remedial class or program or, for those who need remedial work, being required to attend summer school. Some schools are provided an intervention team that comes in to help "fix" their problems. Teachers have little control over these policies, but they certainly feel their effects in their classrooms, as well as in their public image.

The increasing use of test-driven high-stakes policies has brought an outcry of criticism that almost equals the enthusiasm of supporters. The concerns are both technical (e.g., concerns about tests being inaccurate or biased), political (e.g., disagreement that tests will "motivate" improvement), and philosophical (e.g., objections to an overemphasis on a narrow set of measurable outcomes as opposed to the larger democratic purposes of schooling). Most critics worry that the tests have become an end in themselves, rather than the means to achieve a valued educational end. The impact of widespread protest has varied. In some places high-stakes policies have been rolled back, softened, or postponed. Mostly, these protests have generated corrections aimed at fixing specific problems with particular policies; they have done little to stem the popularity and increasing use of high-stakes testing as the cornerstone of school reform.

Can High-Stakes Tests Be Scientifically and Educationally Defensible? In 1999 Congress mandated the National Academy of Sciences to study the ways in which large-scale tests were being used to make high-stakes decisions and to recommend ways of using tests that are scientifically and educationally defensible. The Academy panel investigated three high-stakes uses of testing: tracking, grade promotion, and high school graduation. In particular, they looked at whether tests were used in discriminatory ways and whether they were used accurately to measure students' achievements. The panel established a set of principles for appropriate use of tests:

- The test is valid for the specific purpose for which it is used. For example, tests that might be good for influencing classroom practice are not valid for making decisions about students unless they match the curriculum and teaching that students actually experience.
- Because no test is perfect, no single score can be considered a definitive measure of students' knowledge.
- A single test score should not be used for making consequential decisions in the absence of other information about students' knowledge and skills.
- A test-driven decision cannot be justified if the consequence is not educationally sound.

The panel also warned that differences in test results and consequences among groups of students—such as the lower scores and higher retention rates of low-income students of color must be carefully studied. These differences may not necessarily mean that there is something wrong with the particular test being used, but, rather, reveal troublesome gaps in students' opportunities to learn. Either cause, however, signals a serious problem with a high-stakes policy.

The panel issued a set of findings and recommendations to ensure the accuracy and fairness of high-stakes decisions. Important among these is that accountability for school performance belongs to the whole system, from states to parents, and cannot be imposed only on students. Consequently, high-stakes tests should only be used after changes in teaching and learning ensure that students have a genuine opportunity to learn what is tested. Moreover, special accommodations must be provided to accurately test English language learners and students with disabilities. Neither leaving them out of assessments nor simply testing them like everyone else is appropriate. Finally, if tests are used to make high-stakes decisions about individual children, the system must carefully monitor such practices and study their impact on students.[38]

Can High-Stakes Tests Be Legally Defensible? The civil rights community has also raised serious questions about whether high-stakes testing denies educational opportunity to students based on their race, national origin, sex, or disability. The NAACP Legal Defense Fund held a national conference on the topic on the forty-sixth anniversary of the *Brown v. Board of Education* decision, where representatives of dozens of civil rights organizations, including MALDF (Mexican American Legal Defense Fund), made easing the impact of high-stakes tests on minority students a priority. In 1999 the Office of Civil Rights drafted a report, "The Use of Tests When Making High-Stakes Decisions for Students: A

Resource Guide for Educators," that laid out some of the professional and legal standards for educators and policymakers. The ORC guide applies to testing the legal principles articulated in the Fourteenth Amendment to the Constitution and in federal statues and regulations—namely that intentional discrimination is prohibited, as are programs with a discriminatory disparate impact. Additionally, the guide discusses the legal obligation to provide for the special needs of English language learners and students with disabilities, and the need to ensure Fifth Amendment due process rights for all students subjected to high-stakes testing decisions. Rather than criticize testing per se, the guide makes clear that the OCR, like most civil rights advocates, believes that the appropriate use of testing can advance learning and help safeguard educational opportunity. However, it also insists that good educational results are compatible with the enforcement of principles of nondiscrimination.

Unfortunately, this useful document has never been distributed. When the George W. Bush administration took office in 2001, the OCR placed the guide into a new category on its website—"archival file retained for historical purposes." Although this does not mean that the document will never see the light of day, it adds additional evidence about just how political the testing of students has become.

All of my students are not completely fluent in English, yet they are forced to take the state and district assessment in English. My students are very smart; they are problem solvers and critical thinkers. They are constantly learning about how to better themselves, their community, and their country. They make decisions for themselves when we talk in community circles. In their writing, they demonstrate skills using their own personal experiences. Since I allow my students to use their Spanish when they speak and write, they are able to express their thoughts with meaning and value. They are able to take their writing and thinking to a higher level when they form their own ideas about how to make this world a better, safer, nonviolent society. It infuriates and frustrates me that standardized assessments step in the path of the exciting, high-level critical thinking skills my students have acquired. I will continue to teach my students strategies for taking these tests, but I will also continue to struggle to find ways to incorporate a safe, multicultural learning experience for them.

—Magda Gonzales
First-year teacher, grades 3 and 4

No Easy Recipes

This chapter focused on three important characteristics of classrooms that shape the quality of teaching and learning:

1. Beliefs about students' capability have enormous power. Learning depends on the degree to which classrooms foster students' beliefs in their own competence and their willingness to work hard.
2. Organizing instruction around social interactions enables sociocultural learning processes.
3. Assessment that is integral to instruction not only provides more valid information about what students have learned, it also provides rich occasions for learning.

These three characteristics don't translate into easy prescriptions for teaching practices. However, they matter as much or more than any specific classroom design, curriculum, individual lessons, theories, materials, or elaborate school programs. How teachers enact the preceding items in their classrooms profoundly influences students' willingness and ability to apply their natural learning processes to formal school learning and makes a critical difference in allowing all students in a diverse society to succeed at school.

Digging Deeper

Some of the following scholars and resources can provide readers with a deeper understanding of instructional and assessment theories. Others provide practical, research-based ideas and strategies.

Jo Boaler, associate professor of mathematics education at Stanford, specializes in mathematics education and teacher education, with particular interests in the effectiveness of different teaching environments, the inequitable nature of mathematics classrooms, and situated analyses of learning. Her 1997 book, *Experiencing School Mathematics: Teaching Styles, Sex and Setting,* presents, in a highly readable fashion, the results of a carefully conducted three-year study of the teaching of mathematics in two high schools. Through carefully conducted analyses of interviews with students, observations of lessons, and achievement test data, it provides evidence of the limitations of "traditional" teaching methods, and a resounding endorsement of the approaches of "reform" schools.

John Bransford is Centennial Professor of Psychology and Education and codirector of the Learning Technology Center at Vanderbilt University. Author of seven books and hundreds of articles and presentations, Bransford is an internationally renowned scholar in cognition and technology. He and his colleagues at Vanderbilt have developed and tested innovative computer, videodisc, CD-ROM, and Internet programs including the Jasper Woodbury problem-solving series in mathematics, the Scientists in Action series, and the Little Planet Literacy series—programs that have received many awards. The Young Children Literacy series provides the basis of an exciting "Great

Beginnings" project in Nashville that links homes, schools, and members of the broader community through innovative uses of technology.

Professors **Ann Brown** (deceased) and **Joseph Campione** of the University of California-Berkeley have studied learning in inner-city classrooms. The goal of their research has been to transform grade school classrooms from worksites where students perform assigned tasks under the management of teachers into communities of learning and interpretation, where students are given significant opportunity to take charge of their own learning. A recent description of this work can be found in "Guided Discovery in a Community of Learners," in *Classroom Lessons: Integrating Cognitive Theory and Classroom Practice,* edited by Kate McGilly (Cambridge, MA: MIT Press, 1994).

Professor **Elizabeth Cohen** and her colleagues in the Complex Instruction Project at Stanford University have published several books exploring how schools can teach at a uniformly high level when their students vary tremendously in terms of achievement, proficiency in the language of instruction, and social status. Part of Professor Cohen's solution for teaching to diverse classrooms is Complex Instruction, an approach that focuses on the development of higher-order thinking skills and small-group problem solving. This approach is proving to be particularly effective at promoting equal access to learning opportunities in heterogeneous classrooms. Cohen's most recent books include *Designing Groupwork: Strategies for the Heterogeneous Classroom* (New York: Teachers College Press, 1997) and *Working for Equity in Heterogeneous Classrooms,* with Rachel Lotan (New York: Teachers College Press, 1997).

Constructivist Education Bookstore Online (in association with Amazon .com online bookseller) provides a good list of resources for teachers interested in constructivist approaches to assessment, bilingual education, constructivist pedagogy, and specific content areas. The bookstore is on the Internet at http://www.sunwebdesigns.com/constructivist.

Larry Cuban spent fourteen years teaching social studies in inner-city high schools and seven years as a district superintendent before becoming a professor of the history of U.S. education at Stanford University. His book *How Teachers Taught: Constancy and Change in American Classrooms 1890–1990* (New York: Teachers College Press, 1993) traces the history of teaching in U.S. schools.

The **Cognitively Guided Instruction** group consists of Professors **Tom Carpenter** and **Elizabeth Fennema** of the University of Wisconsin and Professor **Megan Franke** of UCLA. Individually and together, this team has written a number of articles in research journals documenting their work helping teachers learn about children's mathematical thinking and supporting teachers as they develop teaching strategies based on this knowledge. Their article "Cognitively Guided Instruction: A Knowledge Base for Reform in Primary Mathematics Instruction," in the *Elementary School Journal* 97, no. 1 (1996), pp. 3–20, provides an introduction to this work. Other information about Cognitively Guided Instruction can be found on the National Science Foundation site on the Internet at http://red.www.nsf.gov/ABOUT/articles/itaddsup.html.

Kris Gutierrez, a UCLA professor of education, studies how teachers develop classroom interactions that provide the apprenticeship opportunities and scaffolding of students' literacy development. Her research documents constructive patterns of teacher and student talk in what she calls "collaborative/responsive" classrooms. It also describes how students can assume various roles in their own and peers' learning in whole-class as well as small-group activities. An overview of the implications of this work for teachers can be found in "Constructing Classrooms as Communities of Effective Practice," with Joanne Larson, in *Culture and Literacy: Bridging the Gap Between Community and Classroom,* edited by Peter Smagorinsky (Champaign, IL: National Council of Teachers of English, 1998).

Also at UCLA, Professor **Yasmin Kafai** has developed Kids Interactive Design Studios, a design experiment that uses computer and Internet technology to help create classroom learning settings that are compatible with sociocultural perspectives on learning. Kafai also studies issues of gender and technology. Her work is reported in *Minds in Play: Computer Game Design as a Context for Children's Learning* (Hillsdale, NJ: Erlbaum, 1995).

Deborah Meier was principal of one of the most remarkable public schools in the country, Central Park East (CPE) in East Harlem, for twenty years. The East Harlem project has been driven by the core belief that "all children could and should be inventors of their own theories, critics of other people's ideas, analyzers of evidence, and makers of their own personal marks on this most complex world. . . . [Thus], ideas are not luxuries gained at the expense of the 3 R's, but instead enhance them." In her book based on the CPE experience, *The Power of Their Ideas: Lessons for America from a Small School in Harlem* (Boston: Beacon Press, 1995), Meier argues for teaching that connects learning to real-world activities.

The National Center for Fair & Open Testing (FairTest) is an advocacy organization working to end the abuses, misuses, and flaws of standardized testing and ensure that evaluation of students is fair, open, and educationally sound. The center emphasizes eliminating the racial, class, gender, and cultural barriers to equal opportunity posed by standardized tests and preventing their damage to the quality of education. FairTest publishes a quarterly newsletter, *The Examiner,* plus a catalog of materials on both K–12 and university testing to aid teachers, administrators, students, parents, and researchers. FairTest can be found on the Internet at http://fairtest.org.

Fred Newmann, professor and researcher at the University of Wisconsin Center for Educational Research, and his colleagues Professors **Gary Wehlage** and **Walter Secada** developed the concept of authentic pedagogy based on their studies of teaching that emphasizes higher-order thinking, supports the learning of low-income students of color, and fosters high levels of engagement and interaction. A description of authentic instruction can be found in Fred Newmann, editor, *Authentic Achievement: Restructuring Schools for Intellectual Quality* (San Francisco: Jossey-Bass, 1996).

Professor **Annemarie Palinscar** of the University of Michigan developed reciprocal teaching, a dialogue between teachers and students to summarize, generate questions, clarify, and predict the meaning of text. Her book *Teaching Reading as Thinking* (Alexandria, VA: Association for Supervision and

Curriculum Development, 1984) describes the procedures of reciprocal teaching, modifications of the basic strategies, and means of evaluating its effectiveness.

Faye Peitzman, director of the UCLA Writing Project, has collected strategies for teaching the academic subjects to students who are also learning English. In *With Different Eyes: Insights into Teaching Language Minority Students Across the Disciplines* (Reading, MA: Addison-Wesley, 1994), edited with George Gadda, experienced teachers offer practical strategies on how to integrate writing across the disciplines, apply analytical reading and critical thinking tasks to course content, and modify traditional methods of assessing students' subject mastery.

As past president of the American Educational Research Association, University of Colorado Professor **Lorrie Shepard**'s presidential address at the group's 2000 annual meeting in New Orleans provides an extraordinarily helpful explanation of the role of assessment in classroom learning. In her talk, "The Role of Assessment in Learning Culture," Shepard provides a historical overview of testing that shows the connections among tests, ideas of scientific management, and behavioral learning theories; she provides a contrasting framework grounded in cognitive, constructivist, and sociocultural perspectives; and she argues for changes in assessment practices that are consistent with this alternative framework. Shepherd's article is published in *Educational Researcher* 28, no. 7 (October 2000), pp. 4–14.

The book *The Dialogic Curriculum: Teaching and Learning in a Multicultural Society* (New York: Boynton/Cook, 1995), by **Patricia Lambert Stock** of Michigan State University, provides a detailed portrait of inquiry-based, integrated language arts teaching in two twelfth-grade classes where she and her colleagues taught literature by asking students to read and write about subjects that mattered to them. Stock's book describes both teachers' planning and students' reading, writing, and talking in ways that expand their experiences and literacy.

Roland Tharp, professor at the University of California-Santa Cruz, has studied cultural forces in psychological development and change in a variety of settings. His current work is in the research and development of effective educational programs for minority children. His colleague, Professor **Ronald Gallimore** of UCLA, has built on the work he and Tharp began in Hawaii to include teachers in a low-income, largely Latino district in the Los Angeles area. Together Gallimore, his research team, and the teachers work to develop instructional conversations and nonscripted, responsive interactions between teacher and students that will promote reading comprehension and understanding of complex ideas. Tharp and Gallimore's essential ideas are found in *Rousing Minds to Life: Teaching, Learning, and Schooling in Social Context* (New York: Cambridge University Press, 1988). Tharp's most recent book, *Transforming Teaching: Achieving Excellence, Fairness, Inclusion, and Harmony* (Boulder, CO: Westview Press, 2000), translates these findings into specific strategies for teachers.

Notes

1. As quoted in Joel Spring, *The American School, 1642–1990* (New York: Longman, 1990), p. 120.

2. Larry Cuban, *How Teachers Taught: Constancy and Change in American Classrooms, 1890–1990* (New York: Teachers College Press, 1993).
3. Philip Jackson, *The Practice of Teaching* (New York: Teachers College Press, 1987).
4. Larry Cuban, *How Teachers Taught.*
5. Jean Lave and Etienne Wenger, *Situated Learning: Legitimate Peripheral Participation* (New York: Cambridge University Press, 1991).
6. Ibid.
7. Fred M. Newmann, Walter G. Secada, and Gary Wehlage, *A Guide to Authentic Instruction and Assessment: Vision, Standards, and Scoring* (Madison, WI: Wisconsin Center for Education Research at the University of Wisconsin, 1995), p. 8.
8. See Elizabeth Cohen and Rachel Lotan's book *Working for Equity in Heterogeneous Classrooms* (New York: Teachers College Press, 1997) for an elaborated discussion of these issues.
9. Cohen and Lotan's *Working for Equity in Heterogeneous Classrooms* includes a nice review of the sociological literature in this area.
10. See Carol Dweck, "Motivational Process Affecting Learning," *American Psychologist* 41 (1986), pp. 1040–1047, on learned helplessness.
11. Robert Rosenthal and Lenore Jacobson, *Pygmalion in the Classroom* (New York: Holt, Rinehart & Winston, 1968).
12. Derek Mitchell. (Ph.D. diss., University of California, Los Angeles, 2001).
13. Myra Sadker and David Sadker, *Failing at Fairness: How America's Schools Cheat Girls* (New York: Macmillan, 1994).
14. See, for example, Ray Rist, "Student Social Class and Teacher Expectations: The Self-Fulfilling Prophecy of Ghetto Education," *Challenging the Myths: The Schools, the Blacks, and the Poor.* Reprint Series no. 5 (Cambridge, MA: *Harvard Educational Review,* 1971).
15. See, for example, Jere Brophy and Thomas Good, *Looking in Classrooms,* 7th ed. (New York: Longman, 1997), especially Chapter 3.
16. Makeba Jones, "Rethinking African American Students' Agency: Meaningful Choices and Negotiating Meaning" (Ph.D. diss. proposal, Los Angeles, UCLA Graduate School of Education and Information Studies, 1998), pp. 1–2.
17. Claude Steele, "Race and the Schooling of Black Americans," *Atlantic Monthly,* April 1992, pp. 68–78.
18. Ibid.
19. Daniel G. Solorzano, "Critical Race Theory, Race and Gender Microaggressions, and the Experience of Chicana and Chicano Scholars," *Qualitative Studies in Education* 11, no.1 (1998), p. 121.
20. May Garland and Uri Treisman, "The Mathematics Workshop Model: An Interview with Uri Treisman," *Journal of Developmental Education*16, no. 3 (Spring 1993), pp. 14–16, 18, 20, 22.
21. Jo Boaler, "Mathematics for the Moment, or the Millennium?" (*Education Week* 18, no. 29 (31 March 1999), pp. 52, 30.

22. Elizabeth Cohen, *Designing Groupwork: Strategies for the Heterogeneous Classroom* (New York: Teachers College Press, 1994).
23. Newmann, Secada, and Wehlage, *A Guide to Authentic Instruction and Assessment*, p. 35. See also, Fred M. Newmann (Ed.), *Student Engagement and Achievement in American Secondary Schools* (New York: Teachers College Press, 1992).
24. Ann L. Brown, Kathleen E. Metz, and Joseph C. Campione, "Social Interaction and Individual Understanding in a Community of Learners: The Influence of Piaget and Vygotsky," in *Piaget-Vygotsky: The Social Genesis of Thought*, ed. Anastasia Tryphon and Jacques Voneche (East Sussex, UK: Psychology Press, 1996), pp. 145–170.
25. See, for example, Robert Slavin, *Cooperative Learning: Theory, Research, and Practice* (Englewood Cliffs, NJ: Prentice Hall, 1995).
26. "Internet Helps with Homework," Los Angeles Times, 2 September 2001, p. A18.
27. Beau Fly Jones, Gilbert Valdez, Jeri Nowakowski, and Claudette Rasmussen, *Plugging In* (Oak Brook, IL: North Central Regional Educational Laboratory, 1995), on the Internet at: http://www.ncrel.org.
28. More information about the Jasper series can be found on the Internet at: http://peabody.vanderbilt.edu/projects/funded/jasper/intr.
29. "Dividing Lines," *Technology Counts 2001: The New Divides* 20, no. 35 (2001), pp. 12–13.
30. Janet Ward Schofield, *Computers and Classroom Culture* (New York: Cambridge University Press, 1995), pp. 134–190.
31. Ibid.
32. Jane Margolis and Allan Fisher, *Unlocking the Clubhouse: Women and Computing* (Cambridge, MA: MIT Press, 2002).
33. Linda Darling-Hammond, *The Right to Learn* (San Francisco: Jossey-Bass, 1997), pp. 59–60.
34. A noteworthy additional example is the concept of "intelligence," which depends on intelligence tests, which are constructed to match society's existing ideas of who is intelligent.
35. *Validity* refers to whether the information being collected and analyzed is trustworthy for the assessment purpose. Will it lead to correct decisions? Does it provide each student with a fair opportunity to show what he or she has learned? Does it provide information about all important aspects of the performance being assessed? Does the format allow students to show what they can do? Do the instructions make clear what the student is expected to do? Does it guard against the influence of irrelevant factors (e.g., background, language, etc.)? Does the scoring process prevent personal bias? *Reliability* refers to whether the results of the assessment can be trusted to be consistent. Will the results be similar if the assessment is repeated? To be accepted as scientific, assessments must be both valid and reliable. Neither without the other would provide a scientifically defensible basis for educational decisions.
36. Linda Darling-Hammond, *The Right to Learn*, p. 115.

37. Newman, Secada, and Wehlage, *A Guide to Authentic Instruction and Assessment*, p. 8.
38. Jay P. Heubert and Robert M. Hauser, eds., *High Stakes: Testing for Tracking, Promotion, and Graduation* (Washington: National Academy Press, 1999).

CHAPTER 7

Classroom Management:

Caring and Democratic Communities

Janene Ashford
First-year teacher, grade 6

Like most first-year teachers, Erik Korporaal was worried about classroom management as well as about curriculum and instruction. He wondered whether he would be able to control his sometimes-unruly students. Not only were his fourth and fifth graders as rambunctious as any group of 9- and 10-year-olds, but these children lived in a pretty rough urban neighborhood. Tensions between his African American and Latino students often spilled over into the classroom. Many of Erik's more-experienced colleagues used behavior modification systems that meted out rewards and punishment to train the students to follow classroom rules. As a new teacher at the school, Erik was expected to do the same. However, his knowledge of learning and development made him cautious about these strategies—even if they might "work" in the short term to make the children behave. His commitment to social justice also compelled him to bridge the racial differences in his class rather than masking them with firm control.

Erik was determined to build a community in his classroom where students' "good behavior" grew from engaging lessons, from their reflections about ethical actions, and from the caring and respectful relationships that he fostered. Consider again Erik's careful approach to cooperative learning described in Chapter 6. By creating such lessons, he was able to combine his social goals for the class with his academic ones.

Creating a classroom community where the students respect one another and work together to solve common problems makes promoting their academic development easier. I made activities whole-class adventures where finding answers became a quest that involved everyone. I also created opportunities for their collective social development—where students could understand themselves in their social context.

As the year progressed, I saw a definite change. Students were much more polite to each other and exhibited far more respect. The class atmosphere began to change. I have fewer problems with students not getting along. Instead of bickering or competing, they feel responsible for the success of their peers. Success to them is no longer an individual competition, or even a competition between groups. Rather, it means doing well as a whole class. When students have questions about assignments in class, other students jump at the opportunity to help them out. They feel better about themselves for helping a classmate.

This increased cohesion also changed the way many of my Latino students participate. They seem to feel more comfortable in activities and discussion. I believe that their silence at the beginning of the year was a sign that they did not feel connected.

The change also manifested itself outside the classroom. No longer did race and gender strictly define peer groups. Students of different races were friends and began to associate with each other. A much broader peer group also formed that consisted of the entire class. No longer would students split themselves into separate groups on the playground. They began to play together every day during recess and lunch. What I found most remarkable was the group's reaction when somebody felt isolated. Most of the students would take the initiative and try to include this person, and the whole group would become noticeably upset and disturbed if they could not find a way to include someone who felt excluded. The playground monitors were thrilled to see that the students monitored each other's behavior, reminding and keeping in line those students who were breaking the rules.

When I look back to the beginning of the year, I would never have guessed my class could be so close. They are individually and collectively remarkable people. My students' success gives me hope (and higher future expectations) that classrooms, even those divided by powerful social forces such as race, can become communities of learners. By no means are all the problems solved, but every day my students learn more about respecting and relating to one another. I am very proud of the progress they have made.

—Erik Korporaal
First-year teacher, grades 4 and 5

First-year teacher Amy Lee's sixth-grade class—not unlike Erik's—included several children with serious out-of-school problems as well as in-class misbehavior. Hector, for example, had been placed in his aunt's care when the county children's protective services agency decided that his drug-addicted mother was not fit to care for him, and his anger often erupted in the classroom. Amy's school, like Erik's, expected her to follow a discipline system that included a series of increasingly severe consequences for misconduct. The first consequence for misbehavior is that students post cards with their names on them in the front of the class. Hector posted his nearly every day. Amy, like Erik, was determined to use her knowledge of learning, relationships, and community to grapple with her toughest behavior challenges—including Hector.

In the beginning, my students didn't trust me. They were sixth graders on the verge of junior high school; many of them were already hardened and embittered toward school and their teachers. Many had been ridiculed, silenced, demeaned, and misunderstood, and to them, I was just another teacher who would continue to do the same. They waved their attitude like a red flag, challenging me to play their game. They expected me to live up to their low expectations of what a teacher should be. I was determined to prove them wrong.

I wanted to build relationships with my students—authentic relationships. Much of what I had read stuck with me: Be fair; allow your students a voice; teach with care, respect, and kindness. I struggled to be tolerant, giving each student the opportunity to voice his or her side. I touted fairness and mutual respect, always telling my students how much I valued their ideas and insights. However, I had to prove to them through my actions that I was sincere. I gave second chances, and when proven wrong, admitted that I was at fault. At first, none of my efforts made any impact. I think the students believed it was a facade and that soon I would show my true, mean colors. They were wary and did not respond to any of my attempts to know them.

Hector was my biggest challenge. From the first day, he was in my face, resisting any attempts at kindness. Other teachers, some of whom had never even had him in their classrooms, came and warned me about how awful he was.

Every day Hector stayed with me after school for misbehaving. He seemed surprised that I talked with him. His answers were usually short and inexpressive, or he sat like a stone and said nothing. So, at first, I did all of the talking. I told him that no matter how hard he pushed me away, I would not give up on him. I think that this was the key—not giving up. So many of his teachers in the past hit such a point of frustration with Hector that they threw up their hands and walked away. I was very close many times to doing exactly the same. He yelled at me, threw his binder through the air, and sat in class refusing to do the intelligent work that he was capable of. I quietly but firmly reprimanded him in class, and then in our conversations after school shared with him all of the good things that I saw from him during the day. I called his aunt frequently to praise him, and I visited his home.

Slowly Hector came to realize that I was real, and that I really did care. Slowly, he let me into his world. He started to change. He no longer sat like a stone after school and said nothing. In class, instead of reacting quickly and irrationally, I found him expressing himself and calmly telling others "how frustrated I got when . . ." instead of yelling and screaming like before. It was a miracle. Over the next few months, Hector blossomed. He became a real class leader and role model, and the other students noticed. "Wow, Ms. Lee, Hector hasn't posted his card in a whole month. He is really different from last year." He made friends and strengthened his "PR" at school. I was really proud of him; he was proud of himself.

Hector is one of the many students who touched me deeply this past year. I believe that it was the time and effort in building caring relationships that made all the difference. I had many moments filled with frustration, anger, disappointment, and apathy, but fortunately, when I was ready to walk away, the pure joys of teaching revealed themselves. I fell in love with my job this year, because I fell in love with the students I teach.

—Amy Lee
First-year teacher, grade 6

Jennifer Garcia's experience as a first-year high school teacher was challenging in ways similar to Erik's and Amy's, although her students were considerably older. Her school, like theirs, brought diverse students together, including many immigrants. Like many adolescents in low-income city neighborhoods, several of Jennifer Garcia's students grappled with part-time jobs, family responsibilities, and gang activities as they struggled to stay in school.

Like Amy and Erik, Jennifer sought ways to build trusting relationships with her students and to foster a community-like atmosphere. She also knew that she had to consider her efforts to manage students' behavior as part of her efforts to teach them history.

Too often, students do not feel ownership over their learning environment—perhaps because of their experiences with irrelevant curriculum or a perception of powerlessness in the typical student/teacher relationship. By developing a classroom where students help construct the curriculum, I hope to diminish the power issues. In our unit on industrialization, immigration, and unionism, my goal was to bring to life a time period that is often overlooked—one that focuses on poor ethnic immigrants, workers, government scandals, and inner-city living conditions—and to acknowledge the experiences and contributions of a variety of people. This critical multiculturalism acknowledges the contributions and experiences of groups that have been marginalized historically and encourages students to question and challenge the status quo and traditional power relationships.

Hands-on, student-centered activities drew students into the historical theme and time period. They simulated factory life by creating an assembly line along which students constructed, piecemeal, paper airplanes, negotiated a union contract, and reenacted a political machine election. They gathered and analyzed information in cooperative learning groups (e.g., analyzing political cartoons). The students worked well together—supporting each other and offering help when needed. They were able to express their opinions and feelings in the journals they kept. Activities allowed students to empathize with diverse people and challenge their preconceived notions about workers, immigrants, and politics.

—Jennifer Garcia
First-year teacher, high school history

Why should Erik, Amy, and Jennifer expect students to behave well in class, listen to instruction, do homework, study for tests, and so on? Because students enjoy class? Enjoy behaving? Because some external payoff motivates them? Because an authority (a teacher) told them to? Because they want to please? Because they want to avoid punishment?

The remainder of this chapter surveys the legacy of management, discipline, and control that many contemporary teachers still rely on to organize classroom life. It also examines a second tradition—that of caring and democratic classrooms—that leads to alternative ways to create constructive learning environments. This tradition, which is less visible but also has deep American roots, finds considerable consistency with cognitive and sociocultural learning theories. Many teachers like Erik Korporaal, Amy Lee, and Jennifer Garcia are turning to this tradition of caring and democratic relationships to create classrooms in which cognitive and sociocultural learning can take root. They see orderly and productive classrooms as a consequence of caring and democratic learning communities.

Conventional approaches to classroom discipline and management—and the behavioral theories that support them—pervade American schools. Without a critical perspective on the history, philosophy, and politics that underlie these practices, most teachers accept them as common sense. And without theories and research about classrooms as caring and democratic learning communities, few teachers—new or experienced—can sustain efforts like Erik's, Amy's, and Jennifer's. Please note that when we refer to these teachers' efforts to "sustain," we are pointing to their strength of will and knowledge that enables them to persevere with all the challenges they face. Theirs is not a formula or system that guarantees picture-perfect deportment—that no "Hector" will toss a notebook in the air or that no racial epithets will be heard. Theirs is a hopeful struggle—the work of teachers.

Management, Discipline, and Control: Lasting Legacies

Classroom management, discipline, and control dominate the worries of most first-year teachers. There's good reason for that. First, an absolutely endless variety of behavior situations occurs in classrooms, and having experience helps anticipate, recognize, and respond to them. Lacking experience, new teachers, especially, are in for . . . well, some surprises. Second, because in many schools, administrators and experienced teachers place enormous importance on discipline, first-year teachers' reputations often ride on their ability to "control" their classrooms. As a consequence, many new teachers think that without a firm discipline system in place, their classrooms will disintegrate into chaos.

Where does all the concern about classroom management and discipline come from? Why is it that children and adolescents—who by nature are eager and voracious learners—become seen as (and fulfill the prophecy of) unwilling troublemakers who need to be controlled and manipulated into paying attention and learning at school? Why is it that adults—most of whom choose to work with students because they thrive on assisting others develop and learn (and many of whom are experienced teachers)—express as their primary concern and frustration getting students to behave, rather than helping them to learn? Why do the students themselves become educational obstacles—persons and behaviors that must be overcome?

In part, the traditional approach to managing classroom behavior stems from medieval ideas about the role of government in individual lives. St. Thomas Aquinas argued in the thirteenth century that government had a moral responsibility to help individuals lead virtuous lives. Schools, then, according to Aquinas's beliefs, should do more than simply train the intellect; they must also shape character and foster moral development. Teachers must train the wills of the young, as well as their minds. These ideas came to America with its earliest white settlers. From the beginning, then, American public schools were as much or more about socializing children to act right as they were about academic learning.

Classrooms as Smooth-Running Factories

Recall the description in the previous chapter of early-nineteenth-century schools, which were composed of large classrooms with students moving in orderly groups to recite their lessons with monitors. Beginning at this early time, schools tried to match the organizational efficiencies of factories that were producing such abundant manufactured goods.[1] These efficiencies required smooth-running classrooms where many students would all do the same academic work at the same time. In such settings, little movement could be tolerated, and materials other than the most rudimentary texts, slates, tablets, pens, and pencils were either not available, too costly, or thought unnecessary. Neither children nor adults could be left to follow their own propensities to learn and teach. Coercion was a central feature of these public school classrooms.

Training Dutiful Workers By the late 1800s, teachers were expected to transmit to students the values and approved behaviors of the industrialized society: respect for authority, punctuality, following directions, performing tasks with precision, tolerating the boredom of repetitive activity, and so on. Educators could not count on students to adopt these dispositions on their own. As in factory life, teachers had to channel their charges' energies into coordinated, machinelike activity. By the end of the century, the expansion of large-scale, assembly-line production made this school efficiency approach seem even more relevant. At that time, there was little of today's rhetoric or belief that work in the factory or school should be fulfilling, intrinsically interesting, or a midstep in one's upward social mobility. The factory or school meant *work,* and work was one's duty.

Between 1907 and 1927 William Bagley's teacher education textbook, *Classroom Management,* was enormously popular. Bagley made explicit connections between classroom order and assembly lines, and he advised teachers to develop rigid classroom routines to build good behavior habits. For example, Bagley suggested that teachers have students practice packing and unpacking their desks in a particular order, marching to the blackboard, and marching through the cloakroom to get their coats at as they left the classroom. He urged teachers to march the children in lines through the lavatories before recess to develop good habits related to "bodily functions," and to teach them to assume on command a formal pose of attention. Bagley and other educators turned to the expanding field of psychology for help in designing strategies that would produce students' compliance. Edward Thorndike's behaviorist theories led many teachers to reinforce good behavior with rewards that included conveying approval with talk, facial expressions, and gestures. This approach became seen as "scientific," especially as behavioral animal research like that of Pavlov's promised that a regular schedule of reinforcement could actually control behavior.

Throughout the twentieth century, systems for producing student learning and for producing goods and services followed parallel paths. Schools today, as at the beginning of the twentieth century, look to business and industry for scientific and efficient models. Like work-group leaders and middle managers in business, teachers are still expected to be effective business-like supervisors in modern educational organizations. As inappropriate as these teacher roles might be, at least in the earlier part of the twentieth century they fit the prevailing culture and goals of schools. However, more recently Americans have rightfully demanded more from their schools. School attendance has increased tremendously. Teachers have lost or rejected controls over students that had previously supported the factory model of schooling. For example, "firing" students (expulsion or permissible dropping out to a waiting job) is a less available option. When the vast majority of students began to attend high school, teachers increasingly needed to cope with students who would rather be elsewhere.

Managing for High-Quality Work In the 1970s and 1980s, as America's unquestioned dominance of world markets for many products eroded, particularly in those areas that hit closest to American pride—electronic technology and automobiles—much of America's faith in the infallibility of traditional business practices diminished. Some business analysts looked to other countries, particularly Japan and Scandinavia, for their "secrets" and discovered that more cooperative and humanistic production models could produce greater job satisfaction and commitment along with efficiently manufactured, high-quality products. This emphasis on respect for the dignity and worth of workers and students, and the increased productivity and quality it promised, struck a chord with many Americans. That respect and value for working together also seemed like good business was a combination too good to resist.

William Glasser is notable among those who have borrowed from and added to the new enlightened management perspectives to develop strategies to manage students' classroom behavior. He argues that students will act to meet basic human needs (which he asserts are survival, love, fun, power, and freedom) and will prefer productive choices if those choices are available. The key for Glasser is to give students the responsibility for choosing those actions that will fulfill their own needs—to empower them by helping them understand that they can control their lives by experiencing both the benefits and consequences of their choices. Glasser's "choice theory" (until recently called "control theory") emphasizes that the successful teacher should provide students with a "satisfying picture of that activity," "empower" them, and stress cooperation, rather than punishing, telling, overpowering, and enforcing rules.[2]

Drawing from the work of W. Edwards Deming, a widely respected consultant to corporations, Glasser makes his choice theory of discipline an integral part of what he calls "the quality school." In these schools, as in the most successful business organizations, teachers-as-managers use noncoercive practices to help students understand the nature of high-quality work and to persuade students that they can meet their needs by doing such work. In this way, better teaching, which is really better managing, can make all students eager to participate. Glasser's approach is a great improvement over many of the overtly behaviorist classroom management programs finding their way into schools. However, his emphasis on students' choices to meet basic needs within carefully managed classroom environments falls short. Glasser connects the social environment (such as working in groups) directly to its usefulness in meeting student needs. In doing so, he neglects many mediating processes that would explain some of the underlying strengths that led to Amy Lee's effectiveness with Hector, as well as those that would explain why Hector's struggles are far from over.

It was indeed important for Amy Lee to persevere in allowing Hector to make continuously better choices over time, rather than trying to control him through punishment. However, she was also acutely aware that Hector's decision making is far more complex than basic need fulfillment. Hector's decision making was powerfully connected to social *structures* and the school *culture*, two dimensions of his life that neither he nor Amy Lee had entire control over. To some degree, Hector and Amy Lee negotiated acceptable parameters for Hector's behavior; to some degree, Hector gradually allowed additional scaffolding from his teacher and classmates; and to some degree, Hector continues to be in for a rough time at school.

As a social justice teacher, Amy Lee will be aware that other teachers' classes were and will continue to be places that Hector will influence—not always positively. Hector is sure to try to prove to his next teacher that Amy Lee was an exception, a mistake. Others will just as surely respond to him in characteristically unfriendly ways (unless one wants to believe that Hector is forever "cured" of feeling at odds with his environment). Amy Lee is constrained in how influential she can be, but she can continue to struggle on Hector's behalf. She can share how she managed to gain Hector's trust, and she can try to maintain a continuing relationship with him. Depending on the school culture, other teachers will be more or less receptive to learn of their colleague's success with a troublesome student, especially when the colleague has spent extraordinary time and energy in the effort.

Classrooms That "Implant . . . Righteousness, Law, and Order"

From the beginning, schools punished students to manage their behavior. In the early-nineteenth-century public schools that used the "monitorial" method, teachers placed a wooden log around the necks of children who talked too much or didn't do their schoolwork. They punished more serious offenders by hanging them in a sack or basket from the school roof in a place where their classmates could see them. Other schools used a simple "spare the rod, spoil the child" approach. Many viewed strictly enforced behavioral controls as the best way to achieve the common school's goal of suppressing crime and unrest among the lower socioeconomic classes.

Teaching New Immigrants American Values Strict classroom discipline took on a more patriotic tone at the end of the nineteenth century. By that time, society wanted schools to Americanize a flood of newcomers with the habits, manners, and loyalties necessary for a proper social life. Schools responded by adding a considerable dose of patriotism to the curriculum, but Americanization was far more about behavior and discipline than about learning the substance of the American culture. By 1909, 58 percent of the students in the nation's thirty-seven largest cities were foreign born, and many longer-standing residents feared a wholesale corruption of the culture.

The misapplication of Darwin's evolutionary theories to cultural groups—so-called Social Darwinism—confirmed that immigrant students and students of African descent were less socially and morally developed. The superintendent of the Boston schools warned in 1889: "Many of these children come from homes of vice and crime. In their blood are generations of iniquity. . . . They hate restraint or obedience to the law."[3] Because these immigrants came from different parts of Europe than previous waves, racial and religious prejudices were typically at the core of these worries. Prominent educator Ellwood Cubberly wrote in 1909: "These southern and eastern Europeans are of a very different type from the north Europeans who preceded them. Illiterate, docile, lacking in self-reliance and initiative, and not possessing the Anglo-Teutonic conceptions of law, order, and government, their coming has served to dilute tremendously our national stock, and to corrupt our civic life."[4]

Although many considered these unfortunate attributes biological, and therefore unchangeable, reformers hoped that schooling could turn immigrant children toward more constructive ways. In Cubberly's words, "Our task is to . . . assimilate and amalgamate these people as a part of our American race and to implant in their children, as far as can be done, the Anglo-Saxon conception of righteousness, law and order."[5] Here is where G. Stanley Hall's theories played a powerful role. Hall's notion that children's development followed that of the entire race—that is, from presavagery as infants to civilization as adults—included the argument that environments such as neighborhood and school profoundly influenced this development. The unstable and corrupting environments in city neighborhoods pressed individuals toward depravity. Especially vulnerable were children and adolescents—whom Hall described as being at the developmental stage of savage, vagrant, and nomadic life. Unless adolescents were in homes where "industry, intelligence and thrift prevail, where books and magazines abound, where the library table forms the center of an interested group, where refinement of thought and life prevail," they would surely fall into delinquency and moral depravity.[6] Schools, he and many others argued, must provide a countervailing influence through character training and strictly enforced discipline.

Taming the Belligerent The widespread adoption of compulsory education laws in the first half of the twentieth century brought more and more unwilling students into classrooms—immigrants and nonimmigrants alike, making strictly imposed classroom controls seem all the more necessary. Schools couldn't simply fire recalcitrant students the way industry could dismiss unwanted workers, and modern parents and educators increasingly regarded the harsh physical punishment of earlier times as inhumane.

The economic trauma of the depression in the 1930s and World War II in the 1940s dampened quite a lot (certainly, not all) of the country's worries about wayward, troublesome youth. But by the 1950s, popular films like *Blackboard Jungle* heightened fears of an increasingly belligerent younger generation—particularly in city schools. The concept of "juvenile delinquent" gained currency. While favoring minorities, this was a cross-cultural class of antisocial, antischool, antiauthority disruptive youth, vaguely disaffected with modern society. Their lot was to stay in school and be bothersome, drop out to no one's chagrin, or be sent to a variety of "reform" schools, widely understood as one step before prison.

By the 1960s, teachers were taught in their teacher education programs that poor children were "culturally deprived," in part because they came from disorganized families that failed to teach such basics as punctuality, obedience, cleanliness, and respect for personal property. Tellingly, it was often thought that such families did not pass on to their children a value for education. In short, the stereotypical judgments that had previously been associated with race or nationality were partly stripped of their most blatant and odious prejudice. Instead, society adopted a new construction of social science—a nongenetic theory that attributed minorities' huge gaps in education achievement to their culture. In fact, "poor" in the 1960s was also a powerful code word for "race." Often when policymakers referred to "the poor" or "the culturally deprived," they really meant blacks and other minorities or people from isolated rural areas. *Culturally deprived* became one of those reified terms that took on a life of its own. Thus, teachers and the public generally came to see children who were not white, urban, or middle class as requiring a special set of treatments in schools in order to bring them up to the schooling standards that white, middle-class children learned at home. Such children, social scientists and educators reasoned, needed classrooms with fixed routines, unambiguous rules, and firm disciplinary policies.[7]

Matching Offenses with Consequences Since the 1970s college courses, school district workshops, and training from profit-making corporations have offered teachers plans and programs for controlling classroom behavior. Some go so far as to suggest teacher actions to scare or intimidate disruptive students: the "stony stare," verbal reprimands, nonverbal signals (e.g., pointing one's finger or moving close to an offender), and threats of a failing grade. Some build on B. F. Skinner's developments in behavioral psychology to provide more-refined "scientific" methods for using rewards and punishment to shape students' classroom behavior. These behavior modification approaches offer carefully prescribed and scripted lists of foolproof techniques that guarantee correct behavior through conditioning of students' behavior. For example, "Scared Straight" was a widely heralded and heavily criticized program that brought teenagers in contact with hardened, jailed criminals who verbally intimidated the students with horror stories of prison life. Like nearly every other plan to threaten, scare, and punish, this one didn't last long.

Assertive Discipline, developed by Lee and Marlene Canter, is perhaps the most popular of the commercially available, behaviorally grounded discipline programs.[8] The Canters' strategy starts with the premise that teachers have the right to define and enforce rules for student behavior that allow them to teach. Teachers communicate clear expectations for students' behavior and clear classroom rules. They let students know the set of escalating "consequences" (punishments) for undesirable behavior, and that misbehaving students will be identified publicly. Consequences for bad behavior begin with the teacher writing or posting a card with the student's name on the board; the teacher then adds checks for subsequent misdeeds. Persistent misbehavior brings the student's removal from class, phone calls home, a meeting with the principal, and so forth. Whole-class rewards (parties, candy, etc.) for everyone's good behavior are meant to reinforce those behaviors, as well as to bring social control to bear on individual students who might prevent the class from getting its reward.

Assertive Discipline emphasizes consistency in matching consequences to the misbehavior and relies on a consistent sequence of punishments within the class and across the school. This program and other behavioral techniques also emphasize structuring the classroom to minimize disruptive stimuli—for example, by planning and arranging the physical space and daily schedule. Proponents claim that the preestablished punishment routine, along with the proper arrangement of classroom time and space, enables teachers to manage disruptive behavior almost mechanically, without diverting either their or the class's attention from the lesson.

Systematic programs like Assertive Discipline may suppress misbehavior in the short term, but the research on this is not clear. Even if punishment strategies do "work" in this way, however, they don't teach acceptable behavior or even reduce difficult students' desire to misbehave. What we do know about behaviorally oriented discipline schemes is that the "lessons" learned from punishments and rewards tend to be very specific. Even in the unlikely event that all the teachers at a school are wholeheartedly committed to such a program, individual differences are still considerable. And without consistency across the entire system, students may learn that a private disruptive conversation in one teacher's class always brings a punishment, while another teacher has a higher threshold for disruption. Thus, students learn to make judgments based on the teacher's responses—what they can get away with—rather than learning to read the environment and make choices that are appropriate for themselves and for the classroom community. They learn how to avoid punishment, and they learn to make rational choices—deciding sometimes that what they gain from a misbehavior is of greater benefit to them than the punishment is a deterrent. Consistency even within a class is hard to maintain. While it may be clear to the teacher that one child's inappropriate comment made with a smirk is a more serious behavior violation than another's comment made without a smirk, this distinction might be too subtle for students who might simply see favoritism. In fact, attempts—usually unsuccessful—to make the environment totally consistent simply relieve students of the need to "read" the environment, which is a necessary social skill, close to the heart of all behavior decisions.

In more recent years, Glasser and the Canters have embraced more community-like and cooperative classrooms. Yet their approaches remain intensely individualistic—individual students make behavioral choices; the teacher is the center of moral and behavioral authority. Other similar systems that rely more on rewards than punishments, for example, Token Reinforcement or Contingency Contracts, may be somewhat less mechanical and rule-bound while offering more opportunity for cognitive sense-making. However, they, too, have been widely criticized for emphasizing teachers' power and control in the classroom rather than students' learning and problem solving. Substantial evidence exists that giving external rewards for good behavior can actually diminish students' intrinsic motivation to learn or to conform to the social norms of the classroom.[9]

First-year kindergarten teacher Javier Espindola began teaching thinking that the Assertive Discipline strategies used by many veteran teachers in his school would help him motivate his very young students to work productively. Before long, he changed his mind.

I consistently rewarded my students when they demonstrated appropriate behaviors by giving them raffle tickets, candy, stickers, happy faces, stars, etc. When my students were sitting quietly and listening to me or when they were on task writing in their journals, I would give them a sticker or happy face to motivate them to continue that behavior. When I saw them talking with peers and not working, I would put their names on the board or give them a sad face.

At first, these strategies worked. Over time, however, I noticed negative effects. Students who constantly received rewards and/or consequences for being quiet and listening, respecting their peers, and following directions began to refuse to follow classroom directions, work productively, and respect and listen to their peers and me if they did not receive any rewards. Labeling was another problem. For example, at the beginning of the year, Steve rarely followed the classroom rules, always bothered and touched his peers, and interrupted others while they were discussing an activity. Every time Steve broke the classroom rules and directions, I placed his name on the board with a check mark or under the sad face. Soon Steve received a reputation and was labeled as a troublemaker by his peers. One day during a lesson, one of my students was shouting out the answer without raising his hand. I asked my students "Who is shouting out the answer without raising their hand?" A few students shouted out Steve's name, even though he was absent that day! It was evident that Steve's peers had labeled him as the classroom troublemaker, and whenever someone was to blame, they chose Steve. Finally, I felt limited in the activities I could do with my kindergartners. I worried that I would lose control of my students if they were interacting, sharing, and working with each other during group activities.

The first step in removing assertive discipline from my classroom was discussing it with my students. I told them that they were no longer going to receive happy faces, stars, stickers, and candies when they were behaving and performing well or consequences such as check marks, sad faces, or names on the board) when they were behaving inappropriately. I removed from the chalkboard the chart where I posted check marks when students misbehave and stars when they behave well. The students were extremely happy that the chart was gone. Steve said, "No more checkmarks," with a big smile. The next step was to let students know how we were going to solve problems when the classroom rules were not followed. I let them know that we would have discussions after classroom activities to decide what needed improvement. The classroom discussions have been effective in improving students' classroom behaviors without labeling or giving them bad reputations. They enabled my students to learn the behaviors I expected in the classroom in a comfortable environment where they work together without having the pressure of getting rewards or consequences from me.

I no longer feel the need to have complete control of my students. I have implemented group activities that encourage my students to interact, share experiences, and work with their peers. Working in groups, my students were no longer asking for rewards to work productively, they were interested, intrinsically motivated, and best of all they were enjoying learning. Steve's behavior, academics, and social skills improved dramatically. The group activities allowed him to participate freely. He could interact, share his experiences, and work with his peers. Steve became interested and intrinsically motivated; many of the behavior problems he had displayed earlier in the school year disappeared. Steve is no longer seen as the classroom troublemaker but is now is a valuable resource in the classroom. By being patient and not labeling Steve as "troublemaker," I have proven to his peers and myself that everyone is capable of improving his or her academic and social skills in a comfortable environment.

—Javier Espindola
First-year teacher, kindergarten

Can Effective Teaching Prevent Disruption?

The notion that classroom management and discipline will take care of themselves if teachers use effective instructional techniques emerged in the 1970s. The vast majority of classroom management problems were attributed to instructional shortcomings, with claims that mindless curriculum and boring pedagogy added to the need for elaborate management and discipline strategies.

Teachers Who Are "With It" In one of the best-known series of studies on classroom management, Jacob Kounin studied thousands of hours of classroom videotapes. Kounin found that teachers in smoothly running classes consistently used instructional strategies that seemed to prevent disruption. These teachers displayed what Kounin called "withitness." By monitoring students' behavior constantly, they nipped problems in the bud. They didn't hesitate to identify miscreants publicly. They managed multiple activities simultaneously and responded to individuals' needs without disrupting the rest of the class (e.g., moving to stand near an inattentive student without stopping instruction). These teachers also maintained what Kounin called "signal continuity"—that is, a consistent focus for students' attention. They didn't confuse students with "false starts" or disorderly presentation of material, and they provided independent seatwork that was easy enough for students to do alone but challenging enough hold their interest.[10]

Other experts have elaborated on Kounin's initial findings and offered advice about the attitudes and behaviors teachers can develop to enhance their effectiveness. For example, when teachers convey a personal interest and liking for students, it prompts them to imitate a teacher's behavior, adopt her attitudes, and be sympathetic if others misbehave. When teachers are credible—that is, their words and actions are consistent—students will be less likely to "test" teachers with misbehavior. Other experts have offered guidelines that are more general. These include having teachers plan rules and procedures in advance; making those rules and procedures very clear to students; letting students assume some responsibility for determining rules and consequences and lessons; developing cooperative relationships with students; minimizing disruptions and delays; and planning independent activities as well as organized lessons.[11] Most emphasize the importance of starting the year off in a friendly but business-like way, quickly establishing rules and routines.

Very few people would dispute all these commonsense principles. Why, then, are they so often absent from the classrooms of well-intentioned and hardworking teachers? What other conditions exist that make a teacher *not* convey a personal interest and liking, *not* adequately plan, or *not* establish cooperative relationships with students?

Instead of seeing these obvious practices as the *outcome* of a positive social, cultural, and sense-making learning environment, behavioral-minded researchers and educators typically have seen these practices as what *causes* a good classroom environment. They respond by breaking each practice down into its component behaviors, specifying steps, and instituting elaborate systems to train teachers in "effective" teaching. For example, some popular teacher education texts give advice about how frequently to change activities to keep students' attention, how to move about the classroom to make students aware that they are being monitored constantly, and how to use positive language to "cue" desirable behavior. Many texts also provide examples of how to recognize and reinforce good behavior with praise, public recognition, symbolic rewards (like happy faces and stickers), extra privileges, and treats. These management strategies stem from the notion that effective classroom managers can prevent most misbehavior with well-structured lessons, good supervisory techniques, and rewards.[12] Taken individually, some of these recommendations might be seen as mild, useful, intuitive, and spontaneous responses that keep class activities moving along smoothly. However, treating them as "strategies" designed in advance to obtain desired ends and control behavior quickly shifts the focus of a class from learning to discipline.

Teachers Who Make Lessons Interesting Offering the simplistic solution of "make the lesson interesting" hardly addresses the complex problem of student discipline. However, decidedly *un*interesting lessons make any problem, including discipline, worse.

Purdue University researcher Jeff Gregg investigated whether traditional conceptions of curriculum and pedagogy might be at the root of teachers' behavior management.[13] He conducted a fascinating yearlong study of how discipline and control problems came to dominate the "general" (lower-track) mathematics class of a first-year high school teacher. The teacher began the class aware that the students were not "college bound," and she lowered her expectations for their academic performance. However, she still set high (strict and traditional) standards for their behavior, and she pledged to teach them in the same way that she taught the college-bound in her upper-level geometry class. Yet, unlike that class, the general math students had little inclination to comply with her rules, listen to her during instruction, remain silent during seatwork, and do homework each night. They didn't find the math interesting, and they didn't believe that math would have some payoff for them later. Worried about the students' potential to be troublesome, the teacher decided not to joke, "be nice" to students, or give them risky opportunities to participate in "fun" activities. In return, they were even less eager to please her. Together, she and the class reacted to one another in ways that escalated her efforts to clamp down and their efforts to disrupt. Eventually, she gave up trying to enforce her rules, blamed the negative attitudes students brought from home, and decided that she didn't care if they learned or not.

This teacher did not consider that the problems she and her students faced might originate in the commonly accepted view of school mathematics—what Gregg calls "the school mathematics tradition." That is, neither she nor the students thought that "general" mathematics was anything more than (usually boring) rules and procedures. Neither did they consider that math should or could be taught and learned other than with lessons that followed a routine of (a) teacher leads the class as they check their homework, (b) teacher provides instruction on the next topic, and (c) teacher assigns practice problems that the students work on quietly and individually for the remainder of class and finish as homework. The students didn't find this math interesting, and neither, it seems, did their teacher! Like earlier studies, Gregg's research suggests that good behavior is more likely to follow from good teaching. The difference, however, is that Gregg considers the very nature of school knowledge as one root of the problem; a good rule of thumb is that good teaching cannot be based on knowledge or teaching methods that the teacher herself finds boring. It is important to remember that the school culture has much to say about how subjects, especially remedial ones, are defined. Thus, this teacher would have needed far more knowledge and commitment to break from the subject-matter tradition that she followed. Mathematics, stripped down to remedial algorithms and presented without any further inducements (no talk, no fun) creates behaviors other than math learning—that is, discipline problems. In Chapters 4 and 5, we described some curriculum approaches that can keep knowledge-loving teachers engaged and enthused in helping students direct their energy to learning.

In some classrooms, strategies like Glasser's choice theory have replaced more traditional, teacher-dominated approaches to classroom management, much like shared decision making has replaced authoritarian supervision in some companies. However, even enlightened business practices must first serve the traditional interests of businesses, and only then may they address the interests of workers—especially those interests that also increase profitability. Similarly, many enlightened school practices in the early twenty-first century serve first the traditional interests of maintaining conventional schooling relationships and the traditional distribution of opportunities, and outcomes as measured by standardized tests. In all, this can be a very limited view of increased student "productivity."

Caring and Democracy—A Second Legacy

Traditional schooling has had its critics—reformers always looking to make schools better—since the early nineteenth century. For example, Horace Mann believed that physical punishment, generally accepted at the time, undermined character development. Nineteenth-century Boston schools sought women teachers because many progressives believed that women would bring their child-rearing nature into classrooms and make them more nurturing. (Not incidentally, women were cheaper to employ and were thought to be more likely than men to remain in teaching.) Turn-of-the-twentieth-century progressive reformers, including John Dewey, argued for "child-centered," rather than subject-centered schools. Advocacy for caring, child-centered classrooms remains a strong force in American schooling today.

Child-Centered Schooling

Underlying these child-centered impulses is a focus on children's basic goodness as a central organizing principle of schooling. School reformers throughout the nineteenth and twentieth centuries argued that students' essentially good nature would cause them to behave well in school if their needs were being met. Misbehavior follows from instruction that attempts to coerce students, even if it is for their own and society's good. This view echoes Jean-Jacques Rousseau's theories that humans are naturally good, and that it is society that corrupts. Since discipline represents society's efforts to impose itself on the child, Rousseau's followers argued that it has no place in education. Instead, progressive reformers believed that all schooling practices should match children's needs at their current stage of development, rather than preserve the social order.

Johann Pestalozzi (1746–1827), a Swiss educator, translated Rousseau's ideas into pedagogy, and Pestalozzi's ideas had a strong following in the United States throughout the nineteenth century. Pestalozzi wrote about the virtues of "domestic education," explaining that students learn best when schools help them develop self-respect and emotional security. According to Pestalozzi, rather than learning abstractions while sitting obediently at a desk, academic learning should follow from students' engagement, exploration, and activity that connects ideas to real-life objects and events—all under the maternal guidance of a teacher. "Maternal love," in Pestalozzi's view, promised to ensure trust and obedience, elevate moral character, and improve the lot of poor children. Friedrich Froebel (1782–1852) built on Pestalozzi's ideas and developed the first kindergarten curriculum aimed at promoting children's development through self-expression and cooperative play. Froebel saw the classroom as a miniature society, wherein the cooperation children learned at school would make them cooperative members of adult society.

What a contrast these ideas were to the dominant mode in early-nineteenth-century schools! Educational historian Herbert Kliebard recounts that in 1913, Helen M. Todd, a factory inspector, surveyed 500 child laborers and asked if they would prefer to go back to school or "remain in the squalor of the factories." Kliebard notes, "Of the 500, 412 told her, sometimes in graphic terms, that they preferred factory labor to the monotony, humiliation, and even sheer cruelty that they experienced in school."[14]

Meeting Social as Well as Academic and Vocational Needs At the turn of the century, Jane Addams's Hull House in Chicago, and other big-city settlement houses approached the "problem" of immigrants very differently than did Cubberly and other influential educators. Addams argued strongly that reformers must rebuild communities that industrialization had torn apart. In addition to providing education and culture at Hull House, Addams and her colleagues fought for labor laws and health and safety regulations; they ran feeding programs, provided a shelter for prostitutes and battered wives, operated a maternity hospital and a nursery, and more.

The settlement house movement developed an ethic of social service and democratic community that merged political, social, and educational purposes. Hull House and other settlement houses were more like extended families and communities than like schools. Over time, the settlement house reformers persuaded many schools to appoint school physicians and offer classes for handicapped children; they initiated school lunch programs and school libraries in a movement they called "socialized education." John Dewey's friendship and support of Jane Addams's work influenced his thinking that schools might themselves become social centers that modeled themselves after the community at Hull House.

Dewey also wanted schools to provide for the multiple needs of immigrants and especially to respond to the devastating effects of their disconnection from their Old World cultures. But Dewey wanted schools to go further than just administering to needs. The key to social progress, he believed, was for schools to develop in children the dispositions and skills to serve society. Dewey wanted schools to turn immigrant children into "good Americans, public-spirited citizens, and members of the 'great community.'"[15]

"Open" Schools and Classrooms Caring and community have been counterpoints to the dominant theme of management and control throughout the twentieth century. In the 1970s the theme of caring and community emerged perhaps more strongly than it had since the turn-of-the-century progressive reforms, in a movement called *humanistic education.* Spearheaded by a group of humanistic psychologists, most prominently Carl Rogers, Abraham Maslow, and Lawrence Kohlberg, reformers proposed that everyone had the capacity for goodness, cooperation, and decency. If schools treated students humanely and respectfully, these qualities would prevail in classrooms. Closely related to the humanistic movement were the more radical, existential ideas of A. S. Neill, whose school (and the book by the same name), Summerhill, featured "open" classrooms. At Summerhill, students were free to discover and choose for themselves meaningful ways to behave and interact with others in the classroom, and teachers facilitated and mediated students' freedom.[16] These ideas inspired numerous attempts to instill humanist ideas and replicate Summerhill's features in what were and still are often called *alternative* schools.

For humanistic reformers, values, moral development, self-discipline, and personal responsibility assumed a major role in students' learning and behavior. A popular method was a technique called "values clarification," wherein students engaged in discussions and simulation exercises to help them discover and examine the principles by which they choose to live. Interestingly, in the 1990s an emphasis on values would be advocated by another group, also called humanists—though they occupy a niche at the opposite end of the political spectrum. These other humanists, including former secretary of education William Bennett, prescribe fundamental, universal, human qualities and specify how schools should promote them. Often using the term "character education," these contemporary conservative theorists and educators emphasize telling over guiding, control over freedom, and correcting children's errors over teaching them to examine and inquire with confidence. As a final note, much of the alternative and humanistic experimentation, although never widely popular, has taken place in middle class and suburban schools. It has had less appeal in poorer, urban communities.

An Ethic of Care

A compelling exploration of schools and classrooms as caring communities is found in the work of Nel Noddings, a Stanford University professor of education philosophy. Noddings wants an "ethic of care" to shape the social, emotional, and academic conditions in classrooms. She believes that "schools should be committed to a great moral purpose: to care for children so that they, too, will be prepared to care."[17] Because caring encompasses the moral and cultural values of how people relate to others, caring is an alternative to traditional discipline and classroom management. She proposes that behavioral control strategies like Assertive Discipline destroy care. In her view, not only are these strategies manipulative, but in their effort to free teachers from having to talk or interact with students about their behavior, they also foreclose the opportunity to help students learn to be "healthy, competent, moral people."[18] Noddings believes that even in a math or language lesson or on the playing field, the child-philosopher, the child-scholar, the introspective child, and the humanitarian child must be kept together to make a whole child—exactly what does not happen under mechanized discipline systems with predetermined and automatic consequences for undesirable behavior.

Noddings explains that care includes far more than "a warm fuzzy feeling that makes people kind and likeable."[19] Rather, care implies a "continuous search for competence" and includes fostering in students the knowledge and

skills "necessary to make a positive contribution" in whatever field of study or work they might choose. Thus, a caring search for competence has curricular as well as interpersonal implications, as students grapple with questions that are at the core of human existence. According to Noddings: "As human beings, we care what happens to us. We wonder if there is life after death, whether there is a deity who cares about us, whether we are loved by those we love, whether we belong anywhere; we wonder what we will become, who we are, how much control we have over our own fate."[20]

The Power of Relationships

Contemporary reformers like Nel Noddings offer a philosophical perspective that emphasizes caring to fulfill the social and moral purposes of schooling. This work connects in interesting ways to that of psychologists who focus on how relationships are inseparable from cognitive and social development. Consequently, a caring classroom relationship is part of a "search for competence," and, as it is a relationship, there are two people searching. The student's search is his own discovery of what he knows and how he knows it. The teacher's search—an act of care and respect—is also discovering what the student knows and how he knows it. Teachers express care by searching for their students' competence. Far from offering automatic approval for whatever knowledge or interpretation the student arrives at, we can say that the teacher co-constructs the student's competence as he searches for it. And by a wonderful turn of perspective, we can also say that teachers' competence is co-constructed by their students.

Relationships, Meanings, and the Search for Competence In his 1993 book *Developing Through Relationships,* psychologist Alan Fogel explores how relationships are crucial to all development. When we stop to think about it, we can find familiar examples of how individuals and groups shape the meaning of every occurrence. Each new bit of information is understood personally and differently within each social setting and relationship. For example, even a teacher's simplest utterance, "Take out your pencil," means different things to different students—in large part based on their relationships with the teacher: "I'm in trouble, no pencil"; "Great, we are having the quiz I prepared for"; "How rude, he never says please"; "Como?"; "I don't care if I do fail"; "Another 45 minutes to go"; "Should I just get up to sharpen this or raise my hand and ask for permission? Either way some teachers get mad." None of the preceding meanings is independent of the classroom culture or the relationship with the teacher. In this sense, the information "received" is different for everyone in the class, and since the teacher spoke the same four words to everyone, everyone must have created his or her own different meaning. Similarly, the *meaning of* "find the square root of 64" will be constructed differently for everyone in the class, although the "correct" (or *true?*) answer is 8.

Students do not *independently* construct their own meanings. The sociocultural perspectives taken by Vygotsky, Fogel, and others emphasize that meanings are *co*-constructed (or, in Fogel's term, co-regulated) in the relationship. In our preceding example, it was *this* teacher, not another, who spoke *these* words in *this* class where she expected students to have pencils. The teacher and different students share histories of what these words mean. This history might include the teacher's annoyance if students do not have a pencil, the amount of time she waits for students to fish the pencils out of their backpacks, and so on. These are different from the histories the same students might share with other teachers in other classes. The square root problem exists in a similarly rich context of relationships, rules for calculators, access to manipulatives, and so on. Co-construction or co-regulation of meaning—and, therefore, learning—requires relationships where individuals constantly adapt to one another without either being in complete control. There are simply too many meanings in action to try to fix or control most of them. Learning individuals must be willing to accept guidance and expertise from others, and be willing to change.

Over time, teacher and student develop many agreed-upon meanings that allow them to elaborate their thinking and push it even further. Adults—teachers—serve as guides by structuring learning interactions; they connect students' developing meanings with those in the larger culture; they gradually press students to new levels of activity and meaning-making. The following is a brief list of a whole range of teachers' skills or tools that influence the search for competence:

Grasp of theory and facility for translating theory into practice

Knowledge of the subject

Confidence and security

Personal relationships with students

Knowledge of students' cultures

Familiarity, gained over years, with the community

Establishment of a safe, accepting environment that encourages risk-taking with learning

Clearly, these teaching tools are not static. Teachers construct them over time in relationships with students. And students are also in search of competence, their own and their teachers. In this way, a caring classroom helps create caring students.

Beyond Rules and Routines In classrooms that are rigidly structured and bound to the rules of behavioral discipline systems, teachers dispense consequences for "misbehavior" almost automatically. In fact, sometimes these systems advise teachers to avoid "unnecessary" interactions with students. Such teachers might try to assure students, "It's not personal, the punishment is strictly a consequence of your behavior." We think that this is an extreme message to send, because it forecloses the possibility of classroom communities in which students develop their own tools for interaction, interdependence, and problem solving. All classroom interactions are in some way personal.

The relationships among people in and out of classrooms are not incidental to learning. And the importance of relationships goes far deeper than our conventional sense that if a teacher has a "good" relationship with students, students will try harder and learn more. No one would fault the teacher who has the capacity to be popular and friendly. However, these clearly desirable relationship strengths mean far less if the teacher neglects the interactive teaching strategies and cooperative group activities that join cognitive and social learning.

Caring Teachers Complementing Fogel's work are psychological studies that show the importance of relationships between teachers and students who are coping with the difficulties of urban poverty. For example, UCLA researchers Carollee Howes and Sharon Ritchie examined how teachers were able to construct positive classroom relationships with children who lived in difficult circumstances. Some students were homeless, and they all brought to the classroom the behaviors and assumptions about relationships that they developed in response to difficult and sometimes tragic experiences. These children had a very poor learning prognosis. Furthermore, they were often "hostile, aggressive, and distrustful, and not easy to have in a classroom."[21] The teachers established trust with the children in much the same way that Amy Lee did with Hector.

The researchers noted that novice teachers sometimes feel that they must be consistent in their responses to different students to show that they are not playing favorites. However, establishing trust with students who have few safe or reliable relationships with adults requires a teacher who is "sufficiently flexible to individualize" his or her interactions.[22] Also, teachers who repeat key relationship phrases—for example, "I'm going to help you," "Do you need me to help you?," and "I'll help you"—seemed to engender trust.[23] Such repetition signals and establishes a whole category of positive attention that might otherwise be lost as isolated (and meaningless) exchanges.

Expert teachers in the study gave students positive attention and communicated clearly that they believed the children were worthy of affection. However, flexibility and a lack of rigid, behavioral structures should not be mistaken for confusing, inconsistent, or unpredictable classroom practices. Indeed, all students benefit from routines that help them anticipate and organize their daily practices and address disruptions to a safe and productive classroom climate. Howes and Ritchie's research shows that trusting, mutually satisfying relationships and a sense of community at school create conditions where all children—even those in quite desperate circumstances—can learn and develop well.

George Noblit and his colleagues studied how two highly experienced teachers, Martha and Pam, constructed caring relationships with their students in their racially mixed, inner-city school. The two had quite different classroom manners. Pam, an African American teacher, kept her classroom interactions formal and polite, while Martha, a white teacher, encouraged lots of informal exchange. Yet both exercised what Noblit calls a "dogged determination" to develop trustful, caring relationships with troubled students. Like Erik Korporaal and Amy Lee and the teachers that Howes and Ritchie observed, Pam and

Martha used "no magic tricks, no technical fixes—just consistent day-in and day-out, hour-to-hour, even minute-to-minute"[24] attention to creating opportunities for these children to succeed and attain social competence. For example, Martha established daily rituals to communicate her care for Robert, a student who had recently transferred from a special school for students with severe problems. She waited at the door to say "hello" to him; she made sure that she took a few minutes to chat with him about nonschool matters, such as television programs; and she said "good-bye" when he left each afternoon. Martha also insisted that Robert participate in class activities. In time, her regular and obvious commitment and attention helped create a classroom context for Robert that allowed him to behave appropriately, make friends, and achieve more than he ever had before.

In accordance with her style, Pam used a somewhat different approach to developing a caring relationship with John, a painfully shy special education student who had been mainstreamed into her class (see Chapter 8 for a discussion of the terms *special education* and *mainstream*). In response to John's efforts to avoid interacting with her by "hiding" behind other students or his desk, Pam insisted in a stern, but reassuring way that he sit up and participate. She moved his desk so he would be close to her, and she made a practice of standing nearby when he worked in groups with other students. She also often touched his shoulder to show her support. Pam's constancy and her obviously caring actions over the school year helped John feel safe enough to participate and learn.

Martha's and Pam's students recognized the concrete ways that their teachers showed that they cared. Students told Noblit that they knew Martha and Pam were caring because they helped them with their schoolwork "without demeaning them for needing help"; they talked with them and showed respect by listening; they were confident about students' abilities; they tolerated mistakes; and they encouraged them.[25] Importantly (and as we saw with the teachers in Howes and Ritchie's study and with the first-year teachers cited throughout this book), these caring relationships did not just help students "act better," they also assisted their academic development.

Making Classrooms Communities

At the time that I chose to teach the book *Bridge to Terabithia*, I had become quite concerned by a general lack of compassion in the classroom and school communities. Discussions of local violence and death were often glorified with naïve excitement. Many of my students had lost loved ones to violence in the community or in their native countries. In addition, my fourth and fifth graders had trouble finding common ground and seemed to have very different notions of friendship. I felt that I needed to address these issues through the curriculum, and this core literature book offered the collective experience that I thought would most benefit our classroom community. *Bridge to*

Terabithia is primarily about relationships. The plot centers on the friendship of a fifth-grade boy and girl who learn to show compassion.

—Christopher Yusi
First-year teacher, grades 4 and 5

Researcher Mara Sapon-Shevin notes that enacting safe classroom learning communities takes considerable time and patience: Communities don't just happen. No teacher, no matter how skilled or well intentioned, can enter a new classroom and announce, "We are a community." Communities are built over time, through shared experience, and by providing multiple opportunities for students to know themselves, know one another, and interact in positive and supportive ways.[26]

Former teacher Alfie Kohn has written several books that provide teachers with strategies for building classroom communities. In *Beyond Discipline: From Compliance to Community*, Kohn describes class meetings during which students agree on how they will work together to solve the inevitable problems that arise in class. By pondering such questions as "What makes school awful sometimes?," "What can we do this year to make sure things go better?," "Suppose you hurt someone's feelings, or did something even worse. How would you want us, the rest of the community, to help you then?," and "What if someone else acted that way? How could we help that person?" students can construct a safe and caring learning community.[27] Kohn argues that such conversations, combined with lots of collaborative work on academic and social issues, can turn classrooms into places where discipline problems rarely happen.

Kohn draws extensively from the Child Development Project in Northern California, a research group that has worked for the past decade to develop and study community-like classroom practices. The project emphasizes that core values must be experienced, not just taught; thus, participating teachers learn to reflect on their own practice and ask questions that elicit students' thinking. Students are given and accept increasing responsibility for their own learning. Teachers learn how to maintain order without extrinsic rewards and to de-emphasize competition by having students set learning goals and establish classroom rules. Teachers and students collaborate on a curriculum in which they investigate—through literature, science, and history—what it means to be a principled, caring person. They hold class meetings to solve campus and classroom problems. Problem solving is a routine part of classroom community life, rather than a series of responses to crises with meetings or punishment. Students learn to work in cooperative groups in the classroom, and they engage others at home in "family activities."

Project researchers Eric Schaps and his colleagues studied sixth graders who had participated in the program since kindergarten. Compared with peers of the same social class and achievement who had attended conventional classrooms, these students behaved more considerately toward their classmates and worked better together. They also better understood others' perspectives and could better solve interpersonal conflicts. Two years later when the students were in junior high, the positive effects of the program were still evident. Other schools in the project have noted substantial decreases in discipline problems, as well. Research by this group also provides evidence that these strategies work well in central city schools enrolling low-income children of color, as well as in more affluent suburban schools with white and middle-class children.[28]

First-year teacher Cicely Morris provided her African American and Latino kindergartners a series of experiences to establish a culture of care in her classroom that would help them extend caring to the often harsh world outside.

The Peace Builders antiviolence curriculum helps teachers teach social, emotional, and thinking skills to help students avoid violence and give them a strategy for handling conflicts peacefully.[29] Using a combination of stories, role plays, discussions, writing activities, projects, positive reinforcements, and exhibitions, the curriculum addresses the causes, effects, and alternatives to violence at both a global and local level. Peace Builders is organized around four principles that serve as guides for how to develop into an effective peace builder: (1) praise people; (2) give up put-downs; (3) notice hurts and right wrongs; and (4) seek wise people. Lessons and activities focus on these ideas.

—Cicely Morris
First-year teacher, kindergarten

To enact these classroom norms, Morris engages her students in discussions of peace and violence in their own lives, brainstorming ways to support peace, inventing a pantomime to accompany the class-adopted theme song, "I've Got Peace Like a River, " and reading big-book stories like "Tillie and the Wall." Morris calls "Tillie and the Wall" "an allegorical tale of a young mouse who bravely crosses a long-accepted wall that separates her community from another." The story prompts her students to consider the walls in their lives and whether they "fear what is beyond these walls." She also creates a bulletin board on which she recognizes students' peace-building activities and has the students construct links of a giant "peace chain" to help them visualize peaceful acts.

Some may argue that bringing the unpleasantness of surrounding violence to the fore of a curriculum for 5-year-olds is ill-timed and casts a dark shadow on what ought to be the most carefree time of a child's life. This assertion might hold up if these young children did not already suffer from exposure to violence. Several of my students speak very candidly about witnessing domestic violence, homicide, and gang activity. A teacher's silence on these issues is irresponsible. Expecting young children to interpret the violence they witness and extricate themselves from violence in their own responses to conflict [without the help of adults] is a disservice.

> Peace Builders falls squarely in line with my philosophy that includes valuing children, lifelong learning, and the teaching of critical thought. I do not want society's epidemic of violence to curtail the life chances of a single one of my students. This unit attempts to instill the basic value of life—respecting one's own right and the right of others to live in peace. Lifelong learning is addressed by sharing our experiences with violence and ideas on alternatives to violence, and by stressing peace building as a lifelong engagement. Finally, Peace Builders challenges students to arrive at their own conclusions about how the world is and how they desire it to be.
>
> —Cicely Morris
> *First-year teacher, kindergarten*

Morris's approach echoes that of Chicago kindergarten teacher Vivian Gussin Paley. In her book *You Can't Say You Can't Play,* Paley probes the moral issue of children excluding others in the classroom, especially those whom they see as different. According to Paley, schools reinforce children's rejections of others. Sometimes adults accept rejection as a natural behavior and only intervene or take a moral stance in cases of blatant physical or psychological harm. Because acts of rejection are so familiar and frequent (usually painful and cumulative pinpricks rather than violent attacks), teachers may choose to ignore what they see as mild negative behavior. But tolerating rejection is not a minor discipline issue. Unchecked, it lets students develop social attitudes that affect their own and others' well-being and safety. To prevent her students from developing this habit of rejection, Paley implemented a rule that her students proposed when they discussed this problem. That rule forbid them from turning away any student who wanted to play in their group: "You can't say you can't play."

Paley uses storytelling to help her build a more moral world in her classroom. She writes children's stories with characters—including Magpie, a magical bird—and situations that parallel classroom life. Through stories of Magpie, Paley introduces a variety of characters whose torments parallel those faced by students of all ages. In schools and outside, hurtfulness can be a relentless offense against individuals and communities. Within their unique classroom communities, caring teachers will find grade-appropriate responses for each act of rejection, for each slur reflecting on others' race, gender, ability, style, and so on.

Socially Just Classrooms: Doing Democracy

Throughout the nineteenth century, small and often marginalized reform groups worked to make schools instruments of social justice. Particularly interesting are the efforts of African American women educators, often assisted by black churches and sometimes by liberal white groups like the Quakers, to use the schools to improve the social, economic, and political circumstances of the African American community. These women used their classrooms and their leadership to teach reading and writing not only to their students but to community adults as well—a daring act in the nineteenth century. For example, teacher Fannie Jackson Coppin organized tuition-free classes for freedmen coming North and founded a school for children of emancipated slaves. Believing that knowledge is power, Coppin intended her teaching to "uplift" the race. Other well-educated black women educators such as Anna Julia Cooper and Mary McLeod Bethune also went far beyond teaching their students technical skills and attempted to teach in ways that would bring about social and political change. At the root of their efforts was the conviction that education was not about individual gain, but about strengthening the community, a view captured eloquently in the motto of the National Association of Colored Women—"Lifting as We Climb."[30]

In the educational mainstream, first Horace Mann and later John Dewey envisioned schools as agencies of social reform and the democratization of American society. Dewey stressed that classrooms are a part of life, not merely preparation for it, and that to make society more democratic, students must participate in classrooms that are themselves democratic societies. Teachers must give students a chance to learn how their actions affect the success or failure of the group. And students must develop their sense of civic-mindedness by sharing both the pleasant and trying tasks that complex group projects require. "Doing one's part" as a member of a classroom project prepares children to be both leaders and followers.

Beginning with the 1960s' civil rights movement, the struggle for equal educational opportunity for diverse groups of students has brought structural changes in schools: racial desegregation, bilingual education, inclusion of handicapped children in regular classrooms, and heterogeneous (or mixed-ability) grouping. To accommodate these changes, researchers and teachers began developing cooperative small-group learning to improve social relationships and ease tensions in racially mixed classrooms. Elizabeth Cohen's work using specific techniques to eliminate status hierarchies in classrooms (described in Chapter 6) continues this work in contemporary classrooms.

Reformers today speak less about overcoming the "problems" of diverse classrooms than they do about unleashing the educational power in classrooms where diversity is available as a resource. Here too, John Dewey anticipated much of the cognitive and sociocultural theory and research that support this contemporary attitude for learning, development, and community building.

> In order to have a large number of values in common, all members of the group must have an equitable opportunity to receive and to take from others. There must be a large variety of shared undertakings and experiences. Otherwise, the influences which educate some into masters, educate others into slaves. And the experience of each party loses in meaning when the free interchange of varying modes of life experience is arrested. [This] lack of free equitable intercourse which springs from a variety of shared interests makes intellectual stimulation unbalanced. . . . The more activity is restricted to a few definite lines—as it is when there are rigid class lines preventing adequate interplay of experiences—the more action tends to become routine on the part of the class at a dis-

advantage, and capricious, aimless, and explosive on the part of the class having the materially fortunate position. [31]

Critical Pedagogy Responds to Students' "Resistance"

At the end of the twentieth century, critical pedagogy emerged as a theory of education that calls for classrooms to be democratic and socially just communities. Critical pedagogy, introduced in Chapter 4, begins with the assumption that schooling is not Horace Mann's "great equalizer." Rather, schools not only help privileged families pass on their advantages to their children, they make it likely that low-status and low-income children will also follow in their parents' footsteps. When teachers use a critical pedagogy, they ask students to examine historical and contemporary events, institutions, and relationships in order to expose various mechanisms of oppression that are invisible within the official versions of school knowledge and culture. This endeavor requires listening to different voices, versions, and interpretations typically kept out of school.

Critical pedagogy is a tough and unforgiving view of the world that relentlessly seeks liberation of the oppressed by identifying the rawest social sores and refusing to be polite about them. For some, it is difficult to get beyond the vocabulary of critical pedagogy to examine the merits of the ideas. Critical pedagogues tend to use words that approximate how people are affected by ideas and social processes, rather than how democracy-minded, socially concerned people *intend* society to work. Thus, if there are people oppressed by their economic conditions, there must be oppressors. If there are less powerful segments of society, there must be dominant ones. If there are people who find themselves on the margins of society (and they did not place themselves there), others have marginalized them. On the other hand, critical pedagogy is far from a fearsome, subversive perspective bent on destroying the social order. It is a philosophy that seeks to bring clarity to injustice and unjust processes.

One essential ingredient of critical pedagogy is for the teacher to remove himself or herself from the role of oppressor—however benevolent—in the classroom. Brazilian educational theorist Paulo Freire, for example, argued that students must never be manipulated or controlled. And perhaps the most pernicious form of control is in using one's power (authority, charisma, language, etc.) to cause students or their parents to think that they have made unimpeded choices on their own behalf. Rather, critical pedagogues insist that students should be involved in a constant dialogue with their teachers examining experiences that allow students to plan and act on the conditions of their lives—in school and out.

This is extraordinarily difficult, and sometimes seems impossible, given the institutional requirements that teachers must meet—covering the curriculum, assigning grades, enforcing schoolwide discipline policies. However, teachers who struggle to break free from these oppressive relationships will indeed benefit their students in many ways. To the extent they can, teachers may engage students in reflecting on and questioning assumptions and beliefs that underlie what seems to be common sense. Teachers can probe issues of race, class, gender, and the often invisible privileges of white, middle-class people, and of men. They can scrutinize commonsense ideas about learning, knowledge, classroom activities and relationships, and the goals of schooling, including issues of authority, discipline, and control. Although teachers remain officially "in charge," only through common action with their students can they develop new, more emancipatory classroom norms about what they want to accomplish and how they will relate to each other. This shift in classroom life explains why critical pedagogy promises to alter students' classroom behavior—though not necessarily in the usual sense of achieving classroom control.

Although critical educators would never frame their approach as a form of classroom management or discipline (and it surely is not), they do believe that their practices moderate the thinking, structures, and routines that cause many students to be "discipline problems." Further, this shift may cause many teachers to reevaluate what they perceive as a problem. The theory of "resistance," developed by Paul Willis and Henry Giroux, embarks from anthropological studies of schools and classrooms. Both Giroux and Willis found that lower-class students often behave "badly" as an expression of resistance. The students knew, at least on some level, that the way schools responded to them doomed them to limited life chances. Thus, in this view, antischool attitudes and behavior can be seen as healthy (if usually unproductive) rebellion against an oppressive institution, rather than as individual psychological problems—lack of self-discipline, laziness, low ability, and so on—or problems that stem from poor parenting or a disorganized neighborhood. Although critical educators do not believe that all "oppositional behavior" has this political quality, they do believe that many students act to assert their own power over their destiny.

Democratic Classrooms and Diversity

Critical pedagogy and resistance theory are often discussed in highly theoretical and abstract terms that are hard to translate into practice. Yet we can find many examples of educators whose actions embody these theories, who allow all children to preserve, enrich, and value their own culture by contributing to and challenging the schoolwide and community culture. As Professor Gloria Ladson-Billings has said, the classrooms of such educators are "culturally relevant."

Culturally Relevant Classrooms It is easy to have a commitment to "cultural relevance" *as a value* but difficult to act on that value—especially when your students have cultural backgrounds other than your own. However, teaching only those students who share your background is neither desirable nor likely to happen. And teaching all students only from your own perspective is unacceptable. Most teachers of color and teachers for whom English is not their first language have had extensive experience with white, middle-class, mainstream culture, as well as their "own" racial, ethnic, or language group. White teachers are more likely to be monocultural. But whether teachers are monocultural, bicultural, or multicultural, there are both generic and specific dimensions to culturally relevant teaching that they all must acquire. Acquiring these dimensions as part of one's own teaching can be, like foreign travel, daunting at first; but the discovery and adventure are soon difficult to resist. And even though, in our travels, we will not be "natives," we can learn and earn respect.

The generic elements to culturally relevant teaching are really what this book is all about—approaches to schooling, learning, curriculum, and so forth, that are friendly to difference. The specific dimensions to culturally relevant teaching, however, require cultural knowledge that can only be gained by knowing your particular students and their community. Fortunately, increasing numbers of educators are doing scholarly work that can guide teachers' first-hand experiences.

In her book *The Dreamkeepers: Successful Teachers of African American Children,* Ladson-Billings describes the practices of eight teachers (three white and five African American) who created wonderful caring and democratic classroom communities with their inner-city students. These teachers viewed themselves as artists who "mined" knowledge from very capable students, rather than technicians who put knowledge into them. They saw and valued their students' "color," working constantly to help them see how their identity as African Americans connects with national and global ideas and events. All eight teachers saw themselves as part of and "giving back" to the communities where they taught.

In a style that Ladson-Billings calls "we are family," the teachers structured classroom social interactions so that students worked together in ways that we described in Chapter 6. For example, teacher Margaret Rossi used her students' racial identity to accomplish something sixth-grade teachers everywhere struggle with—having students see how "current events" connect with their own lives. At the outset of the Gulf War, for example, Rossi pressed her California students to figure out how events in Kuwait and Iraq affected them. As Ladson-Billings tells it,

> Denisha, a small African American girl who was a diligent student but rarely spoke up in class, raised her hand.
>
> "Yes, Denisha."
>
> In a soft and measured voice, Denisha said, "Well, I think it affects us because you have to have people to fight a war, and since they don't have no draft, the people who will volunteer will be the people who don't have any jobs, and a lot of people in our community need work, so they might be the first ones to go."
>
> Before Rossi could comment, an African American boy, Sean, chimed in, "Yeah, my dad said that's what happened in Vietnam—blacks and Mexicans were the first ones to go."
>
> "I'm not sure if they were the first to go," remarked Rossi, "but I can say they were overrepresented." She writes these words on the board. "Do you know what I mean by this?"
>
> None of the students volunteers a response, so Rossi proceeds with an example.[32]

Notice the several concepts Rossi manages to weave through this culturally relevant lesson, including "disproportionality"—basic to mathematics and statistics—language appropriate to cultural groupings, and respectful affirmations of students' contributions to the group.

> "If African Americans are 12 percent of the total U.S. population, and Latinos are 8 percent of the total U.S. population, what percent of the armed services do you think they should be?"
>
> "Twenty percent total," calls out James, beaming at his ability to do the arithmetic quickly. "Twelve percent should be black, and 8 percent should be Mexican."
>
> "Okay," says Rossi. "However, I would call that 8 percent Latino rather than Mexican, because we are also including Puerto Ricans, Cuban Americans, and other U.S. citizens who are from Latin America. But in Vietnam, their numbers in the armed services far exceeded their numbers in the general population. Often they were the first to volunteer to go. Does it seem as if Denisha's comments help us link up with this news item?"[33]

With Rossi's skillful guidance, the "current events" session evolved into a rich, culturally relevant lesson for students. Ladson-Billings describes the students working busily together by the end of the lesson to create casualty charts revealing how various events in the news might impact their community.[34]

Kindergarten teacher Vivian Paley, mentioned earlier, also grappled with how to build a democratic culturally relevant classroom community in her racially mixed Chicago school. In her book *White Teacher,* she tells how her students' parents helped her realize that the classroom would be a more democratic and caring place if she treated the racial differences of the children in her classroom openly and naturally. In another of her books, *Kwanzaa and Me,* Paley tells how she helped children talk about race and difference in ways that made the classroom safe and comfortable. Beginning with asking an African American parent to come and teach the class about Kwanzaa, Paley regularly invited parents, grandparents, and neighbors of her diverse students to share stories of their culture and to explore with her and the class questions about race, difference, and exclusion. Paley drew on the parents' stories to introduce new fictitious characters—including a former slave named Kwanzaa and an Indian orphan named Kavitha—and events into the running stories she tells. Her characters struggle with moral and relationship issues that parallel the social issues and tone of the classroom.

However, it's not only the content of classroom interactions that matter; cultural relevance also means that teachers understand and respect cultural ways of interacting. A number of studies show that students perform better in classrooms where teachers acknowledge and build on cultural patterns students experience in their families and neighborhoods. For example, African Americans students' use of rhythmic language, alliteration, call and response, and language play can provide a respectful way to engage them in even such mundane curricular topics as phonemic awareness or such lofty ones as poetry forms. Native American children's experience with noncompetitive modes of interaction can provide strong grounding for cooperative learning activities.[35]

Being responsive to cultural style is always more subtle than teaching tips can account for. Teachers can be open about their desire to connect better with their students and overcome handicaps imposed by their own difference. Teachers might acknowledge this cultural difference (which is undoubtedly obvious to all) and invite parents or other members of the students' community into the class to offer their impressions of how the teaching could be more effective for these students. For example, parents might observe that these students would do better with a friendlier, more gentle tone, or they might suggest a more formal and directive approach. Similarly, teachers might observe several successful teachers and note how they "reach" the students. Although teachers must always be on guard against crude stereotypes, they can use culturally relevant modes of interaction to communicate clearly to students that they and their culture belong, are understood, and are respected in the classroom. Such messages can go a long way to counter students' resistance.

Gender-Fair Classrooms Culturally democratic classrooms also consider gender differences. In their book *Failing at Fairness: How America's Schools Cheat Girls,* researchers David and Myra Sadker examine the role that gender plays in the way teachers treat children and the way children treat one another. The Sadkers sent "raters"' to observe fourth, sixth, and eighth graders and their teachers in more than a hundred classrooms in inner cities, rural areas, and affluent suburbs. They studied routine classroom phenomena by asking the following questions: Whom did the teacher call on? How did the student get the teacher's attention? By raising a hand? By calling out? Did the teacher designate the student? What did the teacher say after she or he called on students? What level of help or feedback were students getting? If the teacher praised a student, what was the praise for?

The Sadkers detail how "schoolgirls face subtle and insidious gender lessons, micro-inequities that appear seemingly insignificant when looked at individually but that have a powerful cumulative impact." These "hidden lessons" take many forms and begin early. In elementary school classrooms, girls were shortchanged in class discussion, on the playground, and in the curriculum. Boys received more of four reactions from teachers: praise, correction, help, criticism—all reactions that foster student achievement. "Girls received the more superficial 'O.K.' reaction, the one that packs far less educational punch." Girls also received less time, less help, and fewer challenges. "Reinforced for passivity, girls' independence and self-esteem suffer."[36] David Sadker noted in an interview, "It's not good teaching to reinforce with the boys the idea of 'Act out, threaten to act out, and I will shower you with instructional time to keep you on task.' To girls, teachers say silently: 'Do what's expected, and I'll ignore you.'"[37] The Sadkers suggest that teachers can keep boys from dominating the classroom by waiting longer for answers after asking a question, monitoring cooperative-learning groups, and making comments to girls that encourage academic progress.

Taking this work to heart, first-year high school science teacher Lisa Trebasky considers gender as she makes curriculum and instruction decisions.

If males and females do approach problems differently, which I believe they do, it is essential to create a scientific discourse so that they can share ideas, methods, and ways of understanding. Group discussion and reflection on scientific practices are beneficial for both boys and girls. It is also important for me to be a good role model, showing that women do practice science and do it well. Studying women who have succeeded in science helps break the stereotypes of what scientists are like.

It is not only what I do but also what I do not do that has a tremendous impact. I have high expectations for all of my students, not just the boys. If I challenge a boy to figure out the answer to a scientifically engaging problem for himself, and then go and give the answer to a girl, I send an unconscious message that I do not think my female student can figure it out by herself. I encourage the girls' active participation when it is easy for them to be drowned out by the louder and more aggressive boys. I encourage girls to ask questions and help them use scientific methodology to find answers. I challenge them to think about why there are more men who do science than women.

—Lisa Trebasky
First-year teacher, high school science

Democratic Classrooms and Power

In the introduction to this book we pointed out that "multicultural" is not a philosophy or a strategy or, for that matter, a choice. In a society where there are many cultures, multicultural is simply a description. Similarly, as resistance theory makes clear, the power of students is not something for adults to bestow or deny, or debate whether it is a "good idea" to have. Where there are students, they have power—although that may be power to act out and disrupt; power to shut down and withdraw; or power to learn, care, and contribute. The question worth asking, then, is "What shall students and teachers make of these multicultures and this power?"

Answering that question in the manner of traditional theory and classrooms, we might say that schools want to control students' and their opportunities to disrupt by seeing bad behavior as the student's "problem." As noted earlier, schools prefer to explain (and treat) students' discipline and learning problems as individual (psychological) behavior problems or as individual manifestations of cultural deficits. Rarely are problems attributable to or associated with a clash between students' legitimate cultural attributes and the school's structure and routines. The reason for this preference seems clear: Schools cannot maintain their democratic rhetoric alongside rules prohibiting "bad culture." Thus, schools have a long tradition of responding to students seen as unable or unwilling to fit in as if they have a personal problem. The alternate view here is to affirm, not shut out, students' cultures; to help students use their power in culturally enhancing ways, not suppress their power or turn it against themselves or others.

Classrooms as "Apprenticeships in Democracy" Critical theorists such as Peter McLaren, Ira Shor, and Antonia Darder emphasize the role of culture-related power in the classroom. These educators grapple with the dual dilemma of how to turn resistant students' energies in directions that will benefit them while offering something other than the conventional argument and routes that ask students to give up what makes them different. In a probing and comprehensive argument, Antonia Darder, for example, calls for classrooms to be "apprenticeships in democracy." Darder stresses the need for teachers to take seriously student participation, solidarity, common interest, and voice.[38]

In *Culture and Power in the Classroom: A Critical Foundation for Bicultural Education,* Darder asks teachers to pursue the right of immigrant and nonwhite students to develop and maintain bicultural identities. As a way to support this right, Darder suggests making the classroom a culturally dynamic environment with the goal of helping students construct and determine who they are in relationship to the dominant culture. Given the students' different experience and cultures, there can be no formulas, no "best" cultural curriculum. The curriculum of culture is within the students themselves, and all other learning (such as literacy, science, etc.) will take place in the context of this culture. If students' bicultural identities are not valued, then all other curriculum will be fragmented and resisted.

First-year teacher Ramon Martinez decided that his first graders who lived in poverty in public housing projects were not too young to confront in the classroom some of the conditions they experienced in their daily lives. Using Darder's approach, he sought to counteract the resistance that his students, as young as they were, had already begun to exhibit.

I witnessed firsthand the way that my students' cultural contexts influence their attitudes and actions in our classroom. Since academic and economic success are uncommon in their community, my students are likely to dismiss academic and economic aspirations as unrealistic. In fact, some of my students seem to have already done just that. Once they abandon those aspirations, they are more likely to adopt behaviors that are not conducive to success in school.

The challenge for me is to use my theoretical understanding of students' behavior to provide a more effective learning environment. One of my principal goals this year has been to let the culture of my students inform my teaching practices and shape the culture of our classroom. In particular, I have been influenced by the notion that student participation and the development of student voice are essential components of a culturally democratic learning environment.

My students' familiarity with alcoholism, drug abuse, and gang violence; their mastery of "Spanglish" and code-switching; and their skillful ability to communicate the subtle nuances of everyday life in the projects might not be perceived as knowledge or intelligence by many teachers. However, my students have much to contribute to the construction of knowledge in our classroom. Group discussions, weekly "sharing time," and interactive journals are three ways that I have attempted to validate my students' lived experiences. I have tried to communicate to them that their thoughts, ideas, and experiences are important and worthy of discussion in the classroom. My goal has been for them to feel that they are experts when it comes to their neighborhood and themselves.

For example, although most of my students live in the projects, [when we made our "mural map" of the neighborhood] many of them chose to create large, colorful homes with sloped roofs. Interestingly, one student depicted her building extremely realistically. When I smiled at her house, she insisted that that was how it really looked. I agreed with her and recruited her to make more buildings to fill some of the empty spaces on the map. After she had completed her task, I noticed that one of the buildings had "PR" written on it in large letters. When I questioned her about what the letters were for, she was silent and even seemed a little embarrassed. After an extended pause, she told me that that was what they spray painted on the walls of her building. I quickly realized that she had attempted to imitate the graffiti of "PF" ("Primera Flats"), one of the eight gangs that reside in the housing projects. I realized that her embarrassment was due to her uncertainty as to how I would react to the graffiti. I reassured her that it was perfectly all right to depict things as she saw them.

To a very large degree, these strategies have been successful. My students share their thoughts, ideas, and experiences with me and with their classmates. They seem to perceive that our classroom is a forum for them to share freely and openly. I feel that I have contributed to their empowerment by encouraging them to express and define themselves.

—Ramon Martinez
First-year teacher, grade 1

Building on Students' Powerful Resources Obviously, to help students gain access to their own power, teachers have to be able to recognize it as Ramon Martinez did. This is not always easy, given schools' inclination to interpret hints of student power as negative or valueless. This is a matter about which Ira Shor is very helpful. In his 1992 book, *Empowering Education: Critical Teaching for Social Change,* Shor identifies students' empowering resources that are usually present and worth every teacher's efforts to look for and support. In some respects, the measure of a caring and democratic classroom is revealed by this power in action. In the following list, we offer and build on Shor's specification of ten "student resources for empowering education and critical thought."[39] Recognizing and valuing these student strengths, teachers like Ramon Martinez can reconstruct power relations in elementary and secondary school classrooms to be more democratic and constructive.

1. *"Students have extra cognitive and affective resources"*[40] *that caring and democratic classrooms allow to bloom.* Such classrooms work to diminish the general alienation that draws students into boredom or "defensive silence." These students "can read, write, listen, and debate with more care than they habitually demonstrate; they feel more deeply about experiences and ideas than they let on . . . they are brighter, more articulate, and have more emotional depth" than the typical teacher-centered classroom allows them to risk showing.[41]

2. *Students will talk wonderfully well in caring and democratic classrooms.* Shor notes: "[T]hey can speak passionately about themes that are important to them . . . [and] student speech is rich and colorful when they let teachers hear their authentic voices; they display lively imaginations, interesting thoughts, deep feelings, and humor; city life also makes them verbal in their daily relationships, if not in class; they are used to talking a lot in their private life; their talkative habits can become academic tools in class."[42]
3. *Students will tell their "life and work experiences" in caring and democratic classrooms.* Shor points out that teachers must be aware that students' experiences in "school and family life, in street life, and in relationships . . . are worthy of inquiry, like teenage pregnancy, abortion, drugs and alcohol, suicide, . . . racism, sexual harassment . . ."[43] and, as we have heard from first-year teachers, neighborhood and family violence. Of course, not all is so grim. Students also have warm and enriching experiences—minor satisfactions and major triumphs—to share. Many classrooms take none of this seriously, the grim or the joyful. Importantly, with exceptions for students whose words can dominate or be hurtful, to foreclose the expression of any one student's experience must necessarily dampen the expression of everyone else. The class never loses just one story or one student's insights.
4. *Students desire self-esteem and can find it in caring and democratic classrooms.* Self-esteem is typically seen as a "need," and we may be more accustomed to associating needs with deficits than with power. However, when classrooms support students' confidence, they become powerful actors on behalf of themselves and their classmates. Confidence allows one to ask for help and to help others. Shor's words here remind us that because critical pedagogy hinges on the voices of students, it requires sharp focus and unrelenting attention: "I listen carefully . . . and take notes in class from their comments; I ask them to repeat their statements and to reread their papers aloud . . . so that other students can focus on the words of a peer as serious material for discussion; I also start a class hour with some reference to what students said before . . . to reinforce the importance of their words; I use their themes as problems for dialogue, to indicate the value of their perceptions and lives."[44]
5. *Students have a curiosity that is powerful when it is supported in caring and democratic classrooms.* But in other classrooms, curiosity can be wasteful or destructive. What makes curiosity powerful also makes it risky. It leads into places unknown and reveals vulnerabilities that are intolerable in public settings that threaten, ridicule, or ignore.[45]
6. *Students have powerful democratic attitudes that can be developed in caring and democratic classrooms.* Shor offers a virtual catalog of powerful dispositions that students bring to class. They have "a healthy dislike for bosses, big shots, politicians, and arrogant pundits; they are sensitive to indignity and don't like to be pushed around by arbitrary authorities, haughty supervisors, and bureaucratic chiefs; they resent following

rules they did not make; their democratic values include beliefs in justice, equality, tolerance for differences, fair play, and free speech. [T]hese values compete with antidemocratic ones developed by community and mass cultures, like male superiority, white supremacy, homophobia, narrow-minded ethnocentrism, competitive self-reliance, environmental disregard, excessive consumerism, and glory in military force," and more. Before we float away with the democratic glories of youth, Shor keeps us earthbound. He reminds us of some social conditions that explain why not all power develops positively, and why democratic classrooms are so essential: "[T]hey [students] don't see individuals and groups winning improvements through concerted democratic action, so their orientation to activism is virtually nonexistent; students express cynicism about moneyed power in society but want to live like the rich; they believe in democracy despite few democratic experiences in school, at work, at home, in the street, and in their traditional classrooms."[46]

7. *Students bring differing views of race and racism to school; as a topic, racism is a powerful democratic tool in a caring and democratic classroom.* But ignored, racism destroys a classroom. Perhaps there is no other student attitude that is more futile and dangerous to try to "control" or suppress than racism. We sketch here just a few of Shor's many views and practices as examples of how one democratic teacher approaches racism. (Other places to look for ideas are included in "Digging Deeper" at the end of this chapter.) Shor tells us, "I intervene with questions, comments, exercises, and readings, to raise the profile of the pervasive discrimination faced by people of color and not by whites, and to encourage unprejudiced students to speak up and question their peers; so that I don't remain the leading antiracist voice in class. . . . I try not to lecture students on good and evil; I cannot moralize or sermonize them as if I am a superior teacher who considers them awful or dumb; any superior attitude on my part will only make the racist students defensively cling to their beliefs; . . . I try to treat all students as intelligent people who want to do the right thing; students are generally reluctant to discuss racism while listing it often as a big problem in society needing discussion; one pedagogy I found helpful in regard to racism uses a problem-posing format beginning with a dialogue around the question 'What is "racism"?' . . . What causes racism? What can reduce racism?'"[47]
8. *Students are willing to apply their considerable power to overcoming sexism and homophobia (their own and others) in caring and democratic classrooms.* The Sadkers' studies on the treatment that girls receive in schools, mentioned earlier in this chapter, represents only a fraction of the documented evidence about gender attitudes and inequity. We are so surrounded by differential treatment of men and women—in schools and out—that most teachers will go days or months (some manage an entire career!) without noticing or responding to the misapplication of gender privilege. Whether it is a matter of boys dominating the microscope in science class (while the girls write up the lab notes), a middle

schooler calling his neighbor a "fag," or a group of high school freshmen girls passing along rumors about a classmate's recent date, *not responding* to sexist and homophobic behaviors denies students the opportunity to use their power to change the culture that tolerates these behaviors.

9. *Students are able and eager to explore felt, but usually unspoken, reservations about the American Dream, in caring and democratic classrooms.* Students whose families benefit less from American capitalism have no more facility with its critique than those who benefit more have. Although many students doubt whether they will personally benefit, nearly all seem to have considerable faith that an economic system exists that benefits those who are smart enough, good enough, hardworking enough, or even crooked enough. These beliefs are a source of both power and the undermining of power, and it takes caring and democratic classrooms to help students sort it out. Much of what eventually surfaces as "resistance" may have its origins in the cumulative weight of students' unarticulated sense that America (or simply, school) works in others' favor but not their own. Culturally democratic classrooms help students explore how culture and identity interact with conceptions of worth and merit and how the doctrines of capitalism culturally define worth and merit.
10. *Students express humor and emotion in caring and democratic classrooms.* Shor writes, "[Students] often react with surprise, delight, or shyness when class dialogue is emotional, not just analytic, and when texts convey intensity . . . from humor to sadness to outrage to hope; some take a while to laugh or express strong emotion in class because it is new to them, that intellectual life in classroom should have emotional qualities."[48] Of course, when controlling students is a matter of concern, expressing humor and emotion (especially the noisy kind, like laughter) is the first to emerge as a problem. In fact, emotion and humor are wellsprings of power denied to too many students.

Creating Classroom Communities Is a Struggle

Community and community building were important aspects of my educational philosophy, so I knew they had to be part of my practice from day one. I spent the first week of school doing community-building activities. We did people hunts, made and wore nametags, wrote first-day-of-school creative essays, and did other getting-to-know-you activities. By the second week, I felt my students were getting to know each other and me and were developing a sense of trust and security.

As the days passed, I began to wonder when and if my kids would ever going to "learn." I felt such pressure to make sure my students were academically prepared that, by the third week of school, I had placed the idea of community building on the back burner. I did not see any behavior problems in those first weeks, so I felt comfortable that the time we spent building our community was probably enough. I was ready to get down to "business." I watched them work in partners or in groups, and the work was getting done. That was all that I cared about. What I failed to realize, however, was that they were simply completing the work independently, while sitting next to their partners. There was no negotiation, communication, or interaction taking place. It was every student for him- or herself.

By the fifth week, my students were out of control. They were tattling, bullying, name calling, poking, and excluding one another from activities. They did not value or respect one another, and their antics were affecting the lessons and activities. I spent more time mediating fights than mediating knowledge. I was miserable and angry.

I decided to incorporate a community circle into our schedule. I called the circle to share what I had observed on the classroom and the yard. I used a story, "A Sense of Goose," from *A Second Helping of Chicken Soup for the Soul* as a discussion starter. The story describes how geese function as a community, uplifting one another as they fly in a V formation. Interwoven through the story are italicized messages that make the connection between how geese live and how humans should live. But my students spent more time trying to figure out the vocabulary than to comprehend the meaning. Many did not even know what geese looked like or anything about geese. (I marked this as failure number one.) I found myself losing patience with them because they weren't "getting it." I could not believe that my students were not able to take the meaning from the story and apply it to life and our classroom. I could not imagine taking thirty-two students outside and making them flap their arms in a V formation for them to construct understanding. So I tried to draw it on the chalkboard. (I marked this as failure number two.) Eventually, after a couple of readings a few students understood the meaning, but I didn't want to push it. The idea of community and our classroom as a community of learners was as foreign as another language. I placed the story back into my lesson plan book, feeling defeated. I had my students put the story in their binders, in hopes that one day we would come back to it and really understand its meaning and relevance. They complied and silently sat with bewildered looks as if to say, "What was this crazy lady talking about?" We held a few more community circles before winter break, but we never revisited the story.

Over winter break, I finally had time to read Alfie Kohn's book *Beyond Discipline: From Compliance to Community*. It could not have come at a better time. I began to find answers to why the "A Sense of Goose" story did not make sense to my students. Whatever form of community we had was enforced by me. I was running a very teacher-centered classroom, where all the power of decision making and conflict resolution rested in my hands.

As the year progressed, my students and I began to realize a democratic classroom community. It was an incredible and sometimes difficult evolution from a teacher-centered and controlled environment to a community created and strengthened by students. "Guess what the teacher wants" (under the guise of democracy) evolved into "What should we do?" under guidelines I determined, and then into "I can't/don't need to do it myself, what do you guys think we should do?" Over the next couple of months, my students and I developed and maintained a wonderfully strong community.

Then, once again, I put our community building on autopilot, just as the "change" in sixth-grade students that my colleagues had warned me about occurred. Slowly things crumbled. Best friends were no longer best friends. Rumors and gossip were "destroying" reputations and tearing down trust. Four of my students were put into in-school suspension! I was barely sleeping at night. The "Goose story" began to nag me from the recesses of my mind.

I raced to my classroom and created a space big enough in the center for the thirty-three chairs to be formed into a circle. I stopped the students before they entered and told them to take a seat in the circle. The looks on their faces were priceless. The expression was not the same "What is this crazy lady talking about" look; it was a "something big is about to happen" look. They did as they were told. I sat down, took a deep breath, and let them know we needed a community circle. I then passed around "A Sense of Goose." Expressions of familiarity washed over their faces. Their responses to the story were incredibly insightful. They understood how the geese worked together in communities, took care of and looked after one another. They shared wonderful examples of how humans should work together. They shared relevant and meaningful stories that revealed how profound their connections were with one another and how deeply those connections had been damaged. We sorted through issues in our classroom community by engaging in dialogue, and began the long and difficult process of making change.

—Janene Ashford
First-year teacher, grade 6

Creating a caring and democratic classroom takes time, experience, and patience. Even when teachers gain skill and confidence, and their classrooms are more safe and caring than they might have hoped for previously, new challenges will arise. Next year, Janene Ashford and other teachers like her will be calling upon themselves for even greater measures of care and skill than they thought possible this year. Educational researcher Andy Hargreaves, in his book *Changing Teachers, Changing Times,* offers a valuable perspective on creating better classrooms and a better society. He suggests to us that over the span of a teaching career, teachers' work is not about *solving* learning and social problems, but allowing ourselves to struggle with a "better class of problems." We believe that struggling to care is a better class of problem than struggling to discipline.

Digging Deeper

The group of scholars and educators in this section all explore new theories and practices for making classrooms more caring and socially just. The organizations provide networks of educators working with these approaches in classrooms.

William Ayers is an associate professor of education at the University of Illinois at Chicago. Three of his books provide particularly helpful portraits of teachers' struggles to create democratic schools and classrooms. *To Teach: The*

Journey of a Teacher (New York: Teachers College Press, 1995) provides Ayers's inspiring firsthand experiences. *To Become a Teacher: Making a Difference in Children's Lives* (1995) is an edited collection filled with practical, concrete advice for new teachers (and experienced teachers who are rethinking their practices). *City Kids, City Teachers: Reports from the Front Row* (New York: The New Press, 1996), written with Patricia Ford, contains more than twenty-five essays from educators and writers exploring the realities of city classrooms from kindergarten through twelfth-grade.

The **Child Development Project** group including **Eric Schaps, Victor Battistich,** and **Marilyn Watson** is a comprehensive school-change effort to help elementary schools become inclusive, caring communities and stimulating, supportive places to learn. The CDP's approach to "developmental discipline" and classroom management regards the child as intrinsically motivated to construct a personal and moral system and to conform to adult expectations. Its goal is self-discipline and a strong personal commitment to core values. The Center publishes materials for teachers, including *Ways We Want Our Classroom to Be: Class Meetings That Build Commitment to Kindness and Learning* (Oakland, CA: Developmental Studies Center, 1994). The project is also described in Alfie Kohn's, *Beyond Discipline* (see later in this section).

Professor **Antonia Darder** is a member of the education faculty at the Claremont Graduate School. Her work examines the impact of dominant cultural forces on the lives of students from disenfranchised communities and confronts the cultural values and practices that serve to marginalize black, Latino, Asian, and other bicultural students. In *Culture and Power in the Classroom: A Critical Foundation for Bicultural Education* (Westport, CT: Bergin & Garvey, 1991), Darder offers a set of principles from which to develop a critical practice of bicultural education. The book also provides classroom teachers with a critical perspective that they can use to evaluate their current practices with bicultural students.

Tribes: A New Way of Learning and Being Together, by Jeanne Gibbs, provides teachers with practical strategies to develop cooperative and safe classroom communities. The text presents a process that develops inclusion (caring and support), influence (a sense of value—meaningful participation), and community (positive expectations). Tribes materials are available on the Internet at http://www.tribes.com.

Pennsylvania State University Professor **Henry Giroux** has theorized extensively about the connections between culture, student resistance, and critical pedagogy. Of his many books, teachers might find the following especially interesting: *Pedagogy and the Politics of Hope* (Boulder, CO: Westview Press, 1996); *Postmodern Education: Politics, Culture, and Social Criticism,* with Stanley Aronowitz (Minneapolis: University of Minnesota Press, 1991); *Theory and Resistance in Education* (South Hadley, MA: Bergin & Garvey, 1983); and *Ideology, Culture, and the Process of Schooling* (Philadelphia: Temple University Press, 1981).

Education writer and social critic **Herbert Kohl,** a former teacher, has written many engaging books that tell compelling stories about teachers' work with students in difficult life circumstances. One of his early best-selling books, *36 Children,* relays his own experience teaching in an inner-city school in the 1960s. A more recent book, *I Won't Learn from You and Other Thoughts on Creative Maladjustment* (New York: The New Press, 1994), includes essays and stories about responses to situations where, in Kohl's words, "students' intelligence, dignity, or integrity are compromised by a teacher, an institution or a larger social mindset." In *Should We Burn Babar?: Essays on Children's Literature and the Power of Stories* (New York: The New Press, 1994), Kohl provides new perspectives on well-known children's stories, highlighting instances of racism, sexism, and condescension. He offers powerful ideas for better ways to tell children stories.

Alfie Kohn is also a former teacher, who now works with educators across the country. He has written for most of the major education magazines and journals and is the author of a number of books, including *No Contest: The Case Against Competition* (New York: Houghton Mifflin, 1992), *Punished by Rewards: The Trouble with Gold Stars, Incentive Plans, A's, Praise, and Other Rewards* (Boston: Houghton Mifflin, 1995), and *Beyond Discipline: From Compliance to Community* (Arlington, VA: Association for Supervision and Curriculum Development, 1996).

Gloria Ladson-Billings is an associate professor in the Department of Curriculum and Instruction at the University of Wisconsin-Madison. Her book *The Dreamkeepers: Successful Teachers of African American Children* (San Francisco: Jossey-Bass, 1994) is based on her research on the success of culturally relevant pedagogy.

The National Conference for Community and Justice, founded in 1927, is a human relations organization dedicated to fighting bias, bigotry, and racism in America. The National Conference promotes understanding and respect among races, religions, and cultures through advocacy, conflict resolution, and education programs. It maintains an Internet website (http://members.aol.com/natlconf) that provides links to other human relations, civil rights, human rights, and educational organizations, including sources for anti-hate curriculum materials.

University of North Carolina at Chapel Hill professor **George Noblit** studies caring and community building in schools. Although he grounds his work in a philosophical discussion about morality in schooling, he also provides rich descriptions of teachers developing relationships with students. With **Van O. Demise,** Noblit wrote *The Social Construction of Virtue: The Moral Life of Schools* (Albany, NY: SUNY Press, 1996), which examines the history of two southern elementary schools that merged when segregation ended.

Education professor **Nel Noddings** of Stanford University wrote *The Challenge to Care in Schools: An Alternative Approach to Education* (New York: Teachers College Press, 1992). In it, she lays out the conceptual underpinnings for viewing teaching as creating cultures of care.

Vivian Gussin Paley, a kindergarten teacher to whom the MacArthur Foundation gave one of its prestigious "genius" awards, published her first book, *White Teacher,* in 1979. It has been followed by several others, each addressing fundamental issues of classroom life—children's development, racism, gender, and what it feels like to be the outsider, to be "different." These highly readable books (all published by Harvard University Press in Cambridge, Massachusetts), which include *You Can't Say You Can't Play* and *Kwanzaa and Me*, describe her compelling strategies for building the curriculum and classroom community around the knowledge and traditions of her students' families and neighborhoods.

Rethinking Schools publishes a newspaper regularly, books occasionally, and other materials for teachers seeking practices that match social justice values. Of particular relevance for the issues in this chapter is the organization's book *Rethinking Our Classrooms: Teaching for Equity and Social Justice.* Begun a little more than ten years ago by a group of Milwaukee-area teachers who wanted to help shape reform, Rethinking Schools is committed to equity and to the vision that public education is central to the creation of a humane, caring, multiracial democracy. It emphasizes problems facing urban schools, particularly issues of race. Rethinking Schools is located at 1001 Keefe Avenue, Milwaukee, WI, 53212; the group can also be contacted at 1-800-669-4192 and at http://www.rethinkingschools.org on the Internet.

Myra Sadker (deceased) and **David Sadker,** professor of education at The American University in Washington, D.C., began studying gender bias against women and girls in the classroom as doctoral students in the 1960s. Since that time the Sadkers have completed several studies and written widely on this issue, including a popular book that summarizes their and others' findings, *Failing at Fairness: How America's Schools Cheat Girls* (New York: Macmillan, 1994).

Ira Shor is a professor of English at College of Staten Island, City University of New York. His books *Empowering Education: Critical Teaching for Social Change* (Chicago: University of Chicago Press, 1992) and *When Students Have Power: Negotiating Authority in a Critical Pedagogy* (Chicago: University of Chicago Press, 1996) suggest ways for teachers and students to transform traditional classrooms into more democratic ones. Another of Shor's books, *Critical Teaching and Everyday Life* (Chicago: University of Chicago Press, 1980), can also be helpful to elementary and secondary school teachers.

Teaching Tolerance is a project of The Southern Poverty Law Center. This organization offers a wide range of educational tools including videos, written material as well as a magazine for teachers interested in teaching racial tolerance. Teaching Tolerance is on the Internet at http://www.tolerance.org. The **U.S. Department of Justice** website includes a page called "Hateful Acts Hurt Kids," which is intended for children in kindergarten through fifth grade. It aims to (1) promote discussion among children, parents, and teachers about prejudice, discrimination, and related issues; (2) sensitize elementary school age children to the unfairness and hurt of prejudice; (3) give problem-solving skills to children who may be victims of prejudice; and (4) show children what they can do when they find themselves in the role of bystanders to help prevent or de-escalate hurtful acts, based on prejudice. The site's address on the Internet is http://www.usdoj.gov/kidspage.

Joan Wink, a professor of education at California State University-Stanislaus, wrote *Critical Pedagogy: Notes from the Real World* (New York: Longman, 1997). A primer really, the book introduces the ideas and theorists of critical pedagogy in everyday language, provides examples from Wink's and her students' teaching, and offers practical guidelines for creating lessons. Although it is not a substitute for reading Freire, Darder, McLaren (see Chapter 4, "Digging Deeper"), and others in the original, Wink's book provides a highly accessible overview.

Notes

1. Joel Spring, *The American School* (New York: Longman, 1990), pp. 56–57.
2. William Glasser, *The Quality School* (New York: HarperCollins, 1992).
3. Boston School Committee records, as quoted in Jeannie Oakes, *Keeping Track* (New Haven, CT: Yale University Press, 1995), p. 24.
4. Ellwood Cubberly, as quoted in Oakes, *Keeping Track,* p. 26.
5. Ibid.
6. G. Stanley Hall, as quoted in Oakes, *Keeping Track,* p. 25.
7. See for example, Frank Riessman's *The Culturally Deprived Child* (New York: Harper & Row, 1962) and Harry Passow, Miriam Goldberg, and Abraham J. Tannenbaum (Eds.), *Education of the Disadvantaged* (New York: Holt, Rinehart & Winston, 1967).
8. See, for example, Lee Canter and Marlene Canter, *Assertive Discipline: Positive Behavior* (Santa Monica: Lee Canter & Associates, 1997).
9. See, for example, Alfie Kohn, *Punished by Rewards* (Boston: Houghton Mifflin, 1993).
10. Jacob Kounin, *Discipline and Group Management in Classrooms* (New York: Holt, Rinehart & Winston, 1970).
11. Thomas Good and Jere Brophy, *Looking in Classrooms* (New York: Longman, 1997).
12. Ibid.
13. Jeff Gregg, "Discipline, Control, and the School Mathematics Tradition," *Teaching and Teacher Education* 11, no. 6 (1995), pp. 579–593.
14. Herbert M. Kliebard, *The Struggle for the American Curriculum: 1893–1958,* 2nd ed. (New York: Routledge, 1995), p. 6.
15. Alan Ryan, *John Dewey and the High Tide of American Liberalism* (New York: W.W. Norton, 1995), p. 153. Ryan notes that Dewey was far more nationalistic than Addams, in that he, far more than she, wanted such settings to bring immigrants into the American community, not simply to create community-like settings per se.
16. A. S. Neill, *Summerhill* (New York: St. Martin's Press, 1995, originally published in 1960).
17. Nel Noddings, *The Challenge to Care in Schools: An Alternative Approach to Education* (New York: Teachers College Press, 1992), p. 65.
18. Noddings, *The Challenge to Care in Schools.*
19. Nel Noddings, "Teaching Themes of Care," *Phi Delta Kappan* 77 (May 1995), p. 676.
20. Noddings, *The Challenge to Care in Schools,* p. 20.
21. Carollee Howes and Sharon Ritchie, "Teachers and Attachment in Children with Difficult Life Circumstances" (unpublished manuscript, UCLA, 1997), p. 3.

22. Ibid., p. 18.
23. Ibid., p. 21.
24. George Noblit, "In the Meaning: The Possibilities of Caring," *Phi Delta Kappan* 77 (May 1995), p. 682.
25. Ibid., pp. 680–685.
26. Mara Sapon-Shevin, "Building a Safe Community for Learning," in *To Become a Teacher: Making a Difference in Children's Lives,* ed. William Ayers (New York: Teachers College Press, 1995).
27. Alfie Kohn, *Beyond Discipline: From Compliance to Community* (Alexandria, VA: Association for Supervision and Curriculum Development, 1996), pp. 114–115.
28. Child Development Project, *Ways We Want Our Classroom to Be: Class Meetings That Build Commitment to Kindness and Learning* (Oakland, CA: Developmental Studies Center, 1994).
29. Peace Builders is a commercially available curriculum (Tucson, AZ: Heartsprings, 1995) based on Dennis D. Embry's work in conflict resolution.
30. Michelle Knight, *Unearthing the Muted Voices of Transformative Professionals* (Ph.D. diss., Los Angeles, UCLA, 1998).
31. John Dewey, *Democracy and Education* (1916), in *John Dewey, the Middle Works,* Vol. 9 (Carbondale, IL: Southern Illinois University Press,1989), pp. 84–85.
32. Gloria Ladson-Billings, *The Dreamkeepers: Successful Teachers of African American Children* (San Francisco: Jossey-Bass, 1994), p. 50.
33. Ibid., p. 51.
34. Ibid.
35. Hugh Mehan, "Understanding Equality in Schools: The Contribution of Interpretative Studies," *Sociology of Education* 65, no. 1 (January 1992), pp. 1–21.
36. Myra Sadker and David Sadker, *Failing at Fairness: How America's Schools Cheat Girls* (New York: Macmillan, 1994).
37. David Sadker, as quoted in Millicent Lawton, "Girls Will Be Girls," *Education Week,* 30 March 1994.
38. Antonia Darder, *Culture and Power in the Classroom: A Critical Foundation for Bicultural Education* (Westport, CT: Bergin & Garvey, 1991), p. 67.
39. Ira Shor, *Empowering Education: Critical Teaching for Social Change* (Chicago: University of Chicago Press, 1992), pp. 223–232.
40. Ibid. p. 223.
41. Ibid., pp. 223–224.
42. Ibid., p. 224.
43. Ibid., p. 225.
44. Ibid., p. 225.
45. Ibid., pp. 225–226.
46. Ibid., p. 226.
47. Ibid., pp. 227–229.
48. Ibid., p. 232.

CHAPTER 8

Grouping and Categorical Programs:

Can Schools Teach All Students Well?

Matthew Eide

First-year teacher, high school history

> The way we cut up the world clearly affects the way we organize our everyday life. The way we divide our surroundings, for example, determines what we notice and what we ignore . . . the way we classify people determines whom we trust and whom we fear. . . . The way we partition time and space likewise determines when we work and when we rest, where we live and where we never set foot. Indeed, our entire social order is a product of the ways in which we separate kin from nonkin, moral from immoral, serious from merely playful, and what is ours from what is not.
>
> —Eviatar Zerubavel[1]

Making Distinctions

Documenting and explaining variation has been a controlling purpose of Western science. Humans cannot resist noticing and attempting to make categories for people and things to "fall into." And, as sociologist Eviatar Zerubavel notes, our categories affect how we see the world, how we act, and what we value. Life in schools is just the same—a world of categories and distinctions.

The assessment and evaluation strategies schools use permit us to categorize, compare, rank, and assign value to students' abilities and achievements in relationship to one another and to students in other schools, states, and countries. Policymakers and educators in the United States, as in most Western societies, have made categorizing students a central feature of schooling. However, the educational categories we use are not "real" in any material sense. Rather, they are ideas and abstractions about human attributes and behaviors—what social scientists call *constructs*. In Chapter 2, we characterized *intelligence* as a social construct that schools use to rank and sort students. Today, intelligence rarely stands alone as a single criterion for grouping decisions. Schools weave multiple behavioral and social constructs, including achievement, creativity, motivation, ability, leadership, aspirations, and self-concept, into a complex categorizing web.[2] Even so, intelligence, because of its social and legal acceptance as a signifier of merit, remains as schools' central organizing construct—even as schools attempt to blur distinctions between some categories.

Everyone shares the propensity to categorize, make meaning, and assign values to social and behavioral differences, but different cultures don't necessarily create the *same* categories. Neither do they assign the same meanings and values to categories they may share with other cultures. It is tempting to accept the categories, explanations, and values that one's own culture has constructed as real, true, and "common sense," but clearly they are not. As anthropologists remind us, each culture's meanings and values are simply the particular way a particular group of people has constructed solutions to questions and problems that arise as they create and preserve their society.

For example, differences in how Japanese and Americans characterize and value achievement, noted in Chapter 3, indicate that Americans pay more attention to students' ability and talent than their effort and persistence. In the American culture, a "good" student nearly always means the same as a "bright" or "smart" student. To be a "good" student in Asian cultures is to be "hardworking." Of course, there is no "true" answer to the question of what makes students good, even though both cultures treat the categories they construct and the meanings they assign to them as "common sense."

Americans have decided that schools can most sensibly respond to the differences among students by separating them for instruction. Thus, most schools group students homogeneously (i.e., with others thought to be like them), not only by age but also according to academic "ability," educational "disadvantage," learning and behavioral "disabilities," language "proficiency," educational "aspirations," and college "potential."

Crucially, these distinctions in U.S. schools exhibit strong statistical overlaps with differences in students' race, ethnicity, and social class, with white and wealthy students typically being disproportionately taught in classes for high-ability and college-bound students. Because of these overlaps, no discussion of grouping can take place without paying careful attention to how and why schools assign students with different racial and social class characteristics to particular groups. Defenders of homogeneous grouping practices claim that group assignments are "objective" or "color-blind," and they attribute the disproportionate assignments into college-prep or learning-disabled classes to unfortunate differences in students' backgrounds and abilities. But these claims of objectivity are based on century-old (and older) explanations of differences that are neither scientific nor bias-free. These distinctions intertwine with social and political forces in the history of schooling.[3]

This chapter describes how and why schools classify and group students by ability.[4] It also explores how the multitude of special classes and programs—special education, gifted, compensatory, bilingual—do as much to *create* differences as they do to meet students' special needs. Finally, the chapter describes the theory and innovative practices many schools are using as they struggle against the current culture in order to teach students in heterogeneous (mixed) groups.

Many educators are finding that, unlike homogeneous grouping, heterogeneous grouping supports multidimensional and developmental conceptions of intelligence, sociocultural theories of learning, constructivist approaches to teaching, and a community model of schooling. Heterogeneous grouping also supports education as an instrument of social justice. However, because homogeneous grouping practices are so deeply entrenched in schools and because these practices connect closely to fundamental cultural values and political interests, changing them proves extraordinarily challenging.

History, Diversity, and Homogeneous Grouping

Homogeneous grouping began in earnest at the end of the nineteenth century. Like most traditional school practices, it fit well with and made use of prevailing conceptions of learning, teaching, and schooling. It matched an IQ conception of intelligence, behavioral theories of learning, a transmission and training model of teaching, and the factory model of school organization. Homogeneous grouping also fit with schools' role in maintaining a social and economic order in which those with power and privilege routinely pass on their advantages to their children. In the early 1900s, policymakers and educators saw homogeneous grouping as a way to solve a whole array of problems brought by the growing diversity of students. New immigrants needed to learn English and American ways. Factories needed trained workers. Footloose urban youth required supervision. And schools needed to continue their traditional role of providing high-status knowledge to prepare some students for the professions.

Furthermore, the culture generally was one in which it made perfectly good sense to dislike people who were different. Established American families often did not think much of immigrants; immigrants often thought themselves better than other immigrants from different homelands and better than those more recently arrived in this country. Although there have always been individuals within groups who are free from prejudice, every group at that time thought itself superior to African Americans, and most of the wealthiest Americans thought themselves superior to everyone else. Thus, schools were given the contradictory goals of teaching students to get along while remaining separate—of teaching everyone well, but teaching some students to be better.

After a long debate about how to educate students for such diverse purposes, educators gradually settled on a new view of democratic schooling. They defined *opportunity* as the chance to prepare for largely predetermined and certainly different adult lives. Elwood Cubberly, a prominent educational scholar of the time, wrote, "Our city schools will soon be forced to give up the exceedingly democratic idea that all are equal, and our society devoid of classes . . . and to begin a specialization of educational effort along many lines in an attempt to adapt the school to the needs of these many classes."[5] The superintendent of Boston schools tried hanging onto a few more democratic sentiments. In 1908 he expressed a view close to Cubberly's but not so different from what may be heard today: "Until very recently the schools have offered equal opportunity for all to receive one kind of education, but what will make them democratic is to provide opportunity for all to receive education as will fit them equally well for their particular life work."[6] Concurrently, two phenomena bolstered Cubberly's definition of democratic schooling—the notion of measurable IQ as governing students' "potential" for learning, and the factory model of schooling efficiency.

IQ and Potential By the early twentieth century, industrializing democracies looked for scientific explanations of merit. Differentiating among citizens by using the old indicators of race and family background was functional but not fully comfortable for schools. Intelligence provided a seemingly meritocratic and scientific basis for sorting students into classrooms and improving the quality and efficiency of the schooling enterprise. Highly intelligent students would learn more and faster. Homogeneous grouping would prevent slower students from developing poor self-concepts and attitudes toward learning, by not forcing them to lag hopelessly behind more capable classmates. Since intelligence tests were increasingly accepted as scientific, accurate, and impartial, there could be no claim of unfairness.

Once scores were reified as intelligence and potential (as discussed in Chapter 2), psychological testing helped institutionalize prevailing stereotypes of race and class differences. Test results were consistent with the popular view that poor, minority, and non-English-speaking students were intellectually, morally, and even biologically inferior to Anglo-Americans. Many people who tried to understand school problems adopted a popular distortion of Charles Darwin's evolution theories that explained how darker-skinned, recently arrived immigrants from southern Europe were on a lower rung of the evolutionary ladder. Recall from Chapter 2 intelligence-test pioneer Lewis Terman's words, "Their dullness seems to be racial. . . . Children of this group should be segregated in special classes. . . . They cannot master abstractions, but they can often be made efficient workers." Although these views did not go uncontested, schools enacted the prevailing belief that inherent group differences caused enormous variation in students' potential for school learning. Grouping practices corresponded.

Most current grouping practices don't rely on IQ, at least not exclusively, but the early practices and views set a pattern that continues today. Standardized achievement tests, which help divide students into ability groups based on their potential, are central to qualifying students for compensatory education programs. Standardized language proficiency tests determine the appropriate class level for limited-English students. IQ, in conjunction with other measures, remains basic in identifying students who are gifted as well as those who have cognitive disabilities. Intelligence persists as a widely respected marker in a society that wants to see itself as just and equitable. However, because intelligence has been constructed in a culture characterized by race and class discrimination, using intelligence as an indicator of merit also produces a distribution of power and privilege that is strikingly familiar to the overt racial and social class sorting of earlier times.

Scientific Management Identifying, separating, and treating students differently fit well with turn-of-the-twentieth-century notions of scientific management. As described in Chapter 1, educators quickly embraced the methods of the expanding manufacturing sector of the economy. In the spirit of the age, this approach made wonderful sense to school managers and to boards of education. Consequently, educational managers brought into schools "time-and-motion studies" (picture efficiency experts with stopwatches and charts noting every aspect of school activity, including the passing out and collecting of materials), centralization, authority concentrated at the top, rules for best methods, and so on. They touted this approach as the only way to bring order and efficiency to the schools' disarray. Following the model of the efficient factory, schools increasingly saw children as raw materials out of which they would fashion their product, productive adults. The apex of scientific management was manifest in the assembly line. One line might turn out Fords—all running well and doing what Fords should do; another line would turn out Lincolns—a superior product.

Homogeneous grouping allowed schools to create a structure that permitted specialization and a division of labor. Most teachers and administrators accepted the scientific management perspective that classrooms full of similar students would allow teachers to mass-produce learning. As in the factory, every student would receive a standardized lesson designed for just "this type" of student. In the factory, managers did not value individual differences along the assembly line—differences were defects in the product. So it has been with the schools: Educators often see individual differences within groups as problems.

The Press for Universal Education Over the course of the twentieth century, compulsory education laws and the increased necessity of a high school diploma in the job market drew more and more students to school—even those previously considered uneducable. In less-enlightened times, affluent families closeted away children with serious physical and mental problems or sent them to special schools—often boarding schools. Charitable institutions cared for some of the others. Poor children were often sent to asylums. Frequently, they were an embarrassment and the object of strangers' curiosity, fear, and ridicule.

Milder problems simply went unrecognized or were dismissed as unimportant. When students had trouble fitting in at school, they quit—often with the school's active encouragement. Until midcentury, most of them found jobs and led productive lives. Adults chalked up students' unexplained difficulties at school to their backwardness, having a bad character or upbringing, maladjustment, or just being odd. As the century progressed, however, these attitudes changed, and states and local school systems developed an array of special programs for students who were different.[7]

The 1960s federal War on Poverty legislation provided funding for "categorical" programs (special programs targeted to particular types of students). These programs and other legislation that followed them set particular categories of students in national policy by providing financial incentives for identifying and labeling students in particular ways. *Title I* of the historic Elementary and Secondary Education Act (ESEA) of 1965, for example, provided categorical funding for "educationally deprived" students. Congress saw these students as needing more academic help (most often remedial) than their local schools were currently providing to compensate for the students' impoverished backgrounds. School boycotts and other protests by Hispanic students and communities in the 1960s led Congress to pass the Bilingual Education Act in 1968, supporting programs advancing Hispanic culture and language for Spanish-speaking students. In 1974 *Lau v. Nichols*—a suit brought in behalf of non-English-speaking Chinese students in San Francisco—required that *all* schools provide special assistance to their students whose native language is not English.

Advocacy groups and new legislation increasingly categorized students for special education programs and developed new programs for students whose learning disabilities were attributable to neurological problems. Advocates argued that these students needed help that was different and separate from low achievers whose troubles were thought to result from cultural or economic disadvantage. In 1975 Congress passed the Individuals with Disabilities Education Act (IDEA), after a series of court decisions ruled that disabled students have the right to a suitable free education. IDEA requires schools to provide a "free and appropriate" education to all students with mental retardation; learning disability; impaired hearing or vision; or speech, emotional, or physical difficulties.

Advocates for the "gifted" piggybacked on the trend for categorical funding with the rationale that these students had such significant differences that they could not be fully educated alongside "normal" students. Their efforts were bolstered by faulty views of intelligence held by midcentury mainstream psychologists—for example, that an IQ of 100 was a real representation of "normal" students. Parents, policymakers, and educators alike became convinced that deviation from the norm *in either direction* gave students disadvantages in proportion to the number of points they were from 100. Relying on the appeal of the "bell curve," they reasoned that a student with an IQ of 68 had a similar degree of disability as a student with an IQ of 132 had "extra ability." Borrowing equity-minded arguments used to justify additional services for students disadvantaged by physical or cognitive handicaps, advocates succeeded in reifying "gifted"—changing it from a metaphorical abstraction to a legal and educational category.

Contemporary Grouping Practices: *Ability* by Many Other Names

Educators responded in culturally predictable ways to the new laws and court decisions. They identified students who were "different," scientifically diagnosed the difference, and assigned them to a category. They then grouped students for instruction with others in the same category and tailored curriculum and teaching to the "abilities" of each group, according to what educators thought the groups needed. The increasing importance of legally defined groups increased schools' grouping consciousness, and additional groups have proliferated beyond legal requirements. Soon it was common for high schools to have, taking one high school's example, Special Education English, English as a Second Language, Communication Skills (a remedial class), Regular English (also called College Prep), Accelerated English (a more demanding program than regular, but not as rigorous as honors), and honors/advanced placement classes. Most of these courses were found at each grade level.

Today, ability, previous achievement, postsecondary aspirations, English language competence, and disability status have all become culturally sensible ways to group students. Furthermore, "individual choice," "talent," "motivation," various course prerequisites, and other criteria are also used. However, nearly all grouping assignments are ultimately made and justified by the school's prediction of the student's *ability* to succeed in a particular group. Generally, the intention is to place students in, or encourage students to take, the most demanding courses in which the school thinks they can succeed. These predictions are fraught with difficulties and inconsistencies.

Although the labels differ from school to school, most schools have ways of publicly identifying students and differentiating their opportunities according to their grouping system. First-year teacher Kimberly Aragon's experience, described next, is not unusual.

Grouping pervades almost every area of my K–8 school. Some students enter a "VISTA" (gifted according to various intelligences) program as early as second grade, and, as those students progress, there will be at least one VISTA class in every grade. Every grade, 2 to 8, also has what is called a "SHARP" class. SHARP is an acronym for "Students with High Achievement in Reading Program." Students are placed in a SHARP class based on their previous years' test scores and their grades in English. Although the rest of the students at my school are not labeled as "DULL," the implication of the "SHARP" name is obvious. Moreover, some grades are divided further by placing the Limited English Proficient (LEP) students in one class and all of the rest of the students in another class. In addition, approximately twenty students in grade 1 are pulled out of class for one-on-one Reading Recovery instruction [Title I program]. One-third of the way through this year, the school instituted a middle-school reading elective, which requires ten students who scored in the bottom quartile on the previous year's standardized test to receive extra reading instruction from a credentialed teacher. Those students are then not able to participate in the other electives offered, such as Drama, Spanish, Communications, Art, and Computers. Furthermore, the school's reading philosophy requires that each teacher create ability groups in his or her classroom, based on reading and math levels. As an English teacher, I am required to give each of my seventy students a "Running Record" three times a year and, based on the records, place students in groups in which they are reading material at their instructional level. For instance, if a student's Running Record showed that he could decode 93 percent of the words in a fifth-grade passage, his instructional level, according to the program, is fifth grade, and he should be placed in a reading group that is reading a fifth-grade book.

—Kimberly Aragon
First-year teacher, humanities, grade 8

Sorting by Ability Ability grouping or tracking is the routine sorting of all students into homogeneous groups and classes of "high," "average," and "low" students (or any of the creative euphemisms in vogue, such as "advanced," "accelerated," "opportunity," "basic," "SHARP," "VISTA," etc.). Such sorting typically begins early in elementary school—sometimes even in kindergarten—and it continues throughout the grades.[8] Many elementary schools provide separate classes so that students spend the entire day with others judged to be at the same "ability level." Other schools group students by ability for part of the day for specific subjects such as reading and math. This "regrouping" might include students from more than one class or grade, or, more likely, it may consist of small ability groups (such as reading or math groups) within a classroom. Sometimes ability groups follow a staggered schedule. A kindergarten class may be divided into early- and late-birds (separating the more and less precocious readers) so that each group has time each day to be alone with the teacher.

Nearly all middle and senior high schools ability group some or all academic subjects (typically English, mathematics, science, and social studies) based on students' past grades, test scores, and teacher recommendations. Schools sometimes assign students to blocks of classes all at the same ability level. This typically happens when schools assign a label to the student himself and a high-ability or low-ability student would then go into all classes that match his designation. In recent years, most schools deny this type of assignment exists, and most policies call for assigning students one subject at a time. However, national survey data indicate that 60 to 70 percent of tenth graders who were in honors math also enrolled in honors English. A similar degree of overlap exists between remedial math and remedial or low-level English.[9] Because some subjects like math follow a sequence, students' assignments in earlier grades determine how far they can progress by the time they graduate.[10] Typically, students who will be in the top math classes all through high school are identified by the sixth grade or before. Students not placed in the uppermost ability class by the sixth grade stand only the slimmest chance of completing calculus in high school. This sorting persists even as reforms attempt to interrupt it. For example, the current push to have all students take algebra in the eighth grade is often implemented by sorting students into different levels of algebra, often with different names such as "basic algebra" or "honors algebra." These and many other dilemmas associated with grouping are discussed later in this chapter, after the following survey of the most common kinds of "program" categories.

Sorting for Gifted Programs In the past, exceptionally precocious students often skipped grades if they outdistanced their peers academically. If they remained with their peers, they may have made very exceptional progress, or, if the class offered little intellectual stimulation or opportunity, they may have been discouraged and bored along with the rest of their classmates. About twenty states now provide special funding for gifted and talented students, and nearly all schools have highly visible gifted programs where the highest-achieving students are grouped together for enrichment or accelerated instruction, either in separate classes, in *pull-out* programs, or in gifted *clusters* within regular classrooms. Joseph Renzulli, director of the National Research Center on Gifted and Talented, defines *giftedness* as high ability (including high intelligence), high creativity (ability to formulate and apply new ideas), and high task commitment (motivation and the willingness to stick with a project until it is finished).[11] In many schools, to ensure that "talented" students without strong academic skills can qualify for gifted programs, IQ scores or achievement tests may be augmented by teachers' observations of leadership, creativity, or other special abilities and by parents' nominations.

Sorting by Family Background Today's compensatory programs got their start in the 1960s with the thought that schools could *compensate* students whose poverty, home life, or other life circumstances left them with "cultural deficits." Many experts believed that with intensive remedial help beginning in the earliest grades, students who were already behind when they entered school might catch up with their more-advantaged peers. Today, schools with low-income students have federally funded Title I programs that, at most schools, group the lowest-achieving students for special instruction in reading and mathematics. Schools qualify to participate if they enroll low-income students. But for students to participate in their school's program, they must qualify with low scores on achievement tests. These students are typically in pull-out programs that remove them from the classroom for special instruction while the rest of the students have other, less basic learning activities.

Sorting by Postsecondary Prospects In addition to grouping students by their academic ability or prior achievement in various subjects, high schools also prescribe different sequences of classes, or tracks, for students with different futures. Thus, students heading for college and those expecting to take jobs right after high school will be in different tracks. In some schools, students enroll in programs of study—such as college-preparatory, general, or vocational—that dictate their entire array of courses. The vocational or general (noncollege) track usually coincides with the lower academic levels. College-bound students enroll in the high-ability tracks, since the lower-level courses typically don't satisfy college entrance requirements. Increasingly, schools are recognizing the importance of preparing all students for college entrance. Aware that classes in the vocational track often have low status, low quality, and limited value for gaining college admission, many vocational educators are now working to upgrade these classes. Finally, even *within* the college-prep designation, different course sequences often emerge—designed to prepare some students for the most competitive universities, some for less competitive ones, and some for two-year community colleges.

Most senior high schools offer some advanced placement (AP) classes for exceptionally high-achieving eleventh and twelfth graders bound for the most competitive universities. These courses allow students to pursue college-level study in nearly all the academic subjects. The content of AP courses is similar nationwide, since a major objective is to prepare students for the Advanced Placement examinations, a national test administered by The College Board. This is the same organization that gives the Scholastic Aptitude Test (SAT) that many colleges require for admission. Most colleges give automatic credits to students who receive high scores on AP tests and excuse them from beginning courses in those subjects. AP classes often overlap with gifted and talented programs at the senior high level and with honors-level courses. Increasingly, schools further distinguish these highest-level courses by giving extra weight to grades earned in them when calculating grade point averages.

In the past decade, taking AP classes—multiple AP classes—has become critical for students wishing to attend the nation's most competitive universities. In many states the days have passed when "all A's," or even being "class valedictorian," could assure admission to any university "of choice." Many universities are not just looking for "college prep" courses but are requiring specified numbers of courses in the honors or AP track. Students who have not been programmed for these courses stand little chance. Recent studies in California reveal that most of the state's poor Latinos and African American students attend schools that offer only a small fraction of the courses that wealthier schools offer. Under threat of a lawsuit, the state agreed to add a minimum number of advanced courses to the poor schools, but wealthy schools are already gearing up to add even more. This will perhaps raise the standards for everyone while maintaining the traditional unfair distribution of opportunity.

Sorting by English Language Competence From colonial times, American schools have struggled to educate non-English-speaking populations. Concern about the handicaps faced by the increasing numbers of immigrant students intensified in the early 1970s and fueled support for federal and state assistance. Although the law doesn't require that schools separate students who speak little or no English from their English-speaking peers, *English as a Second Language (ESL)* and bilingual programs nearly always do so.

ESL programs typically take the form of special classes in which non-English-speaking students learn English as a foreign language—without the use of the students' primary language for instruction. Supporters of ESL programs believe that students will do better, both academically and socially, if they use English exclusively for their schoolwork. ESL classes usually occupy one or two hours a day. For the remainder of the time, students attend "regular" classes and learn their other subjects in English. This may mean that these students are in special academic classes where teachers use "sheltered" English and other strategies designed to make instruction in English comprehensible for those with limited English competency. Because ESL and sheltered academic classes use English for instruction, students with different native languages often take these classes together. Finally, the regular classes that these students attend are far more likely to be the low-ability classes (for English speakers) than high-ability classes.

Bilingual education is based on research on second language acquisition showing that students do better in both academic learning and acquisition of the new language if they develop and maintain their native language skills. Advocates of bilingual education argue that students can keep up with their peers in subjects like mathematics and science at the same time that they are learning English. That can best happen if students learn these subjects using their primary language until they are proficient enough in English to understand academic discourse in the subjects. Bilingual classes group students with the same primary language together in separate classes where bilingual teachers teach in the students' language while gradually introducing English.

Most bilingual programs include an ESL component as well as academic instruction in other subjects in the student's native language. Several models of bilingual education rely on separate classes. Bilingual programs called *maintenance* have three goals—learning English, learning academics, and developing literacy in the native language. *Transitional* bilingual programs, in contrast, have only the first two goals, English and academics. Their intent is to shift the student away from the primary language to English as quickly as possible.

Sorting by Disabilities New disability categories surface and old ones disappear as educators, psychologists, and physicians refine their definitions of conditions that fall outside the normal range in physical, sensory, behavioral, or cognitive characteristics. The most current federal Individuals with Disabilities Education Act (IDEA) specifies thirteen categories of disability, and it provides funding to states and local school districts for special programs and services. In 1997 the National Academy of Science reported that 5 million students—about 10 percent of the U.S. school population—qualify for assistance under IDEA. About 90 percent of these students fall into four categories: speech or language impairment, mental retardation (MR), severe emotional disturbance (SED), and specific learning disabled.[12]

Once school personnel determine that a student qualifies for special help, the school is required by law to develop a written Individual Educational Plan (IEP). The IEP states the child's needs, outlines specific learning goals, and specifies the help the school will provide. Students with speech and language problems may need one-to-one instruction provided outside the classroom. Students with long-range illnesses might receive teaching at home or in a hospital. Large school districts often support their own schools for the severely mentally retarded and for the vision- and hearing-impaired. Others may contract with private centers and provide transportation so that students get the help and equipment that typical classrooms can't offer. Students with less-debilitating cognitive and emotional disorders spend all or part of their school day in *resource classrooms*. These are places where small groups of students with disabilities spend time away from the regular classroom receiving assistance from teachers trained in special education and from teachers' aides. However, the law also requires that schools provide special help for disabled students in the *least restrictive environment*. This provision presses schools to *mainstream* students with disabilities into classrooms with peers who have no disabilities for as much of the day as possible.

Cognitive Disabilities Students often lag behind in some school skills. In most cases, this lag is within the normal range of individual developmental differences. However, a growing number of students of normal intelligence who have difficulties, particularly in reading, are identified as *learning disabled (LD)*, and about half of all of those receiving special education services now fall into this category.[13] Students identified as having a learning disability have unusual and specific cognitive disabilities thought to result from an organic cause, such as the brain's inability to process information with the same efficiency as other children. The key to identifying a learning disability is not so much how a student performs in any one area as the discrepancies among different areas of performance. Such students, try as they may, have great difficulty accomplishing certain skills, such as copying correctly, spelling accurately, reading fast, or memorizing details. However, these same students may be skilled at expressing ideas orally and solving problems. Others have more serious difficulty with language, short-term memory, or visual perception. Identified LD students spend varying amounts of their school time in the resource room.

Students with mental retardation are those who score substantially below the normal range on intelligence tests. Categories of retardation range from Mildly Mentally Retarded to those who are designated Severely and Profoundly Retarded. Their disability so restricts their intellectual functioning that they will never reach adult levels. Like LD students, however, those identified as retarded differ widely. Specific intellectual capabilities can differ markedly among students with the same IQ scores. Some students with retardation develop strong social skills that enable them to get along and even learn far better than others who test higher. Seriously cognitively disabled students might join other students for physical education or some electives. For the most part, however, they are taught separately.

Behavioral and Emotional Disorders All students experience occasional mild behavior problems. Some, though, are consistently at odds with their peers and with adults. Sorting typically takes place only when these students are bothersome to others or there are critical concerns about their own well-being. Such misbehavior can result from the complete range of emotional and psychological conditions that affect students. Chronic problems may also result from a mismatch between the behavior standards in class and those of a student's home or play group. Students who seem unable to pay attention are often the first to capture the teacher's notice. Students who fidget and squirm, run around the room, or doze off during a film are hard to ignore. The chronic inability to pay attention, sit still, be quiet, and act cooperatively can be a disability with serious consequences. These students are unable to concentrate on their studies and fall behind academically. Other students often shun them. And they can hardly escape the effects of disapproving and exasperated teachers.

In earlier generations, schools may have labeled older students who consistently acted badly at school "incorrigible" or "juvenile delinquents" and sent them to reform schools, but most such students simply dropped out of school altogether. Today schools categorize many habitually misbehaving students as disabled. For example, attention-deficit hyperactivity disorder (ADHD) now qualifies students for assistance under federal law. Researchers reporting in the *Journal of the American Medical Association* estimate that the disability affects between 3 and 6 percent of the school population.[14] Many advocates view ADHD as a discrete genetic disorder, while others see it as a catchall label for the behaviors just described.

Educators categorize more dangerously unruly and violent students as having other disabilities, for example, as being severely emotionally disturbed (SED). Though such behavior disorders are not themselves cognitive deficits, they often go hand in hand with learning difficulties.

Most students with behavior disorders remain in regular schools, where educators assign them to resource or "opportunity" rooms for a portion of the day or to special daylong classes. Federal law provides guidelines so students with behavioral disabilities are subject to different, and usually less severe, forms of discipline at school than nondisabled students. For example, schools might not be allowed to expel students for behavior that is related to their disability, even if the offense were warranted under the school's expulsion policy.

Dilemmas with Homogeneous Grouping

The traditional reason for homogeneous grouping is that once the school identifies educationally relevant differences, teachers can teach groups of students with meaningful similarities, and students will benefit from instruction in these groups. Historically, grouping has met none of these conditions satisfactorily. Typically, the grouping categories are not educationally relevant; the students within the classes are mistakenly assumed to be similar to one another but are actually different in such important ways that most students do not benefit because of the ability grouping. Further, in the twenty-first century, homogeneous grouping will have to meet an even stricter test. The standard of educating students up to their predicted level of achievement is no longer acceptable when the best evidence about learning indicates that these predictions are consistently and needlessly low. Based on this evidence, many are now demanding that schools educate every student to high academic standards, regardless of presumed intellectual ability, disability, social status, gender, or race. Grouping practices must be judged by whether they help teachers meet this new, ambitious goal.

The Social and Political Construction of Categories

Differences among students are certainly real, and, unfortunately, some students have problems so severe that they interfere with learning or social interactions at school. No one could argue that such differences are merely inventions or reified social constructions. That being said, we need look no further than how school policies define student classifications to see that the definitions are more social and political constructions than they are "facts" about students. For example, states and school districts differ so widely in their definitions of "high," "average," and "low" ability that a student identified as belonging in any one of these categories in one place might wind up in a different category someplace else. Our own research found wide disparities in the cutoff scores that high schools use to decide which students should be admitted to honors, regular, and low-level classes.[15] For example, a student in a generally low-achieving school may require a lower score on a standardized test to get into an honors class than a student in a higher-achieving school.

Similarly, criteria for giftedness constantly change, and they vary from place to place. Who is gifted often gets decided in the halls of the state legislatures. Some states and school districts designate 2 percent of their students as gifted. Others choose 5 percent, and others adjust the cutoff scores to make the number of qualifying students match the available funding. In the 1970s California raised its qualifying score from an IQ of 130 to 132—instantly disqualifying thousands of students who would have been gifted the year before.

Joseph Renzulli, a strong advocate for programs to develop students' talents, argues against "gifted" as a label both because it excludes so many students and because it creates a misleading (and sometimes detrimental) identity for those included. Renzulli told an interviewer that the use of the gifted label is something that he rejects outright, and he relayed his frustration with parents who approach him about their "gifted child": "When a parent comes to me and says, 'I have a gifted child,' I say, 'Wait a minute. Tell me what your child does. Talk to me about their writing, their science, their music. If you begin our conversation by telling me you have a gifted child, you are creating a gulf between us.' "[16]

Disparities in special education categories are also documented widely. Some states require an IQ score of 69 or less for a student to be *mentally retarded (MR),* while others classify as MR any student with a score of 84 or below. Consequently, the proportion of students identified as disabled ranges from 7 to 15 percent among states.[17] For example, in 1996, Georgia identified only about 3 percent of its students as learning disabled while Massachusetts identified more than 9 percent; Alabama identified more than ten times as many students as mentally retarded as New Jersey.[18] Connecticut classified students as severely emotionally disturbed (SED) at forty times the rate that Mississippi did.[19]

Many respond to the fact that categories vary and overlap with modernist enthusiasm for more precision in diagnosing students, more precise categories, and additional categories. However, many researchers question whether the categories actually represent anything real. Louise Spear-Swerling and Robert Sternberg argue in their book *Off Track: When Poor Readers Become Learning Disabled* that the construct of learning disabilities probably causes more problems than it solves.[20] They go further and say that if educators want to help low-achieving students, they would do better to abandon the concept altogether. They claim that distinguishing between LD students—whose achievement is lower than their normal or high IQs would predict—and other low achievers is both inaccurate and unhelpful. Not only do they remind us that IQ is a fundamentally flawed concept, but they point to important research showing that most students identified as learning disabled are no more likely than other students to have biological abnormalities. They believe, therefore, that LD students and others would be better served if special education funding guidelines allowed teachers and other learning specialists to address all students' specific cognitive difficulties, such as in reading. Rather than providing helpful information, most labels make students seem abnormal. Other researchers make parallel arguments about the validity and usefulness of behavioral categories like ADHD.[21]

In the *Encyclopedia of Education and Sociology*, Hugh Mehan, Jane Mercer, and Robert Rueda write that the establishment of disability categories represented a shift from the moral and social explanations for why students succeed.[22] From colonial times until about the 1930s, school failure was attributed to depravity, weak moral fiber, or cultural deficits caused by student's backgrounds and by city life. Then educators began using psycho-medical explanations of deviant behavior, such as *minimally brain injured*. While the cultural deficit explanation emerged again in the 1960s to explain the school failure of students of color and justify compensatory education, true disabilities continued to be considered biological problems. Mehan, Mercer, and Rueda also note that newer categories of attention deficit disorder and "at risk" may supplant more established categories of disability or disadvantage.

Christine Sleeter's analysis of the origins and bases of the learning disabled (LD) category illustrates how educators and the public draw on social and political concerns as they construct the differences that drive grouping practices.[23] Sleeter recounts how the LD category achieved national status in 1963, with the founding of the Association for Children with Learning Disabilities. Frustrated parents drew on European research about students with neurological impairments, and they organized to lobby for special LD programs in U.S. schools. These parents did not want their low-achieving children identified as mentally retarded, but they did want their children to have extra help. By 1979 LD had become the largest special education category. Sleeter argues that this surge did not result from a scientific discovery of a previously unknown biological disorder but from advocacy by white, middle-class parents who wanted to differentiate their low-achieving children from lower-class children and children of color. These more privileged families did not want their children's learning problems to be attributed to low IQ, emotional disturbances, or cultural deprivation. And, in fact, the vast majority of students labeled as LD during the first ten years of the classification's existence were white and middle class. Once established, however, the LD category soon included most students of all racial and economic groups whom schools would formerly have identified as mildly retarded or retarded.

Frequently, special education categories are extremely ambiguous and overlapping. For example, a 1990 research summary distributed by the federally funded ERIC Clearinghouse for Information on Disabilities and Gifted Education describes a category of "Learning Disabled/Gifted" defining such a student as "an extremely bright student who is struggling to stay on grade level."[24] The summary emphasizes that educators may not notice some students in this category because "their superior intellectual ability is working overtime to help compensate for an undiagnosed learning disability. In essence, their gift masks the disability and the disability masks the gift."[25] Moreover, the summary also notes that research has found that very disruptive students may fall into this category: "They are frequently off task; they may act out, daydream, or complain of headaches and stomachaches; they are easily frustrated and use their creative abilities to avoid tasks."[26] Other specialists in gifted education identify a category of "underachieving gifted." Another research summary entitled "ADHD and Children Who Are Gifted" notes the considerable overlap between characteristics of gifted students and those with hyperactivity disorders and cautions about the likelihood of mistaking one for the other—even by professional evaluators.[27]

The Illusion of Homogeneity

In my school, reading groups are based on ability. Students cannot progress to another basal reader or transition to English until they pass test after test. This has become a nightmare. Teachers must accommodate large numbers of students who are "not reading at grade level" because they have not been able to pass the tests. I have been able to successfully "test out" four of my third-grade students who were considered to be reading at the second-grade level. I believed them to be at grade level, but the question remains: Were these students labeled as below grade level based on their ability to pass the test, rather than on their actual reading ability?

—Yvette Nunez
First-year teacher, grades 3 and 4

It's not surprising, given the socially constructed nature of the classifications, that we find considerable heterogeneity within classes designed for specific ability, disability, and language levels. Students who meet the criteria for the class actually display noteworthy differences in learning speed, learning style, interest, effort, and aptitude for various tasks. And even this observation oversimplifies the matter—as if learning speed, style, interest, effort, and aptitude were actual, stable, and reliable facts about students instead of approximations based on very narrow socially influenced impressions. To belie further the appearance of sameness, substantial evidence demonstrates that schools disregard the placement criteria they establish for their classes. A simple comparison of the students' test scores with the placement criteria shows the students don't belong.

Placing students in the correct math class was something I assumed was done with very little discrepancy. I found out over the course of the year that many students had been misplaced and were not aware of it. They knew the course name and number, but they did not know the type of content that would be covered. They just assumed that counselors placed them correctly. Misplaced students are plentiful in my "sheltered" class. It was not until late in the year that I asked students individually whether they spoke Spanish fluently, and if so, whether they considered it their primary language. Three students! Only three students in my entire sheltered course considered Spanish their primary language, and only four others spoke it fluently.

—Marilyn Cortez
First-year teacher, mathematics, grade 9

As Marilyn Cortez discovered, many school systems designate classes for students at a particular ability level but then enroll students whose measured ability ranges far above and below the stated criteria.[28]

Beyond the huge problems inherent in the socially constructed and reified nature of students' classifications, other powerful factors make group assignments no more than rough approximations based on guesswork or bias. These factors include the fallibility of tests, the subjectivity of placement criteria and procedures, and parents' and students' own activism. Moreover, resources, scheduling problems, and other organizational constraints often limit schools' placement options and cause them to disregard their stated requirements.

The Fallibility of Testing Schools risk enormous unfairness when they use tests to rank and sort students. The risks are particularly great when diagnosing learning disabilities. The most common guideline for identifying a student's learning disability is if her achievement lags two years behind her grade level. First, schools use achievement tests, school performance, or both to arrive at a student's achievement level. If her IQ scores show that her intelligence is normal, a low achievement score would indicate a learning disability. (If the student has a low achievement and a low IQ, she may not qualify for some special programs. The reasoning is that she is performing at the anticipated level for a student with low IQ and that special attention would not help her.) However, these test results do not prove that a student has or does not have a neurological disability. Neither do they provide information about what the disability might be.

Difficulties also arise with the measures schools use to identify "gifted" students. Although there is vigorous debate about who is gifted and who isn't, technically, the gifted student is one who meets the state's or the school's criteria. Those criteria often include an IQ score and an array of other criteria, such as artistic talent and leadership qualities. In recent years, many states have expanded the criteria even further in the attempt to make sure that students of color get included in gifted programs. The students who qualify comprise a highly diverse group on many dimensions. Complicating matters further is that intelligence tests are less accurate at the upper end of the curve. Since the normal variations in assessments on tests for IQ are especially wide for bright students scoring in the upper ranges, a given student's IQ may vary from day to day, year to year. On a good day, the student might be gifted. If tested on another day, he could fall short.

Other Attributes Influence Placement Educators engaged in creating homogeneous groups offer mixed explanations of the rigidity or flexibility of group placements. On the one hand, they claim to base placements on merit—that a child's school achievement alone, not irrelevant characteristics like race and social class, determines whether he or she is in a high, average, or low class. On the other hand, some acknowledge that students' own choices, character, and motivation influence track placements, and social indicators such as maturity and cooperation can sway decisions.

Each category has its unique opportunities for inconsistent placements and placements that have little to do with the stated criteria. For example, since the process of identifying gifted students often begins with the teacher's recommendation, students who are outgoing and mature are more easily noticed than shy, immature ones. Similarly, schools frequently fail to follow state criteria when identifying students as disabled.[29] Often schools place capable but bothersome, poorly behaved students in low-ability groups. Although this behavioral criterion is rarely stated explicitly in policy guidelines, it results in high-ability groups being shielded from disruptive and disaffected students.

Parent Activism and Choice Another reason for homogeneous groups not really being homogeneous is that parents can interfere with the criteria that the school sets. The distortion of homogeneity that results from this activism is not random, but skewed to the advantage of white and wealthier families.

Most states and schools provide for parent nominations of potentially gifted students as early as kindergarten. As students get older, parents participate in selecting classes and programs for their children. In many schools, however, savvy parents who want their children enrolled in the "best" classes and special programs also place enormous pressure on educators.[30] In a competitive system that only offers a small percentage of student places in the high-track classes, knowledgeable parents have few options but to pit themselves against others to get what they see as the best educational services. The press to give students the advantages of being in gifted classes is particularly acute, especially among middle- and upper-income families. So much so, that a recent article in the *Washington Post* reported that a third of the students in an affluent Maryland County school district are now in gifted classes: "[I]n Howard, parents can bypass all other criteria by insisting their children be allowed into the more challenging classes. School officials sometimes try to talk parents out of doing so, if they think it's inappropriate, but parents usually get their way."[31]

Gifted students form a quite visible and elite group in the school. Many schools encourage gifted students to associate with one another, since much of the advocacy literature argues that they feel most comfortable and thrive in one another's company. Often schools or parent associations distribute rosters with telephone numbers to parents of gifted students, and educational meetings for parents (who are usually among the more active in the schools) further support the socializing of gifted students with one another. Because these students often come from the ranks of social and economic elites, it's no wonder that many parents work hard to have their children included.

Organizational Constraints Schools often compromise grouping criteria in the face of other organizational constraints. Particularly in secondary schools, administrators juggle many factors that may override accurate placements. For example, they must make sure that each student has a class every hour. Those who want football, beginning string class, or second-year computer drafting often get those classes, even if the student winds up in an inappropriate high- or low-level English class. In addition, since each class must have approximately the same number of students, schools may place borderline students, those who enroll late in school, or others in a higher or lower class. As Hugh Mehan, Jane Mercer, and Robert Rueda observed, "If there are 30 slots for LD students in a school, then there will be 30 kids to fill those slots."[32]

Race and Social Class Bias

My teaching assignment is one of the most diverse that I have ever heard of—two sections of United States History (grade 11), two sections of Math 10–12 (grades 10–12), one section of Driver's Education (grades 9–12), one section of Tutorial (grades 9–12), and the head coach of the men's and women's water polo teams (grades 9–12). The math and tutorial classes are the lowest-level classes in the school.

I see inequities that I had not perceived when I attended high school years before but that, on further reflection, I now realize were present. This high school contains two schools of instruction, even though the two schools are not formally distinguishable. First, there is the advanced placement division. This "school" is composed of the "cream of the crop" of the high school's students. Highly motivated, adequately supported and taught, most of the students are white and are expected to go to college. Then there is the "school" that is not expected to go on to higher education. These students are not motivated or engaged at all by school, are not given the best resources or teachers, and are overwhelmingly Latino and African American. This school's dropout rate is significantly higher than the first school's.

I teach almost exclusively in the undermotivated and unsuccessful school. These students have lost faith in themselves, in school, in peers, in families, and, in some instances, life itself. They have to confront their failure every day at this school. Hearing how many students had been accepted to university, how many teams had won championships, how our music program was second to none, and not participating in these activities because of a lack of previous opportunity or deficient grades/units would keep anyone's self-confidence extremely low. They frequently tell me "I can't do this" or "This is too hard for us."

I could not believe this attitude. When I was given a challenge in school I would complain about it, but I would attempt to do it and would usually succeed. These students would not even try. The most frustrating part of this situation was that I was no more intelligent than these students, I just had learned more about how to make school work for me.

—Matthew Amato Flanders
First-year teacher, grades 9–12

As Matthew Flanders discovered at his high school, African American, Latino, and low-income students are consistently overrepresented in low-ability, remedial, and special education classes and programs. Racially isolated schools serving low-income and minority students typically have smaller academic tracks and larger remedial and vocational programs than do schools serving predominantly white, more affluent students. In desegregated schools, like the one where Flanders teaches, African American and Latino students are assigned to low-track classes more often than white (and Asian) students, leading to separate white and minority schools within these schools.

For example, in a 1990 study for the National Science Foundation, we found a pattern of "racially identifiable" math and science classes in racially mixed schools. That is, one would expect to find in any particular math or science class a similar proportion of white, black, or Latino students as in the whole school. Instead, higher-tracked math and science classes had much larger percentages of white students in classes, and lower-ability classes had far larger percentages of black and Latino students.[33] Similarly, a study by the Educational Testing Service found that while 23 percent of the minority middle-school students in big city districts were in low-track math classes, only 8 percent of white students were.[34] In contrast, 56 percent of white students were in high-track classes, compared with only 36 percent of the minorities. A third study of two hundred school districts in the late 1980s found that schools identified white students as "gifted" more than three times as often as black students.[35]

In part, these placement patterns reflect differences in minority and white students' learning opportunities and achievements in earlier grades. Furthermore, American schools follow white, largely middle-class standards in culture and language styles as they judge ability. White, middle-class students' cultural experiences tend to be compatible with the form and content of much of the curriculum, most tests, and many less formal indicators of ability. By contrast, school personnel sometimes mistake the language and dialect differences of Hispanic and black students for poor language skills, conceptual misunderstandings, or bad attitudes.

Some research, while controversial, argues that low-income African American and Hispanic students (particularly those from large families) often learn to be cooperative rather than highly competitive; that they relate more to people than to things, ideas, and words; and that they often pay more attention to the concrete context of ideas and events than to abstractions. Students from some cultural groups are reluctant to speak up or to outshine other students in the classroom.[36] These and other subtle differences may work against students when they take tests, and when teachers judge their abilities. Students from all racial and ethnic groups have difficulty adapting to expectations for behavior that differ from those of their homes and neighborhoods.

More blatant, if not always conscious, discrimination also takes place. Our recent studies of racially mixed school systems showed that African American and Latino students are much less likely than white or Asian students *with the same test scores* to be placed in high-ability classes. For example, in one West Coast school system, white and Asian students with average scores on standardized test scores were more than twice as likely to be in "accelerated" classes than Latino students with *the same scores.* The discrimination was even more striking among the highest-scoring students. Whereas only 56 percent of very high scoring Latinos were in accelerated classes, 93 percent of whites and 97 percent of Asians with *comparable* test scores were. In three other school systems, we found similar discrepancies between African American and white students. [37]

For the past twenty-five years, researchers have warned that schools often classify and treat students *with identical IQ scores,* but with different racial and social class characteristics, very differently.[38] By the late 1970s the misidentification problem triggered both federal and state court decisions requiring that potentially disabled students receive due process. And in a far-reaching decision, the California courts ruled in *Larry P. v. Riles* that schools could no longer use intelligence tests to identify minority students as mentally retarded. However, substantial problems remain and new ones emerge, including recent evidence that African American boys are disproportionately identified as having attention deficits or hyperactivity.[39] The Office of Civil Rights 1990 data showed that black students were two and one half times more likely than white students to be classified as mildly mentally retarded (MMR).[40]

Parent and student activism further erodes the pretense of unbiased homogeneity.[41] High-achieving, affluent, white parents and students are much more knowledgeable about grouping practices. They are more willing to "push the system" if they are displeased with the course assignments, while parents of low-achieving and midrange students (often nonwhite and lower-income) are frequently less comfortable and skilled at challenging the system. When a status preference or other advantage exists, well-informed, high-income parents will use their considerable political capital on behalf of their children. *Their* culture not only allows but also requires that they do all within their power on behalf of their children. So, for example, these parents might pay a private psychologist to retest their child if the child missed a "gifted" cutoff on the school's test. Similarly, well-off parents have sought out private diagnoses of learning disabled for their children when they think that the identification will help children succeed; for example, by requiring extra teacher attention or allowing extra time to take tests. Sometimes a disability designation is sought out so that a struggling student in a high-ability class will be able to remain in that group.

In all cases, however, the process of discovering a student's disability, identifying it, and deciding what to do is a complex and emotionally wrenching experience for any parent. Parents who are poor, not native English speakers, or cautious about public institutions face additional obstacles. They are the least likely to be active advocates in ways that prompt schools to act on their children's behalf. Consequently, their children may not receive the same careful screening (or repeat diagnostic services) as the children of white, middle-class parents.

Ties to Behavioral Learning Theory and Transmission Teaching

Grouping students according to estimates of their abilities makes it even harder for the schools to break away from unproductive curricula, practices, and behavioral theories of learning and teaching. First, homogeneous grouping requires traditional, high-stakes placements. Grouping does more than determine a student's particular class; it charts the entire pathway or trajectory of the student's school outcomes and life chances. Consequently, educators rely heavily on standardized testing (or at least claim that they do) to bring scientific credibility to the process and protect against charges of bias or capriciousness. More flexible cognitive and sociocultural assessments do not provide tidy cutoff scores. When high-stakes decisions rely on traditional tests, they trigger the entire cycle of behavioral approaches to mastering the small units of information and discrete skills that standardized tests require.

A second tie to traditional learning theory emerges when teachers attempt to match curriculum and instruction to the particular group characteristics of the class. Typically, the curriculum is limited by guidelines specifying *how much* about a topic should be learned as well as *what* should be learned (requiring easily distinguished differences for high, medium, and low groups). By associating so closely the definition of a group with *how much* the group is expected to learn, homogeneous groups foster behavioral and "empty vessel" views of intelligence and learning. As this reasoning goes, students in lower groups are not as smart; therefore, they have lower potential; therefore, they should be taught less.

For similar reasons, homogeneous grouping calls forth transmission approaches to teaching. By assuming that a group is already well suited to learn a specified curriculum, teaching may be seen as a simple matter of delivering (transmitting) knowledge to waiting minds. Much of the rationale for homogeneity depends on teaching students as if they were the same in nearly all respects. Consequently, multidimensional lessons and projects that address multiple learning strengths and styles are not a high priority in homogeneous classes. Teachers have little reason to capitalize on the richness of learning interactions and scaffolding that are possible with diverse learners if they assume that all of their students are the same.

Instead of being separated into more able and lower groups, students should benefit from interactions, not just decoding words but comprehending and understanding the deeper meanings of literature. I have attempted to compensate for ability grouping by *creating new heterogeneous reading groups or literature groups. These groups go beyond decoding to use literature to extend meanings.*

—Yvette Nunez
First-year teacher, grades 3 and 4

Homogeneous grouping masks the essential problem of teaching any group of twenty to thirty-five people. Such instruction always requires, and should require, a variety of teaching strategies. Not all students benefit from the same tasks, materials, and procedures, regardless of grouping strategies. Multiple criteria for success and rewards benefit all students. Unfortunately, conventional grouping practices and the illusion of homogeneity deflect attention from these instructional realities. When instruction fails, the problem is too often attributed to the student or perhaps to a wrong placement.

Self-Fulfilling Prophecies and Processes

My students believe they are in classes for stupid people. They say things such as, "We can't do this. We're only '103' [low-ability class] students." Most of them ask if they can move up, and some even say they are in the retarded classes.

It is important for me to not treat these students as if they cannot handle difficult work. The novel *Always Running* is not that easy of a read for ninth-grade students. Many complex topics are dealt with, and most of the teachers at my high school would tell me it is too difficult for these kids. Yet I pushed them along and helped them get by certain spots. I try to treat these students the same as I do my "college-prep" kids.

One thing that has limited my effectiveness in trying to teach with the same expectations of all my students is the culture of the school. Many teachers believe not only that low-track students will not do the work but that they cannot do the work. Any readings I assign for them to do at home I have to photocopy since they are not allowed their own books. There is only a class set because someone has decided that they will not do any homework anyway, and they will probably just lose the books. Because of this, students rarely get any homework. Many of them tell me I am the only teacher that gives homework.

First semester, I taught my English classes in the print shop. My next room turned out not to be a classroom at all. My students had nowhere to sit, and one of the kids said, "Mr. Alvarez, they always give you the cheap classrooms." She sure was right. Finally, with ten weeks to go in the year, I moved into a [third] room. . . . The room has one window that does not open, no air conditioner, and only one door to let in air. It has been close to ninety degrees every day.

The students are being cheated out of a quality education, and they are seeing a school system that is willing to just throw them anywhere. I look at all the classes that have to endure this environment, and I see they all have one thing in common: They are lower-track classes. The four teachers who were in the print shop and now in the windowless bungalows for the most part have "103" students. I teach all lower-track classes except for one class, the other two English teachers have lower-track classes, and the fourth is an ESL teacher. The school decided that the kids who need the most attention, the most help, should get the worst environment in which to learn. There is no way that the school would put honors kids in these rooms. Many people feel that these kids are already lost so we should not waste any time or resources on them. It is for this reason that I have asked to continue teaching the "103" students. They need someone who has not given up on them.

—Michael Alvarez
First-year teacher, English, grade 9

Some educators argue that remedial and special education programs permit teachers to target instruction to the particular learning deficiencies of low-achieving students. But experiences like Michael Alvarez's reveal targeting of a different sort. The differentiation that accompanies homogeneous grouping provides "less able" students with less access to knowledge than other students have, less-engaging learning experiences, and fewer teachers with reputations for being the most experienced and highly skilled, and other school resources.[42] Further, labeling (even if it is masked in local codes such as "103" students) translates into lowered self-confidence and lowered expectations. Placement in a low class often becomes a self-fulfilling prophecy—a cycle of low expectations, fewer opportunities, and poor academic performance. "Poor performance," then, begins the cycle anew, giving additional justification to the schools to lower expectations and reduce opportunities.[43] Extensive research reveals that in every aspect of what makes for a quality education, kids in lower tracks typically get less than those in higher tracks and gifted programs.[44] Some of the well-documented differences are listed in the following table.

Grouping-Related Differences in Learning Opportunities[45]

Higher-Group Advantages	Lower Group-Disadvantages
Curriculum emphasizing concepts, inquiry, and problem solving	Curriculum emphasizing low-level facts and skills
Stress on students developing as autonomous thinkers	Stress on teaching students to follow rules and procedures
More time spent on instruction	More time spent on discipline or socializing
More active and interactive learning activities	More worksheets and seatwork
Computers used as learning tools	Computers used as tutors or electronic worksheets
More qualified and experienced teachers	More uncertified and inexperienced teachers
Extra enrichment activities and resources	Few enrichment opportunities
More engaging and friendly classroom atmosphere	More alienating and hostile classroom atmosphere
"Hard work" a likely classroom norm	"Not working" a likely classroom norm

Alternative settings for LD students may end up being the lowest track in the school. Often, resource teachers working with disabled students are not subject-matter specialists. Their particular expertise, which is to help students make use of their learning strengths, may not translate into the students' being exposed to the full breadth of the subject to which nondisabled peers have access. Often these students have a heavy dose of "study skills" or "adjustment." Often, too, the attempt is to target very specific deficits relying on independent work. As a result, the special help can put further distance between the learning opportunities of regular and special education students. Moreover, regular classroom teachers may falsely assume that all special needs are taken care of elsewhere and make fewer efforts to tailor instruction to the individual learning needs that all students have.

Limited-English-speaking students in separate programs also tend to have fewer opportunities. Although the evidence is clear that they learn better with support in their own language, the shortage of qualified bilingual teachers frustrates this approach.[46] Many students in these programs must learn from teachers who are not fully able to teach either English or academic subject matter using the students' language. Other students work mostly with paraprofessional teachers' assistants. These assistants may be fluent in the language, but typically they won't have either the subject matter or pedagogical knowledge of a fully qualified teacher.

Finally, grouping practices help shape students' identities, status, and expectations for themselves. Both students and adults mistake labels such as "gifted," "honors student," "average," "remedial," "LD," and "MMR" for certification of overall ability and sometimes personal worth. These labels teach students that if the school does not identify them as capable in earlier grades, they should not expect to do well later. Everyone without the "gifted" label has the de facto label of "not gifted." The resource classroom is a low-status place and students who go there are low-status students. The result of all this is that most students have unrealistically low self-concepts, and schools have low expectations. Few students or teachers can defy those identities and expectations.

Of course, these labeling effects are not just a student phenomenon. They permeate the entire school and social culture. Thus, we have frequent references to "gifted parents." Teachers talk about "my low kids." Parents and educators alike confer greater status on teachers of high-achieving students. For example, at public and professional meetings, a teacher may be more likely to identify herself as an AP calculus teacher than as a teacher of basic math or of average algebra students, even though she might teach all three classes. Teachers of low-ability classes may be admired for how "tough" their job is, but it is often assumed that they are not—or don't need to be—as well qualified. Even highly qualified special education and bilingual teachers are not typically thought of as having the background and training needed to work with highly able students.

First-year teacher Lucy Patrick saw the dynamics of homogeneous grouping at work in an unexpected place—her and a colleague's experiment with creating homogeneous groups within their gifted fourth-grade classes.

Though my teaching partner and I were both teaching gifted fourth graders, we saw a wide range of abilities in both our classes. I especially saw a large discrepancy between students in the area of mathematics. Wanting to address individual differences and needs, I was frustrated, not knowing what to do for a group of students who learned a mathematical concept, while another group of students needed additional explanation or practice.

I felt like the class was a three-ring circus, with one group doing a handout, another group working independently, and the last group still not ready to do their class work. Feeling ineffective, my teaching partner and I decided to divide our classrooms based on math test scores. It seemed like a great opportunity to have two separate groups and teach toward their needs.

Before long we saw the discrepancy between the two groups widening, and I began to reconsider the advantages and disadvantages of having homogeneous grouping based on ability. By separating students, we isolated many of the student leaders into one group, while the other group contained disruptive students. I was meeting my objective to provide additional help to the group that needed it most, yet time spent on management took away from their review or practice, and they fell more and more behind.

Another concern was the effects on their emotional and social well-being. Though we never made it known how we divided the students, the students themselves understood the differences. In my mind, all the students are capable. Yet I am not certain what message the students received, especially when the class work and homework were not the same for the two groups. I saw an elitist attitude building within the higher-track group. I would hear students say, "I already know this," "This is easy," or "The other group isn't doing this." This attitude disturbed me because I had tried to create a fair and supportive learning environment in my classroom and I felt that I had failed.

What I had done with my classroom was create a microcosm of the tracking used in our school in my gifted classroom. I had managed to track the students even more!

As an educator, I want all my students to reach their potential with heterogeneous grouping instead of more homogeneous grouping. I do not think that I would attempt homogeneous grouping again.

—Lucy Patrick
First-year teacher, grade 4

Simply by rejecting the "solution" of ever-greater homogeneity, Lucy Patrick did not solve her original concern. She still must grapple with what to do with a roomful of highly individualistic and competitive youngsters whose various skills, styles, and personalities seemed to create academic and social chaos. Her failed experiment redirected her to think about multidimensional lessons and working with the class to improve their skills at helping their classmates work both independently and in groups.

Disappointing Outcomes

Over the years of schooling, students who are initially similar in background and skills become increasingly different in achievement when schools put them into separate, ability-grouped classes. Students placed in lower-level courses—disproportionately Latino and African American students—consistently achieve less than classmates with the same abilities whom the schools put in higher-level classes. This happens consistently; students with both high *and* low test scores do better when they are in higher-level courses.[47] Recent research on detracked classes shows not only that students who would otherwise be placed in lower-level classes achieve far more in mixed classrooms, high-achieving students can learn more in them as well.[48] Clearly, low-ability classes do not promote learning, even if teachers believe they are tailoring instruction to students' ability levels and academic potential.

Achievement gains from compensatory Title I programs are also disappointing, at least partly because most compensatory programs work like low-ability classes. That is, they classify students as low achievers, create a separate pull-out structure, and provide a low-level, remedial curriculum.[49] Bilingual and ESL programs have generated similar criticisms. First-year bilingual teacher Yvette Nunez observes that separate programs restrict students' access to the natural, real opportunities to interact with native speakers of English.[50]

I am struggling to ground my teaching in my philosophy of learning and still meet the expectations of the district. I want to tear down the system of isolating Spanish speakers from their English-proficient counterparts. I believe in developing primary language skills, not only because these skills will transfer to English, but also because becoming biliterate and bicultural helps one understand the world.

We do not have high enough expectations for all our students to learn a second language. Students are able to learn language when it is applied in meaningful contexts, and an optimal environment includes lots of native-speaking peers.

—Yvette Nunez
First-year teacher, grades 3 and 4

Students' hopes for the future rise or fall in ways that are consistent with their placements. Like achievement differences, this self-fulfilling prophecy accumulates until high school, when wide differences among students are most obvious. One reason for this long-term effect is that placements rarely change. Most students placed in low-ability or even average groups in elementary school continue in these tracks in middle school. Senior high schools usually place these students in non-college-prep tracks or "low" college-prep tracks that offer access to less-competitive colleges or majors, to two-year colleges, or to remedial classes as college freshmen. Although many educators sincerely see low-ability classes as providing an opportunity to catch up, being in a low class most often fosters lower achievement, poor self-concepts, lowered aspirations, negative attitudes, and even dropping out.[51]

Certainly, there are exceptions to these patterns. Many teachers know of students who get inspired and catch on despite their labels and classroom placements. Some, by sheer grit, pull themselves out of low-ability classes and succeed in higher classes. However, exceptions occur in spite of group placement, not because of it, and those who do succeed in spite of the odds often carry bitter memories of their struggle.

Homogeneous grouping is not necessarily good for high achievers, either. In fact, students can become destructively competitive among a very small population of the highest-achieving students—particularly in classrooms that stress individual achievement and grades. Those who are not in the very top sometimes feel like failures when they compare themselves with better students. For other exceptionally bright students, the perception of being gifted as a birthright impedes their discovery that effort and persistence matter more than high scores on tests. Moreover, many studies show that highly capable students do as well in mixed classes as in homogeneous groupings, particularly when teachers use the instructional strategies described in Chapter 6.[52]

Controversy Surrounds Homogeneous Grouping

One highly publicized grouping story came out of Selma, Alabama, in 1990 when Rose and Hank Sanders's high-achieving daughter was put in a low-track class. Rose went to school to straighten out the mistake, as most parents would. It took some negotiating, as it often does, but the principal finally agreed to change the girl's placement. Ordinarily, the matter would have ended here. But the Sanders are not an ordinary family. Graduates of the Harvard Law School, they have a practice together in Selma, and Hank serves in the state legislature. Their daughter's class placement seemed suspiciously like a civil rights violation to them, so they investigated further. When they discovered that nearly all of the school's African American students were in the low track, Rose got on the telephone. She advised every black parent to ask for a class reassignment.

African American school superintendent Norward Roussell agreed to make the grouping system fairer, and he instituted new graduation standards that require all students to take Algebra 1, Biology 1, Geography, and Computer Sciences—courses from which many students had previously been excluded. But Roussell lost the support of white residents and was fired when he tried to make a change. A white city councilman told a reporter that members of the white community feared that the new system would harm their children: "The basic position of the white community was that they wanted an honest program for the gifted students—for the best students. When they saw that being eliminated and the curriculum being watered down, theoretically, to a different level, they objected."[53] Before it was over, African American protesters held daily marches, boycotted white-owned businesses, and occupied city hall. Students boycotted and closed down Selma High School. Rose Sanders was arrested, and ninety-one of the students who staged a "peaceful protest" in the cafeteria were reassigned to an alternative school. Since that time Rose and Hank Sanders have mounted a statewide campaign against tracking and educational inequality in Alabama. More recently, Sanders was appointed the first African American woman judge in the state of Alabama.

Efforts to dismantle homogeneous groups usually trigger controversy. Many educators resist detracking because, despite all of the evidence against tracking, they still believe it helps (or it can help) most students. It is also difficult for many educators to imagine how heterogeneous grouping could work, since so many school traditions and other school practices depend on homogeneous groups. Additionally, as in Selma, many parents of high-achieving students—often the most powerful and active parents in the community—oppose any suggestion to change grouping practices because they fear losing advantages the current system provides their children. And, if resistance to ending tracking is not *caused* by racial attitudes, it is indisputable that most resistance has racial consequences.

To Change or to Fix

Those who hesitate to abandon homogeneous grouping are not necessarily partisan advocates for students currently advantaged by it. The modernist response to the well-supported charges that these practices don't work and aren't fair is to improve grouping practices so they achieve educators' intentions.[54] Certainly, this is the route taken by many schools that are constantly changing criteria, adding or eliminating classes, "recruiting" students of color for the high-track and gifted programs, improving the low-track curriculum, and so forth. For example, a school could assign its most qualified English teacher to the low-ability English class and provide that class with the kind of enrichment typically found in gifted programs.

These suggestions have merit, but educators who have tried them report enormous difficulty in making them stick. Many educators have spent their careers trying to beef up the low-track curriculum, to adopt a more positive disposition toward the capacities of low-track students, and to alter the reward systems that work against teaching these students. They find it extraordinarily difficult to cancel out the negative impact of low-track students' quite accurate perceptions that schools have low regard for their ability and prospects for school success. The argument that educators can fix the technology of grouping underestimates the cultural and political pressures to resist these modifications.

Accommodating Diversity without Sorting

How can democratic schools grapple with differences among students without sorting them into groups that invariably include one category that is high status and advantaged and another category that is low status and at least relatively disadvantaged? Can educators accommodate student diversity without classifying and sorting?

Since the late 1980s policymakers and educators have responded to the problems with homogeneous grouping by recommending that schools begin to dismantle it. The most recent critical voices are those of the directors of the Third

International Mathematics and Science Study who conclude that tracking "fails to provide satisfactory achievement for either average or advanced students."[55] They join an impressive list of tracking critics. In 1989 the Carnegie Corporation's prestigious and influential report *Turning Points* identified heterogeneous grouping as a central feature of reforming middle schools.[56] In 1990 the National Governors' Association proposed eliminating ability grouping and tracking as a strategy to help meet the nation's education goals. The College Board, which criticized grouping in middle and senior high school mathematics because it erects barriers to minorities' access to college, aims in its Equity 2000 project to eliminate mathematics tracking in two hundred racially diverse high schools. Most publishers of standardized achievement tests offer cautions about using their tests to group students. The NAACP Legal Defense Fund, the Children's Defense Fund, the ACLU, and the federal Government Accounting Office have all raised ability grouping, gifted programs, and special education as a second-generation segregation issue. And the U.S. Department of Education's Civil Rights Division has targeted tracking as critical in determining whether racially mixed schools are complying with Title VI requirements for receipt of federal allocations.

These policy recommendations reflect growing support for heterogeneous grouping as necessary to ensure that low-status students have access to high-quality curriculum, teachers, and learning experiences. More and more educators and policymakers believe that schools cannot teach or achieve social justice unless they eliminate discriminatory grouping practices. However, this goal will not be accomplished quickly, and policy reports will simply gather dust unless enlightened teachers understand and act to change the norms and political relations these grouping practices embody. This will require teachers to become very competent in ways that are now less familiar to them and to their communities. They must be articulate spokespersons and persuaders to gather support from their colleagues and communities, a topic we return to in Chapter 10. There is a long, hard road ahead.

Implementing Heterogeneous Grouping

Many schools around the country have altered their grouping practices. The most common reforms include reducing or eliminating ability grouping, adopting schoolwide reform instead of targeting groups of students for compensatory education, including gifted and disabled students in regular classes, and developing two-way bilingual programs.

"Detracking"

I have ideological problems with the entire Advanced Placement program. It is discriminatory and elitist and does not accurately assess a student's academic potential. My AP students received a much more comprehensive education than my other students did. I find this very disturbing. Every student should have access to a college preparatory education. By tracking students, we limit their future choices, and that is the true crime. Every student should be allowed to choose whether they pursue a college education, but by denying them college preparatory classes, we rob them of that choice. My experience with the Advanced Placement program has strengthened my resolve to provide such an education to all of my students. My partner and I will be detracking our classes next semester and offering a curriculum based on AP to everyone.

—Kay Goodloe
First-year teacher, high school history

Kay Goodloe and her teaching partner have joined a large group of educators attempting to "detrack" their schools. Most educators' first step toward mixed-ability classes is to do away with low-level groups and classes. Some of these schools require all students to take a set of core heterogeneous courses in addition to some that remain tracked. Many schools open honors programs to all students who wish to take them—or almost all. Some schools adopt specialized programs like AVID (described in Chapter 4) and The College Board's Equity 2000 that provide schools with strategies for including lower-achieving middle and high school students in classes that prepare for four-year universities. Other schools explore ways for students to earn honors credit within heterogeneous classes (e.g., by doing supplemental assignments and activities). Many schools rearrange their schedules so that students having difficulty keeping up academically can get extra help to master the more challenging curriculum. Some offer "backup" classes, tutorial periods, homework centers, and intensive summer programs intended to provide a "double dose" of instruction. Many racially mixed schools develop multicultural curricula to make knowledge more accessible to all students. Many high schools, for example, diversify their elective offerings to include such classes as African American or Mexican American History, African American or Latin American Literature, Ethnic Literature, and Women's Literature. Affiliation with educational groups that have high status among community leaders such as The College Board and local universities is often useful.

Many teachers in detracking schools adopt the classroom strategies described in Chapters 6 and 7. Such strategies help teachers align their teaching with sociocultural perspectives on learning, and they help students to show their ability in previously unrecognized ways. Using such techniques as Socratic Seminars, experiential curriculum (e.g., project-based science and interactive math), reduced reliance on textbooks, and cooperative small-group learning, these teachers promote instructional conversations and scaffolding in their classes. Teachers in detracking schools also develop multidimensional assignments to challenge students of varying abilities. They stress assessments that provide students with useful information that supports their inclinations to work hard. Many include more multicultural content to make knowledge accessible.[57] A critical pedagogy that draws in students' own backgrounds and experiences can confer expertise on all students in the class. With this equality of status as a common starting point, students with different technical skills in reading, writing, mathematics, and so on can view different skill levels as normal and possibly temporary.

Early evidence from a carefully studied project in Philadelphia shows that when detracking is accompanied by such changes in curriculum, instruction, and assessment, both low- and high-achieving students fare very well. The National Center for the Education of Students Placed at Risk has established a set of urban "Talent Development" middle and senior high schools. The Talent Development schools offer a rich, academic curriculum (such as great literature), provide ample opportunities for students to assist one another, and use authentic assessments in heterogeneous classrooms. Middle-school students in the project showed significantly higher achievement gains than did tracked students in the project's "control" schools.[58] To many observers' surprise, the students with the strongest academic skills seemed to benefit most.

Schoolwide Improvement as "Compensatory" Education

Federal legislation governing compensatory education allows some schools to use federal funding to improve regular programs, rather than create separate ones. This eliminates the need to test and classify students as low achievers in order to qualify for the program. With the extra funds, teachers can adopt fundamentally different approaches to the "regular" classroom that make high-quality curriculum, teaching, and learning available to poor students.

Inclusion of Disabled and Gifted Students

Since the early 1990s a movement called "inclusion" has advocated placing students with disabilities in regular schools and classrooms, integrating the special supports these students need into regular education. Such supports (e.g., another teacher or an aide) are available to all students, not just those identified as disabled. Similarly, many, including advocates for the gifted, have argued that gifted students can be well served in regular classrooms and that the activities shown to be effective for gifted students can be extended to other students in the class.[59] These purposefully heterogeneous classrooms, advocates argue, would not ignore individual differences and needs but would acknowledge and respond to them in shared, more community-like contexts, such as those we described in Chapter 7. Janet Kim's middle-school students and Julie Yu's fourth graders developed such communities.

He didn't speak a word at the beginning of the year. With the support of the special education teacher and a comfortable, caring classroom, he was able to stand up in front of the class during Author's Chair time. He took about ten minutes reading a five-sentence paragraph. He did it on his own with nobody forcing him. He allowed himself to be vulnerable with a class that had a reputation for put-downs and nonstop torment.

He read that paragraph with every pair of eyes fixed on his face—everyone wanting and hoping that he would finish reading successfully no matter how long it took. That was one of the most memorable and amazing moments. We were all so proud.

—Janet Kim
First-year teacher, English, middle school

Aphasia is a language processing disorder. For Michael, it means that he has difficulty processing what he hears and then finding the proper response. I was apprehensive about having Michael in my class. I didn't know how to teach a student with special needs. Still, I tried to be optimistic and hopeful.

I tried to create a safe environment by inviting our special education teacher to the class to talk to students about Michael and aphasia. This helped the students understand why Michael behaved the way that he did. It empowered students by giving them ways to help Michael. We discussed the fact that Michael gets angry and happy and feels sad and lonely, just like we do. Students began to go out of their way to encourage Michael. Some even gave him more "outs" because they knew that he took adaptive PE and had difficulty playing sports. These days, when I give instructions or make announcements, and Michael does not hear or understand, a student who sits near him quietly whispers what I said, "Michael, Miss Yu said that we won't have PE today because we have an assembly in the auditorium. Don't worry, we'll have PE tomorrow." There is always someone willing to help Michael. He has made some great friends this year. I saw his friend Jason patting him on the back, walking toward the line after recess saying, "It's all right Michael. We'll win next time. You did good."

Michael does not need RSP [Resource Specialist Program] anymore. He will pass fourth grade. He has brought out the best in all of us. He has brought out the best in me.

—Julie Yu
First-year teacher, grade 4

Julie Yu and Janet Kim experienced what other teachers and researchers have found. An inclusive classroom can be better for all students, not just disabled or gifted ones, because it helps students become "knowledgeable about differences, supportive of others, and active in changing structures that are oppressive to various groups."[60]

Bilingual Education without Bilingual Tracking

As described earlier, all responsible teachers of students who are not fluent in English advocate giving students substantial support for learning in their primary language until they can be successful in English. Of course, many immigrants have learned with "immersion" or "sink-or-swim" methods, but research demonstrates that this is not a good way for most students to learn either English or other school subjects. Beyond providing primary language instruction in the early stages of English fluency, bilingual specialists support a variety of approaches according to their particular philosophy and the resources that are available at the school. The most important resources may be skilled bilingual teachers who are fluent in the student's language and lots of English-speaking peers.

One method of providing students the primary language support they need without segregating them from English speakers is *two-way bilingual* education. This approach brings native English speakers together with students whose primary language is not English. First-year teacher Steven Branch used a two-way bilingual approach in his classroom, although it wasn't the official policy of the school. He relied on language acquisition theory and sociocultural learning theory to support his practice. Steve's own efforts to become fully bilingual made him a learner as well as a teacher in his classroom.

As of today, I have no idea what the district's bilingual program is. From where I sit, it looks like the students enter kindergarten and all instruction is in Spanish. They go through first, second, and third grade with their academic instruction in Spanish. Then, all of a sudden, in the fourth grade all instruction is in English. It's either sink or swim. Mainly sink!

Bilingualism in the classroom is truly a benefit and should not be suppressed. Code-switching is natural for people learning a second language or who are already bilingual. An example of code-switching is "Yo quiero to go to the store." Students know where and when to switch languages. This knowledge serves as a base upon which students' understanding of languages can be developed. When children (novices) code-switch with other children or teachers (experts), the knowledge of the experts transfers to the novices. This happens until the novice becomes an expert. This phenomenon happens not only in learning situations but at play and work as well.

—Steven Branch
First-year teacher, grade 5

Formalized two-way bilingual programs aim to develop bilingual proficiency in all of the students, as well as promote academic achievement and cross-cultural knowledge and regard. Available evidence suggests that these programs are quite successful. A study of 160 schools with two-way programs (most of them Spanish and English) found these programs to be effective with both English-speaking students and those who are speakers of other languages.[61]

Technical Skills, Norms and Beliefs, Politics and Power

Few teachers entering the teaching profession today have had personal experience in heterogeneous classrooms, and few teaching mentors have "answers" for how to make such classrooms work. But some teachers are powerfully equipped to study the challenges and not settle for replicating the familiar. Teachers like Frank Divinagracia, quoted next, will figure out the technical arrangements for a heterogeneous, socially just classroom because they are well grounded in theory, committed to everyone learning, and willing to struggle throughout their career without always getting it perfect. That is why Divinagracia finds his profession so exciting.

The Environmental Careers Academy expects innovative and reform-minded teaching. This, in itself, pushes me to be more hands-off and more creative. Also, the socioethnic background of my students provides for some dynamic group mixes. In a nontracked class with 25 percent African American, 45 percent Latino/a, and 30 percent Asian, I have the chance to create a challenging learning experience for all of us. In choosing the *Discovering Geometry* book, I had a geometry curriculum that would be centered around investigations and students' conjectures. I wanted to challenge my students to think on their own and in groups. Also, I wanted to give the students more control over the curriculum.

The geometry lessons allowed students to speak and listen to one another and create their own knowledge. As a facilitator, I want them to think for themselves, defend their ideas, and be confident enough to stick to their beliefs. The beauty of it is they have to make their own conclusions and use them for further study. They have to design what they learn in order to apply it. I could see deliberateness in my students' actions, a true yearning to understand. The atmosphere was free and relaxed. They still struggled to learn, but they did so without fear of being wrong.

One young man had a hard time conceiving how to make two angles exactly the same. I began asking questions about the steps he took. Eventually a young woman in the group explained how she was able to [solve the problem]. The young man started to understand. I believe he trusted her observations, and her explanations were probably better than mine.

Because these students are getting a good dose of group work in all their classes, they are used to being challenged and engaged in both their individual projects and their group work. They have been extremely creative and have designed projects such as researching and painting murals, starting a garden, producing a recycling project on campus, and more. The students are thinking critically about their environment and [acting on] its problems.

—Frank Divinagracia
First-year teacher, high school mathematics

Nearly all advocates of ability grouping, in particular those who favor "gifted"/high-track classes, would prefer classes (and teachers!) such as Frank Divinagracia's. For example, Sandra Berger of the Council for Exceptional Children summarized research on curriculum and instruction for gifted students for the federally funded ERIC Clearinghouse on Disabilities and Gifted Education. She concludes that gifted learners are served best by the very same types of educational experiences that make all students successful in heterogeneous classes. Berger advocates "thematic, broad-based, and integrative content" since "concept-based instruction expands opportunities to generalize and to integrate and apply ideas." She points to the need for gifted learners to be challenged by "open-ended questions that stimulate inquiry, active exploration, and discovery." She argues that they learn best in a "receptive, nonjudgmental, student-centered environment that encourages inquiry and independence, includes a wide variety of material, provides some physical movement, is generally complex, and connects the school experience with the greater world." She also emphasizes that teachers must provide multiple ways for gifted students to demonstrate what they have learned: "For example, instead of giving a written or oral book report, students might prefer to design a game around the theme and characters of a book."[62]

Those who advocate heterogeneity conclude that commonly touted benefits to separate gifted classes are attributable to these and similar classroom and instruction characteristics, and they point to the substantial evidence, cited previously, that the benefits occur more frequently in the high classes. Similarly, the most common criticisms of mixed-ability classes—that the classes hold back or are boring for high achievers—can be attributed to the *lack* of these characteristics, not to the particular mix of students.

Confronting Norms and Values

Educators attempting heterogeneous grouping must come to terms with any number of inveterate American values for competition and individualism that bolster and legitimize traditional grouping. These norms imply that "good" education channels the most meritorious students toward even better education and then higher income, power, and status. If heterogeneous grouping is to work well, schools and classrooms must move toward more democratic norms of cooperation, support, and community.

Conventional conceptions of knowledge, language, and culture harbor deep-seated attitudes about race and social class. Extensive procedural and ideological "filters" such as curriculum guides, textbooks, legislative oversight, and typical teacher training, to mention a few, keep the curriculum consistent with mainstream Eurocentric, male, and white versions of valued knowledge. These filters can prevent alternative or competing versions of knowledge from reaching students. Educators trying to create heterogeneous grouping need to rethink how curriculum can include all students.

Researchers Luanna Meyer, Beth Harry, and Mara Sapon-Shevin at Syracuse University argue that inclusive classrooms require norms promoting helping and positive interaction. These norms include the safety to show oneself as an individual and to know one another.[63] If the social context is critical for learning, as sociocultural theory demonstrates, then teachers need to make students' personal and social lives important in their classroom interactions. If students worry about being humiliated if their differences and disabilities are known to others, they won't take the intellectual and social risks that learning requires.

Sociocultural learning theory and social justice values are a starting point for heterogeneity.[64] Changing these fundamental norms requires a careful, daily reflection of the beliefs and values that lie beneath them.

Attention to the Political

The discussion throughout this chapter makes clear that grouping is highly political. Homogeneous grouping and its consequences have meaning and exchange value beyond school. After all, schools and groups are accompanied by public labels, and status differences, and they signal which students should gain access to the university and the status and life chances that higher education can bring. Thus, ability grouping and tracking become part of the struggles for comparative advantage in the distribution of school resources, opportunities, and credentials that have exchange value in the larger society. Efforts to move away from homogeneous grouping nearly always engender resistance from those whose children are advantaged by it.

Educators also worry about the political consequences of abandoning homogeneous grouping: In particular they worry about losing the support of parents of high-track students. In local forums such as school board meetings and in popular practitioner journals, advocates for categorically funded gifted programs lobby strongly against policy changes that may threaten special opportunities now available to high achievers. In many communities, as the story of the Sanders family in Selma, Alabama, illustrates vividly, this political dimension encompasses highly charged issues of race and social class stratification.

The challenge is daunting. Successful heterogeneous grouping will inevitably require that those who may now see themselves as competing—such as advocates for the gifted, for disabled students, for the disadvantaged, and for students of color—make common cause around serving all students well. Building coalitions among these divergent constituencies (and maintaining political credibility) will require that educators guarantee that their new practices will provide all students with opportunities that are at least as rich and rigorous as those they previously enjoyed. No parent would sensibly agree to less. But some parents will also object to changes that take away the *comparative* advantages their privileged children enjoyed with homogeneous grouping—no matter how good the new approach might be. Confronting these issues is a political process that requires astute political leadership by educators.

The Struggle for Heterogeneous Grouping

At our school, the "magnet-gifted" and "resident" classrooms are physically set apart from each other. I have heard my magnet students argue on the playground with resident students. The resident students had been calling the magnet students "nerds" and "dorks," while the magnet students counter by saying that they are "smarter" and that the resident students were "stupid." There is the attitude in my classroom—that they are smarter and better because they "got in" to the gifted program. Others go so far as to say that there are students in our classroom who do not belong in the magnet.

Some staff "joke" about the magnet teachers, "Oh, the magnets are having a meeting" or "We're not good enough to be magnet teachers." Some tension between the two schools centers around resources. As a magnet school, there are more funds available for extra materials or needed equipment.

A main concern for the magnet program is how they can differentiate the gifted program from the regular one. The magnet has special out-of-town field trips and experts who come in and teach (art, music, PE, science, opera). Teachers within the magnet program make it a point to be different from the resident school, regardless of what is best for students. For example, when we were deciding which publishing company to choose for our new language arts program, teachers suggested that we choose a series that is different from the resident school in order to explain to parents how the program is different.

Only after intense and honest dialogue about what is best for all students will this two-school system change. Next year, I would like to bridge the two schools by having students interact more on a social level. Perhaps I can combine magnet students with resident school students in classes. As long as the school is based on merit and "ability," those in power will push for the status quo. It will take the combined efforts of students, teachers, administrators, parents, and community members to come together and engage in thoughtful reflection.

—Lucy Patrick
First-year teacher, grade 4

This chapter has explored how sorting students into categories based on students' presumed abilities requires a school culture that is behavioral and individualistic in its orientation. And in schools where grouping practices position white and privileged students as those with the most merit, Eurocentric versions of valued knowledge dominate. These orientations limit all students' learning, *regardless* of how extensive and well intentioned are the services provided to any particular "special" categories, such as "regular," "gifted," and so forth.

Our educational system has witnessed few events or trends that have required the changes in thinking and attitudes as much as changes in grouping practices will require. Changes of similar magnitude might be the social shifts the country has witnessed in the slow breaking down of legal racial segregation, or gender discrimination, or norms regarding cigarette smoking. For a very long time, knowledge alone about the damage the practices cause was not enough to budge the practices, and now that they have budged, everyone recognizes what a long way we still have to go. But slowly, coalitions of people who see the harm in these practices are finding some success in challenging the status quo. Those who have professional knowledge and those with credible moral standing in the community are joining in. Ultimately, those who benefit from these practices will not be able to marshal political power to hold the practices in place. The status quo does change—by slow, painful degrees, to be sure, but it changes.

Digging Deeper

The scholars, educators, and projects listed in this section conduct research and develop practices to help schools move away from conventional classification and grouping practices.

Vanderbilt University education professor **Alfredo Artiles** writes about the social construction of special education and the overrepresentation of students of color in special education classifications. Of particular interest is *The Knowledge Base on Culturally Diverse Students with Learning Disabilities: The Need to Enrich Learning Disabilities Research with a Sociocultural Perspective,* the special issue of *Learning Disabilities Research & Practice* (May 1997) that Professor Artiles edited concerning these issues.

James Cummins, a professor in the Modern Language Centre at the Ontario Institute on Educational Studies and the University of Toronto, writes about bilingual education and empowering language-minority students. His research focuses primarily on the challenges educators face in adjusting to classrooms where cultural and linguistic diversity is the norm. Dr. Cummins has published several books related to language learning and cultural diversity. His most recent book, *Negotiating Identities: Education for Empowerment in a Diverse Society,* is available from the California Association for Bilingual Education.

Equity 2000 is The College Board's mathematics detracking project. As of 1996, more than 500,000 students at 700 public schools are participating in Fort Worth, Texas; Milwaukee, Wisconsin; Nashville, Tennessee; Prince George's County, Maryland; Providence, Rhode Island; and San Jose, California. Twelve new sites were to be added to the project by 2001. Because of the project, students who might not otherwise be placed on the college track have enrolled in rigorous math courses. **Vinetta Jones** is the director of this New York-based project of The College Board.

Serge Madhere, professor at Howard University, and **Douglas MacIver,** research scientist at the Center for the Social Organization of Schools, direct the Talent Development Middle School project. The project combines a carefully constructed intervention based on a solid understanding of the literature with a controlled, rigorous data collection and analysis strategy. This work documents the outcomes of detracking in the context of the curricular and instructional changes that such a reform requires. It provides a refreshing and optimistic look at what's possible when students in central city schools are provided access to a demanding curriculum within a school where the social organization permits rich learning interactions between teachers and students and among peers.

Hugh Mehan, professor of sociology at the University of California-San Diego, studies the processes by which constructed categories affect students' schooling experiences. With Alma Hertweck and J. Lee Meihls, Mehan is the author of *Handicapping the Handicapped: Decision-Making in Students' Educational Careers* (Stanford: Stanford University Press, 1986). His most recent book, *Constructing School Success* (with Irene Villanueva, Lea Hubbard, and Angela Lintz), was published by Cambridge University Press in April 1996. It discusses the educational and social consequences of a successful educational innovation, AVID, that "untracks" low-achieving students.

The **National Center for Research on Cultural Diversity and Second Language Learning** at the University of California-Santa Cruz maintains an online series of papers on bilingual education through The National Clearinghouse for Bilingual Education (NCBE). The Clearinghouse can be reached on the World Wide Web at http://www.ncbe.gwu.edu.

Jeannie Oakes, a professor of education in the Graduate School of Education and Information Studies at the University of California-Los Angeles, studies inequalities in the allocation of resources and learning opportunities in schools, and equity-minded reform. Her book *Keeping Track: How Schools Structure Inequality* (New Haven, CT: Yale University Press, 1985) describes how tracking and grouping students by ability in school affect the classroom experiences of low-income students and students of color, most of whom are identified as having "low" academic ability or as "slow" learners. *Multiplying Inequalities* (Santa Monica, CA: RAND, 1990) reports the distribution of resources, curriculum, teachers, and classroom learning opportunities in mathematics and science across schools and classrooms enrolling different groups of students. With colleagues, including Professor **Amy Stuart Wells** and **Martin Lipton,** Oakes has also written about ongoing UCLA studies of middle and senior high schools engaged in detracking reforms. Her newest book, written with Karen Hunter Quartz, Steve Ryan, and Martin Lipton, *Becoming Good American Schools: The Struggle for Virtue in School Reform* (San Francisco: Jossey-Bass, 1999), relates the experiences of middle schools engaged in these reforms.

Professor **Joseph Renzulli** is the director of the National Center on the Gifted and Talented at the University of Connecticut. He has written about developing all students' talent and proposes the "schoolwide enrichment model" as a substitute for narrow and specialized programs for gifted students. He details these ideas in his book *Schools for Talent Development: A Practical Plan for Total School Improvement* (Mansfield, CT: Creative Learning Press, 1994).

Professor **Mara Sapon-Shevin** at the State University of New York at Syracuse studies and writes about disabilities and gifted education. A proponent of inclusive education, she has investigated classroom strategies to promote learning in mixed-ability classes. Her work highlights the importance of promoting sharing, understanding, and cooperation among children, both in and out of the school environment. Her book *Playing Favorites: Gifted Education and the Disruption of Community* (Albany, NY: SUNY Press, 1994) examines the ways in which gifted programs can inhibit inclusiveness in classrooms, deskill teachers, and limit their willingness to meet individual needs. Sapon-Shevin contends that many of the strategies of gifted education, that is, curriculum compacting, independent study, mentorships, and thematic instruction, should be part of a regular education program that includes students at both ends of the continuum.

Tom Skrtic is a professor in the University of Kansas Department of Special Education. Skrtic's work focuses on the changes taking place in education and special education and how these changes connect to the challenges of postmodernism. He is editor of *Disability and Democracy: Reconstructing (Special) Education for Postmodernity* (New York: Teachers College Press, 1995).

Robert Slavin, director of the National Center for Research on the Education of Students Placed at Risk, has conducted research and written extensively on ability grouping, tracking, pull-out compensatory programs, and alternatives to these conventional practices. His reviews of the effects of ability grouping on student achievement are the most respected and widely cited in the field. In his book entitled *Every Child, Every School: Success for All* (Thousand Oaks, CA: Corwin Press, 1997), Slavin and his colleagues Nancy A. Madden, Lawrence J. Dolan, and Barbara A. Wasik detail their integrated program for increasing the learning of all students. Built on the premise that all students can and will learn, Slavin's program is designed to provide every student with opportunity, appropriate materials, and instruction to ensure learning.

Education policy writer **Anne Wheelock**'s book *Crossing the Tracks: How "Untracking" Can Save America's Schools* (New York: The New Press, 1992; distributed by W.W. Norton, New York, 1992) describes the knowledge, tools, and philosophies that have been generated by schools that are attempting to develop a "culture of detracking" that works against the traditional tendency to separate students into homogeneous groups. Wheelock and Leon Lynn edited a special issue of the *Harvard Education Letter* (13, no. 1, January/February 1997) on detracking. Wheelock also writes about issues related to special education identification in urban schools.

Notes

1. Eviatar Zerubavel, *The Fine Line: Making Distinctions in Everyday Life* (Chicago: University of Chicago Press, 1993), pp. 1–2.
2. Kenneth Sirotnik, "Equal Access to Quality in Public Schooling: Issues in the Assessment of Equity and Excellence," in *Access to Knowledge: The Continuing Agenda for Our Nation's Schools* (Rev. ed.), ed. John I. Goodlad and Pamela Keating (New York: The College Board, 1994), pp. 159–185.
3. For example, one desegregating school district identified 70 percent of the white students from the most affluent neighborhoods as "gifted." Kevin Welner, *Mandating Equity: Rethinking the Educational Change Literature as Applied to Equity-Minded Reforms* (Ph.D. diss, Los Angeles, UCLA, 1997).
4. Ability grouping and "tracking" are often used interchangeably to describe both ability-grouped classes and differentiated programs of study in which schools place students of different abilities. Some make a distinction by suggesting that "tracking" only applies to permanent assignments to a pathway leading to college or work. In practice, assignment to various

ability levels is quite permanent and often extends to all of a student's academic subjects, K–12.

5. Elwood Cubberly, *Changing Conceptions of Education* (Boston: Houghton Mifflin, 1909), pp. 18–19.
6. Boston School Documents, no. 7, 1908, p. 53, as cited in Marvin Lazerson, *The Origins of the Urban School* (Cambridge, MA: Harvard University Press, 1971), p. 189. Consistent with the American Dream, of course, opportunity also included the possibility that those with extraordinary talents or character could exceed, modestly, social exceptions and could become outstanding examples of their race or class.
7. For a fascinating, detailed history of the links between the growth of universal, compulsory education and special education, see John G. Richardson, "Common Delinquent, and Special: On the Formalization of Common Schooling in the American States," *American Educational Research Journal* 31, no. 4 (1994), pp. 695–723.
8. Although the labels don't always convey it, everyone at a school knows the "ability level" of various groups.
9. Adam Gamoran, "A Multi-level Analysis of the Effects of Tracking" (paper presented at the annual meetings of the American Sociological Association, Atlanta, GA, 1988).
10. Michael Garet and Brian DeLany, "Students, Courses, and Stratification," *Sociology of Education* 61 (1988), pp. 61–77; Brian DeLany, "Allocation, Choice, and Stratification Within High Schools: How the Sorting Machine Copes," *American Journal of Education* 99, no. 3 (1991), pp. 191–207.
11. Joseph Renzulli and Sally Reis, "The Reform Movement and the Quiet Crisis in Gifted Education." *Gifted Child Quarterly* 35 (1991), pp. 26–35.
12. Lorraine M. McDonnell, Margaret J. McLaughlin, and Patricia Morrison, eds., *Educating One and All: Students with Disabilities and Standards-Based Reform* (Washington, DC: National Academy Press, 1997).
13. Hugh Mehan, Jane Mercer, and Robert Rueda, "Special Education," in *Encyclopedia of Education and Sociology* (New York: Garland, 1997).
14. Larry S. Goldman, Myron Genel, Rebecca J. Bezman, and Priscilla J. Slanetz, "Diagnosis and Treatment of Attention-Deficit/Hyperactivity Disorder in Children and Adolescents," *Journal of the American Medical Association* 279, no. 14 (April 8, 1998), pp. 1100–1107.
15. Jeannie Oakes and Gretchen Guiton, "Matchmaking: The Dynamics of High School Tracking Decisions," *American Educational Research Journal* 32, no. 1 (1995), pp. 3–33.
16. Joseph Renzulli, in an interview with Anne Turnbaugh Lockwood, "Beyond the Golden Chromosome," in *Focus in Change,* a publication of the National Center for Effective Schools at the University of Wisconsin, Madison (no. 11, Fall 1993), p. 3.
17. McDonnell, McLaughlin, and Morrison, eds., *Educating One and All.*
18. Mehan, Mercer, and Rueda, "Special Education."
19. Donald L. MacMillan and Daniel Reschly, "Overrepresentation of Minority Students: The Case for Greater Specificity or Reconsideration of the Variables Examined," *Journal of Special Education* 32 (1998), pp. 15–24.

20. Louise Spear-Swerling and Robert J. Sternberg, *Off Track: When Poor Readers Become Learning Disabled* (Boulder, CO: Westview Press, 1996).
21. See, for example, the special issue of *Phi Delta Kappan* (February 1996), and Thomas Armstrong, *The Myth of the ADD Child* (New York: Dutton, 1985).
22. Mehan, Mercer, and Rueda, "Special Education."
23. Christine Sleeter, "Learning Disabilities: The Social Construction of a Special Education Category," *Exceptional Children* 53, no. 1 (1986), pp. 46–54. Also, "Why Is There Learning Disabilities? A Critical Analysis of the Birth of the Field in its Social Context," in *The Formation of the School Subject Matter: The Struggle for an American Institution*, ed. T. S. Popkewitz (New York: Falmer Press, 1987).
24. Susan Baum, "Gifted But Learning Disabled: A Puzzling Paradox," *ERIC Digest #E479* (Reston, VA: Council for Exceptional Children, ERIC Clearinghouse on Disabilities and Gifted Education, 1990.)
25. Ibid.
26. Ibid.
27. James T. Webb and Diane Latimer, "ADHD and Children Who Are Gifted," *ERIC Digest #E522* (Reston, VA: Council for Exceptional Children, ERIC Clearinghouse on Disabilities and Gifted Education, 1993.)
28. Mehan, Mercer, and Rueda, "Special Education."
29. MacMillan and Reschly, "Overrepresentation of Minority Students."
30. For example, researcher Elizabeth Useem found that middle-school students' placement in math classes was "not necessarily based on some objective, highly accurate assessment of students' 'ability' by school professionals" but rather on parents' willingness to take steps to ensure that their children were enrolled in upper-level classes even when school personnel recommended against it or their children resisted it. Elizabeth Useem, "Student Selection into Course Sequences in Mathematics: The Impact of Parental Involvement and School Policies," *Journal of Research on Adolescence* 1, no. 3 (1991), pp. 231–250; also see Susan Yonezawa and Jeannie Oakes, "Making All Parents Partners in the Placement Process," *Education Leadership*, in press.
31. "A New Mix of Gifted Students," *The Washington Post*, 27 July 1997.
32. Mehan, Mercer, and Rueda, "Special Education."
33. Jeannie Oakes, *Multiplying Inequalities* (Santa Monica, CA: RAND, 1990).
34. Anamaria M. Villegas and Susan. M. Watts, "Life in the Classroom: The Influence of Class Placement and Student Race/Ethnicity" (paper presented at the annual meeting of the American Educational Research Association, Chicago, IL, April 1991).
35. Kenneth J. Meier, Stewart Joseph Jr., Robert E. England, *Race, Class and Education: The Politics of Second Generation Discrimination* (Madison, WI: University of Wisconsin Press, 1989).
36. Brenda A. Allen and A. Wade Boykin, "African-American Children and the Educational Process: Alleviating Cultural Discontinuity through Prescriptive Pedagogy," *School Psychology Review* 21, no. 4 (1992), pp. 586–596.
37. Oakes, *Multiplying Inequalities*, 1990.

38. Mehan, Mercer, and Rueda, "Special Education."
39. Luanna H. Meyer, Beth Harry, and Mara Sapon-Shevin, "School Inclusion and Multicultural Education," in *Multicultural Education: Issues and Perspectives,* ed. James A. Banks and Cherry A. McGee Banks (Boston: Allyn & Bacon, 1996).
40. MacMillan and Reschly, "Overrepresentation of Minority Students."
41. Oakes and Guiton, "Matchmaking: The Dynamics of High School Tracking Decisions"; Susan Yonezawa, *Making Decisions About Students' Lives* (Ph.D. diss., Los Angles, UCLA, 1997); Annette Lareau, *Home Advantage: Social Class and Parental Intervention in Elementary Education* (London: Falmer, 1989).
42. Jeannie Oakes, *Keeping Track: How Schools Structure Inequality* (New Haven, CT: Yale University Press, 1985); Oakes, *Multiplying Inequalities.*
43. Oakes, *Multiplying Inequalities.*
44. This is not to say that *particular* classes for lower-ability students are not given wonderful facilities, a solid curriculum, and well-qualified teachers, but such situations are clear exceptions to the rule.
45. Oakes, *Keeping Track;* Oakes, *Multiplying Inequalities.*
46. Jay P. Greene, "A Meta-Analysis of the Effectiveness of Bilingual Education" (Claremont, CA: The Tomas Rivera Policy Institute, 1998).
47. Jeannie Oakes, "Two Cities: Tracking and Within-School Segregation," in *Brown Plus Forty: The Promise,* ed. La Mar Miller (New York: Teachers College Press, 1995.); Jeannie Oakes, *Report to the Court, New Castle County,* unpublished report submitted to the court, 1995; Kevin Welner, Jeannie Oakes, and Gilbert FitzGerald, *Report to the Woodland Hills School District* (Los Angeles: UCLA Graduate School of Education and Information Studies, 1998).
48. Douglas MacIver, Steven B. Plank, and Robert Balfanz, "Working Together to Become Proficient Readers: Early Impact of the Talent Development Middle School's *Student Team Literature Program,*" Report of the Center for Research on the Education of Students Placed at Risk (Baltimore: The Johns Hopkins University, 1998).
49. David J. Hoff, "Chapter 1 Aid Failed to Close Learning Gap," *Education Week,* 2 April 1997, pp. 1, 29; Robert E. Slavin, "How Title I Can (Still) Save America's Children," *Education Week,* 21 May 1997, p. 52; Thomas Kelly, "The 4 Percent 'Structural Flaw,' " *Education Week,* 11 June 1997, p. 44.
50. Jim Cummins, "From Multicultural to Anti-Racist Education: An Analysis of Programmes and Policies in Ontario," in *Minority Education: From Shame to Struggle,* ed. Tove Skutnabb-Kangas and Jim Cummins (Philadelphia: Multilingual Matters Ltd., 1988).
51. Jeannie Oakes, Adam Gamoran, and Reba Page, "Curriculum Differentiation," in *Handbook of Research on Curriculum,* ed. Phillip Jackson (New York: Macmillan, 1992).
52. There is considerable disagreement in the academic community about whether or not high-achieving students benefit academically from high-track placement. Most, however, agree that what benefits might accrue

come about because of the enriched opportunities in these classes, not because the students are separated per se. See for example, the series of articles in the November 1995 issue of *Phi Delta Kappan.*

53. William Snider, "Schools Are Reopened in Selma Amid Continuing Racial Tension," *Education Week,* 21 February 1990.
54. For example, researcher Maureen Hallinan argues that "a more tempered response" is for schools to make grouping practices more consistent with the theories behind those practices, and to balance the inherently negative features of grouping with countervailing policies and practices. See Maureen Hallinan, "Tracking: From Theory to Practice. Exchange," *Sociology of Education* 67, no. 2 (1994), pp. 79–84. See also, Adam Gamoran, "Alternative Uses of Ability Grouping in Secondary Schools: Can We Bring High-Quality Instruction to Low-Ability Classrooms?" *American Journal of Education* 102, no. 1 (1993), pp. 1–22.
55. William Schmidt, "Are There Surprises in the TIMSS Twelfth Grade Results?" *TIMSS United States,* Report No. 8 (East Lansing, MI: TIMSS U.S. National Research Center, Michigan State University, April 1998), p. 4.
56. Carnegie Council on Adolescent Development, *Turning Points: Preparing Youth for the 21st Century* (New York: Carnegie Corporation of New York, 1989).
57. Jeannie Oakes, Amy Stuart Wells, Susan Yonezawa, and Karen Ray, "Equity Lessons from Detracking Schools," in *Rethinking Educational Change with Heart and Mind,* ed. Andy Hargreaves (Arlington, VA: Association for Supervision and Curriculum Development, 1977).
58. Douglas MacIver, Steven B. Plank, and Robert Balfanz, "Working Together to Become Proficient Readers: Early Impact of the Talent Development Middle School's *Student Team Literature Program,*" Report of the Center for Research on the Education of Students Placed at Risk (Baltimore: The Johns Hopkins University Press, 1998).
59. Joseph S. Renzulli and Sally Reis, *The Schoolwide Enrichment Model: A Comprehensive Plan for Educational Excellence* (Mansfield Center, CT: Creative Learning Press, 1985).
60. Luanna H. Meyer, Beth Harry, and Mara Sapon-Shevin, "School Inclusion and Multicultural Education," in *Multicultural Education: Issues and Perspectives,* ed. James A. Banks and Cherry A. McGee Banks (Boston: Allyn & Bacon, 1996), p. 343.
61. Donna Christian, *Two-Way Bilingual Education: Students Learning through Two Languages* (Santa Cruz, CA: National Center for Research on Cultural Diversity and Second Language Learning, 1994).
62. Sandra L. Berger, "Differentiating Curriculum for Gifted Students," *ERIC Digest #E510* (Reston, VA: Council for Exceptional Children, ERIC Clearinghouse on Disabilities and Gifted Education, n.d.).
63. Meyer, Harry, and Sapon-Shevin, "School Inclusion and Multicultural Education."
64. This "starting point" is a moving one, not easily established. It is as much a *commitment* as a *foundation* and requires ongoing experimentation and

theory building. Envisioning what this theory would look like if it actually guided schools would be, and is, at best, a difficult and contentious process, because the contexts for schooling are inhospitable and there is not a long history of sustained significant efforts to effect these kinds of shifts.

CHAPTER 9

The School Culture:

Where Good Teaching Makes Sense

Georgina Acosta

First-year teacher, high school English

Students need committed and capable teachers, but they need more. Students also need a clean and safe environment, and up-to-date books, computers, and facilities, but they still need more. The school's organizational arrangements and routines, attitudes and beliefs, and the relationships among everyone in the building shape what students accomplish in school. In other words, students need a school culture that makes it inevitable that all students receive a socially just and excellent education. So do teachers.

One first-year teacher described how the teachers at two senior high schools approached their concerns about their students' low achievement. She had done a teaching internship at Northern High School, and then she took her first permanent position at Southern High School. In many ways, the two schools, which are only a few miles apart, are similar. Both are large comprehensive urban high schools in medium-sized school systems. Both have racially mixed student bodies. This teacher was so struck by the contrast between the Northern teachers' passion for reform and the Southern teachers' resignation to the status quo that she studied the sharp differences between the two schools.

First she describes Northern High School, where the main concern was addressing the social justice issue of maintaining "two schools" under one roof:

Northern's district used its professional development and reform funds to conduct student and teacher inquiry sessions to address the school's concerns. While participants discuss issues of assessment, literacy, and school culture at length, the guiding focus of these discussions was the "two schools" issue—why do different segments of the student population perform and succeed at different levels? Through these inquiry sessions, Northern has developed and maintained an environment where broader educational issues are discussed openly and honestly, and where participants develop and articulate practical classroom solutions.

For example, at one inquiry session, when someone raised a question about factors outside of the classroom that contribute to the achievement disparities, an English teacher condemned the AP test as the "ultimate canon." He argued that, for teachers, "there are conflicting priorities. Is our goal to build a sense of self—for students—or is our goal to push as many kids into Harvard as possible?" A math teacher responded with his frustration with the current system and how his priorities have been altered, "I refuse to believe that passing a test is a measure of one's intelligence. Let's face it, some of our kids are being prepared to succeed and others are overlooked. I won't be a part of that system anymore."

Several staff members recognized that by not encouraging reform in the area of assessment, the cycle of educational inequality would be perpetuated. A counselor for "at-risk" students explained that not changing would be "most damaging for lower-achieving students—those who don't see themselves as smart because they don't relate to the school environment and don't 'buy into the system.'"

The most striking aspect of Northern's inquiry was the level of comfort in discussing issues of culture and the ways in which teachers' practices can negatively impact students. These are not easy topics to discuss in a group, because individuals tend to become defensive about their teaching practices. I was surprised that this was not the response. Participants explained their frustrations and distress about the impact of some of their classroom practices (particularly assessment). But they did so in a way that demonstrated that they were struggling with these issues and open to change.

At Northern, people honestly want to exchange ideas and hear what others have to say. The environment is safe and supportive enough to deal with these very difficult issues. Teachers are not blaming administrators, and administrators are not blaming teachers. All are working as a group toward addressing how curriculum, school culture, and assessment impact students. Reform is everyone's priority and everyone seems to believe that these issues can and will be addressed in a meaningful way to improve the learning environment for students.

In contrast, Southern High's main concern was with "putting out fires."

Discussions of school culture, classroom practices, and assessment take on an entirely different tone at Southern High School. The sense of school community and commitment to addressing pressing social and cultural problems that exist at Northern simply does not exist to any significant extent at Southern. Teachers are overwhelmed by the requests that are made of them. They honestly have the best of intentions for their students, but they are in an environment that encourages change only at the individual level. The school culture is not one in which teachers develop a sense of community to help and support one another. As an administrator noted, "The school is too busy putting out fires." One teacher shared, "It's not that I don't care but we have to deal with one issue at a time. I try to be creative and 'authentic,' but, realistically, how much can we change? There aren't enough hours in the day to deal with the macro issues. If change occurs, it'll have to be in our classrooms.

A Southern staff meeting provided an interesting contrast to the inquiry session at Northern. The meeting was attended by most of one department and a few administrators. The purpose of the meeting was to discuss the results of the recent state exams and their implications for the department. Overall, the results were not good; students did not perform at levels that the department chair and administration expected.

The results had been distributed two days before the meeting, and people were already comparing the performances of their students—which, incidentally, led to some questions about their teaching effectiveness. (This issue was never addressed specifically during the meeting because bad feelings and tensions were already high.) Teachers seemed more concerned about their own reputations (which they feel are based on assessment results) than they were about advocating for substantive change. The meeting provided a powerful opportunity for the staff to address the broader issues of school culture, the validity of standardized testing versus authentic assessment, and changing practices in the classroom in a meaningful way, but the opportunity was lost in a hostile environment and pervasive feeling of futility.

Teachers and administrators chose instead to focus on the state exam itself. All seemed to agree that in the current system, standardized tests label students and put them in academic tracks that greatly influence their academic and occupational futures. They all agreed that the tests weren't necessarily a fair or accurate measure of potential. But no one offered an alternative or even an argument. They seemed resigned to the current system and believed that a change in classroom philosophies and practices could occur individually, but that schoolwide change and commitment was unlikely. Without that support, no one seemed to want to initiate fundamental changes.

Administrators, who admitted that the day-to-day crises had priority over larger school issues that required substantially more time and energy, called for a change in philosophy and priorities at the district level. The common theme that emerged from this meeting was a denial of responsibility. By the end of the meeting, it had become apparent that, although the staff could be characterized as caring and dedicated, the environment was not conducive to fundamental change. The ability of the staff and administration to work together was almost nonexistent. Each saw its role as separate and distinct. For both groups, other issues took priority over addressing the fundamental problems of curriculum, culture, and assessment. There was a pervasive sense of helplessness—that the broader issues would never be addressed in any meaningful way because no one was willing to accept the responsibility of initiating change.

—Name withheld
First-year high school teacher

Schools as Cultures

Northern High School and Southern High School are dissimilar in many respects, but the heart of their differences lies in their school cultures. School cultures help shape what people see, how they feel, and what they think is possible. Within a culture, people do not tend to see culture as something that shapes or limits; culture is just what is normal. In fact, most people only become aware of culture when they come face-to-face with cultural differences. For example, only when we hear another language do we become aware of another's or our own language difference.[1] Teachers who are new to a school may be more sensitive to the power of the culture than "old-timers" for whom daily practices and attitudes are simply, "the way we do it here." New teachers can make use of their heightened perception, but they also need to be aware that the existing culture does not take happily to those who challenge it abruptly. After all, the culture is normal; challengers are not. That said, new teachers can be assured that patience and struggle do change cultures, and changing the culture is first among the career goals of a teacher who wants to change the world.

Cultures Shape Sense-Making

Yale University psychologist Seymour Sarason has studied the power of the school culture for thirty years.[2] He first realized how much school culture matters when his analyses in the 1960s showed that schools rarely took reforms seriously. The cultural "regularities"—the kinds of opportunities that schools made available to students, the expectations they held for students, and the relationships within the whole school community—blocked any genuine change. These patterns were so deeply ingrained in the schools he studied, few people questioned them. Sarason suggested that a visitor from Mars might ask "Why do you do it this way?" but that few people at the schools would ask such a question. If they did, fewer still would be able to answer. When reforms were proposed, educators and communities saw the way they did things—their cultural regularities—as normal. So, instead of changing their schools to fit the reforms, it made more sense for administrators and teachers to reshape the reforms to fit their schools. Usually, that meant following along with the outward appearances of change, but changing little inside the classroom or in the school relationships in the hopes that the urge behind a particular reform would pass. Usually it did.

Little has changed over the past thirty years, and many studies have echoed Sarason's analysis that few reforms ever take hold in ways that produce the intended results. However, essential reform dilemmas are becoming clearer, and there are hopeful signs that reformers are looking at school cultures to understand what goes wrong and what goes right when schools try to make fundamental changes in their practices. In 1996 the National Commission on Teaching and America's Future issued a challenge, to redesign the nation's elementary and secondary schools. The report, *What Matters Most: Teaching and America's Future,* argued that without a fundamental overhaul of the school culture, teachers cannot teach well, and students cannot learn well.[3]

Some regularities—for example, course offerings, parent conference schedules, and teachers' supervision responsibilities—are matters of policy. But some of the most powerful regularities are not formalized; that is, rarely does anyone consciously decide, "Let's do it this way." For example, at one school the faculty stays late to give students extra help. At another, the parking lot empties shortly after the last bell. At one school the principal freely drops by classrooms and participates in lessons. The students love it, and it pleases the teachers that the principal knows about the class activities. At another school the principal steps into classes and meets a cold reception. Here, the teachers feel the principal is nosy and that she doesn't trust them. Even the students "shape up" and appear to concentrate, waiting for the principal to leave before they and the teacher relax. At some schools, teachers follow the required curriculum to the letter; at others they expand upon the curriculum to meet students' needs better. At some schools, teachers pitch in to help their colleagues—preferring to work on teams and with partners; at others teachers jealously guard their ideas and materials and prefer to work alone. Sarason and other sensible critics of schools emphasize that trying to change individual practices such as these, one by one, is not productive. Broader perspectives are necessary to understand and change schools.

Cultures Where It Makes Sense to Teach All Students Well

Good schools have cultures where it makes sense for faculty to teach all students well and for all students to learn well. The central tenet of the Coalition of Essential Schools, one of the largest reform movements in the United States, is that "good schools do share powerful guiding ideas, principles that are widely accepted even as they take different shapes in practice when people put them to work in their own settings from day to day."[4] So rather than prescribing lists of ideal practices for schools to follow, the Coalition has identified features of a school's culture—guiding ideas—that will move the school toward reform. Among these features are a focus on having students use their minds well, making inquiry central, enabling personalized relationships among teachers and students, and modeling democratic practices. The Coalition's principles and other similar guides draw from a wide array of studies investigating the dynamics of the school culture.[5]

The remainder of this chapter describes four aspects of the school culture that consistently appear on lists of the qualities shared by good schools. These conditions, which have an enormous impact on whether teachers will be able to teach well and students will be able to learn well, foster both high academic quality and social justice. If Sarason's visitor from Mars studied schools for a month, he/she/it would have no trouble identifying the importance of these conditions; we earth dwellers have a harder time recognizing what is in front of our noses. School cultures where teachers can teach well and students can learn well do the following:

1. Press everyone toward learning and social justice.
2. Provide broad and deep access to learning.
3. Build an environment of caring relationships.
4. Support teachers' inquiry and activism.

These conditions—obvious, perhaps—allow teachers and their students to teach and learn in ways that can change the world.

This chapter includes, in addition to observations of their own classes and experiences, several first-year teachers' descriptions of other, more-experienced members of the school community from whom they received valuable guidance, modeling, and mentoring. But those with experience also benefited from the new teachers—drawing on their enthusiasm, reflecting on their difficult questions, appreciating their giving back to their school community, and with their new allies, co-constructing new school cultures. Chapter 10 considers a fifth essential characteristic of a healthy and socially just school culture—respectful connections between schools and the communities they serve.

Press for Learning and Social Justice

During World War II, American schools had an institutional *press* for victory in the war. This press, which was manifest in every aspect of the daily life in schools, helped shape thinking and decisions about school. Students were aware that the geography and history they learned made sense in terms of the war. Students brought money to school to put toward their own federal savings (war) bonds. Clothing, energy use, and meals at school were all influenced by war rationing—not complied with reluctantly, but as a matter of civic responsibility. Games were war games. Conversations often focused on young people who were at or about to go to war.

In the 1970s the popular culture, later labeled the "me generation," was inordinately concerned with self-awareness and personal expression. Encountering one's own and others' feelings and personal revelations were values in the broader culture that also permeated schools. Thus, the curriculum and teaching reflected, more or less, these cultural values; the school's cultural press asked students to look inward, to "find themselves." Later decades exhibit their own unique cultural character.

Similarly, private religious schools have a distinct cultural press that emerges from the religious norms at the school's core. At most of these schools, not everything is religious, but religious values are ever-present reminders in students' daily lives. Adults and usually other students respond very quickly to violations of these norms.

In all of these examples, *press* is an institutional imperative, an alignment, a social consensus, an inevitability that each person in the culture will be immersed in particular cultural values. Some may rebel, some may not "get it," but all will be touched—not just occasionally, but hourly. Although most schools in the 1990s have crafted statements of their purpose or "mission," *press*—the ever-present effort to enact such missions—may be present or absent in varying degrees.[6]

For example, all schools say that learning is their top priority. However, schools differ in how strongly this priority is translated into an institutional press for students' daily and hourly academic accomplishments. In some schools, no matter where one turns—student or adult—there is another reminder that learning is "what we do here and nothing else can take its place."

Likewise, all schools *say* they are equally committed to all of their students. Again, some schools do translate this spoken value into a schoolwide press that elevates social justice from a rhetorical piece of the culture to a defining theme. At many schools, however, other elements of institutional press provide stiff competition to enacting the norms of achievement and social justice. These schools may focus on quiet halls, high attendance at sports events, or a single-minded attention to raising test scores a few points. Some schools proudly point to their success at "keeping the lid on." Some schools in wealthy communities point to their already high test scores to justify all aspects of their school program and answer any critics. Some faculties act like gatekeepers, making sure that students don't get advantages they don't deserve. Some feel powerless to combat race and class loyalties and tensions that tear the school's cultural fabric.

How Convincing Is the Learning Priority?

Is learning publicly recognized and rewarded? Or do sports, clubs, and social events always get the attention? Does the principal spend her time on paperwork, meetings, and building maintenance, or does she find a bit of time for teaching? Does she visit classrooms frequently because she loves to watch learning, or are her visits limited to the teacher supervision requirements? Listen to the principal talk about what makes him proud. Does he describe in detail the rich learning experiences going on in classrooms?

Consider the following description of a fairly well off suburban high school. This school is not "at risk," yet its press for learning seems quite low:

> The bell has rung and the last few eleventh graders are sauntering into their second-period class. Several students present "absence slips" to the teacher, confessing truancy or documenting their real or invented illness or family emergency. Three others present passes, respectively, from the school nurse, the counseling office, and the student government adviser. Another student has forgotten her pass, and the teacher sends her to the office. There are seven students absent. A couple might arrive late. Others will receive summonses from various corners of the school. Only two-thirds of the students actually attend the entire class two days in a row. Over the public address, a student recites the Pledge of Allegiance without error today, though that is not always the case. Another student reads announcements. The senior class advertises, as it will each day for two weeks, its fund-raising computer-dating dance. Two students perform a hastily written skit. They are too close to the microphone, and their garbled speech is nearly unintelligible. However, a few adolescent sexual innuendoes manage to get through, and the class receives them with exaggerated, uproarious appreciation. A single academic announcement—the scholarship society will offer tutoring at noon—arouses no apparent interest. An announcer praises a winning sports team and commends the losers for a great effort. The vice principal issues a warning about lunch passes. He adds that makeup testing for the state achievement test will take place in the library, and therefore the library will be closed for the next two days.
>
> Announcements over, instruction begins.

The students at this school score well on standardized tests, and many gain admittance to top-rated colleges. Some students, particularly those in the highest college-preparatory tracks, undauntedly pursue outstanding education. There is some palpable disdain, however, for many of the top students, especially those with less social appeal. Even some adults at school exercise caution about spotlighting their achievements. The youngsters held in highest esteem by their peers are better-than-average students, but they are as notable for their good looks, cars, and general sociability as for their academic achievements. All students, particularly the large group that simply gets by, would achieve more if their school made its real business seem more important.

Is Learning Time Precious?

Individual teachers vary in their values and methods. And yet, stepping back from these individual differences, one finds school culture differences that influence teachers in one direction or another. For example, one national study found that elementary schools scheduled from eighteen to twenty-seven hours per week for instruction.[7] This range reflects an important difference in learning opportunities. Furthermore, the study found that most classrooms spent only 70 percent of the eighteen to twenty-seven scheduled hours on learning activities—the rest of the time was spent getting ready, cleaning up, disciplining, and socializing. Thus, while an organized and focused teacher will provide more learning opportunities to his students than a disorganized and ill-focused teacher at the same school, the organized, focused teacher will provide more or fewer opportunities depending on what school he is at. The culture makes the difference.

Middle schools and high schools also reveal this combination of individual teacher volition and the school culture. Do teachers hold students until the dismissal bell rings, or do students wander out of class a few minutes early? Does the school generally support "supervised reading" and getting started on homework drills as legitimate classroom activities, or are students engaged in discussion, group activities, research, and other activities that can be done only in the classroom? Are videos and films judiciously selected, edited, and discussed, or, at the start of the period, do the lights go out and the movies go on? Are teachers absent rarely or frequently? When teachers are absent, are substitutes carefully selected to follow well-designed instructions, or are substitutes selected for their willingness to put up with abuse and expected to "baby-sit" the students? Again, each school may have teachers who display the full range of concern for keeping students engaged in learning, but each school will also display a cultural tendency to value student engagement more or less.

Currently, many schools are experimenting with alternatives to traditional schedules in order to provide more focus and concentrated learning time and, in secondary schools, to free teachers from the constraints of fifty-minute lessons. For example, many schools now use "block scheduling," in which each team of teachers has a large chunk of time each day that they can use flexibly, varying the time students spend on particular learning activities and in particular groups.[8]

Not only the schedule matters, however; the prevailing norms about what's most worth spending time on are also important. Some junior and senior high schools excuse students from class for all kinds of reasons. Their sports team may need to get ready for a game or the auditorium may need decorating for a dance. An elementary-school student body may get to spend school time watching cartoons as a reward for having met their candy-sale goal. And there is no end to the ways that schools can spend time on routines. Taking the roll, tardy checks, lining up properly, and practicing good behavior are just a few. Students can lose as much learning time in the teacher's pursuit of quiet and orderliness as they lose because of noise and disorder.

It's a mistake to think that schools can easily limit these time-consuming activities. Each has its roots in school traditions and societal expectations. Americans see social activities and athletics as ways for common schools to help students prepare for community participation. Schools view athletics as a vehicle for teaching fairness, competition, and cooperation. We sometimes justify sports as opportunities for poor, minority, and academically unsuccessful students to find their niches in school (although the only reliable payoffs for schooling come from academic achievement). Bureaucratic routines and record keeping are often a response to legal requirements schools can do little to change.

Does Learning Extend to Everyone—No Excuses?

Where was the radical thinking about student voice and student choice in the curriculum? It was right out the window with the teacher inquiry, the staff support, the familial presence in the classroom, and the progressive district attitude. Nevertheless, I kept hurling my UCLA education at the kids and tried hard to ignore the last hundred years of teaching that were all around me. During the first days, I was incredibly self-conscious about ignoring convention, constantly experimenting, and changing every week. It did not help that my next-door neighbor and mentor was a kindly and smooth twelve-year veteran, heavily steeped in the traditions of spelling tests, rote learning, and textbook-driven curriculum.

After the first month, however, I hit a wave. It was awesome. I seemed to be making progress every week. I nailed some brilliant lessons and produced new ideas. I would sit from 8 A.M. to 10 P.M. every Saturday and just pluck ideas out of thin air. We did group work, hands-on math, and visual social studies; made models, wrote stories, and wrote letters; and did a fascinating unit on the workings of the brain. Then it all began to slip away.

Much to my dismay I discovered that my students had not learned much. My results were fairly standard for the school: 30 percent of the class did very well, 30 percent did passing work, and 30 percent failed. The big question was why. Were my lessons confusing? Was the test too hard? Perhaps I should have given more frequent evaluations. However, the school's answer lay in a conversation I had with one of the older teachers soon after the test. I told her about my result and how discouraged I was over the lack of mastery. She chuckled one of those annoying know-it-all chuckles and said, "We all get those same results. That is just how it is." This immediately reminded me of a similar conversation I had with a teacher during my student teaching. This woman had warned me not to expect to "reach them all." "Take off those rose colored glasses," she said. I sat at a crossroads. What kind of an educator would I be?

—Jeffrey Madrigal
First-year teacher, grade 4

Math reform means working to give each student the opportunity to become a mathematician if he or she chooses. If we assume certain students will fail mathematics, we are not giving all students equal opportunity to succeed in math. If we allow students to fail math because it is not their "strength," we risk having a population illiterate in mathematics. We risk broadening the socioeconomic gap between the privileged and the not so privileged.

I have found this to be a major issue at my school. Students who have the choice to take higher math are encouraged by counselors to take lower-level math courses. The goal is not to get students into college; rather, the goal is to get students to graduate. I began to encourage my students to take higher math. We constantly talked about moving on to algebra next year. I expected them to continue taking math classes beyond the requirements. By the end of the year, many wanted to move on to algebra, and several ninth graders signed up for summer school to "get ahead."

—Name withheld
First-year teacher, mathematics, grade 9

Both of these first-year teachers know that when schools offer students an intellectually rich curriculum and expect them to perform well, students get the message "We believe you can do it." They learn how smart the school thinks they can be. If a school staff believes that all its students can learn challenging subject matter, then schools will work very hard to provide conditions that will enable all students to learn. These efforts pay off.

However, as the preceding two teachers found out, many school cultures foster the belief that only some students can learn very well. Such cultures also promote the assumption that most students will be average, and some will not learn much at all. Many educators and much of the public find these expectations reasonable, given their understanding of students' differences in intelligence. Sometimes a caring faculty intentionally maintains low expectations for children in poverty, thinking they are being kind, even though there is considerable evidence that students learn more—even those in the most-distressed urban schools—when they are offered a challenging curriculum.[9] Frequently, high-achieving high schools are also *under*achieving. So enamored are they with their high averages, they neglect many students who are just getting by.

By contrast, some school cultures are powerfully enriched by teachers who understand that if a student does not succeed, the least likely explanation is that the student lacks intelligence. These teachers concentrate less on what students are lacking and more on what instruction can press all students to achieve. They emphasize and model for their students the hard work and persistence it takes to succeed. Sometimes such teachers become emblematic of their school and community, and over time they define the culture as much as they work within it. First-year middle-school teachers Lily Kim and Suzanne Markoe found an inspiring mentor in veteran teacher Yvonne Hutchinson, who helped them translate their beliefs about students' abilities into rich classroom learning experiences. Here is what they wrote about their mentor:

> Yvonne Divans-Hutchinson teaches eighth- and ninth-grade English at Edwin Markham Middle School in Watts, California. Yvonne was born in Little Rock, Arkansas, in 1943, during the height of racial segregation. When she moved to California, she lived in the Imperial Courts Housing Project in Watts and became a member of the first graduating class of the school where she now teaches. She chose to return to her alma mater and has been teaching there for

> the past thirty years. As one of her respected colleagues stated, "Yvonne is the gatekeeper to Watts. If you want to get out of Watts, if you want to go to college, you need to pass through Ms. Hutchinson; you need to be touched by her."
>
> Yvonne prepares her students for real life by setting high standards and expecting her students to rise to them. Her nickname, "Killer Hutch," came about because of a fight that she broke up, but it has since evolved over the years to describe the type of curriculum that she teaches. One of her students aptly noted that "Ms. Hutchinson helps you to see the deeper side to everything. She makes you think on a higher level." Yvonne challenges her students with engaging literature and demands that they go beyond the literal in analyzing what they read. The students know that they dare not write about what is obvious in what they read. A former student, now a student at the University of California-Berkeley, remarked: "Even now I check all my papers and ask myself if they are good enough for Ms. Hutchinson."
>
> Providing an emotionally safe classroom is also vitally important to Yvonne. To promote respect of different cultures and ethnicities, her students follow a specific routine in calling on each other. When one student wishes to call on another student, he or she must choose someone who differs from him or her in race, ethnicity, gender, or in some other way. Yvonne regularly reminds her students of this policy, and it promotes a respect of diverse cultures in her classroom. Whenever a student dares to utter a racial slur or other form of disrespect to another student, Yvonne will stop the entire class at whatever they are doing because she believes a more important lesson needs to be taught. By the time the class is over, the student and class know not to disrespect another student or culture again.
>
> Instead of seeing her students as so many people see them ("at risk, poverty-stricken, poor, disadvantaged"), Yvonne sees the "thousands of possibilities" that the students possess.[10]

The following questions can reveal a school's press for learning. Can students get by without trying very hard? Are all students—girls as well as boys, minorities as well as whites, poor students as well as more affluent ones—expected to study rigorous subjects like algebra, a foreign language, and advanced science? What percentage of students does the school expect to go to college? (This is a good question for elementary schools as well as high schools.) Does the school keep records of how many students complete college (or even high school)? In what way do the people at this school see questions such as these as relevant?

The Culture of Everyone

Chapter 4 raised the following questions about the school curriculum: Whose knowledge should be represented in what students learn, and whose culture should be represented in what students learn? These questions have political implications because those with the most power in society get to make decisions about what gets taught in schools, and the decision makers tend to favor knowledge that conforms to their own perspectives. These questions also have learning implications, because students learn best when they can make use of their own experiences and cultural backgrounds. Here, we again ask these questions, but this time in order to raise an important distinction between the knowledge a school teaches (the curriculum) and the knowledge a school lives (the culture).

The students attending the school described next will have the chance to make a difference, not just learn about difference. These students will, in Linda Darling-Hammond's words, "find and act on who they are, what their passions, gifts, and talents may be, what they care about, and how they want to make a contribution to each other in the world."[11]

> New teachers at the school where Nancy Parachini is principal encountered a culture that supported their social justice commitments. Teaching multiculturalism or applauding children's various backgrounds and beliefs "has to be at the center of everything," according to Parachini. She has worked with the staff to change the way the school perceives multiculturalism, "even though it might have been done before, it was fragmented, it wasn't a unified focus, a vision." For Parachini multiculturalism means respecting what students bring with them to the classroom; it means planning curricula that suit the strengths and interests of the school's children.
>
> In a school where many cultures are represented, Parachini helps the children in her community to know their roots. She holds that it is important for students to learn to appreciate diversity by understanding first their own uniqueness: "I think that once they can start with themselves, then it becomes a more valuable experience." Nancy Parachini believes that understanding must translate into social action. "It's not just tolerance. It's understanding and a knowledge base that will translate into power [and] social action. Because when there is an imbalance of power, that creates the inequity." By incorporating these ideas into the curriculum, children learn to look at themselves and their surroundings differently. They develop the ability to analyze their relationships and understand the implications of inequity in society at large.[12]

Access to Learning and Preparation for College

> The school district is in such dire straits that the teachers can't make photocopies, we don't have overhead projectors, nor do we have enough space for the children. The lack of resources has actually made me a very creative teacher. I learned this year that I didn't need an overhead nor did I need a chalkboard! I've learned that my students don't need paper or pencil. And I've learned to creatively manage and teach a class without these staples of American education.
>
> —Steven Branch
> *First-year teacher, grade 5*

Money Does Matter

It has become fashionable, especially in politically conservative quarters, to argue that the problems of American schools cannot be solved with money. Tell that to first-year teacher Steve Branch. Despite his ironic bravado about teaching creatively without resources, Branch knows better than most the dual truth that teachers can teach well with very little and that money matters a great deal.

Certainly, upper- and middle-class parents throughout history have understood that if their own children are to become readers, they need classrooms and libraries full of books. Their science learning requires equipment and laboratory space. Their physical development requires things to climb on, toys and sports equipment, and open space in which to play. Their classrooms should be suited to the work the teachers try to accomplish, and students themselves should have suitable workspaces: clean, well-lighted, well-heated, and air-conditioned classrooms with plenty of room for productive activity. Cultural traditions of these same groups likewise have justified the inferior school resources given to poor students and racial minorities by reasoning that it does not pay to put great resources into those students' schools. Moreover, the traditional perspective has guided superficial research "proving" that resources don't matter. Yet researcher Ronald Ferguson's studies of the impact of expenditures on student achievement show clearly that not only does greater school spending yield higher student achievement, spending on teachers matters most.[13] Ferguson's research, however, does not dispute the fact that school spending is more or less effective depending on many other factors within the school culture.

Some Students Get More Teacher Resources In addition to basic facilities and materials, students need enough teachers—qualified ones. Too few teachers means classes will be large and difficult to manage. Hiring less-qualified teachers for less money means that students are unlikely to have teachers with the expertise to teach well. Both matter for student learning.

Considerable research shows that fifteen students, or fewer, per class is optimal at the elementary level.[14] Unfortunately, classes that small are nearly unheard of in any but the wealthiest private schools. Secondary school classes should probably not exceed twenty-five students, although most do. Smaller classes in themselves do not cause more learning, but they strongly affect how teachers can design and carry out lessons. The number of students in a class not only affects the time teachers have available to spend with individual students, but also influences teachers' flexibility in experimenting with teaching strategies. And, though it might sound mundane, teachers also need basic supplies and materials to work with. Books for their students, audiovisual equipment in good working order, hands-on materials, a decent copy machine, access to a computer and a telephone, and whatever might be found in the office of any well-functioning business can make the difference between a teacher feeling able to do her job well and feeling quite overwhelmed.

Some Students Get Better Teachers First, the notion of teacher quality is tricky. There is nothing to say that the newest teacher at the school is the least competent or that "credentials" make a good teacher. However, there is a strong likelihood that highly trained and experienced teachers are valuable resources. Similarly, teachers with good reputations across the school and in the community are not guaranteed to be the best teachers, but they are sure a better bet than those with the worst reputations. All this adds up to the legitimacy and pitfalls of talking about "better" and "the best" teachers.

All students at a school—not just the highest-achieving ones—need access to the best teachers available. A not-so-well-kept secret in many school cultures is that teachers are tracked as well as students. The most-experienced and knowledgeable teachers are often rewarded with the "plum" teaching assignments. New teachers often end up with the classes that the others don't want—usually, the low-ability classes or those with lots of behavior problems.[15] However, schools can make a conscious effort to distribute teacher talent evenly, recognizing that low-achieving students are further disadvantaged when they are consistently placed in classes with less-qualified teachers. Some schools have made it a policy that if they are going to track their classes, students in all of the tracks have access to the "best" teachers.[16]

The combination of well-prepared teachers and small classes is the most potent opportunity schools can offer students. Giving teachers the books, materials, and equipment they need to teach is necessary to maximize their effectiveness and hardly a luxury. In addition to the tangible contribution to learning, the presence or absence of these basic necessities sends a powerful symbolic messages to both teachers and students.

The dismal conditions of schools in poor, urban communities of color have been well documented, and the disparity between rich and poor schools is brought to life for my students by the geographic proximity of my school to areas of Los Angeles such as Palos Verdes and Beverly Hills. The unequal distribution of resources not only perpetuates the existing system of social, political, and economic inequality but sends the message in a very direct way to my students that they don't count as much as the students who have access to computer labs, planetariums, and books! Well-meaning teachers (such as myself) can attempt to compensate for these material deficiencies and be relatively successful in the short run, but it is the long-term effects of an inherently unequal system that will ultimately serve to undermine our good intentions.

—Jennifer Garcia
First-year teacher, high school history

A Rich, Balanced Curriculum

If a school has no French class, no one will learn French at school. No music? No computers? Then no one learns about music or computers at school. When some students take a subject and others do not, the limits on opportunity are just as apparent. These are obvious examples of lack of opportunity. Most are more subtle. For example, all third graders receive reading instruction. Even so, the quantity and quality of that instruction vary. Good sense tells us what will happen when a group of able readers reads stories, and a low group does only worksheets. The latter will have fewer opportunities to read stories. Likewise, if the advanced high school history class requires a research paper and the regular one doesn't, some students won't get to practice research skills.

It matters whether academically rich instruction is available and which students have access to it. Many secondary schools have taken a crude but often effective first step and simply eliminated low-level academic classes. Some require all students to take courses previously considered advanced—for example, algebra in middle school. Other schools open up their honors programs to everyone or provide gifted and honors activities within heterogeneous classes. These actions are supported by considerable evidence that all students—rich, poor, black, Latino, Asian, white, high- and low-achieving—learn better when they are provided rich and challenging curriculum.[17]

While individual teachers may be sensitive to cultural differences and try to bring in academically challenging content that makes use of students' experiences and background, the broader school can do little or much to make this possible. Department, grade level, and whole-school commitments can enable individual teachers to diversify literature; tell multiple versions of history, economics, and other social studies; teach high-level conceptual math; and so on.

A new teacher will not change a school's curriculum single-handedly, but new teachers often find more-experienced teachers in their school who support their efforts (and veteran teachers for the new teacher to support). Like Yvonne Hutchinson, who was described earlier, and Pat Cady, described next, these veterans are not just single teachers whose influence is confined to their classrooms. They are, themselves, cultural features. Their "presence" often creates the space and reveals the possibilities for offering the richest possible curriculum. For example, first-year social studies teacher Kate Castleberry found a mentor in veteran teacher Pat Cady, who scaffolded Castleberry's efforts to create a culturally relevant curriculum in her classes.

> Pat Cady has been a social studies teacher for more than twenty years. He agrees with Noel Ignatiev's ideas in *Race Traitor* that although people look white, acting and participating in the "white club" only furthers racial segregation, degradation, and depression. He therefore is a white Irishman on the outside, yet his actions and beliefs indicate his affiliation with the entire human race. In his teaching, Pat Cady addresses historical perspectives from many points of view and includes innovative scholars who are also concerned with social justice. His unit on the Vietnam era begins with a study of the African American soldier. He has explored Richard Takaki's *A Different Mirror* and James Loewen's *Lies My Teacher Told Me* with his eleventh-grade class. Both books focus on the multicultural historical perspective. By sharing his standpoint and his approach to teaching, Cady continually sends the message that white is not "best" and that all students should share and represent themselves in our history.[18]

Extra Help When Needed

In many schools, both teachers and students expect that some children just won't keep up with their classmates. But some, supportive school cultures are determined not to let students fall behind. They provide extra help, and they keep parents informed if students need more support outside of school. Ideally, in the elementary grades extra help comes within the classroom during regular class time. The routine scaffolding available in daily instruction and student groups should blur the distinction between help and extra help. However, it is normal for situations to occur when students just need extra time with a "knowledgeable other." A special resource teacher, a paid aide, or a parent volunteer may provide an extra boost. Or a peer tutor, either in the same class or from a higher grade, may provide one-on-one assistance. Extra help should supplement classroom lessons and should not substitute a remedial program for the regular one.

Many secondary schools give extra help to master the more challenging curriculum. Some offer "backup classes" for low-achieving students; students enroll in both an advanced academic courses and a backup class in place of an elective. The backup class provides them with additional instruction and time on the material in their advanced course—especially if the backup classes are kept small. Some schools call this a "double dose" of teaching. Other schools operate homework centers or Saturday schools, staffed with teachers, community volunteers, or more-advanced students who provide tutoring to those who need help. Some operate summer programs specifically designed to give students the opportunity to skip to higher-level courses in the fall.

Helping students keep up with the regular curriculum, despite its undisputed benefits, conflicts with some common ideas about standardization and efficiency. It may disrupt schools' orderly progression through the curriculum. It may cost more. On the other hand, not helping students keep up is also costly and inefficient. When schools have students repeat a grade, it adds an additional year's cost for that child's education. And since grade retention does not boost students' school success (in fact, retention likely contributes to dropping out of school), the extra expense is money wasted. If students who don't keep up are simply passed along, schools must provide low-level classes to accommodate them—another ineffective use of school resources. Providing extra help so that students can keep up with the "regular" curriculum is money well spent.

Support for a Multicultural, College-Going Identity

Teachers express a cultural value when they tell all their students, "You can go to college." But too often they leave unspoken their belief, " . . . *if* you act like someone else." Just who that "someone else" might be will vary, but it often conforms to a familiar stereotype of who is a "successful" college student. The profile of such a student is complex, but it likely includes someone who scores high on standardized tests, someone whose parents went to college, someone whose main language is mainstream, unaccented English, someone who has middle-class perspectives and financial support, and so on. Perhaps schools' biggest challenge is to create a school culture that supports college attendance for students whose lives do not conform to this profile. The school culture must position college success as expected and inevitable not just for students who change or for students who are *exceptions* to stereotypes, but for students who have no need or intention to slight their family's background and culture as they acquire the skills and knowledge that are genuinely useful for college success.

For college preparation to be genuinely accessible to students, students must see their cultural identities as integral to college preparation and attendance—not as something they must "overcome." They must develop the confidence and skills to negotiate college preparation without sacrificing their own identity and connections with their home communities. In contrast to commonly held views that low-income students devalue education, studies suggest that they more likely turn away because of a real or perceived lack of opportunities.[19] A recent RAND study of low-income high school graduates who were eligible for the University of California, but chose not to attend found that the students were most deterred by their beliefs that the university is "not for people like me," and that that they weren't prepared for the university's high demands.[20]

In Chapter 6, we pointed to what Claude Steele terms "a stereotype threat" whereby internalized negative labels assigned to racial and cultural groups have deep consequences for how students perform.[21] Students are further affected by their awareness that their individual performance will reflect on other members of their race or culture. To develop college-going identities among diverse students, teachers, communities, and students must confront explicitly all the hidden beliefs and assumptions about who is fit to go to college. Of course, "confronting" means a lot more than talking—for teachers it means entering into the worlds students inhabit and identifying supports, creating programs, and exploring among students, teachers, communities, and colleges every real and potential opportunity for finding and developing students' college-going competence.

Access to Care

A group of student teachers visited the school where first-year teacher Jessica Wingell was teaching. Struck by the caring relationships they found among many teachers and students, they made the following observation:

> Liam Joyce, a white man, is the counselor for "at-risk" students (mostly students of color) at the high school. The night before we talked with him, Mr. Joyce had been at a student's home until 11:00 P.M. talking with the student and her parents. During our conversation, he stopped five or six times to have brief conversations with students. At one point, a student stuck his head in the door and said, "Mr. Joyce, can I talk to you for one second?" Without a hesitation or

a question, Mr. Joyce immediately stepped outside his office. For him, students come first. Mr. Joyce dedicates 99 percent of his time and energy to students and achieving social justice, and the rapport he has developed with his students is amazing.

When one of us asked Mr. Joyce how white educators can bridge the gap between themselves and students of color, he immediately pulled a Latino student in from the hallway. "Michael, I want to ask you some questions." Mr. Joyce then asked Michael questions about whether he trusted him. "Yeah, I trust him," Michael told us. He said that he trusts Mr. Joyce because he "does stuff" for him and shows he cares. "Does it matter that Mr. Joyce is white?" we asked. "No, it don't matter," Michael responded and went on to explain which teachers are "good" teachers. None of what he said had to do with skin color. "Ms. Wingell is good because you know she really wants you to do good," he said, "and she spends time helping you."[22]

Every Student Known by Name

Many schools are attempting to become caring communities—places where teachers can act on their deep commitments to knowing and caring for students. This attention to caring drives other changes in school programs and organization, as well as changes inside classrooms.

Many secondary schools have tried to replace their large impersonal structures with smaller schools-within-schools and teams. These arrangements contrast with the typical bureaucratic structures of secondary schools where students drift through classes without developing stable relationships with teachers or, often, other students. For example, an important middle-school and high school organization is the familiar academic department—social studies, math, English, and so on. School academic departments are simply not designed for teachers' to accommodate students' personal and social needs. When teachers must single-handedly manage large numbers of individual students, only the most motivated and highly skilled students can compete successfully for attention.

Many middle schools divide students into teams—smaller groups that stay together during the day and connect with an interdisciplinary team of teachers. Senior highs are increasingly carving up their large student bodies into similar smaller communities. Within teams and houses, students may have an "advisory" class and a teacher with whom they connect every day, who will support them as they negotiate the complexities of school. These structures allow teachers to monitor their students carefully and to share the burden and expertise of curriculum planning. Ideally, the teams share preparation periods to plan lessons and confer about students.[23]

In some elementary and secondary schools students and teachers stay together for two or three years. Many elementary schools combine students into multiage, multiyear classes where only the youngest students are new to the group each year. Some middle schools use a strategy called "looping," where a team of teachers begins with a group of students as they enter the school at fifth or sixth grade and remains with that group until they move on to senior high.

Caring can be part of the whole school's curricular and extracurricular focus. Many schools have "service learning" programs that engage students in community work—for example, tutoring younger students, working in homeless shelters, and so on. First-year teacher Matt Flanders created a most unusual site for a caring community—his water polo team. Since Flanders took over the team it has become one of the more racially diverse settings on campus. Flanders has sought to create space within this extracurricular activity for students to grapple with issues of success, difference, and common cause. He has also created an ethic of care that not only allows but draws team members toward helping others.

Most of my unsuccessful students felt no connection to the campus community. They did not feel that school was important because they were not involved in it. They did not feel as if their presence mattered, so they sank into the shadows of nonengagement.

I tackled the problem of noninvolvement right away. Water polo had kept me in high school and college, so I knew the value of team involvement in education. My team had been a source of support and friendship for me. Coming full circle, I became head water polo coach. I wanted to do for my student-athletes what my coach had done for me years before. I hired a group of young, energetic assistant coaches to help me out.

We proceeded to coach our team not only in the art of water polo, but in the game of life as well. We provided a place that students could be comfortable as well as mentally and physically challenged. We connected them to the campus, to the school community; both the boys' and girls' teams had winning seasons. However, our involvement with our students did not stop in the pool. We dealt with the issues of alcoholism, drug abuse, pregnancy, sexually transmitted disease, child abuse, and jail time that our student-athletes faced. We helped two team members secure admission to college. We became a big part of our students' lives.

Our teams now include about 5 percent of the student body. Our program in one of inclusion; we do not cut. Our goal is to make the best team and the best group of young people we can. I think that is what draws students to our program. In addition, we have started a middle-school water polo team for our district. Thirty-five children participate twice a week, and they are coached by my senior high school players. Not only are we strengthening our athletic stance for years to come, we are reaching into the broader community and connecting with students to help them be successful in high school.

—Matthew Amato Flanders
First-year teacher, high school history

Safe Zones: It's OK to Be Different

First-year teacher Kate Castleberry found herself in a very diverse high school with a faculty that has been vocal about its commitment to create a school culture where differences among students are acknowledged and respected. Kate, the pep squad coach as well as a history teacher, decided to act. Capitalizing on some of the cheerleaders' interest in promoting better race relations among the school's diverse student body, she and her students proposed Racial Harmony Day. What they wanted was a day of serious inquiry into all aspects of school life. The school principal and most of Kate's faculty colleagues encouraged her to act on her social justice commitment, and they lent their strong support. The Day became a source of pride and of ongoing schoolwide efforts to improve the racial climate.

Racial Harmony Day was not a day to join hands and sing "Kumbaya." It was a time to explore how we thought of others, and our fear and knowledge of different races. Racial harmony is a commitment to stand up for our people and for our brothers and sisters when they are not present.

Racial Harmony Day began as a dream of two juniors. One hundred and sixty students were separated into homogeneous racial groups—African American, Asian/Pacific Islander, Caucasian, Latino, and Middle Eastern. [Pairs of groups met to share] and discuss feelings and questions about stereotypes. Students tearfully faced peers and friends and questioned why their "people" held certain thoughts and beliefs. After each group met with the others, the students broke into small, heterogeneous dialogue groups with a facilitator to discuss unresolved feelings. The day ended with an outpouring of willingness to continue the struggle and journey to racial understanding. A core group of students formed a steering committee to help develop more activities. A week after the event, a lunch meeting reacquainted students who suggested further dialogue at a retreat or sleep-over.

Racial harmony will not happen overnight, but students have taken the first steps toward a society that is fair and accepting of all.

—Kate Castleberry
First-year teacher, high school history

It is extraordinarily difficult in schools to confront honestly and out loud the racism that American teenagers have been raised with. It may be even more difficult to acknowledge a difference and bigotry that exists in every community but that educators have been virtually silent about—difference in sexual orientation. Of course, students have not been silent about this issue; in schools across the country, "faggot" is one of the most common and often tolerated epithets hurled across playgrounds and corridors.

According to research of the American Civil Liberties Union, "[f]or lesbian and gay teens, school is often a nightmare. Harassment from classmates is commonplace, particularly in many schools where teachers and principals tolerate it." A study of Massachusetts high school students published in the journal *Pediatrics* reported that more than 25 percent of self-identified gay teens said they had recently missed school because of fear for their safety, a sharp contrast to the 5 percent of heterosexual teens who had. Nearly one-third of gay teens had recently been threatened with a weapon at school, compared to 7 percent of heterosexual students.

Peer support is difficult to find because lesbian and gay student groups are often discouraged or even prohibited. Survival often means painful self-denial for lesbian and gay youth. It is little wonder, therefore, that the *Pediatrics* study revealed that more than one-third of all gay teens reported having attempted suicide, three times the 9.9 percent for self-identified straight teens.

Indeed, schools rarely offer supportive programs for gay youth. Comprehensive information on sexuality, AIDS/HIV, and other lesbian and gay teen concerns is desperately needed, yet schools choose instead to tolerate, if not actively foster, environments hostile to the development of healthy gay youth. For instance, in one recent study, 53 percent of high school students report hearing homophobic slurs such as "faggot" from their *teachers.*

Perhaps an overriding principle regarding school safety is this: As long as one person does not feel safe—experiences or fears abuse by others—no one can be safe. This principle does not just include students. Teachers themselves are not exceptions. Bullying, harassment, slurs, and physical intimidation in any form and inflicted on any person affects everyone. Further, there can be no distinction between the school's failure to respond to a hurtful act and its approval of that act. We include here part of an open letter from a gay former teacher from the ACLU website.[24]

> [A]s a gay teacher, the silence that hurt the most was over sexuality. In my first year of teaching, a veteran fellow teacher strongly advised me that when I taught sex education, if a kid asked a question about anything controversial, such as masturbation or homosexuality, that I should pause, pick up the district-approved curriculum, and read the officially-approved language to the class. The curriculum, as then issued, contained nothing about homosexuality. Silence. As it turned out, I was spared the educationally awkward moment because the principal did not trust a single adult man in his late 20s to teach about sexuality.
>
> So in my school, as in too many others, gay teachers and students suffered in isolation and silence. Nothing was said about two men or two women building relationships or families. Hallways rang with unchallenged taunts of "fag" or "gay." I still sometimes wonder if one of my pupils, who I recently learned is gay, would have waited until his 30s to come out if he had had any kind of meaningful support at school while growing up.
>
> I'm writing to you today to let you know of a great new initiative designed to break the silence and provide lesbian and gay students with the kind of support they so desperately need in schools. The Lesbian & Gay Rights Project of the American Civil Liberties Union (ACLU) has launched the "Every Student, Every School" campaign, geared to teach educators about the problems caused by homophobia in the schools and how to take positive steps to resolve them.

After Columbine—Care in a Violent Culture

We are used to schools being very safe places. And, in fact, they are. Without denying the very real emotional hurt inflicted on students by the full range of insensitivity that people are capable of, schools are generally safe places—physically safe places. According to the Surgeon General's 2001 report, "Youth

Violence: A Report of the Surgeon General," the public perception that schools are very dangerous places is unfounded. Schools are generally safer places to be than homes and neighborhoods. Of course, any violence is unacceptable and particular concern must be raised at the Surgeon General's finding that some students, namely "senior high school students from racial or ethnic minorities who attend schools in urban districts," are at greatest risk.[25]

What then are we to make of the headlines and on-the-spot television reporting of school violence, of students and teachers suffering injury and even loss of life? Well, it is certainly not acceptable to pass it off by saying, "It doesn't happen that often" or "It probably won't happen here." If there are lessons to be drawn from the shootings at Columbine High School and other well-publicized acts of violence at schools, they are these:

- School violence reflects a violent society, in which violence is a tool available to those who are angry and hurt. When students are helped to talk about these aspects of society and to understand them, then teachers are *doing* something about violence both in and out of school.
- Although watchfulness and security are important, prevention is best accomplished in caring school cultures—cultures that find it intolerable to diminish the dignity or security of anyone for whatever reason. Caring teachers are trusted teachers, and the best safeguard against violence in schools may be students who can approach teachers and report actual or potential violence.
- All physical abuse is violent, and calling it *minor, bullying,* or *normal* does not diminish the violence done.
- There are lots of programs, lots of resources, and lots of caring people. *By working each day to ensure school cultures of care, teachers help to make schools safe as they help students learn more.*

After September 11—Care in a Fearful Culture

The shattering enormity of some local and national events, the September 11, 2001, destruction of the World Trade Center in New York, for example, cannot be left for students to resolve with their limited resources and experiences—perhaps thirdhand accounts of the news, a little commentary heard on television, and some youthful maturity. Young and old alike must find ways to explain and express their anger and fears. At best we hope that our schools help channel these emotions into productive understandings and action. Good teachers will not be immune from anger, fear, and bafflement when horrifying things occur, and we should have no illusions that teachers can know the "correct" ways to respond to these events and then easily turn their personal response into a coherent and healing pedagogy. And yet that must be our goal, our struggle; our surest guide is to listen persistently, question students, bring them information, and demonstrate care.

Third-year high school teacher Mary Hendra wrote the following article for the *Christian Science Monitor* in the days following the attacks of September 11.

I was on my way to school when I heard the news that would rivet the nation, and the world. . . . [M]y reaction went from shock to sorrow. But, there was another thought that went through my head that morning: "What will I teach my students today?"

. . . How could I teach about the Industrial Revolution in world history, and the Gilded Age in U.S. history, and ignore the events of this day? I wondered how I would respond to my students' questions, how we could talk about the event without exacerbating fear?

I have encouraged my students to form their own opinions about events in their history books, and they apply the same principle to the current situation. These opinions include a statement few will want to hear: "I think the U.S. deserved this." Yes, one of my students said "deserved." He did not mean that all those people should have been killed, but he was not alone in citing the arrogance with which America has been involved in world affairs, and he was not alone in thinking this event should be a "wake-up call" to America to rethink its policies.

Looking back, my initial questions on Sept. 11 were the easiest I would confront regarding this event. I have urged my students to question—to think critically, to read critically, and to ask questions about the world around them. So they continue to ask me, "Why would people in other countries be celebrating? Why would people want to cause this destruction? How has the United States created these enemies?"

I also have questions. How do we as a nation critically look at why this might have happened, without being seen as "unpatriotic"? Shouldn't it be a sign of patriotism that we seek to improve our nation? The U.S. has certainly not led a pure and perfect existence, but our democracy has been strong enough to change with the challenges brought by women, African-Americans, social activists, and many others. How can the events of Sept. 11 be molded into an opportunity for humanity's progress?

I wonder, if this tragic event was possible in part because of the freedom and openness of our society, whether restricting that freedom could be the best response. My students, many of whom are first- or second-generation Americans themselves, would probably be among the first to complain of heightened immigration controls. They already ask me, "Why should the U.S. restrict immigration? Immigrants are only looking for a better life."

And if my students look to history for understanding, as I frequently tell my them to do, what can they—and we—learn from Israel's unsuccessful war on terrorism over the past years?

Can we root out terrorism by government-sanctioned violence, regardless of the magnitude of that violence? The more the U.S. is seen as an aggressor, the more resentment it will engender from around the world—and hence the greater commitment it will foster among thousands of individuals who will become willing to put their own lives on the line?

And that implies a question for my classroom: How can I explain to critical teenagers that violence by a government is OK, but violence by an individual is not? What about the violence that was used by imperialist nations to subdue and exploit the African continent?

In the American Revolution, the British were stronger economically and militarily. They had more-experienced generals and stronger supply lines. But the American colonists won. Why? Their commitment to their cause overcame their opponents' strength. As the war progressed and colonists saw what the British were willing to do—the horrendous state-sanctioned treatment of prisoners of war and colonial villages—it did not convince colonists that the fight was futile, it convinced them that to do nothing was no longer an option. Their fight was for their very lives, their way of being, their beliefs. Are we not fighting against people who view this battle in the same way?

My students' questioning has also led me to wonder if the U.S.—because of our power and economic strength—is held to a higher standard than other countries that similarly act in their own self-interest. And whether it should it be.

I believe that asking these questions helps my students understand. I hope they will see adults around them asking questions, too, as we all work through these events and their repercussions. On Sept. 11, my class talked about questions no one yet knows the answers to, but are worth asking anyway. I gave students space to reflect, to put the events outside on "pause" for a few moments.

One student articulated what was probably one of the underlying reasons for much of the questioning that day. "I'm not ready to go to war," she said.

—Mary Hendra
Third-year teacher, high school
Christian Science Monitor
September 25, 2001, edition

If teachers confined their teaching in the aftermath of September 11 to questions that they knew the answers to, these would be very short lessons indeed. So would lessons that were limited to noncontroversial, nonpolitical, and safe topics. In fact, after the attack, many teachers were encouraged to proceed with extreme caution—to acknowledge briefly this "current event" and, for the sake of the children, continue with business as usual.

However, a wiser and more humane alternative is to do as Alfie Kohn urges, ". . . help children locate themselves in widening circles of care that extend beyond self, beyond country, to all humanity."[26] This is a tall order in a social and political environment rife with fear and calls for revenge. Such an environment makes it hard for teachers to feel confident about the appropriate developmental level for such lessons and discussions. They worry about acquiring the range of knowledge and perspectives necessary to be responsive to students' questions and concerns. They wince at their potential vulnerability if they truly encourage students to extend their thinking "beyond self." For example, after September 11, older students quickly became engaged in discussions and arguments surrounding racial profiling, and even the youngest struggled to form impressions about who the bad people were and what they looked like. Politicians, media sources, and others scrambled to learn about the Muslim faith and about the historical and cultural context in which to place and not place the tragic events. Critical thinkers around the world searched for ways to penetrate the meaning and causes of the events without seeming to excuse them. Teachers were no different.

Many teachers are interested in educating their students about the dangers of racial profiling and stereotyping of Arabs and people of Muslim faith and about the historical and cultural context in order to explore the tragic events.

Fortunately, many teachers have found help for grappling with these issues from one another and from the many resources from education and social justice organizations—much of it on the Internet (see last entry in Digging Deeper).

Inquiry and Activism

Professional teaching carries with it the burdens of its history, and it suffers from the low status that society gives to its clients—children. Historically, society has not valued children highly. Neither has it valued those who spend their lives with them. Servants, not professionals, cared for the children of the middle and upper classes. And for most of this century, teaching has been women's work or, in segregated schools, minorities' work. Community leaders saw women as being dependent on their husbands or other male authorities for leadership—not suited for making important decisions. The feminization of teaching also fit well with scientific management theories. Women and minority teachers provided schools with a class of low-status employees—those who occupied the bottom positions on the organizational chart. They carried out the decisions made by those at the top—male administrators.

In 1908, Felix Arnold published *A Text-Book of School and Class Management*, which explicated theories and practices that should guide school administrators and teachers. Among teachers' duties and responsibilities, Arnold listed these obligations to the principal:

> All instructions, when given by the principal, should be rigidly followed. They may be wrong. They may harm the children. They may be against high ethical standards. But they should be followed. The moment a principal delivers his instructions he becomes responsible for whatever happens when they are carried out. Remonstrance and protest are allowable. But as long as the instructions hold, they should be followed.[27]

Mr. Arnold's advice leaves little room for teachers who want to change the world.

Developing school cultures that enhance learning and social justice requires teachers' long-range involvement, rather than their participation in a primarily technical and rational process—for example, sitting on a committee that will disband as soon as a specific policy has been written or a problem "solved." Teachers must be able to engage with one another in an ongoing process of inquiry where they examine the assumptions and values that underlie their own practice as well as the school's.[28]

Teachers' primary visible task is teaching students in the classroom. This typically occupies five to seven hours a day, five days a week, but teachers must also spend time grading, completing administrative paperwork, supervising, tutoring, preparing for classes and parent conferences, cleaning, and telephoning parents. These activities must take place when teachers are not teaching. If attending to students and simply keeping up with lessons consume all of a teacher's time, little time or energy remains for professional activities. And a professional school environment should require that teachers have time for creative, energizing inquiry and learning. Time to read, to work with colleagues, and to participate in inquiry and reform activism may be structured into a teacher's working day, but it is more likely that teachers themselves will have to make the tough decisions on how to squeeze in the time for inquiry and activism.

When I began my first year, I knew that teaching involved more than just planning and delivering a lesson, managing a classroom, grading, and reporting the progress of the students. Teaching included administrative tasks; developing relationships; communicating with fellow teachers, administrators, and parents; and continually striving toward better lessons and instruction. However, I did not understand the constraint that these activities would have on my teaching. With so many constraints, pressures, and demands on teachers, no wonder the profession seems to be conservative and resistant to change. Even though I consider myself one who would like to see changes, I feel pushed toward conservatism because I have so much work. What I want to do on the inside becomes compromised as I deal with the day-to-day reality of the job.

I am finishing my first year of teaching, and these questions are only a few among a mountain that I still ask. Although I have not completely answered them, I know that they are important issues that I need to address if I am to achieve my goals for education. They suggest that in order to achieve my goals for education, I must continue to reflect on my teaching practices through a method of inquiry.

—Jasper Hiep Dang Bui
First-year teacher, English, grade 8

Teaching Together Can Foster Inquiry and Learning

In schools, as in any professional workplace, the most potent force for high levels of performance is a close association and identification with peers. This can take many forms for teachers; a common arrangement is team teaching.

At first, I thought that sharing a room with someone was a horrible thing. I wanted my own class, and I wanted to practice all of the wonderful theories I had learned over the past year. All of my plans were ruined because of a lack of space and because I had to compromise timing, scheduling, and work with this other woman. But, before long, I began to see that we had similar beliefs about how children learn and how we should teach.

The most wonderful thing about it was that we learned an incredible amount from each other not only about teaching, but about every aspect of teaching, including relationships with students, parents, and other teachers. I also learned that two is better than one. We have not only shared ideas and resources, but we are there to constructively criticize and encourage one another as we deal with the many aspects of being a bilingual teacher. It has been so valuable to my students to see that we two teachers are able to work cooperatively and learn from each other. This is consistent with my belief that teachers are not a source of all knowledge, but, like our students, we are learning and changing daily. We have also been able to build a great sense of community among all of our students. They know that there are two adults who care about them, and a whole other class of students who care as well.

—Susie Shin
First-year teacher, grade 1

As discussed in Chapter 6, Deborah Meier provides compelling examples of how teams of four or five teachers working with groups of seventy-five to eighty students can "generate powerful ideas" to drive curriculum and pedagogy in her book *The Power of Their Ideas: Lessons for America from a Small School in Harlem*.[29] In one of many examples of teachers' collegial work, Meier describes the school's graduation committees that coordinate and judge students' portfolios. These final exhibitions demonstrate to faculty, parents, and community members students' competence and readiness for graduation. This public assessment provides a core of authentic work that informs teachers' inquiry into their teaching and their students' learning.

Team teaching is an unbelievable experience. It is not easy; it requires more time to plan (or maybe Megan and I just have not figured it out yet). It requires patience and good listening skills. There are some days that we wake up on the wrong side of the bed, but that is normal. We have learned to deal with it.

Being able to work so closely with Megan makes me realize how important it is to interact, collaborate, and share with other teachers. We were able to work so well together because we believe in the same things about schooling, learning, and community. We have done really great and engaging activities with the kids. We can spend more time doing individual assessments (i.e., running records) while one of us is doing something else. We have a lot of fun together and I think that the kids do, too. It is just really nice to have another adult in the classroom. Our parent meetings are much more successful because there are two of us.

Megan and I have developed a truly special relationship. She has been an awesome person to work with. She has been my shoulder to cry on, my journal to reflect in, my partner in crime, and one of my most influential mentors.

—Wendy Herrera
First-year teacher, grades 1 and 2

Faculties as Inquiring Communities

> My high school is traditional. Most students are used to passively receiving information, memorizing it, and regurgitating it on tests. The school has some teachers who are willing to question and teach students the skills of inquiry, but the lines are clearly drawn. In the faculty lounge, I hear bits of disturbing conversation. Some teachers wonder why education classes are "teaching that school is not meant to teach students how to join the working class. That's what they need—a skill." These teachers are confident that their thinking (and hence teaching) is better suited for their students. A willingness to question and even challenge one's own thinking is not evident in the faculty lounge, and, consequently, it is not found in the classroom.
>
> —Name withheld
> *First-year teacher, senior high*

A productive school culture requires teachers who have the willingness, skills, and opportunities to continuously examine every aspect of their teaching.[30] This inquiry goes beyond the familiar search for "what works" to make conventional school practice "better." It is an inquiry that mirrors the teacher's own sociocultural teaching. Just as students focus on issues that are important to them, teachers' inquiry focuses on their professional life, including their underlying beliefs and their understanding of school values. Enduring democratic change is possible when people are accountable to each other, express themselves authentically, examine aspects of schooling that are typically taken for granted, and negotiate common understandings that support collective action.

Inquiry Has Different Starting Points

Some forms of teacher inquiry are quite specifically focused on curriculum and instruction. For example, teachers in elementary and middle schools who participate in Cognitively Guided Instruction (CGI) projects meet regularly in inquiry groups to examine samples of the mathematics work done by students in one another's classes. A central dynamic of CGI inquiry is the sharing and examination of teachers' own prior knowledge and beliefs about children's thinking and mathematics.

Over time, teachers learn about children's mathematical thinking.[31] As teachers focus instruction on asking students how they solve problems, the teachers become skilled at using children's talk to guide, or target, subsequent instruction. Teachers respond to the children's descriptions with appropriate requests for new information. This pedagogy rests upon sociocultural conceptions of learning—both for students in the classroom and teachers who are learning CGI. As teachers examine with their colleagues these conversations they replicate the same describing/questioning process that occurs in classroom instruction. These inquiry processes are quite different from the typical "in-service" or workshop to which teachers are exposed. Traditional staff development replicates transmission models of teaching. There is little scaffolding over time. Scant attention is paid to the relationships among colleagues who may learn something about innovative practices but may not easily share doubts, expose difficulties, or lend support to colleagues.

Some inquiry approaches are much broader in their reform goals. For example, the Accelerated Schools Project began at Stanford University in 1986 as a comprehensive approach to school change, designed to improve schooling for children in at-risk situations by providing all students with challenging activities.[32] The hope is to counteract the traditional practice of reserving such activities for only those students identified as gifted and talented. Accelerated school communities use a systematic inquiry process to transform their entire school. The transformation begins with the entire school community taking a deep look into its present situation through a process called "taking stock." The school community then forges a shared vision of what it wants the school to be—the kind of dream school that everyone would want for his or her own child. By comparing the vision to its present situation, the school community identifies priority challenge areas. Cadres, which are formed around priority challenges, study the problem, generate and test hypotheses, recommend changes to the whole school community, and assess the results of those changes. Importantly, the change process is a learning process—one that acknowledges and uses the unique cultural backgrounds, interests, and talents of all the people directly involved with the school.

In the early 1990s University of Arizona professor Paul Heckman's work with schools in South Tucson provided a fascinating example of the teacher and community development that can occur when communities of inquiry are central to the school culture. Over the course of the Education and Community Change project's six years, the schools have developed schoolwide structures and activities to promote inquiry and change. These structures and activities include convening regular, small, voluntary "dialogue groups" in which teachers examine their own practices and formulate actions that would further illuminate those practices. Instead of hiring "experts" to conduct traditional professional development workshops, the schools brought in an outside facilitator to promote inquiry by asking critical questions at the dialogue session, to engage in individual conversations with principals and teachers between dialogue sessions, and to work alongside teachers in classrooms. Educators have questioned core regularities of schooling such as the meaning of language learning and literacy, the nature of the subject fields, and what counts as evidence that children have learned. Such questions have led to mixing English- and Spanish-dominant children in bilingual classrooms, the development of learning activities focused on local neighborhood issues, and the exploration of new forms of assessment.[33]

Importantly, the way the Tucson project teachers work together resembles the way they want their students to work in the classroom. A pedagogy guided by sociocultural theory and social justice principles is suitable for all. The goal of fostering individual development within a common educational setting is appropriate for teacher work and student work. More specifically, these schools seek *practices* (such as detracked and multiage classrooms) to foster the goal of common development within a common setting. Second, they seek *activities* that foster information gathering, hypothesis building, dialogue, and experimentation (e.g., researching children's language use and asking for whom the bilingual classes were appropriate). Third, within inquiry projects, teachers look to a *broad pool of potential experts* (other teachers, students, and community members) as the source of vital information and insight to scaffold their learning. Finally, all inquiry activities culminate in some *action* (a product or performance that teachers or students share with individuals and groups outside of the school). In this way, the inquiry activities can bring the press of genuine social concerns and a relevant audience to shape authentic learning and instruction.

Inquiry and Power

It is not easy to define *inquiry*. At its broadest, inquiry is the way of democracy—a way to learn what other people believe and to struggle for common understandings. For similar reasons, inquiry is the mechanism of sociocultural learning—a way to find out what one another knows and to construct, with them, new knowledge.

Some people use the term *critical* inquiry. This adds a political dimension—the dimension of power. Power is always present in relationships, even in the noncoercive, cordial, and cooperative relationships among friends. Typically, when there is a very strong commitment to co-construct understandings (as there often is among close friends), power imbalances do not greatly disrupt the democracy of the relationship. But schools exist in a world of immense status differences associated with gender, race, age, employment, wealth, background, physical power, physical attractiveness, and so on. The goals of inquiry and social justice are closely tied to diminishing the effects of this power when teaching and when teaching decisions take place. Since we live in this world (where people do not and cannot simply leave their status and power "at the door" and proceed to learn and solve problems as equals) it becomes necessary to purposefully, perhaps self-consciously, create the conditions in which people can explore democratic teaching and learning relationships.

Critical inquiry invites and requires the explicit consideration of the power differences that exist in the room and in the broader community. This agreement to consider power and its effects—one could call it a ground rule—lends a different standard of *practicality* to the discussions and problem solving. Typical "practical" approaches result in a quick agreement to follow a program or solution. However, such problems are often "selected" precisely because people can agree to a solution that they (or someone) may already have in mind—usually a course of action that requires fewest changes with the least discomfort. Critical inquiry looks first to the knowledge, routines, and values that exist in the

school community and asks what new knowledge is needed and what alternative values might be explored.

A critical perspective is practical because it seeks to change the culture. Critique of this sort proceeds on the hope (as much as a specific time line) that when people inquire freely and democratically, caring will increase, status differences will diminish, and everyone's full willingness to participate will, over time, address serious problems.

Participating in an "inquiry group" has provided an opportunity for me to reflect with other staff members. Inquiry is an ongoing dialogue session among teachers, administrators, school support staff, and an external "critical friend." There are three inquiry groups at my school, and all but three teachers on campus participate in the inquiry process, by choice. I am part of the "Wednesday Inquiry Group" that meets every other Wednesday, from 12:15 P.M. until 3:00 P.M. During this time an "Inquiry Sub," trained in the arts, teaches my class. My group consists of seven teachers, the school nurse, and a site coordinator. The teachers involved represent all grade levels, kindergarten through fifth, and special education and bilingual teachers. The teaching experience of group members ranges from first-year teacher to those who have taught over ten years. The site coordinator is an "external critical friend" to the school who participates in all three inquiry group sessions and serves as the facilitator for the group.

Inquiry has allowed me to reflect on my teaching practices with a group of teach ers with whom I typically would not have the opportunity to sit and talk. It is a ti when I can meet with other professionals who are at different places in their prof sional careers but struggling with the same educational issues. Topics of discuss centered around our school's two "essential questions": (1) "What can I do to en that the inequitable pattern of student achievement no longer exists?" and (2) "W can I do to ensure that there is student and parent voice in my classroom?" Sti topics of discussion are extremely diverse: racial and ethnic issues, creating an taining a learning community, critical pedagogy, teaching tolerance, discipli school structure, parent involvement, and teaching "growth and developme group also reads and discusses professional articles and books and agrees to tion as a result of these discussions. For example, at one meeting we agreed t tention to how we used "choice" in the classroom. At another meeting, we agre attention to how we call on students in class. After every agreement [on group will observe] we report back our findings at the following meeting. The r ate a new springboard for discussion.

As the youngest member of the group, I am in no way made to feel least experienced. My opinions and viewpoints are listened to and validat expressing my views, even if I think that they will not be embraced by all of of the group. Because this is my first year in the school community as teacher, inquiry is a good place for me to express my opinions. I am n fortable talking in small, intimate settings. This experience has given m in a safe setting to reflect and find my "voice."

When I contribute to my inquiry group, I bring with me the expe cent courses saturated in theory. This theoretical grounding has p my development as a reflective professional because I am able

evaluate my classroom practice from a multitude of perspectives. I have had the opportunity to share books, articles, and my research papers with the group. The positive reaction and interest expressed in my contributions has enhanced my comfort and feeling of inclusion.

—Chrysta Bakstad
First-year teacher, grades K, 1, and 2

Inquiry sessions like those Chrysta Bakstad participated in give educators regularly scheduled time away from their classrooms to struggle through their collective understandings and create new initiatives. The sessions Chrysta describes allowed her and her colleagues to pose questions ("What can I do to ensure that the inequitable pattern of student achievement no longer exists?" and "What can I do to ensure that there is student and parent voice in my classroom?") that, in turn, lead to more questions and challenges to existing understanding. The group sought to forge a sphere of rough equality, where no one voice in the conversation dominated and each group member was viewed as someone who could push forward the group's understanding. Although the conversations ranged broadly, the core concerns stayed with learning and the struggle for equity. Not content to confine themselves to the collective understandings already within the group, Chrysta's group also read and discussed significant work in educational theory. As she describes it, such inquiry can alter relationships among teachers, alter classroom pedagogy, and foster new inquiry settings around the school. Inquiry group discussions can lead group members to examine practices within their own classrooms, experiment with new forms of pedagogy, and then bring the results of this study back to the group for further analysis.

Chrysta Bakstad teaches at a school with a well-established structure for inquiry. Yvette Nunez, however, is at a school that is just beginning to make inquiry a part of its institutional and professional life. Yvette's role in introducing inquiry to her school is just as vital as Chrysta's role in sustaining inquiry at hers.

Bureaucratic nightmares greatly affect my classroom instruction and student learning—testing students out of reading groups, attempting to transition students into English, and ensuring that students are not further distanced from social interaction with native English speakers. I have argued, using sociocultural theory, for doing what is best for my students. But because of the bureaucracy, I have also had to play the game to make sure my students get past the gates. In many instances where the assessment did not reflect the students' capabilities, I had to learn the system to use it to my students' advantage. The next step in my development as a social justice educator is to join the Placement Committee that studies how students are placed in classrooms, so I can express my strong beliefs about the necessity of mixing language

speakers in one classroom and bringing more students of various cultural and linguistic backgrounds into our school.

—Yvette Nunez
First-year teacher, grades 3 and 4

Inquiry groups confront (mostly) taken-for-granted conceptions of intelligence and ability, racial differences, merit, and deeply entrenched traditions of what is valued curriculum and appropriate practice at the schools. At every school, the efforts of inquiry groups to move toward more effective and socially just practices are countered not only by those who actively resist reform but also by well-intentioned educators whose everyday commonsense actions unwittingly reconstruct the dominant culture and schooling ideologies. Inquiry thrives on opportunities to act, and that action takes many forms. Becoming informed about one's own and others' practices, connecting practices with theory, and developing trusting relationships with colleagues are all examples of powerful actions. These are not "getting ready," or warm-ups, or first steps—these are themselves practical achievements that promote excellent learning opportunities and social justice for students.

Necessary But Not Sufficient

Are the best teachers those with the highest salaries? Not necessarily. Will a school that has lots of laboratory science equipment have students who learn science better? Maybe, maybe not. Will a faculty that tries to keep its expectations high for all students have the smartest students? Will faculties who engage in inquiry develop the most powerful strategies for working with students? Will those who connect respectfully with parents have smooth community relationships? There are no guarantees, but evidence indicates that schools whose reform efforts press in these directions are seeing positive outcomes for students. For example, one analysis of nearly a thousand schools undergoing reforms found that schools where faculties developed structures to promote long-term caring relationships, extended a rich curriculum to all students, and stressed teachers working collaboratively made greater gains in student achievement than schools with more traditional practices.[34]

Certainly, the conditions described in this chapter are necessary for a high-quality education. However, any one of these conditions, especially one standing alone, does not create high-quality education. Take, for example, the conflicting claims about lower class size. Some research suggests that smaller classes do not result in more learning, especially if nothing else in the classroom changes. Should we therefore stop worrying about large classes? Absolutely not! Smaller class sizes may be necessary for improved education, even though they may not be sufficient to overcome all the rest of what ails schools. One should also consider the concept of a *tipping point*. For example, having a few people on campus engaged in inquiry groups may not produce a significant cultural change, but perhaps it would take just one more group to shift the culture dramatically—to transform the school into one that is inquiry-driven.

We find another example of the necessary-but-not-sufficient principle in recent responses to students' poor mathematics performance on standardized tests. Research as well as common sense shows that the students who spend the most time studying math learn more math. In response, many schools have increased the time spent on math or have required additional math courses for high school graduation. But these steps may not produce significant results if the culture of schools stays the same, if teaching methods don't change, or if new classes are no more challenging. And if some math teachers do not receive better training, they will not use the added time to advantage. If some students (particularly girls) associate high math performance and academic achievement with being unpopular, or as being too hard, the time the school adds to math classes will accomplish little. Furthermore, an increase in math time may take time away from other subjects. Increased teaching time may upset teachers and exacerbate a salary dispute. Under circumstances like these, the move to improve math education could actually lower overall achievement. Clearly, spending more time on math may be a necessary ingredient for improving math learning, but it is not sufficient in itself.

Each of the school conditions one finds at work within the school culture—each of the regularities—is most powerful in combination with the others. When the school extends important knowledge to all students and focuses its resources and energy on high-quality learning, more students learn better. Caring school environments help keep students and teachers more engaged in school. However, to sustain lasting opportunities, high expectations, and caring, teachers need policymakers and strong administrators who support a professional environment of inquiry. Such a school environment, along with respectful connections with families, can create a school culture that fosters learning and social justice.

Digging Deeper

The resources listed below include scholars whose research provides a solid understanding of the school culture, as well as some innovative education reform projects. Each is struggling to bring high-quality teaching and learning and a spirit of democratic education to schools.

The Achievement Council in Los Angeles has developed tools and approaches to gathering and using data that bring the focus on equity to the forefront of school reform. Their strategy helps schools respond with a heightened sense of urgency about establishing new expectations and opportunities for their students. The Achievement Council can be reached at 4055 Wilshire Blvd., Suite 350, Los Angeles, CA 90010, telephone 213-487-3194.

The Coalition of Essential Schools, a reform movement that links hundreds of schools around the nation and was founded by **Theodore Sizer,** is currently based at Brown University in Providence, Rhode Island. Information about the Coalition can be found at its Internet site http://www.essentialschools.org. Ted Sizer has written about the ideas behind the Coalition in *Horace's Compromise: The Dilemma of the American High School* (Boston: Houghton Mifflin, 1985), *Horace's School: Redesigning the American High School* (Boston: Houghton Mifflin, 1991), and *Horace's Hope: What Works for the American High School* (Boston: Houghton Mifflin, 1996).

Linda Darling-Hammond is a professor of education and codirector of the National Center for Restructuring Education, Schools, and Teaching at Teachers College, Columbia University. Her research, teaching, and policy work focus on issues of school restructuring, teacher education reform, and the enhancement of educational equity. Her book *The Right to Learn* (San Francisco, Jossey-Bass, 1997) provides a comprehensive overview of research and a compelling analysis of how schools can work for all students.

Michael Fullan, dean of the Ontario Institute for Studies in Education at the University of Toronto, is a leading authority on educational change. Books of particular interest to teachers about school culture and reform include his *Change Forces: Probing the Depths of Educational Reform* (London: Falmer Press, 1993) and *What's Worth Fighting for in Your School?* written with Andy Hargreaves (New York: Teachers College Press, 1996). *What's Worth Fighting For* provides action guidelines for teachers and for principals.

Andy Hargreaves is a professor and the director of the International Centre for Educational Change at the Ontario Institute for Studies in Education. His book *Changing Teachers, Changing Times: Teachers' Work and Culture in the Postmodern Age* (New York: Teachers College Press, 1994) addresses the challenges to teachers posed by changes in the culture of schools related to the conditions of postmodernity. Hargreaves shows through teachers' own vivid words what teaching is really like, how it is already changing, and why. Hargreaves is particularly interested in how teachers cope with increased time pressures, feelings of guilt, and other emotions that changed conditions for teaching trigger. He pulls together his and other researchers' work on these topics in the *1997 ASCD Yearbook Changing with Heart and Mind* (Alexandria, VA: Association for Supervision and Curriculum Development, 1997).

University of Arizona professor **Paul Heckman** led an extraordinary inquiry-based school change effort in the barrio of South Tucson. The project departed from the conventional wisdom concerning school reform to create a participant-driven school-based effort. In his book *The Courage to Change: Stories from Successful School Reform* (Thousand Oaks, CA: Corwin Press, 1995), Heckman weaves together the stories of the group of teachers and the principal who reinvented education at their school and made it work.

The **Institute for Democracy in Education (IDE)** was founded by a group of teachers dismayed that the debate over public school reform overlooked the historic purpose of public schooling, that is, the development of responsible citizens. IDE is a partnership of everyone who plays a role in teaching and learning—classroom teachers, administrators, parents, and students. IDE offers a forum for sharing ideas, a support network of people holding similar values, and opportunities for professional development. The Institute publishes a quarterly journal, *Democracy & Education.* Its web site is www.ohiou.edu/ide.

Professor **Henry Levin** founded the **Accelerated Schools Project** in 1986 when he introduced the philosophy and process to two elementary schools in San Francisco. In addition to being director of the National Center, he is also the David Jacks Professor of Higher Education and Economics at Stanford University in the School of Education. The National Center provides leadership and coordination in the development and implementation of accelerated schools across the country. The Center also develops and tests innovations in training, evaluation, coaching, and troubleshooting and studies the workings of the accelerated schools process. The Center can be reached at Stanford University, CERAS 109, Stanford, CA 94305-3084 or on the Internet at http://www-leland.stanford.edu/group/.

Ann Lieberman is a professor at Teachers College, Columbia University, and codirector of the National Center for Restructuring Education, Schools, and Teaching. She studies and writes about the importance of teacher networks for teacher learning and school change. Teachers might be especially interested in reading *Teachers, Their World and Their Work: Implications for School Improvement* (New York: Teachers College Press, 1992).

Making Schools Safe is a training program designed to help educators create a safe and open environment for lesbian and gay students and combat antigay harassment in local schools. The program is not about sex, it is not about morality, and it is not "Gay 101." Instead, it is about safety, equal access, and equal protection. It is about making sure that every student feels that they can achieve their best in school in an environment free of hostility. And it is about taking proactive steps to prevent the antigay attitudes that may exist in a school from turning into harassment and escalating into violence. Making Schools Safe is an initiative of the ACLU Lesbian and Gay Rights Project.

Network of Educators on the Americas is a nonprofit organization that aims to "promote peace, justice and human rights through critical, anti-racist, multicultural education." Its Teaching for Change catalog pulls together books, videos, and posters for K–12 education from a variety of publishers that should help teachers go beyond traditional approaches. The Network can be found on the Internet at: http://www.teachingforchange.org/.

Seymour Sarason, professor emeritus at Yale University, first analyzed schools as cultures in the early 1970s. Recent books of his that provide valuable insight into the power of school culture, especially as it relates to school reform efforts, are the following: *Revisiting 'the Culture of the School and the Problem of Change'* (New York: Teachers College Press, 1996), *The Predictable Failure of Educational Reform: Can We Change Course Before It's Too Late?* (San Francisco: Jossey-Bass 1993), and *Parental Involvement and the Political Principle: Why the Existing Governance Structure of Schools Should Be Abolished* (San Francisco: Jossey-Bass, 1995).

Julian Weissglass is a mathematician at the University of California-Santa Barbara who directs the Center for Educational Change in Mathematics and Science. His *Ripples of Hope: Building Relationships for Educational Change* (Santa Barbara: University of California, Santa Barbara Center for Educational Change in Mathematics and Science, 1997) outlines strategies for teachers interested in working on equity issues together. The title and the theme of the book is inspired in part by Robert Kennedy's words: "Each time a person stands up for an ideal, or acts to improve the lot of others, or strikes out against injustice, he/she sends forth a tiny ripple of hope . . . and crossing each other from a million different centers of energy and daring, those ripples build a current that can sweep down the mightiest walls of oppression and resistance." The Center also publishes other reports and an occasional newsletter, *Many Waters,* for those working for equity in mathematics education. The Center can be reached at 805-893-7722 or by e-mail at weissgla@math.ucsb.edu.

The **World Wide Web** increasingly provides teachers with access to useful resources to help their students grapple with violent crises and fear they bring. For example, in the wake of the September 11 attacks, several established organizations added resources for teachers—including background information, lesson plans, and links to other Internet sites. Here are just a few of the many September 11 sites: Rethinking Schools (http://www.rethinkingschools.org/) has a nice collection of lesson plans and resources that provide teachers with different perspectives and factual information for teaching in the context of these world events. The National Clearinghouse for Bilingual Education (http://www.ncbe.gwu.edu/library/tolerance.htm#geography), whose mission aligns with efforts to promote understanding and respect for cultural diversity, has compiled a list of resources to assist educators in this difficult time. These resources can assist educators and others in preventing cross-cultural misunderstanding and persecution within schools and communities as well as promote healing and respect for differences. Educators for Social Responsibility (http://www.esrnational.org/) has revised *Talking to Children About Violence and Other Sensitive and Complex Issues in the World.* It includes suggestions for when and how to talk to children, ways to respond to revenge and retaliation fantasies, ideas for collective action, anti-Arab sentiment, rage, fear, and more. The National Association of School Psychologists (http://www.nasponline.org/NEAT/crisis_0911.html) has also posted some useful materials. Particularly helpful is that some resources have been translated into Arabic, Farsi, Korean, Spanish, Urdu, and Vietnamese. Advice to Educators from the American-Arab Anti-Discrimination Committee (http://www.adc.org/education/advice.htm) offers the ADC's help to school officials, student groups, and others who want films, speakers, or other help in discouraging hate speech, harassment, and other action that is anti-Arab and/or anti-Muslim. The Center for Contemporary Arab Studies (http://www.ccasonline.org/publications/teachmodule_whoarabs.htm) at Georgetown University offers answers to "Who Are the Arabs?" on their website. This "In the Classroom" section offers lesson plans to help teachers educate students on the Arab culture. The United Nation's "Cyberschoolbus"—a children's website—(http://www0.un.org/cyberschoolbus/

peace/index.asp) has a wonderful Peace Education component, including theory and curriculum.

Notes

1. Cultures permit a broad range of acceptable behavior in some matters, and in other matters, only a very limited range of behaviors is acceptable. A university's culture, for example, may tolerate a wide range of dress for attending class but sharply limit where students can smoke cigarettes. Both of these ranges or limits derive from the culture's general system of beliefs regarding what it must do to preserve its most important values and ways of life.
2. Seymour Sarason, *The Culture of the School and the Problem of Change,* 3rd ed. (Boston: Allyn & Bacon, 1996).
3. National Commission on Teaching and America's Future, *What Matters Most: Teaching for America's Future* (New York: Author, 1996).
4. From the Coalition of Essential Schools Internet site http://www.essentialschools.org.
5. See for example, Edward B. Fiske, *Smart Schools, Smart Kids: Why Do Some Schools Work?* (New York: Simon & Schuster, 1991), Fred Newmann, ed., *Authentic Assessment: Restructuring Schools for Intellectual Quality* (San Francisco: Jossey-Bass, 1996), and Linda Darling-Hammond, *The Right to Learn* (San Francisco, Jossey-Bass, 1997).
6. See Darling-Hammond, *The Right to Learn.*
7. John I. Goodlad, *A Place Called School* (New York: McGraw-Hill, 1984).
8. Jeannie Oakes, Karen Hunter Quartz, Steve Ryan, and Martin Lipton, *Becoming Good American Schools: The Struggle for Virtue in School Reform* (San Francisco: Jossey-Bass, in press); Theodore Sizer, *Horace's Hope: What Works for the American High School* (Boston: Houghton Mifflin, 1996).
9. Council of the Great City Schools, *Charting the Right Course: A Report on Urban Student Achievement and Course-Taking* (Washington, DC: Author, 1998).
10. This is the first of several excerpts in this chapter from a booklet compiled by UCLA teacher education students to honor educators and citizens struggling to promote social justice in and through Los Angeles area schools: John Rogers and Carolyn Castelli, eds., *Building Social Justice for a New Generation: Profiles of Social Justice Fellows from UCLA's Teacher Education Program, 1997* (Los Angeles: UCLA, 1997).
11. Linda Darling-Hammond, "The Right to Learn and the Advancement of Teaching: Research, Policy, and Practice for Democratic Education," *Educational Researcher* 26 (August/September 1996), p. 5.
12. Rogers and Castelli, *Building Social Justice for a New Generation.*
13. Ronald F. Ferguson "Paying for Public Education: New Evidence on How and Why Money Matters," *Harvard Journal on Legislation* 28, no. 2 (Summer 1991), pp. 465–498. Ferguson's studies are supported by other recent analyses showing that money does indeed make a difference, including a 1994 study by Larry Hedges, Richard D. Laine, and Rob Greenwald, "Does

Money Matter? A Meta-Analysis of the Effects of Differential School Inputs on Student Outcomes," *Educational Researcher* 23, no. 3 (1994), pp. 5–14.

14. See Gene Glass, Leonard Cahan, Mary Lee Smith, and Nikola Filby, *School Class Size: Research and Policy* (Beverly Hills: Sage, 1982) and Jeremy Finn and Charles M. Achilles, "Answers and Questions About Class Size," *American Educational Research Journal*, 27 (Fall 1990), pp. 557–577.
15. See Darling-Hammond, *The Right to Learn.*
16. Jeannie Oakes, Amy Stuart Wells, Susan Yonezawa, and Karen Ray, "The Politics of Equity and Change: Lessons from Detracking Schools," in *1997 ASCD Yearbook: Rethinking Educational Change with Heart and Mind,* ed. Andy Hargreaves (Alexandria, VA: Association for Supervision and Curriculum Development, 1997), pp. 43–72.
17. See, for example, Michael Knapp, Patrick Shields, and Brenda Turnbull, *Teaching for Meaning in High-Poverty Classrooms* (New York: Teachers College Press, 1995), Jeannie Oakes, "Two Cities: Tracking and Within-School Segregation," in *Brown Plus Forty: The Promise,* ed. LaMar Miller (New York: Teachers College Press, 1995), and new analyses of the impact of academic coursework on college entrance test scores reported in "Study: Hard Courses Help Urban ACT's," *New York Times,* 15 January 1998.
18. Rogers and Castelli, *Building Social Justice for a New Generation.*
19. See L. Steinberg, *Beyond the Classroom* (New York: Simon & Schuster, 1996).
20. C. Krop, D. Brewer, S. Gates, B. Gill, R. Reichardt, M. Sundt, and D. Throgmorton, *Potentially Eligible Students: A Growing Opportunity for the University of California* (Santa Monica: RAND, 1998).
21. See Claude Steele, "A Threat in the Air: How Stereotypes Shape the Intellectual Identities and Performance of Women and African-Americans," *American Psychologist*, 52 (1997), pp. 613–629.
22. Rogers and Castelli, *Building Social Justice for a New Generation.*
23. One of many recent books exploring these concepts for high school reform is Theodore Sizer's *Horace's Hope: What Works for the American High School* (Boston: Houghton Mifflin, 1996); also see Oakes, Hunter Quartz, Ryan, and Lipton, *Becoming Good American Schools: The Struggle for Virtue in School Reform.*
24. From the American Civil Liberties Union website at http://www.aclu.org.
25. Surgeon General's 2001 report, "Youth Violence: A Report of the Surgeon General," http://www.surgeongeneral.gov/library/youthviolence/report.html.
26. As cited in "September 11 and Our Classrooms," *Rethinking Schools*, 16, no. 2 (Winter 2001/2002).
27. Felix Arnold, *Text-Book of School and Class Management: Theory and Practice* (New York: The Macmillan Company, 1908), p. 22.
28. Considerable research has documented the power of collaborative work among teachers in the process of school change and improvement. See, for example, Michael Fullan, *Successful School Improvement* (Philadelphia: Open University Press, 1992), Judith Warren Little, "Norms of Collegiality and

Experimentation: Workplace Conditions of School Success," *American Educational Research Journal* 19 (1982): 325–340, Judith Warren Little and Milbery McLaughlin, eds., *Teachers Work: Individuals, Colleagues, and Contexts* (New York: Teachers College Press, 1993), and Karen Seashore Louis and Sharon D. Kruse, *Professionalism and Community: Perspectives on Reforming Urban Schools* (Newberry Park, CA: Corwin Press, 1995). Many of the ideas about inquiry presented in this section emerge from our collaborative work with UCLA colleague, John Rogers.

29. Deborah Meier, *The Power of Their Ideas: Lessons for America from a Small School in Harlem* (Boston: Beacon Press, 1995), p. 4.
30. See, for example, Michael Fullan and Andy Hargreaves, *What's Worth Fighting for in Your School?* (New York: Teachers College Press, 1996), Michael Fullan, *Change Forces: Probing the Depths of Educational Reform* (London: Falmer Press, 1993), and John S. Rogers and Robert Polkinghorn. "The Inquiry Process In The Accelerated School: A Deweyan Approach To School Renewal." (Paper presented at the annual meeting of the American Educational Research Association, Boston, 1990).
31. More information about Cognitive Guided Instruction is found in Chapter 6.
32. Christine Finnan, Edward St. John, and Jane McCarthy, eds. *Accelerated Schools in Action: Lessons from the Field* (Thousand Oaks, CA: Corwin Press, 1995).
33. The project is described in considerable detail in Paul Heckman, *The Courage to Change* (Thousand Oaks, CA: Corwin Press, 1995).
34. Valerie Lee, Julia Smith, and Frank Croninger, "Another Look at High School Restructuring: More Evidence that it Improves Student Achievement and More Insight into Why," *Issues in Restructuring Schools* (Newsletter, Center on Organization and Restructuring of Schools, University of Wisconsin, 1995), No. 9, pp. 1–9.

CHAPTER 10

Connections with Families and Communities

Cindy Bell

First-year teacher, grade 2

Teachers and schools are the official and most formal people and institutions that educate, but they are not necessarily the most powerful or influential. Other people and groups will magnify and diminish the possibilities for rigorous and socially just learning communities. Although it is everyone's (parents, schools, communities) responsibility to work together for students' benefit, teachers and schools have the special job and opportunities to make this happen.

Dozens of studies attest to the benefits of parent involvement on children's school achievements and outcomes. Parental "noninvolvement" gets much of the blame when schooling does not go well. When parents participate in their children's education, students' attitudes and achievement improve. Increased attendance, fewer discipline problems, and higher aspirations also are correlated with an increase in parent involvement. So, too, are teachers' confidence about teaching diverse groups of young people, a stronger curriculum, and more positive school and community relations. These positive effects seem to hold regardless of students' socioeconomic status and prior academic achievement.[1] Given these findings, many states and the U.S. Department of Education have mandated parent involvement programs to be introduced into schools' daily operations as a condition for receiving certain state and federal funds.

There is far less agreement, however, about what kinds of connections between families and schools are best, and about how good connections between families and schools might differ across types of communities. Hearing that schools, families, and communities share the responsibility for educating students can get very tiresome. *Cooperation* and *participation* are sometimes just safe, unarguable, "no-brainer" substitutes for genuine school change and improvement. In this chapter, we look at a number of parent and community involvement strategies. As we do in other chapters, we consider whether and how these approaches are consistent with sociocultural perspectives on learning and a commitment to social justice in schools. Perhaps most important, this chapter tries to push pleas for cooperation and participation into a territory where schools often fear to go—sharing, developing, and organizing parents to share the school's power and bring their own power to the common pursuit of social justice and quality education.

We begin by considering two dominant (and contradictory) complaints about parents:

- Parents neglect their responsibilities to participate and support their children's schools.
- Parents are disruptive and overly involved in schools.

We then examine four types of constructive engagement:

- Parents supporting the work of schools
- Schools serving families' and communities' need for health and social services
- Bridging the cultures of home and school through curriculum
- Engaging parents directly in schools through community empowerment.

Each of these strategies depends on teachers' good intentions and hard work, and each has the potential for positive outcomes. However, these strategies don't always result in a supportive and respectful synergy between teachers and parents. When schools focus exclusively on having parents act like teachers or when schools most often treat parents and community members as "clients" for social and health services, they risk positioning families as dependent on the school for expertise or goodwill, rather than as equal partners in their children's schooling. In contrast, when schools draw their families' and communities' cultural strengths into the school or connect with them as community activists, they can create opportunities to bring powerful schooling to students, parents, and communities.

Laments about Parent and Community Involvement: Too Little or Too Much

Too Little Involvement: Low-Income Parents Who Don't or Can't Care

A common complaint in schools serving high-poverty neighborhoods is that parents just don't care—evidenced by their failure to show up at school events, to return paperwork to the school, or to respond constructively to phone calls eliciting their help with academic or discipline problems. Often this lack of caring is framed more sympathetically, as when educators also note that many families *can't* really attend to the school's priorities, given the multiple constraints that poverty imposes on their lives. The complaints lament that school's influence cannot compete with negative influences such as alienated peer groups, drugs, and "dysfunctional " families.

Whether portrayed with anger or sympathy, school failure is attributed to a deficit of proper parenting or commitment to education, or to a variety of other causes that are beyond the school's ability to influence. These explanations of why some parents are not involved in schools have joined notions about genetic and cultural deficits that have been popular for more than a century. As recently as the 1980s, parents' failure to care enough to provide sufficient support for learning has been an official explanation for students' failure to achieve at school. Former education secretary Lauro Cavazos, for example, openly blamed high Latino dropout rates on families that have ignored the problem. He admonished Latino families to take the most important step toward improving education for Latinos by getting actively involved in educating their children.[2]

In fact, studies of parents' attitudes toward schooling consistently show something quite different—that education is a top priority for low-income, culturally and linguistically diverse families. These parents are unmistakably clear in their belief that schooling provides the crucial hope for their children's move into meaningful work and lives undistorted by poverty. How can there be such a large gap between common perceptions and actual commitments to education? Part of the answer lies in the different ways that educators and families in culturally diverse communities define an involved parent. Whereas educators stress participation in organized school events and parents keeping up with the details of lessons, parents often see their involvement role as providing care and support for children at home, encouraging them to do well at school, and instilling family and cultural values.[3] The result may be a school view that parents don't care about education and a parent view that schools don't care about kids.

Much of the challenge rests with finding ways for educators and families, who want much the same thing for students, to stop misreading one another's intentions and find ways to connect their efforts. But this challenge cannot be limited simply to schools holding proper attitudes about parents, or being culturally sensitive; and it goes far beyond "educating " parents to hold correct beliefs about the school. It takes concerted action over time. Teachers and schools must be willing to assume new roles and act in ways that are unfamiliar.

Often low-income parents who grew up in the United States have unhappy recollections of their own schooling that dampen their enthusiasm for getting involved with schools. Teachers may have few resources and little time to pursue parents who work more than one job, who have no telephone or transportation, or who don't speak English. Ugly racial histories in many communities make some parents of color reticent to be a visible presence at school. Immigrant parents may understand little about American schools—they may mistakenly (or correctly) assume that parents are neither wanted nor needed at school, or trust that their children and the school will make all appropriate educational decisions. Parents may have little formal education themselves or have attended schools where parents were not expected to take an active role. For many, language barriers make it difficult or impossible to communicate with teachers.

Schools may not be inclusive environments even for the adults who work there, and teachers and administrators themselves may not feel empowered to make important decisions about students' education and well-being. When that is the case, it may be difficult for them to advocate for parents' inclusion, much less see parents as allies.

Too Much Involvement: Middle- and Upper-Class Parent Power

Many educators levy a different, but equally powerful, complaint about parents—parents who are more typically middle class and more familiar with schools. These parents are too involved, care too much about every little thing (and often the wrong things), and use their considerable knowledge about schooling and their influence to get their way. Nervousness around grades, test scores, and traditional indicators of success (such as scores on weekly spelling tests) emerge even in the earliest grades, and worried parents can make teachers' lives difficult. These parents' involvement and worries about their children may do more than create distractions and burdens for teachers. They may also threaten educational programs and approaches for all students. And in schools with social class or racial diversity, misguided parental involvement can undermine efforts to provide high-quality learning opportunities to students of color, students whose families are poor, and students who have not been designated as destined for high achievement.

This is a side of parent involvement that few educators or researchers discuss openly, since it seems to run counter to the ubiquitous plea for parents to be involved. Because schools need political support—not only for funding and physical resources, but also for credibility—they often respond to parental pressure by acquiescing to their demands, even if it means giving special privileges, abandoning particular practices, or even reining in a reform.[4]

For example, teachers who follow sociocultural conceptions of learning and intelligence and principles of social justice must sometimes withstand the scrutiny of skeptical parents who fear they have much to lose if traditional practices are altered. Many parents who themselves did well with traditional instruction can become apprehensive if their children experience nontraditional classrooms.[5]

In Chapter 5, we discussed the "wars " over curriculum that have triggered many such parent complaints in recent years. We witnessed this recently in an affluent community, when a highly acclaimed principal became the target of parents because she instituted a progressive mathematics curriculum. Importantly, this principal took many of the recommended steps for parent involvement that *should have* smoothed the way for reform.[6] She convened a "transformation" study group of twenty-five community members, teachers, and administrators, paying much attention to developing a process through which difficult school and social issues could be discussed openly. She engaged the transformation study group in reading and talking about research, including the literature on corporate change. She used change ideas familiar in the business world. Despite the principal's efforts to craft a reform process that would include her vocal, upper-middle-class community, some of these parents formed an ad hoc group for "educational accountability" and presented a petition to the board of education demanding that the school return to a basic curriculum and traditional teaching. Some parents demanded that specific books be read and others prescribed specific amounts of time for certain lessons. The innovative math curriculum became a lightning rod for a group of fathers—many with degrees in science and engineering—who blasted the program as failing to prepare their children for the rigors of university. One former student, now attending an Ivy League college, wrote to the local paper blaming the principal for his average math grades in his college class. The principal conceded to parents' demands for more traditional curriculum, but that was not enough. She was fired.

In racially and socioeconomically diverse schools, parent involvement sometimes reflects the racism in the rest of the culture. Some white and middle-class parents' respond to their children's classmates of color or poverty with fear and prejudice. One first-year teacher found herself and her teaching partner in just such a situation.

Last summer, the district decided to install three portable classrooms to absorb the increasing number of children in the district. A group of white, middle-class parents immediately and adamantly opposed the new bungalows, fearing that they would bring transient children of low socioeconomic status from other, less desirable neighborhoods into their children's classrooms (which indeed happened). When the bungalows were installed over their protests, they attempted to rally the neighborhood to turn our school into a charter school. The dissatisfied parents derided teachers in public meetings and sent out inflammatory fliers to convince homeowners without school-age children to vote to change our school to a charter school. The fliers indicated that property values would rise if the measure passed.

Although the charter school proposal died—most teachers and other parents were happy with the school—the problems continued. My teaching partner had one of these parents come to her requesting her child's seat be changed because it was located in the same grouping as Rosa, a Spanish-speaking child who had recently moved here from Mexico. Rosa had done nothing but complete her work and had not been a source of problems in this grouping. The school climate affected our decisions most profoundly during a unit on the migration of groups of people—in this case slaves in the American South. . . . Excitedly, my teaching partner and I prepared everything for the simulation, including a paper rendition of the Ohio River; then, as we were taping it to the floor, she said, "What about the parents? I don't want any more phone calls to our principal. I just know they're not going to go for this." We canceled the simulation.

—Name withheld
First-year teacher, grade 2

What might these teachers have done to ease the parents concerns? Perhaps nothing.

Even when diversity is not an issue, parents often seek educational advantages for their children. In schools with ability-grouped classes, tracking, or with pull-out programs for gifted students, for example, savvy parents invariably (and understandably) want their children enrolled in the "best" classes. Because so many schools permit only a small percentage of student slots in high-track classes, many parents feel they have few options but to push to have their children better educated than others.

The remainder of this chapter provides an overview of strategies educators have used to involve parents in helpful ways. What's striking, but probably not surprising, is that these strategies focus almost entirely on getting parents to be more involved at school and supportive of the school's agenda—not less. Today, programs that assist schools to engage uninvolved parents, especially poor parents, abound. We know of no programs that try, specifically, to help educators manage powerful, overinvolved parents, but we have observed that such parents seem to depend on their *exclusive* role in the school. Informally, we observe that when enough parents are involved, and these parents are representative of the entire school, the parents themselves may effectively subdue the most bothersome, intrusive, or self-serving individuals and cliques.

Forging Helpful Connections

Since the turn of the century schools have attempted to involve parents following two perspectives, and these perspectives have typically reflected the mainstream culture: First, schools have tried to enlist parents to support the school; and second, schools have attempted to provide support for families. However, two other traditions have also persisted. Probably because they can be seen as *counter* cultural, they have never been as widespread: First, some schools have tried to become more compatible with minority cultures; and second, some schools or outside groups have tried to organize parents for broad-based social and educational change.

Parents Supporting the Schools' Agenda

Schools are most active when it comes to getting parents to support the school's agenda for students. Through all manner of communication—letters sent home, pleas at parent meetings, websites, and so on—the theme is that schools can't do it alone; parents must take an active role in their children's schooling. This traditional parent involvement seeks to have parents make sure that children come to school ready to learn—rested, well-fed, with proper materials, and with supervised homework completed. It emphasizes attending parent conferences, back-to-school night, PTA meetings, and other school events. It solicits parents' help at school—all the way from supplying snacks, making photocopies, and supervising on the playground to organizing and contributing to significant fundraising activities that supplement the school's budget. More recently, it has included parents as participants in school governance and other decision-making activities.

Joyce Epstein, research scientist at the Johns Hopkins University Center for the Organization of Schools, has spent much of the past two decades studying these forms of parent involvement and its effects. She and colleague Mavis

Sanders have concluded that although all schools want parents to be involved, most educators need help in developing strategies that work. They argue that such involvement can only be fostered if educators see families and communities as partners and frame their connections as an essential component of school and classroom organization. No longer an optional activity or a matter of public relations, Epstein claims, school, family, and community partnerships that are essential for student learning and success in school take time, organization, and effort to develop.

Through a recently established National Network of Partnerships, Epstein, Sanders, and their colleagues conduct and disseminate research, development, and policy analyses that produce new and useful knowledge and practices that help families, educators, and members of communities work together to improve schools, strengthen families, and enhance student learning and development. They seek greater understanding of partnerships that help all children succeed, though most of their work has focused on schools in high-poverty communities.

Epstein has developed a typology of parent involvement for developing partnerships with families and communities.[7] She claims that each type of involvement has particular challenges that must be met and that each leads to different results for students, families, and teachers. Note that most of these strategies focus on having parents and communities support and enhance the work of schools.

> *Type 1—Parenting.* Assist families with parenting and child-rearing skills, understanding child and adolescent development, and setting home conditions that support children as students at each age and grade level; assist schools in understanding families.
>
> *Type 2—Communicating.* Communicate with families about school programs and student progress through effective school-to-home and home-to-school communications.
>
> *Type 3—Volunteering.* Improve recruitment, training, work, and schedules to involve families as volunteers and audiences at the school or in other locations to support students and school programs.
>
> *Type 4—Learning at home.* Involve families with their children in learning activities at home, including homework and other curriculum-linked activities and decisions.
>
> *Type 5—Decision making.* Include families as participants in school decisions, governance, and advocacy through parent-teacher organizations, school councils, committees, and other parent organizations.
>
> *Type 6—Collaborating with community.* Identify and integrate community resources and services to enhance school and family practices and promote student achievement.

Joyce Epstein's work became extraordinarily popular in the last decade of the twentieth century. In part, this popularity comes from the consistency of this typology with the traditional ways that schools have engaged parents. Types 1 and 2 echo a more than century-long effort to strengthen families in order to improve student learning, school behavior, and socialization into mainstream American culture and child-rearing practices. In essence, these strategies focus on educating parents, as much as involving them.

Types 3, 4, and 5 are similar, but these strategies focus more on teaching parents about and engaging them in the actual work of the school—whether it be the content of the curriculum or the procedures of school life. These strategies have grown in popularity since the 1980s and the Reagan administration's increasing emphasis on families as children's first and most important teachers. This work is consistent with the central premises of schooling. It presumes that the school is a neutral place and that it is the job of families to develop practices that match those of the school so that their children can succeed. The U.S. Department of Education reinforced just this view in its 1987 publication, *What Works,* outlining the practices that promote school success. *What Works* asserted that schools depend on parents in the educational process and that no school can be effective without parental help.

Usually, schools select and follow parent involvement strategies that do not allow parents to have a deep influence over the core practices or resources of the school—even those schools that try to involve parents in decision making. For most parents, the main place they have to learn *about* the school is at the school itself. Further, schools are not likely to offer many opportunities for, or to actively teach, parents how to question conventional practices. Perhaps it is too much to ask of any institution that it energetically encourage a critique that will challenge the institution's own practices. To manage the contradictory goal of encouraging parent participation that does not disrupt the status quo, schools often draw a clear line between the "professional" work and expertise of educators and the "support" role that parents are expected to play. As one school administrator told us recently, "Parents are welcome when educators want them there."

Further, traditional approaches to parent involvement rarely look at the absence of family participation as a collective or structural problem—which is at least partly a school problem; rather, they frame lack of involvement as a problem of individual attitudes or lack of knowledge. Or, in the case of families of color or immigrant families, lack of involvement may be seen as one of many cultural deficits. Only Epstein's sixth type of parent involvement looks beyond developing a two-way relationship between particular families (taken individually) and the schools. Yet even here, when looking to groups and communities, this type of involvement sees schools and agencies as maintaining the role of experts, diagnosing problems, and developing remedies. Families are seen as the solution to problems primarily because they are the source of the problems.

"Fixing" families (to match or be successful in the existing school structures) is a limited strategy. However, we believe that Epstein's sixth type of parent and community involvement—schools serving families' needs—has great potential if schools can make a crucial distinction. This distinction is between *serving* families and *removing obstacles* that stand in the way of families using all the resources and assets that they already possess. This distinction can never be sharply drawn, but it will lead us, later in the chapter, to consider two additional categories of family, school, and community connections: bridging strengths, and bridging action. These are powerful opportunities for parent and community engagement because they reconsider the content of schooling and the distribution of power over schooling.

A Legacy of Services to Low-Income Students and Families

Today's social and schooling problems resemble those at the turn of the nineteenth century. One hundred years ago, approximately two million American children lived in poverty (today the number approaches fifteen million). The public's perception today is also similar to that of a century earlier: Communities are in trouble, children are out of control, and schools are failing to provide students with the right values. Within this rhetoric of decay, educators scramble to respond to the multiple worries about children and the culture.

In the early 1900s reformers in a number of cities advocated to make the public schools "social centers" that would open school buildings up to provide social and educational services to the broader community. Social reformers appealed to more mainstream community interests and established programs that brought a measure of relief to many poor, often oppressed, urban dwellers. Urban centers were polluted, unhealthy, dangerous, and congested, and residents had few common spaces for citizens to gather. In cities throughout the Northeast, schools and other public buildings began keeping their doors open for recreational and educational activities, sometimes dispensing to students and their families health information and care, food and clothing, and perhaps job information.

Today, many low-income area schools have forged similar connections with children, parents, and the neighborhood. They have developed before- and after-school recreation programs, and they offer government-subsidized breakfast and lunch. Often, school faculties, public health officials, social workers, police, and probation officers join forces to help students in various kinds of trouble or need. Teachers make regular home visits or lead activities at community centers to get a better sense of students' lives and to become known as members of the community.

Schools Meeting Families' Needs

Pathetic, needing charity, helpless, and a threat to the health, safety, economy, and morals of established citizens. This was the widespread view about poor and immigrant city dwellers at the start of the twentieth century. Schools and social service agencies (such as orphanages and other community relief agencies) certainly acted with compassion, but it was a compassion closely tied to the self-interests and perspectives of the emerging middle class. One turn-of-the-century reformer declared that "society must, as a measure of self-protection, take upon itself the responsibility of caring for the child."[8] Similar ties mark today's social and school services. Compassion, limited perspectives, and narrow self-interest all guide the charity we dispense. For example, the second-grade teacher quoted earlier whose school's decision to bring in portable classrooms evoked parent protests reported just such a mix of motives.

One mother approached me a number of times with concern about the cleanliness of a child in our class. It was true that Steven often came to school dirty, wearing the same or ripped clothes. This mother came into our classroom, and, while I was occupied with a group of students, put a pair of new shoes on Steven's feet. Steven came up to me and said, "Look! Mrs. Wilson gave me new shoes!" Her behavior was totally unacceptable to me, considering the possible reaction Steven might get from his parents when he walked through the door in these gleaming new shoes. My experience with his parents made me worry about several things: Would his mom suspect him of stealing them? Would she get angry, when her son told her that another parent had given him the shoes, that other people had meddled in their business? Would she see this action as criticizing her for being a bad parent and provider? All kinds of scenarios entered my mind. While Mrs. Wilson might have meant this gesture in the kindest of ways, I saw potential for hurt feelings and conflict.

—Name withheld
First-year teacher, grade 2

Individual acts of charity are just that: individuals acting on behalf of other individuals—often providing critical, even life-saving help, but perhaps offering only short-range help while diminishing another's dignity. Schooling is a public responsibility and an increasing number of school projects are exploring ways to make schools places where low-income families can access health and social services routinely and with dignity.

Today's Full-Service Schools

In 1994 researcher Joy Dryfoos published a book that became enormously popular among school reformers: *Full-Service Schools: A Revolution in Health and Social Services for Children, Youth, and Families.* In the book, Dryfoos documented a growing interest in more formal collaborations among schools, social services, and health agencies to serve better the multiple needs of low-income families. She argues that schools should use the resources of families, communities, and social service agencies to meet simultaneously students' academic, social, emotional, and health needs.

As Dryfoos documents, full-service community schools provide necessary services such as child care, health care, nutrition, and counseling—crucial supports for both parents and children. In addition, these schools bring parents, teachers, community members, and students together in a collaborative effort to strengthen education. Some full-service schools are part of national projects, like those affiliated with the Children's Aid Society and Schools of the 21st Century. Others, like the Molly Stark School in Bennington, Vermont, or the

Polk Brothers Foundation Full Service Schools in Chicago, Illinois, are local initiatives. However, all such schools enlist the aid of various community members and groups to provide health and social services for youth and their families, so educators can focus on their primary mission, teaching. They engage students in community service and service learning. Most are open most of the time—before school, after school, weekends, and summers—and see themselves as family resource centers.

Comer Schools One of the most fully developed strategies for creating full-service schools is the School Development Project created by Yale psychiatrist James Comer. Recalling his own childhood experience as an African American child growing up in a community that, while very poor, surrounded him with a safety net of watchful and caring adults, Comer has sought to create this experience for young people today. Because few such low-income communities of color have weathered the past few decades of urban decay, Comer has given the school the role of the supportive community he remembers.

Comer's "School Development Process" proceeds from a set of key assumptions. First, due to a lack of developmental support in their homes and communities, many of today's children come to school with developmental gaps and "experience deficits" that impair their ability to learn. Second, the School Development Program recognizes and addresses the *experience* deficit that can inhibit development; however, it does not accept the *academic* deficit theory that leads to tracking and lowered expectations of minority and ESL students. The third premise is that students can and are entitled to reach high levels of academic achievement. Fourth, academic learning rests on a foundation of development in six critical areas of human development: physical, psychological, language, social, ethical, and cognitive. Fifth, students with experience deficits will reach their highest potential only if schools provide them with the developmental opportunities they lack. And, finally, schools cannot meet this challenge alone but must mobilize other adults, including parents, to help meet the developmental needs of the students.

Schools following Comer's approach replace the traditional school organization and management with structures and processes that mobilize community adults to support students' learning. Parents, teachers, and administrators are coequal members of a School Planning and Management Team that develops a comprehensive school plan, sets academic, social, and community relations goals, and coordinates school activities, including staff development programs. This team creates critical dialogue around teaching and learning and monitors progress to identify needed adjustments to the school plan as well as opportunities to support the plan. A Student and Staff Support Team, composed of the principal and staff members with expertise in child development and mental health, such as a counselor, social worker, psychologist, or nurse, promotes desirable social conditions and relationships. This team connects all of the school's student services, facilitates the sharing of information and advice, addresses individual student needs, accesses resources outside the school, and develops prevention programs. Finally, through the Parent Team, parents help develop activities to support the school's social and academic programs. Studies of Comer Schools have found significant positive effects of the process on school climate, student attendance, and student achievement.

21st Century Community Learning Initiative During the Clinton administration, the full-service community school movement gained considerable momentum because it suited the national agenda for education reform. This movement speaks to concerns about high-risk youth and those with behavior problems at the same time it incorporates much of the recent work on high academic standards. Following the examples of Comer and similar community-school projects, the Clinton administration and private foundations gave support to about 6,800 rural and inner-city public schools in 1,420 communities—in collaboration with other public and nonprofit agencies, organizations, local businesses, postsecondary institutions, and scientific/cultural and other community entities. This program, the 21st Century Community Learning Initiative, aims to provide youth, parents, and community members with engaging and healthy activities in safe community settings. Schools can stay open longer, providing a safe place for homework centers, intensive mentoring in basic skills, drug and violence prevention counseling, helping middle-school students to prepare to take college prep courses in high school, enrichment in the core academic subjects as well as opportunities to participate in recreational activities, chorus, band and the arts, technology education programs, and services for children and youth with disabilities.

Proponents argue that this massive program gets us back to basics, back to active community involvement in raising and educating all of our children. An often espoused goal is to create a safe after-school and summer haven for children, away from the violence, drugs, and lack of supervision of children that permeate many low-income communities.

Individual Teachers Reaching Out Although it's far more difficult for individual teachers who are not in such schools to make connections that support their students' broader set of needs, some teachers do just that. For example, one first-year mathematics teacher found his teaching role entirely compatible with his concerns for students and their families.

My wife, a law student, and I visited a student's family to discuss immigration paperwork. They truly appreciate that we are trying to help them gain legal residency in the United States. Our conversation ends with so much appreciation and warmth. After we shake hands or kiss each other on the cheek (the way Latino families do) and exchange genuine words of thanks and love, we walk away with mutual trust, or what Luis Moll more meaningfully calls "confianza." I look forward to building more of these trusting relationships as I become a more experienced teacher.

—Anonymous
First-year teacher, high school mathematics

Across the country and each day, teachers like the one just quoted connect with families and communities to help them navigate complicated social processes such as obtaining health care and social services, negotiating the juvenile justice system, and grappling with immigration regulations.

Service, Power, and Deficits

Often, service-oriented schools, programs, and individual efforts are energetic, even heroic attempts to empower families to be effective participants within schools. They are guided by an underlying assumption—sometimes eloquently articulated, sometimes unspoken—that the physical, educational, and social health of families and communities must be self-determining and self-sustaining, which is to say that people must play active roles in shaping their own destinies.

But something is missing from this complex picture of service providing. It has to do with the oxymoron—the contradictory concept—of *empowering others.* Unexamined, this concept of empowerment may presume that one party cannot have power until it is bestowed by another. It may presume that whatever is good and worthwhile (adequate food, clothing, and shelter, skills, for example) necessarily translates into the power to access a high-quality education and a fulfilling life. And the concept often fuels two incorrect impressions. First, the school will readily give up some of *its* power. Second, parents must gain *their* power from the school.

The service-providing model matches well what some have called a "deficit view" of teaching and program design. We prefer a "bridge-building" model. Whereas "service" and "empowerment" are directional—that is, they typically flow from the direction of those who have to those who need—"bridge" implies no such direction. A bridge does not guarantee a two-way flow of respect, of valuing one another's cultures, and of mutual adaptability; but it can allow these processes and dispositions to thrive.

Bridging the Cultures of Schools and Families

As I pass through my community day and night, I feel proud of the countless strengths and positive characteristics it has. I observe hard workers. I see people that have so much imagination. I see a beautiful culture. I see so much life.

—Martha Guerrero
First-year teacher, high school social studies

Recognizing individuals' and communities' assets, strengths, and beauty rather than their deficits does not mean that one is blind to their needs or to their lack of real, meaningful power to determine important elements of their lives. However, if schools are to be useful to families who struggle for a just participation in schools and civic life, we must work to remove obstacles to families using their abundant assets and strengths. Involvement that builds on the cultural strengths and educational resources found in local communities untaps resources that are otherwise lost. These resources include strong loyalties and pride in culture and community; intense interests in a strong education for youth; clubs, churches, and social service agencies; and rich cultural and linguistic heritages. Residents may also have substantial mainstream "school knowledge"—skills, and even college degrees—that are at the heart of the traditional school curriculum.

This perspective—building bridges to people and their strengths—also has its roots in the early twentieth century. Jane Addams and other urban reformers established "settlement house" programs that built on and developed the strengths of immigrant cultures. Addams established Hull House in the midst of the Chicago's burgeoning immigrant neighborhoods. She and a group of well-to-do young women spent their days providing tangible and very much needed services. They cared for children, taught, nursed the sick, and helped immigrant families grapple with horrendous problems in their new lives. But simultaneously, dozens of classes and clubs met at Hull House with the goal of maintaining the immigrants' expression of their cultures, alongside easing them into knowledge of American ways and language.

Addams and her colleagues went beyond the pragmatic "basic skills" of reading and writing and included what they saw as essential cultural tools of mainstream middle-class life and dignity—including the arts, discussion, and political action. Rather than pitying her immigrant neighbors, fearing them, or treating them with a detached professionalism, Addams worked within the community, visiting her neighbors' homes and workplaces. Her personal interaction with her neighbors revealed her belief that social equality is a foundation for community life and individual expression.

Learning with and from Communities

The lesson we draw from Jane Addams's work is that connecting with low-income families is a virtue that includes, but is greater than, providing services for the less fortunate. Addams drew together disparate individuals and groups to form a community with community-minded norms. Hull House was a central gathering place, a community center, an education and research community, and a forum for political action. The norms and ethics of Hull House engaged immigrants in ways that fit their strengths, perspectives, and capacities to serve others. The distinctive feature of Hull House was not that it was a "haven" in a deficient community, but that it was a place where community members could strengthen their own community life.

Contemporary educational philosopher Nel Noddings would probably say that Addams's approach embodies an "ethic of care," in contrast to the "ethic of service" that drives many schools' interactions with families, especially in low-income communities. Importantly, an ethic of care expects all participants to find dignity and understand the conditions that affect them. While an ethic of service focuses on providing a set of fairly prescribed services, an ethic of care stresses the goal of fostering competence in students, families, and communities. A "caring" approach means that teachers and administrators do not assume they know what an individual or community needs. Rather, they listen carefully and act respectfully in response to the knowledge they acquire about the experiences, meanings, and preferences of those in the community. This empathetic response is meant to free educators from the common judgments made about families and communities, such as *incapable, uninvolved, not caring,* and so on. Educators who take this stance, according to Chicago educational reformer William Ayers, see their mission as understanding and responding to the circumstances that shape students' lives and conditions in their communities rather than fixing a student's or community's problems.[9]

Learning from families and community members enhances but does not replace teachers' skills and knowledge. Rather, this knowledge helps form the bridges that link school, community, students, and teachers. Borrowing from W. E. B. DuBois's notion of *sympathetic touch,* such learning relationships between teachers and communities allow teachers to reach back in time to acknowledge the history of their students' and community's social circumstances. In his 1935 article, "Does the Negro Need Separate Schools?" DuBois argued:

> The proper education of any people includes sympathetic touch between teacher and pupil; knowledge on the part of the teacher, not simply of the individual taught, but of his surroundings and background, and the history of his class and group; such contact between pupils, and between teacher and pupil, on the basis of perfect social equality, as will increase this sympathy and knowledge.[10]

DuBois captures two goals of the caring and respectful learning relations that bridge schools and communities: empathetic understanding and sensitive response. First, he helps us see that educators must come to know those for whom they care, followed by a response that demonstrates that knowledge. Second, educators must also embrace those for whom they care as growing persons with a future. It is not enough just to share the question, "Who are we?" We must also share the question, "What will become of us?" Unfortunately, few comprehensive school and community engagement projects evoke images of Hull House or establish conditions for teachers to exercise a *sympathetic touch.* Nevertheless, many teachers, on their own and with the support of like-minded colleagues, do reach out in caring and sympathetic ways. They work to establish relationships that allow them to gain a deep understanding of their students and communities, and they respond by demonstrating that knowledge in their lessons and relationships. And by knowing families and communities over time—by staying and returning to teach and visit and be visited, they care for futures.

Bridging Students' "Multiple Worlds"

Bridging the cultures of neighborhood and school, especially if they are very different from one another, is one of the joys of teaching. This challenge cannot be met solely by settling on the correct curriculum or injecting culturally relevant elements into lessons or becoming familiar with the students' home language, although each of these is worthwhile. The bridges we speak of are not anchored in cement on two sides of a chasm; the bridges are movable and flexible. In this sense, bridging is as much a matter of *navigating* among schools and communities as it is *connecting* them. Since educators are not necessarily more skilled at navigating other people's communities than families and students are at navigating schools, the navigational perspective is a great equalizer. When it comes to navigating multiple worlds, we are all uncertain beginners, and we need one another's help.

Psychologist Catherine Cooper has developed a model that illustrates a complex process of navigating multiple worlds of family, peers, schools, and communities. Cooper has worked with children of migrant farmers in California, immigrants from Southeast Asia, and other students of color. She shows how these worlds provide rich resources for students but the resources are either inaccessible or cannot be turned into usable assets. However, Cooper has also learned that most students have very high ambitions and, with assistance, may use these resources in ways that have high value in school, even if the school clings to many of its traditional practices. To help teachers support this process, Cooper and her team at the University of California-Santa Cruz have developed a "Multiple Worlds Toolkit" with activities and exercises to assist students and families. A wish to bridge the worlds of school and families is clear in the relationships that first-year teachers Mary Ann Pacheco, Zeba Palomino, and Benji Chang developed with parents.

Generally, Latino parents hesitate to approach or question teachers because teaching is highly respected. I made myself very accessible and expressed my interest in their understanding bilingual education, student learning, and the importance of their voices in public education. I also built personal relationships, made phone calls and home visits. I reinforced their cultural beliefs but made them aware of certain characteristics that they might want to help their children develop. For example, during parent conferences, some parents were concerned with their child's tendency to talk excessively. Many times, I reminded them that in higher education, the willingness to initiate conversations, participation in group projects, and dialogue were required of students and highly valued. I told them about the endless number of oral presentations, speeches, and debates I had to deliver throughout my educational career. I emphasized that they should not discourage their child's talk, but that together we could empower their children by helping them be responsible in [their speech].

—Mary Ann Pacheco
First-year teacher, grade 2

Most of my immigrant students come from low-income families, have parents who speak little or no English, and have little or no high school education. Lack of education, language barriers, and time constraints prevent them from making meaningful connections to their children's school. This does not mean, however, that parents do not value education. They simply do not know how to get involved. For example, when I called parents to invite them to Back to School Night, quite a few were surprised and pleased to speak with a teacher in Spanish. The school had never contacted them before. They were not aware of Back to School Night, and they had no idea of their power as parents in their children's education. They rely on their children to relay information about school, but often the students themselves do not have enough information about how to steer their education or they choose not to talk to their families about it.

My job is twofold: I must provide students with the support they need to learn math as they develop their English skills, and I must help students connect their home culture with their school culture so that they can understand and succeed.

—Zeba Palomino
First-year teacher, high school mathematics

I went to work right away to become familiar with my students' backgrounds. I observed and asked questions. I wanted to communicate a sense of respect for my students' diverse communities and put their backgrounds in the forefront of my lessons. I made it a point to be visible off campus, and before and after school. From day one, I talked with parents and guardians outside of class, and sent home the first of my weekly home letters, explaining and requesting a home visit. I eventually visited, and usually shared a meal, at eighteen of my twenty students' homes. In these visits I forged stronger home–school connections and uncovered invaluable information that would shape my curriculum and instruction. I communicated to parents and guardians that they were the experts on their child. I asked about their child's strengths and areas needing improvement.

I used to picture collaboration with families as parents coming to class to help out or at least helping students with their schoolwork every day at home. I now realize that this model was shaped by my middle-class background. My model did not account for working-class families or families at the poverty level, where parents and other family members are always working and cannot "collaborate" with me. My old ideas did not account for families who do have time but do not understand assignments because they were not educated in English. Now I realize that there are many ways to collaborate. Although they may not come in the way that I expected, these collaborative relationships support students in powerful ways.

—Benji Chang
First-year teacher, grade 2

Unlike the resources of middle-class students, the resources in many poor communities are not well matched to today's schools. But resources are available, and they are useful. Mary Ann Pacheco, Zeba Palamino, and Benji Chang all went far beyond schools' typical "parent involvement" strategies to find ways to bridge their students' multiple worlds.

Bridging through the Curriculum

A further step is to connect students' actual schoolwork to their experiences in the community. By engaging students and their families in finding and solving real problems that matter to them at school and outside of school, schoolwork can become less abstract and detached (and thereby more likely to be learned).

In Chapter 4, we referred to researcher Luis Moll's studies that have documented the "funds of knowledge" that impoverished Mexican American students have access to in their homes and neighborhoods. We described in that chapter how teachers Wendy Herrera and Megan Ward used such community resources as they developed elaborate lessons for their immigrant Latino students. In Chapter 7, we described the work of teachers who developed culturally relevant classrooms. These teachers, too, were practicing the type of parent and community connections we describe here.

Veteran kindergarten teacher Vivian Paley, in *Kaawanza and Me,* provides a powerful example of how middle-class white teachers can talk directly and honestly with nonwhite parents, colleagues, and children about their experiences, and incorporate their experiences, cultures, and knowledge into classroom practice. As Paley's work reveals, however, bridging these worlds and building community-based curriculum often requires that teachers learn about and confront the racism and discrimination that many families experience in communities and schools.

Paley's development of kindergarten classroom practices that were sensitive to and incorporated the racism that children and families of color experience in a dominant white society began with a conversation with a former student. As this young African American woman, now in college, shared her painful recollections of loneliness and worry in her kindergarten class, Paley's memory of her as a happy member of her racially integrated classroom was shattered. To learn more, Paley began a series of honest conversations about racism with her students' parents. Their stories were so rich and powerful, revealing enormous joy as well as sadness in family and community memories, that Paley invited parents to bring the cultures and experiences of her diverse students into the core of the curriculum. For Paley, the key was listening along with her students to the rich stories of family traditions and daily life. The *Kaawanza* stories that emerged and that are beautifully retold in Paley's book show how teachers as well as students can bridge multiple worlds of family, neighborhood, and school.

First-year teacher Christina Haug made listening to such stories an integral part of her curriculum.

Kenny, a Latino student, has a close relationship with his grandmother who tells him stories about family members, folk tales, and cultural legends. He is a valuable resource for oral storytelling. He also learns that his culture is not being ignored in the classroom, particularly since he is a racial minority. As he shares family stories, he becomes a teacher for our class, educating us about his home culture and language.

—Christina Haug
First-year teacher, grade 2

Our own experience over the past five years with the Futures project in Southern California provides an example of curriculum that has assisted senior high school students and their families bridge the worlds of home, school, and college going. The Futures project began in the fall of 1997 when our research team joined a local high school teacher in developing his ninth-grade humanities class into a four-year program that would help students navigate the pathway to college. Although the high school was very diverse, and included lots of middle-class white students, this class was made up entirely of low-income, underrepresented students, mostly Latino and African American.

Over four years, in addition to completing their college preparatory coursework, the students in the Futures class joined UCLA researchers in studying issues relevant to the students' own high school experiences and future plans. They investigated questions of student resistance in high school, "hip hop" and popular culture, the influence of parents on education, as well as the influence of language on educational access. They examined patterns of school success and failure, including how students are tracked into different (and seemingly natural) social and academic groups. In the summer of 2000, the students conducted research at the Democratic National Convention. This experience allowed them access to a wide array of national and local leaders concerned with youth access to education, the media, the living wage movement, urban civic engagement, and social justice. The student-researchers have presented their research to university faculty, graduate students, administrators, teachers, community members, and teachers in training.

In addition to making connections between students' lives and the academic curriculum of high school, the project also helped bridge the students' worlds of family and school. Monthly meetings, called "Futures and Families," brought greater family awareness of college pathways, and at the same time, eased parents' feelings of isolation from the school. These bilingual monthly programs helped parents learn about college access for their children, with activities ranging from discussions of admissions requirements and financial aid options to hands-on workshops on deciphering school transcripts and using the Internet to search for colleges. The meetings enhanced parents' awareness of the social and political obstacles to college (such as tracking and SATs). Personal stories of students and alumni of color, as well as school staff, helped these parents develop culturally relevant strategies for overcoming those obstacles. One immigrant father with little knowledge of the American education system came to nearly every meeting, despite his long working hours, because "I learn something new every time." Perhaps most important, the parents learned that they were not alone in their goals for and struggles with their children. As one mother said, "If I didn't have that program, I would have felt like I was by myself [in trying to get her child to college]."

Most of the Futures students have now moved on to college, but the connections among them, their teacher, and their families remain very strong.

Bridging through Community Liaisons

The bridging between home and school that occurred in our Futures project would have been far less likely without the support of an experienced and extraordinarily knowledgeable community liaison, Tere Viramontes. Viramontes, a longtime community member and former parent at the high school, could deftly navigate homes, churches, and community organizations, as well as the school because all of these settings were hers as well. She could share stories of her own struggles with school and family.

When schools integrate parents into the work of the school, other parents gain confidence and competence. Additionally, community representatives contribute enormously to teachers' understanding of families and can foster far more democratic relationships between them. Such respectful links between home and school help students develop academically, socially, and personally. Gina Rodriguez and Miriam Rogers are two other community-based colleagues that enhance the work of teachers at their school. Their stories do much to dispel deficit-laden assumptions about members of low-income communities of color.

> Gina Rodriguez was born in Tijuana, Mexico. Her family immigrated to the United States when she was five. Gina eventually attended and graduated from college, where she majored in political science and was active in a Chicano political organization called MEChA that focuses on gaining access to quality education and other resources. Gina now serves as a facilitator and/or coach for both parents and teachers at her elementary school. She aids in strategic planning, goal setting and gaining access to resources. She also bridges the language and cultural gaps between parents and teachers in order to promote respect and appreciation of one another.
>
> Gina helped parents to realize that they had a right to be involved in their child's education and helped them create a parent center on the school campus where they can come to work on current concerns and issues. One of the strengths of the parent center is that the leadership is shared among all parents. The parents meet weekly and organize major fund-raisers. They also organized the sale and promotion of school uniforms as a way to deal with safety issues. The school staff has become more accepting of parent involvement both inside and outside the classroom. Parent concerns and ideas are now welcomed, respected, and taken seriously, and Gina played a significant role in this transformation.
>
> Miriam Rogers is the parent of a fifth grader and president of the Will Rogers School's African-American Parents group (WRAAP), in addition to her official job as the school's community liaison. Last year, when troubling statistics showed [low academic achievement among] African American students, Rogers brought parents and teachers together to form WRAAP. In addition to

promoting academic achievement, WRAAP's goals are to provide parent voice, seek parent vision, strengthen relations between teachers and parents, and provide a place where parents can feel connected to the school. WRAAP is working to foster relationships of respect and tolerance between African American and Latino children on campus. WRAAP has set up a bicultural parents' meeting and plans to create other bicultural events, forums, and social exchanges. WRAAP has a hotline number for students' questions or concerns.

WRAAP also strives to empower students with information about historical and contemporary African American leaders and current events. Weekly, students receive the WRAAP Sheet that includes a quote for the week, a profile of one important African American leader and his or her contributions, as well as vocabulary pertaining to that leader's field. Recently, students performed at a Teacher Appreciation Breakfast sponsored by the WRAAP group. Students read poetry and literature written by African American authors, and they beamed in the spotlight as they performed. Miriam has helped some of the students in this performance who are thought of as problems in the classroom to express themselves in a more positive and creative light.[11]

Partnering with Families and Communities in Educational Activism

The work of Gina Rodriguez and Miriam Rogers extends beyond bridging individual families and schools. Rodriguez and Rogers also support parents' work as activists on behalf of socially just schooling for all the children in their neighborhoods.

A radically different approach to linking poor parents and schools is to engage low-income families and community members in critically examining their children's schooling opportunities and to take action that promotes change. It contrasts significantly with the more traditional parent involvement strategies described earlier. Rather than treating parents as lacking the attitudes and skills needed to support their children's schooling and developing programs to compensate (with parent education or mental health services), a community organizing approach draws from the collective power of residents to solve public problems. Advocates of parent engagement in community organizing look askance at programs that make families dependent on the expertise and goodwill of educators or other "service providers."

This fourth way of connecting with parents and communities may be the least mainstream—in terms of how many educators engage in it—but it also has a long tradition in American schooling.

A Tradition of Parent Activism

The PTA The forerunner of the PTA—the National Congress of Mothers—can be traced back to 1897. The Congress was founded to act on behalf of children in the home, at school, and in the world. From the beginning, this group focused its advocacy on issues that extended far beyond simply having parents help out with schoolwork or supporting their local schools. That early group voiced public concern over the juvenile justice system, the need for child labor laws, and for federal aid to schools. It promoted cooperation between parents and teachers, advocated for sex education, and lobbied for a national health bureau. By the early 1900s fathers were also urged to join.

In the early twentieth century, the PTA and the National Congress of Colored Parents and Teachers (the latter formed to serve children in segregated states) were well known for their advocacy, with an increasing focus on issues of health, safety, and nutrition. By midcentury they had secured health programs, school lunches, and regulations governing school bus safety. In the second half of the century the groups (integrated in the 1970s) turned to issues of drug addiction, the effects of smoking; child protection and toy safety, violence on television, automobile safety belt and child restraint legislation, the circumstances of children and families in the inner cities, and HIV/AIDS education.

Today, although the national PTA continues to take progressive stands on many of these child and education advocacy issues, local PTA groups often take a far more conservative stance on parent involvement. Most simply meet, raise money, and solicit volunteers to help the school carry out its agenda. While such work provides valuable resources in many schools, it is a far cry from the organization's early twentieth-century parent activism.

Community Schools A second long-standing activist tradition comes out of the "community schools" movement described earlier in this chapter that, like the PTA, began at the turn of the twentieth century. But unlike the PTA, efforts to create "community schools"—loosely defined as places that blur the distinction between communities and schools—have remained mostly local efforts. Only in the most recent years has local community activism around schooling coalesced into national groups that support and inform one another's efforts. We discuss these more recent efforts in a later section of this chapter. For the most part, however, efforts at creating community schools have bucked the national trend throughout the century toward bureaucratic state and national education policies, and away from grassroots control.

In the early 1900s many of the "social centers" included political activities as well as recreation, health services, and hygiene. Much of this activity—to the consternation of the elites who supported these centers—focused on socialist causes and advocacy for minority political views. Some progressive schools—particularly private and special laboratory schools—developed curricula that engaged students in studying community problems and advocating for solutions. However, it wasn't until the Depression years that public schools began taking up social causes. The social reconstructionist curriculum movement, discussed in Chapter 4, argued strongly that schools should develop community-based curricula that engaged schools and students in bettering local conditions. For example, Leonard Covello's tenure as principal of East Harlem's immigrant community's high school was marked by curricula designed to investigate and shape policies in the local neighborhoods, including a campaign for public housing.

It wasn't until the late 1960s that community schools focused on local communities' power over the school itself. In the midst of social activism around civil rights and civic unrest in many of the nation's cities, some local communities—particularly African American communities—sought to wrest control from the education professionals and politicians whom they viewed as part of an oppressive government that had frustrated the quest for equal educational opportunity. The best-known example of the struggle for local control of schools took place in the Ocean Hill-Brownsville neighborhood of New York City. There, activists employed lessons about civil disobedience and power learned from the civil rights movement. Only direct community participation, these leaders believed, would allow schools to shift from being a source of inequality to being a solution to it. Only if local community members were involved in selecting school personnel and curriculum would the schools be accountable for shaping the next generation in ways that would advance the community itself. Although the Ocean Hill-Brownsville experiment collapsed in the face of opposition from traditional power bases, including political interests, business, and unions, it sowed the seeds for a new type of parent and community activism. Today, low-income communities increasingly seek to hold schools accountable for providing high-quality education to their children. And while teachers and community members were clearly at odds in New York's struggle over who would control the schools, increasing numbers of teachers today are making common cause with activists in the communities where they teach.[12]

In the twenty-first century, this new way of connecting with families and communities may prove to be a powerful strategy for social justice school reform.

Contemporary Organizing for School Reform

Truly transformative teaching must be coupled with activism and resistance in the larger community. I have been involved with an activist organization that fights for equitable school reform. Such organizations represent opportunities to create meaningful alliances with other educators, parents, and students. It is not enough for me to encourage my students to become more active. I must walk the talk myself.

—Matthew Eide
First-year teacher, high school history

Researchers Susan Stall and Randy Stoecker define community organizing as "the work that occurs in local settings to empower individuals, build relationships, and create action for social change." It entails building relationships among people that can sustain them through difficult struggles and support political action. Essentially, community organizing "is the process of building power that includes people with a problem in defining their community, defining the problems they wish to address, the solutions they wish to pursue, and the methods they will use to accomplish their solutions."[13]

Grassroots community organizations use somewhat different approaches, depending on the tradition that influences them. These traditions include Saul Alinksy's "self-interest" based model of public confrontation between organized "have-nots" and powerful, more advantaged "targets" whose concessions can provide solutions to community problems, along with more recent adaptations of Alinsky's approach. Other, less confrontational traditions come from women's efforts to extend caring communities beyond the confines of the home. For example, African American women's efforts to preserve home and community during slavery were precursors for women's efforts in the civil rights movement to transform existing local networks into a political force for social change. At the turn of the twentieth century, white women such as Jane Addams sought to extend the protections afforded by homes and families to low-income and immigrant neighborhoods by improving social networks, providing social services, and enriching community life. These feminist organizing traditions have contemporary counterparts in mobilization efforts for safer neighborhoods, child care, and youth programs. Despite their differences, however, most community organizing shares the perspective that power for change exists within networks of people who identify with common ideals and who can engage in social action based on those ideals.

In the past decade, a number of local grassroots organizations—focused originally on issues of housing, jobs, and public safety—have turned their attention to school improvement. Perhaps the best known of these efforts has taken place in Texas, where the Industrial Areas Foundation (IAF) joined forces with educators to improve achievement in public schools in low-income neighborhoods. The IAF, a national group begun over fifty years ago by Saul Alinsky, is a national network of broad-based multiethnic interfaith organizations in economically poor and moderate-income communities. The Texas school reform example reveals the possibilities of educators and parents joining forces and exercising power over schooling, as they initiate services and respectful connections between communities and schools.

Relationships, New Understandings, and Action Analysts of community organizing traditions help us understand how community members come together to act on their common interests. Former civil rights and farmworker organizer Marshall Ganz synthesizes this work into three components of grassroots organizing: relationships, common understandings, and action. Each of these components helps to create bridges among schools, families, and communities.

First, organizers of community-school initiatives spend considerable time talking with parents and educators to learn about their *personal* concerns for their children's school. Then, within this culture of conversation people form relationships based on *common* concerns. IAF organizers, for example, conduct a "situational audit," that gives everyone in the school the opportunity to identify its positive and negative aspects. They identify areas of overlapping self-interest with other parents and, if possible, with educators at a school. Organizers also sponsor "neighborhood walks," in which parents and educators gather at a school and then go out to visit parents at home; the aim is to engage families in conversation about their concerns for the school and community.

Organizers also develop relationships through new and existing networks. Individuals draw from the power of the networks—often described as social capital—and, in turn, contribute to the power of the networks. This individual and collective power becomes a resource for social action. A number of theorists have proposed that belonging to a community creates norms of reciprocity. That is, when people belong to the same social circle, they can count on one another to keep commitments and work on one another's behalf. Leadership development is another key to developing power in these relationships. As networks grow and mature, organizers let go of the leadership. The goal is to locate the responsibility for solving problems in the group and in the leaders within it.

Steady attention to relationships makes it safe for people to trust one another—especially during those important stages when new members might not know one another well or understand fully one another's backgrounds and strengths. Understanding—a second key feature of community organizing—develops as organizers and community leaders shape opportunities for people to engage one another in dialogue about their situations and generate more hopeful alternatives. Such dialogue is constructive. That is, participants are not rushed into simply accepting others' descriptions, analyses, and solutions for problems; they build their own understandings. And because this work is a collective effort, problems that clearly have their origins beyond the reach of individuals are reframed as community, social, or collective problems. This new understanding adds to individuals' identities by fostering a collective identity as people define their shared interests. With common understandings, acting together is not a "strategy" for accomplishing individual concerns; rather, joint action makes sense because the groups' interests and individual interests are seen as indistinguishable. The dialogic pedagogy developed by Paulo Freire in his work with Brazilian peasants, described in Chapter 7, is probably the best example of such generative dialogue. Groups construct a story of who they are, what they do, and why they do it. That "story" points to ways for the group to realize the more hopeful possibilities they've framed.

Third, the emergence of an *activist* community begins when groups pursue a particular objective—often small at first. Perhaps the group acts on a grievance long held by individuals but newly articulated as a jointly held claim. Now the community can strategize about how to use resources at the right moment to achieve its goals. These focused campaigns achieve what the community might call tangible "progress," but they also develop the community itself and increase its capacity to take on larger goals.

All three of these dimensions, relationships, new understandings, and actions, enable communities to gain and use new resources. They both create and result from networks, they frame a story about the network's identity and purpose, and they develop a program of action that mobilizes and expends resources to advance the community's interests.

The Texas Alliance Schools Overall, the Alliance School Initiative in Texas points out sharp differences between school-controlled improvement and parent participation efforts and those that are strongly supported by organizations and leadership outside the schools. In the Alliance Initiative parents communicate first with one another regarding what they want for their children and expect from schools. Organizers who work for local organizations teach parents, teachers, and administrators how to initiate one-on-one conversations about their visions for school improvement. They encourage parents to think differently about the possibilities for their children and to raise questions. They organize door-to-door visits for teachers and parents to meet community members and invite them to school meetings. Alliance schools include parents on core leadership teams making decisions about school improvement. The organizers prepare parents for participation by training them in such matters as how to read a school budget and speak before the school board. Project director Ernesto Cortes explains the rationale behind the Texas project:

> When parents and community members are truly engaged, they are organized to act on their own values and visions for their children's future. They do not just volunteer their time for school activities or drop their opinions in the suggestion box. They initiate action, collaborating with educators to implement ideas for reform. This kind of engagement can only happen through community institutions—public schools, churches, civic associations. These institutions provide the public space where people of different backgrounds connect with one another, listen to each other's stories, share concerns; this is where they argue, debate, and deliberate. In these institutions, individuals transcend the boundaries of their private lives to form public relationships. In the context of these public relationships, parents and community members can initiate conversations around their core concerns and values. These conversations go beyond the discussion of surface problems and complaints. Through these conversations, people develop the trust and consensus needed for action.[14]

UCLA's Parent Curriculum Project Former math teacher Laila Hasan, now a doctoral student at UCLA, has implemented an approach to parent organizing that combines the principles of community organizing with helping parents gain a solid understanding of high-quality teaching and learning. Hasan has worked with parents in very low-income neighborhoods where the once–African American community is being rapidly replaced by immigrant, Spanish-speaking families. The community has some of the state's most dismal schools. Large numbers of underqualified teachers, constant turnover in the ranks of school administrators, and limited curriculum offerings limit students' and families' capacity to grapple with problems of poverty, unemployment, gang- and drug-related violence, and racial tension. School dropout rates are extremely high, achievement rates are extremely low, and college going is a rarity.

During the seminar and after, Hasan and the parents engage in processes explicitly aimed at developing relationships, constructing a collective story of who they are and what they hope to accomplish, and taking action on behalf of their children and their children's schools. Throughout, the parents themselves become the initiators and leaders of the work, rather than acting like traditional students or clients.

Hasan's project begins by engaging twenty to thirty parents at a time in a ten-week seminar in which parents examine the practices at their children's schools and, at the same time, have firsthand experiences with very high quality teaching and learning in academic subjects. In English and Spanish, expert teachers guide the parents through the writing process, science laboratory experiments, algebraic thinking, and historical inquiry. They learn about standardized testing, as well as grading and tracking practices. They learn what to look for when observing in classrooms, and they practice asking hard questions of teachers and principals. They gain experience comparing what they learn in the seminar with what occurs in their children's classrooms. As a culminating project they design and carry out an action project that includes other parents also committed to gaining high-quality teaching and learning in the community's schools. With over 300 program graduates, what began as a series of projects has developed into a significant activist parent presence—they recently became their own nonprofit, community-based organization.

The theory at work here, much like that in the Alliance Schools, is that parent advocacy must be based on an understanding of what a really good school provides, what critical thinking and high standards for learning mean, and what high-quality teaching looks like. The parents come to understand what a really good school looks like, what their rights as parents are, and how they can effect the necessary change and leadership to accomplish it.

After considerable learning and action, the parent group supported one of its own members—a Latina mother—to run for a seat on the school board in a recent election. She won. Her power as an activist parent has now been augmented by her new power as an elected trustee of the school system. What's more, she has an active and powerful parent constituency to assist her as she attempts to transform her growing knowledge of good schooling into policies that will support all the community's children.

Cross-Class and Cross-Race Parent Activist Groups—Parents for Public Schools Both the Alliance School Project in Texas and the UCLA Parent Project focus exclusively on communities and schools that are low income and of color. That's not surprising, since these are the types of neighborhoods where parents are least likely to be involved at school, and where activism for school improvement is most desperately needed. However, there are some examples of cross-class and cross-race organizing efforts for school reform. Perhaps the most notable is Parents for Public Schools (PPS), which began as a local initiative in 1989 in Jackson, Mississippi. A group of twenty parents decided to mobilize parents who reflected the full diversity of their town to build strong public schools and a healthier, more vital community out of their Southern city that had been badly torn by school segregation, desegregation, and white flight.

The Jackson group began by recruiting families one by one. Through information sessions in their homes, they began to cultivate a new sense of the importance of strong public schools to the community and to create an awareness of the sound education being offered in the pubic schools of Jackson. Over time PPS brought racial balance to four primary schools in northeast Jackson and promoted a $35 million bond issue—the first to pass since desegregation.

Soon after the Jackson victory—which was featured in the national news media—parents in other communities began forming PPS chapters, and the organization now has a organizational presence in fifteen states. While individual chapter activities and goals vary, all are committed to public school enrollment, meaningful parent and community involvement, and districtwide improvement.

What's most striking is that the first PPS chapter has brought parents together across race and class lines to combat white, middle-class flight from the public schools, and to publicize the economic, social, and business development benefits that come to cities with strong public schools. In other cities—large and small, urban and rural—PPS chapters have addressed issues such as school safety, building racial and economic bridges, improving facilities, expanding and strengthening curricula, and increasing positive media coverage. What binds these groups together is the belief that parents must become committed owners of, rather than passive consumers in, public schools. Moreover, PPS members must commit to advocate for the improvement of public education for every child, not just their own.

Teachers as Community Activists Teachers are rarely leaders of these organizing approaches to parent and community involvement in education. Yet, increasingly, community organizations are reaching out to teachers who are committed to social justice education to add their voices and their power to that of parents. Many teachers have also discovered that the strategies of community organizing—building relationships, forging common meanings about teaching and learning, and taking action together—are powerful ways for forging connections with parents. First-year teacher Martha Guerrero describes how she integrates such activities into her work as a teacher.

I am not new to East Los Angeles. I have established a relationship with the community as an organizer. I hope that the relationship that I cultivate with my students and parents will allow me to organize community members in the future. I believe that teachers should develop these genuine relationships with the community in order to make changes in the educational and political system.

I interact frequently with my students and their families outside of the classroom. I did countless home visits. I take my students to conferences and work with them on community related issues. I helped organize [one conference] with the theme "Rights Now Youth Conference: Speaking Truth to Power." At the conference students attended workshops related to education and the criminal justice system. We also attended a

Coalition for Educational Justice conference that focused on overcrowding in inner city schools and high-stakes standardized testing.

—Martha Guerrero
First-year teacher, high school social studies

Whose Agenda Is It?

An organizing approach to parent involvement stems from and leads to recognizing that schools belong to poor parents and communities, as much as they do to wealthier and more powerful ones. This is a difficult task. But it is ultimately neither respectful nor effective for educators to ignore the potential power of families as advocates for children. Community liaisons like Gina Rodriguez, and projects like the Texas Alliance Schools and the UCLA Parent Curriculum Project, along with individual teachers have all developed strategies to help parents of lower-status students speak with as much confidence and sense of entitlement about what they want for their children as the parents of high-status children usually have when they speak.

However, such efforts must enable parents—poor, middle class, and rich—to exercise their rightful power over schooling as citizens who are responsible for the education of all children, not simply as parents looking out for their own children's interests. This means that parents who educators consider to be *too* involved, as well as those who seem not involved enough, must develop a very different concept of involvement. They must do more than express their willingness to meet at the same table with parents of different racial groups and socioeconomic positions. Simply coming together to talk isn't enough. People at the table must learn. And then they must act—as citizens.

None of this means that there is no longer a legitimate role for professional educators. In fact, even the most activist citizen parents do not easily develop the knowledge and pedagogical expertise that we've outlined in this book as essential to high quality and socially just education. That is the purview of professional educators who, in partnership with activist citizens, make sure that all voices are represented and heard in ways that are inseparable from good teaching, a safe campus, social justice, and other absolute schooling basics.

Digging Deeper

The scholars and educators listed below all combine research and activism in the attempt to craft constructing positive relationships among families, communities, and schools.

Martin Blank is the Director for Community Collaboration at the Institute for Educational Leadership. He leads the Coalition for Community Schools (CCS) that works to improve education and help students learn and grow while supporting and strengthening their families and communities. Community schools bring together many partners to offer a range of supports and opportunities to children, youth, families, and communities—before, during, and after school, seven days a week. They make schools the center of communities in which children, youth, and families have access to an array of supports and opportunities that improve student learning, strengthen families, and build community. CCS's mission is to mobilize the resources and capacity of multiple sectors and institutions to create a united movement for community schools by sharing information about successful community school policies, programs, and practices; building broader public understanding and support for community schools; informing public- and private-sector policies to strengthen community schools; and developing sustainable sources of funding for community schools. For more information about CCS, visit http://www.communityschools.org/. Blank's book, *Together We Can: A Guide for Crafting a Profamily System of Education and Human Services* (Washington, DC: U.S. Government Printing Office, 1993) is considered a classic text in school-community relations.

James Comer, a professor of pyschiatry in the Yale Medical School, has written a number of books and articles that outline his rationale and approach to the Community Development School process. *In Child by Child: The Comer Process for Change in Education* (edited by James P. Comer, Norris M. Haynes, Edward T. Joyner, and Michael Ben-Avie [New York: Teachers College Press, 1999]), community members, business leaders, school board members, superintendents, principals, teachers, and parents across the country share their experiences as they have tried to create school communities in which all adults help young people develop and learn. In *Waiting for a Miracle: Why Schools Can't Solve Our Problem—And How We Can* (New York: Dutton, 1997), Comer argues that the deteriorated state of America's public schools is a reflection of problems at our cultural core that must be addressed simultaneously with school change. He discusses the causes of these problems and presents a viable approach to resolving them—an approach that focuses on the crucial roles of children, family, and community. Comer provides a detailed blueprint of how sensitively designed programs can and have already begun to make dramatic differences in the classroom.

Joyce L. Epstein is the director of the Center on School, Family, and Community Partnerships and the principal research scientist and codirector of the School, Family, and Community Partnership Program of the Center for Research on the Education of Students Placed at Risk (CRESPAR) and teaches courses in sociology at Johns Hopkins University. Dr. Epstein has over one hundred publications on the effects of school, classroom, family, and peer environments on student learning and development, with many focusing on school and family connections. Her book *School, Family, and Community Partnerships: Your Handbook for Action* (Thousand Oaks, CA: Corwin Press, 1997) guides schools, districts, and states to develop and maintain programs of partnership. Another book, *School and Family Partnerships: Preparing Educators and Improving Schools* (Boulder, CO: Westview Press, 2000), is designed for preservice and advanced education courses.

Pedro Noguera is the Judith K. Dimon Professor of Communities and Schools at the Harvard Graduate School of Education. Previously he was a professor in Social and Cultural Studies at the Graduate School of Education and the director of the Institute for the Study of Social Change at the University of California, Berkeley. Noguera's research focuses on the ways in which schools respond to social and economic forces within the urban environment. He has engaged in collaborative research with several large, urban school districts, and he has published and lectured on topics such as youth violence, race relations within schools, the potential impact of school choice and vouchers on urban public schools, and secondary issues resulting from desegregation in public schools. His articles on these topics have appeared in several leading research journals and edited volumes. Noguera has also done extensive field research and published several articles on the role of education in political and social change in the Caribbean. Noguera served as an elected member of the Berkeley School Board from 1990 to 1994. He has also served as a member of the U.S. Public Health Service Centers for Disease Control Taskforce on Youth Violence, and as chair of the Committee on Ethics in Research and Human Rights for the American Educational Research Association. Noguera was a K–12 classroom teacher for several years and continues to teach part-time in high schools. A sample of Noguera's scholarship can be found in "Where Race and Class Are Not an Excuse," in *A Simple Justice,* edited by William Ayers, Michael Klonsky, and Gabrielle Lyon (New York: Teachers College Press, 2000).

The Right Question Project, Inc. (RQP), a nonprofit organization based in Cambridge, Massachusetts, has developed, field-tested, refined, and shared a different strategy that assists parents and local advocacy groups to learn the skill in formulating questions that focus their advocacy efforts with public institutions. The Right Question Project believes that its strategy—now used in many communities—helps low- and moderate-income people in their encounters with the various outposts of government (including public schools, welfare agencies, the health care system, housing programs, homeless shelters, job training centers, and many other publicly supported agencies, programs, and institutions) in ways that traditional parent involvement does not. First, it helps people to "begin at the beginning" with self-advocacy. That is, ordinary citizens learn to advocate for themselves as they encounter public institutions, agencies, and programs. Second, participants learn to "see a larger system." They move beyond advocacy in one setting to begin to navigate their way through complex bureaucratic systems. Third, they come to "focus on key decisions." Acting on their own and in collaboration with others, they identify and act on key decisions that affect them. Fourth, the strategy assists them to "effect change in institutions and systems." The project calls their process of converting residents into effective citizens "Microdemocracy."

Dennis Shirley is associate dean and a professor of Teacher Education at the Lynch School of Education at Boston College. His book *Community Organizing for Urban School Reform* (Austin: University of Texas Press, 1997) traces the IAF community organizing work in Texas schools. His newest book, *Valley Interfaith and School Reform Organizing for Power in South Texas* (Austin: University of Texas Press, 2002), explores how community organizing and activism in support of public schools in one of America's most economically disadvantaged regions, the Rio Grande Valley of South Texas, has engendered impressive academic results. Shirley focuses the book around case studies of three schools that have benefited from the reform efforts of a community group called Valley Interfaith, which works to develop community leadership and boost academic achievement. He follows the remarkable efforts of teachers, parents, school administrators, clergy, and community activists to take charge of their schools and their communities and describes the effects of these efforts on students' school performance and testing results. Uniting gritty realism based on extensive field observations with inspiring vignettes of educators and parents creating genuine improvement in their schools and communities, this book demonstrates that public schools can be vital "laboratories of democracy," in which students and their parents learn the arts of civic engagement and the skills necessary for participating in our rapidly changing world. It persuasively argues that the American tradition of neighborhood schools can still serve as a bedrock of community engagement and academic achievement.

Notes

1. For a review of this research see Joyce Epstein, L. Coates, K. C. Salinas, M. G. Sanders, and B. S. Simon, *School, Family, and Community Partnerships: Your Handbook for Action* (Thousand Oaks, CA: Corwin Press, 1997).
2. Roberto Suro, "Cavazos Criticizes Hispanics on Schooling," *New York Times*, 11 April 1990, p. B8.
3. Guadalupe Valdez, *Con Respecto: Bridging the Distances Between Culturally Diverse Families and Schools* (New York: Teachers College Press, 1996); Angela Valenzuela, *Subtractive Schooling: U.S.-Mexican Youth and the Politics of Caring* (Albany, NY: SUNY Press, 1999); and Ricardo Stanton-Salazar, *Manufacturing Hope and Despair: The School and Kin Support Networks of U.S.-Mexican Youth* (New York: Teachers College Press, 2001).
4. For a more complete discussion of this issue, see Amy Wells and Irene Serna, "The Politics of Culture: Understanding Local Political Resistance to Detracking in Racially Mixed Schools," *Harvard Educational Review* 66, no. 1 (1996), pp. 93–118.
5. Jan Nespor, "Networks and Contexts of Reform," *International Journal of Educational Change* (in press); Jeannie Oakes and Martin Lipton, "Struggling for Educational Equity in Diverse Communities: School Reform as Social Movement," *International Journal of Educational Change* (in press); Joan Talbert, "Professionalism and Politics in High School Teaching Reform," *International Journal of Educational Change* (in press).
6. This case is described in Jeannie Oakes, Karen Hunter Quartz, Steve Ryan, and Martin Lipton, *Becoming Good American Schools: The Struggle for Civic Virtue in Education Reform* (San Francisco: Jossey Bass, 2000).

7. Epstein et al., *School, Family, and Community Partnerships: Your Handbook for Action.*
8. John Spargo, *The Bitter Cry of Children* (New York: Macmillan, 1906).
9. William Ayers, "Democracy and Urban Schooling for Justice and Care," *Journal for a Just and Caring Education* 2, no. 1 (1996), pp. 85–92.
10. W. E. B. DuBois, "Does the Negro Need Separate Schools?" *Journal of Negro Education* 4, no. 3 (1935), p. 328.
11. John Rogers and Carolyn Castelli, *Building Social Justice for a New Generation,* UCLA IDEA Occasional Paper, 1996.
12. For a discussion of the community schools movement, see John Rogers, *Community Schools: Lessons from the Past and Present* (Los Angeles: UCLA's IDEA Paper Series #1, 1998).
13. Susan Stall and Randy Stoecker, 1997, Internet address: http://comm-org.utoledo.edu.
14. Ernesto Cortes, Jr., "Making the Public the Leaders in Education Reform," *Teacher Magazine,* 22 November 1995.

CHAPTER 11

Teaching to Change the World:

A Profession and a Hopeful Struggle

Cicely Morris
Sixth-year teacher, Kindergarten

It will probably take me a lifetime to develop into the teacher that I want to be.

—Jasper Hiep Dang Bui
First-year teacher, English, grade 8

Teachers entering the profession in the twenty-first century are motivated by all the traditional reasons for teaching—a desire to help, a love of working with the young, pleasant memories of one's own schooling, fun, the intellectual challenge, a passion for the knowledge one gets to teach, an opportunity to "give back" what one has received, a paycheck for an honest day's work—the list goes on. But to these traditional reasons for teaching, many new teachers, like the ones cited throughout this book, will add another reason—teaching for social justice—teaching to change the world.

> *[N]one of us—as an individual—can save the world as a whole, but . . . each of us must behave as though it were in our power to do so.*
>
> Vaclav Havel[1]

> *You must do the thing you think you can not do.*
>
> Eleanor Roosevelt[2]

These words of former president of the Czech Republic and playwright, Vaclav Havel, and those of former American First Lady and Ambassador to the United Nations, Eleanor Roosevelt, capture the spirit of many teachers as they begin their careers. Teachers face daunting challenges that schools, alone, can't overcome, and teachers reach for ambitious goals that they, alone, can't attain. Yet they are determined to use their knowledge and skills to struggle for socially just schooling.

Teachers like those featured in this book are idealists, but they are not naïve about how hard it is to make schools humane and intellectually rich in an age when the gaps between wealthy and poor families grow wider, and racism and anti-immigrant sentiments continue to shape lives. In the face of this struggle, they offer something stronger and more positive than the tired myths of merit, scientific efficiency, competition, and modern progress. They offer new guideposts for creating good schools: the professional knowledge of learning and their vision of social justice that we've outlined in the chapters of this book. These guideposts help today's teachers navigate a fragmented, uncertain, postmodern world in which it is their job—their profession—to keep and encompass difference as essential to the American common good.

These teachers know that they won't make a serious difference if they only choose to teach for a year or two before turning to something more lucrative, more glamorous, or easier. So unlike those who sign up for Teach for America or other short-term stints at teaching, these teachers have chosen to teach for the long haul. This choice means that they must find ways to keep their hope and determination in the face of the pressures that drive many teachers away from schools considered difficult because they serve communities struggling with the challenges of poverty, immigration, limited facility with English, and/or racial discrimination, and that drive others out of the profession altogether.

In the remainder of this chapter, we describe the pressures that plague the teaching profession and detail ways that committed new teachers can maintain their hope, their struggle, and their commitment to change the world.

Teaching: A Vulnerable Profession

We noted in the introduction to this book that over the next decade, public schools throughout the United States will need to hire approximately 2.2 million teachers. Part of the reason is that increased student enrollment and teacher retirements have created a massive teacher shortage. A tidal wave of young children have entered schools just as the current teachers of the baby boomer generation are ending their careers. Teaching has also been the victim of the past thirty years' of revolution in career opportunities available to women and significant reductions in job discrimination facing Americans of color. Members of these groups, who historically have had few options other than teaching, are no longer so willing to choose it over the more lucrative career options now available to them.

Yet the current shortage of teachers is fueled at least as much by high rates of teacher turnover and attrition as it is by insufficient numbers of qualified people being attracted to teaching. Low salaries partly explain why many leave teaching. In 1998, teachers ages 22 to 28 earned an average of $7,894 less per year than other college-educated adults of the same age. From 1994 to 1998, salaries for master's degree holders outside teaching increased 32 percent, or $17,505, while the average salary for teachers increased less than $200.[3] Although low salaries are one important reason that teachers leave the profession, many teachers state that poor working conditions also make it impossible to stay. These teachers point out that deteriorating facilities, overcrowding, insufficient materials, lack of time to meet and plan with colleagues, and the absence of professional autonomy and respect prevent them from doing the job they were prepared to do. While some women leave teaching careers due to family lifestyle issues and child rearing, most teachers who quit are dissatisfied with their jobs and seek better career opportunities in other fields.

This "revolving door" syndrome is felt most acutely in poor urban and rural schools, which historically suffer from a severe shortage of qualified teachers and are often forced to fill vacancies with unlicensed teachers or substitutes. Like other teachers, many teachers in these schools frame their frustrations in terms of the poor working conditions in their schools and the social neglect of schools in low-income communities more generally. However, teachers from high-poverty schools are far more likely than the average teacher to cite students' lack of motivation and problems with discipline as reasons for their dissatisfaction. Furthermore, these teachers are often ill-prepared to connect with students, families, and communities in the ways we've described throughout this book.

Stories also abound that document the ineptness of urban school bureaucracies in recognizing good teaching. For example, in 2001 a large urban school district removed two teachers from their assignment as Advanced Placement teachers. These highly competent teachers managed to inspire a greater number and diversity of students to enroll in their courses and earn college credit through the Advanced Placement program. However, because the school's average Advanced Placement score was lower than it had been when only a few students participated, these teachers were replaced.[4] Or, for another example, in 2001 a school district refused the state's Teacher of the Year's request to a transfer to a high-poverty urban school—one in which the principal had received seven first-year teachers that year, three of whom lacked full-time teaching credentials.[5] Consider that in some urban schools, underqualified teachers on emergency permits outnumber those with credentials. Imagine entering such a school as a novice. Imagine the opportunity presented by a highly qualified mentor willing to transfer to your school and your disappointment at finding that the bureaucracy stood in the way of that transfer. What people and what structures would support your desire to develop innovative curricula? What would give you hope?

Resisting the Pressure to Conform or to Leave

"If they would only let me just teach!" One of teachers' most common complaints is that at every turn they face obstacles to teaching that include school procedures and bureaucracies, inadequate resources, curricula that are ill-suited to students, relentless testing, and so on. These obstacles dissipate teachers' attention and energies that might otherwise be focused on their students. Even so, some teachers believe that school structures generally work well enough for their students who make good progress and derive great benefits from their schooling. Other teachers cope with the obstacles by trying to ignore them; they make the best of difficult situations, try not to fret over things they believe they cannot change, or close their classroom door and immerse themselves in their work with students. Still other teachers are concerned with social justice. For them it will not do to accept or ignore obstacles that they know disadvantage their students. They cannot separate the social conditions of teaching from teaching itself.

To change schools and to change the social conditions that affect schools, in order to do justice for one's students, is a quest that does not have an easily defined end. Veteran teachers who began many years ago cannot say, "My work is done." And teachers just beginning cannot believe that they will struggle for a few years until justice is achieved. How then, can beginning teachers look forward to a fulfilling career in the midst of these challenges? We have no sure answers—no universal guarantees, but we do have the experiences and voices of those whom we call social justice teachers to guide us.

These teachers have figured out ways to stay connected to their profession, their pursuit of social justice, their colleagues, their students, and their communities. Such teachers are not born; our experience with the teachers in this book make clear that they emerge from a commitment to "prophetic pragmatism"; a solid understanding of theory, pedagogy, and the communities where they teach; supportive connections with other professionals engaged in the same struggle, actively pursing socially just education, and finding personal joy and satisfaction in being part of this struggle. We describe each of these teaching career strategies in the remainder of this chapter.

Prophetic Pragmatism

In Chapter 1, we noted that Harvard professor Cornel West argues for a "prophetic pragmatism" as a philosophy that combines faith in democratic processes with a "critical temper." West argues that in diverse cultures like the United States, any democratic process must place its faith in "the abilities and capacities of ordinary people to participate in decision making procedures of institutions that regulate their lives."[6] He cautions, however, that participation itself is insufficient. Rather, the democracy must be one that "keeps track of social misery, solicits and channels moral outrage to alleviate it, and projects a future in which the potentialities of ordinary people flourish and flower." In other words, we should think of democracy as an ongoing struggle, rather than an idyllic or perfect end product. We also introduced Brazilian educator Paulo Freire who paired hope for better social conditions with an active struggle to attain them. As is the case with West, Freire viewed participation in a hopeful struggle as the quality that marks a serious progressive education. People usually think of "hope" as an attitude or a quality of personality, but Freire blurred the distinction between hope and action. For Freire, hope is something one *does* as much as it is a feeling. Throughout this book, we've referred frequently to John Dewey, whose goal was to create schools that were not merely a preparation for democratic life but were themselves sites of democratic living. Dewey, too, linked the ideas of social justice and pragmatism, arguing for schools that acted on bettering society as inseparable from teaching knowledge, skills, and attitudes.

It is hard to feel like your individual efforts matter in the face of socially reproduced inequities that plague low-income communities and distort the lives of so many students and families. Both Dawne Yusi and Georgene Acosta chose to teach as if their efforts did matter—as if they could change the world. By the end of their first full year of teaching, their struggles and their hope had merged in their teaching—in their daily actions. They searched for and found a *prophetic pragmatism*—only to have it slip away and then reappear.

Dawne Yusi had neither illusions nor limits about the struggles of teaching for social justice in her elementary school in a neighborhood torn by a tragic battle between two rival gangs to claim the low-income neighborhood as their "territory."

Teaching is harder than I could have ever imagined. I work at Boulder Avenue Elementary School. It is located across the street from Garden Vista Housing Project, which is home to the Haley Street Boys, the local gang. This year the Haley Street Boys had a gang war with a cross-town rival, causing chaos and heartbreak in the community.

The war began on February 24, when we heard several shots outside the school at 1:30. Many of my students were familiar with the sound of gunshots and immediately knew what was happening. The emergency bell sounded, which signaled us to lock down our classrooms. During a lockdown, all doors are shut and no one may leave the classroom under any circumstances until further notice is given. We did not know how long we would be locked down. I stayed very calm, as an example for students, but inside we were all worried and scared. When I dismissed my students that day, I worried for their safety.

In our class, we wrote in our journals about our feelings and we shared in talking circles. We read stories about violence and peace, and we brainstormed ways to stay out of gangs. We wrote "If I Were in Charge of the World" poetry. One of the students wrote that if he were in charge, "there would be no guns, no drugs, and no gangs." But after a while there was nothing left to talk about. It was time to move on. At the weekly school assembly, the principal taught all the students how to lay flat on the yard to avoid bullets, if they were on the yard when shots were fired.

There is a truce now between gangs, and there haven't been any more shootings in our neighborhood. I worry that I am slowly developing an immunity. What alarms me is that if people become immune to horrendous situations like this and no longer feel any pain, they might also lose the urgency to fight to make things better in the world. However, if I continue feeling so much, I will not be able to keep doing my job.

I need to balance my pain with a critical philosophy of education. I think it is necessary to empower kids to make a difference in their community, and it cannot wait until they're older. It has to be right now. I want to do more. I want to help the kids more, and I want to be an agent of change in the community.

—Dawne Yusi
First-year teacher, grade 5

Yusi's school is in a gang-ridden neighborhood, but a few miles away in one of the city's more affluent areas, first-year senior high school teacher Georgene Acosta met equally difficulty challenges in a similarly pragmatic way.

On the morning of May 1, I returned to work after a two-week spring break. I felt rested, reenergized, and ready to begin a fresh week. About ten minutes into my first period class, the voice of the principal came over the P.A. She began with her usual, "Pardon the interruption. . . ." But this would not be one of her pep talks about the importance of literacy, good attendance, and respectful behavior. "Two students at our school, Eddie Marengo and Richard Rivers, were shot and killed over the break."

In the days that followed, I began to gather various bits of information about the circumstances surrounding these two tragic deaths. I learned that the police gunned down Richard, an excellent student in my eleventh-grade class last year, in his own neighborhood, in the early morning hours. Eddie, a freshman whom I did not know personally, was shot in the back of the head while sitting at a bus stop on Easter Sunday.

In the following days and weeks, I experienced a profound sense of despair. I questioned my effectiveness as a social justice educator and wondered, "Am I contributing enough to end violence in my school and in my community?" While pondering the deaths of these two precious young people, I felt myself falling into an abyss of sadness.

As Jean Paul Sartre said, "Life begins on the other side of despair." I emerged from this abyss with a profound sense of hope. That hope is grounded in my belief that this culture CAN be healed! It CAN be transformed! It CAN nurture and protect its young people. And it CAN give them the tools they need to perpetuate peace!

. . . The tragedies that we uncover in our work in urban schools do not consume us with hopelessness and apathy. Instead those tragedies remind us of our callings and prompt us to take action. We understand that we cannot sit by while attacks are being made against our society's young people.

We must research and analyze the problems that we encounter. We must search for causes and solutions to the problems we find. We must study these solutions and put them to work in our own practices both within and outside of the classroom walls. We must study, we must think, we must ask hard questions and we must work toward even harder solutions. And we must do these things because we believe as Vaclav Havel said that "None of us as an individual can save the world as a whole, but each of us must behave as though it were in our power to do so." We know that there are no quick fixes to the problems that our young people confront on a daily basis. We know that creating meaningful solutions requires commitment, intelligence, dialogue, and most importantly patience. We are up for the challenge. In a culture that is dominated by violence, competition, and greed, we are working together to create a society that is guided by love and defined by its commitment to peace, community, and justice. We focus our energies and utilize our talents in the educational arena because we know that education is one of the most powerful means of helping to construct the kind of society we dream of.

When I think of Eddie and Richard, I feel a deep nameless ache that I know will always be with me. But that nameless feeling helps to sustain my hope. Hope for a world that is worthy of every one of its precious children. We embrace the idea expressed by

Martin Luther King that the universe is on the side of justice and that justice will eventually win. And that is why we teach.

—*Georgene Acosta*
First-year teacher, high school English

Both Yusi and Acosta have learned what John Dewey meant when he cautioned that teachers must not see their work only as a means to some worthwhile end. They know that social justice is not an end state, but rather it is a *way of acting* to achieve that end. To struggle *for* social justice is to engage in social justice. Teachers find their hope—as well as their joy and satisfaction—from the everyday action of working to change the world, rather than from some promise of a better world somewhere in the future. These everyday actions address the practical, here-and-now needs and aspirations of their students and communities.

Theory, Expert Practice, and a Belief in Those You Teach

Social justice is far less a philosophy than it is a commitment to action backed by a solid understanding of educational theory and a command of sound pedagogy. How teachers respond to the daily events of school depends on their theories of teaching and learning, their skill with particular teaching strategies, and their deep-seated views of what their students need and what they are capable of. As Paulo Freire argued, "The idea that hope alone will transform the world . . . is an excellent route to hopelessness, pessimism, and fatalism. . . . Hope is what sustains the struggle for a better world . . . but without the struggle, hope . . . dissipates, loses its bearings, and turns into hopelessness."[7]

Blending Theory and Practice Teachers must defy the myths and metaphors that permeate schools' ordinary routines and conventions. They must be able to see and interrupt inequality in the broader society, not allowing it to be mirrored in schools. They must have a deep understanding of language acquisition and how to scaffold the learning of students whose first language is not English. They must make rich and challenging content in the academic subjects engaging and accessible to all students. To accomplish all this and more, they must integrate the cognitive and sociocultural perspectives on learning we described in Chapter 3 into their everyday teaching actions. They must allow these principles to guide them beneath the surface features of urban schools to engage students in learning for understanding. Further, and perhaps as important, teachers must abandon any wish that their good intentions, social convictions, or their own privileged educational background alone can create good schooling for their students. Children in the most vulnerable communities desperately need teachers with a deep knowledge of subject matter, human development, and language acquisition; they need teachers with the pedagogy, skills, and values that lead to excellence for their students and career fulfillment for themselves—all that we've described in this book.

This, perhaps, explains a great frustration for beginning teachers. Too often, the training of teachers is plagued by the same myth of efficiency that is reflected in commonly held views of teaching K–12 students. Institutions that grant teaching licenses or credentials may offer or require so few course hours that there is just enough time to pass along a few bits and pieces of "practical" teacher knowledge that are then called, "professional training." After obtaining a license or credential, many teachers are afforded too brief a time to act as apprentices. They may observe, have mentors, and be "supervised," but before long (sometimes just a year or less), most teachers are alone with students in the classroom with little opportunity for collegial support, expert mentoring, shared responsibilities, or reflection.

Although the nationwide pressure for supplying urgently needed teachers works against adding to the training and support opportunities for beginning teachers, many teacher education institutions are trying valiantly to address these needs and concerns. Also, at teachers' own initiative, often with colleagues and some early career support from their schools and colleges, they can fashion important opportunities for blending theory, practice, and reflection.

Maintaining consistency between theory and practice is the "trick" to good teaching. It's often difficult to consider Vygotsky's theory of the zone of proximal development when you're planning a geography quiz on Wednesday, your principal's coming to observe you Thursday, and the power goes out for two hours on Friday. It's easy to get caught up in the hectic pace most teachers (including me) keep without stopping to consider the real goals that motivate us. Through personal reflection, reactions from my students, and comments from observers, I seek to keep my classroom practices grounded in the philosophies that I believe.

—Michelle Calva
First-year teacher, grades 4, 5, and 6

Michelle Calva and her colleagues realize that theory and hope are not "cures" for obstacles in the way of their teaching as they would prefer. Practical skills and experience are essential, and sometimes there is simply no substitute for the lack of time imposed by school schedules, crowded classes, and so forth. At some point, their capacity to act on sociocultural theory, their struggle for social justice, and their hopes for their students and themselves are challenged—shoved into the distance by the press (and sometimes panic) of "What do I do now?" For some, the distance is so great that theory and hope are never retrieved. Mastering the "practical matters" of lesson plans, discipline routines, seating charts, learning unfamiliar curricula, test preparation, and more, provide a sense (if brief) of security and protection from the blizzard of unfamiliar demands and responsibilities beginning teachers face.

Sarine Gureghian, quoted next, fought that battle and won. Like Michelle Calva, she found that by holding tight to theory and a strong sense of social justice, she had powerful magnets for attracting the technical competence and experience that keep her vision intact.

It's been a difficult yet transformative year. When I started teaching, I was angry at the Teacher Education Program for not giving me discrete examples and solutions in my search for practical ideas that work in the classroom. Implementing a socially just agenda was difficult when I had discipline cases, district or school guidelines, deadlines, bureaucratic paperwork, on top of tackling issues of literacy, cooperative learning, Limited English Proficient students, and lesson planning. After reflecting on my practice, I realize that all the theory I received has given me a subconscious knowledge that I value and always use. Issues of cultural capital, biculturalism, transformative pedagogy, and the "unschooling" of the mind remain vital concepts needed to build a democratic community of critical learners. Even if the program had handed me lessons, I would choose which ones to adopt and how to alter them based on my philosophy—this is where theory plays the most important role.

—Sarine Gureghian
First-year teacher, grades 1 and 2

Developing Confidence and Respect for Those You Teach Grappling with the racial, economic, and cultural divide that separates many teachers and their students is an essential focus for social justice teacher educators. Bridging this divide requires far more of teachers than simply having taken typical courses in multiculturalism and diversity. Teachers must question commonly accepted beliefs and practices surrounding ability, race, class, gender, language, difference, and so on. They must sit at the intersection of theory and practice, constantly asking, "Whose interests does this practice serve?" or "Why do we do it this way?" Reacting against decades of "deficit" approaches to urban education, social justice teachers must discover and build on the strengths of the communities in which they teach. As education scholar Lilia Bartolome contends, "the most pedagogically advanced strategies are sure to be ineffective in the hands of educators who implicitly or explicitly subscribe to a belief system that renders ethnic, racial, and linguistic minority students at best culturally disadvantaged and in need of fixing."[8]

As first-year teacher Jeffery Madrigal makes clear, summoning up the broad and deep expertise and experience necessary to bolster confidence and respect is not easy, particularly when traditional practices don't connect well with students.

I would summarize my first year as one teacher's journey from progressive optimism, to despair and acceptance of the status quo, and finally back to optimism. However, this final optimism about education is a wiser, realistic, and more-focused optimism.

My initial optimism lasted until about late November. Up until that time, I had been caught up in my own explosion of creativity. However, when I finished patting myself on the back and got down to examining how the kids were doing, I had a rude awakening. The children were doing no better than they had always done. This hurt my ego more than anything. You see I believed that I should be able to get better results than the traditionalist veterans with whom I was working. However, I was not, and in some areas, I lagged. I decided to try to adopt some of the practices of these veterans. I would call this my behaviorist phase. I suppose that I just gritted my teeth and set myself against the apathy and lack of skills that I was finding in my students. I stopped admiring my lessons and began to try to force the students to learn. I tried mastery learning, overlearning, positive reinforcement, punishment, token economies, and so on. I still got sporadic results.

Finally, toward the end of the winter, I began to question my practices. At this point, I reread some literature, and I began to formulate what would eventually become my constructivist direction in teaching. This led to what I would call optimism tempered by a deeper understanding of what general and local communities need in education. Most importantly, it all led to a deeper understanding of what I want out of my educational career.

—Jeffrey Madrigal
First-year teacher, grade 4

As Jeffrey Madrigal came to understand, interactions that promote learning must build on the knowledge, language, and cultures that students bring with them to school. In this way, teaching that is informed by sociocultural theory is teaching that is socially just. More than sixty years ago, John Dewey proposed views similar to those sociocultural and political theorists at the beginning of the twenty-first century:

> [L]earning which develops intelligence and character does not come about when only the textbook and the teacher have a say; . . . every individual becomes educated only as he has an opportunity to contribute something from his own experience, no matter how meager or slender that background of experience may be at a given time; and finally . . . enlightenment comes from the give and take, from the exchange of experiences and ideas.[9]

Participating in this "give and take" is part of being a total teacher. Teachers can no more reject this dimension of teaching—knowledge of and engagement with the community—than they can choose to ignore their classroom environment. For example, in one Latino immigrant community, Ryan Williams spent some of his time as a student teacher learning about resources and capacity in the neighborhoods surrounding the school where they would begin their careers. He and his classmates created an "asset map" of the potential education-related resources. Ryan shared his initial feelings of detachment as he drove to and from the community; he had seen the place as barren, starved of resources. After contacting neighborhood churches, libraries, community groups, and other organizations, the picture softened. Community leaders referred Ryan and his classmates to additional resources that were not obvious at first glance, such as private homes used for tutorials and meetings. Gradually, their deficit conceptions of the community gave way. By the time Ryan began teaching, the detachment he once felt had disappeared. He explained his shift in perspective.

> The green building on the corner that I have passed many times is no longer just a stucco structure but a place where community folks come on Tuesdays, Thursdays, and Saturdays to pick up food items from Ms. Rodriquez. The yellow wooden house across from the liquor store is an after-school site for tutoring. The narrow brown and black Evangelist church provides college access information. Each week this community has at least six Neighborhood Watch meetings at which community members discuss a broad range of issues, including quality education and teenage violence. At one of these meetings, Ms. Garcia, a Neighborhood Watch leader expressed her group's interest in connecting with teachers and the school to discuss how they could work together to provide alternate learning sites for students after school.
>
> —Ryan Williams
> *First-year teacher, grade 4*

The experience opened up new possibilities for teaching. Ryan wants to make sure that he works alongside parents and community members to fully understand and tap into the riches of their urban neighborhoods.

Becoming a Social Justice Professional

The range of understandings, skills, and dispositions that urban teachers require cannot be fully developed even in two years of intensive teacher preparation, nor should they be. Continuous learning is a vital part of high-quality professional practice. Yet the typical conditions in schools provide few opportunities for teachers to continue to learn and develop. Over the years many teachers are encouraged or required to attend "in-service," or "staff-development," but these experiences are typically short-term, packaged lessons that give teachers little encouragement to pay attention to conditions beyond their classrooms. Activities that purport to affect schoolwide or school-community conditions rarely persist long enough to have any influence. If teachers want long-range support for their educational values and activities, they cannot wait for that support to appear as a ready option within the normal course of their workday. However, if this sounds discouraging, it needn't be. No matter how modest the beginnings, there are opportunities waiting for teachers to participate in building a social justice school community that helps to shape their worklives and their personal and professional goals.

Our experiences make clear that teachers who combine their commitments to student learning and social justice remain teaching in urban schools. Rather than seeing professional "development" as a burden imposed by school districts or credentialing entities, they find opportunities that are central to their work satisfaction and their professional identities. Perhaps most helpful are networks of teachers who assume that good teaching—"improved" teaching—is possible only when some conventional (approved or official) practices are resisted and targeted for change, and inequalities in the treatment of students are addressed. These actions do not emerge from a perverse desire to be disruptive for its own sake but are conclusions drawn from social science research and social justice values. In such networks, teachers develop the trust, mutual understandings, and relationship skills they need to build and sustain support for change. These enduring relationships allow teachers to see as "normal" their roles as outsider/reformer, and at the same time build similar insider/reformer relationships within their own schools. These change agent roles are rarely entirely comfortable, but social justice educators are typically welcomed and respected at their schools—especially when their teaching is undeniably competent and their students are engaged and enthused. We have some considerable evidence that those who merge roles as successful teachers, supportive colleagues, and school leaders are among the most powerful change agents in urban classrooms, schools, and communities.

For example, Georgene Acosta belonged to a network of alumni from her teacher education program. The group, with some support from the university, meets regularly to discuss challenges to social justice at their schools, specific lessons, readings, community actions, and participation in various out-of-school teaching activities.

I considered all the amazing work aimed at promoting peace that I have seen among my colleagues at schools around the city. In her Life Skills class Joy Kraft teaches students to see the damaging effects of racism, sexism, classism, and homophobia and helps students devise nonviolent solutions to these social ills. Chris Morrisey has developed Project Peace, a peer-mediation program that he is helping to establish at his high school. These teachers are my heroes. When I face difficult situations as a teacher, they inspire me to work through those difficulties. They renew my sense of hope and courage by reminding me that I am not alone.

—*Georgene Acosta*
First-year teacher, high school English

Professional communities are most helpful when they encourage teachers to learn from one another as well as provide a supportive cushion for the difficulties of teaching. Such networks may bring teachers together who share curriculum interests. Networks of teachers around the country often come together around subject areas, such as the many networks affiliated with the National Writing Project. The Project's goal is to improve the teaching of writing and learning in the nation's schools, and to recognize the primary importance of teacher knowledge, expertise, and leadership in achieving this instructional goal. The Writing Project also connects teachers who share a commitment to social justice. The Project trumpets its belief that access to high-quality educational experiences is a basic right of all learners and a cornerstone of equity. Through its extensive network of teachers, the National Writing Project promotes the value of diversity as well as exemplary instruction of writing in every classroom in America.

One insight drawn from the Writing Project may be important for groups and networks generally; that is to define the affiliate groups' purposes beyond a very general "support for teachers" or "social justice" agenda. Some of the teachers featured in this book have formed a seminar focused on developing curriculum and learning activities that further all students' right to a high-quality education. Their discussions and activities are structured specifically around a Students' Bill of Rights. Just as the Writing Project operates from the principle that the optimal conditions for learning that students require must be made available to teachers (and vice versa), social justice teachers may presume that students will learn and gain from participating in the social change activities that adults such as themselves pursue. This particular emphasis on students' involvement in social justice *activities* parallels much of what we have argued for in this chapter: that a substantial part of urban teachers' work is to blend theory and practice in the cauldron of equity-focused action. The seminar, facilitated by UCLA's Institute for Democracy, Education, and Access (IDEA), invites educators from greater Los Angeles to study and teach together. Teachers participate in finding and developing curricular materials and teaching strategies to help their students study access and equity in their own schools and communities. Teachers meet regularly and contribute the results of their students' research to the online journal *Teaching to Change LA.* Third-grade teacher Salina Gray describes how the seminar helped her develop her teaching.

In the seminar I interact with other socially conscious educators, hear their stories, thoughts, opinions, and experiences. This helps me rethink my own experiences. People are very insightful and honest in responding to the readings and to one another. Nothing has been inflammatory, no propaganda—just views and experiences presented very clearly and objectively. It has been very inspiring to me to question not just my teaching practices, but the educational system that I grew up in. I like to think that I am dramatically different from those who don't respect their students. But I've had to sit and listen and reflect on some of my teaching practices that perpetuate all the things I say that I am fighting against. In the seminar I have evaluated my beliefs as a teacher, asking what education should be, what it means, and what I actually show my students. Do my actions show my values to my students? So, I've become a kinder, more honest Ms Gray. My students have noticed.

In the following quote, Gray describes her students' response to the shift in her curriculum prompted by the discussions in and support from her social justice seminars.

I asked them, "Why do you go to school?" They said, "to get a job" and "to pass the Stanford 9." Now they say "to be the best that I can be," and "to grow up and change the world." The Students' Bill of Rights has affected how they see themselves. Now everyone is really trying to help everyone else. It has been a dramatic change. They were really excited that there were adults who cared about children's rights. They were amazed that they could be valued with the same standards and respect as adults. Since our initial conversations on their rights, and the role of education in their lives, my students place more emphasis on becoming good citizens and leaders. My students look for opportunities to be "teachers." They speak up for themselves now because they realize that their opinions and views are valued and respected. We've had conversations about what makes a "good leader," and reached the consensus that it is more than just getting the grades.

—Salina Gray
First-year teacher, grade 3

Choosing Hope, Taking Action, Finding Joy

In choosing hope over discouragement, and struggle over resignation, teachers who seek to change the world join a venerable American tradition, captured here in the words of escaped slave, abolitionist, and writer Frederick Douglass:

> Let me give you a word on the philosophy of reform. The whole history of the progress of human liberty shows that all concessions . . . have been born of earnest struggle. The conflict has been exciting, agitating, all absorbing. . . . It must do this or it does nothing. If there is no struggle there is no progress. Those who profess to favor freedom, yet depreciate agitation, are men who want crops without plowing up the ground. They want rain without thunder and lightning. They want the ocean without the awful roar of the waters. This struggle may be a moral one; or it may be a physical one; or it may be both moral and physical; but it must be a struggle. Power never concedes anything without a demand. It never did and it never will.[10]

When Douglass wrote the words "the awful roar of the waters," *awful* meant something quite different from the present sense of inspiring fear, extreme unpleasantness, or ugliness. To Douglass, the roar of struggle inspired not fear, but awe, an overwhelming feeling of reverence—grand, sublime, and powerful. Not for the fainthearted, this struggle lifts the spirit of the hopeful as they take action, make demands, plow up the ground.

Frank Divinagracia teaches math at the high school where he was a student. Frank suspects that his students think he is crazy because of his unbridled hope for their futures, but that is an opinion that he can live with.

I like to tell my students, and sometimes they like to listen, about the lives and experiences and words of various activists. I want them to see that people are out there watching out for them and fighting for their betterment. I like telling them how I am like the character in Sandra Cisneros's book *House on Mango Street*. She desperately wanted out of her neighborhood only to discover that the more she learned and grew, the more she knew she had to return home. In returning home she wanted to share with her people all the things that she had learned, and that the shackles that one physically sees are nothing compared with the mental ones we put on ourselves. I think that my students think I am crazy, but I hope one day that my craziness will infect them.

—Frank Divinagracia
First-year teacher, mathematics, grade 10

Fifth-grade teacher Miranda Chavez teaches in a neighborhood of Central American immigrants—most of whom speak little if any English. During her first year of teaching, Chavez integrated into her classwork a study of lead and its impact on health issues, especially for young children. Health department officials met with students and their parents multiple times, as did representatives from the local city councilperson's office. Students studied chemistry to understand the nature of lead. They also went out into their community to collect paint fragments and soil in which children played and then had these samples tested for lead content. As a culminating activity, Chavez invited families to a potluck dinner at which the students presented informational posters they had made—presentations that involved explaining complex chemical processes. The room was packed; almost every parent attended and the evening was conducted exclusively in Spanish. Some parents joined their children in presenting the lead findings, yet a few felt ill-equipped to do so. One parent explained that she "hadn't done anything because she didn't know any English and hadn't attended school herself in her home country." Feeling the tension in the room, Chavez respectfully addressed all the parents, explaining that they had all played important roles in this project, motivating their children and setting rules to ensure that projects were completed successfully. As these students move on to middle school, she continued, parents will play a crucial role in ensuring their children's future success in school. Knowing English and possessing a formal education, she assured parents, were not required. Herself a Central American immigrant, Chavez empathized with parents, yet her message was one of empowerment and therefore social change.

Third-year urban high school teacher Noah Lippe-Klein and now fifth-year elementary teacher Ramon Martinez belong to the Coalition for Educational Justice (CEJ), an activist offshoot of their local teachers' union that has joined forces with a diverse group of civic, legal, and educational leaders committed to eliminating the use of high-stakes testing with low-income children of color. Martinez explains the reason for his activism.

Having been stripped of their home language, my students are now expected to take a norm-referenced, standardized exam, which, in addition to being inherently biased, is administered in a language that they do not understand. Obviously, the test does not provide me with an accurate indication of my students' progress in the various subject areas. The only thing it shows me is what I already know—that my students are Limited English Proficient. High scores on this unfair and inaccurate assessment determine whether schools are rewarded with additional funds to improve their programs. The state's scheme punishes those students who are already at a disadvantage.

. . . It is clear that policymakers at the state and district levels are more concerned with implementing accountability programs than they are with ensuring educational justice. Critical educators must, therefore, step up and take a stand. In defense of educational justice and sound pedagogy, we must engage in individual and collective resistance. If we truly seek to empower our students, we must begin to challenge the educational policies that harm them.

—Ramon Martinez
Fifth-year teacher, grade 1

In 2001 Ramon, Noah, and other members of the Coalition brought over 300 teachers, parents, and students to a school board meeting to seek the board's support in changing the testing program along with the retention policies based on the test results. Since then the Coalition has met with board members and organized antitesting actions at school sites. As a result of these activities, CEJ won a victory when school district officials instructed principals to honor requests from parents who want their children exempted from taking the tests. Since that time CEJ teacher, student, and parent leaders have had meetings with a school board member to organize a grassroots campaign around motions that she will introduce. These motions call for the board to research and adopt a replacement for the current high stakes tests. Contributing to a building statewide pressure to address flawed high-stakes accountability testing, the group is working with activists across the state to have other school boards take similar actions.

Teachers like those cited throughout this book use their professional knowledge and commitments to create public schools where children can both forge a common good and enrich their individual lives. Doing so, they experience deep evidence of children's brilliance that defies typical expectations. Such teachers have seen uncountable combinations of racially and economically diverse students learning together. They have also seen themselves accomplish more than they ever thought they could. They know that if given a chance, they and their students can make common education work.

Sometimes I just sit and think about where I am. I'm a teacher in an inner-city school where I have a classroom of 20 first graders. In June, my first year of teaching will be over. It is scary to think how quickly time went.

When I reflect on this, all I see are faces. When I focus on Reynaldo, I focus on myself. Neither one of us was negotiating, neither wanted to lose. I began to really listen seriously. One deal we made is that whenever he feels like hitting someone he would come directly to me, and we would talk. I can now expect to see him in my class at least once during lunch hour—his way to avoid hitting another student. I am so proud of Reynaldo.

I see Irene who could not speak or write English. There were days when I worked with her using sheltered English strategies and would draw a blank. I felt insecure about my teaching and second-guessed my methods. Then, she started to speak and write in English. Irene taught me not to underestimate the minds of children.

I learn just as much as my students, and my students teach just as much as I teach. Each of my students is amazing. They not only shaped me as a teacher, but as a person. I learned from them that we all have something to learn from each other. I will always see their faces in my mind.

—Hannah Cha
First-year teacher, grade 1

Too Angry and Too Hopeful to Leave

Many of the teachers we've cited throughout this book were first-year teachers in the 2000–2001 school year—as we began writing the second edition of this book. But many others were first-year teachers in 1997–1998 when we began writing the first edition. We've kept in touch with nearly all of these teachers and their "class colleagues." The vast majority continue as classroom teachers. Of those who are not full-time teachers in urban schools, a few have gone on to become administrators in those schools; others are graduate students studying education; still others are curriculum specialists, teacher educators, educational technology experts, or counselors. One is a college professor, another is in the Peace Corps. A few, primarily women, have stopped temporarily to begin their families. Most of them plan to return to teaching.

We conclude the second edition of *Teaching to Change the World* with the experience of kindergarten teacher Cicely Morris. Now in her sixth year, Morris still teaches in the urban school close to the neighborhood where she grew up. During her first year student teaching, she was robbed at gunpoint—a terrifying incident that clarified what she calls "a mission to help children see the range of possibilities for their lives so that they don't see crime or this type of behavior as their only option." She now teaches the younger siblings of the kindergartners she taught during her first year. Still living in the community and buying her groceries alongside her students' parents, Cicely is a deeply committed social justice educator. The longer she teaches, the more opportunities she finds to make her school caring and just. She is always frustrated by conditions familiar to so many who work in urban schools—an unsupportive administration, inadequate facilities, too few community supports, and so on. But she is buoyed by conditions that are not available to many urban teachers. She has the daily support of a partner teacher, monthly discussions with a network of like-minded teachers from across her city, her work as an editor of an online journal focused on social justice teaching, and more.

Why does Cicely stay in teaching? Cicely told us that she was "too angry to leave." In that, she is like many other teachers committed to social justice schooling. Yet more than anger fuels Cicely's commitment to urban teaching. Cicely's anger is paired with hope that is sustained by her connections with her students, her school community, and with colleagues who share her passion for teaching and social justice.

At a time in my career when many of my teaching peers are making the decision to leave the classroom due to burnout and frustration, I am surprised to report that I am experiencing a new sense of hope and commitment to the teaching profession. Despite the struggles I have faced throughout my first five years of teaching, recent changes in my district, my school site, and myself have offered me a "new lease" on my teaching life. I was, once, merely too angry to leave. Now, I am too hopeful to turn away.

At our school, we are experiencing a major overhaul due, ironically, to our designation as a "low-performing" school. Despite the accuracy or inaccuracy of that dubious distinction, it has afforded us a grant to essentially "rethink" and "reinvent" ourselves as a school. This process has involved representation from teachers, administrators, students, and parents in an in-depth collaboration unprecedented at our school. As a result, there is an overall sense that we stand poised at the edge of a sort of new "promised land" for our school and it is exciting for all.

I have also grown to see the immense power of parent/teacher partnerships. I believe that so much of the frustration of the social-justice-minded educator stems from the mistaken perception that we are "lone freedom fighters" in a sea of oppressive administrators, victimized students, and apathetic parents. In the past year, I have co-initiated a parent/teacher collaborative that has helped connect me with authentic hopes, aspirations, frustrations, and expectations of my students' parents. We now share in the struggle of educating in a way that is explicit as opposed to assumed and the results have been astonishing and inspiring. The experience is teaching me that learning to struggle involves learning with whom to undertake the struggle, building alliances that make the struggle feasible and fruitful.

By this school year's end I will have fulfilled my most basic of teaching promises: "I will stay long enough to see my very first class of kindergartners graduate from the fifth grade." However, I see this year not as the end, but the beginning of a new and more powerful commitment: I will stay until we achieve what we are struggling for.

—Cicely Morris
Sixth-year teacher, kindergarten

Notes

1. Vaclav Havel, *The Art of the Impossible: Politics as Morality in Practice* (New York: Knopf, 1997), p. 112.
2. Thanks to Julian Weissglass for reminding us of this quote.
3. *Education Week* (2000). *Quality Counts 2000: Who Should Teach?*

4. Jay Matthews, "Educators Face Pitfalls of Too Much Success," *Los Angeles Times*, 25 July 2001.
5. R. C. Johnston, "System Thwarts Teacher's Bid to Transfer to Needy School." *Education Week*, 11 July 2001.
6. Cornel West, "The Limits of Neopragmatism," *Southern California Law Review* 63 (1990), p. 1747.
7. Paulo Freire, *Pedagogy of Hope—Reliving Pedagogy of the Oppressed* (New York: Continuum, 1997), p. 9.
8. Lilia Bartholome, "Beyond the Methods Fetish," *Harvard Education Review* (1994), Vol. 64 (2) p.180.
9. John Dewey, "Democracy and Education in the World of Today," *Essays* [first published as a pamphlet by the Society for Ethical Culture, New York, 1938], p. 296.
10. Frederick Douglass, speech celebrating West India Emancipation Day, Canandaigua, New York, August 4, 1857, reproduced in Philip Foner, ed. *The Life and Writings of Frederick Douglass*, Vol. 2 (New York: International Publishers of New York, 1976), p. 437.

Bibliography

"A New Mix of Gifted Students." *The Washington Post,* 27 July 1997.

Addams, Jane. "The Public School and the Immigrant Child." In *The Educating of Americans: A Documentary History,* edited by Daniel Calhoun, 421–423. Boston: Houghton Mifflin, 1969.

Allen, Brenda A., and A. Wade Boykin. "African-American Children and the Educational Process: Alleviating Cultural Discontinuity through Prescriptive Pedagogy." *School Psychology Review* 21, no. 4 (1992), pp. 586–596.

Armstrong, O. K. "Treason in the Textbooks." *The American Legion Magazine,* September 1940, pp. 8–9, 51, 70–72.

Arnold, Felix. *Text-Book of School and Class Management: Theory and Practice.* New York: The Macmillan Company, 1908.

Ayers, William. "Democracy and Urban Schooling for Justice and Care." *Journal for a Just and Caring Education* 2, no. 1 (1996), pp. 85–92.

Bartholome, Lilia. "Beyond the Methods Fetish." *Harvard Education Review* (1994), p. 180.

Bauer, Gary L. "National History Standards: Clintonites Miss the Moon." Washington, DC: Family Research Council, 1995; on the Internet at http://www. frc.org.

Baum, Susan. "Gifted But Learning Disabled: A Puzzling Paradox." *ERIC Digest #E479.* Reston, VA: Council for Exceptional Children, ERIC Clearinghouse on Disabilities and Gifted Education, 1990.

Berger, Sandra L. "Differentiating Curriculum for Gifted Students." *ERIC Digest #E510.* Reston, VA: Council for Exceptional Children, ERIC Clearinghouse on Disabilities and Gifted Education, n.d.

Berliner, David, and Bruce J. Biddle. *The Manufactured Crisis: Myths, Fraud, and the Attack on America's Public Schools.* Reading, MA: Addison-Wesley, 1995.

Blau, Sheridan. "Toward the Separation of School and State." Inaugural address, 1997 NCTE Convention, Detroit, MI, November 20–25, 1997.

Boaler, Jo. "Mathematics for the Moment, or the Millennium?" *Education Week* 18, no. 29 (31 March 1999), pp. 52, 30.

Boston School Documents, no. 7, 1908, p. 53, as cited in Marvin Lazerson, *The Origins of the Urban School.* Cambridge, MA: Harvard University Press, 1971, p. 189.

Bransford, John D., Ann L. Brown, and Rodney R. Cocking. eds. *How People Learn: Brain, Mind, Experience, and School.* Washington, DC: National Academy Press, 1999.

Brown, Ann L., Kathleen E. Metz, and Joseph C. Campione. "Social Interaction and Individual Understanding in a Community of Learners: The Influence of Piaget and

Vygotsky." In *Piaget-Vygotsky: The Social Genesis of Thought,* edited by Anastasia Tryphon and Jacques Voneche, 145–170. East Sussex, UK: Psychology Press, 1996.

Bruner, Jerome. *Culture and Education.* Cambridge: Harvard University Press, 1996.

Bureau of the Census. *How We're Changing, Demographic State of the Nation: 1997.* Washington, DC: U.S. Department of Commerce, 1997.

Cahan, Emily D., and Sheldon H. White. "Proposals for a Second Psychology." *American Psychologist* 47 (1992), pp. 224–235.

California Mathematics State Standards—Grade Seven. California Department of Education, 2000.

California State Department of Education. *California's Own History.* Sacramento: Author, 1965.

Carnegie Council on Adolescent Development. *Turning Points: Preparing Youth for the 21st Century.* New York: Carnegie Corporation of New York, 1989.

Cazden, Courtney. *Classroom Discourse.* Portsmouth, NH: Heinemann, 1988.

Cheney, Lynne. "The End of History." *Wall Street Journal,* 20 October 1994, p. A26.

———. "The Latest Education Disaster: Whole Math." *Weekly Standard,* 4 August 1997.

Child Development Project. *Ways We Want Our Classroom to Be: Class Meetings That Build Commitment to Kindness and Learning.* Oakland, CA: Developmental Studies Center, 1994.

Christian, Donna. *Two-Way Bilingual Education: Students Learning through Two Languages.* Santa Cruz, CA: National Center for Research on Cultural Diversity and Second Language Learning, 1994.

Cohen, Elizabeth. *Designing Groupwork: Strategies for the Heterogeneous Classroom.* New York: Teachers College Press, 1994.

Cohen, Elizabeth, and Rachel Lotan. *Working for Equity in Heterogeneous Classrooms.* New York: Teachers College Press, 1997.

Cole, Michael. *Cultural Psychology: A Once and Future Discipline.* Cambridge: Harvard University Press, 1996.

Colvin, Richard Lee. "Spurned Nobelists Appeal Science Standards Rejection." Los Angeles Times, 17 November 1997, p. A25.

———. "State Endorses Back-to-Basics Math Standards." *Los Angeles Times,* 30 November 1997, pp. 1, 18, 19, 26.

Cortes, Ernesto Jr. "Making the Public the Leaders in Education Reform." *Teacher Magazine,* 22 November 1995.

Council of the Great City Schools. *Charting the Right Course: A Report on Urban Student Achievement and Course-Taking.* Washington, DC: Author, 1998.

Crabtree, Charlotte. "A Common Curriculum for the Social Studies." In *Individual Differences and the Common Curriculum,* edited by Gary D. Fenstermacher and John I. Goodlad, 248–281. Chicago: University of Chicago Press, 1983.

Cremin, Lawrence. *The Transformation of the School: Progressivism in American Education, 1876-1957.* New York: Vintage Books, 1964.

Cuban, Larry. *How Teachers Taught: Constancy and Change in American Classrooms, 1890–1990.* New York: Teachers College Press, 1993.

Cubberly, Elwood. *Changing Conceptions of Education.* Boston: Houghton Mifflin, 1909.

Cummins, Jim. "From Multicultural to Anti-Racist Education: An Analysis of Programmes and Policies in Ontario." In *Minority Education: From Shame to Struggle,* edited by Tove Skutnabb-Kangas and Jim Cummins. Philadelphia: Multilingual Matters Ltd., 1988.

Darder, Antonia. *Culture and Power in the Classroom: A Critical Foundation for Bicultural Education.* Westport, CT: Bergin & Garvey, 1991.

Darling-Hammond, Linda. *The Right to Learn.* San Francisco: Jossey-Bass, 1997.

Darling-Hammond, Linda. "The Right to Learn and the Advancement of Teaching: Research, Policy, and Practice for Democratic Education." *Educational Researcher* 26 (August/September 1996), p. 5.

de Tocqueville, Alexis. *Democracy in America*, 2 vols. New York: 1945, Originally published 1835.

DeLany, Brian. "Allocation, Choice, and Stratification Within High Schools: How the Sorting Machine Copes." *American Journal of Education* 99, no. 3 (1991), pp. 191–207.

Delpit, Lisa. *Other People's Children: Cultural Conflict in the Classroom*. New York: The New Press, 1995.

Dewey, John. *Democracy and Education* (1916). In *John Dewey, the Middle Works*, Vol. 9, 84–85. Carbondale, IL: Southern Illinois University Press, 1989.

———. "Democracy and Education in the World of Today." *Essays* [first published as a pamphlet by the Society for Ethical Culture, New York, 1938], p. 296.

———. "How We Think." In *John Dewey, the Middle Works*, Vol. 6, p. 338. Carbondale, IL: Southern Illinois University Press, 1989.

———. "My Pedagogic Creed," 1897. *Early Works*, Vol. 5, p. 93. Carbondale, IL: Southern Illinois University Press, 1989.

———. *School and Society*. Chicago: University of Chicago Press, 1991.

Diegmueller, Karen. "English Group Loses Funding for Standards." *Education Week*, 30 March 1994.

———. "War of Words." *Education Week*, 20 March 1996.

Dividing Lines. *Technology Counts 2001: The New Divides* 20, no. 35 (2001), pp. 12–13.

Douglass, Frederick. "Speech celebrating West India Emancipation Day, Canandaigua, New York, August 4, 1857. In *The Life and Writings of Frederick Douglass*, edited by Philip Foner, Vol. 2, p. 437. New York: International Publishers of New York, 1976.

DuBois, W. E. B. "Does the Negro Need Separate Schools?" *Journal of Negro Education* 4, no. 3 (1935), p. 328.

———. "The Freedom to Learn." In *W. E. B. DuBois Speaks*, edited by P. S. Foner, 230–231. New York: Pathfinder, 1970.

Education Week. *A Better Balance: Standards, Tests, and the Tools of Reform. Quality Counts 2001*. Washington, DC: Author, 2001.

———. *Quality Counts 2000: Who Should Teach*. Washington, DC: Author, 2000.

Epstein et al. *School, Family, and Community Partnerships: Your Handbook for Action*.

Feinberg, Walter "Educational Manifesto and the New Fundamentalism." *Educational Researcher* 26, no. 8 (1997), p. 32.

Ferguson, Ronald F. "Paying for Public Education: New Evidence on How and Why Money Matters." *Harvard Journal on Legislation* 28, no. 2 (Summer 1991), pp. 465–498.

Finnan, Christine, Edward St. John, and Jane McCarthy, eds. *Accelerated Schools in Action: Lessons from the Field*. Thousand Oaks, CA: Corwin Press, 1995.

Freire, Paulo. *Pedagogy of Hope*. New York: Continuum, 1995.

———. *Pedagogy of Hope—Reliving Pedagogy of the Oppressed*. New York: Continuum, 1997.

Gamoran, Adam. "A Multi-level Analysis of the Effects of Tracking." Paper presented at the annual meetings of the American Sociological Association, Atlanta, GA, 1988.

Gardner, Howard. *The Unschooled Mind*. New York: Basic Books, 1991.

Garet, Michael, and Brian DeLany. "Students, Courses, and Stratification." *Sociology of Education* 61 (1988), pp. 61–77.

Garland, May, and Uri Treisman. "The Mathematics Workshop Model: An Interview with Uri Treisman." *Journal of Developmental Education* 16, no. 3 (Spring 1993), pp. 14–16, 18, 20, 22.

Garrison, Jim. "Deweyan Pragmatism and the Epistemology of Contemporary Social Constructivism." *American Educational Research Journal* 32, no. 4 (1995), p. 731.

Glasser, William. *The Quality School.* New York: HarperCollins, 1992.

Glick, Joseph, as cited in Barbara Rogoff, *Apprenticeship in Thinking: Cognitive Development in Social Context* New York: Oxford University Press, 1990, p. 57.

Goldman, Larry S., Myron Genel, Rebecca J. Bezman, and Priscilla J. Slanetz, "Diagnosis and Treatment of Attention-Deficit/Hyperactivity Disorder in Children and Adolescents." *Journal of the American Medical Association* 279, no. 14 (April 8, 1998), pp. 1100–1107.

Good, Thomas, and Jere Brophy. *Looking in Classrooms.* New York: Longman, 1997.

Goodlad, John I. *A Place Called School.* New York: McGraw-Hill, 1984.

Gould, Stephen J. *The Mismeasure of Man,* 2nd ed. New York: Norton, 1996.

Gowen, Annie. "Maryland Schools Remove 2 Black-Authored Books." *Los Angeles Times,* 11 January 1998, p. A6.

Greene, Jay P. "A Meta-Analysis of the Effectiveness of Bilingual Education." Claremont, CA: The Tomas Rivera Policy Institute, 1998.

Gregg, Jeff. "Discipline, Control, and the School Mathematics Tradition." *Teaching and Teacher Education* 11, no. 6 (1995), pp. 579–593.

Harrington, Michael. *The Other America: Poverty in the United States* (1962, reprint). New York: Collier Books, 1997.

Havel, Vaclav. *The Art of the Impossible: Politics as Morality in Practice.* New York: Knopf, 1997.

Heath, Shirley Brice. *Ways with Words: Language, Life, and Work in Communities and Classrooms.* New York: Cambridge University Press, 1983.

Hedges, Larry, Richard D. Laine, and Rob Greenwald. "Does Money Matter? A Meta-Analysis of the Effects of Differential School Inputs on Student Outcomes." *Educational Researcher* 23, no. 3 (1994), pp. 5–14.

Herrnstein, Richard, and Charles Murray. *The Bell Curve: Intelligence and Class Structure in American Life.* New York: The Free Press, 1994.

Heubert, Jay P., and Robert M. Hauser, eds. *High Stakes: Testing for Tracking, Promotion, and Graduation.* Washington: National Academy Press, 1999.

Hiebert, James, and Thomas Carpenter. "Teaching and Learning with Understanding." In *Handbook of Research on Mathematics Teaching and Learning,* edited by Douglas A. Grouws, 65–97. New York: Macmillan, 1992.

Hirsch, E. D. "Address to California State Board of Education," April 10, 1997.

———. "Toward a Centrist Curriculum: Two Kinds of Multiculturalism in Elementary School." Charlottesville, VA: Core Knowledge Foundation, 1992. Located on the Internet at http://www.coreknowledge.org.

Hoff, David J. "Chapter 1 Aid Failed to Close Learning Gap." *Education Week,* 2 April 1997, pp. 1, 29.

Howes, Carollee, and Sharon Ritchie. "Teachers and Attachment in Children with Difficult Life Circumstances." Unpublished manuscript, UCLA, 1997.

Hurd, Paul DeHart. "Science Needs a 'Lived' Curriculum." *Education Week,* 12 November 1997, p. 48.

International Reading Association and National Council of Teachers of English. *Standards for the English Language Arts.* Champaign, IL: Author, 1996.

"Internet Helps with Homework." *Los Angeles Times,* 2 September 2001, p. A18.

Jackson, Philip. *The Practice of Teaching.* New York: Teachers College Press, 1987.

Jefferson, Thomas. *Notes on the State of Virginia,* quoted in Joel Spring, *The American School,* 8–10. New York: Longman, 1990.

Johnston, R. C. "System Thwarts Teacher's Bid to Transfer to Needy School." *Education Week,* 11 July 2001.

Jones, Beau Fly, Gilbert Valdez, Jeri Nowakowski, and Claudette Rasmussen, *Plugging In.* Oak Brook, IL: North Central Regional Educational Laboratory, 1995; on the Internet at: http://www.ncrel.org.

Jones, Makeba. "Rethinking African American Students' Agency: Meaningful Choices and Negotiating Meaning." Ph.D. diss. proposal, Los Angeles, UCLA Graduate School of Education and Information Studies, 1998.

Kelly, Thomas. "The 4 Percent 'Structural Flaw'." *Education Week,* 11 June 1997, p. 44.

Kleibard, Herbert. *The Struggle for the American Curriculum: 1898–1958.* New York: Routledge, 1983.

———. *The Struggle for the American Curriculum: 1893–1958,* 2nd ed. New York: Routledge, 1995.

Knight, Michelle. *Unearthing the Muted Voices of Transformative Professionals.* Ph.D. diss., Los Angeles, UCLA, 1998.

Kohn, Alfie. *Beyond Discipline: From Compliance to Community.* Alexandria, VA: Association for Supervision and Curriculum Development, 1996.

Kounin, Jacob. *Discipline and Group Management in Classrooms.* New York: Holt, Rinehart & Winston, 1970.

Kozol, Jonathan. *Savage Inequalities: Children in America's Schools.* New York: Crown, 1991.

Krop, C., D. Brewer, S. Gates, B. Gill, R. Reichardt, M. Sundt, and D. Throgmorton. *Potentially Eligible Students: A Growing Opportunity for the University of California.* Santa Monica: RAND, 1998.

Ladson-Billings, Gloria. *The Dreamkeepers: Successful Teachers of African American Children.* San Francisco: Jossey-Bass, 1994.

Langer, Judith, as quoted in Deborah Viadero, "Researchers Flag Six Elements of Good Secondary English Instruction," *Education Week,* 14 June 2000; on the Internet at http://www.edweek.org.

Lappan, Glenda, as cited in "Revised Mathematics Standards Provide More Guidance," *Education Week,* 19 April 2000; on the Internet at http://www.edweek.org.

Lareau, Annette. *Home Advantage: Social Class and Parental Intervention in Elementary Education.* London: Falmer, 1989.

Lave, Jean. "Teaching as Learning in Practice." *Mind, Culture, and Activity* 3, no. 3 (1996), pp. 149–164.

Lave, Jean, and Etienne Wenger. *Situated Cognition: Legitimate Peripheral Participation.* Cambridge, England: Cambridge University Press, 1991.

Lee, Valerie, Julia Smith, and Frank Croninger. "Another Look at High School Restructuring: More Evidence that it Improves Student Achievement and More Insight into Why." *Issues in Restructuring Schools* no. 9, pp. 1–9 (Newsletter, Center on Organization and Restructuring of Schools, University of Wisconsin, 1995).

Limbaugh, Rush, as cited in Nash, Gary B., Charlotte Crabtree, and Ross E. Dunn, *History on Trial,* New York: Knopf, 1997, p. 5.

MacIver, Douglas, Steven B. Plank, and Robert Balfanz. "Working Together to Become Proficient Readers: Early Impact of the Talent Development Middle School's *Student Team Literature Program.*" Report of the Center for Research on the Education of Students Placed at Risk. Baltimore: The Johns Hopkins University, 1998.

MacMillan, Donald L., and Daniel Reschly. "Overrepresentation of Minority Students: The Case for Greater Specificity or Reconsideration of the Variables Examined." *Journal of Special Education* 32 (1998), pp. 15–24.

Manzo, Kathleen Kennedy. "Glimmer of History Standards Shows Up in Latest Textbooks." *Education Week,* 8 October 1997.

Margolis, Jane, and Allan Fisher. *Unlocking the Clubhouse: Women and Computing.* Cambridge, MA: MIT Press, 2002.

Mathematics Content Standards for Grades K-12, submitted by Bill Evers, Commissioner to California State Academic Standards Commission, September 15, 1997; on the Internet at http://www.rahul.net/dehnbase/hold/platinum-standards/altintro.html.

Matthews, Jay. "Educators Face Pitfalls of Too Much Success." *Los Angeles Times,* 25 July 2001.

Mayhew, Katherine Camp, and Anna Camp Edwards. *The Dewey School.* New York: Appleton-Century, 1936, p. 65, as quoted in Lawrence Cremin, *Transformation of the School,* New York: Vintage Books, p. 137.

McDonnell, Lorraine M., Margaret J. McLaughlin, and Patricia Morrison, eds. *Educating One and All: Students with Disabilities and Standards-Based Reform.* Washington, DC: National Academy Press, 1997.

McKnight, Curtis C., F. Joe Crosswhite, and John A. Dossey. *The Underachieving Curriculum: Assessing U.S. School Mathematics from an International Perspective.* Indianapolis: Stipes, 1987.

McLeod, Jay. *Ain't No Makin' It.* Boulder, CO: Westview Press, 1995.

McNeil, Linda. *The Contradictions of School Reform: Educational Costs of Standardized Testing.* New York: RoutledgeFalmer, 2000.

Mehan, Hugh. "Understanding Equality in Schools: The Contribution of Interpretative Studies." *Sociology of Education* 65, no. 1 (January 1992), pp. 1–21.

Mehan, Hugh, Lea Hubbard, Irene Villanueva, and Angela Lintz. *Constructing School Success.* Cambridge: Cambridge University Press, 1996.

Mehan, Hugh, Jane Mercer, and Robert Rueda. "Special Education." In *Encyclopedia of Education and Sociology.* New York: Garland, 1997.

Mehan, Hugh, Dina Okamoto, Angela Lintz, and John S. Wills, "Ethnographic Studies of Multicultural Schools and Classrooms." In *Handbook of Research on Multicultural Education,* edited by James A. Banks and Cherry A. McGee Banks. New York: Macmillan, 1995.

Meier, Deborah. *The Power of Their Ideas: Lessons for America from a Small School in Harlem.* Boston: Beacon Press, 1995.

Meier, Kenneth J., Stewart Joseph Jr., and Robert E. England. *Race, Class and Education: The Politics of Second Generation Discrimination.* Madison, WI: University of Wisconsin Press, 1989.

Meyer, Luanna H., Beth Harry, and Mara Sapon-Shevin. "School Inclusion and Multicultural Education." In *Multicultural Education: Issues and Perspectives,* edited by James A. Banks and Cherry A. McGee Banks. Boston: Allyn & Bacon, 1996.

Mitchell, Derek. Ph.D. diss., University of California, Los Angeles, 2001.

Moll, Luis. "Funds of Knowledge for Teaching: Using a Qualitative Approach to Connect Homes and Classrooms." *Theory into Practice* 31, no. 2 (1992), pp. 132–141.

Myers. Miles. "Where the Debate About English Standards Goes Wrong." *Education Week,* 15 May 1995.

Myrdal, Gunnar. *The American Dilemma: The Negro Problem and Modern Democracy.* New York: Harper & Row, 1944.

Nash, Gary, as quoted in "Tragic Side of Mission Era Being Told," *Los Angeles Times,* 2 September 1997.

Nash, Gary B., Charlotte Crabtree, and Ross E. Dunn. *History on Trial: Culture Wars and the Teaching of the Past.* New York: Knopf, 1997.

National Academy Press. *Preventing Reading Difficulties in Young Children.* Washington: The National Research Council, 1998.

National Center for Education Statistics. *Time Spent Teaching Core Academic Subjects in Elementary Schools.* Washington, DC: U.S. Department of Education, 1997.

National Center for History in the Schools. *National Standards for United States History.* Los Angeles: UCLA National Center for History in the Schools, 1994.

National Commission of Excellence in Education. *A Nation at Risk: The Imperatives for Educational Reform.* Washington, DC: U.S. Department of Education, 1983.

National Commission on Teaching and America's Future. *What Matters Most: Teaching for America's Future.* New York: Author, 1996.

National Council of Teachers of Mathematics. *Curriculum and Evaluation Standards for School Mathematics.* Reston, VA: Author, 1989.

National Research Council. *Everybody Counts: A Report to the Nation on the Future of Mathematics Education.* Washington, DC: National Academy Press, 1989.

National Research Council. *National Science Education Standards.* Washington, DC: National Academy Press, 1996.

Neill, A. S. *Summerhill.* New York: St. Martin's Press, 1995, originally published in 1960.

Nespor, Jan. "Networks and Contexts of Reform," *International Journal of Educational Change* (in press).

Newmann, Fred M. ed. *Student Engagement and Achievement in American Secondary Schools.* New York: Teachers College Press, 1992.

Newmann, Fred M., Walter G. Secada, and Gary Wehlage. *A Guide to Authentic Instruction and Assessment: Vision, Standards, and Scoring.* Madison, WI: Wisconsin Center for Education Research at the University of Wisconsin, 1995.

Nieto, Sonia. *Affirming Diversity: The Sociopolitical Context of Multicultural Education,* 2nd ed. White Plains, NY: Longman, 1996.

Noblit, George. "In the Meaning: The Possibilities of Caring." *Phi Delta Kappan* 77 (May 1995), p. 682.

Noddings, Nel. "Teaching Themes of Care." *Phi Delta Kappan* 77 (May 1995), p. 676.

———. *The Challenge to Care in Schools: An Alternative Approach to Education.* New York: Teachers College Press, 1992.

Oakes, Jeannie. *Multiplying Inequalities: Race, Social Class and Tracking on Students' Opportunities to Learn Mathematics and Science.* Santa Monica: RAND, 1990.

———. *Lost Talent: The Underrepresentation of Minorities, Women, and Disabled Persons in Science.* Santa Monica: RAND, 1990.

———. *Keeping Track: How Schools Structure Inequality.* New Haven, CT: Yale University Press, 1995.

———. *Report to the Court, New Castle County,* unpublished report submitted to the court, 1995.

———. "Two Cities: Tracking and Within-School Segregation," in *Brown Plus Forty: The Promise,* edited by La Mar Miller. New York: Teachers College Press, 1995.

Oakes, Jeannie, Adam Gamoran, and Reba Page. "Curriculum Differentiation." In *Handbook of Research on Curriculum,* edited by Phillip Jackson. New York: Macmillan, 1992.

Oakes, Jeannie, and Gretchen Guiton. "Matchmaking: The Dynamics of High School Tracking Decisions." *American Educational Research Journal* 32, no. 1 (1995), pp. 3–33.

Oakes, Jeannie, and Martin Lipton. "Struggling for Educational Equity in Diverse Communities: School Reform as Social Movement," *International Journal of Educational Change* (in press).

Oakes, Jeannie, Karen Hunter Quartz, Steve Ryan, and Martin Lipton. *Becoming Good American Schools: The Struggle for Virtue in School Reform.* San Francisco: Jossey-Bass, in press.

Oakes, Jeannie, Amy Stuart Wells, Susan Yonezawa, and Karen Ray. "The Politics of Equity and Change: Lessons from Detracking Schools." In *1997 ASCD Yearbook:*

Rethinking Educational Change with Heart and Mind, edited by Andy Hargreaves, 43–72. Alexandria, VA: Association for Supervision and Curriculum Development, 1997.

Oh, California. Boston: Houghton Mifflin, 1991.

Orfield, Gary, Mark Bachmeier, David James, and Tamela Eitle. *Deepening Segregation in American Public Schools.* Cambridge, MA: Civil Rights Project, Harvard Graduate School of Education, 1997.

Otto, Roland, as quoted in Richard Lee Colvin, "Spurned Nobelists Appeal Science Standards Rejection," *Los Angeles Times,* 17 November 1997, p. A25.

Parker, Francis. *Talks on Pedagogies.* New York: E. L. Kellogg, 1894.

Pearson, P. David. "Reclaiming the Center: The Search for Common Ground in Teaching Reading"; on the Internet at http://ed-web3.educ.msu.edu.cdpds/pdpaper.rtc 21197.htm.

———. "The Politics of Reading Research and Practice." A presentation at a conference in Houston, Texas, May 15, 1997; on the Internet at http://ed-web3.educ.msu.edu. cdpds/pdpaper. politics.html.

Pyle, Amy. "Attacking the Textbook Crisis." *Los Angeles Times,* 29 September 1997.

Reich, Robert. *The Work of Nations: Preparing Ourselves for 21st Century Capitalism.* New York: Knopf, 1991.

Renzulli, Joseph, in an interview with Anne Turnbaugh Lockwood, "Beyond the Golden Chromosome," in *Focus in Change,* a publication of the National Center for Effective Schools at the University of Wisconsin, Madison (no. 11, Fall 1993), p. 3.

Renzulli, Joseph S., and Sally Reis. *The Schoolwide Enrichment Model: A Comprehensive Plan for Educational Excellence.* Mansfield Center, CT: Creative Learning Press, 1985.

Renzulli, Joseph, and Sally Reis. "The Reform Movement and the Quiet Crisis in Gifted Education." *Gifted Child Quarterly* 35 (1991), pp. 26–35.

Resnick, Lauren. *Education and Learning to Think.* Washington, DC: National Academy Press, 1983.

Rice, Jacob Mayer. *The Public School System of the United States* (1893, p. 34), as quoted in Herbert Kliebard, *The Struggle for the American Curriculum: 1893–1958.* New York: Routledge, 1995.

Rogers, John, and Carolyn Castelli. *Building Social Justice for a New Generation.* UCLA IDEA Occasional Paper, 1996.

Rogoff, Barbara. *Apprenticeship in Thinking: Cognitive Development in Social Context.* New York: Oxford University Press, 1990.

Rosenthal, Robert, and Lenore Jacobson. *Pygmalion in the Classroom.* New York: Holt, Rinehart & Winston, 1968.

Rosser, J. Martin. "The Decline of Literacy." *Education Week,* 15 May 1996.

Ryan, Alan. *John Dewey and the High Tide of American Liberalism.* New York: W.W. Norton, 1995.

Sadker, David as quoted in Millicent Lawton, "Girls Will Be Girls," *Education Week,* 30 March 1994.

Sadker, Myra, and David Sadker. *Failing at Fairness: How America's Schools Cheat Girls.* New York: Macmillan, 1994.

Sapon-Shevin, Mara. "Building a Safe Community for Learning," in *To Become a Teacher: Making a Difference in Children's Lives,* edited by William Ayers. New York: Teachers College Press, 1995.

Sarason, Seymour. *The Culture of the School and the Problem of Change,* 3rd ed. Boston: Allyn & Bacon, 1996.

Saxe, Geoffrey. *Culture and Cognitive Development: Studies in Mathematical Understanding.* New York: Erlbaum, 1990.

Schmidt, William. "Are There Surprises in the TIMSS Twelfth Grade Results?" *TIMSS United States,* Report No. 8. East Lansing, MI: TIMSS U.S. National Research Center, Michigan State University, April 1998.

Schmidt, William. *Facing the Consequences: Using TIMSS for a Closer Look at U.S. Mathematics and Science Education.* Dordrecht: Kluwer Academic, in press.

Schmidt, William, Curtis McKnight, and Senta Raizen. *A Splintered Vision: An Investigation of U.S. Mathematics and Science Education.* Boston: Kluwer Academic, 1997.

Schofield, Janet Ward. *Computers and Classroom Culture.* New York: Cambridge University Press, 1995.

Shavelson, Richard. "The Splintered Curriculum," *Education Week,* 7 May 1997, p. 38.

Shor, Ira. *Empowering Education: Critical Teaching for Social Change.* Chicago: University of Chicago Press, 1992.

Sirotnik, Kenneth. "Equal Access to Quality in Public Schooling: Issues in the Assessment of Equity and Excellence," in *Access to Knowledge: The Continuing Agenda for Our Nation's Schools,* ed. John I. Goodlad and Pamela Keating, rev. ed., 159–185. New York: The College Board, 1994.

Sizer, Theodore. *Horace's Hope: What Works for the American High School.* Boston: Houghton Mifflin, 1996.

Slavin, Robert E. "How Title I Can (Still) Save America's Children." *Education Week,* 21 May 1997, p. 52.

Sleeter, Christine. "Learning Disabilities: The Social Construction of a Special Education Category." *Exceptional Children* 53, no. 1 (1986), pp. 46–54.

———. "Why Is There Learning Disabilities? A Critical Analysis of the Birth of the Field in its Social Context." In *The Formation of the School Subject Matter: The Struggle for an American Institution,* edited by T. S. Popkewitz. New York: Falmer Press, 1987.

Snider, William. "Schools Are Reopened in Selma Amid Continuing Racial Tension." *Education Week,* 21 February 1990.

Solorzano, Daniel G. "Critical Race Theory, Race and Gender Microaggressions, and the Experience of Chicana and Chicano Scholars." *Qualitative Studies in Education* 11, no. 1 (1998), p. 121.

Spargo, John. *The Bitter Cry of Children.* New York: Macmillan, 1906.

Spear-Swerling, Louise, and Robert J. Sternberg. *Off Track: When Poor Readers Become Learning Disabled.* Boulder, CO: Westview Press, 1996.

Spring, Joel. *American Education.* Boston: McGraw-Hill, 1996.

Spring, Joel. *The American School, 1642–1990.* New York: Longman, 1990.

Stall, Susan, and Randy Stoecker, 1997; Internet address: http://comm-org.utoledo.edu.

Stanton-Salazar, Ricardo. *Manufacturing Hope and Despair: The School and Kin Support Networks of U.S.-Mexican Youth.* New York: Teachers College Press, 2001.

Starnes, Bobby, and Eliot Wigginton, eds. *A Foxfire Christmas: Appalachian Memories and Traditions.* Chapel Hill, NC: University of North Carolina Press, 1996.

Steele, Claude. "Race and the Schooling of Black Americans." *The Atlantic Monthly,* April 1992, pp. 68–78.

Sternberg, Robert. "A Waste of Talent: Why We Should (and Can) Teach to All Our Students' Abilities." *Education Week,* 3 December 1997, p. 56.

Sternberg, Robert. "Myths, Countermyths, and Truths About Intelligence." *Education Researcher* 25 (March 1996), pp. 11–16, 13.

Stevenson, Harold, and James Stigler. *The Learning Gap: Why Our Schools Are Failing and What We Can Learn from Japanese and Chinese Education.* New York: Touchstone, 1994.

Stigler, James, and James Hiebert. "Cameras in the Classroom: International Video Survey Examines Mathematics Teaching Practices in Three Countries," Connections

(UCLA Graduate School of Education, Spring 1977), pp. 1–5; also included on the Internet Web page of the Third International Mathematics and Science Study at http://www.ed.gov/NCES/timss/ video.

Surgeon General's 2001 report, "Youth Violence: A Report of the Surgeon General," http://www.surgeongeneral.gov/library/youthviolence/report .html.

Suro, Roberto. "Cavazos Criticizes Hispanics on Schooling." *New York Times*, 11 April 1990, p. B8.

Talbert, Joan. "Professionalism and Politics in High School Teaching Reform." *International Journal of Educational Change* (in press).

Tisn't What You Know, But Are You Intelligent? Preface by Howard W. Haggard. New York: Harper and Brothers, 1927.

"Tragic Side of Mission Era Being Told." *Los Angeles Times*, 2 September 1997.

Valdez, Guadalupe. *Con Respecto: Bridging the Distances Between Culturally Diverse Families and Schools.* New York: Teachers College Press, 1996.

Valenzuela, Angela. *Subtractive Schooling: U.S.-Mexican Youth and the Politics of Caring.* Albany, NY: SUNY Press, 1999.

Villegas, Anamaria M., and Susan. M. Watts. "Life in the Classroom: The Influence of Class Placement and Student Race/Ethnicity." Paper presented at the annual meeting of the American Educational Research Association, Chicago, IL, April 1991.

Waugh, Janet, as quoted in "Kansas Restores Evolution Standards for Science Classes," CNN.com/U.S., February 14, 2001; on the Internet at http://www.cnn.com/2001/02/14/Kansas.evolution.02/.

Webb, James T., and Diane Latimer. "ADHD and Children Who Are Gifted," *ERIC Digest #E522.* Reston, VA: Council for Exceptional Children, ERIC Clearinghouse on Disabilities and Gifted Education, 1993.

Webster's Encyclopedic Unabridged Dictionary of the English Language. New York: Gramercy Books, 1989.

Wells, Amy Stuart. *Time to Choose: America at the Crossroads of School Choice Policy.* New York: Hill & Wang, 1993.

Wells, Amy Stuart, and Robert L. Crain. "Perpetuation Theory and the Long-Term Effects of School Desegregation." *Review of Educational Research* 64, no. 4 (1994), pp. 531–555.

Welner, Kevin, Jeannie Oakes, and Gilbert FitzGerald. *Report to the Woodland Hills School District.* Los Angeles: UCLA Graduate School of Education and Information Studies, 1998.

West, Cornel. "The Limits of Neopragmatism." *Southern California Law Review* 63 (1990), pp. 1747, 1749.

Williams, Luther S. Letter to the California State Board of Education, 11 December 1997.

Wills, John S. "The Situation of African Americans in American History: Using History as a Resource for Understanding the Experiences of Contemporary African Americans," as quoted in Hugh Mehan, Dina Okamoto, Angela Lintz, and John S. Wills, "Ethnographic Studies of Multicultural Schools and Classrooms," in *Handbook of Research on Multicultural Education.*

Yonezawa, Susan. *Making Decisions About Students' Lives.* Ph.D. diss., Los Angeles, UCLA, 1997.

Zerubavel, Eviatar. *The Fine Line: Making Distinctions in Everyday Life.* Chicago: University of Chicago Press, 1993.

Index